THE CAMBRIDGE
ANCIENT HISTORY

VOLUME VIII

THE CAMBRIDGE ANCIENT HISTORY

SECOND EDITION

VOLUME VIII

Rome and the Mediterranean
to 133 B.C.

Edited by

A. E. ASTIN
Professor of Ancient History,
The Queen's University, Belfast

F. W. WALBANK F.B.A.
Emeritus Professor, formerly Professor of Ancient
History and Classical Archaeology, University of Liverpool

M. W. FREDERIKSEN

R. M. OGILVIE

CAMBRIDGE
UNIVERSITY PRESS

Published by the Press Syndicate of the University of Cambridge
The Pitt Building, Trumpington Street, Cambridge CB2 IRP
40 West 20th Street, New York, NY 10011–4211, USA
10 Stamford Road, Oakleigh, Melbourne 3166, Australia

First published 1930
Second edition 1989
Reprinted 1993, 1998

Printed in Great Britain at the University Press, Cambridge

Library of Congress catalogue card number: 75-85719

British Library cataloguing in publication data

The Cambridge Ancient History –
2nd edn Vol. 8, Rome and the Mediterranean to 133 B.C.
1. History, Ancient
I. Astin, A.E.
930   D57

ISBN 0 521 23448 4

CONTENTS

    by C. HABICHT, *Professor in the Institute for Advanced Study,*
    Princeton

      I Asia Minor, 188–158 B.C.   324
        (a) The Attalid monarchy at its peak   324
        (b) Rome's rebuff to Eumenes   332
        (c) Rhodes, 189–164 B.C.   334
     II The Seleucid monarchy, 187–162 B.C.   338
        (a) Seleucus IV   338
        (b) The early years of Antiochus IV   341
        (c) The war with Egypt   343
        (d) Antiochus and the Jews   346
        (e) Antiochus in the east   350
        (f) Antiochus V   353
    III The decline of the Seleucids, 162–129 B.C.   356
        (a) Demetrius I   356
        (b) Kings and usurpers   362
        (c) The catastrophe of hellenism   369
     IV Asia Minor, 158–129 B.C.   373
        (a) The last Attalids and the origin of Roman Asia 373
        (b) Rhodes after 164 B.C.   380
      V Epilogue: Roman policy in the east, 189–129 B.C. 382

11 The Greeks of Bactria and India   388
    by A. K. NARAIN, *Professor of History and South Asian Studies,*
    University of Wisconsin

      I Introduction   388
     II The early rulers   394
    III Menander   406
     IV Successors of Menander   412
      V Conclusion   415
        Appendix I The Graeco-Bactrian and the Indo-Greek kings 420
        in chronological and genealogical group arrangements
        Appendix II Territorial jurisdictions of the Graeco-Bactrian 420
        and Indo-Greek kings

12 Roman tradition and the Greek world   422
    by ELIZABETH RAWSON, *Fellow of Corpus Christi College,*
    Oxford

      I The Roman tradition   422
     II The Hannibalic War   426
    III Contacts with the Greek world in the early second century 434
     IV Reaction and acceptance   448
      V From the battle of Pydna to the fall of Corinth 463
     VI Conclusion   475

BIBLIOGRAPHY

NOTE ON THE BIBLIOGRAPHY

The bibliography is arranged in sections dealing with specific topics, which sometimes correspond to individual chapters but more often combine the contents of several chapters. References in the footnotes are to these sections (which are distinguished by capital letters) and within these sections each book or article has assigned to it a number which is quoted in the footnotes. In these, so as to provide a quick indication of the nature of the work referred to, the author's name and the date of publication are also included in each reference. Thus 'Gruen 1984, 1.40: (A 20)' signifies 'E. S. Gruen, *The Hellenistic World and the Coming of Rome* (Berkeley, 1984), vol. I, p.40, to be found in Section A of the bibliography as item 20'.

MAPS

TEXT FIGURES

PREFACE

The span of time embraced by this volume is short. Some who could recall personal memories of its beginnings – perhaps the news of Hannibal's crossing of the Alps, or of the disaster at Cannae – witnessed events not far from its close; such people witnessed also an astonishingly rapid and dramatic sequence of developments which gave Rome the visible and effective political mastery of the Mediterranean lands. The beginnings of this change lie far back in the history of the Romans and of other peoples, in events and institutions which are examined in other volumes in this series (especially in Volume VII.2); but the critical period of transition, profoundly affecting vast territories and numerous peoples, lasted little more than half a century. In one sense a single episode, it nonetheless comprised a multiplicity of episodes which varied greatly in scale and character and in the diversity of those who, whether by conflict, by alliance, or by the passive acceptance of new circumstances, passed under Roman domination. Furthermore, the Romans themselves experienced change, and not merely in the degree of power and supremacy which they enjoyed. That power, along with the material fruits and practical demands of empire, brought consequences of great moment to their own internal political affairs, to relationships within their society and between them and their Italian neighbours, to their cultural life and to the physical expressions of that life.

It is this elaborate complex of fast-moving change which is examined, aspect by aspect, in the chapters of this volume. A survey of the sources of our information is followed by discussions of the Second Punic War and of the first involvements of the Roman state with people across the Adriatic Sea. There follows a chapter which examines Roman expansion in the West in the subsequent decades, looking successively at Cisalpine Gaul, Spain and Carthage, and concluding with the final destruction of that city in the Third Punic War. After two chapters devoted to the government and politics of Rome itself and to the interaction between Rome and her Italian neighbours, two more consider the contemporary expansion of Roman power in the East. The first of these deals with the great wars against Philip V of Macedon and the Seleucid king Antiochus

III, the second with the overthrow of the Macedonian kingdom and the failure of the final efforts of some of the Greeks to assert a degree of independence, bringing with it the destruction of Corinth in the same year as Carthage. Yet, at least to the east of the Aegean Sea, Roman intervention, albeit on a growing scale, was still only one aspect of the vigorous and often volatile affairs of the diverse peoples of the eastern Mediterranean. The Seleucids and their rivals are discussed at length, in great measure from their own point of view rather than as a mere adjunct to Roman history, though the constantly expanding role of Rome looms ever larger. The Greeks of Bactria and India (upon whom the shadow of Rome never fell) were indeed rivals of the Seleucids but are discussed in a separate chapter which adopts the rather different approach required both by their unique history and by the exiguous and uneven source material. The volume concludes with two chapters which explore the interaction between Roman and Italian tradition on the one hand and the Greek world on the other. The first of these concerns itself mainly with intellectual and literary developments, the second with the material evidence for such interaction at many levels ranging from the basics of economic production to architecture and major works of art.

A few topics have been deliberately omitted from this volume with the aim of avoiding fragmentation and concentrating discussion in other volumes where these topics must occur in any event. Ptolemaic Egypt is examined at length in Volume vii.1 and later events in its history have been assigned to Volume ix, as has consideration of the Bosporan kingdom. Events in Italy between the First and Second Punic Wars are dealt with in Volume vii.2 in a context where they belong naturally, and are not rehearsed again in this volume. Some matters discussed in Chapters 6 and 7 of the present volume necessarily look forward to the tribunate of Tiberius Gracchus in 133 B.C., but the full consideration of that episode, including a review of developments leading up to it, is reserved for Volume ix. Similarly, while Chapter 12 discusses aspects of religion and of literature, the reader who seeks more extended treatment is referred for the former to the appropriate chapters of Volumes vii.2 and ix and for the latter to *The Cambridge History of Classical Literature*. On the other hand the same policy has resulted in two chapters in the present volume having much wider chronological limits than the remainder. These are the chapters devoted respectively to the Greeks of Bactria and India and to the archaeological evidence for the transformation of Italy. In both cases the aim is to preserve the coherence of material which would lose much of its value, not to say its intelligibility, if it were divided.

Two more points of editorial policy require mention. First no obligation was placed upon contributors to conform to an overall interpretation or methodological approach, even in broad terms, though each was asked to signal in text or notes major departures from views which are widely accepted. Second, although each contributor was given the same guidance about footnotes it was felt that differences not only of style but of subject matter, of evidence and of the state of scholarship made it impracticable to insist upon very close conformity to a single model. The resulting variations may not be ideal in aesthetic terms but to a considerable degree they do reflect the requirements of different contributors and the varying character of their subject-matter.

During the preparation of this volume, which has been in train for some time, two events were the cause of especial sadness. Martin Frederiksen, who died in consequence of a road accident in 1980, was the member of the original editorial team who had accepted special responsibility for this volume. Its overall concept and plan and the particular briefs given to most of the contributors owed much to his insight, his care and his enthusiasm. It is a source of much regret that he did not live to nurture and bring to maturity a project which owes so much to his scholarship and wisdom. Less than two years later the grievous blow of Martin Frederiksen's death was compounded by a second tragedy, in the sudden and equally untimely death of Robert Ogilvie. He too was one of the original editorial team and contributed substantially to the initial planning. Thereafter, though he had been less directly involved with this particular volume, it benefited from his general guidance and his perceptive comments on several contributions. Yet another loss which we record with deep regret is that of one of the contributors, Professor H. H. Scullard.

The editors wish to place on record their thanks to several persons, not least to contributors for their patience in the face of the delays attendant upon the completion of a composite work of this nature. Some contributions were received as early as 1980, and the majority by 1984, when there was an opportunity for revision. A. K. Narain consented at a late stage to contribute Chapter 11, agreeing at uncomfortably short notice to add this to an already considerable burden of commitments. Chapter 7 was translated from the Italian by J. E. Powell; thanks are due also to Professor M. H. Crawford, from whose expertise this chapter has benefited greatly. Chapter 13 was translated from the French by Mrs Elizabeth Edwards. Chapter 10 was written in English but Professor C. Habicht acknowledges the assistance of Dr A. S. Bradford. The maps in this volume have been drawn by David Cox of Cox Cartographic Ltd. The index was compiled by Mrs Barbara Hird. Special thanks are due to our sub-editor, Ann Johnston, for her great care and vigilance, and to the staff of the Press for their patience and their unfailing support and encouragement throughout.

A.E.A.
F.W.W.

CHAPTER 1

SOURCES

A. E. ASTIN

I. INTRODUCTION

The period covered by this volume saw a vast expansion of Roman power, an expansion which extended Roman military and political domination over virtually the entire Mediterranean world, from west to east, from Spanish tribes to Hellenistic kingdoms. At the beginning of the period the cities, leagues and kingdoms of the Hellenistic world which lay to the east of the Adriatic lived a largely separate existence, as yet barely touched by Rome; by the end, although (except in Macedonia) the imposition of Roman administration still lay in the future, effective Roman political control was an established fact. This outcome had a profound influence upon the nature of the literary sources which yield both the framework and much of the detail of our knowledge; for the greater part of them have Rome at the centre of their interest and show us the rest of the Mediterranean peoples, both of the west and of the east, primarily in relationship to Rome. Thus although in the western lands there is much archaeological evidence, revealing military constructions, habitations, and a multitude of artifacts, the historical context to which this has to be related is almost entirely Roman. In the east, though the nature of the material is somewhat more complicated, it is still difficult to build up independently of Roman affairs a picture which has much coherence and detail, even for the early part of the period. Admittedly some help can be obtained here from the considerable body of numismatic and of epigraphic evidence. The evidence of coins is particularly useful in resolving a number of chronological problems, especially in connection with some of the dynasts and usurpers whose reigns were short, while for certain of the more remote Hellenistic kingdoms it is fundamental; and the survival of numerous inscriptions, especially inscriptions erected by Hellenistic cities, casts many shafts of light – usually narrow but often intense – upon matters of chronology, political allegiance, administration and royal policies.[1] Nevertheless both coins and inscriptions acquire much of their value as evidence when they are

[1] Section IV below.

I

related to contexts which must be derived largely from literary sources; and for the Hellenistic world, particularly in affairs unrelated to Rome, these are sparse and often fragmented, and frequently permit the reconstruction of only a sketchy outline of events.

Aside from the accidents of loss, which, though erratic, grievously afflict the records of every period of Ancient History, there are two particular reasons for this state of affairs in relation to this period. Firstly, although the Hellenistic world was a world well acquainted with literature and literary composition, and although in the third century it had had a number of distinguished historians of its own, there followed a long period, including the years covered by this volume, during which it produced little major historical writing apart from the work of Polybius, whose central interest was the growth of Roman power and who in several respects was clearly a special case. Admittedly a very large number of local histories and some other monographs on special topics were written in the Hellenistic age[2] and it is plausible to assume that some of them were written in the period now under discussion (all are lost and many cannot be dated); but by their nature these had very limited subject-matter and many probably had only a modest circulation. So apart from these local histories there did not exist for the use of later historians or for transmission to us a substantial body of contemporary historical writing concerned primarily with the Hellenistic world. Secondly, for writers of later generations, living in a Roman empire, it was entirely natural that in the main their concern with this period should revolve around the affairs of Rome.

A partial exception to this widespread practice of treating Hellenistic history simply as an aspect of Roman history is to be found in the work of Pompeius Trogus. Trogus, who in the time of Augustus wrote in Latin a 'universal history' which he entitled '*Historiae Philippicae*', dealt with the Hellenistic period in no less than twenty-eight of his forty-four books. The work is lost but is known in outline from surviving tables of contents (*prologi*) of the individual books and from an epitome made by a certain Justin, probably in the third century A.D. Trogus himself, inevitably and properly, devoted several books to Rome's wars in the east, but even when dealing with the second century B.C. he managed to devote a good deal of space to affairs of the Hellenistic powers in which Rome was not involved. For a number of events these summaries of Trogus are the only evidence; more importantly their sketchy narrative plays a key part in establishing the overall framework of events.

---

[2] It is reasonable to bracket with these the concluding sections of the history of Phylarchus and the memoirs of Aratus, both of which were concerned with European Greece down to 220 B.C. Both were drawn upon by Polybius for his introductory material in books I and II, which covered events to that year.

There is another notable exception to the general pattern of evidence for the period. The uprising of the Jews under the Hasmonaeans against Seleucid domination is an episode of Hellenistic history which is almost entirely outside the orbit of Roman history but which is recorded at some length and in considerable detail. It is the subject of the first two books of Maccabees and is also dealt with in the writings of Josephus. Yet even the *First Book of Maccabees*, which was probably written by a Palestinian Jew *c*. 100 B.C. and is much the more valuable of the two, covers only the years 175–135, while the later, more derivative *Second Book of Maccabees* confines itself to 176–161. Thus although these works provide coherent and fairly detailed accounts (and also throw some incidental light on other aspects of Seleucid history), their subject-matter is limited in time as well as in place, and is a reflection of the importance of the uprising in the Jewish tradition rather than a more general Hellenistic historical record. Much the same may be said of Josephus' accounts of the episode in the introduction to his *Jewish War* and, at greater length, in his *Antiquities*, both written in the Flavian period and both dependent in considerable measure upon I *Maccabees*.

The fact remains, despite these special cases, that the greater part of the evidence for the Hellenistic world in this period is derived from authors who deal also with Roman history and for whom, even in the context of 'universal history', Rome is the true focus of their interest. That is neither surprising nor wholly misleading, for as the period proceeds this point of view approximates more closely to the actual situation which was developing. The history of the Hellenistic world was becoming steadily less distinct and independent, Rome impinged more and more upon it, and the interaction between the two became one of the major political and historical realities of the time, to be superseded by the reality of unchallengeable Roman domination of the whole. All this was to find early expression in both the person and the writings of Polybius, who played a major role in the collection and transmission of much of the information that has reached us.

II. HISTORIANS

Polybius of Megalopolis,[3] born *c*. 200, was one of the thousand leading men of Achaea who were deported to Italy after the battle of Pydna in 168; he was released only in 150 – as also were the others who survived so long. Polybius himself, however, had become well acquainted with P. Cornelius Scipio Aemilianus and Q. Fabius Maximus Aemilianus, both of whom were sons of the victorious Roman general at Pydna, L.

[3] Polybius, like all the authors named in this chapter, is the subject of a special article in *PW*. See also Walbank 1972: (B 39), and, for detailed commentary, Walbank 1957–79: (B 38).

Aemilius Paullus. When the other detainees were assigned to various Italian towns these influential young men arranged that Polybius should remain in Rome itself, and before long his relationship with Scipio in particular developed into a close and enduring friendship (Polyb. XXXI.23.1–25.1). Thus he found himself living in the city, at the heart of the state which within his own lifetime – and he was still only in his thirties – had spectacularly changed the power-structure of the world from which he came; and he was in close touch with men who were likely to be well informed about affairs there and elsewhere. He was stimulated to ask himself how in the short space of time from 220 to 167 Rome had come to dominate the whole Mediterranean world, and he determined to answer this question by writing a history. Although the greater part of that history is now lost, it is, directly and indirectly, a major source of our knowledge and understanding of the period, while for Rome's relations with the Hellenistic states it is the principal source.

The first two books of the history outlined events from 264 to 220 as an introductory background. Sketchy though these are by comparison with the main body of the work, they are invaluable to the modern scholar because of the loss of so much other work dealing with events prior to 220. Polybius' original plan was to write thirty books in all, but some time after he had started he decided to add a further ten books and to take his account down to 146 (Polyb. III.4). The reason given for this change of plan is that he wished to show how the victors used the power they had won, but the surviving passages from the later books do not seem to reflect this intention particularly well and it has often been viewed with a degree of scepticism. There must be a suspicion that he was motivated in part by a desire to include events with which he himself had been closely associated, for in 151 he accompanied Scipio Aemilianus on a campaign in Spain, and shortly after his formal release from detention he was summoned to assist the Romans during the siege of Carthage. Moreover after the disastrous folly of the Achaean war against Rome in 146, which led to the destruction of Corinth, Polybius played a role of great prominence, first as a mediator between the Achaeans and the Romans and then in regulating relationships among the Achaean cities following the withdrawal of Roman troops. Whatever his true motives for the extension, however, the whole history undoubtedly constituted a monumental work which must have taken many years to compile and compose. Indeed the final books were probably published only after his death, the date of which is not known but which may have been as late as 118.

Polybius brought to his history two key concepts, both of which contribute substantially to the value of his work as a source for the period and both of which were facilitated by the circumstances in which he found himself. The first is that though history may be entertaining it is above all a practical, utilitarian matter, intended for the instruction and enlightenment of statesmen and men of office. There is thus a bias (not quite totally sustained) against dramatization and towards solid reliability, with information gleaned as directly and as accurately as possible from actual participants in events. The second is that Polybius' principal theme – the unifying of his world through the imposition of Roman power – required 'universal' history, in other words the recording of events at every stage in all the areas which were to have this unity of domination imposed upon them. It is no surprise that fulfilment of this ambitious objective was uneven or that it was applied most extensively to Greece and the major Hellenistic kingdoms. Nevertheless it did mean that Polybius was seeking out and recording a broad range of information much of which would otherwise not have been passed down. Moreover for both these aspects of his task – indeed for the task as a whole – he was peculiarly well situated. His detention placed him close to the centre of world power; he was in touch with men who were exceptionally well informed about current events and who often were leading participants in them, and after his release he maintained these contacts; in some events he himself had participated in a significant way; he had opportunity to talk with many who had played leading roles earlier in his period; he had access to at least some memoirs, treaties, and other documents, in addition to the earliest histories written by Romans – Q. Fabius Pictor and L. Cincius Alimentus (both of whom wrote in Greek) – and monographs devoted to the Punic wars; and he could meet and talk with many of the envoys, including many Greeks, who now streamed to Rome as the ultimate source of authority and assistance.

Polybius thus had both incentive and opportunity to be well informed and reliable over a broad range of material; and in general his reputation in these respects stands high so far as factual matters are concerned, though inevitably a few particulars are questionable or demonstrably incorrect. The reliability of his judgements and assessments, however, has been the subject of greater debate. First, there is unmistakable evidence of partisanship, apparent for example in the obviously favourable view taken of the Achaeans and the equally obvious dislike of the Aetolians. One instance of a glaring distortion induced by partisanship is the absurd assertion that fear and cowardice were the motives which in 152 induced M. Claudius Marcellus to recommend acceptance of a peace settlement with the Celtiberians. Marcellus, thrice a consul and twice a *triumphator*, was one of the ablest generals of the day; but among the many who disapproved of his conciliatory policy towards the Celtiberians was Polybius' friend and patron Scipio Aemilianus (Polyb. XXXV.3.4, XXXV.4.3 and 8). Once it is recognized, however, that at least in

matters very close to him Polybius' judgement may be affected by
vigorous partisanship it is not difficult to exercise the necessary caution.
More controversial has been Polybius' pervading view that the expansion of Roman power was the product of a conscious desire on the part of
the Romans to extend their domination over other peoples, and that on
certain occasions decisions were taken specifically towards that end. By
and large, however, what is in dispute is not whether Polybius held that
view but whether it is a correct interpretation and accords with factual
information which he himself provides; it is a question about the nature
of Roman imperialism rather than about the value of Polybius' work as
source-material, and as such it is discussed elsewhere in this volume.

In another sense, however, this is but one facet of another question:
whether this Greek ever really understood the character, the motivation,
the ethos of the Romans. In his sixth book, a substantial portion of which
survives, he described and evaluated Roman institutions, including in
this his famous analysis of the Roman constitution as a 'mixed' constitution. Many features of this analysis have prompted discussion and
argument, but however they may be interpreted it remains evident that
the realities of Roman political and constitutional behaviour differed
significantly from the models set out by Polybius in this account. Partly
because Polybius directs attention to formal powers and institutions
rather than to actual behaviour, the highly effective oligarchic manipulation of both executive office and 'popular' organs is lost to sight behind
an appealing picture of a neatly balanced combination of monarchic,
aristocratic and democratic elements, each contributing their own
strengths and checking undesirable tendencies in the others. It is a
picture which conveys little of the actualities of Roman aristocratic
government. Yet it would be unwise to infer too readily from this
constitutional section that Polybius did not understand the nature of
Roman politics and government, or that his assessments elsewhere of
Romans and Roman motives are to be suspected of having been distorted
by Greek preconceptions. He would not be the last writer by a long way
to have created a theoretical model in which his own enthusiasm and
abstractions were allowed to override realities which in day-to-day life he
understood perfectly well. It would be surprising if Polybius were never
mistaken, if he always understood Romans correctly; but for very many
years he lived not just in Rome but in close touch with aristocratic and
political circles. It seems reasonable to treat his judgements with considerable respect.

Only a relatively small part of Polybius' great history has survived.
Apart from fragments of lost books, we have much of book VI, with
Polybius' discussion of Roman political and military institutions, and the
whole of books I–V. The introductory nature and the special value of the

first two books has been mentioned already; books III–V deal with events from 220 to 216, including a great deal of Greek and Hellenistic material which otherwise would be unknown to us. The breaking-off of this continuous narrative in 216 (approximately with the battle of Cannae) results in a sharp change in the precision and detail of our knowledge thereafter, especially in respect of the Hellenistic world. (The record of Roman affairs is much less seriously affected until Livy's narrative also breaks off with 167.) Nevertheless a significant amount of Polybius' material from book VII onwards has survived. This material takes the form either of fragments – extracts and quotations – directly ascribed to Polybius or of passages, some of them of considerable length, in authors who are known to have drawn heavily upon Polybius for certain sections of their own writings, though these two types of Polybian material are not always sharply distinct from one another. The majority of the fragments are derived from sets of extracts from Polybius (and from other historians) made in the Byzantine period, in several cases in order to illustrate a particular theme, such as 'Virtues and Vices', 'Plots against Kings', and 'Embassies'. Such extracts are by their nature isolated and many of them are deficient in indications of context and chronology; on the other hand within each set they are normally in the order in which they occurred in the original text, and the main substance of each extract tends to preserve the wording of the original more exactly than ancient custom regarding quotation would normally require.[4] These sets are therefore a major source for the recovery of material lost from Polybius – and indeed from many other historians who wrote in Greek.

Other fragments are really quotations from Polybius which survive in the works of subsequent writers. Such quotations tend to be less exact than the Byzantine extracts, but they are often related to a definite context and they are fairly numerous, for later writers drew heavily on Polybius' material, especially those who were writing in Greek or were concerned with Hellenistic affairs. Among the Greek writers were Diodorus of Sicily, who in the first century B.C. wrote a World History, and Dio Cassius, a Roman senator from Bithynia who in the Severan age wrote a vast history of Rome down to his own day. It happens that for the period covered by this volume the text of both these works is lost, so we are dependent upon quotations and Byzantine extracts, mostly very similar to those which we have for Polybius himself. Not surprisingly there is a considerable duplication of material which is found also in fragments of Polybius or in Livy, or in both; but there is some informa-

---

[4] These points can be demonstrated by an examination of extracts taken from books which are still extant, both of Polybius and of other authors. For the corpus of surviving extracts: Boissevain and others, 1903–10: (B 1).

tion which has not survived elsewhere, especially for the years after 167, when Livy's text breaks off.

Another Greek writer who preserves quotations from Polybius is Plutarch, who in the late first century A.D. wrote his 'Parallel Lives' of Greeks and Romans. Six of the 'Lives', five Roman and one Greek, are relevant to this volume.[5] Plutarch's principal interest is in the moral characteristics and the personality of each of his famous men. Deeds and sayings are narrated to exemplify these qualities, but he is less concerned with achievements as such, and scarcely at all with policies, political analysis or specific military activity. This is reflected in his choice of material, in the manner in which it is presented, and in the relative importance he assigns to various items. To the frustration of the modern enquirer – especially the political historian – he provides a good deal of minor personal information and anecdote, while other matters are treated with a disappointing vagueness and lack of detail. He usually follows broadly the main sequence of his subject's career but otherwise has no interest in time and date; consequently he provides few chronological indicators and scarcely any which are at all precise. Yet Plutarch is not to be despised. He records a great deal of information, by no means all of which is mere duplication of what can be found elsewhere; and his wide reading enabled him to draw upon many sources. At the same time, in the six 'Lives' presently in question a substantial proportion of his material, including most of that which concerns affairs east of the Adriatic, undoubtedly goes back directly or indirectly to Polybius.

Ancient authors, not sharing the modern horror of plagiarism, by no means always named predecessors upon whom they were drawing, whether for specific statements or for substantial bodies of material. Diodorus, Dio and Plutarch, and others, all have considerable amounts of material which they or intermediaries have taken from Polybius without ascription to him. In some cases this can be established because such a passage has been taken from a section of Polybius which happens to survive, and in this way it is possible to form some idea of the extent of a writer's debt to Polybius and of the manner in which he used Polybian material. By far the most important surviving work which is indebted to Polybius in this way is Livy's history of Rome, surviving books of which include those dealing with the years 219–167. Comparison with passages of Polybius leaves no doubt that the latter was Livy's main source for eastern affairs, that for a very large amount of material concerning Rome's relationships and activities east of the Adriatic he drew directly, extensively, and principally upon Polybius. Moreover, although Livy's

5 *Fabius Maximus, Marcellus, Cato the Elder, Flamininus, Aemilius Paullus, Philopoemen.*

version is not an exact translation of the Greek into Latin, he normally remains close to the content and general structure of his original, despite the touches of vividness and vigour imparted by his own artistry. Thus very substantial amounts of material in Livy dealing with eastern affairs, though not acknowledged to be Polybian, do preserve fairly accurately Polybius' version of events; and, while inevitably there are sections of which the ascription is disputed, the Polybian origin of a great deal of this material can be assumed with considerable confidence. Thus much of Livy's information on these matters goes back to an unusually well-informed writer of the second century B.C. who was a contemporary or near-contemporary of many of the events he describes; and the value of Polybius as a source extends well beyond the actual books and fragments which have survived.[6]

Livy's massive history of Rome from its origins to his own day was almost literally a lifetime's work.[7] So far as is known Livy did not engage in public affairs but devoted himself entirely to literary matters, above all to the writing of his history which is known to have occupied him for virtually the whole of the reign of Augustus. Arranged on a year-by-year, annalistic scheme, it grew in scale as it progressed and ultimately comprised no less than one hundred and forty-two books, of which thirty-five survive. These extant books are I–X, which take the history of 292 B.C., and XXI–XLV, which deal with 219–167 and therefore with a major part of the period covered by this volume. Indeed, since they deal with the Second Punic War and with Rome's major wars against the Hellenistic powers – the very period which Polybius initially took as his subject – they are of exceptional importance, the more so since they are the principal vehicle for much of Polybius' own account. From the lost books (of which XX and XLVI–LVII are relevant to this volume) there are only a small number of fragments, but there are epitomes. One of these epitomes, generally known as 'the *Periochae*', is a very brief summary of the main items (as they seemed to the compiler) in each book; the result is longer but not a great deal longer than a table of contents might be expected to be, and precise chronological indications are usually lacking. Nevertheless these summaries exist for all 142 books except CXXXVI and CXXXVII. Portions of a different epitome, similar in type but somewhat briefer, were found in a papyrus from Oxyrhynchus. Though much damaged, this included summaries of books XXXVII–XL (which are extant) and of books XLVIII–LV. In addition several other short historical works are derived from Livy to such an extent that they are not far

[6] Nissen 1863: (B 23) is the foundation study of this relationship between Polybius and Livy.
[7] Klotz 1940–1: (B 13); Walsh 1961: (B 40); Ogilvie 1965, 1–22: (B 25); Luce 1977: (B 15). Commentaries relevant to this period: Weissenborn-Müller 1880–1911: (B 43); Briscoe 1973: (B 3) and 1981: (B 4) (books XXXI–XXXIII and XXXIV–XXXVII).

removed themselves from being epitomes. These include the relevant
parts of Eutropius' *Breviarium* and of Orosius' *Historiae adversum Paganos*,
and the biographical *De Viris Illustribus* attributed to Aurelius Victor.

Livy's principal intention and achievement was artistic – the creation
of a grand design and its realization in a lively, polished and often
powerful narrative. Only rarely did he engage in the primary research
which his modern counterparts regard as an essential function of a
historian. His method for any particular episode was to follow one
account selected from those available to him, with only occasional
mentions of variants found in other accounts. Generally he seems to have
followed his chosen account quite closely, but to have re-written it in his
own accomplished style and to have given it some vivid and dramatic
expression – as he did with Polybius. For the period of this volume he
used especially (apart from Polybius) two of the so-called 'Sullan
annalists' of the early first century B.C., Valerius Antias and Claudius
Quadrigarius, though there are traces of other sources, such as the
account of the military campaign of Cato in Spain in 195 which certainly
goes back to Cato himself. Since Valerius and Claudius were both prone
to exaggeration and elaboration (not to mention cavalier alteration) in
the interests of dramatic effect, family glory, or Roman chauvinism,
there has been a tendency to treat with scepticism any material in Livy
which does not come from Polybius, and in some extreme cases to
discount completely all such material. It is more realistic, however, while
maintaining a sensible degree of caution about such details as casualty
figures and highly dramatic battle scenes, to recognize that Valerius and
Claudius were themselves drawing upon a great body of second-century
material, much of it well informed and derived from contemporary
accounts and records. The broad framework can be taken to be generally
sound, and so can much of the detail. Year by year, for example, Livy
reports elections, the allocation of provinces, recruitment and assignment of troops, triumphs, donatives, booty, dedications of temples, and
prodigies and their expiation. Much of this is probably derived from the
annales maximi, the public record made by the *Pontifex Maximus*, the
archive of which was probably written up and published in the later
second century.

Livy's twenty-five books are not, of course, the only source of
information for the great age of Roman expansion. Apart from the
fragments of Polybius and such authors as Diodorus, Dio and Plutarch,
there are other minor historical works and, scattered through a great
variety of literature, a substantial number of anecdotes. Nevertheless the
role played by Livy's account in the work of the modern historian of that
period is central, indeed it is fundamental. Its importance is well brought
out by comparing the periods before and after Livy's text breaks off.

After 167 there is no continuous narrative, except for the Third Punic War and some wars in Spain, nor is it possible to reconstruct such a narrative or even a truly coherent picture of events. Information is particularly thin and fragmentary for the years between 167 and 154, and there are many uncertainties of sequence and chronology. Some improvement in chronology and structure is evident from about 154 because of Rome's record of warfare. From that date until 133 Rome was engaged in an almost unbroken sequence of wars in Spain, and from 149 to 146 she was committed also to her final war against Carthage, the Third Punic War. We have narratives of these wars written by Appian. Appian, a Greek of the second century A.D., wrote accounts of Rome's wars, arranging them on a geographical or ethnic basis (Italian, Samnite, Macedonian and Illyrian, Syrian, etc.). Although much of his work is lost some books and a number of fragments survive, including the *Iberica* and *Libyca*. For the years prior to 167 he has little of value which is not also in Livy or Polybius, but his narratives of these later wars provide both a valuable framework and much useful detail. Although his treatment of the Spanish wars fluctuates in scale and detail it does seem to be in the main reliable and chronologically accurate, while his account of the Third Punic War is close to that which was given by Polybius, from which it is almost certainly derived through an intermediate source. Apart from Appian, the outline of events after 167 is derived largely from the epitomes of Livy, already mentioned, and such brief histories as those of Eutropius and Orosius, which themselves are based largely upon Livy's work. Thus even for the years after 167 such record as has come down to us is still strongly influenced by Polybius and Livy, even though the actual text of each is lost.

III. NON-HISTORICAL LITERATURE

The sources considered so far have been largely the historical literary works which constitute the principal basis for the political and military history to which the greater part of this volume is devoted. However, the volume also contains substantial sections dealing with the social, economic and cultural history of Rome and Italy,[8] and even for political and military history not all the sources are literary and not all the literary sources are historical. Naturally historical and narrative works contribute much information regarding social, economic and cultural matters, just as non-historical works of all types and of all periods contain numerous anecdotes and incidental details relating to the political and military affairs of this period; but the contemporary non-historical

---

[8] Aspects of social and economic history in the Hellenistic world are discussed in *CAH*[2] vii.i.

Roman literature does require some separate mention, even though it
receives extended treatment in Chapter 12.

In the later third and second centuries B.C. Rome experienced a literary
awakening and a cultural transformation of very considerable magnitude. This resulted in a substantial output of Roman literary composi-
tions, the bulk of which are now lost except in so far as there are
quotations and comments in writings from the late Republic onwards.
This included many historical works, beginning with the histories in
Greek written by Fabius Pictor and Cincius Alimentus, and proceeding a
generation later to Cato's *Origines* which initiated a vigorous and fast-
expanding historical tradition in Latin; but there was also a great output
of verse and drama, most notably from the versatile genius of Quintus
Ennius, and the first steps in non-historical prose literature, including
published speeches and various handbooks. All this historical writing, all
the verse, much of the drama, and nearly all the other prose writings are
known to us only in fragments or at second-hand;[9] of complete works we
have only twenty-one comedies by Plautus, six comedies by Terence, and
a handbook concerned with agricultural matters by Cato. Yet the total
volume of what survives, whether complete, in fragments, or by way of
comment, though only a small fraction of what once existed, is quite
considerable and constitutes an acceptable basis for studying the literary
and intellectual aspects of Roman cultural history in the period.

How far these sources contribute to our knowledge of social and
economic history is more debatable. On the one hand the fragments offer
little in their substance and frequently lack adequate context (many
survive as quotations only because they illustrate interesting points of
vocabulary or grammar). On the other hand Cato's agricultural handbook illuminates many aspects of the organization and practice of
agriculture, and also of economic and social attitudes, though it must
always be kept in mind that it is a work with limited purposes and
markedly particularist tendencies which leaves quite untouched many
more aspects of agriculture as well as of social and economic life.[10] The
value of the comedies in this respect, however, is the subject of perpetual
controversy. They are all known to be adaptations of Greek originals;
how much 'Romanization' has there been, then, in the portrayal of details
of everyday affairs, of life-styles, of economic transactions and resources,
and, above all, of social relationships? Some modification there certainly
was, if only in consequence of the use of the Latin vocabulary with its
own connotations, but whether the resulting picture is reliable remains
highly debatable. Indeed it may be asked how far it is realistic to expect
even a moderately faithful reflection of contemporary Roman life in

[9] Peter, *HRRel.* 1²: (B 27), and *ORF*⁴: (B 16) for fragments of historical works and speeches
respectively.   [10] White 1970 *passim*: (H 120); Astin 1978, chapters 9 and 11: (H 68).

comedy of the type presented by Plautus and Terence. The fact is that the greater part of the literary material for Roman social and economic history of the period is found in the historical works discussed in the first two sections of this chapter, or in anecdotes and incidental items in the main body of Latin literature from the Ciceronian age onwards; and this is supplemented by the non-literary evidence.

IV. NON-LITERARY EVIDENCE

The main categories of non-literary evidence available to the historian of the ancient world are documents written on papyrus, coins, inscriptions, and the enormous range of material remains, from great buildings to tiny domestic articles, which are recorded and studied by archaeologists. Papyrus documents, which survive almost exclusively in Egypt, are of relatively little importance for this volume and may be passed over here.[11] Similarly, not a great deal need be said here concerning the material evidence supplied by archaeology – though for very different reasons. By its nature it is found everywhere, exists in vast quantities, and varies enormously in kind, physical magnitude and state of preservation. It can illuminate numerous facets of history: economic conditions, means of production and cultivation, trade, social organization, urbanization, prosperity (or otherwise) reflected in the scale and type of public buildings, military methods as reflected in equipment and constructions, and even the working of political institutions as reflected in their physical setting. However, this type of evidence is not always as easy to interpret and apply as might be expected at first sight. Frequently there are problems of dating, of a sequence of building, of identification of context, of establishing the relationship between items from the one site or from adjacent or similar sites; accurate record-keeping is not easy and has not always been as assiduous or sustained as might be wished; and usually such evidence cannot supply its own historical setting but yields its full evidential value only when it can be related to contexts supplied from literary sources.

Coins, too, are found almost everywhere.[12] They were issued by all the major states of the Mediterranean world and by many of the minor ones; and they can yield a variety of information which is of interest to the historian, though to determine it with sufficient reliability often requires a great deal of specialized and complex study. They can play an important role in resolving problems of chronology. In many instances, a careful

[11] For discussion of papyrus as evidence in the Hellenistic period see *CAH*² VII.i.16–18 and 118–19.
[12] Coinage of the Roman Republic: Crawford, 1974: (B 88). Hellenistic coinage is poorly served in consolidated publications but there are numerous specialized studies of particular aspects: see the Bibliography, esp. section B(c).

examination of die-marks, mint-marks and stylistic features has enabled numismatists to determine the correct sequence of issues, and when these results are combined with the evidence of associated finds, whether of other coins in hoards or of other datable articles, at least approximate dates and sometimes quite precise dates can usually be determined. A minority of Hellenistic coins actually have a particular year indicated on them, by reference to a local era. Coins whose actual or approximate dates have been determined can then be used to fix *termini* for the dates of other objects found with or over them; or sometimes they yield even more direct information, such as the date of the death of a ruler or the length of his reign. The designs used on coins are often useful testimony to special concerns or ideals, whether political, religious or general ethos, of the issuing states, and in the case of an autocratic ruler the choice of symbols is often a guide to aspects of his policy or to the 'image' of himself that he wishes to promote among his subjects. All these aspects of coinage are particularly relevant to many events discussed in Chapters 10 and 11 below. The volume of a particular coinage, provenance, variations in the magnitude of issues, and changes in the production or even the structure of a coinage can all be reflections of important economic or political developments. Thus the radical restructuring of Roman coinage in the late third century is in great measure a response to the pressures and demands created by the Second Punic War. Nevertheless, numismatic evidence has to be used with considerable caution and is fraught with uncertainties and controversies. Interpretations which relate the results to a historical context often have substantial subjective and conjectural elements, and frequently the historical evidence is illuminating the numismatic at least as much as *vice versa*.

Lastly there are inscriptions, writing which was displayed on wood, stone or metal, though naturally most of those which survive are on stone or metal.[13] Metal, in the form of bronze sheets, was more often used in Italy than in the east, especially for the publication of formal state or city documents; which is one reason why comparatively few such documents survive in the west, whereas they are common in the Greek-speaking world. However, there was almost certainly a more fundamental difference in practice in this period, for we have only quite a small number of inscriptions of any kind from Rome and Italy until the late Republic, and it is under the Principate that they really proliferate. The contrast clearly represents something more than an incidental difference

---

[13] *CIL* I collects Latin inscriptions of the Republican period; *ILLRP* is the most important selection of these. New publications are listed in *L'Année épigraphique*. For Greek inscriptions *IG* and *IG*² include Europe only. *OGIS* is a basic collection of eastern inscriptions, but many Hellenistic documents are most accessible in collections for particular localities: see Bibliography, esp. section B(b).

in survival rate (often related to the extent and nature of re-use in more recent times) or in intensity of exploration, though these are certainly relevant to some of the differences in numbers of inscriptions we have from various towns and areas in the Hellenistic lands.

The numerous inscriptions surviving from the Hellenistic areas, though only a small part of what once existed, throw much light on both private and public affairs. There are many types. Some were erected by individuals – epitaphs, dedications, thank-offerings; others by public authorities, which usually means city authorities (even in the kingdoms) – dedications, public notices and regulations, decrees and resolutions (including those honouring distinguished persons), treaties, and in some cases even communications and instructions received from rulers. This last group, which began with letters from kings,[14] came in time to include also letters and edicts from Roman magistrates and decrees of the Roman Senate, with the paradoxical result that most of the surviving examples of documents of this kind from the period of the Republic are Greek translations.[15] These contribute substantially to the understanding of Roman attitudes and policies in the east, and also of Roman institutional procedures. The range of topics illustrated or illuminated by other inscriptions is extremely wide: technical points of chronology, city organization, royal interference, taxation, trade, prices, social ideals and values, relationships between cities, political allegiances, and policies of kings and dynasts – all from contemporary documentation undistorted by literary adaptation or by transmission at the hands of a succession of copyists.

Like every other class of evidence, inscriptions have their limitations and often require the application of special expertise. Many are not closely dated; lettering is often worn and difficult to read; and most are damaged with resulting loss of part of the text, sometimes a substantial part, not infrequently leaving many or most of the surviving lines of writing incomplete. Such problems are eased by the expert's familiarity with the language, conventions and style used in inscriptions, and with the stereotyped phraseology that constantly recurs and enables many gaps to be filled by 'restoration'; but the damage remains considerable, and in any case by far the greater part of the inscriptional documentation that once existed has been lost totally. Furthermore, almost all inscriptions, especially public inscriptions, are in a sense isolated documents. We hardly ever have other documents to fill out the particular chain of action or the detailed circumstances to which they belong, and if literary sources supply a context at all it is nearly always a broad context, lacking specific detail to which to relate the particular document and by which its

---

[14] Collected and studied by Welles 1934: (B 74).   [15] Sherk 1969: (B 73).

full significance might be identified. This is why it was said earlier in this chapter that the shafts of light cast by inscriptions are usually narrow but often intense. In that intensity, however, lies their particular value. They afford glimpses of detail which are scarcely ever provided by the literary sources and which often afford a closer insight into organization and into prevailing attitudes and motivation. Inscriptions figure extensively in several chapters of this volume and it will quickly be seen that their contribution is both important and distinctive.

CHAPTER 2

THE CARTHAGINIANS IN SPAIN[1]

H. H. SCULLARD

I. PUNIC SPAIN BEFORE THE BARCIDS

The story of the expanding and often conflicting interests of Phoenicians, Carthaginians, Greeks and Etruscans in the western Mediterranean has been told in earlier volumes. With the decline of Tyre the string
of trading posts, which the Phoenicians founded from Gades on the
Atlantic shore of Spain round to Malaca, Sexi and Abdera along the
south-west Mediterranean coast, gradually passed into Carthaginian
hands. The process was apparently peaceful, but to us is quite obscure in
detail. The Phoenician decline afforded greater freedom to the Spanish
kingdom of Tartessus in the middle and lower Baetis valley. This rich
realm which flourished in the seventh and sixth centuries B.C. derived its
wealth from its great mineral resources and its control of the tin trade-
route to Brittany and Cornwall. It traded with Phoenicians and
Carthaginians, and especially with the Greeks. The Phocaeans in particular had good relations with the Tartessian ruler Arganthonius, and
founded a colony at Maenake, but the shadow of Carthage over the west
gradually grew longer.

After the failure of Pentathlus of Cnidus to drive the Phoenicians
completely out of western Sicily, Carthage gradually took over from the

---

[1] The literary sources for early Punic expansion in Spain are extremely meagre. This is due in large
measure to the success of Carthage in excluding the Greeks from the southern parts of the peninsula,
which therefore remained largely unknown to their writers (only a tiny chink in the curtain is
provided by the Greek navigator Pytheas, whose *Periplus* is reflected in Avienus' *Ora Maritima*).
The archaeological material is also sparse and difficult to interpret: is it the result of sporadic trade, or
settlement, or domination? For the conquest by the Barcids (237–218 B.C.) we have Polybius' brief
accounts which are pro-Barcid (11.1.5–9, 13, 36, 111.8–15, 17, 20–1, 29–30, 33–5, 39), together with
some further details, mainly based on the later annalistic tradition, in Diodorus, Appian, Dio
Cassius, Zonaras, Livy, Valerius Maximus, Frontinus, Nepos, Justin, Orosius, Plutarch, Polyaenus
and Strabo. Polybius drew on the Greek writers who recorded the Hannibalic War; though he
contemptuously dismissed Chaereas and Sosylus as gossip-mongers, he probably relied largely on
Silenus, who like Sosylus had accompanied Hannibal on his campaigns. On the causes of the
Hannibalic War Polybius quoted and criticized Fabius Pictor whose view reflected the position of
the anti-Barcid faction at Carthage. Both Silenus and Fabius were probably used by Coelius
Antipater, on whom Livy and the annalistic tradition in part depended. The literary sources are
collected in Schulten 1935, III: (B 33).

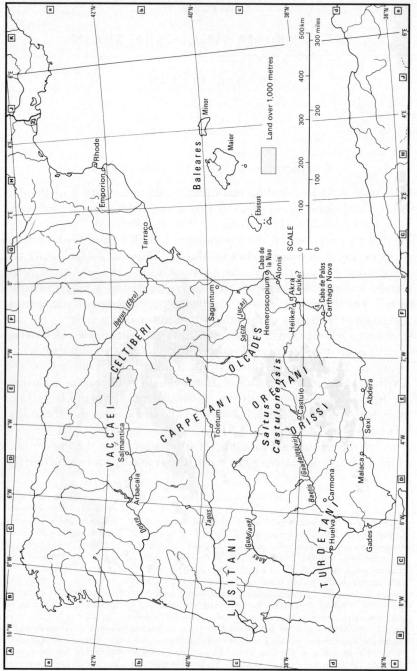

Map 1. Carthaginian Spain.

Phoenicians and became the champion of the Semitic settlements against the Greeks. Their Punic leader, Malchus, checked the Greeks in Sicily and then went to Sardinia, where Phoenician settlements existed at Caralis, Nora, Sulcis, and Tharros, while a strong hillfort was built *c*. 600 B.C. on Monte Serai a few miles inland from Sulcis. Malchus suffered a serious defeat at the hands of the native population; there is also evidence that the fort at Monte Serai was damaged. However, it was soon rebuilt and the Carthaginians established their control over the Phoenician settlements. But their penetration of the island was slow (though they succeeded in preventing any Greek colonization), and even by the early fourth century their grip was much weaker in the east than in the south and west. Sardinia was valuable as a source of minerals, agricultural products and manpower, and also as a staging-post on the way to Spain. An even nearer foothold was provided by the Balearic Islands: the Carthaginians sent a settlement in 654 to Ebusus (Ibiza), where they seem not to have been preceded by the Phoenicians.

A turning-point in Carthaginian relations with the Greeks was the battle of Alalia (*c*. 535), where with their Etruscan allies they smashed Phocaean sea-power: one result was that the Phocaeans together with other Greeks were barred from Tartessus and southern Spain, though they retained their influence along the coast of Catalonia and southern France. All this time Carthage was also extending her control in North Africa itself, until before the end of the fifth century it stretched from Cyrenaica to the Atlantic, although the stages of this advance unfortunately cannot be traced in detail. However, the terms of her first treaty with Rome in 509 demonstrate that before the end of the sixth century[2] she was able to close the Straits of Gibraltar to all foreign shipping and had established a commercial monopoly in the western Mediterranean.

In southern Spain the Carthaginians entered into the inheritance of Tartessus and the Phoenicians. They had apparently destroyed the centre of the Tartessians by the end of the sixth century, but how far they and the Phoenicians before them had penetrated into the Guadalquivir valley is uncertain. Finds on the coast at Toscanos and Almuñecar, with Phoenician settlements of the latter part of the eighth century and fresh settlers arriving early in the following century, reveal the importance of this area to Phoenicians and Carthaginians. From here their influence spread inland to the Guadalquivir valley, as finds (such as alabaster jars, splendid carved ivories, and Phoenician pottery) at Seville, Carmona and Osuna indicate, but it is uncertain how far this reflected an actual movement of population or merely penetration by traders; many of the burials in which these goods were found are native Spanish, but some

---

[2] For the date see *CAH*[2] VII.ii, ch. 8.

possibly are Phoenician.[3] Nor can we judge the extent of assimilation between native and intruder or the degree of the later Carthaginian political control, if any, in the Baetis valley. The Atlantic coast of Andalusia also received Phoenician goods and settlers. Whether Tartessus lay in the area of Gades (with which the ancient writers identified it) or further north at Huelva, there appears to have been no Phoenician settlement at Gades before the eighth century: its great days belong to its development by the Carthaginians in their exploitation of the Baetis valley and the Atlantic trade-routes. Two incidents have been related to the downfall of Tartessus.[4] Vitruvius (x.13), in discussing the invention of the battering-ram, records how it was used by the Carthaginians in capturing a fort near Gades: here perhaps Gades has been confused with Tartessus. Secondly, the difficult trade-route over the mountains from Maenake to Tartessus, mentioned by the Massiliote *Periplus* (Avienus, *Ora Maritima* 87), looks like an attempt to secure the continuance of trade when the Carthaginians had closed the easier sea-route through the straits. However, whatever resistance the Carthaginians encountered, they succeeded in destroying both Tartessus and Maenake so thoroughly that their names disappeared from history, to be succeeded by Gades and Malaca.

The development and exploitation of Carthaginian control in southern Spain for the next two centuries or so remain very obscure. Their tightening grip is indicated by their second treaty with Rome: whereas in the earlier agreement of 509 the Romans were forbidden to sail along the African coast west of the Fair Promontory, in the second they agreed not to plunder, trade or colonize beyond the Fair Promontory in Africa and Mastia (Cartagena) in Spain. Thus the Carthaginians claimed control of the southern coast of Spain as far north as Cabo de Palos; north of the Cape, however, Massilia in the fifth or fourth century was able to found two new colonies, Alonis and Akra Leuke (Alicante). Gades became the centre of Punic control in Spain and probably enjoyed some special privileges, such as Utica had in Africa. The Blastulo-Phoenician towns of Malaca, Sexi and Abdera (so-called after the neighbouring native Iberian tribe) also had some degree of freedom. The Iberian tribes of Andalusia probably enjoyed much the same conditions as they had under the 'rule' of Tartessus. What the Carthaginians wanted from them was their manpower: in all the great battles fought between the Carthaginians and the Greeks in Sicily in the fifth and fourth centuries Iberian mercenaries played a major part. So too they exploited the mineral wealth of Andalusia: gold, copper, iron and especially silver – later one mine alone at Baebelo provided Hannibal with 300 lb of silver a day. Natural products

[3] Cf. Whittaker 1974, 6off.: (C 65).
[4] See Schulten 1922, 44–5: (B 53); *CAH*[1] VII, 775; Schulten and Bosch Gimpera 1922, 87: (B 34), on lines 178–82 of the *Ora Maritima* of Avienus.

included corn, oil, wine, esparto grass and salt-fish. Their stranglehold on the straits allowed them to seek the tin of Brittany and the gold and ivory of West Africa, but occasionally they appear to have allowed controlled access beyond the Pillars of Heracles: at any rate the famous voyage of Pytheas (in the 320s B.C.) which started from Gades is not likely to have been launched without their permission. But in general for some two centuries Pindar's words (*Nem.* IV.69) were true: 'we may not go beyond Gadeira toward the darkness'. Thus the Greeks knew and recorded little about Punic Spain and so our ignorance also is great.

The Carthaginians maintained their command of the sea (until challenged by Rome), but they appear for a time to have lost their grip on southern Spain. If the fate of an empire can depend on a single preposition they will have lost all their influence, since Polybius (II.1.6) records that in 237 Hamilcar Barca 'set about recovering (ἀνεκτᾶτο) the Carthaginian possessions in Iberia'. The date and extent of this diminution of power cannot be determined. Perhaps Andalusia successfully asserted her independence during the First Punic War, but Gades seems to have remained in Punic hands, since when Hamilcar sailed there we hear of no resistance. The loss of the Spanish mines in particular was a severe blow and is reflected in the debased quality of the silver coins that Carthage issued during her first war with Rome. But it may be that often too strong a contrast is drawn, and that in the earlier centuries southern Spain should not be regarded as part of a Carthaginian empire, still less as an *epikrateia* in the sense of a province, but rather as a sphere of influence or a protectorate, while the word 'empire' is first really applicable only to the military conquest by the Barcids.

II. HAMILCAR AND HASDRUBAL

When the First Punic War ended Hamilcar Barca remained undefeated in Sicily and was then given full powers by the Carthaginian government to negotiate a peace settlement with Rome. During the subsequent war against the rebellious mercenaries in Africa he won the confidence of the army and overshadowed his political rival, Hanno the Great, although the latter had a share in the final success. According to the annalistic tradition they then conducted a joint campaign against the Numidians, but Hamilcar's political intrigues led to a threat of impeachment which he averted by leading his army to Spain without the authority of Carthage. This alleged charge against Hamilcar, which is not recorded by Polybius, should be rejected as part pf the anti-Barcid tradition.[5] The

---

[5] See Appian, *Hisp.* 4–5. 13–18, *Hann.* 2.3–4; Diod. Sic. xxv.8; Nepos, *Ham.* 2.5. This account of Hamilcar's activities is regarded by De Sanctis 1907–64, III.i. 338 n. 16: (A 14), as a reduplication of a temporary overshadowing of Hamilcar immediately after the end of the First Punic War. Cf. Walbank 1957–69, I.151: (B 38).

development of Hamilcar's political rivalry with Hanno cannot be traced in detail, but he had the support of Hasdrubal, a popular leader and his own son-in-law, and as the Barca family seems to have been 'new men', some personal and political clashes were probable. Hanno and his supporters may well have wished to limit Carthaginian expansion to Africa, but the idea that Hamilcar went to Spain against the wishes of the Carthaginian government must be rejected. The loss of Sicily and Sardinia had weakened the economic life of the city; fresh sources of minerals and manpower must be sought, and where better than in Spain where they abounded? Such a move would not be likely to antagonize Rome since Spain was far from her sphere of interest. No doubt Hamilcar's personality was the driving force that secured the adoption of this policy, but it was certainly not carried against the wishes of a majority of his fellow-citizens, and any opposition that existed would soon be weakened when money and booty began to pour in from the peninsula.

Equally suspect is the tradition that Hamilcar deliberately planned to build up Punic power in Spain as the first step towards a war of revenge against Rome. True, this view is advanced by Polybius (III.9.6–10.7), who finds the three αἰτίαι of the Hannibalic War in the wrath of Hamilcar, the Roman seizure of Sardinia, and the success of the Carthaginians in Spain.[6] The belief that Hamilcar decided to use Spain as a base of operations against Rome (rather than merely as a means of compensating for recent Carthaginian losses) gains some support in the story that before setting out for Spain Hamilcar, after sacrificing to Zeus (Baal), asked his nine-year-old son Hannibal whether he wanted to go on this expedition with him, and when the boy eagerly agreed he bade him take an oath at the altar that he would never be the friend of Rome (μηδέποτε Ῥωμαίοις εὐνοήσειν). The story was later told by Hannibal himself to Antiochus III of Syria, and (by whatever channels it ultimately reached Polybius) there is no good ground to reject it. Rather, its negative form should be noted: 'not to be well disposed to' is very

[6] According to Fabius Pictor (Polyb. III.8), the causes of the Hannibalic War were the attack on Saguntum by Hannibal and the ambition of Hasdrubal (Hamilcar's son-in-law) which led him to govern Spain independently of the Carthaginian government, as did Hannibal later; thus Fabius blames not Hamilcar but his successor Hasdrubal (for his love of power) and Hannibal (for his attack on Saguntum). This anti-Barcid Fabian view may derive from the attempted self-justification of those Carthaginians who, after the war had been lost, tried to blame Hannibal and Hasdrubal for having caused it (and it would gain favour when in 195 the anti-Barcid party were plotting to exile Hannibal). Polybius rejects Fabius' view (including his suggestion of Hannibal's independence of Carthage) and pushes the causes of the war further back to the time of Hamilcar. He also (III.6.1ff.) records that 'some authors who have dealt with Hannibal's activities' (probably the second-century senatorial historians at Rome) alleged that the causes of the war were Hannibal's attack on Saguntum and his crossing the Ebro; but Polybius regarded these episodes as merely the beginnings (ἀρχαί), not the causes (αἰτίαι) of the war.

different from the oath of eternal enmity which the later tradition records (e.g. ἄσπειστος ἐχθρός or *hostis*).[7] Whatever Polybius may have thought, an attempt to re-establish Punic influence in the western Mediterranean was not necessarily the same as planning a war of revenge against Rome, a view for which Hamilcar's subsequent conduct in Spain supplies little evidence.

To whatever extent Punic power in southern Spain had been lost, the Carthaginians decided to regain, consolidate and extend it. Gades was still in their hands and thither Hamilcar Barca sailed in 237, taking young Hannibal and his son-in-law Hasdrubal with him. In the course of the next nine years (until 229) he proceeded to conquer or reconquer southern and south-eastern Spain, but Polybius gives little detail of his campaigns: 'he reduced many Iberian tribes by war or diplomacy to obedience to Carthage [not, be it noted, to himself] and died in a manner worthy of his great achievements' (II.1.6–8). Diodorus (xxv.10.1–4) adds more: Hamilcar defeated the Iberians, Tartessians and some Celts and incorporated 3,000 survivors into his own army; he then routed an army of 50,000 men, tortured the captured commander but released 10,000 prisoners. He founded a large city which he called Akra Leuke from its situation. While besieging Helike he sent most of his army and his elephants to winter in Akra Leuke, but was tricked by a false offer of friendship by the king of the Orissi who had come to help the besieged. He was routed, but in his flight he saved the lives of his sons, Hannibal and Hasdrubal: he diverted the pursuit by plunging on horseback into a large river where he perished. Akra Leuke is usually located at modern Alicante, and Helike at modern Elche (ancient Ilici). This identification has, however, been questioned on the ground that Hamilcar would hardly have founded Akra Leuke at Alicante which is only some 12 km north-east of Elche while the latter was still unconquered, nor would he have leap-frogged past Cartagena which was a much stronger position than Alicante (although it should be noted that we do not know whether he was seeking the best possible harbour or a reasonably good site as far north as possible). Further, the Orissi lived in the area of Castulo on the upper Baetis. Thus, it has been argued, Akra Leuke should be placed in this mining area in the interior. If this view is accepted, it would mean that Hamilcar had not advanced further north along the coast than the old Punic 'frontier' at Cartagena, which had been mentioned in the second treaty with Rome in 348 (Polyb. III.24.4). The question must

---

[7] Appian, *Hisp.* 9.34; Livy XXI.1.4. Errington 1970, 26ff.: (C 15), in rejecting 'the wrath of the Barcids' as a cause of the Hannibalic War, argues that this view was part of an oral tradition (it was not in Fabius or Silenus) which circulated in Rome about the time of Polybius. He is inclined to accept the basic fact of Hannibal's oath (unless the story was invented by Hannibal himself in order to persuade Antiochus of his genuine hostility to Rome), but agrees with those who believe that in any case it is evidence only for Hannibal's hatred of Rome and not for Hamilcar's intentions in Spain.

remain open unless fairly secure sites can be established for Akra Leuke and Helike in the Castulo area.[8]

The Romans took little interest in these events in Spain until, according to one writer alone (Dio Cassius XII.fr.48; a damaged text), in 231 they sent ambassadors to investigate. Hamilcar received them courteously and neatly explained that he was fighting the Iberians to get money to pay off the remainder of his country's war-debt to Rome; the Romans were left somewhat nonplussed. This episode should not be dismissed on the ground that, because the Carthaginians had agreed in 241 to pay their indemnity in ten years, their obligations were completed in 231, since we do not know how the extra indemnity imposed in 237 after the cession of Sardinia was to be paid: ten annual instalments seem more probable than a lump sum. How the story reached Dio is uncertain: it was not in Polybius (and therefore presumably not in Fabius), but it could derive from Silenus via Coelius; indeed, since it involved a rebuff to Rome it is more likely to have been recorded by Silenus than by Fabius. But whether true or false, it should not be used to suggest any keen Roman interest in Spain at this date, since Dio expressly states the contrary: μηδὲν μηδέπω τῶν Ἰβηρικῶν σφισι προσηκόντων.[9] If true, however, it points to Massilian rather than any Roman concern. Massilia had long been a friend of Rome, at least from early in the fourth century; later this friendship was sealed in a formal alliance, probably between the First and Second Punic Wars, possibly earlier but certainly before 218. Now Massilia had commercial links with the Spanish tribes, especially through her trading colonies in Emporion, Alonis (near Benidorm), Rhode and Hemeroscopium (near Denia), the last of which, originally a Phocaean settlement, was some fifty miles north of Alicante; she would not welcome the prospect of Carthaginian expansion northwards. Rome's interest in Massilia was not commercial (indeed it was Rome's lack of overseas trading interests that made her so acceptable a friend to Massilia), but rather as a source of information about the Gauls whose threatening movements were giving Rome increasing anxiety from 237 onwards. Conflicts with the Ligurians and a thrust by the Boii against Ariminum (236), not to mention troubles in Sardinia and Corsica, forced Rome to consider the defences of her northern frontier. Massilia was in

[8] For the rejection of the identification of Akra Leuke with Alicante: Sumner 1967, 208ff.: (C 56), who tentatively suggests Urgao (quae Alba cognominatur: Plin. HN III.10) between Cordoba and Castulo, and for Ilici he suggests I(n)lucia in Oretanis (Livy XXXV.7.7). These seem possible, but what then was the ancient name of Alicante?

[9] It has been accepted by the majority of modern scholars, but rejected by Holleaux 1921, 123: (D 33), and recently by Errington 1970, 32ff.: (C 15), though not by Sumner 1967, 205ff.: (C 56). Badian 1958, 48: (A 3), and Hoffmann 1951, 69ff.: (C 25), are agnostic. Two differing views of Roman policy towards Spain are given by Errington, who believes that 'it was directed by nothing more potent than apathy' (p. 26), and Sumner, who thinks that it was 'entirely concerned with the curbing of Carthaginian expansion' though Roman interest in Spain was 'not strong or sustained' (p. 245).

an excellent position to provide Rome with news of current movements and would be glad if Rome cleared the Tyrrhenian Sea of pirates. She may well therefore have drawn her friend's attention to the activities of their potential common enemy in southern Spain in 231, as she almost certainly did in 226. If so, Rome could scarcely refuse the token gesture of sending an embassy to Hamilcar. Spain may have lain far beyond the practical limits of Rome's political horizon and Carthage was weak, but some Roman senators at least may have thought it prudent to keep a weather-eye open, even though the stories that Carthage was trying to stir up trouble for Rome in Sardinia are almost certainly later annalistic inventions.[10]

Hamilcar had laid a solid base for a Carthaginian empire in Spain. His personal position, as a colonial governor, accepted by the home-government, was vice-regal. His increasing success is emphasized by the coinage which he minted at Gades. At first he could issue only debased billon coins and some bronze, but before long he had acquired sufficient wealth by mining and plunder to enable him to issue a coinage of fine silver, together with some gold and bronze; these mostly copied normal Carthaginian types, though the gold boldly displays a head of Greek Victory, while the execution of the bronze varies between very good and crude. It was reserved for his son Hannibal to place the father's portrait in the guise of Heracles-Melkart on the magnificent silver issued later at New Carthage.[11]

At some point the Iberian city of Saguntum made an alliance with Rome, doubtless not without some Massilian prompting or co-operation. Some of those scholars who accept the Roman embassy to Hamilcar in 231 also place this new concordat in this year.[12] The precise date is of less importance than whether it fell before or after the 'Ebro treaty' of 226, since this inter-relationship vitally affects the whole tradition regarding the causes of and responsibility for the Second Punic War. A *terminus ante quem* of 220 is implied by Polybius III.14.10; in another passage (III.30.1), he is unfortunately vague and merely places the alliance 'several years before Hannibal's time' ($\pi\lambda\epsilon\acute{\iota}o\sigma\iota\nu$ $\check{\epsilon}\tau\epsilon\sigma\iota\nu$ $\check{\eta}\delta\eta$

[10] Zon. VII.18; Eutropius II.2.2; Orosius IV.12.2 (*Sardinia insula rebellavit, auctoribus Poenis*). This tradition is rejected by Meyer 1924, II.385–6 and 387 n. 2: (C 37). Nor should the closing and speedy re-opening of the temple of Janus (traditionally in 235) be connected with a renewed Roman fear of Punic intrigues, as is argued by Norden 1915, 53ff.: (B 24). He probably rightly applies Ennius' lines '*postquam Discordia taetra Belli ferratos postes portasque refregit*' to this event, but it does not follow that Ennius saw a Carthaginian threat arising as early as 235. In any case the Janus incident, through a confusion between T. Manlius Torquatus (*cos.* 235) and A. Manlius (*cos.* 241), may belong rather to 241 and apply to the end of the First Punic War and the revolt of Falerii. See further: Meyer 1924, II.389: (C 37); Fraenkel 1945, 12ff.: (H 179); Timpanaro 1948, 5ff.: (B 37); Latte 1960, 132 n. 3: (H 205).

[11] See Robinson 1956, 34ff.: (B 130) and n. 37 below.

[12] E.g. Taubler 1921, 44: (C 58); Schnabel 1920, 111: (C 52); Otto 1932, 498: (C 40); Oertel 1932, 221ff.: (C 39); Gelzer 1933, 156: (H 45).

πρότερον τῶν κατ' Ἀννίβαν καιρῶν), which could mean either before Hannibal became commander in 221, or before he had dealings with Saguntum, or before the Hannibalic War. But the exact meaning of this phrase is of little importance, since Polybius is clearly saying 'some time before 221–219'. The crucial problem is whether πλείοσιν ἔτεσι refers to a time before or after 226, the year of the Ebro treaty. Since Rome was involved with a Gallic invasion in 225/4 and is unlikely to have concerned herself with Spanish affairs then, the Saguntine alliance probably fell in or before 226 or else in 223/2. In favour of a date after 226 is Polybius' remark (ΙΙ.13.3) that the Romans took an interest in Spain only after the treaty.[13] On the other hand Polybius as we shall see, refers to later Roman intervention in Saguntum as a short time (μικροῖς χρόνοις) before 220/19. In view of the contrast between μικροῖς and πλείοσι it seems difficult to refer the latter to a period as recent as 223/2 for the Saguntine alliance, though some scholars accept this:[14] a date earlier than 226 may seem preferable.

However, not only the date but also the nature of this agreement with Saguntum is controversial. For long it was regarded as a full formal treaty, a *foedus*, but this makes it difficult to understand Rome's later delay in going to Saguntum's aid during its protracted siege by Hannibal in 219: could Rome have neglected her formal legal obligations for so long? All that Polybius actually says (ΙΙΙ.30.1) is that the Saguntines had placed themselves in the *pistis* (= *fides*) of the Romans, as proof of which he advances the fact that at the time of an internal dispute they sought the arbitration of Rome and not of Carthage. A *deditio in fidem* imposed no legal obligations on Rome and left her free to decide how to react to any future requests for help. Thus earlier during the Mercenary War Utica, in rebellion against Carthage, had asked for Rome's help, though in vain. When Saguntum appealed, Rome may well have thought it was wise to have a foothold in Spain which committed her to nothing beyond her own wishes, and if the initiative came from Saguntum, it is easier to explain Rome's otherwise somewhat strange commitment. Indeed it has

[13] Heichelheim 1954, 211ff.: (C 24), argued for a later date on the supposition that the Saguntine coinage was influenced by the Roman victoriate and by Massiliote types which were later than 226. But this argument is weakened now that the issue of victoriates has been shown to start only c. 211 rather than soon after 229: see Crawford 1974, 7ff., 22ff., 28ff.: (B 88). Thus the Saguntine silver may also date only from the period of the Roman recovery of the city in 212. However, the assumption of the priority of the victoriate may be wrong and it may even be of Spanish origin and based on the early Saguntine silver: cf. Hill 1931, 120 (B 96); Crawford considers (p. 33) that one early victoriate (his no. 96) was issued by Cn. or P. Scipio in Spain before 211. Further, the remarkable Saguntine coin (Hill, pl. 21, no. 12), bearing a head of Heracles, is obviously influenced by the Barcid silver; it would seem therefore to belong to the period of Punic occupation (219–212), and it is significant that its weight corresponds to that of the victoriate standard (3.41 g; cf. Hill, p. 121). Jenkins, however, would date it in the early to mid second century (*SNG Copenhagen: Spain and Gaul* (1979), nos. 251–5), but why should the Saguntines have revived a Barcid type then?

[14] E.g. Reid 1913: (C 45); Badian 1958, 48ff., 92–3: (A 3).

even been argued that the Saguntines came into Roman *fides* in some less formal way than by a strict *deditio*. In any case, if there was no *foedus*, Rome incurred moral, but no legal, obligations. Provided that the word σύμμαχοι, which Polybius applies to the Saguntines, does not necessarily presuppose a *foedus*, then a *deditio* is likely.[15]

Hamilcar was succeeded in the governorship (στρατηγία) of Spain by his son-in-law and admiral, Hasdrubal, who was first chosen by the troops and afterwards received confirmation of his appointment from the people of Carthage (Diod. Sic. xxv.12). Fabius Pictor (Polyb. III.8.2) believed that Hasdrubal's love of power was one of the causes of the Hannibalic War and records that after he had acquired great δυναστεία in Spain he crossed to Carthage and tried to overthrow the constitution and establish a monarchy, but the leading politicians united to force his return to Spain, where he then governed without any regard to the Senate at Carthage. This attempted *coup* will fall soon after Hasdrubal's appointment to Spain in 226 if δυναστεία means his command (*imperium*) as it probably does, or else later in his governorship if the word means 'a great empire'. But the story is doubtful and could have arisen from the fact that on one occasion after 237 Hasdrubal had already been sent back to Carthage to crush a Numidian uprising.[16] However, if Hasdrubal's monarchic attempt be questioned, the story may reflect something of the political and constitutional tensions that had been emerging during the Mercenary War when the election to a supreme military command had already been left to the army. In the famous chapter (VI.51) in which Polybius compares the constitutions of Rome and Carthage, he observes that just before the outbreak of the Hannibalic War, the Carthaginian constitution was weakening because the function of deliberation was shifting from the Council to the people.[17] The nature of these political reforms and popular movements escapes us, but they may reflect the power of the Barcid faction. The anti-Barcid tradition has clearly exaggerated the ambitions of this group in depicting their leaders in Spain as completely independent rulers, and it may be in this hostile context that Hasdrubal's alleged *coup* should be placed.

On assuming his command in Spain Hasdrubal first avenged

[15] No *foedus*: Reid 1913, 179ff.: (c 45); Badian 1958, 49ff., 293: (a 3); Errington 1970, 41ff.: (c 15). *Deditio*: Dorey 1959, 2–3, 6–7: (c 13). No formal *deditio*: Astin 1967, 589ff.: (c 2). Polybius (1.40.1) does apply σύμμαχοι to the people of Panormus, though it was a *civitas libera* (Badian 1958, 293: (a 3)), but in a general military rather than a legal context, while he applies the word to Saguntum (III.15.8, 21.5) in a context of legal obligation. Polybius of course may not have fully understood the position. But *non liquet*.

[16] Diod. Sic. xxv.10.3. So De Sanctis 1907–64, III.i. 409 n. 55: (a 14). But Taubler 1921, 71: (c 58), accepts both episodes and thinks the account told by Polybius (Fabius) represents an attempt by Hasdrubal to seize the στρατηγία of Africa which Hamilcar had held during the Mercenary War.

[17] Polyb. VI.51.6. See Poechl 1936, 61ff.: (H 19); cf. Brink and Walbank 1954, 117–18: (b 2), and Walbank 1957–79, I.734: (b 38).

Hamilcar's death by a punitive expedition against the Orissi which took him to the upper Guadiana. The extension of his control enabled him ultimately, it is said (Diod. Sic. xxv.12), to increase his forces to 60,000 infantry, 8,000 cavalry and 200 elephants, but he also strengthened his position by diplomacy. He married an Iberian princess, established good personal relations with many of the chiefs, and moved his headquarters from Akra Leuke to Mastia, where he founded Carthago Nova (Cartagena) on a peninsula which commanded a fine harbour; here his communications with Africa were easy and there were rich silver mines close by. In the new city on a hill (Monte Molinete), commanding the entrance to a lagoon, he built himself a fine palace and his power was certainly vice-regal. It is possible that, like a Hellenistic monarch, he even issued silver coins with a diademed portrait of himself and on the reverse a Punic warship. If so, he was the first of the Punic commanders in Spain to make so bold a proclamation, but the coins may well have been issued later by Hannibal's brother, Mago, and thus it would be safer not to use them as evidence for Hasdrubal's regal pretensions.[18] However, he certainly consolidated and extended the Carthaginian hold over Spain, before he was killed in 221 by a Celt who had a personal grudge (or else by an Iberian slave who was avenging his own master).[19] He had probably not reached as far north as the Ebro, but this river became the central point of negotiations which he carried out with the Romans at their request.

Late in 226 the Romans 'sent envoys to Hasdrubal and made a treaty (συνθήκας) in which no mention was made of the rest of Spain, but the Carthaginians engaged not to cross the Ebro in arms (ἐπὶ πολέμῳ)'. Such is Polybius' meagre statement (III.13.7) about an episode which has provoked much discussion both in antiquity and among modern scholars. It will be best to consider Polybius' view first, unencumbered by the allegations of later writers, since their accounts are often confused by propaganda and misunderstanding arising from recriminations about the dispute over Saguntum and the causes of the Hannibalic War.[20]

---

[18] This rare issue is attributed by Robinson 1956, 37–8: (B 130), to Hasdrubal and a mint at New Carthage, but the distribution of the finds (two from Seville and one each from Malaga, Granada and Ibiza, with none from the three large hoards of Barcid coins discovered near Cartagena) suggests the likelihood of a mint at Gades and the attribution to Mago, who later campaigned in this area (at Ilipa and the Balearic Islands). True, Hasdrubal had been trierarch to Hamilcar, but perhaps he would not wish to express his earlier subordinate position. Mago too was involved in naval operations.

[19] Celt: Polyb. II.36.1. Iberian: Diod. Sic. xxv.12 and Livy xxI.2.6, etc.

[20] It is not possible here to refer to all the minor distortions and variations given in the 'apologetic' Roman annalistic tradition. Only the main differences from the better tradition will be mentioned. The historical fact of the treaty is accepted here despite the doubts expressed by Cuff 1973, 163ff.: (c 10), who is inclined to dismiss it as a fabrication of Roman propaganda, whose purpose will have depended on its date, ranging from 220 to provide a formal ground for hostilities or a deterrent to aggression, to second-century Catonian propaganda.

First, the nature of the contract. It was clearly negotiated between Hasdrubal and a senatorial commission, but was it accepted by the Carthaginian and Roman states? In later arguments the Carthaginians refused to discuss it, denying either its existence or their ratification of it (Polyb. III.21.1); the Romans in reply brushed aside the question of ratification but bluntly underlined the fact that Hasdrubal had made the treaty (ὁμολογίας) with full authority (αὐτοτελῶς: III.29.3). If the Carthaginians had granted Hasdrubal such authority, they may have done so for convenience and in good faith, but it was in fact a useful device by which they could later repudiate any such agreement (a trick which the Romans themselves often used later in Spain when the Senate repudiated agreements made by Roman generals, such as Hostilius Mancinus, with Spanish tribes). The instrument may from the Carthaginian side have been a 'covenanted' form of oath (*berit*), a unilateral pledge, given with or without conditions. The form of such an understanding is revealed in the contract between Hannibal and Philip V in 215, and differs from the earlier treaties between Rome and Carthage which were bilateral agreements confirmed by the oaths of both parties. E. J. Bickerman, who made this suggestion,[21] recalls how Laban set up a pillar to delimit his and Jacob's boundaries; neither should pass over the mark 'for harm' and Jacob swore by the Pachad of his father Isaac (Genesis 31.53). If this view is accepted, Hasdrubal's agreement did not bind the Carthaginian government, but the Romans may well not have understood this practice. Since they themselves later insisted on regarding it as a valid treaty, it must presumably have been ratified in Rome, though the procedure can only be surmised. If it contained no corresponding commitment on the part of Rome, there was nothing for the Roman people to swear to, and it may have been transmitted to Rome in the form of a statement by Hasdrubal concerning the negotiations and his undertaking. The Roman commissioners presumably reported to the Senate in writing or in person. Since the Senate regarded it as a binding treaty, they may have ordered a copy (in bronze?) of Hasdrubal's letter to be lodged in the Roman Record Office for keeping with the copies of the earlier treaties with Carthage. Thus some reliable information was presumably available to Polybius when he investigated all the treaties between the two states, and his factual statement of its content must be accepted even if his interpretation may be questioned.[22]

Polybius' bare statement of the content, however, affords room for much speculation. Has he given the complete text or only the part which he considered relevant to his argument? Was there some *quid pro quo*, either formal or informal, such as a reciprocal clause which limited

[21] Bickerman 1952, 1ff. and esp. 17ff.: (c 5).
[22] Cf. Errington 1970, 34ff.: (c 15), and for the lodging of treaties Scullard, *CAH*² VII.ii.

Roman activity south of the river (as recorded by Livy xxi.2 and Appian, *Hisp.* 7.27, though in *Hann.* 2.6 and *Lib.* 6.23 Appian follows Polybius in giving only Hasdrubal's obligation)?[23] Even if the undertaking was given unilaterally by Hasdrubal, was it granted only conditionally? If there was no formal reference to Spain south of the river in the agreement, may not the Romans have unofficially assured Hasdrubal by a gentleman's agreement that they had no interest south of the river and would not interfere there? And when the Carthaginians agreed not to cross the Ebro in arms, was the ban purely military, with the implication that they could cross for peaceful purposes into an area where Massilia had active commercial interests? Such questions make it difficult to see why both parties agreed to this rather strange arrangement. If Hasdrubal had no actively hostile intentions against Rome and if his conquests were still well to the south of the river, he presumably felt that a recognition by Rome of a Carthaginian empire which might reach to the Ebro was a satisfactory settlement, particularly if in fact he had no intention of trying to incorporate the area between the Ebro and the Pyrenees.

Polybius' explanation of Rome's attitude seems to combine truth and error. He says (II.13.3–6) that the Romans suddenly woke up to Hasdrubal's increasing power, but were at the moment unwilling to challenge this because of the threat of a Gallic invasion of Italy; they therefore decided to conciliate him while they dealt with the menace to their northern frontier. The falsity of this explanation is the implication that Hasdrubal was becoming a threat to Rome: this is part of the propaganda story of 'the wrath of the Barcids', and there is no evidence that he was plotting with the Gauls. On the other hand the Romans were facing a crisis which culminated in the Gallic invasion of Italy and its repulse at Telamon in 225. At such a time the Romans might be thought not to want to bother about Hasdrubal unless they had any reason to regard him as an urgent threat. But there was another interested party, namely Massilia, who, if the Roman embassy of 231 is accepted, had already jogged Rome's elbow about events in Spain. In 226 the position was more urgent for both Massilia and Rome. Massilia had more to fear in Spain, where Hasdrubal was consolidating a powerful empire on the foundations laid by Hamilcar, and Rome, faced by a more serious menace from the Gauls, could not afford to offend Massilia. Thus, although no

---

[23] Heichelheim 1954, 217ff. (C 24), accepts the clause in App. *Hisp.* 7.27 that bound the Romans not to attack the tribes south of the river (μήτε Ῥωμαίους τοῖς πέραν τοῦδε τοῦ ποταμοῦ πόλεμον ἐκφέρειν) because he detects a Semitism in this phrase which derived, he believes, from the original Punic text. Badian 1980, 164: (C 3), accepts Polybius' denial that any concessions made by the Romans were connected with Spain: rather they might concern trading concessions or remission of the indemnity.

ancient source specifically says so, it was almost certainly Massilian pressure on Rome that led her to send the embassy in 226.

The choice of, and agreement upon, the Ebro as a limit for Hasdrubal has also caused surprise. Why was a river so far north chosen, when the Massiliotes obviously would want to keep him as far south as possible and to maintain control over as many of their coastal colonies as they could? Some scholars have been so puzzled by this point that they have supposed that the Hiberus of the treaty was not the Ebro but another river of the same name further south, but the attempt to substitute the Jucar (of which the usual ancient name was Sucro) can be considered to have failed, while the hunt for a Hiberus among the streams around Cabo de la Nao is very speculative.[24] It must be supposed that the Ebro was agreed as the result of some hard bargaining and a compromise. If the Romans really did not consider Hasdrubal a potential menace to themselves, they might have been content to agree to the Pyrenees as a line of demarcation, though in the interest of general security they would no doubt like to keep him at arm's length. But on behalf of their Massiliote friends they had to press for a line as far south as possible. If Hasdrubal insisted on the Ebro, they had at least won security for Massilia's most northerly colonies at Emporion (Ampurias) and Rhode (Rosas). An unknown factor is how far northwards Hamilcar's power did in fact stretch. It is generally assumed to have been confined to the south of say Cabo de la Nao; if so, Hasdrubal won a considerable concession by receiving implicit agreement to his expansion to the Ebro. On the other hand he may well have already been probing north of Alicante in sufficient strength to suggest a growing interest in this wider area, which included Saguntum. This city cannot have been mentioned in the treaty in the light of Polybius' explicit statement that southern Spain was not referred to. Naturally if Rome had not at this time accepted the friendship of Saguntum, no specific reference would be relevant, whereas if the friendship had been formed before the Ebro treaty, Saguntum's position must have been passed over in tactful silence in the agreement itself whatever may have been said unofficially in the preceding discussion. The status of the city became a burning issue only when it was threatened by Hannibal: it was then soon enveloped by a confusing cloud of propaganda which has distorted the later tradition by asserting either that it *was* included in the Ebro treaty or else that the city lay north of the river, beyond the limit set in the treaty.

[24] Jucar: Carcopino 1953: (C 7) and 1961, 18ff.: (A 11). Rejected by Walbank 1957–79, I.171: (B 38) and *id. JRS* 51 (1961) 228–9; Cassola 1962, 250: (H 35), and Sumner 1967, 222ff.: (C 56). Sumner, however, though rejecting Carcopino, has sought a Hiberus in the vicinity of Cabo de la Nao (1967, 228ff.).

III. HANNIBAL AND SAGUNTUM

On the death of Hasdrubal in 221 the army in Spain enthusiastically conferred the command on Hannibal, now aged twenty-five, and this appointment was quickly confirmed by the Carthaginian government by a unanimous vote (μιᾷ γνώμῃ): Polybius thus emphasizes (III.13.4), against the view of Fabius Pictor, the support that Hannibal received in Carthage. But Hannibal, who had enjoyed Hasdrubal's confidence in Spain, reverted to the more warlike policy of his father, although he followed Hasdrubal's example of marrying a Spaniard, a princess from Castulo. There is no good reason to suppose that Hannibal was at this moment determined on war with Rome: he was following Hamilcar's policy of empire-building in Spain itself. He at once launched an attack on the Olcades who lived around the upper Guadiana (Anas) and captured their chief city, Althaea.[25] After wintering in New Carthage he turned in 220 against the highland tribes of the central plateau and advanced northwards over the Sierra Morena on a line later taken by the Roman road via Emerita (Merida) to Salmantica (Salamanca). He defeated the Vaccaei, captured Salamanca and reached the Douro, where he successfully besieged Arbacala (modern Toro).[26] Plutarch tells how after the surrender of Salamanca on the terms that all the free population should leave, wearing only one garment apiece, the women managed to smuggle out some arms and then pass them to their menfolk, who succeeded in fighting their way to freedom. However, though they were ultimately rounded up, Hannibal, impressed by the courage of the women, restored the town to the inhabitants. From this northerly point he then turned south, taking a more easterly route than on his approach, through the territory of the Carpetani and neighbouring tribes who faced him in battle at the Tagus near Toledo. Soon after he had crossed the river he found the enemy were close behind him, so he doubled back northwards and faced his opponents as they tried to get across. His cavalry caught some of the Spaniards in the river itself, while his forty

---

[25] So Polyb. III.13.5; Livy (XXI.5.4) names the town Cartala. Both historians derive their accounts of Hannibal's Spanish campaigns from a common source, probably Silenus who accompanied Hannibal, though Livy used an intermediary, probably Coelius Antipater. In opposition to the usual location of Althaea, Gómez 1951, 12ff.: (C 19), places it at Aldaya some 22 km north of Valencia and 25 km from the coast.

[26] Polybius (III.14.1) gives Ἑλμαντική and Ἀρβουκάλη; Livy (XXI.5.6) gives Hermandica and Arbocala. Plutarch (Mor. 248E = Polyaenus VII.48) gives a fuller account of the capture of Σαλματική, which he derived perhaps from Hannibal's other companion chronicler, Sosylus, since the form of the name differs from that in Polybius (= Silenus?). Clearly Salamanca is meant. Gómez 1951, 35ff.: (C 19), however, removes Hannibal's campaigns from central Spain and believes that he was conquering the area behind Saguntum. He places Elmantica and Arbacala near Chelva, which lies some 60 km west of Valencia, and the battle of the Tagus (= the Valencian Tajo) a little further east.

elephants patrolled the bank and trampled to death the others as they endeavoured to struggle out. He then re-crossed the river himself and routed the whole surviving force, whether or not they numbered the 100,000 attributed to them.[27] Central Spain was thus conquered and although the loyalty of the Vaccaei and Carpetani was guaranteed mainly by the hostages that Hannibal held, and though the Celtiberians of the upper Tagus and Douro and the Lusitanians were still unvanquished, nevertheless Hannibal and his predecessors had won a vast empire from which they could draw immense supplies of manpower and mineral wealth.

Hannibal's next move was not to plan an attack upon Italy, but to expand his empire up to the Ebro, as the Romans had allowed Hasdrubal to contemplate. But there was one overriding difficulty: Saguntum, where a clash of Punic and Roman interests had flared up. It was an Iberian city of the Arsetani, as the Iberian character of its coinage shows, though the Romans might believe that its name indicated that it was a colony of Greek Zacynthos. However, it shared one weakness of Greek cities: it suffered from *stasis* in a clash of policy between pro-Roman and pro-Punic factions. An episode led to the need for external arbitration and, though the Carthaginians were close at hand, the pro-Roman party naturally turned to their Roman allies. A settlement followed in which 'some of the leading men' (that is, leaders of the pro-Punic faction) were put to death. Polybius gives no details of the cause of this episode beyond attributing to Hannibal, in a subsequent report which he sent to Carthage, the complaint that the Saguntines (i.e. of course the pro-Roman faction), relying on their Roman alliance, were wronging some of the peoples subject to Carthage (Polyb. III.15.8). For more detail we have to rely on later authors. Appian (*Hisp.* 10.36–38) names the wronged tribe as the (otherwise unknown) Torboletae (the Turdetani, given by Livy XXI.6.1, are too far from Saguntum; possibly the Edetani are meant). He alleges that the incident was provoked by Hannibal, who persuaded the Torboletae to complain to him that they were being attacked by the Saguntines; when the latter insisted that Rome rather than Hannibal himself should be the arbitrator, he used their rebuff as an excuse to attack the city. Whatever be thought of Hannibal's part in provoking the episode, the factor which led the Saguntines to ask for Roman arbitration was clearly a quarrel with a neighbouring tribe which, if not settled quickly, might, so they feared, have serious consequences.

Polybius dates this episode 'a short time before' (μικροῖς ἔμπροσθεν

<hr>

[27] Polyb. III.14.5–8. Livy's account (XXI.5.8–16), though probably deriving from the same source as Polybius, is confused and has misunderstood the movements of the armies. See Walbank 1957–79, 1.318: (B 38). The attempt by Meyer 1924, II.403 n. 1: (C 37) to reconcile the two versions is hardly conclusive.

χρόνοις) the events of the winter of 220/19 which he is describing
(III.15.7). It should therefore be placed not earlier than 221 and it should
not be regarded as the occasion of Rome's first alliance with Saguntum.
This original agreement had been made, as we have seen, several years
(πλείοσι ἔτεσι) before Hannibal's time, as Polybius states when he reverts
to Saguntine affairs in a later chapter (30.1). In this latter passage
Polybius is referring back to the arbitration episode of 15.7 when he
records that the Saguntines in a state of *stasis* (στασιάσαντες) turned for
arbitration to the Romans rather than to the Carthaginians, although the
latter were 'quite near' (ἐγγὺς ὄντων). The proximity of the Carthaginians
again suggests that the incident was recent (e.g. 221 or 220). To sum up,
Polybius seems to believe that many years before 220/19 (whether earlier
or later than the Ebro treaty of 226 he unfortunately does not specify)
Saguntum had made an alliance with Rome, and relying on this agreement had appealed to Roman arbitration in *c.* 221/20 at a time of internal
stasis, and as a result some leading Saguntines were put to death.

The subsequent course of events is difficult to determine amid much
misunderstanding and misrepresentations by the ancient sources.
Polybius records that in the past the Saguntines had sent frequent
messages to Rome (συνεχῶς): as allies, they duly kept Rome informed of
any developments in Spain. But the Romans had paid little attention until
they acted as arbitrators in the Saguntine *stasis*; in 220 a message arrived
which induced them to send an embassy to investigate and to meet
Hannibal when he returned to his winter quarters at New Carthage after
his very successful campaign. If the arbitration can be placed as late as
220, it could have been handled by these ambassadors on their way to
New Carthage,[28] but it perhaps falls better into 221. At any rate the
Romans were at last stirred to confront Hannibal in person: according to
Polybius (III.15.5) they requested him to keep his hands off Saguntum
(Ζακανθαίων ἀπεχέσθαι), which was protected by their *fides* (πίστις), and
not to infringe Hasdrubal's treaty by crossing the Ebro. Since the main
issue was Hannibal's attitude to Saguntum which lay 100 miles south of
the river, it would have been needlessly offensive of the Roman ambassadors to have brought the Ebro into the discussion, and Polybius is
probably wrong in saying that they did. His error, if such it be, could
have arisen from a false transference to the negotiations in 220 of a similar
request made at Carthage in 218 (see below); it is less likely that he was
confused by the later annalistic tradition which, in an attempt to brand
Hannibal as a treaty-breaker, falsely linked his attack on Saguntum with
his crossing of the Ebro by the barefaced placing of the city to the north

[28] Cf. Sumner 1967, 232ff.: (c 56). Livy, Appian and Zonaras place the Roman embassy in 219
after Hannibal had started to besiege Saguntum, but Polybius' date of the autumn–winter of 220/19
before the siege should be preferred.

of the river (though some scholars do believe that in a later passage, III.30.3, he may for the moment confusedly have implied that Saguntum *was* north of the river). But whatever the reason for Polybius' slip, it is better to eliminate any reference to the Ebro treaty in these earlier discussions, the more so since Polybius himself records no reference to this treaty in the reply of Hannibal, who confined himself to blaming the Romans for interfering in Saguntum which they had seized treacherously: παρεσπονδημένους probably implies a breach of faith rather than of a legal treaty, since it is difficult to establish that any formal treaty was in fact broken. However, although the Ebro treaty contained no reference to southern Spain, Hasdrubal may have been led to believe that the Romans had no intention of interfering there (see above pp. 29–30). On the other hand, Hannibal knew very well that Saguntum was an ally of Rome and that any threat to it would involve Rome's concern. He therefore reported to Carthage that the Saguntines trusting in their Roman alliance had attacked a tribe under Punic protection, and he sought instructions. He received unanimous support, apart from the opposition of Hanno (Livy XXI.10ff.), and was apparently given a free hand. Polybius adds (III.15.12) that the Roman envoys, who now believed that war was inevitable, also went to Carthage to make the same protest there, but the tradition of this visit is very confused and is open to question.[29]

Hannibal would no longer tolerate Roman interference in an area where they had apparently given his predecessor a free hand. Embittered by the bullying to which Carthage had been subjected at the time of the seizure of Sardinia, he determined not to see his country humiliated a second time. In the spring of 219 he therefore advanced against Saguntum as champion of the cause of his subjects, the wronged Torboletae. Relying on help from Rome, the Saguntines refused to surrender, but tragically for them no help came: although Rome's northern frontier had just been secured against Gallic threats, she was involved with the Illyrians. The Senate was unwilling to face war on two fronts, and decided to clear up the Adriatic, where Demetrius of Pharos was attacking Illyrian cities which were under Roman protection. Thus the two consuls of 219 were sent to Illyricum, not to Spain. Saguntum lay on a steep plateau about a mile from the coast (it is now some three miles distant, owing to coastal changes); it ran for some 1,000 yards from east

---

[29] Cic. *Phil.* v.27; Livy XXI.6.4ff., 9.3ff.; App. *Hisp.* 11.40–43; Zon. VIII.21. Confusion may have arisen from a later Roman embassy to Carthage and also from a muddle between Carthage and Carthago Nova. See Sumner 1967, 238ff.: (C 56), who also suggests that Livy's unlikely account (XXI.19.6ff.) of how the final Roman embassy to Carthage in 218 returned to Italy by way of Spain and Gaul may be a false transference of the return of the ambassadors from New Carthage in 220/19 (on the assumption that they had not gone to Carthage itself). Livy's whole account of the Saguntine affair is chronologically muddled, since he places the Saguntine embassy to Rome in 218 instead of 220. He himself tried to straighten out the general chronological confusion in XXI.15.3ff.

to west but was only some 120 yards wide. The weakest point in its
almost impregnable walls was at the western end; there was a slightly
more accessible approach just to the west of the citadel, and here
Hannibal concentrated his attack (as did Marshal Suchet in 1811). The
blockade continued for eight months without thought of surrender,
though Hannibal was ready to offer relatively lenient terms. At one point
Hannibal himself left to overawe the Oretani and Carpetani who, annoyed at his severe levying of troops, had seized his recruiting officers
(Livy XXI.11.13). The siege continued relentlessly, however, and more
than heroism and desperation were needed to resist the assault indefinitely: Saguntum fell in the late autumn of 219.

What happened when news of the fall of the city reached Rome is open
to doubt. According to Polybius (III.20.1–6) there was no senatorial
debate on the question of war (it had been agreed a year earlier, he adds,
that Carthaginian violation of Saguntine territory would be regarded as a
casus belli), and he dismisses as barber-shop gossip rather than history the
statements of Chaereas, Sosylus and other historians who recorded such
a debate. Rather, the Romans immediately (παραχρῆμα) appointed ambassadors and sent them in haste (κατὰ σπουδήν) to Carthage to deliver
an ultimatum: either Hannibal and other Carthaginian leaders must be
handed over or else war would be declared. But Polybius can hardly be
accepted at his face-value. In the first place it is extremely unlikely that in
219 the Senate had agreed to regard an attack on Saguntine territory as a
casus belli. If it had done so, its inactivity throughout the whole siege and
the following winter until at the very earliest 15 March 218 (the first
possible date for the despatch of the final embassy to Carthage) is difficult
to explain. True, both consuls of 219 became involved in the Adriatic and
it might not have been easy to switch some forces to the western
Mediterranean (though the war was effectively over by late June when
Pharos was captured). Since the consuls of 218 did not start for their
provinces until late August, there is a very long gap between Roman
words and Roman deeds. Behind Polybius' statement may lie the fact that
many Roman senators, perhaps a majority, felt that an attack on
Saguntum might or should lead to war, but a clearcut vote for war in such
circumstances is not likely to have been taken in 219 even before
Hannibal advanced against Saguntum. Further, the sudden burst of
energy after months of allowing Saguntum to resist unaided, as reported
by Polybius, looks suspiciously like an attempt at self-justification. If
therefore the question of war had not been irrevocably decided by the
Senate in 219, and since senatorial opinion can hardly have been completely unanimous, some debate is likely on reception of news of the
city's fall, and in fact such a debate is recorded by Dio Cassius (fr.55.1–9;
Zon. VIII.22). This tradition appeared not only in pro-Carthaginian

historians such as Sosylus but also (since Dio's source is pro-Roman) in the Roman annalistic accounts and could have reached him by way of a writer such as Coelius Antipater. Livy may well have omitted to record the debate either because he could not believe Rome could have hesitated when once Saguntum had fallen or out of respect for Polybius' criticism.

In the debate, according to Zonaras, L. Cornelius Lentulus, probably the consul of 237, urged an immediate declaration of war and the sending of one consul to Spain, the other to Africa, while Q. Fabius Maximus counselled a more cautious approach and the despatch of an embassy. Not only the debate, but even the names of the speakers may well be historical facts: it is unnecessary to suppose that Dio's source has invented a Cornelius and a Fabius as prototypes of P. Cornelius Scipio and Fabius Cunctator who later in the war urged an offensive and defensive strategy respectively. Internal political differences in Rome cannot be considered at length here, but the Cornelii may have been eager to start the war as soon as it appeared inevitable (the Cornelii Scipiones certainly pressed forward its vigorous prosecution later in Spain and Africa), while it has been suggested that their political allies, the Aemilii, stimulated by Massiliote pressure, had long urged the checking of Punic aggrandizement in Spain, both in 231 and 226 (and the Scipios, at any rate later, had personal links with the Massiliotes: *nostri clientes*, Cic. *Rep.*1.43).[30] A more cautious policy was advocated by Fabius who, while perhaps agreeing with the general opinion that Hannibal's activities constituted a ground for war, nevertheless wished to attempt negotiations on the basis of disavowal of Hannibal by Carthage before war was finally declared.[31] The prospects of success for such a move might seem small, but some latent, if not open jealousy and opposition to Hannibal must have survived at Carthage, and an appeal to Hanno and the anti-Barcid faction might help to weaken the city's resolve at so critical a moment. At any rate Fabius may have thought so and personal contacts may have provided him with the means to learn something of current political feeling at Carthage, since he is said to have had a *paternum hospitium* with the father of Carthalo who later commanded the Punic garrison at Tarentum in 209 (Livy XXVII.16.5). Further, another Fabius, the historian Pictor, took the anti-Barcid view (which Polybius strenuously rejected) that Hasdrubal and Hannibal had been acting independently of the Carthaginian government (see n. 6 above). This or other possible debates probably involved discussion of the wider question of the ultimate objective of Roman policy: was this to be limited to crushing Hannibal and Punic power in Spain and then a negotiated peace, or was it to aim at the destruction of Carthage as a Great Power? At any rate Fabius' attempt at compromise was finally accepted to the extent

[30] See Kramer 1948: (C 30).   [31] Fabius' policy: Rich 1976, 109ff.: (H 20).

that war should be declared only if Carthage refused to disavow Hannibal. Five senatorial *legati* were sent to Carthage to convey the ultimatum which Polybius wrongly asserted was despatched immediately after news of the fall of Saguntum had reached Rome. If the Romans had acted more speedily the war might have been fought in Spain or Gaul rather than in Italy. The legation chosen was a weighty one: it was led probably by M. Fabius Buteo rather than by Q. Fabius Maximus;[32] in 218 Buteo, the oldest living *censorius*, and perhaps the *princeps senatus*, had greater authority than Fabius Maximus. He was accompanied by the two consuls of 219, M. Livius Salinator and L. Aemilius Paullus, together with C. Licinius (probably the consul of 236) and Q. Baebius Tamphilus, one of the commissioners sent to Hannibal in 220.

The interval between the reception of the news of the fall of Saguntum and the despatch of the embassy has been much debated: the longer the delay, the less credit to the Senate. The extremes of the time-gap are 15 March 218 (the two consuls of 219 could not serve as legates until their consulships had ended) and a date late in August when at last the consuls for 218 left for their provinces.[33] One suggestion is that news of Saguntum's fall did not reach Rome until mid-February and the ultimatum was sent soon after 15 March, thus reducing the Senate's delay to about a month, while on another view the Senate normally regarded itself as entitled to postpone wars until the new consuls entered office (*ad novos consules*).[34] On the other hand, a possible reason for placing the despatch of the embassy late in this period between mid-March and late August has been found in the puzzling insistence on the Ebro treaty by the Roman embassy when it met the authorities in Carthage: Polybius (III.21.1) says that the Carthaginians refused to discuss the treaty (on the grounds that either it did not exist or else had not been made with their approval) and therefore implies that the Romans wished to discuss it. But why? It was not relevant since it was not violated by Hannibal's attack on Saguntum (the two were only linked in later misrepresentations which placed the city north of the Ebro). It has therefore been suggested that the embassy did not leave Rome until news came (in June?) that Hannibal had in fact crossed the Ebro probably in late May or early June.[35] On this

[32] Fabius Buteo: Scullard 1973, 274: (H 54).

[33] Calculations are hampered by uncertainty about the state of the calendar. Thus the position would be complicated if 218 happened to be an intercalary year, which is quite uncertain, or if in 218 the Roman calendar was a few weeks ahead or behind the Julian. See Sumner 1966, 12: (C 55); Errington 1970, 54ff.: (C 15). Nor is it certain whether a *trinundinum* was obligatory between promulgating a *rogatio* for war and voting on it: cf. Sumner 1966, 20: (C 55), and Rich 1976, 29: (H 20).

[34] See respectively Astin 1967, 577ff.: (C 2), and Rich 1976, 20ff., 28ff., 107ff.: (H 20).

[35] See Hoffmann 1951, 77ff.: (C 25) (despite the objection that Polybius believed (III.37.1) that news of the discussion in Carthage reached Hannibal just before he left New Carthage). Scullard 1952, 212ff.: (C 54), suggested a modification of this view, namely that the Roman embassy may have left late in May when news came that Hannibal was on the war-path, having left New Carthage (late April or early May) with a large army, and was heading north towards the Ebro.

supposition the silence of the Carthaginians becomes clear: they obviously would not wish to discuss a treaty which Hannibal had just broken.

Whatever the exact date of the delivery of the Roman ultimatum, the Carthaginians replied to the brusque alternative of disavowing Hannibal or accepting war by refusing all discussion of the Ebro treaty and concentrating on the treaty of 241 which they claimed covered only those who were allies of either Rome or Carthage at the time of the treaty. To prove this they read out the terms of the treaty several times (the actual list of allies probably formed an annexe to the treaty),[36] and the name Saguntum certainly did not appear. There was no question that Rome's 'alliance' with Saguntum was made after 241, but the Romans brushed the matter aside and said that now Saguntum had fallen their ultimatum must be accepted. Polybius has clouded the issue when he says (III.21.6) that a treaty had been broken by the capture of Saguntum. He then turns aside to examine all the earlier Romano–Punic treaties, and when he returns to discuss the Roman embassy of 218 he says (29.1) he will give not what the Roman ambassadors actually said at the time, but what was usually thought to have been the Roman case (as argued in 152–150 B.C.?). This was to harp on the validity of Hasdrubal's covenant and to assert that peoples who became allies after the treaty of 241 were covered by it since otherwise it would have specifically forbidden all future alliances or laid down that subsequent allies should not enjoy the benefits of the treaty. As to war-guilt, therefore, Polybius condemns the Carthaginians in regard to Saguntum, but he equally condemns the Romans for their previous unjust seizure of Sardinia. Amid so many confusing claims and arguments, at least the outcome of the embassy is clear: Fabius dramatically declared that he carried war and peace in the folds of his toga. When the presiding sufete told him to offer which the Romans wished and when Fabius said 'war', the majority (πλείους) of the Carthaginian council cried out 'we accept'.

Meanwhile Hannibal had wintered in New Carthage and had sent some of his Spanish troops on leave. He visited Gades to pay his vows to Heracles-Melkart and also had been issuing a large amount of silver coinage to pay his troops. The first series, from triple to quarter shekels, showed the laureate head of Heracles-Melkart with what are almost certainly the features both of Hamilcar (bearded) and Hannibal himself (beardless); on the reverse was an African elephant. These magnificent coins were followed by shekels and triple shekels with Hannibal's head, without laurel wreath and Heracles' club, and the ordinary Carthaginian type of horse and palm-tree on the reverse (this series may possibly have been issued by his brother Hasdrubal after Hannibal's departure). The

---

[36] See Taubler 1921, 63ff.: (c 58).

Barcas were displaying themselves as Hellenistic rulers, with even a suggestion of the divine.[37] In order to secure the loyalty of Spain and Africa, Hannibal interchanged some troops between these two countries and thereby separated the soldiers from their own people; Africa was thus apparently within his command. He instructed Hasdrubal to administer Spain in case he might be separated from him (ἐὰν αὐτὸς χωρίζηταί που); does this rather naive expression suggest that Hannibal was trying to keep his future movements as secret as possible? He had also been in touch with Gallic tribes, both in Cisalpine Gaul and in the Alps, and when he heard that they were willing to co-operate, he set forth from New Carthage in the spring of 218 (late April or early May) with a large force which, however, probably fell short of the 90,000 infantry, 12,000 cavalry and 37 elephants attributed to him. He crossed the Ebro when the spring flooding had subsided.[38] His avowed and immediate objective must have been north-eastern Spain between the Ebro and the Pyrenees. If his intention at this point was to reach Italy, as it may well have been, he will not have advertised the fact: the Romans must be kept guessing. In the event he took two and a half months to reduce much of northern Spain and he did not succeed against the coastal cities of Tarraco and Emporiae. It remains uncertain whether this long period was owing to unexpectedly tough resistance or to a deliberate delaying tactic to hoodwink the Romans and then to make a hurried dash forward at the last moment just before the winter closure of the mountain passes. In any case he must have masked his intention of attacking Italy as long as possible, and he could not of course have carried it out that year if his campaign in northern Spain had not ultimately been successful. By the end of July or early August he had reached the Pyrenees, and the road to Rome stretched out before him.

Hannibal left behind in Spain an immensely strong base. The wealth that he and his predecessors had acquired in the peninsula was spectacular; it was the reply of Carthage to the loss of Sicily and Sardinia. The resources of Numidia and Mauretania would have been easier to develop, as some Carthaginians such as Hanno seem to have argued, but this area lacked the mineral wealth that Spain could offer and in the Barca family

[37] See Robinson 1956, 39: (B 130). This view, that these and other heads with very individualized features (cf. nn. 18 above and 41 below) represent the Barcids, has been accepted by Richter 1965, 281: (B 192), Blázquez 1976, 39ff.: (B 81), and many others, but rejected by de Navascués 1961–2, 1ff.: (B 120), and Villaronga 1973: (B 141). It is difficult to believe that the great variation of feature and the presence or absence of symbols (e.g. diadem or club) can refer only to Heracles-Melkart *simpliciter*.

[38] In view of the necessary preparations Proctor 1971, 13ff.: (C 44), sets Hannibal's departure from New Carthage not earlier than mid-June, after assembling the army at the end of May. But the prolonged interchange of troops may not have been confined to the winter of 219/18: see De Sanctis 1907–64, III.ii.13 n. 21: (A 14).

Carthage found the instruments to conquer, administer and exploit the peninsula. The political opponents of the Barcids might accuse them of building a 'private empire' in Spain, but despite their semi-regal position they remained loyal citizens of their motherland, and if Hannibal's practice was not a novelty they often consulted a council (συνέδριον) which seems to have contained representatives of the Carthaginian government.[39] Spain, however, was sufficiently far away from Carthage to allow the Barcids to act with reasonable independence, and far enough away from Rome to prevent the Senate becoming unduly interested.

The Barcids seem to have lost no time in exploiting the mineral wealth of Spain to the full: at any rate Hamilcar's first debased billon coinage was soon replaced by silver and even gold. Though the gold mines of north-west Spain were far from his direct control (and indeed were not fully worked until the Augustan conquest), there was also gold in Andalusia: Strabo (III.2.8) enthuses over the great abundance of gold, silver, copper and iron in Turdetania, and his statement that gold was previously obtained from what in his day were copper mines is confirmed by modern analysis of the ancient slag heaps at Rio Tinto which contained 13 grains of gold per ton (indeed the modern mining company at Rio Tinto has obtained gold and silver ores, as well as its main production of copper).[40] The result of this exploitation is seen in the wealth accumulated in the capital of New Carthage when stormed by Scipio in 209 B.C.: he captured 276 golden plates, each weighing about a pound, 18,300 lb of silver in bullion and in coin, a large number of silver vases and quantities of copper and iron, besides a vast amount of munitions, armour and weapons (Livy XXVI.47). As we have seen, one mine (Baebelo) alone provided Hannibal with 300 lb of silver a day; this was in the area of New Carthage which in Polybius' time produced at least 25,000 drachmas per day.

This great wealth provided the sinews of war, both equipment and mercenaries. The growth of the Barcid armies in Spain cannot be traced in detail, but Hasdrubal is said to have had 50,000 infantry, 6,000 cavalry and 200 elephants (Diod. Sic. XXV.12), Hannibal in 219/18 interchanged some 14,000 infantry, 1,200 cavalry and 870 Balearic slingers from Spain with a roughly similar force from Africa: he is said to have started *en route* for the Pyrenees with 90,000 infantry and 12,000 cavalry. He also left in Spain a fleet of 50 quinqueremes (though 18 lacked crews), 2 quadriremes and 5 triremes. The army figures, though seen by Polybius

[39] Polyb. III.20.8, 71.5, 85.6, VII.9.1, IX.24.5.
[40] See Rickard 1928, 129ff., esp. 132–3: (G 26); and for Roman workings see Richardson 1976, 139ff.: (C 24). Healey 1978, 26: (I 20), provides a diagram of the San Dionisio lode at Rio Tinto, showing a thin gold and silver lode above the copper. Strabo explains how the inhabitants of Turdetania also obtained gold from the dry auriferous sand.

himself on the inscription left by Hannibal on the Lacinian Cape, may be
slightly exaggerated, and the proportion of Spanish mercenaries cannot
be estimated, but they indicate the general level of the Barcid achievement. But more than mere numbers was needed. Among the Spanish
tribesmen the unit of loyalty was small; it could be strong (as witness the
desperate resistance of Saguntum to Hannibal), but there was no independent Iberian nation and little national feelings so that the
Carthaginians found it easy to recruit them as mercenaries. Further, it
was a Spanish tradition (noted by Caesar and Plutarch) for bands of
followers (*devoti*) to swear total allegiance to a leader, to serve as his
bodyguard and never to survive him. Ennius (fr.503 v) seems to have
emphasized the loyalty of a Spaniard who refused a Roman demand to
abandon the Carthaginian cause. Thus with good pay and charismatic
leadership the tribesmen might be welded into a fine and loyal fighting
force, since they apparently had no difficulty in accepting a leader from
overseas (thus after his capture of New Carthage and the battle of Baecula
they readily hailed Scipio Africanus as king: Polyb. x.40). Carthage
meant less to them than did their Barcid commanders, who in the later
years of occupation placed their portraits – and that in a divine setting –
on the coins which their troops received as pay. Hasdrubal Barca had a
gold shield bearing his portrait, which was later captured by the Romans
and dedicated in the Capitoline temple.[41]

For years the Barcid conquest of Spain had been accomplished by
diplomacy and assimilation as well as by war: both Hasdrubal and
Hannibal had married Spanish wives, while Hannibal had lived in the
country for 19 years. He may not indeed have been averse to trying to
increase his prestige by appealing to the superstitions of the natives. He it
was who was probably responsible for the first issue of the coins
depicting his father and himself in the guise of Heracles-Melkart, and the
story that before he crossed the Ebro he dreamed that he received a
promise of divine guidance may have been told to enhance his authority
still further. The story was recorded by Silenus, who was with him at the
time, and it may well have circulated among his troops in 218.[42] But

---

[41] Cf. n. 37 above. Gold shield: Plin. xxxiv.14. Livy (xxv.39.17) refers to such a shield of silver,
weighing 137 lb. The coins with a laureate diademed head of Melkart, and an elephant on the reverse
(Series 8 of Robinson 1956, 52–3: (B 130)) are recognized by Robinson as Barcid. A hoard found
fairly recently in Sicily confirms that they certainly belong to the later years of Hasdrubal, but raises
some (though not insuperable?) difficulties in the assumption that they portray the features of
Hasdrubal Barca: cf. Scullard 1970, 252–3: (H 77).

[42] See Cic. *Div.* 1.49; also Livy xxi.22.5–7; Val. Max. 1.7. ext. 1; Sil. Ital. iii.163ff.; Dio Cassius
xiii.56.9. Polybius (at iii.47.8, 48.9) may have been alluding indirectly to this as well as to similar
stories of divine guidance for Hannibal. The view of Norden 1915, 116ff.: (B 24), that the council of
the gods figured in Ennius is not very probable. The story told how Hannibal was summoned to a
council of the gods, where Jupiter ordered him to invade Italy and provided a divine guide who
warned Hannibal when on the march not to look back. Hannibal disobeyed and saw behind him a

whether or not supported by any popular belief in their divine mission, the Barcids doubtless lived like princes, if not as Hellenistic monarchs (in whose tradition Hamilcar and Hasdrubal had founded cities). The latter, in his palace on the citadel of New Carthage, in command of a great army and fleet, with his ships in one of the best harbours in the whole Mediterranean, in control of the local silver mines and holding hostages from many Spanish tribes, must have appeared an impressive figure to his contemporaries, while all the Barcids made a strong impact on later generations. Thus, for instance, Polybius rejected the anti-Barcid tradition of Fabius Pictor, praised the gallantry of Hamilcar, and on the whole judged Hannibal with impartiality, and even Cato, the bitter enemy of Carthage, said that no king was worthy of comparison with Hamilcar Barca.[43] But however spectacular the achievement of the Barcids, in the event the rich resources of the peninsula were denied to Hannibal fighting unaided in Italy, thanks to the brilliant initiative of members of another family, the Cornelii Scipiones, and to the strength of the Roman navy: the efforts of his brothers Hasdrubal and Mago to keep him supplied from Spain were too little and too late.

trail of destruction caused by an enormous beast: his guide told him this meant the desolation of Italy and he was to go on unworried (*ne laboraret*). However, Meyer 1924, II.368ff.: (C 37), thought that Hannibal's disobedience must have led to his destruction which therefore originally figured at the end of Silenus' account; in consequence the story was suppressed by later Roman writers (starting with Coelius). But we do not know that Silenus' history went down to 202 B.C. (the latest attested event is in 209), and it is unlikely that as a companion of Hannibal he would have told a story which implied that Hannibal was responsible for his own downfall. Meyer has been influenced by the tragic legend of Orpheus' disobedience which he cites, but in fact in its original form this story may have had a happy ending, namely the recovery of Eurydice, and Orpheus' backward look and its consequence may be only an addition by an Alexandrian poet: cf. Guthrie 1935, 31: (I 17), and Bowra 1952, 117ff.: (H 171). In any case, in Hannibal's dream we are in the realm of Hellenistic invention rather than of primitive taboo, of the gods of Olympus rather than of the underworld, and it is not impossible that a story that Hannibal's march had been commissioned by a council of the gods was circulated to encourage the troops, and then written up by Silenus in the more extravagant vein of Hellenistic invention which Polybius condemned.

[43] Polyb. IX.21–26, XL.19; Plut. *Cat. Mai.* 8.14.

CHAPTER 3

THE SECOND PUNIC WAR

JOHN BRISCOE

I. THE CAUSES OF THE CONFLICT[1]

In 241 Carthage had no alternative to accepting the Roman peace terms and surrendering possession of the whole of Sicily to Rome. Three years later the Senate took advantage of Carthage's difficulties in the Mercenary War to seize Sardinia.[2] Polybius rightly regarded the latter action as unjustified and the subsequent Carthaginian resentment as a major cause of the Second Punic War.[3] But even without that additional provocation many Carthaginians, and particularly Hamilcar Barca, the father of Hannibal, would not have been prepared to accept the outcome of the First Punic War as definitive. It was Hamilcar who laid the foundations for a new Carthaginian offensive by re-establishing Carthaginian power in Spain. In 229 Hamilcar died and was succeeded in Spain by his son-in-law Hasdrubal, with whom Rome concluded the Ebro treaty in 226, which made the river Ebro the northern limit of Carthaginian power in Spain and, implicitly at least, renounced Roman claims south of that limit. The treaty, however, contained the seeds of a new conflict, for its terms were flatly inconsistent with the Roman alliance with Saguntum, concluded several years before the Ebro treaty.[4] Saguntum lay south of the Ebro, and while Rome was to claim that the alliance overrode the Ebro treaty, the Carthaginians saw the Ebro treaty as giving them the freedom to proceed against Saguntum.[5]

Hannibal succeeded his brother-in-law in 221. In 220 the Saguntines, fearing an attack, asked Rome for help and the Senate, which had ignored several previous appeals from Saguntum, sent an embassy to Hannibal urging him to refrain both from attacking Saguntum and from crossing the Ebro in defiance of the treaty.[6] Hannibal countered by accusing

---

[1] The events leading to the outbreak of the Second Punic War have been dealt with at length in the previous chapter. What is presented here is a brief and necessarily dogmatic statement of the view which underlies this chapter. [2] See *CAH*[2] VII.ii, ch. 11 (e).

[3] Polyb. III.10.4, 15.10, 28.2, 30.4. [4] See pp. 25–7.

[5] Several writers, including Polybius himself on certain occasions (see especially III.30.3), twisted the facts by placing Saguntum north of the Ebro; see pp. 34–5.

[6] Polyb. III.15. For most of the events preceding the declaration of war references are given to Polybius alone. Livy XXI.4–15 is based on a totally confused chronology and is best left out of account.

Rome of interfering in internal Saguntine affairs. We need not doubt that Hannibal was looking for a reason to reopen the conflict with Rome and as soon as he was sure that the rest of the Carthaginian empire in Spain was secure,[7] he was happy to take the opportunity of attacking Saguntum. The Senate had concluded the Ebro treaty partly as a security against the possibility of the Carthaginians joining the Gauls in an alliance against Rome. It could now reassert the validity of the Saguntine alliance, and the Senate was confident that the conflict, when it came, would take place in Spain and that its timing could be controlled by Rome.[8]

The Roman embassy had gone on to Carthage to repeat the message it had delivered to Hannibal. In the spring of 219 Hannibal embarked on the siege of Saguntum; it fell eight months later.[9] Polybius vehemently denies that the Senate took time to decide its response and asserts that it immediately despatched an embassy to Carthage to declare war unless the Carthaginians agreed to surrender Hannibal and his leading officers.[10] In fact it seems very likely that a debate took place, with one side, led by L. Cornelius Lentulus (cos. 237) wanting an immediate declaration of war, the other, led by Q. Fabius Maximus, the future Cunctator, urging negotiations.[11] The result – effectively a victory for Lentulus, not a compromise – was that a conditional war-vote was passed and five ambassadors despatched to present the ultimatum.[12]

The Roman failure to help Saguntum earlier was criticized by Roman writers themselves, and to many it has seemed strange that complete inactivity during the siege should have been followed by a declaration of war once the town had fallen. In fact once Hannibal had begun to besiege Saguntum there was little that Rome could do. The consuls had already gone to Illyria[13] and it would have been difficult to raise a sufficient force and get it to Spain in time to be of any use. The Senate clearly did not envisage Hannibal moving outside Spain and in that case it was up to Rome to make the first move. There is nothing particularly surprising in the decision to go to war being postponed until the beginning of the following consular year: decisions to embark on wars seem regularly to have been taken at the beginning of a consular year.[14]

Hannibal had probably already resolved on taking the initiative by marching on Italy, whether or not Rome declared war.[15] He had sent

---

[7] Polyb. III.14.10.   [8] Polyb. III.15.3.

[9] Polyb. III.17.1. For the chronology see Walbank 1957–79, I.327–8: (B 38). I am not convinced by the argument of Astin (1967, 583ff.: (C 2)) that the siege may have begun as late as May 219, with the news of the fall of Saguntum not reaching Rome until shortly before the Ides of March 218.

[10] Polyb. III.20.

[11] Dio fr. 55; Zon. VIII.20. The story is rejected by Harris 1979, 269–70: (A 21).

[12] Polyb. III.20.8; cf. Livy XXI.18.1–2.   [13] See p. 93.

[14] See in particular Rich 1976, 38ff.: (H 20).

[15] I reject the view of Hoffmann 1951: (C 25) that the embassy to Carthage was sent only after Hannibal had crossed the Ebro.

messengers to Gaul before he had heard of the Roman ultimatum to Carthage.[16] The Senate, however, thought that the initiative still lay in their hands. No further decisions were taken until the return of the embassy from Carthage. It was then decided that one of the consuls, P. Cornelius Scipio, should go to Spain, the other, Ti. Sempronius Longus, should proceed to Sicily and launch an invasion of Africa.[17] At this point the Senate may still not have realized that Hannibal's ambitions extended outside Spain. Once it was known that Hannibal was in fact marching on Italy, there was no advantage in trying to meet him in Spain, which may explain the fact that Scipio did not leave until July at the earliest – if, indeed, the delay did not arise merely from practical problems in raising his army, caused particularly by the diversion of the legions originally assigned to him to deal with a Gallic attack on the settlers of Placentia and Cremona.[18]

We can do no more than speculate on the plans that Hannibal had when he began his march. It is clear from subsequent events that he had no intention of destroying Rome as such. He did not march on Rome after his victories at Trasimene and Cannae in 217 and 216 respectively,[19] and doubtless realized that to capture the city would be a very different proposition from victory in the open field. We may note that the treaty between Hannibal and Philip V of Macedon (Polyb. VII.9) clearly envisaged Rome's continuing existence after a Carthaginian victory. He wanted, no doubt, to bring Rome to a position where he could conclude a settlement that would recover Sicily and Sardinia for Carthage and ensure that Rome would not again be able to hinder Carthaginian expansion in the western Mediterranean. What is not clear is whether Hannibal intended to do this by significantly weakening Rome's degree of domination over Italy. In the early battles he went out of his way to treat captured Roman citizens and allies in different ways,[20] and he may have realized that permanent limits could not be set on Roman expansion if she retained control over the whole of Italy. But it is unlikely that he had any very detailed knowledge of the political geography of Italy or any very precise idea of the system to be established when Rome had been defeated.

The Carthaginian reaction to Rome's ultimatum had shown that Carthage accepted full responsibility for Hannibal's actions. But Hannibal cannot have been certain of the degree of continuing support he would receive from the home government once he had arrived in

---

[16] Polyb. III.34; Walbank 1957–79, 1.365: (B 38). Cf. Livy XXI.23.1.

[17] Polyb. III.40.2. Polybius' statement that these decisions were taken only after it was known that Hannibal had crossed the Ebro is to be rejected: see Sumner 1966, 14: (C 55).

[18] Rich 1976, 37: (H 20); on the Gallic attack see Polyb. III.40.6–14; Livy XXI.25–26.2; Walbank 1957–79, 1.375–7: (B 38).

[19] Polyb. III.86.8; Livy XXII.51.1–5; cf. Lazenby 1978, 85–6: (C 31).   [20] See n. 169.

Italy. The Barcids had powerful opponents in Carthage, and even if Hannibal felt confident that peace would not be concluded over his head, he must have realized that for military reinforcements he might have to rely on the support he could attract in Italy and whatever further troops his brother Hasdrubal could send from Spain.[21]

The narrative that follows treats the operations in the different theatres of war separately. It is hoped that the gain in clarity will compensate for the loss of a synoptic view of each year's events. The sources for the war, mainly Polybius and Livy, are full and detailed, though when we do not have Polybius as a control Livy's narrative must be treated with caution. References to other sources are given only when they add something to the information provided by Polybius and Livy.[22]

II. THE WAR IN ITALY

Hannibal left Carthago Nova, it seems, sometime in May, and reached the Rhône in September.[23] Scipio, with an army destined for Spain, arrived by sea at the mouth of the Rhône at the same time. Hannibal, however, succeeded in crossing the river well inland – probably at Beaucaire rather than further north[24] – and the only military contact was a cavalry skirmish of which the Romans got the better. Scipio now sent the major part of his forces to Spain under the command of his brother Gnaeus, while he himself returned to Italy.[25]

There has been enormous controversy about the route by which Hannibal crossed the Alps. The balance of probability is in favour of the view that Hannibal arrived in Italy in the area of Turin (in mid-October, about a month-and-a-half after crossing the Rhône), and if this is so the choice for Hannibal's pass lies between Mt Genèvre, Mt Cenis and, the solution preferred by the two most recent writers, the Col de Clapier.[26] Hannibal had incurred considerable losses on his journey from Spain, though, as so often with troop numbers, the precise extent of the casualties cannot be measured.[27]

The Gauls that Hannibal had encountered on his journey had demonstrated a mixture of friendship and hostility. Those of the Po valley, only

[21] See below, p. 56.
[22] The best detailed military narrative is that of De Sanctis 1907–64, III.ii: (A 14). See also Lazenby 1978: (C 31).
[23] Proctor 1972, 13ff.: (C 44), has shown that to date the start of the march in April, with the arrival in Italy in September (thus Walbank 1957–79, 1.365: (B 38)), does too much violence to Polybius III.54.1. But Proctor himself pushes that passage too far in insisting on applying it to the middle of November. For the dates here suggested see Rich 1976, 33: (H 20).
[24] Lazenby 1978, 35–6: (C 31); for other views cf. Walbank 1957–79, 1.377–8: (B 38).
[25] Polyb. III.41–46, 49.1–4; Livy XXI.26.3–29, 32.1–5.
[26] Proctor 1972, 165ff.: (C 44); Lazenby 1978, 33ff.: (C 31); cf. Walbank 1957–79, 1.382ff.: (B 38).
[27] For details see Walbank 1957–79, 1.366: (B 38).

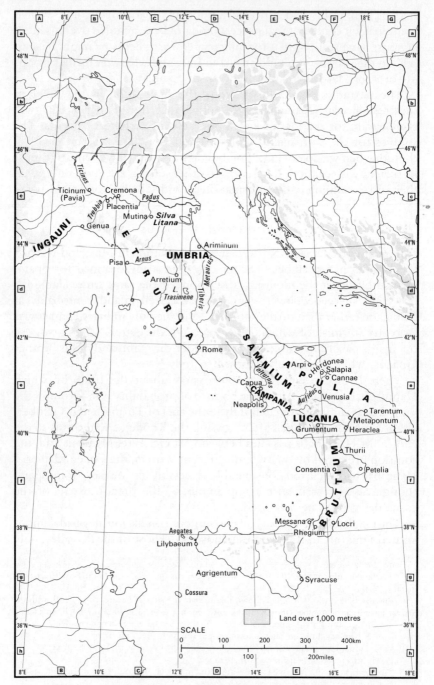

Map 2. Italy and Sicily in the Second Punic War (for Campania see Map 3).

recently subjugated by Rome, welcomed him as a liberator. The Boii and the Insubres had already revolted, attacked the Roman settlers at Placentia and Cremona and besieged them in Mutina.[28] The first clash with Roman forces took place at the River Ticinus near Pavia, a skirmish of cavalry and light-armed troops of which the Carthaginians got considerably the better and in which Scipio himself was wounded. The Romans retreated eastwards to Placentia where Scipio was joined by Sempronius Longus, who had been urgently recalled from Sicily. A little west of Placentia there occurred the first major battle of the war, at the River Trebbia (December 218–January 217). The result was a major victory for the Carthaginians and well over half the Roman army was destroyed.[29] Livy's story[30] of an attempt by Hannibal to cross the Appennines immediately after the battle of the Trebbia and of a drawn battle between Hannibal and Sempronius is to be rejected.

Sempronius returned to Rome to preside over the election of C. Flaminius and Cn. Servilius Geminus as consuls for 217. Flaminius took up position at Arretium (Arezzo) but Hannibal proceeded over the Appennines, along the River Arno and past Flaminius southwards towards the heart of Etruria. Flaminius pursued him but Hannibal concealed his army in the hills at the north-east corner of Lake Trasimene and, with the assistance of early morning fog (the date in the Roman calendar was 21 June, probably 8 May (Jul.)), the Roman army was caught in an ambush. It was, as the *praetor urbanus* announced at Rome, a great defeat. Flaminius was killed and some 15,000 of his army died with him. The battle was the last time until 207 that Roman and Carthaginian forces met in the northern part of the peninsula.[31]

Rome was faced by a major crisis. One consul was dead, the other at Ariminum (Rimini) cut off from the capital.[32] It is now that there begins the period of Roman strategy dominated by Q. Fabius Maximus, the period of attrition and of avoiding full-scale battles. Initially Fabius' conception was not unchallenged but from the defeat at Cannae in 216 until 210 it was on Fabian principles that the campaign in Italy was conducted. That is not to say that there were no formal battles in this period. It was only in the immediate aftermath of Trasimene and Cannae that the Fabian strategy was applied in its most extreme form. The policy was rather that pitched battles were to be avoided in circumstances chosen by Hannibal and favourable to him. It would not have precluded

[28] For the attack on the colonists see n. 18; for the welcome for Hannibal from the Gauls of northern Italy: Polyb. III.60.11; Livy XXI.39.5. Some, however, were unwilling to commit themselves completely to Hannibal (Polyb. III.69.1ff.; Livy XXI.52.3ff.), and later Hannibal was afraid of Gallic attacks on his life (Polyb. III.78.1–4; Livy XXII.1.3).

[29] Polyb. III.64–74; Livy XXI.46–48, 52–56.   [30] XXI.58–59.9.

[31] Polyb. III.77–85; Livy XXII.2–6. For the date cf. Ovid, *Fast.* VI.763ff.; for the problems associated with the battle see Walbank 1957–79, 1.415ff.: (B 38), Lazenby 1978, 62ff.: (C 31).

[32] Livy XXII.8.6, 31.9.

a full-scale battle in circumstances chosen by the Romans and where
Hannibal would have been at a disadvantage – but Hannibal was too
good a general to allow that ever to happen. Fabius' natural caution made
him extremely reluctant to commit himself, but M. Claudius Marcellus,
though a supporter of the fundamental strategy, showed much more
initiative in taking opportunities when they arose. In both 215 and 214 he
was not afraid to engage Hannibal when the latter was attempting to
capture Nola in Campania, and in the years following 210 he was clearly
determined to force Hannibal into accepting a battle. But the basic view
was that Hannibal could not be defeated decisively in open conflict. After
Cannae the aim was to concentrate on winning back towns and areas that
had defected, and by putting a vastly increased number of troops in the
field to force Hannibal either to divide his own forces or to leave his allies
without support. If Hannibal were unable to replenish his army from his
allies in Italy, and as long as Rome continued her maritime domination
and her armies in Spain could prevent reinforcements coming to Italy by
land, Fabius could be confident that eventually Hannibal's forces would
be so reduced that either the Romans would be able to defeat him by
overwhelming numerical superiority or Hannibal would be forced, prior
to such a defeat, to abandon Italy. But the cost of the policy was heavy. It
meant enormous demands on Roman and Italian manpower, enormous
financial sacrifices, and it meant accepting that Hannibal could not be
prevented from ravaging large parts of the Italian countryside, the loss in
corn production being met by imports from Sicily, Sardinia and, eventually, Egypt.[33]

Immediately after the battle of Trasimene Fabius was appointed
dictator with M. Minucius Rufus as his *magister equitum*. As the surviving
consul could not come to Rome, Fabius and Minucius were appointed
directly by the people, instead of the dictator being nominated by a
consul and the *magister equitum* by the dictator.[34] Hannibal proceeded
from Trasimene to the Adriatic coast and it was in Apulia that Fabius
embarked on his strategy, keeping close to Hannibal but avoiding a
pitched battle. From Apulia Hannibal moved into Samnium and thence
into the *ager Falernus*, the plain between the River Volturnus and Mount
Massicus. Fabius remained in the mountains watching him ravage the
plain. But when Hannibal had to leave the plain to find winter quarters
elsewhere, Fabius succeeded in blocking all his exits and it was only by
the extraordinary stratagem of driving a herd of oxen, with blazing

[33] Compare the perspicacious assessment of the Fabian strategy by De Sanctis 1907–64,
III.ii.220ff.: (A 14). Relations between Fabius and Marcellus: p. 70; Marcellus' positive attitude:
De Sanctis, *op. cit.* 287, 473. For the events of 215 and 214 referred to see Livy XXIII.44 and XXIV.17;
for the imports of grain: Thiel 1946, 56: (H 60).
[34] Polyb. III.87.6–9; Livy XXII.8.6–7; Walbank 1957–79, I.422: (B 38).

THE WAR IN ITALY

faggots tied to their horns, up a mountain, and thus diverting Roman attention, that Hannibal was able to escape with the main part of his army.[35] Fabius followed Hannibal back to Apulia, but was then summoned to Rome, allegedly to deal with religious business. The latter may well have been a pretext, discontent with Fabius' policy, particularly the fact that it involved allowing Hannibal to ravage the *ager Falernus* at his will, being the real reason. Fabius left Minucius in charge with instructions not to take any risks. But Minucius was eager to discard the Fabian strategy and succeeded in winning a minor victory.[36] Opposition to Fabius' policy, both in the field and at Rome, was increased by this success, and the assembly took the extraordinary step of conferring on the *magister equitum* an *imperium* equal to that of the dictator.[37] When Fabius returned to Apulia, he chose to divide his army rather than accept Minucius' alternative suggestion that the two men should command on alternate days. It was, of course, not long before Hannibal was able to entice Minucius into a rash venture, from which he had to be rescued by Fabius.[38]

The six-month term of the dictator elapsed before the end of the consular year, and the armies of Fabius and Minucius reverted to the consuls M. Servilius Geminus and C. Atilius Regulus (who had been elected to replace the dead Flaminius).[39] For 216 the new consuls were L. Aemilius Paullus and C. Terentius Varro.[40] Polybius reports that it was decided to give the consuls a force of eight legions of 5,000 men each, which, with the same number of allied troops, meant a total force of 80,000. There is no need to doubt these figures and it is the size of the Roman army that made the third Roman defeat particularly devastating. Hannibal occupied Cannae, by the River Aufidus, an important supply base for the Romans in Apulia. Hannibal was thus able to draw the Romans into battle on flat terrain that favoured the Carthaginian superiority in cavalry. In the battle, which took place at the end of June, Paullus fell, and out of the huge Roman army only 14,500 escaped death or captivity.[41]

Polybius, perhaps misled by the desire of the Scipionic family to absolve Paullus (Scipio Africanus' father-in-law and Scipio Aemilianus' grandfather) from blame for the disaster at Cannae, makes Varro responsible for the decision to engage, against the advice of Paullus. Livy goes

[35] Polyb. III.88–94.6; Livy XXII.12–17. On these events see Ungern-Sternberg 1975, 1 ff.: (C 59).

[36] Polyb. III.94.7–10, 100–102; Livy XXII.18, 23–24.

[37] Livy XXII.25–26, to be preferred to Polybius' statement (III.103.4) that Minucius was appointed a second dictator. See Dorey 1955: (C 12); Walbank 1957–79, 1.434: (B 38). See further p. 70 below.   [38] Polyb. III.103.5–105; Livy XXII.27–30.

[39] Livy XXII.31.7, 32.1–3, to be preferred to Polyb. III.106.1–2.

[40] See further p. 69 and Additional Note p. 79.

[41] Polyb. III.106–117; Livy XXII.41–50.

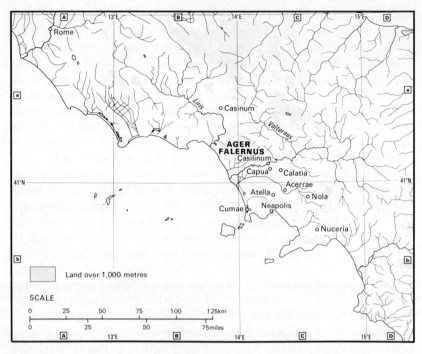

Map 3. Campania.

further and portrays Varro as the spiritual successor of Minucius, bitterly
opposed by Paullus who wanted to continue the policy of Fabius. But it is
clear from Polybius (III.106.7, 108.1) that it was the Senate as a whole
which took the decision to face Hannibal again in a pitched battle, and
that if there was any disagreement between the consuls, it was purely
tactical, not strategic. The hostile picture of Varro is belied by the
Senate's vote of thanks to him after the battle, in sharp contrast to the
treatment of those soldiers who escaped death or captivity, and to his
employment in a number of responsible positions in subsequent years.[42]

   The battle was not only a disaster in itself, but also led to the defection
to Hannibal of a large part of southern Italy, including part of Samnium.
The peoples who defected did not, for the most part, fight for Hannibal,
but their resources were no longer available to Rome.[43] The defection of

   [42] Vote of thanks: Livy XXII.61.14, other references in *MRR* 1.247. Subsequent employment:
Walbank 1957–79, 1.448: (B 38). Add his presence on diplomatic missions in 203 and 200 and his
membership of the *iiiviri* for the supplementation of Venusia in the latter year. On the *legiones
Cannenses* see n. 157.
   [43] Polyb. III.118.3 and Livy XXI.61.11, but both lists are anachronistic and contain peoples who
did not defect immediately after Cannae. At the extreme tip of Italy Rhegium remained loyal to
Rome throughout the war. For details of the status of various cities and peoples see De Sanctis 1907–
64, III.ii.211ff., 223ff., 274: (A 14); Walbank 1957–79, 1.448, II.29, 100: (B 38), Salmon 1967, 299: (H
151).

Capua, narrated at length by Livy, caused the greatest anger at Rome.[44] In Campania Atella, Calatia, and the Sabatini followed Capua and Hannibal captured Nuceria, Acerrae, and Casilinum. But Nola held out and the Roman forces under the dictator M. Iunius Pera and the praetor M. Claudius Marcellus did their best to restrict Hannibal's successes. Varro meanwhile returned to Apulia to attempt to hold the position there.[45] Hannibal was anxious to gain control of a port but repeated attempts on Naples and (the following year) an assault on Cumae by Capua and the Carthaginians were all unsuccessful.[46]

The firmness with which the crisis was met prompted Polybius to devote the whole of book VI of his history to explaining the qualities of a constitution of a state that was able to climb out of such an abyss. If we may believe Livy, the Senate refused to ransom those captured at Cannae and took emergency measures against a possible attack on Rome itself. As we have seen, however, that did not form part of Hannibal's plans.[47]

L. Postumius Albinus, who was already holding a praetorship, and Ti. Sempronius Gracchus, Iunius Pera's *magister equitum*, were elected to the consulship for 215, but before Postumius could take up office, he was killed in a battle with the Boii in the Silva Litana, north of Bologna. Fabius Maximus was chosen to replace him.[48] The year opened with Rome holding her position. As we have seen, an attack on Cumae failed and several towns in Campania and Samnium were recovered, though an attempt to retake Locri was unsuccessful. Hannibal failed in his renewed attempts to capture Nola – though the substantial victory over Hannibal ascribed to Marcellus by Livy is open to grave suspicion.[49] It was soon afterwards, however, that Syracuse defected.

For 214 Fabius was re-elected to the consulship with M. Claudius Marcellus as his colleague. Matters in Italy were now in a position of stalemate. Ti. Sempronius Gracchus defeated Hanno near Beneventum but later suffered a reverse in Lucania. A further assault on Nola by Hannibal was repulsed by Marcellus and he and Fabius together captured Casilinum. Fabius also had a number of successes in Samnium and Hannibal's hopes of taking Tarentum were foiled. In the following year, when Gracchus held a second consulship in company with Fabius' son, the Romans recaptured Arpi in Apulia.[50]

[44] Livy XXIII.2–10. See Ungern-Sternberg 1975, 25ff.: (C 59).

[45] Livy XXII.61.11, XXIII.14.5ff., 15.2–3, 17.1–6, 19–20.3, 22.11, XXVI.16.5, 33.12.

[46] Livy XXIII.1.5ff., 14.5, 15.1–2, 35–37.9 (215). XXIV.13.7 (214).

[47] Livy XXII.55–61.10. See p. 46.   [48] See p. 70.

[49] Livy XXIII.37.10–13, 39.6ff., 41.10–14, 43.6ff. For the defection of Locri in 216 cf. Livy XXIII.30.8. Livy XXIV.1.2–13, dating the defection to 215, should be rejected. On Marcellus' alleged victory see De Sanctis 1907–64, III.ii. 255 n. 104: (A 14).

[50] Livy XXIV.14–16, 17 (for doubts see De Sanctis 1907–64, III.ii.260 n. 119: (A 14), 19, 20.1–2 (for doubts see De Sanctis, *op. cit.* 274 n. 135), 20.3–5, 20.9–15, 46–47.11 (for doubts about the details of Livy's account see De Sanctis, op. cit. 273 n. 132).

The Roman recovery in the years 215–213 had been remarkable and in three years Hannibal had achieved little. Early in 212, however, he scored a significant success with the capture, by stealth, of Tarentum, and this was followed by the defection of Metapontum, Thurii and Heraclea. But the citadel of Tarentum remained in the hands of the Roman garrison, under the command of M. Livius, and since this could control the inland harbour (the Mare Piccolo), Hannibal was deprived of a substantial part of the advantage of the possession of Tarentum.[51] The consuls, Ap. Claudius Pulcher and Q. Fulvius Flaccus, began to besiege Capua. Fulvius had earlier inflicted severe losses on Hanno, who had been sent north by Hannibal to thwart the consuls' plans, and had fought a drawn battle with Hannibal himself. On the debit side Ti. Sempronius Gracchus was killed in an ambush in Lucania.[52] An indication of the Roman recovery is that from the winter of 212/11 onwards, with one possible exception, Hannibal retreated to the extreme south of Italy at the end of each year's campaign.[53]

The next year, the consulship of P. Sulpicius Galba and Cn. Fulvius Centumalus saw more dramatic events. In an attempt to raise the siege of Capua Hannibal undertook the march on Rome which he had forgone after Trasimene and Cannae. He had no serious hope of taking the city and when he discovered that Rome was adequately defended without the armies of the consuls of the previous year being withdrawn from Capua, he rapidly returned to the south. Soon afterwards came the fall of Capua, symbolically the most important reversal of Hannibal's successes after Cannae. Meanwhile, the citadel of Tarentum was still in Roman hands and an attempt by a Punic fleet to cut off its supplies failed.[54]

In 210 Marcellus held a third consulship with M. Valerius Laevinus, who had been the Roman commander against Philip of Macedon since 215 and had just concluded the important alliance with the Aetolian League.[55] The Romans recaptured Salapia in Apulia and two Samnite towns. But Cn. Fulvius Centumalus, the consul of the previous year, was killed in an attack by Hannibal at Herdonea. A Roman fleet was defeated by the Tarentines but the garrison under Livius continued to hold out in the citadel. Meanwhile Marcellus was eager to bring Hannibal to a fixed battle. After an indecisive conflict in Lucania Marcellus pursued him

---

[51] Pol. VIII.24–34; Livy XXV.7.10–11, 15.6–17; App. *Hann.* 34–35, 142–149.

[52] Livy XXV.13–14, 16–17, 19.1–8, 22.5–13. The story of the defeat of the praetor Cn. Fulvius Flaccus at Herdonea (Livy XXV.21) is to be rejected as a doublet of the defeat of Cn. Fulvius Centumalus in 210: De Sanctis 1907–64, III.ii.459: (A 14); Brunt 1971, 652: (H 82). The story of one M. Centennius obtaining a force of 8,000 men from the Senate and losing virtually all of it in a battle with Hannibal in Lucania (Livy XXV.19.5–17) is also highly implausible (cf. Münzer, *PW* III.1928).

[53] De Sanctis 1907–64, III.ii.470: (A 14) thinks that Hannibal spent the winter of 210/9 in Apulia.

[54] Polyb. IX.3.1–9.11; Livy XXVI.4–14, 20.7–11.   [55] See pp. 97–100.

through Apulia, though remaining careful to avoid any possibility of an ambush.[56]

In 209 Fabius held his fifth consulship, Q. Fulvius Flaccus his fourth. Fabius recaptured Tarentum, though afterwards he was nearly caught in an ambush by Hannibal. Marcellus was still looking for the chance of a full-scale engagement with Hannibal: when he obtained one he was defeated. Livy's story of a subsequent victory that was *nec incruenta* probably conceals an indecisive result. Hannibal then returned to Bruttium.[57] In the following year Marcellus was again consul with T. Quinctius Crispinus as his colleague. Their principal aim was the recapture of Locri. But first a Roman force sent from Tarentum to Locri was ambushed by Hannibal near Petelia, and then the consuls themselves were caught in another ambush near Venusia. Marcellus was killed immediately and Crispinus fatally wounded. Hannibal obtained possession of Marcellus' signets, but his attempt to use them in order to retake Salapia was foiled. He was, however, able to raise the siege of Locri and the Roman forces in the south, though numerically superior, made no attempt to confront him.[58]

The year 207 was a critical one and the last in which engagements of moment took place in Italy. The consuls were C. Claudius Nero and M. Livius Salinator. Hannibal's brother Hasdrubal, who had escaped from Spain after the battle of Baecula, was marching towards Italy, and Rome was again faced with the prospect of fighting in the north. Claudius was appointed to face Hannibal, Livius Hasdrubal. The aim of the two brothers was to meet in Umbria. But Hasdrubal's messengers were intercepted and Nero, who had begun by fighting not unsuccessfully against Hannibal at Grumentum and Venusia, took the bold decision to march with part of his forces to join Livius in the north. When Hasdrubal discovered that he was facing the combined forces of the two consuls, he decided to avoid a battle and instead to attempt to proceed down the Via Flaminia to his planned meeting-place with Hannibal. The Roman armies pursued him and at the battle of the River Metaurus the Carthaginian forces were massacred and Hasdrubal himself fell. Immediately after the battle Nero returned to the south and Hannibal retired to Bruttium, unable to embark on any further aggressive actions.[59]

In 206 there was virtually no military activity in Italy, but Lucania returned to Roman control. In 205, while Scipio was in Sicily, his colleague in the consulship, P. Licinius Crassus, faced Hannibal. But

---

[56] Livy XXVI.38.6–39, XXVII.1–2. Cf. n. 52.   [57] Livy XXVII.12.2, 12.7–15.1, 15.4–16.
[58] Polyb. X.32–33; Livy XXVII.25.11–28. On the unwillingness of the Roman commanders in the south to launch a united and full onslaught on Hannibal see De Sanctis 1907–64, III.ii.476, 488 (concerning 207): (A 14).
[59] Polyb. XI.1–3.6; Livy XXVII.38–51. Cf. Lazenby 1978, 182ff.: (C 31).

both armies were afflicted by disease and no conflicts occurred. Alarm was caused, however, by the landing of an army under Mago at Genua and the making of an alliance between Mago and the Ligurian tribe of the Ingauni. Two Roman armies were sent north to meet the threat. In the south Scipio recovered Locri, despite an attempt by Hannibal to save the city. The subsequent behaviour of his *legatus* Q. Pleminius almost destroyed Scipio's career and ambitions. In 204 the consuls M. Cornelius Cethegus and P. Sempronius Tuditanus inflicted a reverse on Hannibal in Bruttium and regained a number of towns, including Consentia (Cosenza). In 203 Roman forces defeated Mago and the Carthaginian commander was seriously wounded. Soon afterwards both he and Hannibal were ordered to return to Africa to face the army of Scipio. Before Hannibal left, the consul Cn. Servilius Caepio had regained further areas of Bruttium. The war in Italy was at an end.[60]

III. SPAIN

We have seen that the Senate's original expectation was that the war as a whole could be fought in Spain.[61] That hope was soon dashed but when P. Cornelius Scipio failed to prevent Hannibal from crossing the Rhône he nevertheless sent the greater part of his troops on to Spain under the command of his brother Gnaeus.[62] The immediate aim now was to keep the Carthaginian forces in Spain occupied and thus prevent reinforcements being sent to Hannibal.[63] In fact the campaigns in Spain, with the exception of the catastrophe of 211, represented an unbroken run of success and the result was to drive the Carthaginians right out of the country and leave a considerable area under Roman control. In 218 Gnaeus Scipio brought the area north of the Ebro, both the coastal strip and the hinterland, into Roman control and defeated Hanno, the Carthaginian commander in the area. Hannibal's brother Hasdrubal, who had been left in overall command in Spain, came north, killed a number of soldiers and marines wandering in the fields near Tarraco and perhaps attempted, without success, to secure the defection of some of the tribes that had just joined Rome.[64]

    [60] Livy xxviii.11.11–15, 46.7–13, 15, xxix.5–9, 16.4–22, 36.4–9, 38.1, xxx.18–19.6, 19.10–20. On Mago's departure from Spain see p. 60.
    [61] See p. 45. For events in Spain see particularly Scullard 1970, 32ff.: (H 77); Lazenby 1978, 125ff.: (C 31).   [62] Polyb. iii.49.4; Livy xxi.32.3.
    [63] Cf. Polyb. iii.97.3. Livy's statement (xxi.32.4) that the aim in 218 was to drive Hasdrubal out of Spain is exaggerated and anachronistic.
    [64] Polyb. iii.76; Livy xxi.60–1. I follow De Sanctis 1907–64, iii.ii.240–1 n. 59: (A 14), and Walbank 1957–79, i.409: (B 38) (*contra* Walsh 1973, 235: (B 41)) in regarding Livy xxi.61.4–11 as a doublet. But I prefer to make Hasdrubal's incitement of revolt among the Ilergetes and others part of his first expedition north of the Ebro rather than to reject it altogether.

In 217 Hasdrubal launched both naval and land expeditions north of the Ebro. Gnaeus, helped by a Massiliote contingent, defeated the Punic fleet at the mouth of the Ebro and captured twenty-five ships. He followed up this victory with lightning raids which took the Roman fleet south of Carthago Nova and to the island of Ebusus (Ibiza). But Livy's claim that subsequent land expeditions went as far as the *saltus Castulonensis* (the Sierra Morena) is open to serious doubt. The inhabitants of the Balearic Islands (Mallorca and Minorca) sent embassies to Gnaeus seeking peace. Subsequently the Ilergetes revolted and Hasdrubal recrossed the Ebro but was diverted by an invasion by the Celtiberians acting at Scipio's behest. On news of the naval battle of the Ebro the Senate sent Publius Scipio to join Gnaeus and the two brothers advanced to Saguntum.[65] In 216 the Carthaginian position became even more difficult. Hasdrubal, who had retreated to south-west Spain, had first to deal with a rebellion among the Tartessii and was then ordered by the authorities in Carthage to join Hannibal in Italy, Himilco being sent to Spain as a replacement. The Scipios' task was to keep Hasdrubal in Spain, and when the two armies met just to the south of the Ebro, the Romans won a convincing victory which put an end to any prospect of Hasdrubal joining his brother in the immediate future and consolidated the Roman position in Spain.[66]

The events of the next four years are not easily determined. It seems, though, that in 214 and 213 a revolt by Syphax of Numidia led to a considerable part of the Carthaginian forces being withdrawn, thus enabling the Scipios to make further headway in southern Spain. In 212 Saguntum was recaptured and either then or earlier the important town of Castulo joined Rome.[67] Thus in seven years the Scipios had not only prevented the Carthaginians from sending reinforcements from Spain to Italy but had succeeded in extending Roman control deep into the territory under Carthaginian domination.

The next year, however, disaster struck. Now faced by three separate Carthaginian armies, under Hasdrubal, his brother Mago and another Hasdrubal, the son of Gisgo, the Scipios decided to split their armies,

[65] Sosylus, *FGrH* 176F1; Polyb. III.95–96.6; Livy XXII.19–22. On the alleged expedition as far as the *saltus Castulonensis* cf. De Sanctis 1907–64, III.ii.242–3 n. 62: (A 14). It was while the Scipios were near Saguntum that the Saguntine Abelux defected to the Romans and, deceiving the Carthaginian commander at Saguntum, succeeded in bringing to the Roman camp all the Spanish hostages held at Saguntum by the Carthaginians. The episode is, however, given unwarranted prominence by the sources: cf. Walbank 1957–79, 1.432: (B 38).

[66] Livy XXIII.26–29. I see no need to follow De Sanctis 1907–64, III.ii.244–5, 246 n. 7: (A 14) in placing the events described in chs. 28–9 in 215 nor in rejecting the statement that Hasdrubal was ordered to join Hannibal in Italy.

[67] App. *Hisp.* 15–16, 57–61, to be preferred to Livy XXIII.49.5–14 (s.a. 215), XXIV.41–42 (s.a. 214), XXIV.49.7–8 (s.a. 213). See De Sanctis 1907–64, III.ii.247–8 n. 76: (A 14). Livy (XXIV.42.9) dates the capture of Saguntum to 214, but also says that it was in its eighth year under Carthaginian control.

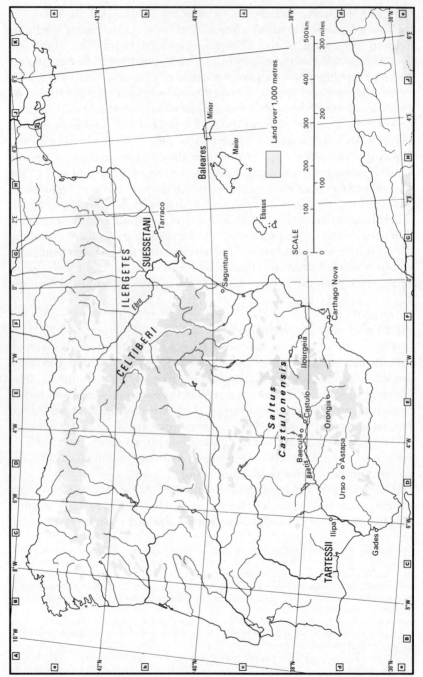

Map 4. Spain in the Second Punic War.

Publius at Castulo taking on Mago and Hasdrubal the son of Gisgo, and leaving Gnaeus at Urso to face Hasdrubal the brother of Hannibal. The Romans were relying on the support of a large number of Celtiberian mercenaries and these Hasdrubal persuaded to desert. Publius, attempting to cut off a force of Ilergetes and Suessetani who had come from north of the Ebro to join the Carthaginians, was caught by the Carthaginian generals; in the ensuing battle Scipio himself was killed and his army fled. Gnaeus, guessing what had happened, attempted to retreat but was pursued by all three Carthaginian armies, and he too met his death, though much of his army, together with that part of Publius' forces which had not been involved in the latter's final battle, survived. But the work of seven years had been undone and had it not been for the work of an *eques Romanus*, L. Marcius Septimus, in organizing the remains of the Roman armies, the Romans might have been driven out of Spain entirely and the route to Italy left open.[68]

A new commander had to be found. Initially C. Claudius Nero was sent and he appears to have succeeded in holding the situation.[69] In 210 it was decided that the assembly should elect a *privatus cum imperio* to the Spanish command, and the young P. Cornelius Scipio, son and nephew of the two dead commanders, was chosen. He arrived in the autumn and held an assembly at Tarraco of the peoples under Roman control.[70] In 209 Scipio embarked on his first major campaign, the siege of Carthago Nova, the main Carthaginian supply base in Spain and itself of great strategic importance. Scipio captured the city by sending a wading party across the lagoon that lay to the north of the city and which, as Scipio had discovered, frequently ebbed in the evening. Before the attack he told his troops that in a dream Neptune had promised his aid, an episode that played an important part in the development of the 'Scipionic legend'. Scipio's success meant the capture of a huge amount of booty, both material and human, and eighteen ships. The human booty included a considerable number of artisans who had worked in the Carthaginian armouries. The Carthaginians had been holding their Spanish hostages at Carthago Nova and these Scipio released. Several Spanish chieftains, including the Ilergetan leaders Andobales and Mandonius, now defected to Scipio.[71] In 208 Scipio advanced inland and met Hasdrubal at Baecula, north of the River Baetis (the Guadalquivir). Scipio was victorious but

[68] Polyb. x.6.2–7.1; Livy xxv.32–39; App. *Hisp.* 16.60–63, De Sanctis 1907–64, 445ff.: (A 14). For the date *ibid.* 446 n. 4. The achievements of Marcius have perhaps been exaggerated: Walbank 1957–79, II.136: (B 38).   [69] Livy xxvi.17; App. *Hisp.* 17.65–67.

[70] Livy xxvi.18–20.6; on the chronology cf. De Sanctis 1907–64, III.ii.454 n. 18: (A 14).

[71] Polyb. x.2–20; Livy xxvi.41–51; on the chronology cf. De Sanctis 1907–64, III.ii.468–9 n. 38: (A 14); Walbank 1957–79, II.14–15: (B 38); on the Scipionic legend see n. 147.

Hasdrubal was able to escape with most of his army and, despite a guard put on the Pyrenees, reach Gaul and the route to Italy.[72]

In 207 Hasdrubal was replaced by Hanno, who joined Mago in Celtiberia. Scipio sent Iunius Silanus against them and in the ensuing battle Hanno was captured. Hasdrubal the son of Gisgo had split up his army and retired to Gades (Cadiz). Scipio sent his brother Lucius to attack the town of Orongis (Jaen), south-east of Castulo. In 206 came the decisive battle at Ilipa, just to the north of Seville. Hasdrubal fled to the west coast, and reached Gades by sea. What remained were mopping-up operations. Ilourgeia and Castulo, which had gone over to Carthage in 211, were captured. Ilourgeia had slaughtered refugees from the armies of the Scipios and received the severest punishment.[73] Further south Marcius Septimus captured Astapa, whose inhabitants committed mass suicide. At this point Scipio fell ill and rumours of his death caused both a revolt by Andobales and Mandonius and a mutiny in the Roman army. When the rumours proved false the Ilergetan leaders abandoned their plans and the mutiny was quelled, the ringleaders being executed. Meanwhile the remnants of the Carthaginian forces in Spain were at Gades under the command of Mago. Another Hanno had collected some Spanish mercenaries, but he was defeated by Marcius, while C. Laelius inflicted a naval defeat on Adherbal. Hopes of the surrender of Gades itself, however, were thwarted. News of the severity of the punishment of the mutineers led to another outbreak by Andobales and Mandonius and a punitive expedition by Scipio. After the defeat of Andobales, he and Mandonius again asked for Roman mercy and, somewhat surprisingly, were granted it, a conclusion which casts doubt on Livy's statement that Scipio set out *ad caedem Ilergetum*.[74] Scipio, who had earlier crossed to Africa to visit Syphax, next went to the west of Spain to meet Massinissa.[75]

Mago now received instructions from Carthage to sail to Italy. On reaching Carthago Nova he attempted to attack the city, but was severely repulsed and forced to return westwards. Gades, however, refused to admit him and he eventually crossed to Minorca (the inhabitants of Mallorca would not allow him to land) and from there to Genua. Gades surrendered to the Romans.[76]

Scipio returned to Rome to stand for the consulship of 205. In Spain the command was taken over by L. Cornelius Lentulus and L. Manlius

---

[72] Polyb. x.34–40; Livy XXVII.17–20; on the chronology cf. De Sanctis 1907–64, III.ii.468–9 n. 38: (A 14); on Hasdrubal's escape see Walbank 1957–79, II.252: (B 38).

[73] Polyb. XI.20–24; Livy XXVIII.1–4.4, 12.10–16, 19–21. On the identification of Ilourgeia, called Iliturgi by Livy, see Walbank 1957–79, II.305: (B 38).

[74] Polyb. XI.25–33; Livy XXVIII.22–34.

[75] Syphax: Polyb. XI.24a.4; Livy XXVIII.17.10–18. Massinissa: Livy XXVII.16.12, 35. See below pp. 62–3.   [76] Livy XXVIII.36–7; on Mago in Italy see p. 56 above.

Acidinus. Andobales and Mandonius revolted yet again and were yet again defeated. This time Andobales was killed in battle and Mandonius executed. Until 200 there is no further information on events in Spain.[77]

IV. SICILY AND SARDINIA

Sicily and Sardinia were the prizes won by Rome as a result of the First Punic War and its aftermath. They were finally organized as provinces in 227 but in Sicily the kingdom of Syracuse, like the city of Messana, remained an independent state, bound to Rome by treaty.[78] The loyalty of the Syracusan king Hiero to Rome was unwavering. In 218 he intercepted Carthaginian ships and warned the Roman commander of a plan to capture Lilybaeum. In 216 and 215 he provided corn, money and light-armed troops, and urged Rome to invade Africa. In 216 Carthaginian ships ravaged his kingdom.[79] But in 215 Hiero died and was succeeded by his son Hieronymus. The latter, inspired by two of his advisers, made approaches to Hannibal, who in his turn sent Hippocrates and Epicydes, two Carthaginian citizens of Syracusan origin, to conclude an alliance. Before long (214), however, Hieronymus was assassinated.[80] Accord was eventually reached between the various factions in Syracuse, but Hippocrates and Epicydes claimed that the council were planning to deliver the city into Roman control and Adranadorus, who had been the power behind Hieronymus, was killed on suspicion of plotting a *coup*. In the election of new magistrates Hippocrates and Epicydes were chosen. By now (late 214) M. Claudius Marcellus had been appointed to command in Sicily, and as the result of a complex series of events Hippocrates and Epicydes eventually overcame the desire of the upper-class leadership to maintain peace with Rome, and Syracuse declared for Carthage. In spring 213 Marcellus began to besiege the city. In addition a Carthaginian force under Himilco had landed in Sicily, captured Agrigentum, and was seeking to bring about the defection of other towns. In 212 Marcellus captured Syracuse, aided by a plague which virtually destroyed the Carthaginian army. The treatment of the city was harsh, the booty enormous.[81] There remained only mopping-up operations against Carthaginian forces in Agrigentum (spring 211). Following Marcellus' return to Rome a new Carthaginian force landed and secured the allegiance of several states, but they were soon recovered.[82]

---

[77] Livy XXVIII.38.1, XXIX.1.19–3.5. It is uncertain how far a permanent organization of Spain was undertaken at this time, but at least some peoples were probably paying a fixed tribute in these years. Cf. Schulten 1930, 308ff.: (G 28) (for financial payments see Livy XXIII.48.4ff.).

[78] *CAH*[2] VII.ii, ch. 11 (b).   [79] Livy XXI.49.2–6, XXII.37, 56.7. XXIII.21.5, 38.13.

[80] Polyb. VII.2–5; Livy XXIV.4–7.9. For the chronology see Walbank 1957–79, II.2: (B 38).

[81] Polyb. VII.14b, VIII.3a.3–7, 37, IX.10; Livy XXIV.21–39, XXV.23–31.11, XXVI.21.1–13; Plut. *Marc.* 13–21. For the chronology see Walbank 1957–79, II.3.5–8: (B 38).

[82] Livy XXV.40.5–41.7, XXVI.21.14–17.

Marcellus' treatment of Syracuse gave rise to an embassy of protest to Rome, but although many senators seem to have agreed that Marcellus had gone too far, the Senate voted to ratify his actions.[83]

Little happened in Sicily after this. In 210 M. Valerius Laevinus, through the treachery of the Numidian Muttines, recaptured Agrigentum and transported to Rhegium a number of exiles who had been engaging in brigandage in Sicily. Laevinus also devoted his attention to the re-establishment of Sicilian cereal farming.[84]

As far as Sardinia is concerned, there were clearly many people who were discontented with Roman rule, and in 217 the consul Cn. Servilius Geminus demanded hostages. In 215, on the initiative of anti-Roman forces in the island, the Carthaginians sent Hasdrubal 'the Bald' to attack it, but his fleet was wrecked by a storm off the Balearic Islands. Later in the same year Manlius Torquatus defeated the Sardinian leader Hampsicora, and when Hasdrubal's fleet eventually arrived Manlius won a victory over the combined Carthaginian and Sardinian forces. Another attack on Sardinia came in 210, but nothing more than ravaging was achieved.[85]

V. THE FINAL CAMPAIGN IN AFRICA

Until 204 Roman activity in Africa itself was confined to a series of lightning raids.[86] A full-scale invasion by Ti. Sempronius Longus had been planned for 218 but Hannibal's arrival in Italy had prevented its implementation.[87] The policy of taking the war to the enemy, even if it had been possible after 218, was one entirely alien to the Fabian strategy, and in 205 Scipio's plans for an invasion of Africa were vehemently resisted by both Fabius and Q. Fulvius Flaccus.[88]

Before we come to the details of Scipio's campaigns something must be said about the tangled history of the Numidian princes Massinissa and Syphax. In 214 or 213 the Scipios made an alliance with Syphax, king of the Masaesyli, who had revolted from Carthage. In the ensuing conflict the Carthaginians were aided by Gala, king of the Massyli and father of Massinissa.[89] In 210 Syphax sent an embassy to Rome which was warmly received while Massinissa was active in the service of Carthage. In 206 both Scipio and Hasdrubal the son of Gisgo visited Syphax in person to solicit his support. Syphax pledged his loyalty to Scipio, but later married Hasdrubal's daughter and transferred his allegiance to Carthage. Fortu-

[83] Livy XXVI.26.5–9, 29–32; Plut. *Marc.* 23: see below p. 78.
[84] Polyb. IX.27.11; Livy XXVI.40.
[85] Livy XXII.31.1, XXIII.34.10–17, 10–41.7, XXVII.6.13–14.   [86] See below pp. 66–7.
[87] Polyb. III.40.2, 41.2–3, 61.8–10; Livy XXI.17.6, 51.6–7.
[88] See below p. 73.   [89] See above p. 57.

nately for Rome, however, Massinissa had also changed sides. In 206 he had made approaches to the Romans and met Scipio himself, though without openly proclaiming his defection from Carthage. Before long, however, Syphax, inspired by the Carthaginians, occupied the kingdom of the Massyli and Massinissa was forced to flee with only a small band of supporters.[90]

In 205 Scipio had been assigned Sicily with permission to cross to Africa if he saw fit. In that year the invasion was restricted to another in the series of lightning raids, under the leadership of C. Laelius. Massinissa urged Laelius to persuade Scipio to launch a major invasion as soon as possible.[91] In 204, following the episode at Locri, Scipio did invade and landed near Utica. A cavalry force under Hanno was defeated by Massinissa and Scipio began to besiege Utica. In the following spring the decisive series of events began. Hasdrubal and Syphax had camped near Scipio, who had had no alternative to placing his winter quarters on a narrow, rocky peninsula.[92] Their camps, however, were constructed of wood or reeds. The details of the camps were discovered in the course of counterfeited peace negotiations, and a night attack on them resulted in the camps being destroyed by fire and large numbers killed. The Carthaginians recruited fresh forces and persuaded Syphax to rejoin the conflict. The armies met at the 'Great Plains', about 120 km west of Carthage, and Scipio was victorious. After the battle Laelius and Massinissa pursued Syphax and captured him. Massinissa was restored to his kingdom.

Meanwhile the Carthaginians had taken the twin decisions to recall Hannibal and Mago from Italy and to launch their fleet against Scipio's ships, which were engaged in the siege of Utica and quite unprepared for a naval battle. Scipio, who had camped in sight of Carthage at Tunis, was forced to use a wall of transport ships in defence. Sixty transports were lost but a major disaster was averted.[93]

Carthage now opened peace negotiations and a provisional agreement was reached. Carthage was to abandon all claims to Italy, Gaul, Spain, and the islands between Italy and Africa. Her rights to expand in Africa itself were to be limited and Massinissa's possession of both his own kingdom and parts of that of Syphax were to be recognized. In addition Carthage was to surrender prisoners and deserters, give up all but twenty

[90] Polyb. XI.24a.4; Livy XXV.34.2ff., XXVII.4.5–9, 5.11, 20.8, XXVIII.16.11, 17.10–18, 35, XXIX.29.5–33; App. *Hisp.* 37.149–150. It should be emphasized that the initial approaches to the Romans by Massinissa preceded Syphax' attack and that it was not until 204 that Syphax declared publicly against Rome (Livy XXIX.23). In 205 Scipio was hoping for support from both Syphax and Massinissa; cf. Brisson 1973, 277: (C 6). For the chronology cf. De Sanctis 1907–64, III.ii.519 n. 122: (A 14).   [91] Livy XXVIII.45.8, XXIX.3.6–5.1. See below p. 67.

[92] Livy XXIX.23–29.3, 34–35. On Scipio's exposed position in the winter of 204/3 cf. e.g. Scullard 1970, 123–4: (H 77).   [93] Polyb. XIV.1–10; Livy XXX.3–15.

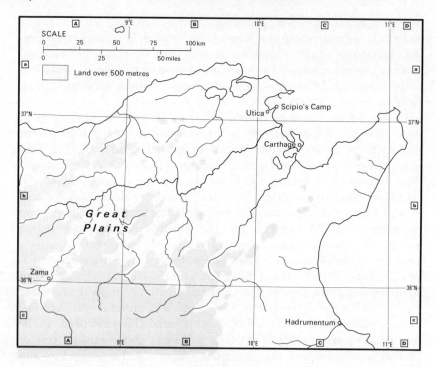

Map 5. North Africa.

ships and pay a substantial indemnity. The Senate accepted the terms but
during the truce the Carthaginians, who were suffering from an acute
shortage of food, attacked a convoy of Roman supply ships which had
been driven ashore near Carthage, and followed this with an attack on the
ship carrying the Roman envoys sent by Scipio to protest about the
earlier incident.[94]

Hannibal had now returned to Carthage, and at a meeting with Scipio
he offered peace on the terms of Rome possessing Sicily, Sardinia, Spain,
and the islands between Italy and Africa. But Scipio was determined that
Carthage should be weakened enough to eliminate the possibility of any
further aggressive actions, and so rejected Hannibal's offer. There
followed the final and decisive conflict, the battle of Zama.[95]

The peace settlement concluded after the battle contained the following terms. Carthage was to remain free within boundaries as they were

---

[94] Polyb. xv.1–2; *PRyl.* 491; Livy xxx.16, 21.11–25.10; App. *Pun.* 32.134–137. Livy wrongly says
that the Senate rejected the terms. See Walbank 1957–79, 11.441–2: (B 38). On the terms cf. De Sanctis
1907–64, 111.ii.535–6: (A 14).

[95] Polyb. xv.4–14; Livy xxx.29–35. For the problems associated with the battle see Walbank
1957–79, 11.446ff.: (B 38); Lazenby 1978, 220ff.: (C 31).

before the war. Restitution was to be made of the goods seized during the earlier truce. Prisoners and fugitives were to be handed over and Carthage was to surrender all her elephants and her fleet, with the exception of ten triremes. Carthage was to launch no attack outside her own territory without Roman permission. Massinissa was to have all lands possessed by his ancestors – the seed of later disputes. An indemnity of 10,000 talents was to be paid in fifty annual instalments.[96] Despite some resistance Hannibal persuaded the Carthaginians that there was no alternative to accepting these terms. There was also opposition at Rome from the consul of 201, Cn. Cornelius Lentulus, eager to command in Africa himself. But the assembly ratified the peace and ordered that Scipio should administer it.[97]

VI. THE WAR AT SEA[98]

Unlike the First Punic War the Hannibalic War was primarily a land conflict: for the most part the activities of the Roman and Carthaginian fleets form part of the story of the various theatres of land engagements and several have already been mentioned as such. It would be wrong to conclude, however, that sea-power was not an important factor in the war. Indeed, it is clear that Rome's continuous numerical dominance in the western Mediterranean was of vital importance to the whole course of the war. It was this dominance which made it impossible for Hannibal to transport his army by sea in 218, and equally impossible for Hasdrubal to do so ten years later. Only once did reinforcements reach Hannibal by sea but Rome could transport her troops to Spain and safely import supplies of grain from Sicily, Sardinia and Egypt.[99]

Neither side, however, made the best of its naval resources. The only year when Carthage made a major maritime effort was in the Sicilian theatre in 212, and then the Carthaginian admiral Bomilcar completely failed to exploit the fact that, for once, the Roman fleet was outnumbered.[100] In the years following the recapture of Syracuse persistent rumours of a major new Carthaginian naval offensive failed to materialize. Partly, no doubt, Carthage was simply unable to find the manpower for new ships, but another factor may well have been sheer lack of confidence in their ability to match the Romans at sea.[101] In 204, again,

---

[96] Polyb. xv.18; Livy xxx.37.1–6; App. *Pun.* 54.234–238; Walbank 1957–79, 11.466–71: (B 38).

[97] Polyb. xv.19; Livy xxx.37.7–12, 40.7–16, 42.11–43.4.

[98] The fullest and most penetrating account of naval matters during the war is Thiel 1946, 32–199: (H 60).

[99] Livy xxiii.41.10; Thiel 1946, 64,71–2: (H 60). The only other (unsuccessful) attempt to send reinforcements to Hannibal by sea was in 205 (Livy xxviii.46.14; App. *Hann.* 54.226–227; Thiel, *op. cit.* 150). On grain imports see n. 33.

[100] On the naval side of the siege of Syracuse see Thiel 1946, 79–90: (H 60).

[101] Livy xxvii.5.13 (210), 22.8 (208); Thiel 1946, 109–11: (H 60).

Carthage failed to use her fleet to attack Scipio's exposed camp near Utica and even in 203 they launched their attack on Scipio's fleet too late.[102]

As to the Romans, they may be criticized for allowing Bomilcar to sail unchallenged into the harbour of Syracuse on several occasions in 213 and 212, for the fact that Mago was able to make an attack on Carthago Nova in 206 with a fleet consisting largely of transports, and for making no effort to prevent either Mago from reaching Genua in 205 or Hannibal from crossing to Africa in 203.[103] In fact the number of ships actually in commission in 206 and subsequent years dropped sharply. In part this may have been owing to the Senate's belief that victories over the Carthaginian fleet in 208 and 207 had removed all threat from the Carthaginian navy. It is certainly true that the Romans did not have a 'naval mentality'. They naturally thought in terms of land engagements and saw the maritime arm as something to be employed only when they were forced to do so by the actions of the enemy. But as far as the latter years of the war are concerned it may be that Rome simply could not raise the manpower needed to put all the ships it possessed into active service.[104]

It will be convenient to mention here some of the more significant naval events which have not been touched on in other contexts. Of particular importance is the fleet which was based at Lilybaeum – from 217 until his death in 211 under the continuous command of T. Otacilius Crassus. In 217, according to Livy, a Punic fleet making for Lilybaeum and Italy was scattered by a storm. Three ships were captured by Hiero, who warned the praetor M. Aemilius that a further thirty-five ships were on their way to Lilybaeum. This fleet was then defeated by Aemilius off Lilybaeum. Subsequently the Romans captured the island of Malta which was held by a Carthaginian garrison. In 217, after the Roman victory in the naval battle of the Ebro, a Carthaginian fleet tried to make contact with the land army near Pisa and captured some Roman transport vessels off Cosa. They were deterred from further actions, however, by a Roman fleet under the consul Cn. Servilius Geminus, which subsequently ravaged the island of Cercina off the African coast, raided the coast itself, and placed a garrison in Cossura (Pantelleria). In 216, after Cannae, one Carthaginian fleet attacked the territory of Syracuse, while another stood off the Aegates Isles, ready to move on Lilybaeum if Otacilius went to the assistance of Syracuse. Later the praetor P. Furius Philus made a raid on Africa in which he was wounded. In 215 another raid on Africa was launched by Otacilius and he subsequently captured

[102] *Ibid.* 159–66. [103] *Ibid.* 8off., 89, 143–4, 148–9, 171–3.
[104] *Ibid.* 139ff.; Brunt 1971, 666ff.: (H 82). Brunt also suggests that in earlier years the 'paper strengths' of the various squadrons were well above the actual numbers in commission. He may have a point, but his own estimates of the numbers seem too low.

seven Carthaginian ships. Otacilius' next raid was in 212 when he captured a large number of grain transports.[105] After Otacilius' death the Lilybaeum squadron was placed under the command of M. Valerius Laevinus, the consul governing Sicily as a whole, and he launched a further attack on Africa under the command of M. Valerius Messalla.[106] In 208 rumours of a Carthaginian naval assault on Sicily and Italy led to an increase in the size of the Roman fleet but the alarm proved unfounded.[107] In both this year and 207 further raids were made, and in both years considerable victories were achieved over Carthaginian fleets.[108] In 205 Carthaginian transport ships were captured off Sardinia[109] and in 203 the Sardinian squadron intercepted some of Mago's transports on their return journey to Africa.[110]

VII. THE WAR AND POLITICS AT ROME

There were, of course, no political parties at Rome, and political analysis must investigate the activities and positions of individuals or groups of individuals. Modern writers have taken widely differing views of the nature of political divisions during the war and what follows cannot claim to be more than a personal picture of the situation.[111]

The discussion proceeds from a number of assumptions.

(i) Political activity is not something that can be carried on in isolation and individuals are bound to group together, even if, as at Rome, such groups are not necessarily long-lasting and there may be a constant kaleidoscopic process of persons joining and leaving such groups.

(ii) Committed adherents of these political groups were only a minority in the Senate and no group could command a consistent majority there. Similarly the number of votes that each group could control in the *comitia* (in the case of elections, in the upper classes of the *comitia centuriata*) was limited. To secure support for a particular view, to secure the election of a particular candidate, were things that had to be worked for on each occasion. It has been claimed that during the Second Punic War the assembly chose consuls simply on the grounds of military ability, and that a choice between different groups did not come into the matter.[112] The arguments which follow are sufficient, it is hoped, to

---

[105] Polyb. III.96.7–14; Livy XXI.49–51.2 (Thiel's doubts (44ff.) concerning the authenticity of the events described in this passage do not seem to me to be justified: Thiel 1946, 44ff.: (H 60)), XXII.31.1–7, 56.6–8, XXIII.21.2, 41.8–9, XXV.31.12–15; Thiel, *op. cit.* 52–4, 58–9, 70, 86.

[106] Livy XXVII.5.8–9; Thiel 1946, 113–14: (H 60).　　[107] See n. 101.

[108] Livy XXVII.29.7–8, XXVIII.4.5–7; Thiel 1946, 130–2, 134–5: (H 60).　　[109] See n. 99.

[110] Livy XXX.19.5. A Carthaginian fleet had plundered Sardinia in 210 (see p. 62) and it was not protected by a standing squadron until 208 (Livy XXVII.22.6–8).

[111] On the politics of the period see particularly Patterson 1942: (C 41); Scullard 1955: (H 24) and 1973, 39–88: (H 54); Cassola 1962, 259ff.: (H 35); Lippold 1963, 147ff.: (H 13).

[112] Patterson 1942: (C 41).

refute this position. What is true, however, is that no group could hope to secure the election of someone who was believed to be militarily incompetent and that proven military ability might well help a candidate to secure election even though other factors favoured his opponents. In 217 the *lex Genucia* forbidding iteration of the consulship within ten years was suspended for the duration of the war.[113] This made the election of untried men more difficult and helps to explain the political pattern which will be outlined below.

(iii) In the pre-Gracchan period it is reasonable to regard the *gens* as an important political unit and to assume, as a working hypothesis, that those closely related to each other worked together politically. But such an assumption cannot be extended to all the members of long-established and, by the late third century, widely spread families such as the Cornelii or the Sempronii. We shall see that Sempronius Longus, the consul of 218, has a different allegiance to that of Sempronius Gracchus, the consul of 215 and 213, and that in 201 a Cornelius Lentulus is clearly opposed to Cornelius Scipio.[114]

(iv) Though individual cases of collegiality or succession in office can prove nothing (and in particular the influence of presiding officers at elections must not be overestimated[115]), when members of two different *gentes* are found a number of times in close connection with one another, that does constitute evidence for association between the two families.

(v) Though the main aim of political groups may often have been no more than securing office for their members, there may be occasions when they differed on matters of substance and when the *comitia*, in voting for candidates for office, were choosing between policies as well as between men.

From the point of view of Roman strategy the war falls into three clearly defined phases. First, the period of meeting Hannibal in open conflict with the three disasters of the Trebbia, Trasimene and Cannae. Secondly, the period from Cannae until 205, when Roman policy was fundamentally defensive, and thirdly, the final period of the invasion of Africa, first planned, it will be recalled, in 218. The significant point is that it is in the first and third of these periods that the consulship is held by the Scipios and those associated with them. In the intervening period, there is only one instance, and that not certain, of a 'Scipionic' consul. This should not be regarded as a coincidence, and we may conclude that the 'forward strategy' was that advocated by the Scipios and opposed by other leading

[113] Livy XXVII.6.7.
[114] For both the importance of the *gens* and the limits of its influence see particularly Livy XXXV.10.9.
[115] On the role of the presiding officer see particularly Rilinger 1976: (H 21).

families. In 205 Scipio's proposal to invade Africa met with strong opposition from Fabius and Q. Fulvius Flaccus.[116] That does not mean, however, that all those opposed to the Scipios were members of one group: all that united them was opposition to the Scipios and the failed strategy. (It is not, of course, being suggested that in the immediate aftermath of Cannae supporters of the Scipios were still arguing in favour of the strategy that had failed. But both the strategy and those who had supported it were discredited.)

We may now examine the consular colleges of the war in more detail (see Table, pp. 525–8). In 218 the consuls were P. Cornelius Scipio and Ti. Sempronius Longus: the sons of the two shared the consulship in 194. The original plan, as we have seen, was to fight the war outside Italy – Scipio was to go to Spain and Sempronius to invade Africa. Fabius, moreover, may well have been opposed to going to war at all.[117] The consuls of 217 were C. Flaminius and Cn. Servilius Geminus, of 216 L. Aemilius Paullus and C. Terentius Varro. Nothing can be surmised about the allegiance of Servilius, but Paullus' daughter was married to Scipio Africanus and in the second century the close relationship between Aemilii and Cornelii Scipiones is beyond doubt.[118] We have already noticed the unacceptability of the picture of Varro presented by both Polybius and Livy,[119] and Livy's portrayal of Flaminius as an upstart demagogue opposed by virtually the whole of the rest of the nobility[120] is equally unconvincing. In fact both Flaminius and Varro may well have had the support of the Scipios.[121] It is probably true that they were men willing to make a wider popular appeal – at least to those whose votes mattered in the *comitia centuriata* – than was normal for the governing class and that the Scipios were less opposed to this than were their political opponents. Flaminius was certainly no friend of Fabius, with whom he had clashed violently over his law for the viritane assignation of *ager publicus* in Picenum in 232.[122] M. Minucius Rufus, the *magister equitum* of 217, whose views on strategy were clearly close to those of the consuls of 218–216, may also be linked with the Scipios.[123] There is nothing strange in both Fabius and Minucius being elected at the same time by the assembly, any more than in two consuls of different

---

[116] Livy xxviii.40–45.   [117] See above p. 45.

[118] See in general the genealogical table in Scullard 1973, 309: (H 54). Observe that the father of Paullus' daughter-in-law, C. Papirius Maso, and Scipio's brother-in-law M. Pomponius Matho were consuls together in 231 (see further Additional Note pp. 79–80).

[119] See above pp. 51–2. Notice also that Polybius seeks to put the blame for the Trebbia on to Sempronius Longus and to absolve Scipio: iii.70.1ff.; Walbank 1957–79, 1.404: (b 38). For the complex issue of the elections for 216 see Additional Note pp. 79–80.

[120] Livy xxi.63, xxii.1.5–8.

[121] I accept in its essentials the view of Scullard 1973, 44ff.: (H 54).   [122] Cic. *Sen.* 11.

[123] Another Minucius, Q. Minucius Thermus (*tr. pl.* 201, *cos.* 193), was a strong supporter of Africanus at the end of the war (Livy xxx.40.9–16, 43.2–3).

views or factions being elected as colleagues. Nor should we reject the story of the equalization of the *imperium* of Fabius and Minucius:[124] in an emergency constitutional oddities are always possible. The unpopularity of Fabius' strategy, together with Minucius' broader appeal, produced a situation where there was enough support to downgrade Fabius but not enough for the complete deposition of a man of proven military ability. The bill for the equalization of *imperium* was tribunician and was therefore passed in the tribal assembly where support for Minucius may have been stronger than in the *comitia centuriata*[125] (we may note that it was proposed by a Metilius and that in 220 Flaminius as censor had given his support to a *lex Metilia de fullonibus*[126]).

We now move into the period when the offensive strategy is completely abandoned and in which, until the second consulship of M. Livius Salinator in 207, there is no consul whom there is any reason to link with the Scipios. But it would be wrong to think that all the consuls of this period were closely linked to and supported by the great Cunctator. It does appear that in the first three years after Cannae Fabius was able to ensure that the consulship was held by himself or his close associates. In 215, following the death of the consul-elect L. Postumius Albinus, M. Claudius Marcellus was elected as colleague for Ti. Sempronius Gracchus, but was subsequently declared *vitio creatus* by the college of augurs, of which Fabius was the senior member (he had been elected in 265), and Fabius himself was elected in Marcellus' place. In 214, when it appeared that T. Otacilius Crassus and M. Aemilius Regillus were about to be elected, Fabius intervened and secured the election of himself and Marcellus instead.[127] Otacilius was married to Fabius' niece, while Otacilius and Marcellus were half-brothers.[128] It is reasonable to think that Marcellus accepted his removal from office in 215 on the assurance of Fabius' support for the elections for 214. As for Otacilius, he may well have been no more than a competent second-rater whom Fabius, despite his relationship to him, did not regard as of sufficient calibre for the consulship.[129] In 213 Fabius' son held the consulship together with Ti. Sempronius Gracchus. As Gracchus had been consul with Fabius himself in 215, we may classify him as a Fabian ally.

It is at this point that a break comes. The three years of Fabian dominance meant that senior members of other leading families, though serving as praetors, had not held the consulship. This naturally led to resentment, and the lack of any striking success by Fabius helped to

[124] See above p. 51.   [125] Livy XXII.25.3. See further p. 73 below.
[126] Pliny, *HN* XXXV.197.   [127] Livy XXIII.31.12–14, XXIV.7.12–9.3.
[128] Livy XXIV.8.11; Plut. *Marc.* 2.2ff.
[129] The claim attributed to Fabius (Livy XXIV.8.14–16) that Otacilius had been incompetent as fleet commander at Lilybaeum is not justified. See Thiel 1946, 71 n. 117: (H 60).

create a change. It is wrong, however, to think of the non-Fabian consuls of 212–210 as a united group. They were: in 212 Q. Fulvius Flaccus, who had held his first consulship as long ago as 237, and Ap. Claudius Pulcher, the senior member of the senior branch of the patrician Claudii; in 211 Cn. Fulvius Centumalus and P. Sulpicius Galba; and in 210 M. Valerius Laevinus (whose colleague was M. Claudius Marcellus). These consuls have been described as constituting a 'Fulvio-Claudian' group,[130] but though relations between Fulvii, Sulpicii and Valerii Laevini[131] can be traced over a considerable period – the consul of 212 was married to a Sulpicia and the son of the consul of 210 was the half-brother of M. Fulvius Nobilior, the consul of 189[132] – there is no reason to link the Claudii, and Ap. Claudius Pulcher in particular, with them. The consuls of 212 may have been united by nothing more than common rivalry with Fabius. We may note their strong differences over the treatment of the leaders of the Campanian revolt following the fall of Capua.[133] Claudius and Fulvius probably canvassed for office with a pledge to achieve more than Fabius and his friends, but there was no difference in their basic approach to the war.[134]

Marcellus' success at Syracuse made him a political force in his own right and his election to the consulship of 210 need not be seen as a Fabian success, particularly as Fabius himself seems to have been defeated by M. Valerius Laevinus. The accusations of the Sicilians against Marcellus were supported by M. Cornelius Cethegus, which causes no surprise, and Marcellus was criticized in the Senate by T. Manlius Torquatus, who had withdrawn from consideration for the consulship of 210.[135] Manlius' political position must be left uncertain.[136]

In these years Marcellus appears to have been eager to confront Hannibal in a pitched battle and eventually met his death in an ambush in 208.[137] But of course the dangers of open conflicts were by now far less

---

[130] Scullard 1973, 61ff.: (H 54).

[131] These three families, together, with the Postumii and the Manlii, form the core of what I have elsewhere called the 'Fulvian group'. Relations between members of this group, and opposition to the Scipios and their supporters, can, I believe, be traced over a period of more than fifty years. (The refusal of Laevinus to nominate Fulvius Flaccus as dictator in 210 (Livy xxvii.5.15ff.) is probably to be regarded as pique at the rejection of his proposal to nominate M. Valerius Messalla and is not a counter-indication to the picture here presented.)

[132] Cf. Münzer, PW vii.246 (Sulpicia); Polyb. xxi.29.11 (Fulvius and Valerius Laevinus).

[133] Livy xxvi.15–16.4; cf. p. 77.

[134] The feeling that new men were needed perhaps explains why Sulpicius who had held no previous curule office could be elected for 211 and why P. Licinius Crassus could become pontifex maximus and censor in 212 and 210 respectively (see below).

[135] Livy xxvi.22.12, 26.8, 32.1.

[136] In 231 both Manlius and Fulvius Flaccus were deprived of their censorship by the augural college. Scullard 1973, 37: (H 54), thinks this alienated Fulvius, but strangely regards Manlius as still 'Fabian' (58, 65). The only reason for regarding him as 'Fulvian' is the position of other Manlii in the second century. [137] See p. 55 above.

than they had been after Cannae and, though Fabius himself held a fifth consulship with Q. Fulvius Flaccus in 209, both the need for a Fabian strategy and the period of Fabian influence were coming to an end.

The first overt sign of change[138] is the election of M. Livius Salinator to a second consulship in 207. He had been consul in 219 with L. Aemilius Paullus and convicted of *peculatus* during the Second Illyrian War. C. Claudius Nero, his colleague in 207, had been a prosecution witness at his trial and Paullus too had nearly been brought down.[139] The Livii and the Aemilii seem to have had close links over a long period[140] and it is reasonable to see the trial as an anti-Scipionic move. Livius, though, may have felt that his allies had not done enough to help him at his trial, and he is not necessarily to be viewed as a whole-hearted Scipionic supporter in the latter years of the war. In 203 Salinator advocated delaying discussion of Scipio's peace terms until the return of one of the consuls.[141] (Little can be made of the fact that it was Laevinus and Marcellus, the consuls of 210, who brought him home from self-imposed exile, whilst the Scipionic censors (see below) made him return to public life. Nor is it easy to see what significance is to be attached to the fact that Salinator was the son-in-law of Pacuvius Calavius, the leader of the revolt of Capua[142].) Nevertheless the news that Hasdrubal was on his way meant that an open battle could not be avoided and that would create a desire to make use of the services of an experienced consular who had not been involved in the defensive strategy of the Fabian period. The Fabians and Fulvians perhaps found Livius, with his now much looser ties with the Scipios, more acceptable than a younger man from the heart of the Scipionic bloc, and the Scipios did not have sufficient strength to impose their own choice on the assembly.

But though Livius is the first consul with the slightest Scipionic links since 216, the resurgence of the Scipios in other ways begins earlier. In 212 P. Licinius Crassus, who had not yet held the praetorship, became *pontifex maximus*, defeating two senior consulars, Q. Fulvius Flaccus and T. Manlius Torquatus, for the post, and in 210 he was elected censor.[143] He was Scipio's colleague as consul in 205 and all his actions as *pontifex maximus* show him in conflict with those who, on other grounds, can be regarded as opponents of the Scipios.[144] In 210, as we have seen, the

---

[138] I am unable to assess the position of T. Quinctius Crispinus, consul in 208.

[139] Livy XXII.35.3, XXVII.34.10.

[140] The first Livius to hold the consulship had M. Aemilius Paullus as his colleague. The next is our Livius, with L. Aemilius Paullus as his colleague. In 236 M. Livius Salinator was *decemvir sacris faciundis* with M. Aemilius Lepidus. In the next generation there is a M. Livius Aemilianus, possibly a son of Paullus adopted by his colleague. This is a case where evidence of collegiality can properly be used to demonstrate links between a major and a minor family.   [141] Livy XXX.23.1.

[142] Livy XXIII.2.6, XXVII.34.5–6.   [143] Livy XXV.5.2–4, XXVII.6.7–18.

[144] See Briscoe 1973, 80, and 1981, 22–3: (B 3 and 4).

future Africanus was elected to the command in Spain. It may be that there was no opposition, and the prestige of his father and uncle increased his attractiveness. But the decision did mean the replacement of C. Claudius Nero and the appointment cannot be regarded as anything other than a Scipionic success. The election was made in the tribal assembly which was, in principle at least, more democratic than the *comitia centuriata*.[145] It was suggested earlier that the Scipios had a broader 'popular' appeal than their opponents and it is remarkable that though Scipionic successes in the centuriate assembly were rare, they had a great deal of success in the election of aediles held in the tribal assembly. Of the ten known patrician curule aediles between 217 and 213 six are Cornelii. Between 216 and 202 we know the names of 13 curule aediles from plebeian *gentes* and six came from families closely connected with the Scipios.

In 206 comes the real resurgence of Scipionic control of the consulate. In that year the consuls were Q. Caecilius Metellus, a consistent supporter of Scipio against his opponents in the final years of the war,[146] and L. Veturius Philo, son of the man who had held the censorship with Crassus. In 205 come Scipio and Crassus, and in 204 P. Cornelius Cethegus and P. Sempronius Tuditanus. The latter's position is uncertain: no other Sempronius Tuditanus can plausibly be regarded as Scipionic and the allegiance of the Sempronii Longi cannot prove anything about a Tuditanus.

Scipio was determined to carry the war to Africa, but, as we have seen, his plan was strongly opposed by Fabius and Fulvius Flaccus. They were doubtless alarmed by the growth of Scipio's personal prestige, and the stories of Spaniards saluting Scipio as a king and the popular belief that he was divinely inspired increased that alarm.[147] But there is no need to doubt that Fabius and Fulvius genuinely believed that an invasion of Africa would create unnecessary dangers and that the first task was to drive Hannibal out of Italy. The following years see a series of attempts by his opponents to deprive Scipio of the final victory. In 204 Fabius wanted him recalled because of the Locri scandal, in 203 Cn. Servilius Caepio attempted to cross to Sicily, in 202 both consuls wanted the command in Africa, and in 201 Cn. Cornelius Lentulus obstructed the confirmation of the peace concluded with Carthage by Scipio.[148] Throughout, tribunes loyal to Scipio defended his interests and carried the matter to the tribal assembly which gave him continual support. It

[145] See p. 70 above. [146] Livy XIX.20.1, XXX.23.3, 27.2.
[147] Cf. p. 68. On the salutation see Polyb. x.10.2-9; Livy XXVII.19.3-6. On the Scipionic legend: Scullard 1970, 18ff., 233ff.: (H 77); Walbank 1967: (H 79).
[148] Livy XXIX.19.4ff., XXX.24.11 (though the story is not above suspicion), 27.1 (Livy's statement that Claudius Nero was given *imperium par* to that of Scipio should be rejected), 40.7ff.

would be wrong, though, to think that the consuls of 203–201 were motivated merely by personal ambition and animosity towards Scipio. A consul could reasonably expect to command in a major theatre of war and the continued prorogation of Scipio's command negated this principle.

It will be noticed that the consuls of the last three years of the war included a Cornelius Lentulus and two Servilii, a family which had had close links with the Caecilii Metelli[149] and one of whose members had held the consulship in 217. It may be that in fact neither the Lentuli nor the Servilii had been Scipionic supporters at any point during the Hannibalic War. But it could be that though they had earlier been connected with the Scipionic group, the growth of Scipio's personal prestige and power led them to join his opponents.

VIII. MANPOWER AND FINANCE

There can be no doubt that one of the vital factors in Rome's eventual success in the Hannibalic War was her reserves of manpower from Roman citizens, Latins and Italian allies, especially in comparison with the difficulties which the Carthaginians had in recruiting their own citizens and their over-dependence on foreign and mercenary troops.[150] The unreliability of casualty figures and uncertainties about the number of legions in action year by year[151] – though the basic authenticity of the legion lists in Livy should not be doubted – make it impossible to form a meaningful estimate of the total number of men under arms during the war, but a recent calculation suggests that the total at any given time, including those serving with the fleet, reached a peak (in 212) of about 240,000.[152] That is not to say that the figure was reached easily. Many legions may have been under strength and, as we have seen, lack of manpower provides part, at least, of the explanation for Rome's failure to realize the full capacity of its fleet.[153] Many emergency measures were taken: after Cannae criminals, debtors and slaves (*volones*) were enrolled, and in both 214 and 210 the rich were compelled to give their own slaves to the state as rowers and to provide their pay as well.[154] In 216 and 212 those under the normal military age were enrolled and Livy's language suggests that the minimum census qualification was ignored (it was doubtless in the course of the Second Punic War that the minimum

[149] Badian 1964, 36: (A 4).   [150] Cf. Livy XXIX.3.12.
[151] For the different views cf. Toynbee 1965, II.647ff.: (A 37); Brunt 1971, 645ff.: (H 82).
[152] Brunt 1971, 422: (H 82); cf. De Sanctis 1907–64, III.ii.288: (A 14).
[153] See above p. 66.
[154] Livy XXII.57.11, XXIII.14.3, XXIV.11.7–9, XXVI.35, XXXIV.6.12–13. I see no reason to believe that Roman *proletarii*, other than freedmen, were not utilized for naval service, as claimed by Thiel 1946, 12 n. 28: (H 60).

qualification for the fifth class was lowered from 11,000 asses).[155] In 208 maritime colonies not normally liable for military service were compelled to provide soldiers.[156] The demands made by the Senate in relation to losses suffered bore particularly heavily on communities liable to a fixed levy. In 209 twelve Latin colonies claimed that they were unable to provide the soldiers demanded from them.[157]

The war was expensive of money as well as men. It was the shortage of silver and bronze that was responsible for the reform of the Roman monetary system about 212.[158] We have seen that the masters who provided slave rowers had to pay them as well. Heavy imposts of *tributum* were levied throughout the war,[159] but even that did not give the *aerarium* sufficient for all its military needs. In 215 the Scipios had to find the money to pay their troops by levies on Spanish peoples. For other supplies needed for Spain the companies of *publicani* submitted bids on condition that the state would pay when money was available. The contractors were dispensed from military service and the Senate agreed that the state should bear any losses arising from storms (two *publicani* were said to have taken advantage of this last condition by using old ships and falsifying the records of the goods being carried in them). The following year contractors offered of their own accord a similar procedure for the upkeep of temples and the provision of horses for magistrates. Owners of slaves manumitted as *volones* similarly offered to wait until the end of the war for their money, and trustees of the property of widows and orphans loaned money to the treasury. In 210 voluntary contributions were made by all sections of the Roman people and use was made of a previously untouched gold reserve.[160] In 204 it was agreed to treat these contributions as loans and repay them in three instalments.[161]

IX. SUBJECTS AND ALLIES

Polybius and Livy give lists of the Italian communities which defected from Rome in the aftermath of Cannae. The lists contain the names of a number of peoples whose defection in fact occurred later than 216, but the immediate toll is still formidable.[162] The remarkable thing, though, is that it was not more serious. In Italy the defections were limited to the

---

[155] Livy XXII.57.9, XXV.5.7–9. The census figure for the fifth class attributed to Servius Tullius in Livy I.43.7 is plausibly regarded as the Second Punic War figure. By the time of Polybius (VI.19.2) it was 4,000 asses.   [156] Livy XXVII.38.3–5.

[157] Livy XXVII.9.7–10.10, XXIX.15. In these circumstances it seems impossible to believe that the remnants of those defeated at Cannae, later joined by those defeated under Cn. Fulvius Centumalus in 210, were really forced to remain in Sicily for the duration of the war without being permitted to see active service. See Brunt 1971, 654–5: (H 82).

[158] See Crawford 1964 and 1974, I.28ff.: (B 86 and 88).   [159] Livy XXVI.35.5.

[160] Livy XXIII.48.5, 48.6–49.4 (cf. Badian 1972, 16ff.: (H 32)), XXIV.18.10–15, XXV.3.8–4, XXVI.36, XXVII.10.11.   [161] Cf. Briscoe 1973, 91: (B 3).   [162] See n. 43.

south, together with some but not all of the Samnites.[163] Despite
complaints about the demands that the war was making on them, no
community of Roman citizens, no Latin town joined Hannibal.[164] Notwithstanding Hannibal's victory at Trasimene, Etruria remained fundamentally loyal: in the later years of the war there were constant suspicions
of attempts at defection in Etruria and military precautions were taken,
but nothing of any substance occurred.[165] Nor did Hannibal gain all that
much military assistance from the states that did defect. This was largely
because their own resources were fully stretched in resisting Roman
efforts to recapture them, but that apart they saw Hannibal as a means of
gaining their independence from Rome: they were not willing to fight
outside their own territory for Hannibal's interests.[166] Similarly, though
the Gauls of the Po valley welcomed Hannibal as a liberator in 218[167] and
the control established in that region by Rome in the 220s was lost, they
made no independent attempt to embarrass Rome and did not even
succeed in capturing Placentia and Cremona, the twin symbols of Roman
occupation, during the course of the war.[168] Hannibal enrolled Gallic
troops in his army at the beginning of the war, but after Cannae, when he
was operating entirely in the south of Italy, it was impossible for further
reinforcements to reach him from the north.

From the point of view of both manpower and supplies the loyalty of
the allies was essential to Rome's survival. Hannibal realized this as well
as anyone, and we have seen that in the early battles he went out of his
way to treat captured Roman citizens and allies in different ways.[169] But
his attitude to those who resisted him was uncompromising. One may

[163] On the Samnites see Salmon 1967, 297ff.: (H 151) (with a list of southern peoples who
remained loyal to Rome).
[164] Complaints: Livy XXVII.9. The assertion attributed by Livy (XXIII.12.16) to Hanno that no
individual Roman or Latin had defected is exaggerated. Roman citizens were clearly among
deserters from the army: see n. 181.
[165] See in particular Harris 1971, 131ff.: (H 136); contra Pfiffig 1966: (C 42). I am not convinced by
the argument of Thiel 1946, 147: (H 60), and Pfiffig 1966, 205ff.: (C 42) (following Mommsen) that
the voluntary contributions from Etruscan cities for Scipio's fleet (Livy XXVIII.45.14ff.) were really
penalties imposed on these cities for actual or presumed disloyalty.
[166] See Salmon 1967, 298: (H 151), quoting the agreement between Hannibal and Capua that no
Capuan should serve with Hannibal against his will. See also Hannibal's guarantee to Tarentum
(Polyb. VIII.25.2; Livy XXV.8.8). One may note that not a single Nucerine was willing to serve with
Hannibal (Livy XXIII.15.5). There are indications that in some cases the upper classes remained loyal
to Rome (Livy XXIII.14.7, XXIV.2.8, 3.8, 47.12; Plut. Marc. 10.2), but it would be wrong to see the
choice between Rome and Carthage as a class issue. Cf. in general Ungern-Sternberg 1975, 54ff.:
(C 59).   [167] But cf. n. 28.
[168] See Briscoe 1973, 84: (B 3). For Gallic support for Mago cf. Livy XXIX.5, XXX.18. That the
Gauls of the Po valley gave their support to Hasdrubal is not specifically attested but can be assumed.
[169] Polyb. III.69.2, 77.3, 85.3; Livy XXI.48.10, XXII.50.6, 58.2, XXIII.15.4,8. The story of
Hannibal's crucifixion of the guide who took him to Casilinum instead of Casinum (Livy XXII.13.5–
9) is not a counter-example, as the story itself is highly suspect: cf. De Sanctis 1907–64, III.ii.125: (A
14); Ungern-Sternberg 1975, 18ff.: (C 59). For Hannibal's reputation for cruelty see Walbank 1967,
151: (H 79).

mention in 218 his massacre of the Taurini; in 217 his slaughter of all those of military age who came into his hands in Umbria and Picenum and his massacre of the inhabitants of Gerunium; in 216 his destruction of Nuceria; in 213 his treatment of the family of Dasius Altinus, who had fled from Arpi to the Roman camp;[170] in 210 his devastation of those parts of Italy which appeared about to rejoin Rome following the recapture of Capua[171] and his destruction of the town of Herdonea, the population being transplanted to Metapontum.[172]

But the record of the Romans' treatment of defectors is far grimmer reading yet. Roman policy was to deter by punishment, not to conciliate by humane treatment. In 216 Nolan traitors were executed by Marcellus,[173] in 212 Thurian and Tarentine hostages at Rome who had escaped from captivity were recaptured and thrown from the Tarpeian rock: the severity of this action seems to have been an important factor in the subsequent defection of Tarentum.[174] Laevinus sold all the inhabitants of Agrigentum into slavery, Fabius did the same to 30,000 Tarentines.[175] But it was for Capua that Roman anger was particularly intense.[176] Despite the doubts of his colleague Ap. Claudius Pulcher, Q. Fulvius Flaccus ordered the execution of the leaders of the rebellion in Capua and other Campanian towns. The Senate decided that Capua should cease to be a self-governing community and all its land was declared *ager publicus populi Romani*. Later the Senate decided that the populations of the secessionist towns in Campania should be transplanted, some beyond the Liris, others beyond the Tiber.[177] Though some Campanian land was let or sold, what we know of Campania in the second century B.C. indicates that in fact this massive transplantation was never carried out.[178]

Scipio was as fierce as anyone in wreaking retribution on Rome's enemies. He ordered his troops to kill all they encountered in Carthago Nova.[179] Ilourgeia, whose inhabitants had killed those who had fled thither after the defeat of the Scipios in 211, was razed to the ground and every living human being butchered.[180] It was Scipio, too, who executed the leaders of the Locrian rebellion and who went so far as to crucify Roman citizens among the deserters handed over by Carthage as part of the peace treaty after the battle of Zama.[181]

The hesitation of an Ap. Claudius Pulcher was unusual, and the

[170] Polyb. III.60.10, 86.11, 100.4; Livy XXIII.15, XXIV.45.13–14.
[171] Livy XXVI.38.1–5; Diod. Sic. XXVII.9; cf. Polyb. IX.26; De Sanctis 1907–64, III.ii.457: (A 14); Salmon 1967, 300 n. 2: (H 151).
[172] Livy XXVII.1.14. Appian (*Hann.* 57.239) states that the town of Petelia was given to the Bruttians, but does not record the fate of the original inhabitants.
[173] Livy XXIII.17.2.   [174] Livy XXV.7.10–8.2.   [175] Livy XXVI.40.13, XXVII.16.7.
[176] Livy XXVI.1.3, 13.9.   [177] Livy XXVI.15–16, 33–34.   [178] Cf. Briscoe 1973, 132: (B 3).
[179] Polyb. X.15.4–5.   [180] See above, p. 60.
[181] Livy XXIX.8.2, XXX.43.13 (the corruption at the beginning of the sentence cannot cast doubt on *Romani in crucem sublati*).

execution of leaders of a rebellion was not something that would be challenged in the Senate. The accusations against M. Claudius Marcellus which found some sympathy at Rome concerned his carrying off large quantities of works of art from Syracuse.[182] Fabius behaved with more circumspection at Tarentum, though his treatment of the inhabitants was far more severe than that inflicted by Marcellus on the Syracusans.[183]

Despite their utter dependence on the support of their Italian allies the Senate would not countenance any change in the existing structure of the Italian confederation. After Cannae a proposal that two senators from each Latin town should receive Roman citizenship and become members of the Roman Senate was, Livy says, shouted down.[184] To the Roman governing class, it seems, any change in the existing situation would have been a partial victory for Hannibal. It was, moreover, on allied land that most of the fighting took place. When troops were no longer operating on *ager Romanus* the Senate was concerned to see that Roman citizens could resume agricultural production – *ut in agros reducendae plebis curam haberent.*[185] It is perhaps not mere chance that there is no mention of doing anything to help the allies in a similar situation.

X. CONCLUSION

It would go far beyond the scope of the present chapter to attempt an assessment of the results of the Second Punic War. The effect on agrarian developments in the second century of the devastation of large parts of Italy and the continuous absence on military service of many small farmers will be treated elsewhere. The fact that Rome won the war without making a single concession to her allies doubtless helped to harden the Senate's attitude towards any changes in subsequent years. Despite the differences between individuals and groups the war was won by the traditional governing class. The overall direction of the war belonged to the Senate, and its eventual success will go a long way to explaining the increasing power of the Senate in the second century. All the successful commanders in the war were members of established *nobilis* families. It may not be entirely coincidental that in the second century the domination of the consulship by those with consular ancestors is particularly striking.[186]

As to foreign policy, some will hold that the victory over Carthage led the Senate to look immediately for fields for fresh conquests. Those, like

---

[182] See above p. 62.
[183] Livy XXVII.16.8. One may note that L. Pinarius received no criticism for forestalling a possible rebellion at Enna by butchering its citizens at an assembly (Livy XXIV.37–39.9: *aut malo aut necessario facinore* (XXIV.39.7) is, of course, Livy's own comment).   [184] Livy XXIII.22.4–9.
[185] Livy XXVIII.11.8.   [186] Cf. Scullard 1973, 9: (H 54).

the present writer, who incline to the view that the declaration of war on Macedon in 200 was not undertaken for reasons of aggressive imperialism, see a different link with the Hannibalic War. The presence of Hannibal on Italian soil for sixteen years, winter and summer, made a profound impression on the minds of the Senate, and fear of another foreign invasion was uppermost in the minds of many senators not only in 200 – when it was not entirely irrational – but also at other critical moments in the next 50 years, though after 196 it is highly unlikely that any of Rome's potential enemies seriously considered launching an invasion of Italy.

ADDITIONAL NOTE: THE ELECTIONS FOR 216 B.C.

Livy's account of the election of C. Terentius Varro and L. Aemilius Paullus as consuls for 216 (XXII.33.9–35.4) has given rise to a great deal of controversy.[187] It is not possible here to discuss the different views in detail; the following merely sets out the problem and the interpretation accepted by the present writer.

(i) Livy begins by saying that the Senate wrote to the consuls asking one of them to come to Rome for the elections. The consuls replied that this was not possible and suggested elections under the presidency of an *interrex*. The Senate, however, preferred a dictator to be appointed. L. Veturius Philo was appointed and he chose M. Pomponius Matho as his *magister equitum*. They, however, were declared *vitio creati*, and resigned on their fourteenth day in office. An *interregnum* then began.

The fact that the consuls could have held the elections shows that we are still in the consular year 217/16. But when at 33.12 Livy says *ad interregnum res rediit* the year is at an end, as is confirmed by the following sentence *consulibus prorogatum in annum imperium*. It is, then, probably that the consuls suggested that the elections should be held by an *interrex* because they did not think there was sufficient time for a dictator to hold them. The dictator and his *magister equitum* are clearly Scipionic supporters. Philo was censor in 210 with the young P. Licinius Crassus, his son consul in 206 with Q. Caecilius Metellus. Africanus' mother Pomponia was probably the sister of Matho, and the latter's consular colleague in 231 was C. Papirius Maso, whose daughter married the son of L. Aemilius Paullus. The responsibility for declaring that the dictator and his *magister equitum* had been *vitio creati* will have lain with the augural college, and the influence of Fabius must be suspected. His motive will not have been so much to avoid the election being conducted by a Scipionic supporter, for, as we have seen, the influence of the presiding officer must not be exaggerated. There was, rather, a positive advantage in having the election conducted by an *interrex*. For it seems that an *interrex* put one name to the *comitia* at a time, which had to accept or reject it. The process would continue until someone obtained a majority.[188] It was thus easier to block an election than to get someone elected,

[187] For bibliography see Sumner 1975, 250 n. 1: (c 57). Gruen 1978 (c 20A).

[188] Accepting the arguments of Staveley 1954–5: (H 26) (though not his interpretation of this election).

and Fabius may have hoped that he would have to step in at the last moment.

It cannot be excluded, however, that Livy's statement that the dictator and his *magister equitum* had to resign because they were *vitio creati* is mistaken. There is no mention of their abdication in the *Fasti*, and it could be that they simply failed to hold the elections before 14 March when their office came to an end with the consular year.[189]

(ii) Livy goes on to say that the elections were held under the second *interrex* P. Cornelius Asina. Varro, strongly opposed by the *patres*, was gaining support by his attacks on Fabius, but was defended by his relative, the tribune Q. Baebius Herennius. None of the three patrician candidates (P. Cornelius Merenda, L. Manlius Vulso and M. Aemilius Lepidus) could gain a majority and Varro alone was elected. Against his will L. Aemilius Paullus was persuaded to stand and, under Varro's presidency, was elected. Now the Baebii are a family linked with the Aemilii over a long period,[190] and Baebius' support for Varro constitutes further evidence for the view that Varro had the support of the Scipionic group. We can, then, reject Livy's picture of the conflict as one between plebs and *nobiles* and with it that part of Baebius' speech which is a wholesale attack on the *nobiles*, though it is probable enough that Baebius should have criticized the invalidation of Philo's dictatorship (34.10).

The first *interrex* could not hold the elections.[191] Livy's words *prodici sunt a patribus* appear to apply to both *interreges*, but at v.31.8 he clearly envisages each *interrex* nominating his successor. If that happened in 216, it may seem puzzling that C. Claudius Centho should have nominated a Cornelius. Claudius, however, may have been more hostile to the Fabii than to the Scipios and again the influence of the *interrex* should not be overestimated: there is no need to hold that the *interrex* himself decided whose names to put to the *comitia*.[192] After the election of Varro, the *interregnum* was at an end and Paullus was elected in the ordinary way. The two original Scipionic candidates, P. Cornelius Merenda and M. Aemilius Lepidus, will have retired in his favour, though he may still have been opposed by L. Manlius Vulso.

---

[189] Cf. Sumner 1975, 252: (C 57).   [190] Cf. Briscoe 1973, 70–1: (B 3).
[191] Asconius p. 43C.   [192] Thus Staveley 1954–5, 207: (H 26).

CHAPTER 4

ROME AND GREECE TO 205 B.C.

R. M. ERRINGTON

I. THE EARLIEST CONTACTS

The Romans had had state-to-state contacts, both friendly and un-
friendly, with Greek communities and kings of the Greek world east of
the Adriatic for many generations before the first trans-Adriatic military
adventure in 229 B.C. At a different level, Italian traders were no
strangers to the opposite coast of the Adriatic, and Greeks had maintained regular contacts with Italy even before the founding of the first
permanent colony in Italy at Cumae in the mid eighth century B.C.; the
Greeks of the colonial foundations of Italy had long been naval allies
(*socii navales*); many Greek cities of Sicily were since 241 part of the first
Roman province. Greek culture, the Greek language, the Greek way of
life were thus all familiar to many, above all upper-class, Romans long
before serious political engagement on the Balkan peninsula was even
contemplated.

One must nevertheless beware of overemphasizing the nature and
intensity of the earliest contacts with the eastern Greeks. Before 229 there
was no Greek state east of Italy with which Rome had a contact which
was more intense than *amicitia* – and *amicitia* was a global term for
relationships which extended from the level of polite and distant friendliness to something approaching a recognition of common interests, in
which case the relationship might conceivably be defined by a treaty.
Amicitia could mean much or little; but for the eastern Greeks before 229
it meant without exception little.

At the religious and cultural level Rome was not above making a
dedication in the Greek shrine at Delphi in 394, after her success at Veii.
The dedication was made in the treasury of Massilia, which later claimed
to have maintained a friendship with Rome since the Phocaean settlers
put in at the mouth of the Tiber on their way to Massilia in the early sixth
century.[1] And the contact with Delphi was not forgotten: it was (among
other places) to Delphi that Rome turned for help in the dark days after

---

[1] Livy v.28.1–5; Diod. Sic. xiv.93.3–4; Justin xliii.3.4, 5.1–3.

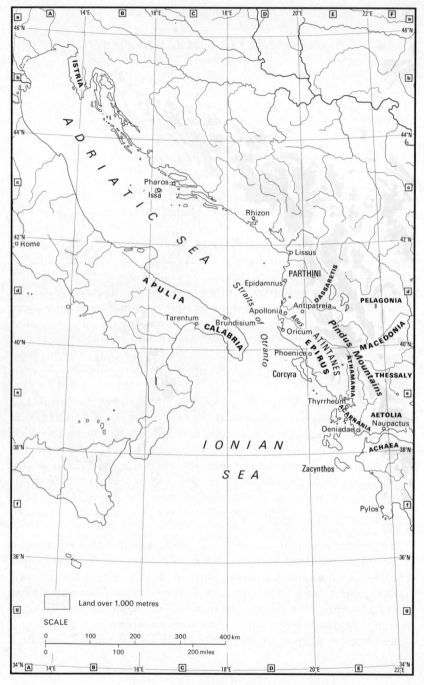

Map 6. The Adriatic.

the battle of Cannae, when the future historian Fabius Pictor was despatched to consult the oracle.

Experience of a quite different kind had been gathered with the northern Greek monarchies of Epirus and Macedon. Alexander I of Epirus had crossed to Italy in 333/2 B.C. while his brother-in-law Alexander of Macedon (Alexander the Great) was invading Persia. His proclaimed aim was to help the Greek city Tarentum against its native neighbours, which he duly did; in the course of this he is also alleged to have made a treaty and *amicitia* with Rome, though his premature death prevented this from becoming effective.[2] Rome doubtless regarded this as an Italian affair, but the ease of Alexander's crossing and his contact with the Greek cities of southern Italy will have served to make Rome more aware of this overseas neighbour. Contacts of a diplomatic character are also alleged for Alexander the Great. According to Strabo, Alexander sent a complaint to Rome about pirates operating from the Roman colony of Antium, a complaint which was apparently taken seriously by the Romans only when repeated several years later by Demetrius Poliorcetes. Clitarchus recorded that a Roman embassy, of which neither purpose nor date is mentioned, was sent to Alexander. This has often been regarded as a late invention, but the presence of Alexander of Epirus in Italy might well have stimulated the Roman Senate's curiosity about the activities of his brother-in-law.[3] However this may be, rather more than fifty years later another king of Epirus, again in the first instance claiming to be aiding Tarentum, gave Rome a shock which must have ensured that in the future events and developments across the Adriatic would be watched: Pyrrhus' invasion of Italy and Sicily threatened for a while the whole structure of the Roman system of controlling southern Italy and stimulated a treaty of mutual help with Carthage. The danger did not last long; but while it lasted it seemed serious enough. One side-effect of the defeat of Pyrrhus was that it put Rome on the map for the Greek world. Ptolemy II Philadelphus was sufficiently impressed to choose this time to send presents to the Senate and to form an informal friendship; the Romans returned the diplomatic gesture. Around 266 the Greek city of Apollonia on the eastern coast of the Adriatic, for reasons which are unknown to us, sent envoys to Rome, who were officially received and officially well treated by the Senate: their visit was remembered and recorded as a famous occasion on which the Senate protected the rights of foreign ambassadors even against insulting behaviour by its own members.[4]

[2] Justin XII.2.1–15.
[3] Strabo v.3.5 C 232; Pliny, *HN* III.57 (= Jacoby. *FGrH* 137 F 31).
[4] Dion. Hal. XX.14; Liv. *Per.* XIV; Zon. VIII.6.11 (Ptolemy); Val. Max. VI.6.5; Dio X, fr. 43; Liv. *Per.* XIV.

A feature common to all these contacts, with the exception of the alleged embassy to Alexander the Great, is that the initiative in each case seems not to have come from Rome. The Roman role was essentially passive; and this will doubtless have been the case also with the earliest friendly contacts with the Greek island of Rhodes about 305. Rhodes was a trading state and will have regarded it as useful to be on friendly terms with the most powerful state in Italy.[5] Nor, it seems, was anything specific demanded of Rome by those who sought these contacts. It was sufficient that the friendship was established. Thus, even by the end of the First Punic War (241), during which Rome had established control over the greater part of Sicily and was in alliance with Hiero of Syracuse, who ruled the rest of the island, her official contacts with Greek states beyond the geographical limits of Italy and Sicily remained very limited. This did not mean, however, that the Senate was blind to developments across the Adriatic: the experience of the two Epirote kings, Alexander and Pyrrhus, had made this impossible henceforth; and no doubt the frequent crossing of Italian traders to the Balkans and the friendship with Apollonia will have served as sources of information. Moreover, the long war in Sicily and the development of the Roman navy which this caused had made the Senate more than ever aware of the potential importance for Roman security also of territories which, though not physically part of the Italian mainland, were near enough to be danger-ous; this, still in a Carthaginian context, expressed itself very soon after the end of the war in Sicily in the conquest of Sardinia and Corsica, which until then had been controlled by Carthage. The Straits of Otranto are, however, no wider than the distance from Corsica to Italy: for a Senate which had had its eyes opened to the possibilities of naval power, the eastern coast of the Adriatic must have become more interesting.

Rome was not the only state to have learned from the events of the Pyrrhic War and the war in Sicily. If Rome had learned that overseas territories were also neighbours who not only provided profits for traders but also needed watching or protecting, the inhabitants of such territories had also become more aware of Rome. Our source tradition is very fragmentary, but we still have the examples of Apollonia and Ptolemy Philadelphus, who soon after the Pyrrhic War took the initiative in opening formal friendly relations with Rome. Contacts of another kind also began to develop. One of the factors which had led to the

---

[5] Polyb. xxx.5.6–8. This interpretation owes most to Schmitt 1957 1ff.: (E 77). Polybius depicts the Rhodians in 168/7 as claiming that they had participated with the Romans in their most glorious and finest achievements for some 140 years without a treaty. In this exaggerated form the claim is patently untrue, but since all attempts to amend the text are unconvincing it seems necessary to assume an initial contact between the two states *c.* 305, perhaps in connection with Demetrius' siege of Rhodes, which the Rhodian ambassadors to Rome in 168/7 (or Polybius on their behalf) inflated into major active co-operation throughout the whole period. For detailed commentary see Walbank 1957–79, III.423ff.: (B 38).

opening of the First Punic War was the appeal of the Mamertines of Messana, which Rome rather surprisingly had accepted. The acceptance and readiness to act on this appeal were noted by the historiographers and later written up into an integral part of a view of Roman foreign policy, much in favour at Rome, whereby Rome's desire to help the weak who appealed was depicted as being a major factor in Roman decision-making in the field of foreign policy.

It was unlikely that the example of the Mamertines would remain isolated, once it had been seen to be successful; and the Senate could reasonably expect other similar more or less reasonable and hopeful appeals to arrive in Rome. This development is in detail uncertain and not undisputed. It is, however, unlikely that our very fragmentary sources for the third century record all instances, particularly if no Roman action followed. But even the few instances where we do have a mention in a source are not so clear that they are undisputed. A very late source, Justin's epitome of Pompeius Trogus, records a garbled and rhetorical account of an appeal by the Acarnanians, a western Greek people, who were being attacked by their neighbours the Aetolians. The precise date is uncertain, but seems to be in the thirties of the third century. According to this account the Senate sent *legati*, who unsuccessfully tried to negotiate and then returned home.[6] Many scholars have regarded this episode as apocryphal and more particularly (after Maurice Holleaux) as a confusion with some of the events of Rome's war against the Aetolians early in the second century. But as long as we do not attribute political aims to the Senate, it seems at least conceivable that Justin may have preserved a real event which was not mentioned by Fabius Pictor (who is probably Polybius' chief source for this period) because of its relative triviality, because of the lack of success for the Romans, and because, in a critical phase of political developments in 212, Rome allied with Aetolia at the cost of Acarnania. It was normal practice in the Greek world for a threatened community to seek the intervention of a Great Power; since Rome's defeat of Pyrrhus and Carthage and as a result of the regular activities of Italian traders doing business across the Adriatic, Rome was no longer a strange and unfamiliar state to the Greeks of western Greece, but – in a moment of panic, as the Mamertines in Sicily had found – almost a natural source of help. The Acarnanian appeal and the Roman attempt to conciliate thus seem not impossible.

II. THE ILLYRIAN WARS

No far-reaching aspect of Roman foreign policy is affected by acceptance or rejection of the Acarnanian incident. At the most we have to do with a

---

[6] Justin XXVIII.1.1–2.14.

nuance of the Roman attitude towards playing the 'honest broker' in disputes in which Rome had no essential interest. The next case, however, is of more substance, since it is directly related to the first Roman military intervention across the Adriatic which is known as the First Illyrian War.[7] Before discussing this it will be advisable to indicate the political situation on the east coast of the Adriatic at this time. Throughout the third century the dominant political feature of the western Balkans had been the kingdom of Epirus: it was kings of Epirus, Alexander and Pyrrhus, who had invaded Italy; it was the kingdom of Epirus which controlled the coastline south of Oricum, that is, controlled the eastern coastline at the Straits of Otranto, where the Adriatic is narrowest, where Italy is nearest. In 232 the dynasty which had provided the kings of Epirus, the Aeacides, died out and Epirus changed, not without severe internal difficulties, into a federal republic. At about the same time, possibly under pressure from movements of Celtic tribes, which in the 220s also threatened Italy, the Illyrian monarchy of the Ardiaei under King Agron, which occupied the Dalmatian coast southwards from near Split, began to extend its regular raiding activities to the south. We hear of raids on Messenia and Elis in the Peloponnese, of support (paid for by Macedonia) for Acarnania against the Aetolians, and of a plundering attack of major importance, verging on warfare, on the young Epirote Republic, whereby Phoenice, the chief city of one of the federal units, the Chaones, was taken and plundered. There can be no doubt that the Illyrians represented a considerable factor in the affairs of the communities of the southern sections of the eastern Adriatic seaboard and, insofar as events around the Straits of Otranto could not be totally ignored by the Roman Senate, in Roman affairs. Roman interest became particularly active when, at the capture of Phoenice, many Italian traders who were in the town at the time were killed or taken as slaves; and the appeals of the Italian trading community to the Senate, which in the past had not been taken seriously, were listened to at last.

Our sources offer different versions of Roman reasons for taking military action against the Illyrians in 229; and modern historians vary equally, depending on which ancient source they prefer to follow. The accounts are unfortunately incompatible. Polybius, whose version is the lengthiest and is probably based both on Greek sources and on the history written by the Roman senator and historian Fabius Pictor, links Roman actions to the appeals of the Italians after the capture of Phoenice. According to his version, the Senate sent two of its members, the brothers C. and L. Coruncanius, whose father had ended his distin-

---

[7] Sources for the First Illyrian War are: Polyb. II.2–12; App. *Ill.* 7.17–8.22; Dio XII, fr. 49; Zon. VIII.19; Florus I.21 (II.5); Orosius IV.13.2; Eutropius III.4.

guished career as *pontifex maximus*, to investigate. They travelled to the island of Issa, which was being besieged by Queen Teuta, who had succeeded her husband Agron towards the end of 230. Teuta received them haughtily and replied that she could not control the private affairs of her subjects, though she was willing to control the public sphere. The younger Coruncanius replied, in a virtual declaration of war, that Rome would teach her the necessity of also controlling their private affairs. As the Coruncanii were sailing away, Teuta gave orders for the younger, who had spoken the threats, to be murdered. She then sent out an expedition to the south, which captured Corcyra, where Demetrius of Pharos was put in charge of the garrison, and began to blockade Epidamnus. This blockade and the siege of Issa were still going on when the Roman expedition arrived at Corcyra.

Appian's version, based on Roman sources which we cannot identify, is different. Agron had, before his death, already captured part of Epirus, Corcyra, Epidamnus and Pharos and had begun the siege of Issa. The people of Issa appealed to Rome with accusations against Agron, and the Senate sent out ambassadors. The ships carrying the Issaeans and the Roman ambassadors were intercepted on the high seas by Illyrian pirates and the leader of the Issaean delegation, Cleemporus, and a Roman, Coruncanius, were killed. As a result of this incident the Romans sent their military expedition. At about the same time Agron died and entrusted the kingdom to Teuta, who was to serve as regent for Pinnes, his infant son by another woman. It was thus against the newly appointed Teuta that the Romans fought.

There are aspects of these two accounts which are incompatible, and, were Appian's account the only one we had, it would, though brief, be convincing enough. It has no room for the interview of the Coruncanii with Teuta; Appian gives the ambassador from Issa, Cleemporus, a name which is rare but also on another occasion attested for Issa, which is a reasonable indication of authenticity.[8] On the other hand, Polybius shows neither here nor elsewhere knowledge of Pinnes. These details cannot have been invented by Appian or his source, since in themselves they serve only to complicate an otherwise quite brief report: a simplifier or abbreviator might well have left them out, but would hardly have invented them. Polybius' version, on the other hand, has the hallmark of having been 'written up', particularly the dramatic confrontation between the Coruncanii and Teuta, where Teuta is depicted with all the prejudices of the hellenistic female-stereotype, as wilful, passionate, thoughtless and proud. Moreover, Polybius is not very well informed about Illyrian affairs before the outbreak of the war, above all he does not

[8] See Derow 1973: (D 20).

know about Pinnes and he makes Agron die before the Romans reach Issa for their interview, which then takes place with Teuta. Plausible reasons for the variations between Polybius and Appian may be imagined if Appian is right and Polybius wrong, but not *vice versa*. Teuta was the chief person against whom Rome fought, therefore it would not be unnatural for someone who was not well informed in detail to depict Teuta also as a secondary cause of the war, if he thought Agron was already dead. The omission of the appeal of Issa may be attributed either to ignorance or to the fact that Rome took so long before helping Issa, despite her military operations in Illyria, that Fabius wished to disguise the delay in responding to the appeal. But in any case, even Appian does not make the appeal of Issa into a cause of the war. It thus seems likely that in certain critical areas Polybius' source was guilty of romanticizing his ignorance.[9]

What, then, seems to have happened? The appeals of the Italians after the capture of Phoenice were doubtless real enough, and may well have influenced the Senate, particularly since Phoenice lay just in that critical area of Epirus near the Straits of Otranto which the Senate needed to watch. This, however, does not mean that when Agron attacked Issa the people of Issa did not appeal to Rome, the only power which might be willing and able to help; nor that Rome did not use the opportunity given by the appeal to investigate the suspicious activities of the Illyrians. The appeal could, under the circumstances, be regarded as tailor-made. When the ships were attacked and Cleemporus and one of the Coruncanii (doubtless the younger, as Fabius Pictor will have known) were killed, the nuisance-value – and potential danger – of the Illyrian pirates was demonstrated in a dramatic way which also affected the Senate intimately. The disrespectful, overly powerful neighbour needed to be punished and above all weakened. In the last resort, therefore, the picture is not greatly changed by accepting Appian's facts against Polybius'. The Senate's ultimate motivation was precisely that suspicion of strong neighbours which had played a significant role in the development of Rome's position of dominance within the Italian peninsula and which (much more recently) had led to Rome's taking control of Sardinia and Corsica from Carthage. Illyria cannot of course be compared with Carthage; but the principle of making apparently strong neighbours weaker, especially at a time when militarily there was not much else for the consuls to do, was equally applicable.

[9] This account is a modified form of the results of a recently re-opened discussion over the relative value of Appian's and Polybius' versions of these events, through which Appian's version has been at least partially rehabilitated and the weaknesses of Polybius' made clearer: see Petzold 1971: (D 49); Derow 1973: (D 20). The best earlier discussion with the older literature is Walbank 1957–79, I.153ff.: (B 38).

The importance of the Straits of Otranto to Roman thinking and the limited aims of the war emerge from the course of events. The consuls of 229, Cn. Fulvius Centumalus and L. Postumius Albinus, were both sent out with forces appropriate to their status and to the Senate's perhaps exaggerated view of the difficulties of the Illyrian objective: in all 20,000 soldiers, 2,000 cavalry and 200 warships were engaged. The Romans did not head straight for Issa, where the Illyrian royal forces were occupied with the siege, but concentrated in the first instance on the straits: Fulvius sailed to Corcyra, which was immediately betrayed by its Greek commandant Demetrius of Pharos, who seems to have estimated for himself good chances of benefiting from co-operation with Rome, just as he had earlier joined the Illyrians when his Greek neighbour Issa resisted them. From Corcyra Fulvius sailed to Rome's old friend Apollonia, where Postumius joined him with the army. Apollonia had no alternative to strengthening its friendly connection and through an act of *deditio*, which implied a formal unconditional surrender to Roman discretion (*fides*), put itself at the disposal of the Romans. They did not, however, delay at Apollonia, but pressed on to Epidamnus, where the Illyrians were driven out and the town was also formally received into Roman *fides*. The inland tribes of the Parthini and the Atintanes were also impressed by Rome's presence and secured themselves Roman favour by offering submission in terms which the Romans interpreted as *deditio*. Only then did the Romans go to Issa and deal with Teuta, on the way taking several Illyrian towns. Their mere appearance at Issa put an end to the siege; Teuta fled to the fortress of Rhizon (on the Gulf of Kotor) and the war was effectively over. Fulvius returned to Rome in the autumn with the larger part of the fleet and the army, leaving Postumius to spend the winter in Illyria and organize a settlement with Teuta. They clearly did not expect that this would require the presence of large forces of Roman troops.

Our sources vary in detail over the terms of the treaty. Polybius' version is handicapped by his knowing nothing about Pinnes; he thus concentrates solely on Teuta, whereas Appian does not mention Teuta as a party to the treaty at all. Appian records the explicit renunciation by the Illyrians of Corcyra, Pharos, Issa, Epidamnus and the Atintanes, and the provision that Pinnes should retain 'the rest of Agron's kingdom' and be *amicus* of Rome. 'The rest of Agron's kingdom' must, however, have been restricted by the fact that Demetrius of Pharos was given 'some places' as a reward; Polybius adds that Teuta was also granted 'a few places' on condition that she withdraw from Illyria, and he mentions an agreement to pay a tribute (*phoros*). This latter no doubt relates to the kingdom of the Ardiaei under Pinnes, from which Teuta was to withdraw. A last clause, which both authors record, and on which Polybius comments that 'this affected the Greeks most of all', stated that the Illyrians were not allowed to sail south of Lissus with more than two unarmed *lembi* (the *lembos* was their own type of light ship).

If we put all this together we gain a picture of a Roman attempt to weaken and obtain influence in Illyria, but not to destroy or to control it. Demetrius was a friend of Rome and was given some territories, doubtless near Pharos; the energetic Teuta was removed from the regency and confined to a few less important places, probably around the Gulf of Kotor; the independence of the kingdom of the Ardiaei was weakened by its having to make payments to Rome (which, even if these were merely a war-indemnity, also brought Rome some profit from the operation), by the Roman recognition of Pinnes as Rome's friend, and by the provision that warlike or piratical expeditions south of Lissus were not to take place. South of Lissus, in the strategic area around the eastern shore of the Straits of Otranto, Rome now had a group of friendly states, all of which had formally put themselves at Rome's disposal: Epidamnus, Apollonia, Corcyra (these being critically important harbour towns), the Atintanes and the Parthini. They would doubtless be quick to report a breach of the treaty by the Illyrians or other threatening activities in the area. The federation of Epirus, whose coasts controlled the narrowest part of the straits and which under severe pressure had allied with Illyria shortly before the Romans arrived, was too weak to require special treatment.

When the agreement was complete and before leaving for Rome Postumius sent envoys to the Aetolian and Achaean Leagues to explain the terms of the treaty. These were the most powerful states in southern and western Greece and they had tried to help Epirus against the Illyrians before the Romans arrived. Shortly afterwards the influential cities of Corinth and Athens also received visits from Roman representatives. At Corinth they were present, no doubt deliberately, at the time of the Isthmian Games in spring 228. This was one of the major Panhellenic festivals, where Greeks from the whole Greek world would be present; Polybius records that the Romans were even allowed to participate in the games which, if true, amounted in effect to their recognition as 'honorary Greeks'. The defeat of the Illyrians and the solution imposed by Rome would, with this publicity, rapidly become known in every Greek state.

Rome's interest in Illyria was limited and the settlement seems in general to have functioned, though it did not prevent a further short Roman intervention from being necessary ten years later. The key was the separation of powers: Demetrius, Teuta, Pinnes and the Ardiaei, the friends of Rome, all were intended to keep a check on each other and to ensure than any threat in the area would be recognized in time to prevent its becoming serious. The weakest aspect of these separated powers was the ambition of Demetrius of Pharos. The sources record a series of events and incidents, unfortunately only in an inadequate chronological framework, which illustrate how Demetrius 'stretched' the terms of the settlement – the phrase which crops up more than once in our hostile sources is 'abused Roman friendship', and this doubtless represents the Roman point of view – through a series of incidents, of which none in itself would have justified Roman action, but which cumulatively provoked the brief military action in 219, on the eve of the Hannibalic War, which is known as the 'Second Illyrian War'.[10]

Some time during these ten years Demetrius married Triteuta, the mother of Pinnes, and formally took over the regency of the Ardiaei. Demetrius' own influence was thereby greatly extended, and the fundamental weakness of the Ardiaei after 228 – that there was no competent regent for Pinnes – was relieved. But one of the pillars of the separation of powers, which was the heart of the Roman settlement, was demolished. Demetrius then renewed the Illyrians' now traditional friendly contact with Macedonia and contributed a body of 1,600 men to the army of allied Greek states which in 222, under the Macedonian king Antigonus Doson, fought and defeated Cleomenes III of Sparta at Sellasia, where the Illyrians played an important part in the allied victory. This event in itself was not contrary to the Roman settlement of Illyria; but the fact that not only the Illyrians but also Epirus and Acarnania, who had been allies of Agron, contributed troops to the Macedonian army will presumably have been reported back to Rome by the Greek friends.

During the 220s Rome was seriously occupied in Italy by the Gallic invasion; and the Senate was also observing events in southern Spain, where the Carthaginians were successfully rebuilding their influence and power. Under the circumstances the Adriatic could attract serious attention only if an actual major breach of the treaty, or events which could be interpreted as such, took place. After the war with the Gauls the Romans made an expedition against the Histri in Istria in 221 – and it was said at Rome, though perhaps later than 219, that Demetrius had had something to do with the activities of the Histri which provoked Roman action.[11] Despite the obvious readiness of Rome to engage in Adriatic affairs Demetrius seems to have seen no implication for his own position. In 220, together with another Illyrian dynast Scerdilaidas, he sailed with a fleet of 90 *lembi* not only south of Lissus but as far as Pylos in Messenia. Here the two leaders split their forces. Demetrius sailed round the Peloponnese to the Cyclades with 50 ships, where he plundered and ravaged the islands; Scerdilaidas with the remaining 40 returned home. Polybius, reflecting the Roman view of his source Fabius Pictor, de-

---

[10] Sources for the Second Illyrian War: Polyb. III.16, 18–19; Dio XII, fr. 53; Zon. VIII.20.11–13; App. *Ill.* 8.23–24.   [11] App. *Ill.* 8.23.

scribes this as a clear breach of the treaty; and indeed, even if the ships
counted as being Demetrius' and Scerdilaidas' own, raised from the
subjects of their own territories (which is not related by any source),
Demetrius, as successor of Teuta in the regency for Pinnes and thereby
effectively the ruler of the Ardiaei, must have been regarded by the
Senate as being bound by the 'Lissus clause'. The two dynasts seem to
have been aware of this and to have tried to keep their provocation as
slight as possible, in that although they sailed south of Lissus, they seem
to have made no attack on any friend of Rome. Their first recorded
landfall is Pylos; and Demetrius' raiding expedition into the Aegean, far
from the normal haunts of the Illyrians, may have been intended in the
same sense, as an operation so far away from the area of Roman interests
that, although the treaty was technically broken, it was broken in such a
way that the Senate might not feel obliged to retaliate.

If we knew more about a further area of Demetrius' activities we
might understand better why he thought Rome would not react to his
breach of the treaty. Polybius accuses him of ravaging and destroying
'the cities of Illyria subject to Rome'. This phrase can only mean the
towns in or near the territory of Rome's friends, the Parthini and the
Atintanes, which counted as being Illyrian (although the Atintanes had
from the time of Pyrrhus to the end of the Epirote monarchy constituted
part of the state of Epirus).[12] Names which recur in the later events are
Dimallum (or, in Polybius, Dimale)[13] near Antipatreia, and Eugenium
and Bargullum, whose precise location is unknown. Polybius clearly
exaggerates by saying that Demetrius destroyed these places: he says that
in 219 Demetrius garrisoned Dimallum and was able to expel his
opponents and instal his friends in 'the other cities' – which excludes
their previous destruction. But the time-scale of this political and military activity among Rome's friends is quite uncertain. It could be
connected with Demetrius' first contacts with Macedonia, which may go
back to 224 or 225; or it might be quite a recent development arising out
of his successful co-operation with Macedonia in 222, perhaps, as
Polybius' phrasing seems to imply, as late as autumn 220.[14] We know for
certain merely that it was before 219, since he was then in control of
Dimallum and was able to provoke *coups d'état* in the other cities. If,
however, this activity which, if successful, would effectively destroy
another separatist pillar of the Roman settlement of 228, had in 220
already been going on for some years and had provoked no Roman

[12] Hammond wishes to distinguish between Illyrian Atintani and Epirote Atintanes (1967, 600:
(D 31A)); but see Cabanes 1976, 78–80; (D 12).

[13] The precise location of Dimallum and the correct form of the name are now established by the
find of stamped tiles at the fort of Krotine: see Hammond 1968, 12–15: (D 32).

[14] Polyb. III.16.2 with Walbank 1957–79, 1.325: (B 38).

reaction, this would help to explain why he and Scerdilaidas had risked sailing south of Lissus with a large armed fleet in 220.

The precise reasons why in 219 the Senate decided to send both consuls of the year, L. Aemilius Paullus and M. Livius Salinator, to Illyria, why it decided that now and not later (or earlier) the moment had come to chastise Demetrius, we shall never know. The fact that all recent consuls had enjoyed military command and that no other sector was available where the consuls of 219 could do likewise – affairs in Spain had not yet reached the point where war with Carthage was certain – may easily have helped to exaggerate the danger of Demetrius. Polybius adds the thought, which however must have been developed in the light of later events, that they saw that Macedonia was flourishing and acted for this reason. But Macedonia was not particularly flourishing in 219. The recently acceded young king Philip V was still labouring under beginners' difficulties; and in the event Macedonia was not involved in the war, which was once again solely concerned with Illyria: merely to remove Demetrius of Pharos from Illyria and to take no further action would be a remarkably inadequate way of responding to a perceived threat from Macedonia. We have, in fact, no reason for disbelieving the Roman tradition – Fabius Pictor was a contemporary senator – that the Senate, doubtless under the influence of the well-connected and militarily eager consuls, decided that Demetrius had abused his position as Rome's friend. The thought that, should war with Carthage break out in Spain, it would be helpful to have the Adriatic made safe may have also played a part.

The events of the war were brief and unspectacular, though the consuls had sufficient influence in the Senate to persuade their peers that triumphs would be appropriate. Dimallum, which had been garrisoned by Demetrius while he himself went to defend Pharos, fell after a seven-day siege, whereupon 'all the towns' also gave up – this can only mean those which had recently come into the control of Demetrius' friends. The Romans then sailed to Pharos, where they took the town by a stratagem and, according to Polybius, destroyed it (though he probably means just the military installations, since Pharos crops up later as a Roman possession). Demetrius, however, escaped to Macedonia. With the capture of Pharos and the flight of Demetrius the *status quo* of 228 was automatically restored. No new principles were employed in settling affairs in 219: the damaged Pharos and captured Dimallum joined those communities which had a special friendly relationship (*amicitia*) with Rome and were expected to behave as Rome's friends; the kingdom of the Ardiaei remained under Pinnes, who may have been required to pay another indemnity or to raise his tribute payments. Otherwise nothing changed: the restoration of the separation of powers in Illyria had been achieved by defeating Demetrius and undoing his work of consolidation. Roman objectives had been met.

III. THE FIRST MACEDONIAN WAR

The total defeat of Demetrius of Pharos had restored the *status quo* in Illyria; but Demetrius had escaped the fiasco of Pharos and had found refuge at the Macedonian court. Philip V, who in 221 at the age of seventeen had succeeded Antigonus Doson, was in 219 heavily engaged on two fronts. The first was military. The Greek League which Doson had created in order to fight against Cleomenes of Sparta continued to exist after Cleomenes' defeat and Doson's death; and in 220 Philip undertook to lead it against the Aetolian League (the 'Social War'). This war was in its second year when Demetrius joined Philip. Philip's second front was an internal political one. He had inherited advisers from Doson, and it was presumably they who had encouraged him to undertake the Social War, so continuing Doson's hegemonial policy among the Greeks: but Philip felt himself increasingly controlled and dominated by them. In 218 Philip equipped a fleet and operated with it against Aetolia in the Adriatic; and this tactical change may possibly have resulted from Demetrius' advice. In the same year his dissatisfaction with his inherited 'friends' broke out into a serious dispute, in which the most irritatingly influential of Doson's advisers were eradicated. Thereafter it quickly became clear that Philip's aspirations were more grandiose than Doson's. Even a total defeat of the Aetolians could bring him little power or glory, and this began to seem increasingly unlikely. The very next year showed the direction of his thoughts: as soon as the news of the Roman defeat at Trasimene reached him, he began negotiations to end the Aetolian war, which he managed to do on the basis of the *status quo* in the 'Peace of Naupactus'. His hands were then free to involve Macedonia in the great events of the Mediterranean world. As Polybius records, he was in this doubtless closely advised by Demetrius of Pharos, who had largely taken the place of the Macedonian advisers.

Macedonia had in the past never seriously tried to control the coast of the Adriatic. The Pindus Mountains were such a major barrier in the west that whenever Macedonia had extended its direct control over neighbouring areas, it had been to the south into Greece, to the east into Thrace or to the north into Paeonia, but not to the west. The Epirote monarchy had usually been a friendly neighbour, a tradition which after 232 the Federation continued; the Illyrians could be (and were) used as mercenaries or allies; and from a further control of the lands west of the Pindus, it seemed, Macedonia had little to gain. But the Aetolian war, the war between Carthage and Rome and Demetrius' self-interested advice combined now to direct Philip's attention to the Adriatic. Another factor may also have played a part. Scerdilaidas, the Illyrian dynast based perhaps at Scodra, who had participated with Demetrius in the expedition south of Lissus in 220, had, like Demetrius, been allied with Macedonia, and in 218 had helped Philip during the Social War. The Social War produced little profit for him, however, and in 217, doubtless under pressure from his men but possibly resenting Demetrius' influence over Philip – it was scarcely in his interest that Demetrius be restored to Illyria, should Philip have this in mind – he began raiding not only with ships in the Adriatic but also by land in the Macedonian border districts of Dassaretis and Pelagonia, where he took several towns.

Scerdilaidas could not anticipate that the war with Aetolia would end virtually overnight, as happened in late summer 217; he thus could not expect that Philip would quickly be able to retaliate. Before the winter Philip recovered the territories which had been occupied by Scerdilaidas earlier in the year and captured some more towns. At about the same time the Senate, despite the serious contemporary events in Italy, showed that it had not forgotten the lands east of the Adriatic. Livy records for 217 embassies to Philip, asking for the delivery of Demetrius, which Philip refused, and to Pinnes, reminding him that an instalment of indemnity had not been paid and offering to accept hostages, should he prefer to postpone payment even further.[15] It is possible that the Roman reminder about the Illyrian payments may have caused Scerdilaidas' sudden breach of his alliance with Philip and his search for funds in piracy and his raids on Macedonia. He clearly had a good relationship with Rome, which he did not wish to jeopardize: he had not been punished by the Romans in 219, despite having sailed south of Lissus with Demetrius in 220; in 216 he appealed to Rome for help against Philip. After 217 Pinnes is not mentioned again in our sources, instead the dynasts Scerdilaidas and his son Pleuratus seem to be the only recognized powers in Illyria; and their status as Roman friends might well go back to 219. This raises the possibility that Scerdilaidas himself might have suggested to Rome the danger which Demetrius represented in 217 as adviser to Philip.

In any case, the key to Roman interest lay as before in the Illyrian coast: as long as Hannibal was in Italy, it was important that the Straits of Otranto remain in friendly hands; and should Philip abandon traditional Macedonian policy and, following the self-interested advice of Rome's enemy Demetrius, engage in Illyria, the Senate must inevitably take notice of his activities. Events of 216 seemed to suggest that Philip was trying to replace the Illyrians as the effective power on the Adriatic

---

[15] Livy XXII.33.3, 5. Livy has perhaps made two embassies out of one.

seaboard. He even followed Demetrius' advice about the type of ship which he should construct: a fleet of 100 Illyrian-type *lembi* was built during the winter and deployed in spring 216 in the Adriatic. Scerdilaidas informed the Senate about this, and they detached a mere ten ships from the fleet which was now stationed at Lilybaeum in Sicily. Philip, who seems to have been hoping to take Apollonia, panicked when he saw the Roman ships arriving and abandoned his plans. There was no engagement: he simply went home. With an informant as vulnerable and reliable as Scerdilaidas there was no need for the Roman ships to stay in eastern Adriatic waters. A detachment of 25 ships was detailed off to guard the Italian coast between Brundisium and Tarentum; but their main purpose will doubtless have been to guard against any development of Carthaginian naval authority. Should Philip unexpectedly seem to be dangerous, they would also be in a position to deal with him.[16]

Had Philip been content to restrict himself to Illyria the situation might not have seriously changed for a long time, though Rome would doubtless have protected her strategically situated friends if necessary. But in 215 a single incident changed the Roman appreciation of Philip's activities. During the summer the Roman fleet guarding Calabria intercepted a suspicious ship which was sailing eastwards. It turned out to be a Macedonian ship; on board were an Athenian, Xenophanes, and three high-placed Carthaginians, Gisgo, Bostar and Mago. A search of their possessions brought documents to light, the most important of which was the draft of a treaty between Hannibal and Philip. The Romans thus learnt at an early stage of planned co-operation between Philip and Hannibal. Polybius records the oath of Hannibal in a Greek translation of the Punic original. We have no reason for believing that it is not authentic, and it must represent either the copy of the draft document which was captured with Xenophanes (though it is not clear why a non-Roman draft document should have been preserved in the Roman archives), or, perhaps more likely, the official Macedonian copy, plundered from the Macedonian archives in 168 by the victorious Romans and made available to Polybius through his friendship with Scipio Aemilianus.[17]

The contents do not give much idea of the balance of power between the two generals, though it would be reasonable, with the source tradition, to see the initiative as lying with Philip. Even after Cannae Hannibal could be grateful for a diversion of Roman strength to Illyria, if it were offered, though there is no reason to believe that he would have gone to much trouble to organize it. But the preserved document contains no promise of action, either by Hannibal in Illyria or by Philip in

[16] Polyb. v.109; Livy XXIII.32.17.
[17] Sources and exhaustive literature in Schmitt 1969, no. 528: (A 32).

Italy. It comprises only a series of very general clauses which committed neither side to any immediate action. A general 'friendship' clause ruled that neither party nor his allies nor subjects might act in a hostile way against the other party, his allies or subjects, and that they were to be allies in war against the Romans 'until the gods give us the victory'. Philip was to help 'as necessary and as we shall from time to time agree'. The only concrete measures which were foreseen concerned the establishment of the peace treaty after the victory. Here the interests of Philip were finally to find recognition: the Romans were to be bound not to wage war against Philip, they were no longer to 'possess' (κυρίους εἶναι: here the hostile interpretation of Rome's trans-Adriatic friendships) Corcyra, Apollonia, Epidamnus, Pharos, Dimallum, the Parthini and Atintania; Demetrius of Pharos should receive back all his friends and relatives who had been interned in Italy since 219. The substantive part of the treaty ends with a pledge of mutual support in any future war with Rome and in general, so long as existing treaties with other 'kings, cities, peoples' were not affected by it.

The treaty thus represents merely a framework within which friendly co-operation could take place. Hannibal bound himself to nothing until he had won the war with Rome; and Carthage, it seems, possibly not even to this, since Philip's envoys appear not to have visited Carthage and it is a moot point whether Hannibal and his councillors who swore the oath (which Polybius also records) had bound the Carthaginian state at the same time.[18] The interests of Philip and Demetrius were to be taken care of in the peace treaty with Rome, which Hannibal hoped to be able to dictate. This did not amount to very much, though it doubtless reflects Hannibal's confidence after Cannae. Nor did the Roman Senate apparently think that it amounted to much, although it certainly required that more attention be paid to Philip than hitherto. There was, however, no panic action nor reason for it. The fleet in Apulia was strengthened by the addition of thirty ships and was put under the direct command of the praetor M. Valerius Laevinus. Laevinus was instructed that, should investigations confirm Philip's plans to co-operate with Hannibal, he was at once to cross 'to Macedonia' and ensure that Philip stayed there. Appropriate funds were also made available.[19] This reaction was typically sensible and to the point: the possibility that Philip would cross to Italy was remote, but if the evidence of the documents proved correct, it had to be taken into account. The modest and practical response of the Senate contrasts sharply with the later Roman tradition, which Livy's Roman sources related. They, clearly without knowledge of the document itself, invented treaty-terms to suit an exaggerated fear and perhaps

---

[18] This is denied, with some probability, by Bickerman 1952: (E 7).
[19] Livy xxiii.38.7.

to justify Rome's later severe treatment of Macedonia: according to this version Philip was to attack Italy with 200 ships; when the war was over, Italy and Rome should belong to Carthage and Hannibal, and Hannibal would sail to Greece and wage war with whomever the king wished; all states and islands which neighbour on Macedonia should become part of Philip's kingdom. The exaggeration is obvious; the Senate's disposition of a mere fifty ships in case of need, recorded by the same Livy, is sufficient comment.

Events showed that the Senate had been right not to over-estimate the danger from Philip. The fifty ships were adequate to achieve the limited Roman aims. In the spring Philip moved again into Adriatic waters, this time with 120 *lembi*. He first attacked and took Oricum, but not before the people of Oricum had sent an appeal to Laevinus. In accordance with his instructions from the Senate, he crossed the Adriatic and chased Philip's small garrison without difficulty. At the same time news arrived that Philip was attacking Apollonia; Laevinus managed to put some of his men into the town, who succeeded in beating off Philip's attack with such thoroughness that Philip felt it necessary to burn his new fleet at the mouth of the River Aous and to retreat overland to Macedonia. The only thing he had achieved was the permanent stationing of the Roman fleet in Illyrian waters: Laevinus wintered at Oricum.[20]

Philip's burnt boats prevented his undertaking a naval expedition in 213. *Lembi* were in any case no match for the heavy Roman quinqueremes, as he had already decided at Apollonia. But he had, it seems, no difficulty in withdrawing home overland in 214 and was loath to let one disaster colour his strategic thinking. It is not certain whether Demetrius was still alive; but he had clearly recommended his Illyrian plan so convincingly that Philip seems to have felt fully committed to it. Probably in 213 he crossed the Pindus Mountains again, managed to take control of the Parthini, Dimallum and the Atintanes, and crowned his achievement by capturing the fortress of Lissus, which may have been part of Scerdilaidas' territory. In any case, these successes, which neither Laevinus, who had few land troops, nor Scerdilaidas was able to prevent, put a land-barrier between Scerdilaidas and the Roman base at Oricum; and Lissus was in any case of great strategic importance. But despite these ostensible successes, Philip could not join Hannibal without a fleet; and insofar as Laevinus controlled the sea, so he continued to fulfil his function. The question was, however, how long Roman credibility in the area would survive when, despite a substantial Roman naval presence, Philip was able without difficulty and without provoking retaliation, to take control of some of Rome's friends and of a major fortress.

[20] Livy XXIV.40.

If effective resistance were to be offered, the Romans had two possibilities: either Laevinus' force must be strengthened, above all by the
provision of adequate numbers of legionaries who could tackle Philip on
land; or Rome could look for new local allies, since her inland friends
were obviously alone unable or, without effective Roman help, unwilling to offer serious resistance to Philip. Under the strained circumstances
of the Hannibalic War, when fighting was already going on in Italy,
Spain and Sicily, the second alternative was the obvious one for the
Balkan sector. This, however, if it were to be effective, meant alliance
with a major Greek power already hostile to Philip; and this implied that
Rome would run the risk of becoming involved in the political struggles
of the Greek states. No Greek opponent of Philip could be expected to
share the extremely limited Roman war objectives. Within Greece the
struggle against Macedonia had a long history, in which all kinds of local
factors, the future importance of which no contemporary Roman could
foresee, had played and might again play a part. To take sides with one or
more Greek powers against Philip meant inevitably taking sides in
internal Greek affairs. So far Rome had avoided this through the very
limited nature of the actions against Illyria and by avoiding any formal-
ized relationship with the friends across the Adriatic. If the pressure of
the Hannibalic War now made the search for a formal military alliance in
the Balkans virtually inevitable, then in the long term it was unlikely that
Rome would avoid being sucked into the complex political affairs of the
Greek states, which would bring with it an extension of commitments
and interests far beyond the very limited war objectives which Laevinus'
standing orders of 215 laid down.

Moreover Laevinus had little choice as to whom he should approach.
Philip's predecessor Antigonus Doson had organized a majority of the
Greek states into an alliance which had fought with Antigonus against
Cleomenes of Sparta and under Philip against the Aetolians. This alliance
still existed. Of the western Greek states Epirus, Acarnania and the
Achaean League were members of this alliance and allies of Philip:
whether he could use them for an aggressive war against Rome is
questionable; but Rome could certainly not hope to win them for a war
against Philip, and only a western Greek state could be interested in co-
operating with Rome on and around the coasts of the Adriatic. There
was thus no alternative to approaching Philip's old enemy of the Social
War, the Aetolian League, once it became necessary to seek an ally. The
Aetolians were the only Greek state of any military importance which
was not friendly with Philip; and contact with the Aetolians was duly
taken up during 212. The date when the negotiations were completed
cannot be certainly established. Livy sets the treaty in 211; information
from Polybius (who, whether at first or at second hand, is Livy's source)

seems to indicate 212, but since his own account is lost, this cannot be regarded as wholly conclusive; and an inscription found at Thyrrheum, the chief town of Acarnania, which originally bore the full published text of the treaty, is badly damaged and does not help to decide the problem of the date.[21] The precise date is less important, however, than the terms, which are recorded, albeit in abbreviated form and with some mistakes, by Livy from his literary source (Polybius or perhaps Coelius Antipater); and some few sections are preserved in Greek translation by the Thyrrheum inscription, which allows us to expand some of Livy's abbreviations.

The terms, as we can reconstruct them, were as follows: the Aetolians should immediately wage war on Philip by land; Rome should provide not less than 25 quinqueremes; as far north as Corcyra, any cities which were conquered by the Romans should belong to the Aetolians; moveable property (including persons and animals) should belong to Rome; any cities which were conquered jointly by the Aetolians and Romans should, as before, go to the Aetolians. In this case, however, the moveable property should be shared; cities which came over to the allies without being conquered might join the Aetolian League under certain specific conditions, which are unfortunately lost; the Romans should help Aetolia to capture Acarnania; if peace should be made by either party, it should be valid only on condition that Philip should not wage war on the other party or its allies or subjects. A further clause provided that certain specifically named friends and allies of the parties to the treaty, Elis, Sparta, Attalus of Pergamum, Pleuratus and Scerdilaidas, might also co-operate *eodem iure amicitiae*. It was some two years before the treaty was ratified by the Senate, probably because the senators wanted to hear Laevinus' personal explanation of the (for Rome) unusually unfavourable terms, which his military activity in the Adriatic and perhaps an illness prevented from happening until 210. It was then published on the Capitol in Rome and at Olympia and presumably at Thermum, the Aetolian federal shrine, by the Aetolians; but this delay did not prevent the war from continuing as if the treaty had been ratified at once.

The most striking aspect of these terms is Rome's lack of interest in gaining territory in the Balkans. In this respect the treaty represents a direct continuation of previous Roman policy in this area. The 'Corcyra' limitation was certainly not intended to limit this seriously: it probably meant no more than that Rome did not want to be committed to handing over to the Aetolians the territories of Rome's friends which had already been lost to Philip (the Parthini, Dimallum, Atintania) or which might

---

[21] Thorough recent discussions of the date by Lehmann 1967: (B 14) (212); Badian 1958: (D 6) (211); sources and literature to the treaty in Schmitt 1969, no. 536: (A 32).

still be captured by him, should they be recovered during the war. On the other hand the Roman claim to moveable property – a type of division of booty which is known from all areas and all periods of the ancient world – meant no more than that Rome wished to try to recover the costs of the war or even, if the opportunity arose, to make a profit. Acarnania had long been a thorn in the side of Aetolian expansionist aims; it was an ally of Philip, however, and thus caused the Romans no difficulty in accepting what can only have been an Aetolian demand. The clause about peace-making is clear and requires little comment; it meant in practice that Aetolia was bound to continue fighting until Rome's interests were met. The provision about the allies is clear in principle but obscure in detail. Its aim was to broaden the basis of the formal alliance against Philip; but what it meant in practice – for instance, what provisions were envisaged about division of the spoils, should further states become involved in the war – is unknown, although some agreement about this will have been necessary. It probably amounted in general to participation in the division of the 'moveable property', which must have stood in some kind of proportion to the level of participation. No Greek state was going to go to war with Philip just for the fun of it.

The Aetolian alliance meant that the Romans, who thereby committed at least half the Adriatic fleet to joint operations, could no longer maintain their hitherto passive role towards Philip, merely reacting when his actions seemed dangerous. No ally could be won for such a programme. The implication of the Aetolian alliance was that Rome must go onto the offensive, but that the details of the offensive would in practice largely be laid down by the Aetolians. And since, according to the treaty, the Aetolian League was to receive all conquered land and cities, it is not surprising to find that the military operations resembled those of the Social War: they took place largely at the cost of Philip's allies in areas, above all in central Greece, into which the Aetolian League wished to extend its influence. Acarnania was expressly mentioned as a war objective in the treaty; but Aetolia also aimed to strengthen its position in Thessaly and Phocis; and since these actions inevitably involved Philip in defending his southern Greek allies (or abandoning them and with them all claims to credibility among the Greeks, which he was not prepared to do), he was soon fully employed in the south and therefore could not operate in the west and threaten Italy. Laevinus was satisfied to accept this traditional Aetolian strategy since operations in central and southern Greece were far more likely to provide booty, which, according to the treaty, came proportionately to the Romans, than, for instance, operations in the north-west against Epirus, which had already recently been seriously plundered by the Aetolians during the Social War.

The greatest allied successes came in the first two years of co-operation.[22] Oeniadae, Nasus and Zacynthos were taken and became Aetolian. The desperate will of the Acarnanians to resist to the last man prevented their conquest by Aetolia, which the treaty foresaw; but Anticyra in Phocis and Aegina in the Saronic Gulf were taken in 210 by Laevinus and his successor, the pro-consul P. Sulpicius Galba (the Aetolians promptly sold Aegina for 30 talents to King Attalus of Pergamum, who now sent a fleet to the war). The capture of Aegina, however, marked the end of major conquests. The Senate seems to have been so well satisfied with the results of the alliance that Sulpicius was instructed to send his legionaries home and to retain only the *socii navales*, the Italian allies who manned the fleet, and the sources mark a return to more sedate activity by the Romans. Philip, who since 214 had no fleet, tried urgently to exploit this with Carthaginian naval support, but this did not amount to much in practice. In 209 Bomilcar, the Carthaginian admiral, reached Corcyra; in 208 he ventured as far as the mouth of the Corinthian Gulf before deciding not to risk a battle with the Romans.[23] Rome clearly did not need to take this feint very seriously.

The conquest of Greek cities, the sale of their populations and the general disruption of normal inter-state relationships which the renewed war in thickly settled central and southern Greece produced affected others besides the combatants in the war, whether because the balance of power in the Greek world was being upset, or because commercial opportunities were being damaged by the war, or because of fears that the war might spread and involve ever more areas and cities. Outsiders had indeed tried to bring the Social War to an end. And in 209, the year after the capture of Aegina and its sale to Attalus of Pergamum, a group of non-participant states took the initiative to explore with the combatants the possibilities of peace. Their motives were doubtless mixed. Rhodes and Chios may have been concerned about their trade; this may also have been a factor with Ptolemy IV, though he may have been more concerned about Attalus' intentions, since he cannot have been pleased at the Pergamene possession of Aegina, only a short distance from his own Peloponnesian base at Methana. Athens had freed itself from more than a generation of close Macedonian control only in 229; Philip's anti-Aetolian operations in Euboea, Epicnemidian Locris and southern Thessaly might well have re-awakened fears of Macedonian actions to re-establish control of Athens and its important harbour Piraeus. But neither the Aetolians nor the Romans (who did not participate in the conference) were interested in peace with Philip in 209. For the Aetolians, the war was far too profitable strategically, for the Romans far too convenient for it to be brought to an end merely for the sake of a few

----

[22] For detailed discussion of the military details see Walbank 1940, 68ff.: (D 54).
[23] Livy XXVII.15.7, XXVIII.7.17–18.

Greek non-participants, even if they were Roman *amici*.[24] In 208 another attempt was made. Livy mentions only Rhodes and Ptolemy this time, but it may be that in abbreviating Polybius he has omitted Chios and Athens. But this time Philip, who in the meanwhile had achieved some successes, felt himself strong enough to refuse talks. This will have pleased Rome well enough, since it was Aetolia and the other allies who were suffering from Philip's new strength.

A third attempt in 207 by the non-participants, this time joined by Mytilene and Amynander of Athamania, came closer to success. The Aetolians were wearying, since Philip had by now rebuilt his fleet and recaptured Zacynthos. Then, as he had done during the Social War, he had penetrated into the Aetolian heartland and plundered the Aetolian federal sanctuary at Thermum (it may have been on this occasion that his Acarnanian allies removed to their capital Thyrrheum the stone which contained the Aetolian treaty with Rome). Sulpicius Galba managed once more to sabotage the peace talks, but Roman inactivity, which had already allowed Philip to recover Zacynthos and to penetrate into Aetolia, was wearing the patience of the Aetolians. Moreover, given that Philip was again operating in north-west Greece it was increasingly important that he should be contained, since Hannibal, albeit now lacking long-term prospects of success, was still in Italy. Without a stronger Roman commitment the Aetolians were beginning to think of peace, even though this involved breaking their treaty with Rome. The successes of the first two years of co-operation had by 206 lost their gloss through a series of defeats and losses and wearisome indecisive action; and in 206 the non-participants finally managed to persuade the Aetolians to make peace with Philip – but, ominously, a separate peace, against the wishes of Sulpicius Galba, who spoke against it at the Aetolian assembly. From their peace treaty they gained merely peace: the precise terms are not recorded, but it is probable that they simply confirmed the *status quo*. They had, in order to achieve this, broken a decisive clause of their treaty with Rome. But strategically they were in any case no longer able to fulfil Roman expectations, since it seemed that they were no longer a match for Philip on land. Whether they made peace or not, the Romans would have had to commit themselves more deeply in the Balkans, so long as they considered it important to keep Philip in check. If the Aetolians had fought on, they would probably have been defeated: a defeated Aetolia was useless to Rome; it might indeed even have been dangerous to the insecure Roman position in Greece to allow Aetolia to be defeated.

The Aetolian peace with Philip was probably agreed in autumn 206.

[24] Sources for the attempted negotiations: Livy XXVII.30, cf. Polyb. X.25 (209); Livy XXVIII.7.14 (208); Polyb. XI.4.1; App. *Mac.* 3.1 (207). See Habicht 1982, 138–9: (D 30).

The Senate, however, seems to have retained hopes that, despite this, Aetolia would return to the fray in the next campaign, if Rome showed a greater commitment. In 205 a new commander, P. Sempronius Tuditanus, was sent to the Balkans with 10,000 infantry, 1,000 cavalry and 35 warships. The force was inadequate to fight Philip by itself and cannot have been intended to operate alone. We may compare the 20,000 infantry, 2,000 cavalry and 200 ships which had been sent against Teuta in 229. Livy indicates that an attempt was made to bring the Aetolians back into the war; but even winning back the Parthini and an attack on Dimallum could not persuade them to take up arms again, despite clear indications that the Romans were angry at their breach of the treaty. In 205 the Senate had no interest in continuing the Balkan war alone; by then the fighting against Carthage in Spain was over and the successful Roman commander in Spain, P. Cornelius Scipio, was consul and hoped to cross to Africa and defeat Carthage there. Under these conditions, if the Balkan war was to continue, its burden needed more than ever to be carried chiefly by the allies; if this was impossible, the risk from peace was less in the circumstances than the risk from an all-Roman commitment, expensive in both money and manpower. The final reckoning with Philip for his stab in the back of 215 could be postponed. And when it became clear that the Aetolians, despite the new Roman demonstration of military commitment, were still not to be moved, Tuditanus accepted the good services of the officers of the Epirote federation (despite Epirote friendship with Philip) when they suggested peace negotiations.

The negotiations took place at Phoenice, the main town of the Chaones, one of the states forming the Epirote confederacy. They seem to have made no attempt to meet the theoretical risk that Philip might even now try to join Hannibal in Italy.[25] The terms which Livy records for the bilateral peace treaty concern solely the possessions of the two parties in Illyria, since this was still the only area, it seems, which affected Rome: of Rome's friends of the Illyrian Wars, three, the Parthini, the Atintanes and Dimallum had been taken by Philip in 213 or 212.[26] The peace terms foresaw that, of these, Philip should give up the Parthini and Dimallum, but that if the Senate should agree he might retain the Atintanes. Two other places, Bargullum and Eugenium, the locality of which is unknown but which must have been in the same general area – perhaps they were villages or forts already taken by Tuditanus in 205 – should also be Roman. Otherwise Philip might keep his conquests. These and perhaps a general peace formula, whereby neither party should attack each other or the allies of the other, seem to have concluded

---

[25] Livy XXIX.12.1; App. *Mac.* 3.1.
[26] Livy XXIX.12. Literature on the peace in Schmitt 1969, no. 543: (A 32). See Habicht 1982, 138–9: (D 30) for a critical discussion.

this hastily patched-up treaty, which was quickly ratified in Rome.

After his account of the terms of the treaty Livy adds two lists of states which, he says, were *foederi adscripti* ('written into the treaty'): Prusias, king of Bithynia, the Achaeans, the Boeotians, the Thessalians, the Acarnanians and the Epirotes were 'written in' by Philip; the Ilians, Attalus of Pergamum, Pleuratus, Nabis the ruler of Sparta, the Eleans, the Messenians and the Athenians by Rome. The precise significance of this procedure is uncertain, but it is clear that it meant that the named communities must at least have participated explicitly in the general terms of the peace as Roman *amici*, although they cannot have been affected by the specific territorial terms agreed between Philip and Rome. There has been a great deal of inconclusive discussion about the authenticity of these lists – inevitably inconclusive, since neither the full significance of the procedure is known nor, thanks to the loss of Polybius' account, the level of participation of the individual states concerned. In particular Ilium and Athens have often been suspected of being added by later Roman writers, since they have been regarded by modern historians as 'neutrals'. Moreover, it has been argued, Roman self-justification may have played a part: Roman legend traced Roman origins to Troy, the predecessor town of Ilium; and an appeal or appeals by Athens to Rome played some part in the renewed outbreak of war against Philip in 200. Ilium, however, was certainly not neutral, since at this time it was controlled by Attalus of Pergamum and may even have provided some ships or troops for Attalus; and Athens had already shown her fear of aggression by Philip when she was aligned with the states that had from 209 onwards tried to persuade the combatants to negotiate a peace. Of these, Athens was the only mainland Greek state and might well have sought some modest protection against Philip by associating itself explicitly with the peace treaty on the Roman side. It thus seems not altogether unreasonable to accept the Livian list of *adscripti* as authentic, even though we cannot appreciate the precise significance of the procedure.

One thing it must mean, however, and that is the recognition of these states as Roman *amici*. The course of the First Macedonian War had broadened Roman knowledge of and extended Roman contact (both friendly and hostile) with Greek states of central and southern Greece and of Asia Minor, and had thus opened up an area of potential interest and possible involvement far wider than the narrow limits set by the operations in Illyria in 229 and 219 and by the initial aims of the war against Philip. The list of *adscripti* documents some of these implications; and we should probably envisage that informal assurances will have been given to the *amici*. Nevertheless the formal terms of the Peace of Phoenice reflect merely the urgency of bringing military operations in the Balkans to an end, and remain firmly within the framework of Rome's traditionally limited interest in Illyria. This time Rome even sacrificed one inland Illyrian community, the Atintanes, as the price of peace. Thus apart from the coast the Roman position appeared formally even less substantial than in 219. The critical harbour towns, Corcyra, Oricum, Apollonia, Epidamnus, nevertheless remained Roman friends; and Scerdilaidas' son and successor Pleuratus would doubtless keep watch from Scodra on Philip's activities. Even without the Atintanes the checks and balances which had characterized Roman policy towards Illyria since 228 were still functional. The peace treaty and the watchfulness of the *amici* should manage to guarantee the peace at least until Hannibal had been driven out of Italy. Should it then seem desirable to adjust Rome's relation with Philip, the Senate would be able to choose its own moment.

CHAPTER 5

ROMAN EXPANSION IN THE WEST

W. V. HARRIS

I. INTRODUCTION

Between the end of the second war against Carthage and the fall of Numantia in 133 Roman power engulfed northern Italy and vast territories in Spain, as well as defeating Carthage once more, destroying the city and establishing a province in northern Africa. These developments can conveniently be considered in a single chapter. This does not mean any detraction from the important differences which distinguished these three areas and Roman behaviour in them. In addition, due attention will be paid both to the internal workings of the state and society of the conquerors and to the expansion carried out in the east in the same period. Only when studied as a whole can the vastly complex process we call Roman imperialism be understood.

The Roman Senate had already made its crucial decisions about the Gallic area of northern Italy and about Spain before 202. In the case of the Gauls, the decision to exact obedience dated from before the Hannibalic War, and in 206 the two pre-war colonies in the plain of the Po, Placentia and Cremona, had been resettled. At about the same date the Senate had decided to begin sending a regular series of governors, two at a time, to Spain. In the year after Zama, with the Carthaginians now committed to a treaty which effectively prevented them from re-establishing their power in Spain, Rome could in theory have withdrawn from its Spanish possessions – though such an action would have had no appeal at Rome. Northern Italy, however, required attention more urgently.

II. THE SUBJUGATION OF CISALPINE GAUL[1]

In 201 there was not even a geographical expression to apply to the area which the Romans later came to call Gallia Cisalpina (among other labels). It was not a single political or even ethnic unit, and its popula-

[1] The main literary source for this section is Livy; Polybius and also Diodorus Siculus, Strabo and Zonaras contribute. The important epigraphical and archaeological evidence is mentioned in later notes.

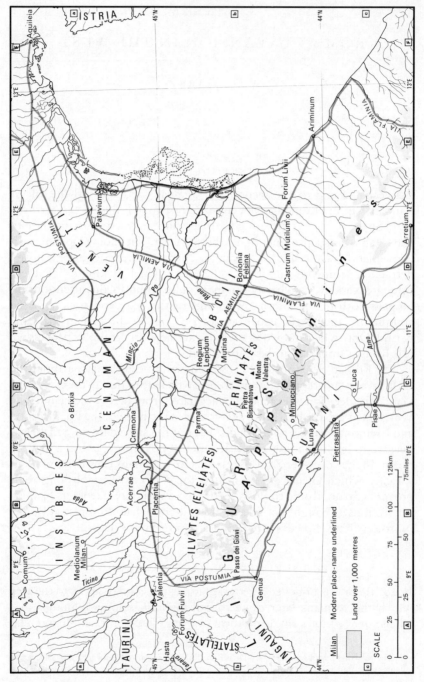

Map 7. Northern Italy.

tions lived in several different ways, as well as having different relationships with Rome. The Ligurians, though they had some level territory on both sides of the Appennines, were largely hill people with a more pastoral, less agricultural, economy than could be found in most other parts of Italy, with hunting, too, relatively important.[2] There must have been rudimentary political institutions at the tribal level, since quite large armies sometimes took the field, but no organization bound all Ligurians together. There are no Ligurian inscriptions in this period, there is no coinage. The quantity and quality of their metal work is scarcely known (no territory was more thoroughly plundered by the Romans); they were probably short of iron.[3] They had very few settlements larger than villages, and had lost two important places, Pisae and Genua, to Rome before our period begins. Population, however, was probably quite dense by the standards of the ancient countryside, for otherwise such long resistance to Roman legions would be hard to understand.

The main Gallic tribes, the Boii, Insubres and Cenomani, were more advanced in some respects. Polybius libels them in saying that they had no *techne* whatsoever, as we know from preserved metal ornaments, equipment and weapons.[4] Iron weapons were commonplace. Similarly Polybius is wrong to represent them as essentially nomadic,[5] though it is no doubt true that there was a significant pastoral element in their economy too. The Gauls tilled the soil extensively, it almost goes without saying.[6] Once again, Polybius' assertion that the Gauls lived in unfortified villages is partly unjust. Acerrae, Mediolanum, Felsina (Bononia) and Brixia, at least, must have had fortifications.[7] The silver coinages produced by the Gauls of Northern Italy are imitative but they prove the existence of a certain degree of civic organization.[8] Though none of the handful of extant Gallic inscriptions is likely to date from before the arrival of the Romans, some Gauls were literate, since they addressed letters to the Roman Senate. And while very little is known of

---

[2] The importance of stock-raising: Diod. Sic. v.39.4 (from Poseidonius?) (also mentions hunting). Flocks: Strabo IV.202; cf. v.218. These and other texts bearing directly on ancient Liguria are collected in Forni and others 1976: (B 211).

[3] They used bronze shields: Strabo IV.202.

[4] Polyb. II.17.10. In fact he knew about their horns and trumpets (29.6), necklaces and bracelets (29.8, 31.5), but in 33.3 he gives an unduly belittling account of the Gallic sword. The best guide to the archaeology of the North Italian Gauls in this period is Peyre 1979: (H 164).

[5] II.17.11. For later wool production among the Insubres see Strabo v.218.

[6] Polyb. II.15 may have little relevance to the pre-Roman period, but see II.34.10, III.44.8; cf. Toynbee 1965, II.256: (A 37).

[7] Polyb. II.17.9. On Acerrae and Mediolanum: II.34. On Bononia: cf. Livy XXXIII.37.3–4. It is impossible to suppose that Brixia, being the capital of the Cenomani (Livy XXXII.30.6), lacked walls.

[8] On these coins see Pautasso 1966, 1975: (B 123 and 124); Peyre 1979, 99–101: (H 164). All or virtually all of these silver coins were minted north of the Po. Considerable quantities of bronze and silver coins appear in Livy's accounts of the booty collected from the Gauls (cf. *ESAR* I.128–32).

the political organization even of the larger tribes, these plainly maintained stable control over fixed and quite sizeable territories.[9]

The Boii and the Insubres had regained their freedom from Rome
when Hannibal arrived, though the Cremona and Placentia colonies
remained. The Cenomani for their part appear to have taken open action
against Rome only in 200 – which, if true, shows how badly informed
they were about the outside world. During the Hannibalic War they may
have been influenced by their neighbours to the east, the Veneti, who
continuously preserved the alliance which they had made with Rome
before 225. (Since the latter offered no armed resistance to Rome in the
second century, while becoming more and more subject to Rome, not
much will be said about them in this section.) After the withdrawal of
Mago's forces in 203 the reimposition of Roman power in northern Italy
had a high priority, and each year from 201 to 190 the Senate assigned one
or both consuls to that region, until the Gauls had been subdued.[10] In the
majority of years more legions served there than in Spain, and even after
190 the North Italian legions were usually as numerous as those in Spain,
down to 172.[11]

One reason behind this policy was that in Roman eyes it was necessary
to punish the Insubres and Boii for their defection. According to a
common interpretation, however, the main aim was simply the defence
of existing Roman territory.[12] And the Gallic wars, perhaps even the
Ligurian wars, did have something of this character. Gallic troops had
been all too visible in Roman Italy on various occasions since 225, and it
may have been felt, whether this was realistic or not, that they were still
dangerous. But there were other motives, still more important than
these. Roman society in this period was directed towards very regular,
virtually annual, warfare, towards the expansion of Roman national
power, and towards the material benefits which were part of successful
warfare.[13] So deeply ingrained were these traits that even the fearful trial
of the Hannibalic War did not alter them. The plain of the Po had been a
potential area for Roman conquest since the 260s, for though it was both
poorly drained and heavily wooded by the standards of later centuries, it
was a very attractive territory, as indeed the massive Roman and Italian
immigration of the second century demonstrates. The relative back-
wardness of the Gallic and Ligurian populations had some obvious
advantages from the Roman point of view – their fortifications and

---

[9] Livy XXXII.30.6 (*in vicos*), however, suggests some fragmentation among the Cenomani.
[10] The best detailed accounts of these events are still those of De Sanctis 1907–64, IV.i.407–17:
(A 14) and (in spite of many faults) Toynbee 1965, II.252–85: (A 37); see also Hoyos 1976: (H 161).
[11] On the disposition of legions see Toynbee 1965 II.652: (A 37).
[12] E.g. De Sanctis 1907–64, IV.i.407: (A 14); Scullard 1973, 89–90: (H 54).
[13] For this view see Harris 1979, 9–130, 210–11: (A 21).

military organization were weak. Thus it was entirely to be expected that Rome would quickly return to attacking these peoples.

The precise political situation among the Gauls in 202/1 has some obscurities to it. A Carthaginian leader named Hamilcar still seems to have been present,[14] but his influence and significance may have been very limited. When the consul of 201 P. Aelius Paetus, assigned to the *provincia* Italy, arrived in the north, he supposedly received reports of attacks on allied lands before he invaded the territory of the Boii;[15] in any case his expedition resulted in heavy Roman casualties in a battle at Castrum Mutilum (probably Modigliana, in the Appennines above Faenza). Another puzzle, already mentioned, concerns the Cenomani, who, if we are to trust the sources, were now on the verge of rebelling against Rome for the first time, at a very inopportune moment.[16]

In the latter part of 201 Rome was moving quickly towards war against the king of Macedon, and for 200 Gaul was initially no more than a praetorian *provincia* lacking legionary troops. This, however, was the year when not only the Boii but also the Insubres, Cenomani and Ligurians made their most vigorous effort to expel the Romans from Gallic territory. So at least said the Roman annalistic tradition, and it is probably true that contingents of all these peoples combined; however, the Cenomani were not unanimous, and not all the Ligurian tribes were involved – the Ingauni, for example, having freely made a treaty with Rome the year before,[17] are likely to have kept it. In any case this force sacked the Latin colony Placentia and attempted to do the same to its twin Cremona, only to be heavily defeated there by the army of L. Furius Purpurio. The victory was considered important enough to earn him a triumph, even though he thus became the first praetor to celebrate one for more than forty years.

Henceforth the pressure all seems to have come from the Roman side, though Rome incurred some serious losses along the way. One of the consuls of 200 led a plundering expedition, and the following year a praetor initiated an attack on the Insubres – which resulted in heavy Roman casualties.[18] In 199 and 198 the consuls who were assigned to the northern region did 'nothing noteworthy', Livy tells us; the second of them, Sex. Aelius Paetus, took up most of his year re-establishing Placentia and Cremona, which must have required some military operations against the Insubres.[19] But the reason why events were moving relatively slowly is plain: the war against Philip V was still unsettled. The

---

[14] Livy XXXI.10.2, 11.5, 21.18, etc.   [15] Livy XXXI.2.5.
[16] A conflict between generations among the Cenomani may explain their erratic behaviour (cf. Livy XXXII.30.6).   [17] Livy XXXI.2.11.
[18] Livy XXXII.7.5–7 (more than 6,700 killed); Zon. IX.15; cf. Harris 1979, 258: (A 21).
[19] Cf. Zon. IX.16; Livy XXXIII.21.6–9.

fact that Paetus had retained in the north two legions which were supposed to have been disbanded[20] may suggest that he was impatient for activity. In 197, with Flamininus still in possession of the Macedonian command, both consuls campaigned in this region. They inflicted severe defeats on both Gauls and Ligurians, though the Cenomani submitted without much fighting and never again took up arms against Rome (a praetor who tried to provoke a war with them in 187 was restrained by the Senate); C. Cornelius Cethegus celebrated a triumph over the Insubres and Cenomani, Q. Minucius Rufus only an unofficial triumph 'on the Alban Mount' over the Boii and Ligurians. Cethegus' army fought its main battle on the River Mincio, among the Cenomani, and though Insubrian casualties were heavy[21] he may not have advanced into Insubrian territory. Minucius, after reaching Genua and campaigning in Liguria (see below), crossed the Appennines and plundered the land of the Boii, who were unable to persuade the Insubrians to help them by sending an army southwards and were so unnerved by the Roman attack that they could not put up a concerted defence. This chain of events makes Polybius' allusion[22] to the 'fear' that was felt at Rome with regard to the Gauls in early 197 impossible to take at face-value; if the consuls had feared a Gallic attack, Minucius in particular would have had to follow an entirely different strategy.

The Insubres had clearly been much weakened even before the consul of 196 M. Claudius Marcellus (son of the man who had won the *spolia opima* against the Gauls in 222) attacked them, since he was able to penetrate as far as Comum, on the northern side of Insubrian territory, where he captured the town as well as inflicting a severe defeat on the Insubrian army. The Boii too, though they defeated Marcellus in one battle, had to surrender Felsina and the surrounding *castella* – at least for a time – to the combined forces of Marcellus and L. Furius Purpurio (now commanding in Gaul again as consul).

With Spain claiming increased Roman attention in 195, only one consul, L. Valerius Flaccus, went north (against the Boii), but early the next year he commanded in the final defeat of the Insubres near Milan. Both consuls were sent north each year from 194 to 192, the Boii still showing considerable resilience.[23] In 192, however, their state began to disintegrate as the elite, including what Livy calls the 'senate', deserted to the Roman side; some 1,500 persons were involved.[24] In the following

---

[20] Livy XXXII.9.5, 26.2.   [21] Livy XXXII.30.11–12.
[22] Polyb. XVIII.11.2, echoed by Zon. IX.16. Livy explains the attacks simply by saying that the Gauls had defected (i.e. in 200) (XXXII.28.9).
[23] But it is quite uncertain how much value should be attributed to the Roman casualty figures: 5,000 killed in the main battle of 194 (Livy XXXIV.47.8), more than 5,000 (including allies) in the main battle of 193 (Livy XXXV.5.14).   [24] Livy XXXV.22.4, with a 'doublet' in 40.3.

year the subjugation of the Boii was completed by the consul P. Scipio Nasica.

It was a foregone conclusion that Rome would force the Insubres and Boii to capitulate within a few years. Only a prolonged demand for many legions in the east could even have delayed the event. The defeat of Hannibal, as well as the ruthlessness and persistence of Rome, must have dispirited the Gauls, and the betrayal of the Boii by their own rulers in 193 shows how far demoralization had progressed.

The devastation Rome caused in the conquered areas was certainly intense, even though in the case of the Insubres it is hard to gauge. Polybius was exaggerating when he wrote that he had himself seen that the Gauls (he is concerned mainly with the Boii and Insubres) had been driven out of the plain of the Po 'except for a few places near the Alps', for there is plentiful evidence that many Insubres continued to inhabit their ancestral territory.[25] No new colonies were settled on Insubrian land. Many other Insubres, however, had been captured and sent into slavery; and it is very possible that the Insubrian treaty with Rome, about which very little is known,[26] designated some of their territory as Roman *ager publicus*. At all events the treaty must have imposed burdens on the Insubres, as must also have happened even in the case of the less stubborn Cenomani.

Some Insubres survived, with the advantages as well as the disadvantages of a Roman treaty. The Boii on the other hand were dealt with brutally, since they had put up a somewhat longer resistance, and perhaps also because their territory was more accessible from the south and hence more desirable for settlement. The survivors had about half of their land confiscated by Scipio Nasica;[27] presumably this was the more valuable half of their territory and much of the rest of it was too poorly drained or too heavily wooded to sustain a dense population. Polybius implies, and Strabo plainly believed, that the expulsion of the Boii was total.[28] This was the effect as it seemed a generation after the remnant had been reduced to living on unsatisfactory land outside the Roman settlements. The archaeological and onomastic evidence shows a very marked contrast between Cenomanic and Insubrian territory on the one hand and Boian territory on the other; the latter area lacks significant Gallic survivals of the second century or later.[29]

[25] Polyb. II.35.4. Strabo v.213 merely says that they 'still exist'. For the archaeological and onomastic evidence see the relevant items in Chilver 1941, 71–85: (H 159); Mansuelli 1965: (H 163); Peyre 1979, 63–4, 72–81: (H 164). Without doubt they continued to mint coins after the conquest.
[26] Cic. *Balb.*32 is the only source.   [27] Livy XXXVI.39.3.
[28] Polyb.II.35.4; Strabo v.213, 216; cf. Plin. *HN* III.116.
[29] On the archaeological evidence, or rather lack of it, see Arslan 1971–4, 47, and 1976–8, 445–6: (H 157–8). The 'Celto-Italian' dialect of Emilia, Toynbee 1965, II.664 n. 1: (A 37), is a myth, and the religious survivals mentioned by Peyre, 52: (H 164), who realizes that the surviving Boians were few and impoverished, are minor and very dubious.

The most useful part of the land of the Boii passed into the hands of Roman, Latin and probably Italian-ally immigrants. At the same time as Cremona and Placentia were gaining no fewer than 6,000 new families of colonists between them (190), it was decided to found two new colonies on Boian land.[30] In the event only one, Bononia, was established quickly (189); it had 3,000 'Latin' colonists, each of them with a relatively large land-grant of 31 acres (43 for a cavalryman). Next in order probably came the small settlements of Forum Livii (188) and Regium Lepidum, the latter founded when M. Aemilius Lepidus, the consul of 187, constructed the trunk road from Ariminum to Placentia. Parma and Mutina followed in 183, with 2,000 male citizen colonists each.[31] 183 was also the year when, faced with some possible opposition in the extreme north-east of the north Italian plain, Rome decided to establish the Latin colony of Aquileia. The long-term effects of all this settlement will receive attention in a later section (ch. 7, pp. 197–243). Here only the overall political and economic effects can be noted. They are obvious enough: the colonies and other settlements, together with the Insubrian and Cenomanian treaties, finally secured Roman control over the Gallic section of the Po plain; they also represented a massive transfer of resources from Gauls to the Romans and their Italian allies.

The Ligurian wars progressed more slowly. Even in the 170s fighting still occurred in the Appennines as far east as the hills south of Mutina, and Mutina itself was captured by Ligurians in 177. It was not until 155 that the whole of what can be regarded as 'Cisalpine' Liguria was indisputably in Roman hands.

On the coast Genua had been rebuilt in 203, and two years later it was partially secured by means of a treaty with the Ligurian people immediately to the west, the Ingauni. This site provided an important harbour and access of a kind to the Po valley through the Passo dei Giovi. It was now the Ligurians to the east and south-east of this line (which must have been in common use long before the Via Postumia was built in 148) who were the objects of Roman attention: in the main, the Ilvates, Apuani and Friniates. The territory in question, it is worth recalling, was quite extensive, running southwards as far as Pisa and eastwards almost as far as the line of the Via Flaminia (which was built in 187 to connect Arretium and Bononia).

In 197 the consul Q. Minucius Rufus conducted a vigorous campaign, subjugating the Celeiates and Cerdiciates (who probably lived on the path northwards from Genua), and the Ilvates immediately to the east.[32]

---

[30] Livy xxxvii.47.2.

[31] Mutina must have been mainly Boian in the years before 191, in spite of Polyb.iii.40.8 (he anachronistically calls it a Roman colony) and Livy xxxv.4.3–4.

[32] An advantageous consequence for Minucius which can be inferred from *ILLRP* 517 is that he became *patronus* of Genua.

His triumph was the last one over Ligurians for sixteen years. This was not because the Senate failed to pay attention to Liguria. Throughout this period and down to the start of the Third Macedonian War in 171, one consul usually campaigned in Liguria each year, often both; each of them commanded two legions and a comparable number of allies. The first to make much impact after 197 was Q. Minucius Thermus (not a close relative of Minucius Rufus), who as consul in 193 allegedly had to defend Pisa against a massive attack, before taking the offensive in the following year.[33] The place name 'Minucciano', some eighteen miles east of La Spezia, probably derives from him – a detail which underlines the absurdity of his claim to have forced all Liguria to surrender.[34] Since he was refused a triumph on his return in 190, the Senate evidently did not believe any such claim.

With Antiochus III and the Aetolians defeated, consular wars in the north became more acceptable again in 188 and 187. The consuls of 187, C. Flaminius and M. Aemilius Lepidus, are said by Livy to have defeated and disarmed Ligurian Friniates – all of them, supposedly – and Flaminius also defeated the Apuani, 'who by their attacks were making it impossible to cultivate land at Pisa or Bononia'.[35] Mention of fighting at the mountains Ballista and Suismontium (Valestra, Pietra Bismántova) shows that Lepidus had penetrated deep into the Appennines above his Ariminum–Placentia road and his settlement at Regium Lepidum, and though the vowing of two temples while he was on campaign suggests some difficulties, this is the last we hear of resistance by the Friniates for several years. The Apuani, however, defeated a Roman army in 186 and continued to resist thereafter. It seems to have been the achievement of M. Sempronius Tuditanus (*cos.* 185) to make the land-route to Luna (near the River Magra, at the north end of the coastal plain) truly secure against them. The other consul of 185 extended the war to the Ingauni in western Liguria.[36]

The year 182 apparently marked an increase in Roman effort in Liguria, since a proconsul as well as both consuls spent the year there, each with two legions. One of the consuls, L. Aemilius Paullus (who was later to command at Pydna), attacked the Ligurian Ingauni, the reason or pretext being piracy,[37] and defeated them severely. The Ingauni capitulated, and Paullus returned to Rome and a triumph in which the

[33] Livy XXXIV.56.2, XXXV.3.1, 21.10–11; at about the same time other Ligurians were plundering the territory of Placentia (XXXIV.56.10).

[34] Livy XXXVII.2.5. He was attacked by Cato in a speech 'On Fictitious Battles' (*ORF*⁴ fr. 58, pp. 26–7).

[35] Livy XXXIX.2.5; but the Apuani cannot have got as far as Bononian territory.

[36] Livy XXXIX.32.2–4. What happened in the Ligurian wars in 184/3 is quite obscure; cf. Harris 1979, 259: (A 21).

[37] Plut. *Aem.* 6, probably derived from Polybius; cf. Livy XL.18.4, 28.7.

prisoners were naturally more conspicuous than the gold and silver.[38] Other Ligurians wanted to surrender, but were put off by the Senate.[39]

The consuls of 181, still in Liguria in 180 with instructions to make war on the Apuani, introduced a radically new policy of deportation. They transported some 40,000 adult males, and presumably a great number of women and children, from Liguria to Samnium. The two cousins named Q. Fulvius Flaccus continued this policy as consuls in 180 and 179, the one sending about 7,000 more Apuani to Samnium, the other settling 3,200 mountain Ligurians in the plains to the north. On the territory of the Apuani Rome now founded the Latin colony of Luca (180),[40] and three years later Luna, a citizen colony of the large new type with 2,000 male colonists.[41]

The conquest of all of Liguria east of Genua being nearly complete, the more active of the consuls of 178, A. Manlius Vulso, was sent instead to fight in Istria, where a war had been in the making since 183 and where a praetor had fought in 181.[42] Two years of consular campaigning imposed Roman power. The most interesting details concern the plunder seized by the consul C. Claudius Pulcher in 177: 5,632 prisoners (a useful figure since we have few prisoner totals for 'normal' wars in the second century) and the equivalent of about 350–370,000 *denarii*, some of this perhaps from Liguria.[43]

The Ligurian Friniates continued to resist, even capturing Mutina for a time in 177/6 by means of a surprise attack. But shortly afterwards they lost their main stronghold at Valestra-Monte Fósola.[44] The last phase of the war is obscured by a lacuna in Livy's text covering the activities of the consuls of 175, both of whom triumphed over the Ligurians.

When we next hear what Roman commanders were doing in Liguria, the focus has changed to the Statellates in southern Piedmont but the policy of deportation continues. Those of the Statellates who survived the attack of M. Popillius Laenas (*cos.* 173), fewer than ten thousand, surrendered to him. He promptly sold them into slavery, though this was not the customary treatment of peoples who made a formal *deditio* – hence an opening for Popillius' political enemies. The most important facts about this case are that though the Senate tried to make Popillius free the

---

[38] Livy XL.34.8.   [39] Livy XL.34.9–12.

[40] Livy XL.43.1 implies that the land was provided by Pisa, but the territory of Luca went further than that of Pisa can ever have done.

[41] Livy (XLI.13.5) says that each colonist received 51½ *iugera* (32 acres); scholars have generally followed De Sanctis 1907–64, IV.i.568 n. 204: (A 14) and Castagnoli 1946–8, 55: (H 84) in scaling this down to 6½ *iugera*, but this figure can hardly be reconciled with centuriation as far south as Pietrasanta.   [42] For the pretexts invoked cf. Livy XL.18.4, 26.2.

[43] Livy XLI.11.8, 13.7 (it seems unlikely that much of this silver coinage was collected in Liguria, which had produced little before – whereas Istria, after a long period of peace, was now overwhelmed); on the value of the victoriates included see Crawford 1974, 628–9: (B 88).

[44] Livy XLI.18.1–3, 9–13.

prisoners and give them back their land,[45] he not only made war on some more Statellates in 171, but in the end obtained a compromise under which many of them remained slaves and most of the rest were deported northwards across the Po.[46] Somewhere in that region they were 'assigned' land, while between them and their homeland Rome set up the new communities of Hasta and Valentia.[47] Besides the activities of M. Popillius and his brother Caius (*cos.* 172), a ten-man commission of 173 – in which the senior man was M. Aemilius Lepidus (*cos.* 187, 175), already powerful in Northern Italy – engaged in what was in effect a rival programme of individual land distributions, both in Cisalpine Gaul and in Liguria, for the benefit of Romans and Latins.[48] There for the moment, with a new war due to begin against Macedon in 171, Roman expansion in Liguria rested. After Pydna there were still more campaigns, but without Livy we know scarcely anything about them. There were at least three more triumphs: two over the Eleiates Ligurians, in 166 and 158, one over the Apuani in 155.[49]

These Ligurian wars are problematical and interesting, though they are not commonly so regarded by historians. What is most puzzling is why it took Rome so long – till 180 if not 175 – to produce decisive effects. It was not shortage of manpower, since four legions, with auxiliaries, were often used, and the Ligurians probably could not field much larger armies. The usual belief is that the land itself, and particularly the steep-sided valleys within the Appennine range, formed the chief obstacle.[50] The terrain was without doubt more confusing and more arduous for an attacking force than was the plain of the Po. On the other hand Rome possessed, from the late 190s, the great strategic advantage of being able to attack eastern Liguria from both sides of the Appennines at once. In fact the mode of life of the Ligurians was a serious additional obstacle (as it later was with the Celtiberians): a stock-raising semi-pastoral economy gave the Ligurians enough mobility to make them awkward enemies. But once a wholehearted Roman effort began, only real guerrilla warfare in the modern sense could have prevented the Roman conquest. Hence we must ask why the thorough-going Roman drive began only in 181. The reason cannot be that the Ligurians

[45] Livy XLII.8.8, 9.6, 21.1

[46] This result is described in Livy XLII.22.5–6; those who qualified as not having been enemies of Rome since 179 (this clearly excluded many Statellates) were freed and transported to land north of the river (there were 'many thousands' according to Livy). The name of Aquae Statiellae shows that some remained.

[47] Toynbee 1965, II, 668: (A 37). Forum Fulvii in the same area probably followed in 159.

[48] Livy XLII.4.3–4.

[49] See the *Acta Triumphalia* for these years. Another in 166 seems to have been over the 'Ligurian' Taurini in the area of Turin, who were not properly called Ligurians: Walbank 1957–79, 1.177: (B 38).   [50] See already Florus 1.19.4.

suddenly seemed to offer a greater threat then, since their comportment was unchanged and there had been no trouble in Pisan territory since 187. All through the 180s they had been a threat to the Roman immigrants in the plain of the Po, as they had long been a threat to Pisa and to Roman traffic to and from Spain; but there was clearly an additional factor at work in 181.

What appears to have happened is that soon after the Roman occupation of Boian territory was completed by the colonies of 183, and colonies had been planned for some other desirable and (in Roman eyes) available sites (Saturnia in 183, Aquileia and Graviscae in 181), the most desirable section of Ligurian territory became the target of Roman greed for land. Luca, Luna and land of the Statellates were the latest, and as it turned out almost the last, places in Italy which Romans and Latins settled before the Social War.

It would be absurdly anachronistic to suppose that when the Romans conquered northern Italy they had anything like the 'unification of Italy' in mind,[51] since Italy as a political concept, in so far as it existed, did not include Ligurians or Gauls. As for the 'natural frontier' at the Alps, it seems likely that the notion was devised only after the conquest – perhaps by Cato.[52] Even as a geographical concept Italy probably did not extend into the northern regions until the second century.[53] In the event, however, the wars against the Gauls and Ligurians were the first important step in the Romanization and Italianization of a large section of the peninsula.[54]

III. SPAIN[55]

Simultaneous with the decisive conquest of northern Italy was the conquest of a large area of Spain, a sequence of events which shows, more plainly perhaps than any other, the Romans' drive to expand and their determination in the face of obstacles to expansion.[56]

---

[51] The treaty clauses which forbade the bestowing of Roman citizenship on any Cenomanian or Insubrian (Cic. Balb. 32) are significant.

[52] Orig. fr. 85; cf. Polyb. III.54.2. Livy XXXIX.22.7, 54.10–12 may show that Venetia was claimed as 'Italy' in the 180s. Cisalpine Gaul was of course commonly called Gaul down to 42 B.C. and even later.

[53] Geographically, Cisalpine Gaul was part of Italy to Polybius (I.13.4, II.14.3–12, III.54.2, etc.), though it had not been so to outsiders in 215 (VII.9.6).   [54] See below, ch. 7, pp. 197–243.

[55] The main literary sources for this section are Livy and Appian, Hisp. (all references to Appian are to this work); Polybius, the fragments of Cato's Origines and speeches, Lucilius, Cicero, Diodorus Siculus, Strabo, Valerius Maximus, Velleius Paterculus, the elder Pliny, Plutarch, Florus, Ptolemy the geographer, Festus, Cassius Dio and Cassiodorus also contribute. The important archaeological, epigraphical and numismatic evidence is mentioned in later notes.

[56] The best detailed narratives remain those of De Sanctis 1907–64, IV.i.428–71, and IV.iii.222–79: (A 14), and (for the wars of 154–133) Simon 1962: (G 29). Still very useful is Schulten's commentary on the sources: Schulten 1935 and 1937: (B 33). Spanish publications have proliferated since about 1960; Blázquez and others 1978–80, II.51–98: (G 11) provides a serviceable narrative of this period.

The Spain which Rome subdued between 218 and 133 was far from
being capable of repelling the onslaught of a Roman army of even
moderate size. Not that the territory was entirely primitive or without
exploited resources; rather, it resembled Oscan Italy in the period of the
Samnite wars. On the coast lay several cities of mainly Punic or Greek
character. Inland, while the Celtiberians and Lusitanians inhabited
regions comparable in size with Etruria or Samnium, there were at least
twenty other independent peoples that possessed considerable territories. From the archaeological evidence scholars have concluded that
scarcely any substantial cities existed away from the coast; Numantia is
the most impressive.[57] Yet the literary sources often speak of cities and
towns, and though they certainly exaggerated – Cato cannot have
captured 400 towns – we should also allow for the inadequacies of the
archaeological record, which tells us little or nothing about, for example,
the existence of wooden buildings or the pre-Roman remains of such still
inhabited sites as Toledo or Sigüenza. However, small hill-top *poblados*,
not large towns, were characteristic of inland Spain about 200. We have
very little evidence for complex political institutions, though the sources
sometimes refer to local kings and senates, but we ought not to assume
that the tribal institutions were crude or primitive by Italian standards.[58]
While it was mainly the Greek and Punic cities that devised their own
coin-types before the Roman conquest, some Iberians in adjacent regions
were minting imitative coins.[59] As to literacy, it was obviously very
sparse among the pre-Roman Iberians, but to judge from the inscriptions
– which are admittedly difficult to date – Iberian was being written to a
significant extent in certain areas, for example at Ullastret (near
Emporion) and among the Edetani.[60] The existence of the Iberian group
of alphabets is itself significant.

With regard to metal resources, the pre-Roman Iberians not surprisingly had a fair knowledge of how to exploit them. Even the silver
objects which Carthage and Rome neglected to take away show that
Iberian craftsmen had real skill.[61] Iron weapons and equipment appear in
numerous Spanish burials, and it was notoriously from the Iberians that
the Roman army learned a major improvement in efficient sword de-

[57] The area within Numantia's second-century fortifications was 93 hectares (=229 acres):
Schulten 1914–31, II.96–103: (B 198); but only about 11 ha were really built up (with some 2,000
houses, according to Schulten, II.178). On Spanish towns of this period in general see Blázquez 1964,
181 n. 40: (G 8); García y Bellido 1968, 7–30: (G 17); Martínez Gázquez 1974, 156–7: (G 22).
[58] On the political culture of pre-Roman Spain see Maluquer de Motes in Menéndez Pidal 1954,
145–51, 251–2, 318–24: (G 23); Blázquez and others 1978–80, 1.183–203: (G 11).
[59] The chronology of these coins in the standard handbook, De Guadan 1969, 122–8: (B 89) is too
low because in practice he ignored the discovery that the Roman *denarius* dates from 211 B.C. Hoard
evidence, e.g. from Les Ansias: De Guadan, *op. cit.* 93; Crawford 1969, no. 104: (B 87), shows that
Emporion coins were being imitated by *c.* 210.
[60] See Maluquer de Motes 1968: (G. 21).   [61] Cf. Raddatz 1969: (B 189).

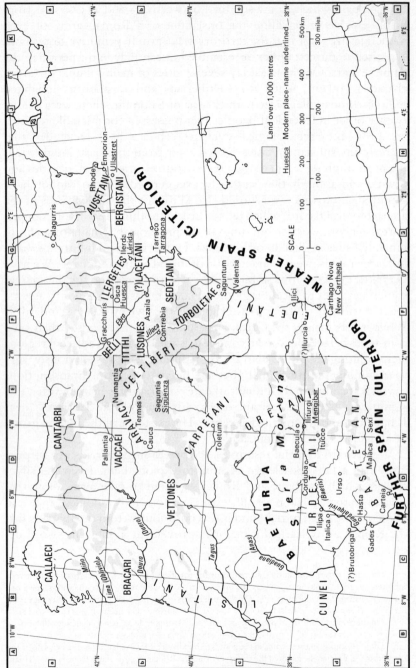

Map 8. Spain in the second century B.C.

sign.[62] This chapter is not the context for a full survey of the cultures of
the Spanish peninsula at the moment of the Romans' first arrival, but we
ought to avoid the stereotyped view of a barbarian Spain being conquered by civilized Romans.[63] Reality was more complex than that, and
we must attend both to the more 'primitive' aspects of Roman behaviour
and to the variegated local conditions, political and material, which
affected the lengthy process of Roman conquest.

A war in Spain had been part of the Senate's original design for the
conflict with Carthage in 218. After the Romans had shown remarkable
tenacity in maintaining forces there, the reward came in 206 with the
victory of Scipio Africanus' army at Ilipa. The Senate soon let it be
known, next year at the latest, that it intended to send a regular series of
annual magistrates to govern the new territory.[64] This, not 197, was the
date of the first Roman annexation as that term is usually understood.[65]
From the beginning there were two provinces, Hispania Citerior
(Nearer) and Ulterior (Further), though a precise dividing line between
the two may not have been drawn until 197.[66] Scipio's main effort had
been in the valley of the Guadalquivir (Baetis), where the right bank of
the river as well as the left was evidently under firm control after Ilipa; the
lower reaches of the river were guarded by the town of Italica, founded in
206. Further to the east, a continuous but not very wide strip of coastland
stretched northwards to the Ebro.[67] In the north-east, some thirty
peoples had given hostages in 205, and the appearance of the Ilergetes as
Roman allies shows that strong influence, if not control, extended as far
to the north-west as Osca (Huesca).[68]

As to what Roman control meant, here too we know little about the
earliest phase. Gades had a treaty with Rome which probably contained a
provision that Roman *praefecti* should be sent there, a provision which
the Senate cancelled in 199.[69] But neither Senate nor people ever voted on
this treaty, and Gades was probably alone or almost alone in having one.
Other Spaniards were not favoured with such guarantees of their rights.

[62] Basic information about indigenous Spanish metallurgy: Maluquer de Motes in Menéndez
Pidal 1954, 109–22, 257–69, 355–60: (G 23); Blázquez 1968, 210–11, 218–20, 228, 236, 245–9: (G 9).
The Spanish sword: Walbank 1957–79, 1.704: (B 38).
[63] Found in some standard accounts, e.g. De Sanctis 1907–64, IV.i.408: (A 14).
[64] App. 38.152.
[65] Harris 1979, 136: (A 21). For the contrary view: Bernhardt 1975, 420: (G 5); Knapp 1977, 62:
(G 20).
[66] Cf. Livy XXXII.28.11. Sumner's theory that Nearer and Further Spain did not become distinct
provinces until long after 197 is to be rejected: Sumner 1970 and 1977: (G 30 and 31); Develin 1980,
364–7: (G 12). On the coast the two provinces were divided just west of New Carthage (Livy
XL.41.10).
[67] The narrowness of this territory is suggested by Scipio's campaign against 'Ilurcia' after Ilipa;
it was probably at Lorqui, north-west of Murcia and only 30 miles from the coast: Walbank 1957–79,
II.305: (B 38). [68] Livy XXIX.3.5. The Ilergetes: Livy XXXIV.12.1, Frontin. IV.7.31.
[69] Livy XXXII.2.5, with the interpretation of Badian 1954: (G 3); Knapp 1977, 209–10: (G 20).

With regard to revenue-gathering in the newly acquired territories, it is best to assume that the fixed *vectigal stipendiarium*, known later, was imposed from the start and that each community was responsible for delivering a fixed sum or its equivalent in goods to Roman officials each year. As for garrisons, the two legions in Spain were probably amalgamated in 201,[70] and in 197 even these troops were to be withdrawn, leaving only Latin, Italian and Spanish allies. This decision was, as we shall see, a serious mistake.

The years 198 to 196 are, because of Livy's negligence, obscure ones in the history of Roman possessions in Spain. The background is plain enough. After Scipio's departure several of the peoples whom the Romans already aspired to control rebelled, including the Ilergetes and Ausetani north of the Ebro, and the Sedetani further south. By 199, however, serious fighting had ended, and in the following year, now that the Senate presumably felt that Spain was secure, a desirable constitutional change was made: two new praetorships were created, an increase from four to six, so that a praetor could rule each of the two Spanish provinces each year.[71] In further recognition of the imagined calm in the Spanish provinces, the Senate decided that the legionary part of the army in Spain should be shipped home. On the most probable reconstruction it was the beginning of this repatriation of the legions which provoked the rebellion; the cause can hardly have been, as is often said, the realization by the Spaniards that they had now been annexed. In any case by the summer the rebellion was on, and it required the efforts both of the new praetors and of their predecessors, Cn. Cornelius Blasio and L. Stertinius. The latter pair's stay in Spain was prolonged into the winter of 197/6, and it was probably during 197 that they won the victories which they celebrated on their return home;[72] all or most of their legionaries are likely to have returned with them. Livy's account of the Spanish events of 197 is too scrappy to show us the scale or the geographical range of the rebellion,[73] but the delayed return of the proconsuls of 199–197 seems to guarantee that the rebellion was widespread in its first year.[74] One of the governors of 197/6, C. Sempronius Tuditanus in Further Spain, died of wounds after his army suffered a defeat. The new praetors sent to Spain in 196 were each given a legion and additional allied troops, and after his

[70] Livy xxx.41.4–5.

[71] However, most or all of the praetors who governed the Spanish provinces were given proconsular power (Jashemski 1950, 41–7: (H 12); McDonald 1953, 143–4: (A 24)), at least when their praetorships expired; cf. Develin 1980, 352–3: (G 12).

[72] Blasio and Stertinius returned to Rome only early in 196, as is evident from Livy xxxiii.27.1–5 and from the *Acta Triumphalia*; *contra* Briscoe 1973, 299: (B 3).

[73] Cf. Briscoe 1973, 290: (B 3).

[74] It is striking that Stertinius (who had been in Further Spain) brought home as plunder a larger quantity of silver than any other commander in the war of 197–174 (50,000 lb: Livy xxxiii.27.4).

return the governor of Nearer Spain, Q. Minucius Thermus (on whom see above, p. 115), celebrated a triumph rich in plundered silver. As to the geography of the rebellion, the first definite details we hear concern places south of the Guadalquivir, including Punic towns on the coast; 'all of Baeturia' was involved.[75] Who rebelled in Nearer Spain is unknown, but in 196 the fighting there seems to have been against the Torboletae (inland from Saguntum).[76]

In spite of the success achieved by the forces of Q. Minucius Thermus (*pr.* 196) in this conflict in Nearer Spain, the Senate took the striking step in the winter of 196/5 of deciding to send one of the consuls-elect, with two extra legions, to rule the province. By lot, though presumably not by accident, this turned out to be a man of exceptional energy, M. Porcius Cato. It looks as if there was genuine cause for alarm about the Spanish possessions. And indeed when Cato arrived he met opposition even at the ports of Rhode and Emporion in the extreme north-east; if Livy is to be believed, the Ilergetes of King Bilistages were the only obedient Spaniards left north of the Ebro.[77] However, we need to guard here against exaggerations designed to dramatize Cato's success, exaggerations which without doubt derive from Cato's own writings.[78] He claimed among other things to have conquered more towns than he had spent days in Spain, and the fighting which occurred under his successor shows that his claims to have pacified his province were also overstated.

It remains true, however, that Cato's impact on Spain was considerable, and his effect on Roman perceptions of Spain may have been still more important. He defeated or disarmed several peoples north of the Ebro, business which took several months.[79] Crossing the river in 194, he then according to many historians took his army some 300–400 miles south-west to fight against the Turdetani.[80] In spite of the fact that 'Turta' is mentioned in two of the few relevant fragments of Cato's writings,[81] we should recognize this as an impossibility – especially as conditions were still turbulent in the north-east and Cato's next move was deep into Celtiberian territory. The latter fact hints at the most probable solution: Cato too fought against the Torboletae.[82] He then

---

[75] Livy xxxiii.21.7–8. But '*Baeturiam omnem*' looks like an exaggeration, since Roman power hardly extended to the River Guadiana.

[76] Livy xxxiii.44.4. Livy never realized that some of those whom he found referred to in his sources as Turdetani/Turduli were separate from the Turdetani of Further Spain and more accurately known as Torb-/Turboletae.   [77] Livy xxxiv.11.6, cf. 13.8.

[78] Even if Livy did not rely primarily on Cato's own writings, and even if some sections (e.g. xxxiv.17.1–4) do not derive from Cato. On the source question see Astin 1978, 302–7: (H 68); Briscoe 1981, 63–5: (B 4).

[79] On the controversial chronology of his campaigns see Briscoe's same note.

[80] Following Livy xxxiv.17.1; so Astin 1978, 41 n. 32: (H 68).

[81] *ORF*⁴ frs. 40, 41 (p. 23).

[82] See further Sumner 1977, 127: (G 31); Briscoe 1981, 80: (B 4).

became the first to lead a Roman army in an invasion of Celtiberia, presumably reaching that region through the valley of the Jiloca. He failed to capture either Seguntia (Sigüenza) or Numantia, however, and returned – obviously down the valley of the Ebro – to deal with the apparently still rebellious Lacetani and Bergistani in Catalonia. His successes in all these areas were important, and on returning to Rome he celebrated a triumph (which was not, however, richer than some previous ones earned in Spain). During his stay he was also active in increasing Roman revenues, and by this means as well as by his publicity concerning the resources of Spain (see below, p. 130), he doubtless made it much more valuable in Roman eyes.

It was not for several more years, not until 188, that the conquerors' efforts increased, if we measure them in terms of the manpower used; but the impetus of Cato's campaigns was carried forward. In 193 several new peoples appear in the sources, at war with Rome: the Lusitanians (first mentioned while supposedly plundering the province of Further Spain); the Oretani, who lived around the upper reaches of the Guadiana (Anas); and still further north, the Carpetani, Vettones and Vaccaei, all of whom suffered a defeat that year at Toletum (in Carpetanian territory) at the hands of M. Fulvius Nobilior, the praetor in Further Spain. There should be no doubt that the latter pressed aggressively northwards, and on his return to Rome he won an *ovatio*, followed at the next election by the consulship. His successor in Further Spain, L. Aemilius Paullus, also fought against the Lusitanians (191/90):[83] the stereotyped details and the shortage of clear geographical references in Livy's narrative make it impossible to say much that is certain about this campaign.[84]

By 188, with the North Italian Gauls under control and Antiochus defeated, the Senate made a somewhat greater commitment of troops to Spain. The praetors of that year received an extra allotment of allied troops, though it was not enormous (6,400 men in all) and neither were the results. Lusitanian raids continued to cause trouble in allied and subject territory, if we should believe Livy. But in 187 a more serious reinforcement took place: in fact the number of legions in Spain was doubled. The praetors sent in 186 (C. Calpurnius Piso, L. Quinctius Crispinus) achieved an unusual degree of mutual co-operation and were able to fight successfully on the River Tagus in the land of the Carpetani. On their return to Rome (184), they were both voted triumphs over the Lusitanians and Celtiberians, the first full Spanish triumphs since 194. But neither of these two peoples was near to final defeat, and in 183 the Celtiberians appear to have penetrated far into Roman-controlled terri-

---

[83] Livy xxxvii.46.7–8 ('*in Bastetanis*'; cf. Knapp 1977, 66 n. 12: (G 20)), 57.5–6.

[84] *ILLRP* 514, an interesting text of a decree of Paullus, provides little to go on, though we can infer from it that the provincials of Hasta had been rebellious.

tory.[85] The first praetor who carried out a really successful invasion of Celtiberia itself was Q. Fulvius Flaccus, who ruled Nearer Spain from 182 to 180. This was clearly in accordance with a policy determined in Rome, since both Spanish armies had been extensively reinforced in 182,[86] and Flaccus had at least two ex-praetors in his army as military tribunes (a sure sign that an important campaign was expected).[87] After defeating the Celtiberians to the south of their own territory he advanced northwards along the valley of the Jiloca, contending mainly with the Lusones (a subdivision of the Celtiberians), until the majority of the Celtiberians surrendered.[88] In the following year he attacked the 'further' part of Celtiberian territory which had not been surrendered.[89] This campaign was taken over by Ti. Sempronius Gracchus (180–178), who succeeded in imposing a degree of control in the rest of Celtiberia. Though the places he captured in 'the furthest parts' of Celtiberia (Livy's phrase) are unidentifiable, it is certain that he defeated some of the Aravaci, the most north-westerly and in the long run the most formidable of the Celtiberians. Gracchus also imposed a political settlement, to be discussed below. The triumph which he celebrated in February 177 included the unusually large amount of 40,000 pounds of silver in its booty.

Events in Further Spain in these years are more difficult to follow. The praetors of 186 had triumphed over the Lusitanians, but Livy tells us nothing about the campaign.[90] There was fighting with the Lusitanians again in 181, and then in 179 L. Postumius Albinus, co-ordinating his plans with Gracchus, advanced deep into Lusitanian territory in order to attack the Vaccaei, who lived far to the north in the region of Valladolid and were the western neighbours of the Aravaci. He defeated both Lusitanians and Vaccaei,[91] and in 178 his triumph, which took place the day after Gracchus', was 'over Lusitania and Spain'.

Gracchus' successor in Nearer Spain, M. Titinius Curvus (178–175), also celebrated a triumph, but gaps in Livy prevent us from knowing where he fought. It was not against the Celtiberians, since they remained quiet under the Gracchan settlement until a short-lived rebellion in 175/4. Yet somewhere or other – perhaps within the area already well controlled by Rome (in view of the charges brought against him in 171) – he established his claim to a triumph. It was the last full triumph of the war.

Since Scipio's departure, Spain had been without warfare only in 204–200, 191 and possibly 188/7, periods which coincide to a significant

[85] Livy XXXIX.56.1.   [86] Livy XL.1.7.   [87] MRR 1.385.   [88] Livy XL.33.9 (181).
[89] Livy XL.39.1.
[90] Though it is possible that the events he describes in XXXIX.30–31 as taking place in Carpetania and near Toletum concerned the Lusitanians.   [91] Livy XL.50.6; Per. XLI.

degree with important Roman fighting in other theatres. This supports the view – which it would be difficult to contest in any case – that the main military pressure came from the Roman not the Spanish side during all or almost all of the period from 202 to 174. This is the impression which the Romans create by their progressive involvement with new peoples – the Celtiberians and others during Cato's command, the Lusitanians from 193, the Vettones and Vaccaei from the same year. The Carthaginians had shown that a Spanish empire could be held, in consequence of the political disunity of the Spanish peoples, without constant advances to the north and west.[92] It is true and important that Spaniards did sometimes invade territory which the Romans regarded as subject to themselves. Roman sources were naturally prone to invent or exaggerate such stories, and the precise circumstances in which the Lusitanians intruded into Roman territory (if they did) in 193 and 190 cannot be recovered. In 186 both Celtiberians and Lusitanians supposedly attacked the territory of unspecified Roman allies, but this was probably no more than a convenient pretext. Celtiberian raids into the territory of the Ausetani (183) and Carpetani (181) are also to be regarded with suspicion. And if all these stories were true, they would not by themselves explain Rome's regular Spanish wars and relentless advance.

The Roman conquest up to this point had proceeded at a moderate pace by comparison with what happened in some places. This should no doubt be traced in part to the determination of the indigenous population to resist. In addition the Celtiberians, like the Ligurians, had a largely pastoral economy[93] which made them difficult to pin down and destroy. But though reliable figures are lacking, our Roman sources do not give the impression that any Spanish people could mobilize a force of overwhelming size.[94] Nor does guerrilla warfare, in any precise sense of the phrase, have much to do with it, though modern scholars often say that the Spaniards fought in this fashion. Some Spanish peoples must have been elusive opponents, but more relevant is the fact that the Romans did not commit forces that were enormous in relation to the extent of the land itself; it was only from about 187 to about 172 that four legions were regularly in Spain[95] – previously there had only been two, that is to say a nominal complement of 10,800 citizen troops for the whole peninsula. Italian allies too were an essential component in each of the two armies. Though the figures we have in Livy are incomplete it has been calculated from them that in the period 197–187 each legion was supplemented by an average of 7,900 allied troops (including 400 cav-

[92] Schulten 1930, 307: (G 28).   [93] Schulten 1914–31, I.191–2: (B 198).
[94] On Celtiberia cf. *ibid.* 245–6.
[95] The increase: Afzelius 1944, 40–1: (H 80) (it may have happened in 185). The number was probably reduced about 172; cf. Brunt 1971, 661–3: (H 82), who puts the change slightly earlier.

alry), while in the period of four legions the allies amounted to 6,300 (including 300 cavalry) for each legion.[96] To be added to these figures are the contingents of Spanish allies who often served in thousands on the Roman side.[97] All the same, the total force was remarkably small until about 187 in relation to the size of the peninsula. The Senate rated rapid expansion in Spain less important than expansion in northern Italy (which was also the reason why a consul was only once sent to Spain in this period). But what is really remarkable is that so *many* Romans served in Spain, given the size of the citizen body and more particularly the number of *assidui* qualified for military service. It is probable that in the period of four legions as many as 20% of the eligible *iuniores* were in Spain and suffering casualties at any given time,[98] as sure a sign as any of Rome's profound commitment to imperial power.

Here in the 170s expansion came to a halt for twenty years. One reason must have been a military preoccupation with Macedonia in and after 173. It seems likely, too, that the Senate felt that a satisfactory limit had been reached by the activities of the most recent governors, so that little individual or collective gain would result from further campaigns. Gracchus evidently saw his role as the glorious one of bringing an important enemy, the Celtiberians, to submission, and though this was somewhat premature – in spite of the scholars who carelessly state that Gracchus completed the war in Celtiberia or in Spain as a whole – it was an understandable claim. He had after all compelled not only the Belli and Titthi but also the Aravaci, or at least those in the main Aravacan town, Numantia, to accept treaty terms (unknown to us in detail) which were acceptable to the Roman Senate.[99]

The extent of the power the Romans had achieved in Spain by 174, as far as it can be known, was as follows. North of the Ebro, it extended, as before 197, to the Ilergetes, while in the river valley itself the limit was further west, at Calagurris (Calahorra) or a little higher.[100] To the south of the river, all or most of the Celtiberians, and all who lived between the latter and the south-east coast, were subject to Rome. So were the Carpetani and Vettones, whose territories lay astride the River Tagus further west; and so probably were their northern neighbours, the Vaccaei. Yet none of these three peoples was completely subdued, and

---

[96] Afzelius 1944, 66–75: (H 80).

[97] Cf. Afzelius 1944, 90–1: (H 80); Balil 1956, 120–4: (G 4); Brunt 1971, 663–4: (H 82).

[98] Cf. Harris 1979, 44: (A 21).

[99] It was misleading of Simon 1962, 12: (G 29), to say that the Aravaci were free under Gracchus' settlement, since though Appian is somewhat unclear on the subject (43.179, 44.183), Gracchus definitely made a treaty with them (Polyb. xxxv.2.15, etc.).

[100] Presumably Calagurris took its additional name Nasica from P. Cornelius Scipio Nasica (*cos.* 191) after he served as one of the *patroni* of the provincials of Nearer Spain in 171; Gabba 1954, 298–300: (H 130) = 1976, 106: (H 42).

evidence is lacking that anything like provincial government had been imposed on them.[101] The Lusitanians remained independent, it seems; there are few Lusitanian placenames in the sources for the period down to 174, and in fact Roman control beyond the River Guadiana was probably limited to the Cunei in the extreme south of Portugal. That the Cunei were Roman subjects before 153, and hence before 174, we know from Appian.[102] The limit of Roman power probably lay along the Guadiana for a long distance. As to where the northern boundaries of the provinces were, it is entirely possible that they remained without definition.

In Spain, as elsewhere and always, Roman armies plundered the inhabitants with great thoroughness. Metals, and above all silver, made the gathering of booty in Spain especially profitable. The amounts of silver and gold which Livy reports as having been carried in triumphs between 200 and 174 represent only a fraction of what was seized, but all the same the total of uncoined silver easily exceeded 100 tons, a very large quantity by the standards of the time.[103] Among moveable assets of other kinds, the plunder will have included very numerous slaves, though enslavement was usually such a routine matter that the sources do not trouble to mention it; casual references confirm the obvious fact that some of these slaves were exported.[104] But the strongest attraction of all, for those with any vision, were the workable deposits of silver, especially near New Carthage and in the Sierra Morena. As Gibbon wrote, 'Spain, by a very singular fatality, was the Peru and Mexico of the old world.'

The sources about Spain in this period seldom reveal any interesting details about the forms of Roman domination, but there are questions worth discussing about immigration and about taxation. Three new cities appear after Italica – Gracchuris, Iliturgi and Carteia – but none of them is likely to have been inhabited mainly by immigrants. Carteia, on the bay of Algeciras, was founded as a Latin colony in 171 – the first outside Italy and hence an important innovation. Its primary members were the children of Roman soldiers and Spanish women, though their freedmen and the local inhabitants of the district were also, Livy says, able to enroll.[105] Who inhabited Gracchuris, which was founded on the upper Ebro by Ti. Gracchus in 178 (he thus became the first Roman to name a city after himself), the sources do not tell us; scholars usually

---

[101] Thus in the 150s Appian still seems to contrast the Vettones with those who are Roman subjects (56.235, 58.243–244).   [102] App. 57.239.

[103] *ESAR* I.127–37 catalogues the evidence (though with some inferior textual variants). On the importance contemporaries attached to booty cf. Harris 1979, 209 n. 6: (A 21).

[104] Acts of enslavement: Blázquez 1962–3, 19–20: (G 6). Export: Liv. *Per.* XLIX; App. 77.331.

[105] Livy XLIII.3.4. Why exactly the Senate said it was to be called a colony of freedmen is unclear; cf. Galsterer 1971, 8–9: (G 15); Humbert 1976, 225–34: (H 138).

suppose that it must have been indigenous Spaniards,[106] but a mixed population, with some Italian blood in it, is more likely, for otherwise Gracchus would have been creating a potential danger to the security of the province. The third site, Iliturgi (Mengíbar, on the south side of the upper Guadalquivir), is more problematical still: its status as a Gracchan foundation depends on a solitary inscription which may not be trustworthy.[107] If Ti. Gracchus really did establish such a town (presumably it was not a formal colony), its population too was probably made up of both Spaniards and Italians. Other immigration in the period before 174 cannot be measured, but quite a lot of Italians were probably attracted to the mining areas. The immigration is likely to have centred at New Carthage, because of the silver mines nearby,[108] while other immigrants probably concentrated at the main ports, Emporion, Tarraco and perhaps Gades.

How the exploitation of the silver mines was organized has been debated. It is evident that Rome must in some way have relied on contractors (*publicani*), and the considerable investment which must have been required[109] suggests that large companies were involved. These are likely to have been Rome-based and to have made their contracts over five years with the censors. In the developed Roman system, and probably from the beginning of the Roman occupation, slaves naturally provided the manual labour.[110] What the surviving sources do not make clear is whether there was a system of subcontracting by the companies of *publicani*, as Polybius may imply when he says that in his time the mineworkers near New Carthage contributed 25,000 drachmas to the Roman people *each day*.[111] An alternative possibility is that the Roman governors rented mining rights to contractors who had migrated to the locality. In any case, as Polybius' account makes clear, the revenues to the state from the area of New Carthage alone were enormous, the equivalent of 36.5 million sesterces a year.[112] Private profits must also have been on a generous scale.

The other public revenues drawn from the Spanish peoples were a fixed tax in cash, the *stipendium*, and a 5% levy on grain. Attempts to deny that any Spaniards paid *stipendium* in this sense in the early second century

---

[106] E.g. Brunt 1971, 215 n. 8: (H 82); Knapp 1977, 108–9: (G 20). In the case of 'Complega' (in or near the territory of the Celtiberian Lusones), Gracchus seems to have given some rights and land to the landless after defeating an attack (App. 43.179).

[107] The text is '*Ti. Sempronio Graccho/deductori/populus Iliturgitanus.*' For the view that the inscription is ancient (though not of 178 B.C.) and correct see Degrassi 1967, 34–8: (B 48); Galsterer 1971, 13 n. 53: (G 15); Knapp 1977, 110: (G 20); ancient and incorrect: Wiegels 1982: (G 36); not ancient at all: García y Bellido 1959, 449 n. 6: (G 16).   [108] Cf. Strabo III.147.

[109] Cf. Badian 1972, 33–4: (H 32).   [110] Diod. Sic. v.36.

[111] XXXIV.9.9 = Strabo III.148: cf. Richardson 1976, 142: (G 24); Harris 1979, 69: (A 21).

[112] A perfectly credible figure; cf. the 300 lb of silver a day which Hannibal received from a 'Baebelo' mine (Plin. *HN* XXXIII.97).

are ill-founded: the sources are no more silent than we would expect about such a mundane matter, and the natural presumption is that Rome started to gather taxes in the period after the battle of Ilipa, gradually (perhaps slowly) extending the obligation to more and more Spanish peoples, rather than waiting until the 170s.[113] The minting of Iberian '*denarii*' began at the latest about 197,[114] and it seems plain that such coins, minted on the Roman standard, must in the first place have been designed principally as a means of paying tribute to Rome. The uniformity not only of the weight-standard but also of the types between widely scattered mints, together with the chronology, establishes this.[115] To use the names that appear on the coins themselves, Bolscan (Huesca), Iltirta (Lérida?), Cese (Tarragona), Ausescen (north of Tarragona) and Icalguscen/Icaloscen (somewhere in the south) are the main places.[116] The only reason to doubt that Rome imposed money taxation on the peoples of Spain from the earliest period is that there was simply not enough money in the economy; but the Romans realized that this problem could be overcome at least in many areas by means of these local '*denarii*'. It may possibly have been in other areas that the 5% levy on grain production was exacted. Unfortunately the only text which mentions this levy – in the setting of the 170s – gives us very little clear information about it.[117] But there is no good reason to doubt that grain was already being exacted in the first years.[118]

It is a waste of time to try to 'calculate' the profits Rome made from the Spanish provinces in the second century, the evidence being entirely inadequate; it is almost equally far-fetched to claim that they were not profitable at all.[119] Silver must have tipped the balance. Not that other natural resources were lacking: the astute Cato, as we know even from our very fragmentary evidence, was greatly impressed not only by the silver, but by the sources of iron and salt and even by the fishiness of the Ebro.[120] It might be comforting to imagine that the greed which was

---

[113] Otherwise Bernhardt 1975, 422: (G 5); Richardson 1976, 148–9: (G 24). Already in XXVIII.25.9 Livy refers to *stipendiariae civitates*, and Florus (1.33.7), for what he is worth, says that Scipio Africanus made Spain a *stipendiaria provincia* (the natural reference in these texts is to taxation).

[114] Knapp 1977, esp. 8–11: (B 106).

[115] For this interpretation cf. Albertini 1923, 21: (G 1); Schulten 1935, 153: (B 33); Knapp 1977, 17–18: (B 106); Dominguez Arranz 1979, 294: (G 13). Knapp is tempted by the alternative theory that the Iberian *denarii* were minted to pay Spanish auxiliary troops, but this would hardly account for the uniformities mentioned in the text.   [116] Knapp 1977, 2–3: (B 106).

[117] Livy XLIII.2.12; it seems that the task of collecting it was farmed to the local communities. Plut. *C. Gracch.* 6 refers to a case in which, presumably, more than 5% had been exacted by a Roman governor.

[118] Richardson 1976, 150: (G 24) notwithstanding; it is hardly surprising that with his province in chaos, as it was on his arrival, Cato had to rely for grain on purchase (a course he naturally rejected) or violent seizure (Livy XXXIV.9.12–13).

[119] As said by Van Nostrand, *ESAR* III.123 and Badian 1968, 8: (A 5); see further Harris 1979, 69: (A 21).   [120] Cato, *Orig.* frs. 93, 110 ('pisculentus').

obviously an important reason why Rome maintained and expanded its Spanish empire in the second century was somehow disappointed, but in reality it is likely that Rome profited both in the public and private sectors.

The following years, from 173 until about 155, were relatively though not entirely peaceful in Spain. During the Third Macedonian War Roman governors in Spain restrained themselves or were restrained by the Senate; but in 170 some part of Nearer Spain evidently saw a quite serious rebellion, most of the details of which are lost in a gap in the manuscript of Livy.[121] After the manuscript finally breaks off, we know that Rome fought against the Lusitanians in the period 166–160.[122] But the most interesting known events in this period concern the conduct of provincial governors and the repercussions of this conduct at Rome. In 171 delegates from several peoples in both Spanish provinces petitioned the Senate about the 'greed and cruelty' of three recent governors. The Senate had a committee of five assessors (*recuperatores*) appointed for each of the accused, with senatorial *patroni*, including Cato, to represent the provincials.[123] The *triumphator* M. Titinius Curvus was acquitted, the two others evaded judgement by going into 'exile' at nearby Praeneste and Tibur. What is of most interest here is the faint beginning of a wish on the Senate's part to restrain provincial governors. The restraint was of the lightest, and the motives may have been entirely prudential, yet two ex-praetors had their political careers ended and even Titinius failed to reach the consulship he could otherwise have expected. When the case was over, the Senate issued three prohibitions concerning Spain which presumably correspond to some of the practices complained of: Roman magistrates were no longer to set their own prices for requisitioned grain, or to compel Spaniards to sell the contracts for gathering the grain levy at their own prices, or to impose *praefecti* in Spanish towns to collect money. All this suggests that a system of corruption had already grown up in the Spanish provinces which fell not far short of what was inflicted on many provincials in the late Republic.

Similar events seem to have occurred in the 150s, probably contributing very substantially to the renewed fighting in Spain. We know at any rate that in 153 'several praetors' were condemned for *avaritia* in the provinces, that at about the same date a consul was found guilty of a similar offence, and that it was a Spanish case, that of Ser. Sulpicius Galba (governor of Further Spain, 151/50), which led directly to the creation of a senatorial court on provincial misgovernment by the *lex Calpurnia* of

---

121 Livy XLIII.4.1–4; cf. *Per.* XLIII; Flor. 1.33.14.
122 Liv. *Per.* XLVI.
123 Livy XLIII.2.1–11. *MRR* 1.419 erred in calling these *patroni* a 'special commission'.

149.[124] It is reasonable to suppose that exploitation by officials helped to provoke a rebellion in Spain.

The new series of wars began, as far as the Romans are concerned, with an invasion of Roman territory by the still independent Lusitanians about 154. It appears that they defeated the governors of both Spains in a single battle.[125] Where this took place we do not know, but according to Appian's narrative (our most important source on Spain from this time onwards) the Lusitanians intruded in the first two years of the war into several sections of the further province, in southern Portugal and Andalusia as well as somewhere further east. They also led the Vettones to rebel.[126] They even crossed to North Africa, in search of plunder and perhaps of land; but there the praetor L. Mummius, who had failed against them in Spain, followed and defeated their expeditionary force (probably in 153).

The success of the Lusitanians may, as Appian says, have encouraged the Aravaci to rebel in 154. Another account he gives is that the Belli (Celtiberians like the Aravaci) got into a dispute with Rome about the degree of fortification allowed to them by the Gracchan treaty, and subsequently took refuge with the Aravaci. In any case the Senate must have believed the area to be quite disturbed since it sent one of the consuls of 153, Q. Fulvius Nobilior, to govern Nearer Spain.[127] This Celtiberian war was called 'the fiery war', Polybius says, because of its extreme violence.[128] Awareness of what it was like contributed to the unprecedented recruiting difficulties which arose at Rome in 151. In spite of dissension among the Celtiberians themselves and the unusual size of his army,[129] Fulvius' year in Spain was a failure. It was only his successor, M. Claudius Marcellus (*cos.* 152), who, after a period of armistice in which the Celtiberian peoples sent ambassadors to Rome, brought the rebellion to an end in 151, when the Aravaci and the anti-Roman dissidents among the Belli and Titthi surrendered to him.[130] Though he exacted an indemnity of 600 talents, his hope of gaining credit for completing the war seems to have led him to give the rebels relatively

[124] Liv. *Per.* XLVII. The consul (L. Cornelius Lentulus Lupus, 156): Val. Max. VI.9.10; Festus 360L. It is not known where he served; Liguria is more probable than Spain. On Galba and the *lex Calpurnia* see MRR 1.456–7, 459.   [125] App. 56. 234; Simon 1962, 13 n. 6: (G 29).

[126] App. 56.235.

[127] However, the conversion to consular governors resulted in part from the fact that with all Italy, even Liguria, now secure, there was often little for the consuls to do except in Spain. Fulvius and his colleague were the first consuls to enter office on 1 January instead of 15 March, the reason being that he was needed quickly in Spain (Liv. *Per.* XLVII, Cassiod. *Chron.*).

[128] Polyb. XXXV.1.

[129] His army: App. 45.184; cf. Polyb. XXXV.2. The campaign: Simon 1962, 25–30: (G 29).

[130] Polyb. XXXV.2–4 describes the embassies to Rome. Marcellus was elected consul contrary to law (since he had held the office in 155), no doubt because of his reputation as a general and perhaps because he was regarded as an expert on the strength of his command in Spain in 169/8; cf. Astin 1967, 38: (H 67).

SPAIN 133

favourable terms in other respects.[131] The next governor, L. Licinius
Lucullus, had to find other opponents and out of his desire for fame and
for money, Appian says, fought against the Vaccaei. He also remarks that
the Senate had not voted in favour of a war against the Vaccaei, who had
not attacked the Romans or done any injury to Lucullus himself.[132]
Lucullus also fought against the Cantabri still further north and 'other
previously unknown peoples'.[133] This kind of aggressive marauding was
tacitly permitted by the Senate,[134] but Lucullus' attacks were not followed up.

Meanwhile in Further Spain the successors of Mummius had also
taken the offensive to some degree, aided in late 152 by Marcellus. The
forces of M. Atilius (praetor in 152) captured a city which Appian says
was the Lusitanians' largest, 'Oxthracai'. Ser. Sulpicius Galba, whom he
describes as even more avaricious than L. Lucullus though he was about
the richest man in Rome, was responsible for a notorious massacre of
Lusitanians.[135] And though the Lusitanians still put pressure on Rome's
subject territories, the silence of the sources about any fighting with
them in 149 and 148, when Carthage was claiming Roman attention,
suggests that the initiative was now mainly in Roman hands.

In fact fighting began again at a somewhat awkward moment for
Rome. The Lusitanians acquired a new and exceptionally effective
leader, Viriathus, with whom they attacked Turdetania in the further
province, this probably in 147. Viriathus proceeded to defeat at least
four more commanders within Roman territory, and it was not until 144
that Q. Fabius Maximus Aemilianus (*cos.* 145) succeeded in putting
Viriathus' forces to flight (we should be sceptical about the thorough
defeat which Cicero says C. Laelius, governor of Nearer Spain in 145/4,
inflicted; Appian knew nothing of it).[136] Even at the end of 144,
Viriathus had withdrawn only to Baecula (Bailén),[137] just to the north of
the Guadalquivir, while Fabius Aemilianus spent the winter at Corduba.
There was plenty of fight left in Viriathus' Lusitanians, and in 143 they
advanced southwards once again. After two years of campaigning by
Fabius Servilianus (*cos.* 142), brother by adoption of Fabius Aemilianus,
Viriathus finally seemed to be passing his zenith. Nevertheless after

131 App. 50. The indemnity: Strabo III.162, citing Poseidonius, *FGrH* 87 F 51. On the credit to
be gained from completing a war cf. Harris 1979, 34: (A 21). It is evident that Marcellus' attitude
aroused the resentment of L. Licinius Lucullus (*cos.* 151) and his subordinate Scipio Aemilianus (see
esp. Polyb. XXXV.3.4–5).
132 App. 51.215. These statements probably derive from Polybius: cf. Walbank 1957–79, III. 640,
648: (B 38).   133 Liv. *Per.* XLVIII.
134 It is very possible that Lucullus celebrated a triumph: Degrassi 1947, 559: (B 47).
135 Oxthracai: App. 58.243; cf. Simon 1962, 34–5: (G 29). Galba's greed and wealth: App. 60.255.
The massacre and its aftermath in Rome: Simon, *op. cit.* 60–7.
136 Cic. *Off.* II.40. See Münzer, *PW*, 'Laelius (3)', 406.
137 Appian in fact calls the place Βαικόρ (65.278).

Servilianus' departure for Rome, Viriathus cornered a Roman commander at an unidentifiable site named Erisane and compelled him to surrender (141/40).[138] Fabius Aemilianus, who was apparently the officer in question (he had returned to Spain as his brother's legate), conceded very favourable terms to the Lusitanian leader, including the right to rule all the territory he currently controlled.[139] Even more remarkably, the Roman people confirmed the agreement. So at least Appian says, and in fact such an attitude on the part of the assembly fits well with the recruiting difficulties experienced at Rome in early 140: service in Spain was now generally unpopular.[140] But in practice the Senate could by this date declare war independently of the people, and with the encouragement of the new governor of Further Spain, Q. Servilius Caepio (cos. 140), it did so, ruthlessly disowning the treaty. Caepio drove Viriathus, who possessed only a small force, out of Carpetania and then turned instead to fighting the Vettones and even the Callaeci. The latter, who lived in the far north-west, now appear for the first time as enemies of Rome. In any case during 139 Caepio arranged or encouraged the assassination of Viriathus – a curious incident as well as a brutal one, since it appears that Viriathus had previously been negotiating with the new governor of Nearer Spain (M. Popillius Laenas, cos. 139).[141]

While Viriathus was still strong, his success had encouraged some of the Celtiberians to rebel once again; this was in 144 or 143.[142] The war lasted somewhat more than a decade, during which a long series of consuls still found the Aravaci difficult opponents. The measure of their powers of resistance is given by the willingness of Q. Pompeius (cos. 141) and C. Hostilius Mancinus (cos. 137) to make concessions. Pompeius, though provided with very substantial forces,[143] made no progress against Numantia or Termes (some fifty miles to the south-west),[144] the main centres of resistance, and in 139 his position seems to have become so difficult that he led the Aravaci into a peace settlement by promising them somewhat favourable terms.[145] Perhaps, like Marcellus twelve

[138] App. 69.293–294.

[139] The normal opinion is that the officer who surrendered was Servilianus, not Aemilianus (Schulten 1937, IV.118–19: (B 33); MRR 1.480). This, though many writers seem unaware of the fact, follows from the decision of J. Schweighäuser (1785) and others to excise several lines from App. 68.291 or transfer them to the end of 65.278 (which entails some other textual changes). In fact the MS text (followed by Viereck-Roos) is readily intelligible, though Appian did make the unremarkable mistake of saying (68.291) that Q. Pompeius A.f. (cos. 141) was the successor of Servilianus, whereas he really took over Nearer Spain (there is also some confusion in 70.296). On the treaty see further Simon 1962, 123: (G 29).

[140] Ratification: App. 69.294. The year 140: Harris 1979, 49: (A 21).

[141] On the assassination: Simon 1962, 130–3: (G 29). Caepio may have triumphed on returning to Rome: Degrassi 1947, 559: (B 47).   [142] App. 66.279–280.   [143] App. 76.324–325.

[144] 'Termestinos subegit' in Liv. Per. LIV. is erroneous, as App. 77.327–8 shows.

[145] App.79. It seems that they nominally surrendered but were not disarmed, and were subjected to the relatively mild indemnity of thirty talents. See further Simon 1962, 115–16: (G 29).

years earlier, he entertained the vain hope of gaining credit for having completed the war; perhaps he came to the conclusion that conquering the Aravaci was not worth the effort. In any case, though the Senate's repudiation of the new agreement may have been caused in part by personal feuds against Pompeius,[146] it took the traditional attitude in wanting the obstinate resistance of the Aravaci broken. There were plenty of magistrates willing to try, first M. Popillius Laenas (*cos.* 139) and next C. Hostilius Mancinus (*cos.* 137). Both failed, Mancinus disastrously so. To avoid the probable slaughter of his army he surrendered to the Numantines with a solemn oath and on equal terms.[147] If the Numantines had known more about the mentality of Roman senators, they would have realized that they could obtain no solid result from such restraint. Mancinus' treaty too was rejected by the Senate, which to appease divine anger attempted to hand him over, naked, to the Numantines. Since it was not yet known for certain whether the Senate would disavow Mancinus, his successor as governor of Nearer Spain, M. Aemilius Lepidus Porcina (*cos.* 137), plundered the territory of the Vaccaei on the pretext – admitted by Appian to be spurious[148] – that they had helped their neighbours the Aravaci against Rome. The Senate, interestingly, tried to make him desist, the reason being that enthusiasm for wars in this particular region had declined steeply except among those, such as Porcina, who stood to gain extensively and directly.[149] In fact the next governor of Nearer Spain did not take action against the Aravaci either. The decline in enthusiasm for warfare was very selective, however, as can be seen in the other Spanish province.

The campaigns of D. Iunius Brutus (*cos.* 138), who reaped the benefit of the earlier wars with the Lusitanians by invading their territory in depth, show that no fundamental change had yet occurred. Brutus first advanced by rapid and very violent steps to the Douro (Duero), then to the Rivers Lima (Oblivio in Latin) and Miño, where he defeated the Bracari. Beyond the Douro lived the Callaeci, from whom Brutus eventually took an honorific surname; he did not, however, subdue the whole north-west.[150] Instead he turned in 136 to helping his relative Lepidus Porcina make war against the Vaccaei around the upper Douro.

By 134 there remained independent only the peoples who lived in the mountain range parallel to the north coast, and of course the Aravaci of

---

[146] On these see Gruen 1968, 36–8: (H 11). The statement in some texts of Liv. *Per.* LIV. that it was the Roman people which invalidated the agreement is simply the result of an unwise emendation (read '*ob infirmitatem*', not '*a populo R. infirmatam*').

[147] Equal terms: App. 80.347.   [148] App. 80.349.

[149] Appian says, in connection with Porcina, that 'some men took their governorships not to benefit the state, but for fame or material gain or the honour of a triumph' (80.349). The Senate's attitude: 81.351. After his return Porcina was fined: 83.358.

[150] In spite of Florus 1.33.12; see other sources in Schulten 1937, IV.135–40: (B 33).

Numantia. It seems to have been agreed at Rome that the northern region should be neglected, and it went untouched in the generation after the fall of Numantia when it could have been conquered. The Numantines had to be suppressed, but the task required a general of exceptional élan even by Roman standards. This had to be – at least in the judgement of many Romans – the conqueror of Carthage, Scipio Aemilianus, even though it was illegal for him to become consul again;[151] and he will not have resisted the opportunity to score another spectacular military success. Elected consul for 134, he decided that he needed a larger army than the two legions, with auxiliaries, which the governors of Nearer Spain normally commanded. Four thousand additional troops were raised by means of his personal and political connections and from among volunteers, and to judge from the 60,000 men his army eventually contained he also acquired a large number of new allied troops in Spain itself.[152]

After elaborate preparations, including another campaign against the Vaccaei (134), Scipio closely besieged Numantia for many months, until after frightful suffering the survivors surrendered in the summer of 133.[153] 'Having chosen fifty of them for his triumph, Scipio sold the remainder and razed the city to the ground.'[154] The Senate sent out the usual commission of ten legates to organize both the territory conquered by Brutus and that of the Numantines.[155] The latter had been so reduced by the end of the siege that at his triumph, celebrated *de Numantinis* in 132, Scipio was able to distribute only seven *denarii* to each of his soldiers.[156]

Thus a number of quite separate wars took place in Spain between 154 and 133. Some of them, most obviously the two wars fought by the Celtiberians, were rebellions against Roman power. The Lusitanians too, once they came under the leadership of Viriathus, drew considerable support from inside what Rome had regarded as pacified territory, some of it even from south of the Guadalquivir. In 141 Fabius Servilianus plundered five cities in Baeturia 'which had collaborated with Viriathus', and three of the latter's most trusted friends (who eventually betrayed him to the Romans) came from Urso (Osuna); Itucce (Martos) was no doubt only one of many places that oscillated between one allegiance and

[151] Liv. *Per.* LVI; cf. Astin 1967, 183–4: (H 67).
[152] The 4,000: App. 84.366. The 60,000: 92.403, 97.419. Among those present at the siege of Numantia were Polybius, C. Gracchus, Jugurtha, Marius and the future historian Sempronius Asellio.
[153] On the campaign (relatively well attested in the sources) see especially Schulten 1914–31: (B 198).
[154] App. 98.424. The physical evidence for the destruction: Schulten 1914–31, II.171–3: (B 198).
[155] App. 99.428.   [156] Plin. *HN* XXXIII.141.

the other.[157] On a number of occasions – exactly how many we cannot tell – Lusitanians invaded lands which the Romans regarded as subject to themselves. But from time to time the Romans themselves pushed forwards, both against the Lusitanians and Callaeci, who were added to the further province, and against the Vaccaei. It is imaginable, though not attested by the sources, that all the fighting against the Lusitanians was based on a defensive policy, but that cannot apply to the other two peoples.

Perhaps the most remarkable feature of this series of wars was the ability of the Aravaci and particularly of the Numantines to go on resisting. This is all the more extraordinary since in the final war (144–133) they had little support, as far as we can tell, even from other Celtiberians, and according to Appian they had only 8,000 troops (he seems to be referring to the Aravaci as a whole) even in 144, before new casualties began.[158] The reasons for this capacity to resist have already been discussed in relation to the 180s and 170s (p. 126). Appian emphasizes the difficulty of the terrain and simply says that the Aravaci made excellent cavalry and infantry.[159] Undoubtedly the semi-pastoral nature of the local economy also made a great difference. In addition it is likely that the Roman army in Nearer Spain was itself becoming less effective in these years – there were certainly few reasons for first-rate legionaries to want to serve there.[160]

Like the other wars described in this chapter the Spanish wars of 154–133 obviously caused death and devastation on a large scale, but no extant writer was interested in assessing the damage. The behaviour of some Roman commanders became even more ruthless: in 151 L. Licinius Lucullus ordered the killing of some 20,000 men at the Vaccaean city of Cauca, almost the whole adult male population, in spite of their already having surrendered.[161] The following year Ser. Sulpicius Galba was responsible for a similar massacre in Lusitania, after having pretended sympathy for the hard economic circumstances of those whom he intended to slaughter; but it is true that after he returned to Rome he only with difficulty repelled an attack in the law courts which was based, in

---

[157] Baeturia: App. 68.288. Urso: Diod. Sic. xxxiii.21. Itucce: Diod. Sic. xxxiii.7.5–6 (he calls it 'Tucce', but the identification is guaranteed by App. 66.282, 67.284). Cf. App. 65.278 (Fabius Aemilianus in 144 plundering one city and burning another, south of the Guadalquivir).

[158] App. 76.324, 97.419. According to the Livian tradition (*Per.* LV; cf. Flor. 1.34) there were 4,000 Numantine troops at the time of Hostilius Mancinus' defeat.   [159] App. 76.323–324.

[160] Comments in the sources on the indiscipline of the legions, though part of the rhetorical furniture of Roman historiography and hence suspect, are very frequent in this period: App. 78.334, 83.359; Dio fr. 78; and on 134 B.C. the many texts collected by Schulten 1937, 63–8 (B 33). Lucil. 398–400 Marx are lines written by a man who, like Polybius, witnessed the siege of Numantia, and it is probable that the Roman army Scipio found there in 134 was most unimpressive. For a clear instance of incompetence in command see App. 82 (Lepidus Porcina at the Vaccaean city of Pallantia).

[161] App. 52.

part at least, on this incident.[162] Nor was such extreme violence entirely new to the Romans; yet taken with their behaviour towards Carthage and towards the Achaeans in 150 and succeeding years, these actions suggest that the Roman aristocracy now accepted unscrupulousness and ultra-violent reactions even more readily. Mass enslavements continued of course to be normal.[163]

Eventually it should be possible to gain a clear impression of some of the effects of the conquest from the archaeological evidence. At present, however, the lack of firm chronology on many sites prevents this. Not that there can be much doubt about the widespread destruction of indigenous settlements in the second century. That which took place in the middle and lower valley of the Ebro must mostly date from the early part of the century;[164] the archaeologically best-known site among those of any size in this region is Azaila, which was destroyed about the time of Cato, though it was repopulated again later.[165] In the area fought over in 154–133, Numantia, the site of Schulten's famous excavation, was simply one of a number of sites that ceased for a while at least to be inhabited.[166]

Some of these communities must have declined because of the economic conditions created by Roman control rather than because of the wars of conquest themselves. Strabo remarks, somewhat vaguely, that in Lusitania between the Tagus and the far north-west – that is, in the territory conquered by Brutus Callaicus in 138 and 137 – the Romans 'humbled' the inhabitants and made most of their cities into villages, though they improved some of the cities by 'synoecizing' them.[167] The change from cities to villages was presumably both an economic and a political matter; part of the 'humbling' may have resulted from the outflow of taxation to Rome or even from the fact that the Lusitanians were now no longer able to carry out large plundering raids against neighbouring populations – which had certainly been a traditional practice of some economic significance.[168]

The Romans and Italians did not, however, seize the agricultural resources of Spain for direct ownership on a grand scale as they had done in Cisalpine Gaul and in Liguria. Immigration to Spain still seems to have been heavy only in the mining areas, and there was little formal colonization of immigrants. Corduba and Valentia are the only real possibilities.

---

[162] The incident: App. 59–60; for precedents: Harris 1979, 52 n. 3: (A 21). The sources on the trial: Schulten 1937, 103–6: (B 33).   [163] E.g. App. 68.291, 77.331, 98.424.

[164] For a useful account of these sites see Pellicer Catalán 1962: (B 187).

[165] See Beltrán Lloris 1976: (B 151).

[166] The archaeology of Numantia: Schulten 1914–31: (B 198), and also Wattenberg 1963, 11–29: (B 205). See further Wattenberg 1959, 181: (G 34), on the Aravacan and Vaccaean regions. The Lusitanian evidence is more obscure, but it is significant that 'Oxthracai' (above, p. 133) cannot be traced.

[167] Strabo III.154; the statement probably derives from Artemidorus of Ephesus or from Poseidonius.   [168] Strabo III.154 provides a very instructive account.

Of the former, Strabo says that it was originally inhabited by 'chosen men' of both the Romans and the local people. It was founded in some sense by M. Marcellus (*cos.* III 152), perhaps during his praetorship in 169/8 rather than, as is generally assumed, his less peaceful second tour of duty in Spain. Its territory was remarkably large.[169] Valentia (138) was probably settled by Romans and Italians who had fought in the war against Viriathus, and though there is no clear evidence for other veterans having stayed permanently in Spain in the second century, it is likely that some did.[170] The presence of Roman armies must also have led to the arrival of contractors to deal with supplies, traders to handle plunder, and assorted parasites. Some no doubt settled permanently in such places as Corduba and Tarraco. As for the mining districts, Diodorus recounts in his discussion of the Spanish silver mines how after the conquest 'a great number of Italians swarmed to the mines and took away great wealth because of their avarice. For they buy a great number of slaves and turn them over to those who are in charge of the mine workings. . . .'[171] This almost certainly comes from Poseidonius, who visited Spain about 90. But the migration to the mines had obviously begun quite quickly after the Roman conquest, and their great reputation at Rome is confirmed by a mention in I *Maccabees*, a text written in the 150s.[172] The 40,000 slaves mentioned by Polybius as working at the silver mines of New Carthage[173] imply the presence of a considerable number of free immigrants as well. We should probably think of a total of immigrants amounting to many tens of thousands by 133. In 122 it was possible to take 3,000 of 'the Romans from Iberia' to the Balearic Islands as colonists.[174]

The political forms of Roman domination are known to us only from very fragmentary evidence. Specific information is meagre about the degree of intervention in judicial affairs by the governors of the Spanish provinces,[175] and about the presumable tendency of Rome to favour aristocratic regimes among the subject peoples. What did Roman governors of Further Spain think of the agricultural communism of the Vaccaei, probably still in operation in the 90s (since Diodorus probably

[169] Strabo III.141; he gives no date for Marcellus' action. The silence of Polyb. xxxv.2.2 (who mentions that Marcellus wintered there in 152/1) slightly favours 169/8, and cf. Galsterer 1971, 9: (G 15).   [170] Brunt 1971, 218–19: (H 82).   [171] v.36.3–4.   [172] I *Macc.* 8.3.

[173] Strabo III.147–148 = Polyb. xxxiv.9.9 (on the number see Walbank 1957–79, III.606: (B 38)). A scholar who studied the silverware finds of late Republican Spain concluded that a prosperous class existed in northern Andalusia by about 100, and he associated this with the silver-mining in the Sierra Morena (Raddatz 1969, 169: (B 189)).

[174] Strabo III.168; cf. Gabba 1954, 299: (H 130) = 1976, 106: (H 44). The notion that the immigrants were primarily Osco-Umbrian (propounded on philological grounds by Menéndez Pidal in Alvar and others 1960, LIX–LXXXVI: (A 1), and in earlier publications) appears quite unproved; cf. Knapp 1977, 155–7: (G 20).

[175] An inscription of 87 B.C. throws some light on this: Fatás 1980: (G 14).

took his description of it from Poseidonius)?[176] Perhaps official interference in local political matters was quite rare in the period of the conquest.[177]

Several new cities were created in the period 155–133. Strabo says that Corduba was a colony, but this is usually dismissed, largely because Velleius wrote that C. Gracchus' colony at Iunonia was the first colony outside Italy.[178] However, Carteia and Valentia show that Velleius was wrong, at least as far as Latin colonies were concerned, and Corduba may be another instance; in any case it became a conspicuous success as a centre of Romanization. So too was Valentia (Valencia). About this foundation the Epitomator of Livy says that Brutus Callaicus 'gave lands and a city' to 'those who had served under Viriathus'.[179] This statement is clear, but it is extremely difficult to believe that such a site would have been bestowed on recent rebels.[180] We should reluctantly conclude that 'under Viriathus' is a mistake and that the beneficiaries of Brutus' action were really the men who had fought *against* Viriathus. This is all the more likely because the foundation belongs to a date when some veterans were in desperate need of land, and because Valentia very probably did have colonial status, which (like the name itself) is more likely to have been awarded to veterans than to newly surrendered rebels.[181] Brutus also founded another settlement, which he named Brutobriga. Its exact site is unknown, but it is to be sought near the coast somewhere just to the west of the lower Guadalquivir, and it had the evident aim of securing Roman influence over the local population.[182] Brutus had in fact been preceded in this policy by Q. Caepio (*cos.* 140), who, after having arranged the assassination of Viriathus and defeated his successor Tautalos, awarded some land and, according to Diodorus, a town to the Lusitanians who had surrendered.[183] But the total of new towns created by the Romans was in this period still quite limited.

---

[176] Diod. Sic. v.34.3.

[177] On Iberian coinage after the conquest see De Guadán 1969, 128–53: (B 89); Knapp 1977, 4: (B 106).

[178] Vell. Pat. 1.15.4. Against Corduba as an actual colony: Brunt 1971, 215: (H 82); Griffin 1972, 17–19: (G 19).

[179] Liv. *Per.* LV. The notion that the Valentia in question may have been at one of the Valencias other than 'Valentia del Cid', still to be found in Simon 1962, 138: (G 29), is refuted by Torres 1951, 114–16: (G 32); Galsterer 1971, 12: (G 15); Wiegels 1974: (G 35).

[180] Wiegels 1974, 164: (G 35).

[181] For these and other relevant arguments cf. Wiegels 1974: (G 35); Knapp 1977, 125–31: (G 20). The status of (Latin) colony depends on an Italian inscription, *ILLRP* 385.

[182] On the site: Steph. Byz. *s.v.* Βρουτοβρία; Wiegels 1974, 170–2 (G 35) (who suggests that this is where Viriathus' veterans were settled). On the coin-types: Grant 1946, 381: (B 93); De Guadan 1969, 128, 216: (B 89). On the geographical limits of the -briga termination: Untermann 1961, map 3: (C 60).

[183] App. 75.321; Diod. Sic. XXXIII.1.4. It was probably called Caepiana and in Lusitania: Ptolem. II.5.5; Tovar 1974–6, II.216: (B 223).

Another form of Roman profit-making, less important for Roman policy than plunder or silver mines, but still of interest, came from the increased trade between Italy and Spain in the second century. The main kind of evidence available consists of sherds of black-glazed pottery, and quite apart from the difficulties of dating this material precisely and of showing that any particular item was imported and not merely a local imitation, the economic significance of the trade is dubious. In any event such pottery was already being imported to some sites in the extreme north-east – Emporion, Rhode and Ullastret – in the third century. In the second century quite a substantial trade, though not of course on an 'industrial' scale, grew up with places further south and inland.[184] Italy also began to export a certain quantity of wine to the more accessible parts of Spain.[185] On the analogy of other areas in and on the fringes of the second-century empire a considerable number of Roman and Italian *negotiatores* were present (the shortage of literary evidence, apart from that which concerns mining, is of minor significance).

Can any long-term changes in Roman policy in Spain be discovered by 133, apart from the obvious one that the conquest stopped short of the far northern part of the country? It has already been suggested that some Roman commanders began to show an even higher degree of ruthlessness in warfare. Some of them, from the time of the elder Gracchus onwards, were also ready to help certain elements in the Spanish population by including them in new towns. This was hardly an altruistic policy; and the occasional willingness of the Senate from the 170s onwards to restrain the avarice of provincial governors was based at least as much on political considerations as on concern for the well-being of the provincials. It is a mistake to suppose that Rome made frequent grants of its citizenship to Spaniards in this period; on the contrary, they were probably limited to a handful of men.[186] Schulten's judgement that the Romans treated the indigenous population 'little better than cattle' is exaggerated,[187] but the time of far-sighted measures was still in the future.

Much has been written about the Romanization of Spain,[188] but for the second century the evidence concerning actual changes in the behaviour and attitudes of the local populations is sparse. In coastal towns such as

[184] For Emporion and Rhode: Sanmartí-Grego 1978: (B 195). A modern survey of black-glaze in the rest of the peninsula is lacking; by way of example see Ramos Folques and Ramos Fernández 1976, 18: (B 191), on Illici (Elche), and Beltrán Lloris 1979: (B 152) on Azaila.
[185] Consult, with caution, Beltrán Lloris 1970, esp. 328, 608: (B 150) and Blázquez 1974, 31 n. 35: (G 10).
[186] Frequent grants: Blázquez 1964, 325: (G 8) and others; see instead Knapp 1977, 161–3: (G 20).
[187] Schulten 1930, 324: (G 28).
[188] Note especially Sánchez-Albornoz 1949: (G 27); Blázquez 1964: (G 8); García y Bellido 1972: (G 18).

Emporion, Tarraco and Gades, in the new towns and in the mining districts, local populations must soon have come under powerful Roman influence, and the indigenous culture lacked the prestige and self-confidence which allowed the Greeks to maintain long-term resistance to cultural Romanization.[189] However, traces of the Romanization of the local populations are hard to find anywhere in the second century. Even in the late Republic, Punic language and religion continued in the south-coast towns;[190] Iberian and 'Celtic' inhabitants of sites which were not subjected to direct Roman influence continued to use the local languages for inscriptions (to the exclusion of Latin, apparently, for several generations). Local deities went on being worshipped, and even local political structures persisted.[191] But the full detail of first-century developments falls outside the scope of this chapter; for the present many of the local populations of Roman Spain retained the same cultural character as before simply because of the Romans' lack of any interest in direct exploitation of their territory.

Submissiveness towards Rome was widespread after 133, as indeed it had long been in the coastal region and in the north-east. In the succeeding generation some of the Lusitanians, some of the Celtiberians, particularly Aravaci, and some Vaccaei continued to offer armed resistance.[192] But harsh experience had convinced most of the peoples under Roman power that freedom had been truly lost.

IV. ROME AND CARTHAGE[193]

Under a treaty very advantageous to Rome (above, pp. 64–5), Rome and Carthage remained formally at peace for fifty-two years (201–149).[194] Rome's power over the Carthaginians was now considerable, and if the latter honoured their obligations – which without a fleet they were very likely to – Rome had nothing to expect but the annual arrival of 200

[189] The importance of Tarraco as a Roman base has been underlined by archaeological investigation of its early second-century fortifications: Hauschild 1979: (B 170).

[190] See Koch 1976: (C 28).

[191] Late inscriptions in local languages (other than Punic) and other evidence for the survival of the languages: García y Bellido 1972, 470–91: (G 18). The survival of cults and other religious phenomena: Blázquez 1978–80, II.118–26: (G 11); of local political structures: Blázquez 1964, 337–40: (G 8).   [192] Sources in Schulten 1937, IV.144–54: (B 33).

[193] The main literary sources for this section are Polybius, Livy and Appian, *Pun.* (all references to Appian here are to this work); Aristotle, Plautus, the fragments of Ennius and of Cato's speeches, Nepos, Diodorus Siculus, Varro, Fenestella, Strabo, Valerius Maximus, Velleius Paterculus, the elder Pliny, Plutarch, Justin, Diogenes Laertius, Aurelius Victor, Orosius and Zonaras also contribute. The important archaeological, numismatic, epigraphical and papyrological evidence is mentioned in later notes.

[194] The best detailed discussion of Roman–Carthaginian relations in this period is Gsell 1913–28, III.297–407: (C 21). Also especially useful are Astin 1967: (H 67) and Sznycer and Nicolet in Nicolet 1977–8, II.545–626: (A 27).

talents (payable for fifty years) and diplomatic appeals resulting from the inevitable conflict between Carthage and its neighbour to the west, Numidia.

The Roman Senate continued to support its tested ally Massinissa, king of the Massylii in eastern Numidia and now of some of the Masaesylian territory in western Numidia which had previously belonged to Syphax. There were obvious strategic reasons for this support. But at the end of the war, and for some years afterwards, moderation was observed. Part of Syphax's lands went to his son Vermina.[195] Nor, as we shall see, was every single territorial dispute between Carthage and Massinissa decided in favour of the latter. From the point of view of the Roman Senate, Massinissa too was under a serious obligation to respect Rome's wishes, not least because of Scipio Africanus' and its own announcements of the king's royal power.[196]

Successive rulers of Carthage tried to conciliate Rome in all circumstances, understandably failing to realize that in the end another war was extremely probable. In 200 the city contributed 400,000 *modii* (about 2,700 tons) of wheat, half of it for the army in Greece. The indemnity was paid regularly. Even when an awkward incident did occur, it showed how essentially submissive the Carthaginian leaders were.

This incident was the election of Hannibal as one of the annual sufetes (chief magistrates) for 196/5, with the support of the mass of the voters against the entrenched oligarchs.[197] In office he concentrated his efforts on internal matters, proposing various democratic reforms, but his enemies wrote to 'the leading men' at Rome, with whom they had formal relations of hospitality,[198] that he was in secret communication with Antiochus III. Rome accordingly sent a mission to Carthage in the summer of 195; after Hannibal, who had now left office, had fled to the eastern Mediterranean, this mission obtained assurances of obedience from the Carthaginian senate.[199] The claim that Hannibal had been negotiating with Antiochus before his flight should be regarded, as it was by Scipio, with extreme scepticism.[200] In any case it is evident that the other Carthaginian officials behaved impeccably from the Roman point of view. Hannibal was only one annual magistrate,[201] and even he did nothing worth mentioning to subvert the treaty with Rome while he was

[195] Livy xxxi.11.8, 19.5–6   [196] Livy xxx.15.11–12, 44.12. Cf. xlv.13.15.

[197] On this episode see Livy xxxiii.45.6–49.7, and also Nepos, *Hann.* 7; Val. Max. iv.1.6; Justin xxxi.1.7–2.8; Zon. ix.18.11–12.   [198] Livy xxxiii.45.6

[199] Livy xxxiii.49.1 refers to the 'senate', the meaning of which is unclear in a Carthaginian context.

[200] Livy xxxiii.47.4; Val. Max. iv.1.6. However, he may have been disdainful rather than unbelieving. Though this section of Livy derives from Polybius, it is not clear what the latter thought of the Carthaginian charges.

[201] And perhaps one of four sufetes a year rather than two, as is usually thought: Huss 1977: (c 27).

Map 9. North Africa at the time of the Third Punic War.

at Carthage. He did not take any considerable number of followers with him to the east, and his complete inability to raise support against Rome in his home territory is apparent from his activities at Antiochus' court. There was still a 'Barcid faction' at Carthage in 193,[202] but it was not strong enough to advocate anti-Roman policies in any effective way, even if it wanted to. The mere appearance of a Tyrian emissary from Hannibal sent the government into such a paroxysm of nervousness about Roman reactions that it despatched a mission to report the matter to Rome.

This mission also complained about 'the injustices of Massinissa'.[203] Livy's account of what had happened is somewhat problematical, since he can be convicted of importing at least one detail – the story of the

---

[202] At least according to Livy xxxiv.61.11. On the difficult question of Livy's sources in this section see Walbank 1957–79, III.490–1: (B 38).   [203] Livy xxxiv.61.16.

Numidian dissident Aphther – from a sequence of events which we know from Polybius to have taken place much later.[204] Furthermore he muddles up elementary facts about North African topography, putting Leptis in the region of the Emporia ('Markets'), that is the Gulf of Gabès, where neither Leptis Minor nor Magna was to be found. Yet a real territorial dispute between Carthage and Massinissa had probably been going on. In the treaty of 201 Rome had put Carthage in a most vulnerable position by prescribing among other things that Massinissa was entitled to any land or cities that had ever belonged to him or to his ancestors 'within boundaries to be assigned in the future'.[205] The boundaries had been settled by Scipio Africanus,[206] with the precious territory in the Gulf of Gabès either awarded to Carthage or (less probably) unassigned. In any case this is a probable enough region for a dispute to have arisen. The Senate now sent Scipio on a new embassy – which, however, decided to do nothing; the evident intention was to keep the dispute in suspense until the conflict with Antiochus was resolved, without in practice alleviating Carthaginian difficulties.[207] Carthage was of course forbidden by treaty to make war on Massinissa, even in its own defence.[208] Not that Carthage was in severe financial difficulty, for two years later the city offered Rome a quantity of grain and some ships for the Syrian–Aetolian War and, still more impressively, the immediate payment of the outstanding indemnity, an amount equivalent to 187.2 million sesterces, even now a very large sum by Roman standards (and one should recall that until 187 the Roman treasury was still in debt because of the Hannibalic War). Massinissa too offered a supply of grain, with some troops and elephants.[209] The Senate kept itself free of obligations by paying for the grain (whether the troops were accepted is unclear, except that six Punic ships served with the Roman fleet in Greece). The important question, however, was the balance of the indemnity. This offer was an attempt to buy favour and a degree of independence, and from the Roman point of view it was better to refuse, thereby keeping Carthage in the position of debtor.[210]

For almost two decades after this, though relations between Carthage and Massinissa no doubt continued poor, Rome offered the king no great encouragement to attack. On one occasion, in 182, he did so, seizing an

---

[204] In the 170s at the earliest: Polyb. xxxi.21.   [205] Polyb. xv.18.5.

[206] Livy xxxiv.62.9 (Carthaginians speaking). Though the Numidians accused them of 'lying about the boundary-making of Scipio' (sect. 11), that phrase seems to imply that he did establish boundaries somewhere.

[207] This is probably the occasion mentioned by App. 67, when the Senate told the legates to favour Massinissa, who consequently gained territory.

[208] Cf. Walbank 1957–79, II.468–9: (B 38).   [209] All this: Livy xxxvi.4.

[210] The refusal also shows how confident the Senate was about the results of the Syrian–Aetolian war.

area (unidentified) which for a time had supposedly been his father's.[211]
When the Senate came to adjudicate the matter the following year, it
appears from a somewhat unclear sentence of Livy's that Carthage was
successful.[212]

If a Roman embassy went to North Africa in 174, as Livy asserts,[213] it is
most unlikely that it was able to find any evidence of clandestine
negotiations between Carthage and King Perseus; that was simply a piece
of later Roman propaganda. But this was in fact a period of renewed
pressure by Massinissa, who perhaps saw an opportunity in the approaching war between Rome and Macedon (he was certainly informed
about affairs in the Greek world as well as at Rome).[214] According to the
charges made by Carthage to Rome in 172, he had forcibly taken more
than seventy 'towns and forts' in their territory in the previous two
years.[215] It is often said that the Senate resolved this dispute in
Massinissa's favour,[216] but in fact it postponed a decision to give the
Numidians time for consultation, and we are prevented from knowing
what was decided the following year by a long lacuna in the manuscript
of Livy (after XLIII.3.7). Meanwhile the Senate tested the spirit of its
North African allies by summoning assistance from them against Perseus. Carthage eventually sent one million *modii* of wheat (about 6,700
tons), half that amount of barley.[217]

In the context of 162/1 Polybius reports that 'not long before' – a
vague expression – Massinissa had seized the territory in the Emporia
district which belonged to Carthage, though Carthage was able to retain
the towns. Both sides 'often' sent missions to Rome about this, the
Senate always deciding in Massinissa's favour. In the end Carthage lost
the cities too, and also in some undefined way 500 talents of revenue. It
has been judged that this story goes back only a year or two earlier than
162/1; more probably the period was longer, and Polybius may have been
referring all the way back to the dispute of 174–172.[218]

There is therefore no definite reason to think that Rome's decisive
victory at Pydna had the immediate effect of making Rome strongly
favour Massinissa's interests against those of Carthage.[219] In fact the
Senate's attitude towards the Numidian king was somewhat ambiguous

[211] Livy XL.17.1–6.
[212] Livy XL.34.14. Interpreted otherwise by Gsell 1913–28, III.318: (C 21), and some others. The
Carthaginian hostages now released were probably replaced by new ones: Walbank 1957–79, II.471:
(B 38).   [213] Livy XLI.22.1–3.   [214] Cf. Walsh 1965, 154–5: (C 62).
[215] Livy XLII.23.2 (from an annalistic source); nothing in Polyb. XXXI.21 contradicts this (in spite
of Walsh, *op. cit.* 157).
[216] E.g. Walbank 1957–79, III.490: (B 38). The nearest thing to support for this is Livy XLII.24.7.
[217] Livy XLIII.6.11. Massinissa's contributions: 6.13.
[218] 'Often': Polyb. XXXI.21.5; compare 'finally', sect. 8. Walbank 1957–79, III.491: (B 38), prefers
the shorter interval (cf. Walsh 1965, 159: (C 62)), but the story seems too complex to fit into such a
period.

just after the Third Macedonian War: while it professed itself thoroughly pleased with his assistance during the war, his expressed wish to visit Rome in person and the Senate's declining to invite him[220] both suggest that he had reason for nervousness. Kings seemed to be at a discount, as Eumenes of Pergamum discovered a year or so later. In the short run, however, it was only Carthage that had to fear new developments in Roman policy. During the 160s it was constantly Carthage which lost when the Senate gave its verdicts, and presumably this happened again in the major controversy which broke out in 162/1, a controversy about which we know nothing except that it began with the 500 talents of lost revenue.[221]

As we are now approaching the large historical problems involved in the Third Punic War, a survey of Carthaginian affairs and particularly of the Carthaginian economy will be helpful. 'It was considered the richest city in the world', says Polybius, thinking of the final period of its existence,[222] a judgement which may have become anachronistic only in the 160s. As a state Carthage had of course lost enormous revenues as a result of Roman and Numidian aggression. Gold and silver coins seem to have been issued in smaller quantities in the second century (if that is significant).[223] Yet there were some positive developments in both public and private finance. The treasury, which as we have seen was well off in 191, benefited from greatly reduced military expenditure, and the absence of mercenaries no doubt explains why its precious-metal coins were of increased purity.[224] Presumably the state also benefited to some extent from long-distance trade in Carthaginian hands, and though the evidence is too haphazard and fragile to justify any notion that this trade increased in the second century, it certainly did reach out to some noteworthy places, such as both the Red Sea and the Black Sea.[225] Three second-century coin hoards from sites in Yugoslavia which are dominated by Carthaginian and Numidian issues[226] suggest Carthaginian imports from that area (slaves perhaps). They also imply some considerable involvement of Carthaginians in trade with Numidia itself, which is probable in any case, in spite of the political disputes, and somewhat supported by a difficult text which derives from the early imperial writer

---

[219] As argued by De Sanctis 1907–64, IV.iii.10–11: (A 14).

[220] Livy XLV.13.17, 14.4.

[221] The importance of this dispute is to be inferred from the elaborate introduction Polybius provided (XXXI.21).   [222] Polyb. XVIII.35.9.

[223] Jenkins and Lewis 1963, 53: (B 101).   [224] Robinson 1937–8: (B 128).

[225] A Carthaginian merchant in the Red Sea: *Sammelbuch* III.7169. Another at Istrus: Lambrino 1927–32, 400–6: (B 177); cf. Rostovtzeff 1941, 1462 n. 20: (A 31). It was about 200 that the Carthaginians reached the Azores: Pfeiler 1965, 53: (B 125).

[226] Crawford 1969, nos. 142, 145, 146: (B 87). Further information about the distribution of Carthaginian coin finds: Jahn 1977, 414: (B 98).

Fenestella.[227] An inscribed Rhodian amphora-handle recently found at Carthage[228] indicates second-century wine imports. The Romans and Italians themselves certainly traded with Carthage on a significant scale.[229] Though there is always the danger of exaggerating the importance of long-distance trade in an ancient state, some Carthaginians probably prospered in the second century.

The same may well have been true of landowners, who were probably responsible for most of Carthage's exports. A strange passage in a late source tells us of Hannibal's efforts to encourage olive production after 201,[230] and the grain Carthage periodically provided for the Romans strongly suggests a regular surplus (a million *modii* of wheat represents the net yearly production of as much as 40,000 acres). The Black Sea merchant just mentioned dealt in grain. And unless Carthaginian agricultural productivity had an excellent reputation at Rome, it would be impossible to understand why, after 146, the Senate ordered the translation of Mago's 28-volume handbook on farming into Latin.[231]

As for population trends, they are very hard to make out. Strabo's total of 700,000 for the population of the city in 149 is impossibly high, and since other elements in his description are also much exaggerated[232] it is doubtful whether any value can be extracted from the figure by any such expedient as supposing that it applied to Carthaginian territory as a whole. Beloch's guess of 200–300,000 for the city itself is plausible.[233] More to the point are two other observations: first, the Carthaginian state as a whole did not dispose of sufficient manpower, even if it could mobilize its population, to rival Rome and Italy. Secondly – and this comment is subject to amplification as the results of excavations become known – construction of a new quarter within the city during the second century[234] implies that some population growth took place.

What may be Polybius' most important surviving statement about the Third Punic War is that the Roman Senate had decided to begin a new war 'long before' it was formally voted in 149.[235] This vague expression might take us back only a few years beyond 149, say to 153, which is in effect the date which Appian (unfortunately not reproducing Polybius in

---

[227] Fenestella fr. 9 (Peter, *HRRel.* II, p. 81): there was no trade between *Italici* and *Afri* (and the context shows that by the latter he meant Numidians and Gaetulians) until after 146; this can only have been because such trade was dominated by Carthaginians.

[228] Lancel 1978, 310: (B 179). There are others, not so well dated: Gsell 1913–28, IV.154: (C 21); Ferron and Pinard 1955, 61–8: (B 165); Lancel and others 1977, 26, 91: (B 178).

[229] For the pottery evidence from Carthage see Fulford 1983, 8: (C 16). The main literary evidence is Polyb. XXXVI.7.5 (cf. App. 92.434); Plaut. *Poen.* 79–82; *ORF*⁴, Cato, fr. 185 (p. 75). Cf. *ILLRP* 1177. The Cani Islands coin hoard may also be relevant: Crawford 1969, no. 132: (B 87).

[230] Aurelius Victor, *De Caes.* 37.3.   [231] Plin. *HN* XVIII.22; cf. Varro, *Rust.* 1.10.

[232] See Gsell 1913–28, II.21 n. 3: (C 21).   [233] Beloch 1886, 467: (A 6).

[234] See Lancel 1978: (B 179).

[235] Polyb. XXXVI.2.1. There is no sound reason to doubt this; cf. Harris 1979, 235 nn. 2, 4: (A 21).

a dependable way) assigns to the decision.[236] It might alternatively take us back further, perhaps even as far as 162/1, the date of a major new Carthaginian dispute before the Senate.

However, before coming to the reasons behind this Roman war decision, we must review what is known about Roman–Carthaginian diplomacy in the years from 157 to 151. The task is more difficult than it seems, for Polybius is almost entirely missing, and our other sources, principally Appian and the *Epitome* of Livy, are contaminated by more or less obvious falsehoods, especially the *Epitome*. The main reason for this was of course the desire of contemporary and, even more, later Romans to justify Rome's conduct.

Five Roman embassies went to Africa in this period, according to the *Epitome*. They are to be dated to 157, 153, 153/2, 151 and 150. The first was merely one of the series of missions sent to investigate territorial disputes between Carthage and Massinissa;[237] its results are unknown but are likely to have been favourable to the Numidian side. Hostility between the two African states evidently continued to intensify, since about 154 the commander of the Carthaginian auxiliaries, Carthalo, who was one of the leaders of the faction Appian calls 'the democratizers' – the opponents of appeasement – organized some attacks, which, however, seem to have stopped short of regular warfare.[238] The Roman mission which came to help the Numidians in these circumstances must be the one datable to 153 of which the *Epitome* says that it somehow discovered 'an abundance of ship-building material' at Carthage.[239] It is in fact not likely to be true that an abundance of such material had been collected, at least not for warships, above all because it is plain from what happened later that in the period before the war Carthage did not build any warships beyond the ten triremes which the treaty of 201 permitted, even if it had that many.[240] Livy and his source were already at this point mired down in Roman propaganda. His next story accentuates this: the general Arcobarzanes, a probably fictitious Numidian ally of Carthage, is dragged in, and Cato appears arguing in favour of declaring war against Carthage on the grounds that it had prepared an army against Rome.[241] It is quite possible, as we shall see, that Cato was already in favour of declaring war, but if so this is not likely to have been his reason.

Next comes the Roman embassy which is perhaps the most problematical one of all (153 or 152). This was sent essentially on a spying

---

[236] App. 69.314. In 74.343 (149 B.C.) he says that this was 'long before'.
[237] Liv. *Per.* XLVII middle.
[238] App. 68.306–307; but the whole story is undermined by the lack of any specific Roman reaction. [239] Liv. *Per.* XLVII end.
[240] See Harris 1979, 235 n. 1: (A 21). This was in spite of the fact that Carthage consciously broke the treaty with Rome in 151, and needed ships more than anything else for defence against Rome.
[241] Liv. *Per.* XLVIII.

mission.[242] Our information about what took place is very unsatisfactory, but the overall result is clear – namely that Rome allowed Massinissa's depredations to continue, but found no *casus belli* which the majority of the Senate held to require an immediate war or justify one. Almost everything else is obscure: the *Epitome* says that the mission was sent to spy out what Carthage was doing, Appian that it was sent in response to yet another Carthaginian appeal, this one provoked by Massinissa's laying claim to 'the Great Plains and the region of fifty towns which they call Tysca', that is to say the fertile plain which opens out around the upper River Bagradas (in the vicinity of Jendouba). In fact both accounts of the purpose of the embassy may well convey parts of the truth. The *Epitome* omits to mention Cato's participation, which is described by Appian and by Plutarch (in an otherwise poorly informed section).[243] This famous story may be a complete fiction; whether it is does not matter much – except for the reliability of Appian. There are further discrepancies between our two main sources. At the end, the *Epitome* says, the Roman mission was forced to flee to avoid 'violation', a classic Roman propaganda motif, absent from Appian's account. The latter asserts that the returning ambassadors reported to the Senate an alarming growth in Carthaginian resources.

Now we reach an obscure sequence of events which is jumped over by Appian, perhaps for the good reason that it did not take place. The *Epitome* relates that Massinissa's son Gulussa visited Rome to give an alarmist report about Carthage, and that the Senate responded (this will have been in the winter of 152/1) by despatching ten *legati* to investigate – which would have been a very unusual use of such a commission.[244] They eventually reported that they had found an army and a fleet at Carthage (the latter was certainly not true and is not likely to have been reported), whereupon the Senate threatened Carthage with war if it did not disband its forces. All this is probably Roman fiction designed to put blame on Carthage.

At all events the Carthaginian government's policy of avoiding outright war with Massinissa had been discredited by the complete or partial loss of the Great Plains. The 'democratizers', under the leadership of Hamilcar surnamed the Samnite, now established their dominance in a more decisive fashion and banished some forty supporters of the policy of appeasing Massinissa. When the king besieged a Carthaginian town called Oroscopa,[245] the new government sent a force of 25,400 troops

---

[242] *Ibid.* (*legatos mitti Carthaginem qui specularentur quid ageretur*); App. 68.309–69.313.

[243] Plut. *Cat. Mai.* 26.   [244] Cf. Mommsen 1887–8, II.692–3: (A 25).

[245] Evidently a hill-top site near the eastern end of the Great Plains; near Vaga (Béja), according to Walsh 1965, 159: (C 62).

under Hasdrubal to oppose him.[246] Lacking substantial military experience they fought a disastrous campaign from which only very few
returned home. While they were already in severe difficulties another
Roman mission arrived (the date is now spring or summer 150, it
appears) – with the purpose of settling the dispute, according to Appian.[247] In fact it will have been obvious to these Roman senators that a
new Roman–Carthaginian war was on its way, for here was a large
Carthaginian army in the field contrary to the treaty of 201. The Roman
mission had been told to spur Massinissa on if he was succeeding, and this
no doubt encouraged Gulussa to slaughter the Carthaginian army after it
had surrendered and disarmed.

It was this armed Carthaginian resistance to Massinissa's forces that
now provided the *iusta causa* which, according to P. Scipio Nasica and the
majority of Roman senators, had previously been lacking. This was a
very important preliminary in any Roman war with a powerful enemy:
the gods had to be satisfied as did Roman opinion and Rome's allies in
Italy and elsewhere.[248] How important it was considered on this occasion
can be judged from Polybius' statement that the Senate almost gave up
the notion of fighting the war because of its disagreements about the
effect on outsiders' feelings.[249] Even in a period of great Roman aggres-
siveness, the weight of senatorial opinion remained on Nasica's side until
Massinissa, with Roman encouragement, more or less forced Carthage to
provide technical justification for the war. Even then, Nasica himself was
not satisfied,[250] presumably because he thought that the justification had
been obtained in an excessively deceitful way. But the technical justification really was there, as the Carthaginians in effect admitted after their
expedition had failed; this does not, however, reveal to us why the
Romans fought the Third Punic War.

The war might have started in 150, since Carthage had without much
doubt fought against Massinissa by late 151. It is possible that some
senatorial opinion was still hesitant, more possible still that well into 150
the Senate was content to allow Carthage to use up its military resources
against the Numidians, since the latter offered no threat to Rome's
immediate interests.[251] Normal procedure was to await the assumption of
office by the new consuls, in this case on 1 January 149. The extremely
evasive replies which the Senate gave to the two Carthaginian embassies
sent to Rome during 150 show that it was uninterested in negotiation.
These missions brought news that the failed generals had been con-

---

[246] App. 70.319; later the force is said to have been as large as 58,000 (73.337), but neither figure is
very reliable.   [247] 72.331.
[248] Cf. Walbank 1957–79, III.654: (B 38); Harris 1979, 168–75: (A 21).
[249] Polyb. XXXVI.2.4.   [250] Liv. *Per.* XLIX; Zon. IX.26.
[251] It seems more than doubtful that Rome delayed in order to tell the Carthaginians that it would
not make war if they burned their fleet and dismissed their army (Liv. *Per.* XLVIII); they had neither.

demned to death and that Carthage was once more docile. How, they asked, could Carthage make amends? The first mission was told, according to Appian, 'If you satisfy the Romans', the second that the Carthaginians knew well what they must do.[252] In reality Rome was already beginning the practical preparations for what was to be an unusually large expedition, and the leaders of the Senate cunningly intended that Carthage would receive news that war was entirely certain, and that the Roman fleet was on its way, at almost the same time.[253] Late in 150 Rome had gained a further logistic and psychological advantage when Utica sent to Rome to make a formal submission (*deditio*).[254] Shortly afterwards, early in 149, the Senate voted to declare war.

Before we look more closely at the underlying reasons for this Roman policy, it is worth continuing for a moment with the diplomatic exchanges, for Roman conduct in the interval before fighting began is indicative. Before the news of the war declaration reached Carthage, five emissaries were sent to Rome empowered to offer surrender, and this they in fact did. The Senate's reply was deliberately misleading. They were told in essence that the Carthaginians could recover their freedom if they surrendered 300 sons of powerful families as hostages and if they 'obeyed the commands the consuls imposed on them';[255] furthermore, the Senate's reply made no mention of the city of Carthage itself. Carthage duly turned over the young hostages, but it did no good, for the Roman expedition continued on its way to Africa. Roman policy was now war, on the best terms possible, but in any case war. With the consuls already at Utica, the Carthaginians enquired once again, and were told to surrender all armour and artillery. In folly and desperation they handed over 200,000 sets of armour and 2,000 catapults,[256] only to be summoned to receive the consul's final demand. They must now give up their city for destruction and move at least ten miles inland. By this humiliation, as the Epitomator says with unusual precision, the consuls on the Senate's orders drove the Carthaginians to fight.[257]

Coming now to consider the fundamental reasons why the Roman Senate decided to make war – a decision made well before 149, perhaps in 153 – we must pay attention not merely to the prior diplomacy but to the mentality of the leading men and its basis in the Roman system.

---

[252] App. 74.344, 346. Polyb. XXXVI.3.1 confirms that there had been a Delphic response at Rome.
[253] As in fact happened: Polyb. XXXVI.3.9; App.76.352–353.
[254] Liv. *Per.* XLIX cannot be right, against Polybius and Appian, in putting this after the war vote.
[255] Polyb. XXXVI.4.6.
[256] Polyb. XXXVI.6.7; Diod. Sic. XXXII.6.2. Strabo (XVII.833) and Appian (80.375) exaggerate. The demand for disarmament was normal and natural (cf. Walbank on 6.5) in such circumstances.
[257] Liv. *Per.* XLIX (*compulerunt*). Some scholars, most notably Astin 1967, 274: (H 67), have argued that the Senate did *not* intend to drive the Carthaginians to resistance. Clearly there could be no certainty, but probability is heavily against this; after all, Rome could have caused Carthage further severe political or economic damage by other less provocative means.

A theory which deserves to be dismissed quickly holds that Rome's essential reason for beginning the war was fear – fear not of Carthage but of Massinissa, whose growing power the Senate supposedly felt compelled to resist.[258] There never was any support for this theory either in the sources or in general probability, and successive critiques have made it untenable.[259] If Rome had wanted to restrain the very aged Massinissa, there were many much easier methods. What remains instructive nonetheless is the difficulty which drove scholars to accept this theory: the difficulty of believing that Carthage itself was a source of profound fear to Rome in the 150s.

For this, in the eyes of most modern historians, has been the only other possible explanation, namely that Rome gradually became aware in the years before the war that Carthage was regaining its military strength and spirit and so once more becoming a significant threat to Roman security. So the Senate was motivated by fear, 'fear of a Carthage economically resurgent and rearming; fear of a people who had shown themselves restive and impatient . . .'.[260] Even after disarmament in 149, scholars have pointed out, Carthage had the will and resources to hold out for three years. May the Romans not have feared that the Carthage in which the 'democratizers' had gained some power by 153 might soon become so powerful that Rome would only be able to disarm it at enormous cost and real risk?

Yet this theory too has serious weaknesses, and such fears are only a fraction of the most likely explanation. In the first place, it remains unproved that Carthage's economic or military resources had improved in any dramatic fashion in the immediately preceding years. Even the arms surrendered in 149 may well have been old, and it must be reiterated that Carthage had built no new fleet. The interesting ship sheds discovered on the island in the centre of the old military harbour cannot date, as far as the main structure is concerned, from any date after 201.[261] Until 151 – after the decision had been made – scarcely a single Carthaginian citizen had done serious military service for fifty years. And from some points of view Carthage had grown still weaker, while Rome had grown incomparably stronger, since the end of the Hannibalic War. Revenues had been lost to the Numidians, and as for soldiers, the catastrophe which overcame the Carthaginian army under Hasdrubal in 150 showed how enfeebling fifty years without military experience had been. In any case almost all of this army had been destroyed before the Senate finally

---

[258] Kahrstedt in Meltzer and Kahrstedt 1879–1913, III.616–17: (C 36); Gsell 1913–28, III.329–30: (C 21); Hallward 1930, 476: (C 22).

[259] De Sanctis 1907–64, IV.3, 18–19: (A 14); Walsh 1965: (C 62); for other contributions see Astin 1967, 273: (H 67).   [260] Astin, op. cit. 52; see also 274–6.

[261] See Hurst 1979: (B 174). It seems more likely that the original construction pre-dated 201, and that repairs were carried out in 149–147.

voted for war. As for a navy, if Carthage had tried to build one of any size, the Romans would probably have tried to burn it, as they burned the Syrian warships in 163. Most of the territories from which Carthage had historically recruited mercenaries were now closed off, and the North African allies, to judge from the hasty desertion of Utica in 149, were demoralized. What remains very difficult to judge is the temper of the Carthaginians themselves at the time when the real Roman decision was made. A group of 'democratizers', including Hamilcar 'the Samnite' and Carthalo, no doubt existed, but its efforts were directed against Massinissa not Rome. More remarkable is the continued existence and (except for a period in 151/50) dominance of those who favoured the appeasement of Rome and Massinissa (these were separate groups, according to Appian).[262] It is undeniable that if Rome had given its natural allies at Carthage a modicum of support against Massinissa, they would have been able to maintain the now long-standing foreign policy of submissiveness to Rome without even the minor interruption of 153. No doubt most Carthaginians hated Rome, but they had shown very little inclination to translate this hatred into political action.

Irrational fear of Carthage may conceivably have infected the Roman Senate. Information may have been poor, especially about Punic resources, though there was probably some contact with leading Carthaginians in addition to the diplomatic exchanges.[263] Cato attempted to rekindle hatred of Carthage, in part by recalling atrocity stories,[264] and he may have been saying such things before 153 and having some effect. The extreme violence of Rome's policy towards Carthage (submission and disarmament were not enough) might possibly have been based on fear. There is no doubt that other Romans besides Cato had created a hostile stereotype of the Carthaginians. Since the latter were obviously not barbarians like the Celts or Spaniards – their material culture was quite on a level with that of Rome – this stereotype had among other functions that of hindering any kind of peaceful settlement. The Carthaginians were cruel and above all untrustworthy, according to the clichés which go back at least to Ennius and probably much further.[265] But in the years 201–150 the Roman attitude towards the Carthaginians was not simply one of blind detestation, as Plautus' *Poenulus*, probably produced in the 190s, demonstrates.[266] In the end it is hard to believe that

[262] App. 68.305.
[263] Ties of *hospitium*: Livy xxxiii.45.6 (195 B.C.). Scipio Aemilianus would logically have had the best connections (cf. App. 72.329, 101.473). D. Iunius Silanus' knowledge of Punic (Plin. *HN* xviii.22) may be relevant.   [264] *ORF*⁴ frs. 191–5 (cf. 187) (pp. 78–9).
[265] Ennius, *Ann.* 221, 274–5 (ed. Vahlen). For later texts see Burck in Vogt 1943: (c 61); Walbank 1957–79, 1.412: (B 38).
[266] The play is not free from hostile clichés (see lines 112–13, 1125), but on the whole it is surprisingly sympathetic; Hanno is even allowed to speak Punic, a passage more likely to have come from Plautus himself than from his Greek model.

the Senate was carried away by irrational fear, a motive which modern historians have generally been far too ready to attribute to the Roman Senate.[267] Fear, both rational and irrational, had some effect; but there are other still more important factors to consider.

Before we leave this theory, however, it is worth considering briefly a complex chapter of Polybius in which he describes Greek reactions to the Third Punic War.[268] Four points of view are represented, in two pairs, the first two consisting mainly of opposing arguments about political justification, the second two of opposing arguments about the legal justification of the war. The first pair of arguments is what concerns us here, and it would be particularly interesting to know which, if either, of the arguments was accepted by the highly knowledgeable and intelligent Polybius himself. Did he, that is to say, hold that in starting the Third Punic War the Senate was merely trying to defend Rome, or did he reject this and privately interpret Rome's policy as an example of a more extreme love of power which had infected the Senate since the decisive battle of Pydna? Both answers have won support;[269] here it can only be said that the form of the argument (A is capped by B) favours the latter interpretation, which is perfectly consistent with Polybius' known opinions – and Polybius can hardly have believed that Carthage was really capable of challenging Rome's hegemony.

As with Rome's other wars, so with this one, any valid explanation must be based on a thorough analysis of the behaviour and mentality of Roman aristocrats and also of other citizens. This means that we should discard the notion of a Roman leadership reluctant to go to war and recognize that war was generally known or believed to produce some highly desirable results. Hence the amazing regularity with which Rome went to war in the middle Republic. In the case of Carthage it was obvious that any commander who succeeded in inflicting a decisive defeat on Carthage would gain glory to rival that of Scipio Africanus, not to mention any contemporary, while the war would provide parallel opportunities for other officers. Being the richest state on the immediate fringe of the annexed empire, Carthage was expected to enrich its conquerors handsomely. The habit of going to war was enormously strong, and when at some time between 162 and 153 the Carthaginians came once more to the surface of Roman minds – because of the intensifying conflict with Massinissa and presumably also because of the expected ending of the indemnity – it became very likely that Rome would find some way to pass through a victorious war before coming to a new settlement. That settlement would reflect a further growth in Roman power, whether it resulted in an annexed province or not.

[267] Harris 1979, 163–254: (A 21).   [268] XXXVI.9
[269] The former: Walbank 1957–79, III.663–4: (B 38); the latter: Harris 1979, 271–2: (A 21). See also Musti 1978, 54–7: (B 22).

No explanation of the Third Punic War which heavily emphasizes Roman commercial interests has much appeal to historians now.[270] Familiar and in large part convincing arguments tell against such a theory: no independent group of merchants or financiers exercised sufficient power at Rome in this period to bring on an important war. In the short and medium terms the harming of Carthage might actually have had negative effects on Roman and Italian businessmen, since there was a substantial trade between Italy and Carthaginian Africa.

A thorough rejection of all economic explanations of the Roman war decision would also be a mistake. Public and individual profits were an entirely normal and expected part of successful warfare, and the private profits would fall to senators as well as others. Appian writes that after war was voted, 'every single citizen and ally rushed to join what was a splendid expedition with a predictable result, and many offered to enlist even as volunteers'[271] – all this in marked contrast to what had happened two years earlier in the case of the Celtiberian war – and most of the reason lay in the expectation of booty. This is exactly the period in which certain senior magistrates made themselves remarkable even among members of the Roman upper class by the avarice they showed while holding office in Spain. Senatorial hopes for profit were an encouragement to another war against Carthage. Such a war was likely to lead to long-term benefits as well, an indemnity or perhaps provincial revenue, and if the city was destroyed, as had been resolved by 149, to the confiscation of land as Roman *ager publicus*. In the event this land and its products, as in the case of Corinth, became in good part another perquisite of Rome and well-to-do Romans.[272]

The destruction of Corinth, an act with even less 'political' justification, shows at least that 146 was a hard year for commercial cities. An intriguing fact perhaps takes us further: when the consuls of 149 told the Carthaginians that they must move their city ten miles inland, they were apparently alluding to Plato's advice that if a city was to avoid being full of trade and the moral consequences of trade, it must be 80 stades (10 miles) from the sea.[273] In any case the Senate aimed either to provoke a war, the most desirable result, or, the next best thing, to destroy the city's trade by sea. This was an effective way of ruining Carthage, but it may also have had some positive promise for large Italian landowners, including Roman senators and their non-senatorial friends. Before 149 Carthage probably exported grain and other farm products over a wide area, and Numidian external trade was still dominated by Carthaginians.

[270] Among older historians Mommsen 1921–3, II.23: (A 26), and De Sanctis 1907–64, IV.3, 21–2: (A 14), attributed some importance to this factor.

[271] 75.351. For emphasis on booty later in his account see 115–16, 127.609, 133.631.

[272] Harris 1979, 95 n. 2: (A 21).

[273] Plat. *Leg.* 704b–705b, brought into the discussion by Meltzer 1891: (C 35).

On the fiscal side, payments to Rome were to cease in 152. After 146, by contrast, Rome drew provincial taxation from Carthaginian territory and also revenue from *ager publicus*, some of which naturally passed before long into the hands of wealthy Romans. Meanwhile a certain vacuum in long-distance trade is likely to have been filled by Romans and Italians, who within a few years were also established in great numbers in Numidia. In short, many forms of economic advantage came with the political advantage. That Roman writers have nothing to say about this aspect of the matter in the context of the 150s follows naturally enough from their source material and their presuppositions.

The expedition which the consuls of 149 took to North Africa was quite exceptionally large. There is no reason to reject Appian's statement that they took 80,000 infantry and 4,000 cavalry,[274] figures which imply a force of eight legions with a normal complement of allied troops. Some scholars have preferred to suppose that the consuls took the normal force of two legions each,[275] but they then have to explain that many of Appian's 'infantry' were really sailors or marines. Yet the number of warships used was relatively small – since there was no opposing navy to speak of – namely 50 quinqueremes and 100 'half-ships' (*hemioliai*, with one-and-a-half banks of oars). Even if Appian did mistakenly include the crews of these ships in the 'infantry', that would hardly account for many more than 25,000 men (he cannot have included the crews of the miscellaneous non-military vessels which also participated in the crossing). The 84,000 could have been made up of eight citizen legions of 5,000 men, each with 500 (instead of the usual 300) cavalry, and 40,000 allies. Presumably the size of this force resulted both from awareness that Carthaginian territory contained a large population and from the Senate's willingness to accommodate the legitimate ambitions of an exceptionally large number of men.

No hindsight is needed to see that the war had to end in Carthaginian defeat; the military resources available to Carthage had been too slight even before the forced disarmament, and internal political tensions were too strong. It is true that the city itself was effectively fortified, [276] and that it was a rare event in antiquity for first-rate fortifications to be overwhelmed by frontal assault. An elaborate effort was going to be necessary. But even the best fortifications had no chance against a determined Roman army, and the city's size brought a further disadvantage – its defence required a large force, which in turn could only be fed if a large hinterland was also defended.

---

[274] 75.351.
[275] De Sanctis 1907–64, IV.3, 34 n. 55: (A 14); Brunt 1971, 684: (H 82).
[276] The fortifications are described in App. 95–96. For the archaeological evidence see Duval 1950: (B 164); Reyniers 1966: (C 46).

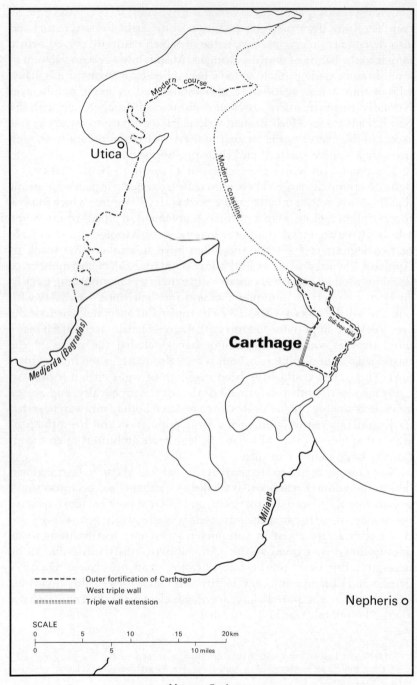

Utica

Medjerda (Bagradas)

Carthage

Sidi-bou-Saïd

Miliane

Nepheris o

- - - - - Outer fortification of Carthage
========= West triple wall
========= Triple wall extension

SCALE

| 0 | 5 | 10 | 15 | 20km |

| 0 | 5 | 10 miles |

Map 10. Carthage.

In reaction to Rome's final demand the Carthaginian senate declared war, freed the slaves, established a reconciliation with the Hasdrubal who had recently been among the generals condemned to death (see above p. 151), and gave him official command of the forces outside the city (where he already had 20,000 men). Carthage then set about re-arming as quickly as possible. The consuls, L. Marcius Censorinus (in command of the fleet) and M'. Manilius (infantry), went into action in a dilatory fashion, at least in part because of the supply difficulties of their monstrous expedition.[277] Though Censorinus' forces succeeded in breaching the city wall, the Romans made no decisive headway, and indeed lost a good part of their fleet to Carthaginian fireboats. In the last part of the year, Censorinus having returned to Rome for the elections, Manilius decided to attack Hasdrubal's army at Nepheris, a site about twenty miles south-east of Tunis. The logic of this must have been that Manilius wanted to supply his army from Carthaginian territory during the winter, and could not expect to do so without defeating Hasdrubal. Appian's narrative is dominated by hero-worship of Scipio Aemilianus, who was serving as a military tribune under Manilius, so that it is hard to judge the result of this manoeuvre, but in any case the Romans suffered serious casualties and Hasdrubal was not dislodged. A similar attempt in the winter (149/8) also failed. In fact Polybius' glorification of Scipio resulted in a unanimous ancient tradition to the effect that the Romans achieved nothing of consequence before he arrived as consul in 147. The truth was that Manilius did important work during 148 in extending Roman control in the surrounding territory.[278] Though according to Appian Carthaginian morale improved as time passed without a decisive Roman victory,[279] tension within the city was so acute that when the city commander, whose name was also Hasdrubal, was accused in the senate of treachery he was immediately slaughtered.

The first Roman commander to force his way into Carthage itself was L. Hostilius Mancinus, a legate under the consul of 148, L. Calpurnius Piso Caesoninus; this must have been early in 147, shortly before Scipio's return to Africa. Mancinus established a bridgehead somewhere in the Megara, that is on the promontory of Sidi-bou-Said in the north part of the city.[280] It appears, however, that this gain had to be surrendered. In any case Scipio now succeeded in instituting a really thorough blockade of the city, with appalling consequences among the defenders. During 147 the latter managed to construct and put into action a fleet of more than negligible size.[281] Much more important, however, was the Roman

---

[277] Cf. App. 94.446. Of the cities which joined Rome, only Utica was close.
[278] Liv. *Per.* L end; Oros. iv.22.8; Zon. ix.27.   [279] App. 111.522.
[280] Zon. ix.29; cf. Plin. *HN* xxxv.23; App. 112–113.
[281] Fifty triremes plus small boats: App. 121.575–576. Strabo (xvii.833) exaggerates again.

capture of Nepheris at the start of the winter, with large Carthaginian casualties; this allowed them to bring the rest of the countryside under control.

The end was near. Hasdrubal, who had previously taken over the city command from his murdered namesake, now made an unsuccessful attempt to capitulate.[282] However, it was not until the beginning of the next spring that the final assault began. Scipio's soldiers forced their way into the city from the south and gradually drove the defenders back on the Byrsa and the temple of Eshmoun. Once Scipio himself had arrived at the Byrsa, six days were devoted to burning and destroying the city. With most of it under Roman control, the survivors succeeded in surrendering; Appian gives their number as 50,000.[283] The vast majority of these prisoners-of-war became slaves in the usual way. In spite of the destruction, the city was carefully plundered of portable objects,[284] but Scipio, imitating his father's behaviour after the battle of Pydna, ostentatiously refused a share. Shortly afterwards the remains of the city were effectively destroyed, and finally its site was cursed. The latter action was perhaps not only an exaggerated precaution (some Punic enemies of Rome survived) but also the result of an unconscious realization of the awfulness of what had been done. As for the destruction itself, it had precedents in other captured cities,[285] and was soon followed by that of Corinth; what makes the Carthaginian case stand out, in addition to the size and former power of the city, is the fact that this policy, having been decided in advance, was retained in the period after Carthage had made its original surrender. This was, and remained, unusual behaviour even in the history of Roman warfare.[286]

Carthaginian territory was now annexed as the province 'Africa'.[287] The area in question had of course been much reduced by the Numidians, and Rome seems to have been content with this at first: the sons of Massinissa retained the Great Plains and the Emporia.[288] The procedure followed in the annexation was unusual: it appears that the province was annexed by means of law, under which *decemviri* (ten commissioners)

---

[282] Polyb. xxxviii.7–8; cf. Diod. Sic. xxxii.22; Zon. ix.30; Astin 1967, 72 n. 2: (H 67).

[283] App. 130.622. Florus (1.31.16) gives 36,000, Orosius (iv.23.2–3) 55,000.

[284] To judge not only from general probability, but from the survival of the Carthaginian libraries (Plin. *HN* xviii.22) and from the restitution of objects plundered from Sicily; see Astin 1967, 76: (H 67).

[285] To mention only quite recent cases: Haliartus (171), seventy Epirote towns which had ceased resistance (167).

[286] Cf. Livy xxxvii.32.12: Diod. Sic. xxxii.4.5. However, the towns of Epirus were not at war with Rome, and Piso had destroyed towns in North Africa which had surrendered in 148 (Diod. Sic. xxxii.18; cf. App. 110.519). See further Dahlheim 1968, 16: (H 86).

[287] Cf. App. 135.641; Vell. Pat. ii.38.2.

[288] On the frontier cf. Romanelli 1959, 43–6: (C 48). The area seems to have been somewhat less than 25,000 sq. km. (9,000 sq. miles) and was thus slightly smaller than Sicily.

were appointed,[289] instead of ten *legati* appointed by the Senate. The suspicion must arise that the author of this law was C. Livius Drusus, the consul of 147 (rather than some otherwise unknown tribune of 146).[290] In any case what we seem to be witnessing here is part of a struggle over the economic and other rewards of the conquest, the author of the law desiring to minimize the role of Scipio and his friends; this is scarcely surprising, since Scipio had won the consulship illegally and in the face of bitter opposition.[291]

The commission of ten, in conjunction with Scipio, saw to the destruction of all the towns which had remained loyal to Carthage, and rewarded those which had supported Rome – above all Utica, which received the territory 'from Carthage to Hippo' (that is, to Bizerta). Much of Carthage's own land, however, became Roman *ager publicus*. Finally they imposed a poll-tax on all adults in the province and a tribute (*stipendium*) based on land, with exceptions for the cities which had taken the Roman side.[292] Then Scipio returned to Rome with his army and duly triumphed over the Carthaginians and Hasdrubal.[293]

Rome's annihilation of Carthage and most of its inhabitants was a brutal act – and this would still be true if there were something more than a grain of truth in the apologetics of the ancient and modern writers who have argued that the policy was, or was imagined to be, necessary to Rome's security. But it is important to realize that this brutality differed only in degree from what was normal in Roman warfare.

The war also had the incidental effect of ruining an entire culture. Not of course that everything Punic disappeared, any more than everything Latin would have disappeared if Hannibal had destroyed the city of Rome. The language and even the religion had long later histories.[294] But the high culture of the great city had disappeared. About this culture we admittedly know very little, less perhaps than scholars with an urge to write the history of Carthage have admitted. The political system, however, had been an object of interest and respect, together with very few other barbarian constitutions, to Aristotle, Eratosthenes and

---

[289] Harris 1979, 134 n. 3: (A 21). There were of course only five annexed provinces before this date.

[290] Suggested by Gelzer 1931, 265 n. 9: (c 18); Astin 1967, 74 n. 1 : (H 67). Livius had wanted the African command himself (App. 112.533).

[291] He is also the first known Roman magistrate to have obtained his *provincia* by a vote of the people (App. 112.532), an important precedent.

[292] For these arrangements: App. 135.640–641. There is some uncertainty as to whether the pro-Roman cities other than Utica received land: cf. Romanelli 1959, 46 n. 2: (c 48). The other main source of information is the *lex agraria* of 111 B.C. (*FIRA* I, no. 8 = *Remains of Old Latin* (ed. Warmington) IV, pp. 370–437), lines 43–96. See further Haywood in *ESAR* IV.3–5.

[293] Only 4,370 lb of silver were carried in the triumph: Plin. *HN* XXXIII.141; cf. Astin 1967, 342: (H 67); but there was plenty of other booty (App. 135.642).

[294] See especially Millar 1968: (c 38); Bénabou 1976: (c 4). For Punic after 146 see Röllig 1980: (c 47).

Polybius.[295] Hellenization had had significant effects, increasingly perhaps in the last century of the city's existence, with the strange result that a certain Hasdrubal became a philosopher *à la grecque*, moved to Athens about 163/2, studied with Carneades and in 127/6, under the name of Cleitomachus, became head of the Academy. While still at Carthage, he had taught philosophy,[296] an activity which no well-bred Roman could or would have undertaken at this date. Beyond this, there is not a great deal to recount[297] about the high culture which produced libraries worth giving to the Numidian princes. It was murdered, with very little regret, by the Romans.*

[295] See Arist. *Pol.* 11.1272b; Strabo 1.66 (Eratosthenes); Polyb. vi.51.

[296] Diog. Laert. iv.67. See Von Arnim, *PW* 'Kleitomachus (1)', 656–9. Politically, he went over to the Romans: Momigliano, 1975, 5: (1 27).

[297] For other items see Momigliano, *op. cit.* 5–6.

* This chapter was substantially completed in 1981.

CHAPTER 6

ROMAN GOVERNMENT AND POLITICS, 200–134 B.C.[1]

A. E. ASTIN

I. THE CONSTITUTIONAL SETTING

The constitutional arrangements with which Rome emerged from the Second Punic War differed scarcely at all in form from those with which she had embarked upon that great struggle. Their essence remained the threefold structure of magistrates, Senate, and assemblies of the citizen body, the structure which the Greek observer Polybius was shortly to characterize as a 'mixed' constitution.[2] Of the magistrates the most senior and powerful were the two consuls. Invested with *imperium*, consuls could be placed in command of armies; they could exercise jurisdiction; they could issue instructions, particular or general, in the form of edicts, and could employ coercion and punishment to enforce their will. They could propose legislation to the assemblies; one of them conducted most of the meetings at which magistrates, including their own successors, were elected; and when one or both were in Rome it was normally a consul who presided over the deliberations of the Senate and gave effect to its most important decisions. On the other hand they were elected officials, the term of their office was limited to one year, early re-election was not permitted, and in various directions their freedom of action was restricted by the powers and authority of other bodies.

All magistrates were elected by the citizen body – consuls, praetors and censors in the *comitia centuriata* (the assembly organized into 193 voting-units known as centuries), the remainder in the *comitia tributa* or the almost identical *concilium plebis* (in which the voting units were the

---

[1] The purpose of this chapter is to examine the nature of Roman politics in the period and certain changes which were taking place. It is not a comprehensive survey of those internal events which could be termed political. The principal source is Livy, whose account of events to 167 survives almost intact; thereafter epitomes provide a basic framework. Other evidence, frequently anecdotal and fragmentary, comes from many authors but especially Cicero, Plutarch, Gellius and Appian; fragments of speeches, of which Cato's are the most important, in *ORF*[4]. For the *lex Voconia*, which is not discussed here, see Astin 1978, 113–18: (H 68).

[2] For constitutional matters Polybius' analysis in the sixth book of his *Histories* is fundamental. Comprehensive modern studies are rare: Mommsen 1887–8: (A 25) remains definitive; De Martino 1958–67: (A 13) is valuable but at times controversial; in English Greenidge 1901: (H 10) is still a useful shorter treatment.

thirty-five tribes, in one of which every Roman citizen was registered).³ Declarations of war and ratification of treaties were matters for the approval of the *comitia centuriata*; legislation could be enacted only by vote of the citizen body, the *populus*, usually in the more convenient procedure of the tribal assembly; and both forms of assembly – but usually the tribal – might be used for major judicial hearings, especially when it was proposed to inflict a penalty on a major public figure. Although the citizen body was dependent upon the initiative of a magistrate to convene an assembly and to lay before it proposals for acceptance or rejection (but not amendment), and although the assembly as such did not deliberate, it did not vote without hearing argument. A voting assembly was normally preceded by a meeting (*contio*), summoned by a magistrate who invited speakers to address it; and it is clear that convention expected him to bring forward speakers both for and against whatever was being proposed.

Yet it was by no means the entire citizen body which listened to argument and cast its votes, nor by any means a representative portion of it. Organization and order would surely have broken down, the voting procedures have been made unworkable if the greater part of the adult male citizens had attended simultaneously to cast their votes in an assembly. Even at the end of the Hannibalic War they numbered at least 140,000, and probably more than 240,000; by 189/8 the recovery in population had taken them permanently beyond the quarter-million mark.⁴ Probably lack of interest kept many away, distance and cost many others, inhibiting the poor and leaving greater opportunity to the more prosperous. Furthermore, in addition to the skewing of actual composition which was produced by social factors, the structures of the assemblies themselves prevented participation on an equal basis, even though every Roman citizen was entitled to vote. In the *comitia centuriata* the division of citizens into several classes according to the value of their property, the allocation of a larger proportion of the voting-units to the wealthier classes, and a procedure which took the votes of the 'highest' centuries first and stopped the counting when a majority had been reached, ensured that the wealthy exercised a disproportionate influence and that *de facto* the poorest groups were virtually disfranchised. The disparities were much less marked in the tribal assemblies, where wealth was not a formal consideration, but even here the likelihood that many of

³ The total number of regular magistrates remained small, as follows: consuls, 2; praetors, 4, soon to be increased to 6; curule aediles, 2; plebeian aediles, 2; quaestors, at least 8 (but some believe the number had already been or was soon to be increased, perhaps to 12); tribunes of the plebs, 10. There were also military tribunes, both elected and nominated, and a few minor magistrates. A pair of censors was elected every five years and held office for eighteen months. For elections and assemblies see esp. Taylor 1960 and 1966: (H 29 and 30); Staveley 1966: (H 27).
⁴ Brunt 1971, esp. 13–14 and 61–74: (H 82).

the poorer inhabitants of Rome itself were confined to the four 'urban' tribes probably meant that in practice a disproportionate number of the individual votes cast in rural tribes came from wealthier members.

The only formal body suitably structured for debate and deliberation was the Senate, the three hundred members of which included most of the men who had held magistracies. It was so structured because in principle it was largely an advisory body (though not exclusively so since it controlled expenditure from the state treasury, the *aerarium*).[5] The fundamentally advisory nature of most of its resolutions is reflected in the language in which its decrees (*senatus consulta*) were cast, carefully avoiding direct commands. Nevertheless in many fields the Senate was in practice taking the effective decisions for the state: that is how the sources present it, and there is little doubt that often it thought of itself as doing this and that it was so thought of by others. The Senate decided what armies should be levied and where they should be sent; it authorized provisions, supplies and funds; it instructed magistrates about action to be taken in a variety of matters; it appointed envoys to foreign powers; and it received and responded to the embassies which came to Rome in ever-increasing numbers. Its advice on legislation and on decisions about war and peace, about treaties, and about other matters where the formal decision lay with an assembly, was not always the effective decision to the same extent as in other matters; for the necessary votes in the assembly had to be obtained, and furthermore it was possible in principle, though unusual in practice, for a proposal to be placed before an assembly without prior consultation of the Senate. Nevertheless it is clear that, at least in the early decades of the second century, the Senate was normally consulted and its recommendation accepted. Only once is a recommendation for war reported to have been rejected. That was the proposal to declare war on Macedonia in the spring of 200, immediately after the conclusion of the Hannibalic War; and even then the initial rejection was soon reversed.[6]

Polybius, his attention caught by the distribution of functions between magistrates, Senate and assemblies, interpreted Rome as an example of a 'mixed' constitution, combining elements of monarchy, aristocracy and democracy in a constitutional balance of which the stability was maintained over a long period by the restraints which these elements exercised over each other. Yet he too saw that in the Roman governmental system of this period the role of the Senate was central, that his aristocratic element predominated. In his discussion of how the constitutional balance would eventually collapse, he predicted that the people (the *demos*) 'will no longer be willing to obey or even to be the equal of the leading men'.[7]

---

[5] Polyb. vi.13 and 15–17.   [6] Livy xxxi.6.3–8.1.   [7] Polyb. vi.57.8.

It would be misleading to suggest that the Senate was 'the government' of Rome in this period – for Rome had no 'government' in the modern sense, but rather a governmental system. Nor is it to be forgotten that the Senate had no role in the electoral process, or that many of its decisions, particularly concerning extra-Italian matters, were effectively shaped by the actions and the recommendations of Roman commanders and envoys. Nevertheless in the constitutional structure it was the body which dominated a large part of the major decision-making of the governmental process.

Two further groups of officials are relevant to the manner in which these constitutional arrangements operated. There were first the ten tribunes of the plebs, elected each year in the *concilium plebis*. These could intervene to protect a citizen against a magistrate, indeed they could veto almost any act of public business in Rome; they could impose penalties, often leading to judicial hearings before the assembly of the plebs, and they could introduce legislation to that assembly. The actual exercise of these independent and potentially far-reaching powers was kept in check by various forms of social and political pressure, and by the ability to use one tribune's veto against another's proposals. In practice almost all the known tribunician legislation of the first half of the second century seems to have had the approval of the Senate, and in some cases the tribunes were virtually agents for that body; and sometimes tribunes could be persuaded or pressured into withdrawing a veto with nothing achieved. Nevertheless, none of their powers was merely notional; all were in use in the years covered by this chapter, and their existence was an important element in the constitutional and political scene.

The other officials who must be mentioned here are the censors. These were peculiar among Roman magistrates in their term of office (eighteen months instead of the normal twelve) and in their discontinuity – for pairs of censors were elected only at intervals, which at this time had been stabilized at five years. Originally established to conduct the census and register the citizens by their tribes and centuries, they had acquired important additional responsibilities which included making up the rolls of the senatorial and equestrian orders (with the power to omit existing members whom they judged unsuitable), and arranging numerous public contracts. In a state with few public servants, the range of such contracts was great, including recurrent contracts for state services, the lease of public lands and properties, the collection of rents and some taxes, and non-recurrent contracts for repairs to public properties and the construction of new buildings. Furthermore the censors' exercise of these various powers was largely unfettered, for, except that the repair and construction projects required the allocation of funds by the Senate, most of their decisions were subject neither to approval nor to appeal.[8]

As was mentioned at the beginning, these constitutional arrangements were in form essentially those with which Rome had entered the Second Punic War. Unorthodox arrangements necessitated by the emergencies of the war years were brought to an end. Particularly striking is the strict observance of the rule which required an interval of ten years between tenures of the same magistracy; and no further private individual was invested with *imperium* without election to praetorship or consulship. Yet there may also have been some force at work deeper than the understandable desire to revert to pre-emergency arrangements. Despite the continuity of form there were changes in practice, not all of which were obvious responses to the requirements of expanding empire. With obvious hesitation the number of praetors was increased, eventually settling at six each year;[9] and the recent practice of extending a magistrate's authority for a year, or even two, as a promagistrate was used frequently in Spain and soon emerged as the normal device for meeting a need elsewhere for more commanders than were available as magistrates. But also no more dictators were appointed – perhaps another reflection of a conscious pursuit of system and order. As will be seen later, the convention that certain magistracies should be held in a fixed sequence and with an interval of two years between election to each was soon to be reinforced by law, and before long other requirements were added. Symptoms such as these reflect not merely constitutional tidiness but current political attitudes; they raise questions about the nature of political activity and its relationship to constitutional forms at this period in Roman history.

II. THE NATURE OF ROMAN POLITICS

The nature of political life is a topic important for the understanding of any state; unfortunately, in the case of the Roman Republic it is also a matter of considerable controversy, not least in respect of the years with which this chapter is concerned. The sources and the distribution of power, as exercised both through and alongside the constitutional organs of the state, the issues over which the participants in political life divided and disputed, the coherence and continuity, indeed the very *raison d'être* of such groupings as they formed, and the extent to which all these matters may have been related to the concerns of the poor or to

[8] Special studies include Suolahti 1963: (H 28), Pieri 1968: (H 18) and Nicolet 1980: (H 51). The present writer has further studies in preparation.

[9] Livy XXXII.27.6 (6 in 198), XL.44.2 (4 and 6 in alternate years under the *lex Baebia* of 180); reversion to 6 every year not recorded but effected by 173, probably by 175.

other potential sources of tension in Roman society: all these have been much debated, not without progress but certainly without achieving a clear and generally accepted consensus.

In the later nineteenth century and the early decades of the twentieth it was widely assumed that the essence of political life in the middle and later Roman Republic was a contest between advocates of change and defenders of the *status quo*, mainly in respect of the location of power and the dominating authority of the Senate. Political figures, although recognized to have belonged mostly to established families and not to have been organized into political parties in the modern sense, nevertheless were thought to have been associated loosely in two broad groupings which were respectively conservative and reformist in their outlook and inclinations. This kind of interpretation, however, was inadequately supported by positive evidence (which might have been expected to be plentiful) and often relied on an uncritical acceptance of political language at face-value, with insufficient sensitivity to its nuances and shifting shades of meaning or to the overtones of polemic and propaganda. Eventually a radically different analysis was put forward and has exerted a strong influence on virtually all subsequent discussion.[10]

Attention was directed to the considerable degree of family continuity among those who held high office and were prominent in public life. Examination of the lists of known magistrates, combined with some remarks by Cicero and others, confirms that in the middle and late Republic it was unusual to win election to the consulship unless one's father had been at least a senator, and that a substantial proportion of consuls were descendants of former consuls or praetors. Moreover, a few families held a clearly disproportionate number of consulships, in some cases sustaining the achievement over many generations. The conclusion was drawn that there were factors at work which enabled members of a small number of families to sustain political prominence for long periods and to exercise exceptional influence.

The source of that influence was identified as lying not in any special legal privilege but in the elaborate network of social relationships, based on personal relationships of many kinds, which permeated Roman society. It was a society in which the lesser constantly looked to the more powerful for assistance and protection (not least in legal matters), a society in which there was a strong sense of the obligation created by the receipt of favour, both between equals (between whom *amicitia*, 'friendship', might mean anything from personal affection to an essentially political relationship) and between unequals, such as patron and client –

[10] Gelzer 1912, trans. Seager 1969: (H 8 and 9).

to say nothing of numerous other relationships, such as those between landowner and tenant or creditor and debtor. Thus the means existed to influence, even to determine numerous votes – which for long were cast openly and orally – to mobilize voters in support of oneself or a friend or an ally.[11] Furthermore, those who enjoyed most success in the exploitation of such means could often transmit power to their descendants, since these might inherit both their wealth and *de facto* the patronage of their *clientelae*.

This transmission of social and political power was assisted by the concept of *nobilitas*, which, whatever its precise content, is generally recognized to have had a hereditary aspect. The term, it was argued in the new analysis, was not a loose reference to high standing but indicated descent from a former consul. Thus a *nobilis* enjoyed a defined and distinctive status (but a social status, with no recognition in law) which itself conferred prestige and was a considerable electoral asset. Also, it has been suggested, those who possessed that status had an incentive to maintain its social and political value by restricting the rise of new men to the consulship. Restricting, not preventing; for there was always some upward movement of new men who were the first in their families to attain the consulship, though probably only a very few of them had been also the first in their families to become senators.

In such a context politics was primarily the expression of personal competition in which each sought to surpass others in the acquisition of honour and power for himself and his family. The means to that honour and power were the tenure of high public office, the established status and lasting prestige which resulted from such tenure, and the enhanced role in the deliberations of the Senate which was open to those who achieved such status; and the means to attain such office – and for some families the means to the near-hereditary enjoyment of power – lay, it was argued, in the development and exploitation of a network of social relationships through which votes could be controlled.

The idea that a major source of political power was a network of social connections which tended to be passed from one generation of a powerful family to the next prompted a further influential hypothesis.[12] Attention was drawn to a number of instances in which members of two or

---

[11] The censors of 179 altered the method of tribal registration and those of 169 restricted the registration of ex-slaves to one tribe (Livy XL.51.9, XLV.15.1–7). It is often assumed that in both cases the motives were political, and especially that the change in 169 was an attempt to limit the influence which former owners could derive from their ability to direct the votes of their freedmen. However, since the change made in 179 is reported very briefly and imprecisely, with no mention of controversy, it is possible that it was essentially technical and administrative. The censors of 169 did disagree about their action, but their difference was resolved by sortition and seems to have provoked neither tribunician intervention nor public outcry; it is conceivable therefore that they were more concerned with social esteem than political manipulation.

[12] Münzer 1920: (H 15); Scullard 1973: (H 54).

more families were clearly associated with each other in public life in more than one generation; and to the instances which are unmistakable can be added others which are probable. An explanation was sought in the importance of kinship as a social connection, combined with the suggestion that *amicitia*, in the sense of political 'friendship' or alliance between persons of high status, was also a relationship which was often transmitted from one generation to the next. The conclusion was drawn that leading families (i.e. not only individual members of them) formed groups or 'factions' which cohered closely, often for several generations. Families so associated would support each other and exploit their social resources to their mutual benefit in competition with other, rival groups. Efforts have been made to identify such groups of families, to detect symptoms of their rivalries, and to reconstruct the ebb and flow of their political fortunes, along with occasional dissolutions and regroupings. But whatever the details, the supposition that political groupings were primarily of families rather than of individuals and that they often endured for generations would make it even more difficult to avoid the conclusion that, whatever short-term disagreements arose about particular decisions of state, the underlying source of continuing political conflict was to be found in the competition for office, honour and influential status, not in policy or programme, or in ideology or philosophy. For such groupings are unlikely to have correlated closely with divisions of the latter kind, whereas it is especially in electoral competition that they could have expected to benefit from the exploitation of social allegiances to muster support for each other.

Interpretations along these lines have provoked a rash of criticisms, some of them well founded.[13] Insecure and sometimes grossly inadequate criteria have all too often been used in attempts to identify political alliances. The term '*nobilitas*' may have been misunderstood in some modern studies, or its connotation may have changed during the last century of the Republic.[14] Insufficient allowance has been made for the range of relationships which could be described as '*amicitia*'.[15] There is a suspicious lack of political vocabulary which can be related to the concept of family-based factionalism. The extent to which the consulship was dominated by 'consular' families has been overstated, for in every generation there were several consuls who were not the direct descendants of consuls, and more with no consular forebear for several generations past. Similarly there were only a few families which supplied one or more consuls for a number of generations in succession, and the notion that in certain families all male children were virtually 'born to the

---

13 Astin 1968: (H 3); Broughton 1972: (H 4); and the studies indicated in the next six notes.
14 Afzelius 1945: (H 1); Brunt 1982: (H 6).   15 Brunt 1965: (H 5).

consulship' overstates the advantage they enjoyed.[16] Likewise the proportion of votes in the assemblies which could be controlled by social
pressure and explicit direction has often been exaggerated, giving the
impression that exceptions were insignificant; whereas it is clear that the
effectiveness of control varied, down to the point where many voters had
to be swayed by canvassing, by argument, by emotive rhetoric, by
displays of liberality, or by outright bribery; and that notwithstanding all
these there were some instances in which the decisive factor was the
independent judgement of individual voters regarding the qualities of
the candidates.[17] Furthermore, among those who were active in politics
the nexus of personal and kinship relationships was certainly not so
straightforward that each individual could be located unambiguously in
a self-contained faction, with no ties or obligations to anyone outside it.
On the contrary, in the relatively small social group from which the
Roman senators were drawn relationships must always have been both
complex and shifting, fraught with cross-ties and conflicting
obligations.[18] Finally, on a different level of consideration, to some
historians, even to some who have embraced the concept of family
groupings, it has seemed *a priori* implausible to identify aristocratic
competitiveness as the overriding determinant of political division, to
suppose that lasting divisions bore no substantial relationship to great
issues of policy implicit in the expansion of empire; or alternatively, to
suppose that they were not shaped in considerable measure by the social
and economic contrasts of Roman society.[19]

   These criticisms warn against thinking of Roman politics in terms
which are unduly rigid and schematic, or are too preoccupied with the
operation of a single factor. In particular political co-operation – and
rivalry – between families, and even between individuals, was subject to
more variation, to greater fluidity and complexity than many discussions
of factional politics have allowed. Nevertheless the criticisms do not
refute the fundamental contentions that aristocratic ambition and competitiveness were major characteristics of political life, and that the
patronage system and the social nexus based on kinship and mutual
obligation were major sources of political power and important contributors to the restraint (though not the nullification) of the popular
elements in the constitutional structure. Nor do they dispose of some
striking features which seem best explained by this kind of analysis. First,
a state in which legislation could be effected only by popular vote in
popular assemblies, to which popularly elected officials had direct access,
was nevertheless predominantly an oligarchy in which most major

---

[16] Hopkins (with Burton) 1983, ch. 2: (H 49).
[17] Astin 1967, esp. 28–9 and 339: (H 67); Millar 1984: (H 14).
[18] Astin 1967, esp. 80: (H 67).   [19] Finley 1983, *passim*: (H 7).

decisions were taken, without answerability to an electorate, by a Senate of some three hundred men, or by officials who for the most part were responsible to the authority of that Senate. Second, though at times the continuity and dominance of 'consular' families has been overstated, it remains an astonishing fact that although officials were elected in popular assemblies, and although any citizen qualified by age and military service was entitled to seek the offices in progression (at least if he had the equestrian census qualification), still in the last two centuries of the Republic about two-fifths of those who reached the consulship were sons of former consuls, and more than half were sons or grandsons; approximately one-third of the consuls had one or more sons who were elected to the consulship; and among the families represented in the consular lists it is not denied that there were a few who had success manifestly disproportionate to their number.[20] Third, despite the theoretically powerful popular institutions of the Republic, in the early second century there is a singular lack of evidence for the shaping of politics by a conflict of programmes or by economic and social disparities, or for particular measures and controversies having roots in such broadly-based divisions (though the seeming absence of serious economic discontent in these years was related to other factors which will be examined in a later section of this chapter). Such features demonstrate that, although in occasional situations of high enthusiasm the personal judgement of voters could be decisive, in general voting was strongly influenced – and the political independence of the assemblies was significantly restrained – by forces considerably greater than those of the purely constitutional biases and limitations, forces which were created by taking advantage of an elaborate network of social relationships.

The combination of oligarchic predominance and popular electoral institutions had a further consequence which tended both to reinforce the pattern as a whole and to create ample scope for political competition conceived in personal terms. For this combination tended to divorce electoral contests, especially for the magistracies in the strict sense but also for the tribunate of the plebs, from most major decisions of state. The latter were largely in the hands of the Senate; and since there were approximately three hundred senators and membership was essentially for life, not only was their record not subjected to the test of re-election but the composition of the Senate could not be affected more than marginally by the outcome of any election. Even a presiding consul was able to exert only a very limited influence on the topics and outcome of senatorial deliberation. A candidate offering himself for election could dwell upon his personal merits and qualifications, could undertake to

[20] Hopkins (with Burton) 1983, ch. 2, esp. 55–60: (H 49).

perform his duties effectively, could point to his record of liberality and promise to subsidize public entertainments. If he was seeking the praetorship or consulship he was especially likely to commend himself as experienced and competent in warfare, and as the candidate most fitted to command an army and to be entrusted with a campaign. But he had little incentive to offer policy or programme, for election even to the consulship did not give him the power to deliver upon such promises.[21]

It is not surprising, therefore, that political activity was not uniform in kind and that it took place at more than one level. Aristocratic personal competition was a major component, manifested in such displays as triumphs, dedicatory temples and games, and in elaborate funeral rituals; and it was given its major political expression in contention for magistracies. In that contention, played out in the electoral context of the assemblies, much could be achieved through the active support of friends, kin, family, dependants, and all who could be influenced, directly and indirectly, through the chain of obligation. Since success was deemed to bring added distinction to the family as well as to the individual – exemplified by the *ius imaginum,* by which families kept and on occasion displayed in public 'portraits' of ancestors who had held curule office[22] – this reinforced the natural tendency for close kin to aid each other and for the immediate family to operate as a unit in electoral situations.

These were not the only assets needed. A scion even of one of the greatest consular families required a reasonable measure of talent and early achievement if, in his quest for high office, he was to hope for sufficient family and social support, for recommendation by distinguished senators, and for acceptance by the voters as an adequate candidate. For the quest was highly competitive, and the competition was for more than mere triumph over rivals, or for getting ahead in a race for grandiose titles and symbolic honours. Magistrates exercised considerable power in matters of public importance (without support by professional civil servants) for a full year. In the case of the senior magistrates that power was very great indeed. It might have to be applied in a wide range of fields, and it frequently involved command of a Roman army in active campaigning – which in the strongly militaristic ethos of Roman society was a potent source of individual glory and prestige and hence was itself the object of considerable ambition. The electoral process did not guarantee the success of the most competent; for, errors of electoral judgement apart, competence did not suffice, but neither did social connections and distinguished ancestry. Yet still, when personal

---

[21] Astin, 1968: (H 3).
[22] Polyb. VI.53.4–8; Walbank 1957–79, 1.738–9: (B 38); Mommsen 1887–8, 1.442–9: (A 25). The phrase *ius imaginum,* though convenient, does not itself have ancient authority.

qualities and competence are added to the considerable complex of factors which affected electoral struggles, it serves only to reinforce the point that most such contests were essentially personal in character.

On the other hand there were also decisions to be taken about the internal and external affairs of Rome. Sometimes a citizen assembly did have a real decision-taking role in these, but much more often the effective decision lay with the Senate, which alone was a deliberative body. A major characteristic of its decisions, however, was pragmatism; of competing political theories or long-term social programmes there is no sign. In particular all internal government was in a broad sense conservative, seeking to preserve and maintain, to ensure order, to react to problems as they arose but not to initiate unprompted change in social or political organization. Consequently, although individuals with similar temperaments and preconceptions may often have found themselves aligned for or against a particular proposal, and, although some junior senators may have seen advantage for themselves in giving regular support to some powerful leader and patron, there was no incentive to form semi-permanent groupings committed to political programmes, nor was there a consistent basis upon which to do so.

It is no cause for surprise that from time to time the politics of personal competition and aristocratic rivalry intruded into these pragmatic deliberations, became blurred with debates unshaped by 'party' affiliation, and sometimes perhaps swayed the Senate's judgement. The political participants, after all, were the same and are unlikely to have achieved or even attempted a total compartmentalization of their motives. Yet fundamentally senatorial deliberation was a different kind of political activity from the selection of annual officials; it was a process for resolving a different kind of conflict and reaching different types of decision. Given its essentially distinct institutional setting and the absence of conflicting ideologies there was little reason why divisions among senators about particular issues should be founded upon permanent groupings or why they should be identified with those divisions which sprang from rival ambitions and found their essential expression in electoral contests.

III. OLIGARCHIC STABILITY

(a) The politics of competition

The fearful crises and strategic necessities of the Second Punic War caused a few talented individuals upon whom Rome placed exceptional reliance to be appointed to unusual terms of office and to achieve extraordinary fame. There had been Q. Fabius Maximus and M. Claudius

Marcellus, with their recurring consulships and (in Claudius' case) proconsulships; and later there was P. Cornelius Scipio, conqueror of Carthaginian Spain and victor at Zama.[23] Scipio had gone to Spain in 210 with a special grant of *imperium*, even though he held no magistracy. On his return in 206 he was elected to the consulship of 205, and thereafter as consul and proconsul he commanded Roman armies until he brought the war to an end in 201. For almost ten years, virtually without interruption, he had been invested with *imperium*. Flamboyant, the centre of adulation, still only in his mid-thirties, ambition not yet slaked, he re-entered Rome in a magnificent triumph, parading his achievement even in the very name he assumed: Africanus. It is small wonder that when he sought the censorship in 199 he was elected over many distinguished competitors.[24]

But those defeated competitors are significant. In an oligarchic system in which men competed for brief tenure of formal power, in which great value was placed upon military glory and high status, and in which personal fame could magnify political power, Scipio had drawn uncomfortably far ahead in all of these. It is a reasonable guess that many senators were resentful and that some were disposed to co-operate to reduce his influence, though modern attempts to find the reflection of such a struggle in the identities of those elected to high office depend on much conjecture. But whether or not it happened in conscious reaction to Scipio, there are unmistakable signs of a collective senatorial concern to prevent further instances of early and spectacular advancement, and of extraordinary and lengthy exercise of magisterial power – a concern to contain the careers of even the most able and ambitious within a limiting framework. That the senators of this time feared usurpation and monarchy is improbable, but they almost certainly resented and distrusted pre-eminence so marked that it threatened to restrict opportunities for others and to distort the conventional pattern of competition for office and power. Rules suspended during the earlier part of the Punic war had already been reinstated, namely a prohibition upon election to one curule office while holding another, and another upon holding any one magistracy twice within ten years.[25] The latter rule made second consulships rare, long before they were prohibited altogether in or soon after 152.[26] But it is probable that what actually precipitated the first new rules was the spectacular rise of yet another brilliant individual.

Titus Quinctius Flamininus had already distinguished himself in junior appointments, but when he put himself forward for the consulship of 198 he was still only about thirty years of age and had held neither the curule aedileship nor the praetorship. Two tribunes who threatened to

[23] Scullard 1970 and 1973: (H 77 and 54).   [24] Livy XXXII.7.2.
[25] Inferred from the lists; cf. *MRR* for these years; Astin 1958, 19 n. 6: (H 2).
[26] Astin 1967, 39: (H 67).

block his candidature because he had held neither of these offices gave way when the Senate affirmed that the *populus*, the citizen body, should be free to elect anyone who was legally eligible.[27] Nevertheless new restrictions on eligibility for office followed quickly, and in the general field of appointments some changes in practice can be discerned – all probably effected without controversy, though by no means all were related directly to Flamininus' case. Prior tenure of the praetorship became a required qualification for those who sought the consulship, almost certainly with effect from 197, since that year marked the end of a series of consuls who had not held the praetorship.[28] At the same time the number of praetors was increased to six.[29] The purpose must have been to provide elected magistrates to govern the two additional provinces which had been acquired in Spain; but the converse of this was that it removed the need to confer promagisterial authority on private individuals, a practice which now ceased. Furthermore the increase had the effect of enlarging the pool of ex-praetors just at the moment when the choice of consuls was restricted by law to the members of that pool. From 196 plebeian aediles were brought into line with their curule counterparts by no longer being allowed to proceed to the praetorship without an interval of at least one year.[30] It is noteworthy too, though it cannot have been the subject of a law, that emergencies and special situations were never again met by the appointment of a dictator (until Sulla's unorthodox exploitation of the office); the dictator of 202 was the last.

A new burst of similar legislation began in 181, when the *lex Baebia* attempted to reduce the number of praetors by providing for four and six in alternate years; but this cumbersome arrangement was soon superseded or repealed and the number reverted to six.[31] Meanwhile, in 180, a tribune named L. Villius carried the *lex Villia annalis*, which prescribed minimum ages for the curule aedileship, praetorship and consulship. Moreover at this time, and almost certainly by this same law, it was made a requirement that there be an interval of at least two years between entrance upon successive curule magistracies.[32] Finally, nearly thirty years later still, there came the restriction which prohibited second consulships altogether; the circumstances in which this was done will be described in a later section of this chapter.

These restraints and limitations, so far from being designed to impose a collective uniformity, were essentially an instinctive attempt – possibly even a conscious attempt – to safeguard opportunities for the exercise of ambition in the contest for position, for glory and for power. That

---

[27] Livy XXXII.7.8–12.   [28] Astin 1958, 19–30, esp. 26–7: (H 2).   [29] Livy XXXII.27.6.
[30] Mommsen 1887–8, 1.531–3: (A 25); Astin 1958, 27: (H 2).
[31] Livy XL.44.2; six every year by 173, probably by 175.
[32] Livy XL.44.1; Astin 1958: (H 2).

contest found expression in many ways beyond immediate electoral competition, and took forms often shaped by the circumstances of the age. Thus almost constant warfare and frequent victories, in the eastern lands, in Spain, in northern Italy and Cisalpine Gaul, encouraged many to claim triumphs; and the number of claims which were disputed creates the suspicion that objectors and claimants alike were as much aware of political considerations as of formal merits.[33] With the triumphs came booty, much of it expended in the name of the commander. Cash donatives to troops increased steadily, creating an expectation which could not be disappointed without political damage. Thus in 179, although a campaign against the Ligurians is said to have yielded almost no money, the troops received three hundred asses each, with the usual bonuses for centurions and cavalry; and in 167 it was with the greatest difficulty that troops disgruntled with their donative (in fact it was probably exceptionally large) were dissuaded from using their votes in an assembly to prevent L. Aemilius Paullus celebrating his triumph over Macedonia.[34]

Booty paid also for temples vowed to deities in the heat of battle, and for games similarly vowed and increasingly lavish in scale. It does not require much cynicism to find a political dimension to the ten days of games which in 186 L. Cornelius Scipio Asiaticus suddenly announced, probably for the first time, that he had vowed four years previously when he was engaged in the war against Antiochus.[35] Lucius was almost certainly looking ahead to his candidature for the censorship of 184. Games were also staged by the aediles, and even before the end of the Hannibalic War these were having a marked effect on the electoral prospects of the organizers.[36] To the income from booty could be added resources derived from empire, often obtained as 'contributions' from provincial and even Italian communities in order to fund ever more lavish spectacles. In consequence the Senate at least twice saw fit to limit the amount of public money which might be spent on victory games. On the second of these occasions, in 179, it also decreed that the commander who was giving the games (Q. Fulvius Flaccus) 'should not invite, compel or accept contributions for these, or do anything contrary to that decree of the Senate which had been made concerning games in the consulship of Lucius Aemilius and Gnaeus Baebius' (=182). Livy commented that 'the Senate had passed this decree because of the lavish expenditure on games by the aedile Ti. Sempronius, which had been

[33] E.g. Livy XXXI.20.1–6 (200), XXXI.47.4–49.1 and 8–11 (200), XXXII.7.4 (199), XXXIII.22.1–23.9 (197), XXXV.8.2–9 (193), XXXVI.39.4–40.10 (191), XXXVIII.43.1–44.6 (187), XXXVIII.44.9–50.3 (187), XXXIX.4.1–5.6 (187), XLV.35.5–39.19 (167).
[34] ESAR 1.127–38 (collected data); Livy XL.59.2 (for 179); Astin 1978, 118–19 (Aemilius Paullus): (H 68).   [35] Livy XXXIX.22.8–10.   [36] Mommsen 1887–8, 1.532: (A 25).

burdensome not only to Italy and the Latin allies but also to the provinces outside Italy'.[37]

There were other manifestations of this competitive expenditure. Funeral ceremonies, always ostentatious in the leading families, might now last three or four days and include theatrical performances, the public distribution of meat, elaborate public banquets, and above all increasingly expensive gladiatorial games.[38] But such expenditure was not confined to funerals. At the start of the electoral contest for the censorship of 189 the favour of the populace inclined very much towards M.' Acilius Glabrio, 'because he had distributed many largesses, by which he had placed a great part of the people under obligation to himself'.[39] Before long bribery was a cause for serious concern. In 181 legislation against bribery was carried on the proposal of the consuls, who acted on the authority of the Senate. In 166 the Senate held a special debate because elections had been marked by much bribery, and there was further legislation in 159. At least one of the laws made bribery a capital offence.[40]

Another area into which the rivalries of political figures intruded was that of prosecutions. The bringing of prosecutions and the presentation of defences against them were important activities among senators in that period. Many of the leading figures are known to have played some part in such proceedings, though probably few of them to anything like the same extent as M. Porcius Cato (*c.* 235–149; *cos.* 195; *cens.* 184). In the course of his long career he was prosecuted (and acquitted) no less than 44 times, not to mention the numerous prosecutions he himself initiated or supported.[41] It would be unreasonable to assume that such judicial clashes were primarily or frequently political in their motivation, or that they were normally expressions of rivalry and personal resentment more than of genuine concern about the substance of the charges. The fragments of Cato's speeches, for example, afford several glimpses of issues and arguments closely akin to undoubtedly genuine concerns which he displayed elsewhere in his career; and such matters as corruption, the abuse of magisterial power, and extortion in the provinces, all of which gave rise to prosecutions, were serious and growing problems of the day. Yet it is not likely that the participants maintained a rigid separation between these concerns on the one hand and their rivalries and contests for power on the other. It is suggestive, for example, that on at least three, probably on four, occasions, Cato's judicial opponent was a Minucius Thermus;[42] and that in 140 P. Cornelius Scipio Aemilianus was

---

[37] Livy XL.44.10–11.   [38] Astin 1967, 339: (H 67).   [39] Livy XXXVII.57.10–11.

[40] Livy XL.19.11; *Per.* XLVII; Obsequ. 12; Polyb. VI.56.4.

[41] Plut. *Cat. Mai.* 15.4, 29.5; Pliny *HN* VII.100; Aur Vict. *De Vir. Ill.* 47.7.

[42] Astin 1978, esp. 59, 109, 111: (H 68). His opponent was not the same on each occasion, since at least two Minucii were involved.

prosecuted by a man whom two years before he as censor had attempted to downgrade to the lowest citizen status.[43] Two other examples, however, are especially striking.

The first of these is the prosecution of M.' Acilius Glabrio in 189 for alleged mishandling of booty won from Antiochus. One of the principal witnesses against him was Cato. At the time Cato and Glabrio were both among the candidates for the censorship, with Glabrio, as was mentioned earlier, much the most favoured to win the plebeian place because of his extensive largesses. Misappropriation of booty is certainly a matter likely to have roused genuine indignation in Cato, whom Glabrio evidently considered to be chiefly responsible for this attack on him; but that there was a powerful political motive at work, as Livy assumes in his account of the episode, seems amply confirmed by the fact that the prosecution was abandoned as soon as Glabrio withdrew his candidature for the censorship. Furthermore there is reason to believe that an unsuccessful prosecution of Cato at about the same time, arising out of his consulship several years previously, also had some connection with the censorial elections.[44]

The other striking example consists of the accusations and prosecutions which in the 180s were directed against the Scipio brothers, Africanus and L. Cornelius Scipio Asiaticus.[45] These events constitute a notoriously difficult and complex episode, accounts of which conflict on almost every point of substance and betray an underlying history of confusion, speculation and fabrication. There is no possibility of a reconstruction which would be beyond dispute. Nevertheless the salient features can be identified with some plausibility. In 187 tribunes demanded that Lucius Scipio submit accounts concerning 500 talents which had been received from King Antiochus. Lucius apparently insisted that this was not part of the indemnity required from Antiochus, and that it was booty and therefore not subject to account. Africanus intervened in the argument, dramatically tearing up the account books in front of the senators. Another tribune then imposed a huge fine on Lucius, who was threatened with imprisonment (probably for non-payment of a surety pending the actual hearing of the charges to which the fine related). From this imminent humiliation only one tribune was willing to save him by interposing the veto. Probably at this stage an *impasse* had been reached and for the time being the affair lapsed; for a year or so later Lucius gave his magnificent victory games, the vowing of which he seems only now to have seen fit to report![46] In 184, however, another tribune made a

[43] Cic. *Orat.* II.268; Astin 1967, 120 and 175–7: (H 67).
[44] Livy XXXVII.57.12–58.1; *ORF*[4], Cato frs. 66 and 21–55; Astin 1978, ch. 4. esp. 59–60: (H 68).
[45] Principal sources: Polyb XXIII.14; Livy XXXVIII.50–60; Gell.IV.18 and VI.19. Astin 1978, ch. 4, esp. 60–2 and bibliography there: (H 68).   [46] Livy XXXIX.22.8–10.

new attack, evidently against Africanus himself and perhaps concerning his private dealings with Antiochus. It seems that Scipio effectively dispersed the assembly which was to hear the case by dramatically withdrawing from it as soon as he had completed a highly emotional speech in which he reminded his hearers of his great services to Rome. But he had placed himself in a difficult position, for he had defied a tribune and refused to answer the charges made against him. He left Rome and settled at Liternum, where he died a year later.

There are traces of a tradition, insecure in detail but surviving in several sources, which attributed much of the responsibility for these attacks on the Scipios to Cato. With this in mind, attempts have been made to interpret them as part of a long-drawn-out struggle between major political factions, or as the surface expression of a fundamental clash of cultural aspirations. There is little evidence to support such far-reaching hypotheses, which to some extent are derived from misconceptions, especially concerning Cato's cultural outlook. Furthermore the accusations made against the Scipios are not necessarily to be dismissed as mere technical excuses for mounting political assaults. It is not impossible that there was substance in the charges, and in the motivation which prompted them there may have been a substantial measure of genuine concern about impropriety in the handling of public funds. Yet a suspicion persists that there were other, more political motives at work, particularly in the case of an attack launched so long after the event as the one directed at Africanus in 184. It is possible that this attack (though scarcely the earlier one as far back as 187) was intended to influence the outcome of the censorial election of 184,[47] in which Africanus' brother Lucius and Cato's close associate L. Valerius Flaccus, were rival candidates for the patrician place.

On the other hand political motivation need not have been wholly or even in part the pursuit of specific political objectives. Africanus had friends and supporters, but it is plausible to conjecture – possibly implausible to suppose otherwise – that much resentment was engendered by his successes and eminence, by his flamboyance and arrogance, not to mention the reflection of all this in the ostentatious extravagance which characterized the public appearances of his wife.[48] The 'trials of the Scipios' were perhaps another manifestation of that spirit which generated in the oligarchy of this period a strong sense that in the competition for advancement, power and glory there were limits to the degree of success which could be tolerated in any individual.

[47] The timing is possible, since the attack on Africanus could have been initiated in the tribunician year which began on 10 December, whereas at this time the consular year still began on 15 March.
[48] Polyb. xxx.26.1–5.

(b) Mores

In the year 184 the election of M. Porcius Cato and L. Valerius Flaccus to the censorship brought into sharp relief another characteristic of the political climate of the early second century. For much of their activity as censors gave expression to a considerable concern with *mores*, that is with standards of conduct, which in practice meant largely the conduct of individuals in the upper strata of Roman society. This was no innovation. Censors had long since acquired a recognized responsibility to concern themselves with *mores*; but Cato and Valerius evidently placed a distinctive emphasis upon this aspect of their duties. In doing so they were acting from a concern which was not theirs alone but which has left many other traces in the history of these years.[49]

This special concern with *mores* reflected the tensions generated by changing circumstances. On the one hand the two great struggles against Carthage, especially the second of them, had placed a high premium on long-established military virtues, on social discipline, on the authority of the *res publica*, and upon the fostering of a strong sense of corporate responsibility. On the other hand those same struggles had enlarged the dimensions of Roman experience and initiated a process which repeatedly brought new opportunities for the exercise of power, for the acquisition of wealth, and for personal indulgence in the fruits of affluence. Roman commanders and provincial governors found themselves exercising virtually untrammelled authority; victories brought booty and indemnities, sometimes on a spectacular scale; the annexation of provinces created a regular flow of taxation and opened up new possibilities for private investment. Not a little of the new wealth passed directly into private hands, and much of the large portion which went to the state quickly found its way into general circulation. Simultaneously the same processes made wealthier Romans more aware of the possibilities of different, more comfortable life-styles, and gave them access to more varied, more exotic and more luxurious products. In such circumstances it was inevitable that changes in *mores* and social values, and reactions to those changes, should have consequences which are visible in several areas of public life.

One such area was the prosecution of public figures and the nature of alleged offences. Acilius Glabrio and the Scipios, as has been seen, were attacked on the score of improper handling of public resources. In 190 Cato accused Q. Minucius Thermus not only of claiming an unmerited triumph but of beating allied officials, allegedly for having made inadequate arrangements to supply him. At about the same time Cato also

---

[49] Astin 1978, ch. 5 *passim*: (H 68).

accused Thermus of having executed ten men without trial or opportunity to plead in their own defence.[50] In 171 three former governors of the Spanish provinces were prosecuted for maladministration and extortion.[51] The next year an ex-praetor, C. Lucretius Gallus, was convicted and subjected to an enormous fine for having grossly maltreated Greek allies during the war against King Perseus of Macedonia.[52] In 154 or 153 Cato accused another Minucius Thermus, alleging outrageous and deceitful conduct inspired by greed; and in 149 he spoke vehemently in support of an attempt to prosecute Ser. Sulpicius Galba, who was said to have massacred a large number of Lusitanian captives and sold many others into slavery.[53] Furthermore some of these cases highlighted the inadequacy of the existing judicial machinery to cope with some of the situations now arising. In 171 it had been necessary to create a special temporary court, and in 149 the dispute surrounding Galba was centred upon a proposal to set up another. Since Galba managed to prevent this it is probably not a coincidence that 149 was also the year in which a tribunician law, the *lex Calpurnia*, established a standing court for the trial of extortion cases.[54]

The actions of censors are another area in which the concern about *mores* can be seen at work. For the most part censors discharged their responsibility in the field of *mores* by retrospective action against individuals whose conduct they judged to have been gravely at fault in some respect. In practice they concerned themselves mainly with senators and *equites*. The normal and almost the only sanction was to remove an individual from his order and usually also in effect to deprive him of his vote in the *comitia* by enrolling him in the lowest possible category of citizens.[55] Probably most pairs of censors took such action against several senators and *equites*, and in the early decades of the second century almost all are known to have done so. The initiative in these cases, the grounds for action and the determination of the facts were all entirely in the hands of the censors themselves and at their discretion. When grounds are recorded they usually refer to particular actions rather than categories of conduct, but known cases include instances of dereliction of military duty, abuse of magisterial power, neglect of family cults, perjury, and indulgence in extravagance and luxury.[56]

An atmosphere of euphoria following the Hannibalic War probably explains why the censors of 199, quite exceptionally, expelled nobody

[50] Livy XXXVII.46.1–2; *ORF*[4], Cato frs. 58–65 and 182–4; Astin 1978, 59 (esp. n. 27) and 63: (H 68).   [51] Livy XLIII.2.1–12.   [52] Livy XLIII.8.1–10.
[53] *ORF*[4], Cato frs. 177–81 and 196–9; Astin 1978, 111–13, with further references there: (H 68).
[54] Cic. *Brut.* 106; other refs. in *MRR* 1.459.
[55] E.g. Ps. Ascon. 189 St.; Cic. *Rep.* IV.6 ('imposes almost nothing except a blush').
[56] Mommsen 1887–8, II. 377–82: (A 25); Nowak 1909: (H 17); Schmähling 1938: (H 23).
[57] Livy XXXII.7.3.

from the orders.[57] Those of 194 and 189 effected a few expulsions but are reported to have acted with moderation.[58] In 184, however, Cato and Valerius sought the censorship with a declared intention of exercising severity, 'cutting and searing the hydra-like luxury and softness' which they alleged were afflicting Roman society.[59] The number of expulsions from the Senate, though not large in an absolute sense, increased sharply, and the same can safely be assumed to have happened to the equestrian order. In several instances expulsion was accompanied by scorching public denunciation. Most striking was the expulsion of a former consul, L. Quinctius Flamininus, for an outrageous misuse of his authority while he was in Cisalpine Gaul. His expulsion will have had all the more impact because Flamininus was the first former curule magistrate for at least twenty-five years, and probably for nearly a century, to suffer this ignominy. Criticisms of an *eques*, L. Veturius, included neglect of a cult and gluttony to a degree which had rendered him unfit for cavalry service. A more direct attack on luxury and extravagance – prominent targets of Cato in many fragments of his speeches and in anecdotes about him – was the imposition of heavy financial penalties upon those who possessed certain very expensive items of property: ornaments, women's clothing and vehicles valued at more than 15,000 asses, and slaves under the age of twenty who had been purchased since the previous census for 10,000 asses or more. This financial penalty, linked to an adjusted census assessment, was probably a device peculiar to these particular censors, but in general terms their more stringent attitude seems to have prevailed for several censorships thereafter. In 169/8, for example, when the censor Ti. Sempronius Gracchus went through the streets at night on his way home, citizens are said (no doubt with picturesque exaggeration) to have extinguished their lights for fear that they would be thought to be indulging themselves immoderately.[60] A generation later, P. Cornelius Scipio Aemilianus, as censor in 142, looked for similar severity, though he was thwarted by an unco-operative colleague.[61]

The concern with *mores*, and with luxury and extravagance in particular, was by no means an idiosyncrasy of Cato and Valerius and a few other individuals. The promise to 'cut and sear hydra-like luxury and softness' did not impede the election of Cato and Valerius and seems rather to have brought them large numbers of votes. And at various times in this period both Senate and assembly actively supported sumptuary legislation.[62]

---

[58] Livy XXXIV.44.2, XXXVIII.28.2; Plut. *Flam.* 18.2.

[59] Plut. *Cat. Mai.* 16.6–7. For this censorship see esp. Livy XXXIX.42.5–44.9 and 52.1–2; Plut. *Cat. Mai.* 17–19; ORF⁴, Cato fr. 69–127; Astin 1978, ch. 5, *passim*, for further references and discussion, and appendix 6 for some alternative views: (H 68).

[60] Plut. *Ti. Gracch.* 14.4.   [61] Astin 1967, 116–21: (H 67).

[62] For the sumptuary laws and for the wider issues discussed in the remainder of this section see esp. Astin 1978, 93–103: (H 68); Clemente 1981: (H 85). Principal sources for the laws: Macrob. *Sat.* III.17.2–6; Gell. II.24.1–7.

As far back as 215 a *lex Oppia* had imposed restrictions upon the ownership of gold by women, upon the wearing of multi-coloured garments by them, and upon their use of animal-drawn vehicles. That had been primarily an economic measure in response to a serious financial situation, but such restrictions pointed the way towards the later sumptuary legislation which was introduced to control expenditure on 'luxuries' for social rather than for economic reasons. Indeed the latter concept came to the fore when the *lex Oppia* itself, seen by many as an outdated wartime measure, was repealed in 195; for there was vigorous though unsuccessful opposition to the repeal, led by two tribunes and by Cato, who was consul in that year.[63] The first true sumptuary law, however, the *lex Orchia*, which placed restrictions on expenditure for banquets, was enacted in 182, and it was introduced on the recommendation of the Senate. The *lex Fannia* of 161, which strengthened and elaborated the provisions of the *lex Orchia*, was put forward by a consul 'with the consent of all orders', which means that this too was recommended by the Senate; indeed earlier in that same year a decree of the Senate had required leading citizens who were to entertain each other during the Megalesian games to take an oath before the consuls that they would not exceed specified expenditure limits. A third law, the *lex Didia* of 143, which extended sumptuary restrictions to the whole of Italy, presumably also had substantial support at all levels.

The reasons for this concern about luxury and extravagance were no doubt mixed. They are likely to have been more numerous and subtle than the modern historian can hope to comprehend. There are three reasons, however, which can be conjectured with some plausibility. Probably there was a widespread assumption that indulgence in luxury was liable to undermine traditional military virtues, above all physical and mental hardiness. Then a love of luxury was almost certainly considered to be a powerful stimulus to avarice, hence as a major contributor to the growth of corruption and extortion. And there was probably a deep-seated inclination to associate lavish and self-indulgent expenditure with the wasteful dispersal of personal and family fortunes, disapproval of which had been given expression in legal provision to restrain *prodigi* since very early times.[64]

All these activities concerned with *mores* – prosecutions, rhetorical exhortation and denunciation, censorial actions, sumptuary legislation – were more than tolerated by the Roman elite. They sprang almost entirely from that elite, the very group to which they were primarily applicable. They were essentially measures of self-regulation – measures

---

[63] Livy xxxiv.1–8; Zon. ix.17; Val. Max. ix.1.3; Astin 1978, 25–6: (H 68); Clemente 1981, 5–6: (H 85).

[64] *Dig.* xxvii.10.1 pr. (Ulpian); *Epit. Ulp.* 12.2–3; *Pauli Sent.* 3.4a.7; Watson 1975, 78–80: (H 119).

not merely embodying idiosyncratic attitudes of Cato and a few others, but favoured, or at the least accepted by a considerable portion of the elite itself.

There were contradictions and illogicalities inherent in this state of affairs. Throughout this elite which was seeking to restrain certain types of expenditure, the level of wealth was rising significantly; almost all its members – Cato included – were increasing 'non-productive' expenditure on the comforts and adornments of life; acceptable social values and standards were changing as the context and scale of the Roman world changed. Already the Romans of the early second century must have looked back with a mixture of astonishment and moral uplift, as later generations certainly did, to the story of an eminent ex-consul, P. Cornelius Rufinus, who is alleged to have been expelled from the Senate in 275 because he possessed ten pounds' weight of silver table-ware;[65] whereas the Senate's decree of 161 attempted to limit the amount to be used at any one banquet to one hundred pounds' weight.[66] Nevertheless it was because changes were taking place that the self-regulatory process, long familiar, acquired fresh impetus in the early decades of the second century and was a significant element in the outlook of the elite in that period. Fundamentally it was a reaction – perhaps in considerable measure an instinctive reaction – in defence of accepted social values and standards of conduct when new circumstances seemed to threaten their rapid modification or even their destruction. Furthermore, whether or not the issues were generally thought through with care and logic, these were values and standards which had helped to mark off and distinguish the elite in society, to sustain its sense of corporate identity and obligation, to facilitate the transmission of wealth and influence, and to preserve stability and continuity. It is no wonder that the prospect of swift and far-reaching change provoked response.

(c) Economy and society

In the early decades of the second century the character of Roman political life does not appear to have been determined to any substantial degree by conflict (or the potential for conflict) arising from the great economic and social disparities which existed in Roman society. There are a few particular measures which might be construed as showing that from time to time those in power were conscious of the need to remove some immediate sources of discontent as they arose. Thus in 193 a serious problem of debt arose in consequence of very high rates of interest made

[65] Numerous refs. collected in *MRR* 1.196.
[66] Gell 11.24.2. On senatorial wealth and expenditure see Shatzman 1975, esp. chs. 2, 4 and 5:
(H 55).

possible by evasion of the laws governing usury. The Senate and magistrates responded with new regulations, followed by new legislation, and in 192 by the imposition of heavy fines on some usurers.[67] In 188 fines were inflicted on dealers in grain who had been holding back supplies, presumably in an attempt to force up the retail price.[68] Whether the heavy fines similarly imposed on 'herdsmen' in 196 and 193 had much bearing on the interests of the poorer sections of the population is doubtful; these were rich men, operating on a large scale, whose principal offence may have been to defraud the state.[69]

The one episode which does have something of an appearance of social conflict is the so-called 'Bacchanalian conspiracy'. In 186 the Senate, through the consuls, rigorously suppressed, with many executions, an apparently widespread and organized Bacchic cult. This cult, which had flourished for a number of years, practised secret nocturnal rites which were alleged to have degenerated into sexual depravity and ritual murder, and to have become the setting for a variety of other crimes. In pursuit of its complete suppression the Roman authorities took further action in 184 and 181. Probably the participation of many thousands of men and women in this cult did in some way reflect social frustrations – though the participants were by no means drawn exclusively from the poor. Also the cult was indeed an organization which operated independently of the normal framework of social and legal constraints. Nevertheless there is no indication that it had political objectives, pursued social or economic change, or set itself to supplant the established authorities.[70]

It is not difficult to identify reasons why social and economic disparities were not major political factors in these years. To start with, although the investment of new wealth in Italian agriculture had already begun, the processes which it set in train, and which were ultimately to make land reform the centre of a political explosion, were not yet having a severe effect upon large numbers of the peasants who farmed on a small scale. They were not yet causing the disruption and dispossession which were to have far-reaching consequences in the last third of the century. On the contrary, though the wealthy were enlarging their holdings and in many cases working them primarily with slave labour, at this stage they were not so much supplanting their poorer neighbours as filling a

---

[67] Livy xxxv.7.2–5, 41.9–10. On the nature of the problem and the possible relevance of a proposed *lex Iunia* see Astin 1978, 54–5 and 319–23: (H 68).

[68] Livy xxxviii.35.5–6.   [69] Livy xxxiii.4–2.10, xxxv.10.11–12.

[70] It is sometimes assumed *a priori* that an episode of this kind must have been fundamentally economic or political, and therefore such an explanation is superimposed, though the evidence itself does not demand it. Principal sources: Livy xxxix.18–19; *ILLRP* 511 = *ILS* 18. See Scullard 1973, 147: (H 54); Tarditi 1954: (H 58); Toynbee 1965, 387–400 (A 37); Cova 1974: (H 37). See also p. 227 of this volume.

vacuum. The enormous population losses and the general disruption of the Second Punic War left them considerable opportunities to expand their activities without creating immediate widespread pressure on the peasants. Further opportunities for rich and poor alike had been brought about by the great increase in Roman public land, *ager publicus*, following confiscations from rebellious Italian allies in the south and newly conquered peoples in the north. Any Roman citizen was permitted to farm or pasture animals on public land, up to prescribed limits and subject to a small rental, though presumably those with substantial resources were best placed to take advantage of this. Also, considerable tracts of public land were distributed to the citizens of the new colonies and other settlements which Rome established in these years. These settlements could themselves be the means of relief to any who were distressed or dispossessed, but it is unlikely that the provision of relief was a major motive for their creation or that the need for such relief was especially marked at this time. In fact it seems to have been difficult to find sufficient settlers for the colonial ventures of the first quarter of the century.[71]

A second major factor which was masking the potential social tension was the great inflow of new wealth, which, though primarily concentrated in relatively few hands, was filtering through society and creating new opportunities for the poorer sections.[72] It was not all invested in the acquisition and development of agricultural enterprises. Much was spent on goods and services and on buildings, in the towns and in Rome itself. It was expended – and thus put into circulation – by private individuals enlarging their dwellings and enhancing their mode of life, by successful generals distributing donatives and celebrating their victories with games and dedicatory temples, and by the state itself as it maintained and equipped its armies, purchased a multitude of services from contractors, and undertook extensive public works. The censors of 184 – Cato and Valerius – incurred enormous expense, probably 6,000,000 *denarii*, on the renovation of the sewer system, and in addition they are known to have constructed a new road, a mole or causeway, two business buildings and a basilica.[73] Their activity seems to have initiated a period in which censors continued to contract for public works on a very large scale: the censors of 179 had at their disposal for this purpose funds equal to the entire *vectigalia* received by the state in one year, and those of 169 had half the *vectigalia* of a year despite the cost of the Macedonian war then being

[71] Astin 1978, 240–2, and refs. and bibliography there: (H 68).

[72] *ESAR* I, chs. 3 and 4, for a useful collection of data. For an assessment of the archaeological evidence see Ch. 13 of this volume.

[73] Livy xxxix.44.5–7; Dion. Hal. III.67.5 (= Acilius fr. 6); Plut. *Cat. Mai.* 19.3, *Cat. Min.* 5.1; Aur. Vict. *De Vir. Ill.* 47.5; Ps. Ascon. 201 St.

fought.[74] The consequences of expenditure on this scale cannot have failed to be far-reaching: in the direct demand for labour and supplies and the indirect requirements of a whole range of support provision – food (itself requiring transportation, harbour and warehouse facilities, and marketing), shelter, clothing, shoes, tools. Not surprisingly, there are signs that the population of Rome in particular was expanding. It is significant both that Latins and Italians moved to Rome in substantial numbers and that this extra population could be accepted without major difficulty – for when the authorities were induced to require them to leave the initiative and urging came not from within Rome itself but from the parent communities whose populations were declining.[75]

Nevertheless the vastness of economic and social disparity was potentially a powerful political factor which could emerge to interlock with others and become one of the important elements in the shaping of political struggles – as did happen before the second century was out. The factors which concealed this growing potential in the earlier part of the second century were palliatives, not preventatives. The expenditure on goods, services and construction could not always be increasing. By its very nature it was liable to fluctuations, both short- and long-term, and it had encouraged a considerable and not easily reversible concentration of poorer citizens in the urban setting of Rome itself. Investment in agriculture – the most secure and most socially regarded form of investment[76] – with expansion of holdings, an increasing use of slave labour and direct management, and the enclosure, often illegal, of much public land, could not long continue without engendering serious problems for many of the free peasantry who farmed on a modest scale. The problems were exacerbated by the recurring levies for the considerable and predominantly conscript armies which the state now normally had in being and which often took men away from family farms for long periods. Furthermore the opportunity to move to new settlements disappeared when colonial foundations ceased in the 170s. That probably happened because the colonies had been conceived primarily in terms of military needs which by then seemed to have been met, while the demands for agrarian resettlement had not yet developed very markedly. By the time such demands became acute most public land which was suitable for settlement had been taken into use in other ways.

IV. FORCES FOR CHANGE

It has been seen that in the years following the Second Punic War the Roman political scene was characterized by an apparent stability. The

[74] Livy XL.46.16; XLIV.16.9.   [75] Livy XXXIX.3.4–6, XLI.8.6–12, 9.9–10.
[76] Astin 1978, ch. 11, esp. 250–61: (H 68).

predominantly oligarchic pattern of government, though not so exclusive as to prevent the rise of new political figures, did not seem threatened by the theoretically powerful popular elements in the constitutional structure. To some extent, especially in elections, it was necessary to court the favour of those citizens who played a part in the popular institutions; but their independence was considerably restricted, and the oligarchic structure was correspondingly sustained, by a variety of constitutional and social devices. From time to time there were domestic problems which required administrative action or new legislation, but these seem to have been perceived as isolated episodes and not to have persisted or coalesced into a long-term issue. At this stage the inflow of wealth, though it bore within it the seeds of disruption, helped to obscure the potential importance of economic and social tensions as political factors. The political attention of senators was engaged principally with foreign and military affairs, and with their own ambitious and mutual competition for honour and office, for distinction and esteem, conducted within a framework of conventions and rules which was actually reinforced by the legislation of the early second century.

This seeming stability, however, was closely associated with factors which were not constants – with factors which, if not exactly ephemeral, were by their nature liable to change. That is the case, for instance, with the complex diplomatic and strategic questions which were prominent in the earlier decades of the second century. The phase in which these were a major preoccupation of political life did not last beyond, at the latest, the subjugation of Achaea and the destruction of Carthage in 146, perhaps not really beyond the end of the Third Macedonian War in 168. Of course military problems and occasional crises continued to occur – as in Spain between 153 and 133, and later in the Jugurthine, Cimbrian and Mithridatic Wars. The age of conquest was not yet ended and there were still decisions for the Senate to take in this field. But fundamentally all this took place in a world which Rome now dominated, in which she was no longer treating with Hellenistic powers or engaging in the complexities of diplomacy and of strategic interest. The very magnitude of Roman success had diminished the role of such matters among the preoccupations of political life.

There were changes also in the manner in which men pursued the competition for advancement and distinction. Two trends can be discerned. One was a growing tendency to take greater advantage of the popular elements in the constitution by means of self-projection and direct appeal to the electorate at large. The other was an increasing readiness to find technical means of circumventing conventional or legal obstacles, or actually to override them. No doubt this was always done on the ground of expediency in the immediate public interest, though it can usually be seen to coincide with the ambitions of some eminent senator.

In practice these two tendencies often went together, and neither was wholly novel. Scipio Africanus, when he was sent to Spain in 210, and Titus Flamininus, when he was elected consul for 198, both overrode convention, the former certainly, and the latter probably, less by means of social manipulation than by personal appeal to the electorate. In 184 Q. Fulvius Flaccus stirred up great controversy by seeking election to a vacant praetorship while he was in office as curule aedile; and the Senate judged his prospects of success so good that it decided to leave the praetorship unfilled rather than risk such a questionable appointment.[77] Finally, the legislation of the 190s and 180s which sought to control by law the sequence of offices and speed of careers itself reflects an awareness that contrary tendencies, illustrated by the cases of Scipio, Flamininus and Fulvius, were at work in the contemporary political scene.

Attempts to circumvent or set aside constitutional impediments are a consequence only to be expected from the increasing elaboration of artificial restrictions upon career patterns. In a social environment which placed a high premium on the competitive pursuit of public office, and in which this was the route not only to a sense of achievement and success but to power, status, and the military glory which Roman society esteemed so highly, it is no surprise that from time to time men of ambition sought to override seemingly unnecessary formal impediments which slowed their advance or denied them attractive opportunities. Nor is it surprising that there was sometimes impatience with restrictions which prevented the election of an apparently excellent candidate because he did not meet some formal condition. It was understandable that in the face of a serious military situation the voters might wish to elect to the consulship someone with an outstanding military reputation despite the fact that he was below the minimum age, or had not been praetor, or alternatively had held a previous consulship within the last ten years – not to mention the total exclusion, from c. 151, of anyone who had had previous experience in the consulship. It is perhaps more remarkable that such rules were sustained for decades than that ultimately they were set aside in a number of instances; but when they did begin to be overridden, precedents were set and the inhibitions which reinforced rules and conventions were gradually eroded.

Two early instances of this development were the second consulships of C. Marcius Figulus and P. Cornelius Scipio Nasica Corculum. These men entered on the consulship of 162 but were obliged to resign when it

[77] Livy xxxix.39.1–15.

was announced that there had been a fault in religious procedure at the election. Magistrates who resigned because they had been declared *vitio creati* were nevertheless deemed to have held the office in question, so these men do appear in the consular lists under this year, and when they appear again later they are each designated 'consul for the second time'. They should therefore have been subject to the rule which prohibited tenure of a second consulship less than ten years after the first. Yet Marcius was re-elected consul for 156, Nasica for 155. Plainly Marcius had successfully advanced technical arguments to the effect that his aborted consulship in 162 did not count, and thereby he became the first exception to the ten-year rule in more than half a century, to be followed immediately by Nasica.[78]

Three years later there was another instance. In response to news of a serious military situation in Spain, M. Claudius Marcellus, who had held his second consulship as Nasica's colleague as recently as 155, was elected consul for 152. Since Marcellus was one of the foremost generals of this period and was now sent to take command in Spain, it is evident that he won his third consulship so soon after his second because the intention of the law was subordinated to expediency.[79]

Five more years brought an even more striking instance. P. Cornelius Scipio Aemilianus was a son of L. Aemilius Paullus, who had conquered Macedonia in 168, and by adoption was a grandson of Scipio Africanus. Ambitious to prove himself worthy of such a distinguished inheritance, he had already won for himself a considerable reputation of military skill and daring, first in Spain, then in Africa, where the Third Punic War had begun in 149. But the Punic War had not brought the quick and easy victory which had been expected. At the end of 148 there was still little visible progress, and there were even some reports of Roman reverses. In reaction the *comitia centuriata* elected Scipio to be one of the consuls for 147; subsequently a tribune intervened to ensure that he received the command in Africa. But Scipio had not been praetor (in fact he had returned to Rome at that time to stand for the aedileship) and he was several years below the minimum age for the consulship. Moreover his election was strongly opposed both by the presiding consul and by the Senate; not until there was a threat by a tribune to use his veto to block the consular elections altogether if Scipio's name was not accepted did the Senate assent to the temporary repeal of the legal obstacle.[80] Nor was

[78] *MRR* 1.442; Astin 1967, 36, n. 2, 38–9: (H 67).

[79] Astin 1967, 37–40: (H 67). It is generally agreed that the total prohibition of second and subsequent consulships was a reaction to this episode. A proposal to this effect was supported by Cato, who died in 149: *ORF*[4], Cato frs. 185 and 186.

[80] Most detailed of the many sources: App. *Lib.* 112. The election: Astin 1967, ch. 6: (H 67). The military events: Ch. 5 of this volume.

this all. Thirteen years later rules were again set aside for Scipio, who in the meantime had destroyed Carthage, assumed his adoptive grandfather's *cognomen*, Africanus, and in 142 been censor. In 134 he again entered upon a consulship for which he was not eligible – this time because since the election of Marcellus for 152 all second consulships had been prohibited by law. Again he was elected by supposedly popular choice to take charge of a war protracted beyond expectations, in this case the seemingly endless struggle against Numantia in Spain (which he captured in 133); and again he was probably elected against the wishes of a majority of his fellow-senators, whose attitude may be inferred from the fact that they denied him cash and conscript reinforcements for his campaign.[81]

Thus in achieving his consulships Scipio not only overrode legal obstacles but defied the Senate, certainly on the first occasion and probably on both. Moreover in 134 when that body denied him money and permission to levy reinforcements he responded by recruiting clients and volunteers, by drawing upon the private fortunes of himself and his friends, and by obtaining assistance from Hellenistic monarchs. Nor was he the only eminent senator successfully to defy the Senate and thereby impair its authority. In 143 Appius Claudius Pulcher celebrated a triumph which the Senate had refused him. When there was a threat of physical intervention to enforce a tribunician veto against the proceedings, he thwarted it by having with him in his triumphal chariot a daughter who was a Vestal Virgin, so contriving that the tribune could not touch him without doing violence to her sacred person.[82]

Equally significant is Scipio's evident ability to ride to success on a wave of popular enthusiasm – which no doubt he did much to encourage. In theory this tactic was always open to candidates, for in principle every citizen had the right to vote as he thought fit; and probably an effort to appeal directly to the judgement and emotions of voters at large was made in most contests. In practice, however, its significance was usually restricted by a combination of structural, procedural and social factors. Presumably the degree to which it was restricted varied from election to election, but only occasionally did such direct appeal become the overwhelmingly decisive feature. More than most, Scipio Aemilianus seems to have had considerable success in exploiting this possibility afforded by the constitutional structure. When he was canvassing for the censorship of 142 he was criticized by his principal rival, Appius Claudius, because he was being escorted by 'men who frequented the Forum and were able to gather a crowd and to force all issues by shouting and inciting passions'.[83]

[81] Livy, *Per.* LVI; App. *Iber.* 84; Astin 1967, 135 n. 5 and 182–4: (H 67).
[82] Cic. *Cael.* 34; *Val. Max.* v.4.6; Suet. *Tib.* 2.4; cf. Oros. v.4.7; Dio fr. 74.2.

There are other indications in this same period of a growing sense that
those in the assemblies could be won over and that social pressures could
be outweighed by personal appeal and emotive incitement; and that this
could be a potent means to political achievement. The process could be
assisted by shielding the act of voting from social supervision. In 139 a
lex Gabinia introduced the written ballot in place of open voting in
elections;[84] two years later a *lex Cassia*, powerfully supported and perhaps instigated by Scipio Aemilianus, made the same provision for all
popular trials except where the charge was treason (*perduellio*).[85] Earlier,
in 145, a tribune named C. Licinius Crassus had failed to carry a proposal
that vacancies in the priestly colleges should be filled by popular election
instead of co-option. Yet the principal speaker for the opposition, C.
Laelius, is himself known to have used arguments calculated to appeal to
the independent judgement and the religious emotions of the voters,
while Crassus symbolized the 'popular' nature of his proposal by turning
around on the *rostra* to address the mass of the people, instead of
conventionally facing the more restricted space of the *comitium*.[86]

Alongside and increasingly interacting with the changing practice and
attitudes of competitive politics were social and economic problems. By
the middle years of the second century these were developing to a degree
which made them potentially influential factors in the shaping of political
contests. In the city itself, for example, a special arrangement in 144 to
repair the existing aqueducts and construct a new one undoubtedly put
vast additional funds into circulation, but it was also a reflection of the
growing problems of the large urban population.[87] A harbinger of
trouble to come was the serious difficulty with the grain supply in 138.
This gave rise to agitation by a tribune, C. Curiatius, and to a popular
outcry against the consul Scipio Nasica (son of the consul of 162 and 155)
when he rejected a plan under which the state would have purchased
grain through special *legati*.[88]

Probably most tribunes, whatever their real motives may have been,
had always claimed to be carrying out their historic function, 'to perform
the will of the plebs and especially to seek after their wishes'; but it is
symptomatic of growing problems that from the 150s onwards more
incidents are recorded in which this took on substance.[89] Attention has
been drawn already to the actions of C. Licinius Crassus in 145, to the
ballot laws, and to the dispute about grain in 138. The latter year saw also

---

[83] Plut. *Aem.* 38.2–6, *Praec. Reip. Ger.* 14.
[84] Cic. *Leg.* III.35, *Amic.* 41; Livy, *Ox. Epit.* LIV.
[85] Esp. Cic. *Brut.* 97, 106, *Sest.* 103. Astin 1967, 130–1: (H 67).
[86] Cic. *Amic.* 96; ORF[4], Laelius frs. 12–16; cf. Varro, *De Re Rust.* 1.2.9. Plut. *C. Gracch.* 5.4–5
attributes the innovation to Gaius Gracchus. Astin 1967, 101–2, esp. 101 n. 2: (H 67).
[87] Frontin. *De Aquis* 1.7; Astin 1967, 108–10: (H 67).
[88] Val. Max. III.7.3.   [89] Polyb. VI.16.5. Taylor 1962: (H 59).

a massive demonstration at the funeral of a popular tribune, conceivably Curiatius himself;[90] and tribunes, including Curiatius, were prominent in the disputes now arising in connection with the military levy.

Rome's recruiting problems in the middle decades of the second century sprang from a mixture of causes which even at the time were probably not easy to analyse and evaluate.[91] They included the fluctuating but often considerable number of men required, the arduous and relatively unprofitable nature of some of the campaigns, and the long periods of service demanded of many soldiers, which added to the dislocations increasingly being caused by the accelerating investment of wealth in agriculture. While some Romans perceived the problem as a shortage of manpower, it is likely that this was not the case in an absolute sense. More probably the difficulties sprang rather from the inadequacies and obsolescence both of the recruiting system and of the terms of service in relation to the conditions which now prevailed. The net effect, however, was that, except when the prospect of an easy campaign with much booty attracted volunteers, the pressures increased upon those who were subject to the compulsory levy. As a result, manifestations of resistance from time to time developed into overt political clashes.

Occasional minor episodes earlier in the century probably reflect little more than the ordinary problems and resentments incidental to any system of enforced recruiting, though in 169 difficulties related to the heavy demands of the Third Macedonian War gave rise to mutual recriminations among the magistrates and to exceptional action by the censors of that year.[92] From 151 onward, however, there are symptoms of a more acute malaise. Fragmentary evidence for that year records an initial reluctance to serve which amounted almost to a boycott of the levy; there was tribunician intervention, which the consuls must have defied since the tribunes went so far as to imprison them; and for the first time the drawing of lots was introduced into the procedure of the levy.[93] Six years after this sensational episode the Senate forbade Scipio Aemilianus' brother, Fabius Maximus Aemilianus, to recruit for his army in Spain anyone who had served in the recent wars in Africa, Macedonia and Greece.[94] In 140 the Senate, at the prompting of Appius Claudius Pulcher, decreed that there should not be more than one levy in the year.[95] In 138 deserters from Spain were publicly scourged on the orders of the consuls, perhaps in connection with fresh disputes about recruiting. Curiatius and another tribune, S. Licinius, demanded that

[90] Livy. *Ox. Epit.* LV.
[91] Astin 1967, 162–4 and 167–72: (H 67); Brunt 1971, chs. 22–3: (H 82). Rich 1983: (H 53) denies both that there was a real problem and that contemporary Romans believed that there was one.
[92] Livy XLIII.14.2–10.
[93] Polyb. XXXV.4; Livy, *Per.* XLVIII; App. *Iber.* 49; Oros. IV.21.1; cf. Val. Max. III.2.6.
[94] App. *Iber.* 65.   [95] Livy, *Ox. Epit.* LIV.

each tribune should have the right to exempt ten persons from the levy, and the consequent escalating conflict led once again to the brief imprisonment of consuls.[96] Finally, in 134 the stated ground for the Senate's refusal to allow Scipio Aemilianus to take any but volunteers to Spain was that otherwise Italy would have been stripped of men.[97]

Thus the difficulty experienced in military recruiting was not merely a technical or an administrative issue but was something which impinged upon political life. Some perhaps saw in it an excuse for obstructing political opponents. The growing pressure of an increasingly unpopular levy produced resentment and attempts to defy consuls and Senate; it led consuls to try to ignore the veto of tribunes, and to a diminution of the prestige of their office by the consequent symbolic imprisonment; and it eroded the authority of Senate and consuls by forcing them, in one major instance and probably in two, to accept compromise.

Lastly, there were the consequences of the considerable investment in land and agriculture: on the one hand extension and consolidation of powerful vested interests, on the other changes in modes of operation and in the patterns of rural life which brought disruption, dislocation and distress to substantial numbers of humbler citizens.[98] Herein were a conflict of interests and a source of social discontent such as could scarcely fail to become potent political factors – especially in the context of constitutional arrangements which made elections and legislation subject to the popular vote, however successfully that may have been contained and guided in earlier decades. This development, which was to lie at the heart of a political cataclysm in 133, is amply attested in general terms but manifested itself in only one particular political event prior to that year. That event was the unsuccessful attempt by C. Laelius, probably when he was consul in 140, to effect some kind of land reform, details of which are not recorded. Even then it is not certain that the full measure of the problem had yet been grasped, for the one source which mentions Laelius' proposal assumes that his motive was a concern about the decline in manpower available for military service. No hint survives that his aim was to relieve distress or pre-empt an outburst of discontent, though the silence may be accidental.[99] A further dimension to the changing situation was brought forcefully to attention in 136 by a slave rebellion in Sicily so serious that it took several years to quell, and then only after consular armies had been deployed against it. Yet the scale and initial success of the rebellion suggests that there had been little aware-

---

[96] Livy, *Per.* LV; *Ox. Epit.* LV; Cic. *Leg.* III.20; Frontin. *Strat.* IV.1.20.   [97] App. *Iber.* 84.
[98] See further Ch. 7; also Astin 1967, 161–5: (H 67); *id.* 1978, 240–2: (H 68); Toynbee 1965, II, esp. chs. 6–8 (A 37); Brunt 1971, chs. 17 and 20: (H 82).
[99] Plut. *Ti. Gracch.* 8.4–5; Astin 1967, 307–10: (H 67). A slightly earlier date is possible but less likely than 140.

ness even of the dangers of the accumulation of numerous resentful and poorly supervised slaves.[100] The agricultural changes of the second century were not an event but a process spread over a substantial period of time. It is more than likely that an understanding of these changes in all their aspects came slowly and developed unevenly. Just a few years before the epoch-making events of 133 there may still have been only a few who realized the full implications and appreciated their political significance. But whether or not it was widely understood, there was here an emergent political factor of major proportions and far-reaching implications.

V. CONCLUSION

Superficially the political scene just before 133 closely resembled that of the early second century. The constitutional structure was almost unchanged: in form and standing the senatorial and equestrian classes were much as they had been; the governmental system had its popular elements but remained predominantly oligarchic in practice; while 'new men' made their way into the Senate and a few even to the highest offices, many of the leading men were from families which were prominent early in the century. Yet this continuity also embraced deep and significant changes. As a focus of attention the interplay of Mediterranean powers had faded, to be superseded by the comfortable exploitation and easy extension of empire. The new opportunities, new pressures, new temptations, new wealth, to which those who dominated the governance of that empire were already exposed in the early decades, had proliferated steadily. Ambition, rivalry and expedience, lubricated by wealth, were combining to erode some of the inhibitions and conventions which restrained political conduct, including some of the rules introduced early in the century precisely to combat such tendencies. Even the authority of the Senate and the consuls was subjected to challenges which were damaging to the esteem in which they were held. Underlying all this were the military commitments of empire, the inflow of wealth, and the increased investment in land and agriculture. For these induced social and economic changes of a kind which could not fail in time to exert a major influence upon the debates and contests of political life, and which in some respects had already begun to do so by the middle years of the century.

---

[100] Principal source: Diod. Sic. xxxiv/xxxv.2 = Poseid. fr. 108 *FGrH*. For further refs. and consideration of the date see Astin 1967, 133–4: (H 67).

CHAPTER 7

ROME AND ITALY IN THE SECOND CENTURY B.C.

E. GABBA

I. THE EXTENSION OF THE *AGER PUBLICUS*

The end of hostilities in the Hannibalic War was accompanied by a series of severe punitive measures against the allied communities which had defected to Hannibal. In 211/10 B.C. punishment had already been meted out to Capua:[1] the aristocratic ruling class had been practically annihilated, the city had lost every trace of autonomy and even its citizenship, all public and private real property had been confiscated and the entire *ager Campanus*, with the sole exception of lands belonging to those who had remained loyal to Rome, thus became 'public land of the Roman people', *ager publicus populi romani*. It had also been decided to deport the entire population; this decision does not seem to have been carried out, although some measures to limit the right of abode must have been taken.[2]

The turn of Tarentum had come in 208; the city had been sacked at the time of its capture, but as a whole it was punished only by the confiscation of part of its territory. The treaty that bound the Tarentines to Rome may have been made rather more onerous.[3]

The confiscation of territory also represented the main punitive measure against all the other allied communities which had forsaken Rome. In 203 the dictator Sulpicius Galba with his *magister equitum* M. Servilius Pulex spent part of his magistracy conducting investigations in the various Italian cities that had rebelled.[4] The enquiries were presumably followed by decrees of confiscation and by amendment of the individual *foedera*, the treaties with the cities. It is not easy to determine the extent of the territories that became Roman *ager publicus*. The *ager Campanus* must have been the only territory to become Roman *ager publicus* in its entirety, complete with buildings, although it is thought by some that Telesia also had all of its territory confiscated. Evidence relating to earlier periods suggests that the amount of land lost by

---

[1] Livy XXVI.14–16, 33–4; De Sanctis 1907–64, III.ii.303–4: (A 14).   [2] Livy XXVIII.46.6.
[3] Livy XXVII.21.8, 25.1–2, XXXV.16.3, XLIV.8.6; Plin. *HN* III.99; Vell. Pat. I.15.4; De Sanctis 1907–64, III.ii.457: (A 14).   [4] Livy XXX.24.4.

rebellious allied communities was probably proportionate to their responsibility for the rebellion and their participation in the war against Rome (one-quarter, one-third, half, two-thirds). According to the calculations of Beloch,[5] which are widely accepted, the lands now confiscated may have amounted to as much as 10,000 km², although other historians put the figure at about 7,500 km². In any case, the increase in Roman *ager publicus* must have been very large throughout southern Italy, even though it may be difficult to quantify and to locate;[6] some cautious conclusions in this regard may be drawn from the geographic location of the extensive post-Hannibalic colonization of the south and also from the geographic data concerning the assignments which resulted from the land law of Tiberius Gracchus in 133 B.C., although it is naturally very difficult to determine whether the *ager publicus* recovered and assigned under the Gracchan law was being worked at that time by Romans or by allies.

It is not easy to state with certainty what significance the confiscation of such vast and widely dispersed lands had in concrete terms. At the political and constitutional level this tremendous increase in territory had very serious consequences for the Roman state. The need to punish obliged it to resume the policy of territorial expansion that had been consciously terminated in the middle of the third century B.C. in order not to jeopardize the political structure of the city state. It was for this reason that the Senate had unsuccessfully opposed the assignment of land in the *ager Gallicus* and *ager Picenus*. This was followed by unavoidable expansion in Cisalpine Gaul.

On the practical level, even the implementation of the decrees of confiscation was problematic. The Roman state certainly did not have the resources to verify, measure and mark boundaries in dozens of areas, so that in many cases accurate surveys were probably never carried out to determine the area of land confiscated. This situation of confusion and uncertainty goes a long way towards explaining the serious difficulties in distinguishing between public and private land later encountered by the Gracchan agrarian commission set up to recover *ager publicus*. It is therefore plausible to suppose that a large proportion of the lands expropriated as a result of the Hannibalic War were not seriously examined with a view to planning their use until the Gracchan era, simply because of the practical and technical inability of the Roman government to occupy them; this would also explain the vast scale of uncontrolled private occupation that had developed in the meanwhile.

The likelihood that the expropriated agricultural areas were scarcely

[5] Beloch 1880, 62ff., 73: (H 125); Frederiksen 1981, 267: (H 89).
[6] Toynbee 1965, II.117–21: (A 37); Brunt 1971, 278–81: (H 82).

or never surveyed makes it probable that in many cases these lands remained in the hands of their previous owners, although on a different legal basis, and that the original owners were able to re-occupy them *de facto* or even *de iure*. The further they were from Rome, the looser was the control. The situation in the rich and easily accessible *ager Campanus* was far from clear a few years after its confiscation. Quaestorian sales had occurred in 210 and again in 205; by the later year it was already necessary to attempt to define the boundaries of the public part of the land by offering a large reward to anyone proving that it belonged to the state.[7] Illegal occupation by private individuals (whoever they may have been) is again recorded in 173, when the consul L. Postumius was given powers to recover land; in 172 it was decided that the censors would grant leases on land recovered by the state.[8] In 165 the praetor P. Cornelius Lentulus prepared a bronze map of the state lands following a further exercise in land recovery and complex surveying and administrative operations.[9]

Elsewhere the situation seems to have remained completely unresolved, except in areas where there is evidence for the founding of colonies or for land assignations. The lack of accurate information does not necessarily indicate negligence on the part of the Roman government, even though we happen to learn that in 186 B.C. the colonies of Sipontum and Buxentum had been abandoned, only a few years after their foundation:[10] in many cases the government deliberately took no action. In several instances it may be assumed that after having confiscated part of an allied community's land as a punishment, the Roman government granted the use of this *ager publicus* to the community under the treaty concluded with it and, of course, collected the corresponding rent.[11] (This arrangement probably lies behind the subsequent violation of the allies' 'rights and treaties', *iura ac foedera*, by the Gracchan agrarian law.)[12] The possession of Roman *ager publicus* would in general have been granted mainly to Latins.[13] Further, some communities allied to Rome would have received allotments of *ager publicus* in Cisalpine Gaul.[14] It should also be borne in mind that it was not in Rome's ultimate interest for her punitive measures to have too profound an effect on the existing economic and social order within the allied communities or, above all, for the upper classes among the allies to lose their dominant political position. The limited use of Roman *ager publicus* in Etruria and Umbria for colonization and land grants (despite its extent) can probably be explained in terms of Rome's conscious desire, of which there is also

[7] Livy XXVII.3.1, XXVIII.46.4–5. Tibiletti 1955, 251 n. 1 (H 117); Frederiksen 1981, 275–6 (H 89).
[8] Livy XLII.1.6, 9.7, XLIII.19.1–2.   [9] Gran. Lic. 9–10 Flemisch; Cic. *Leg. Agr.* II.82.
[10] Livy XXXIX.23.3–4; Tibiletti 1955, 249 n. 3: (H 117)
[11] Tibiletti 1955, 259 n. 2: (H 117).   [12] Cic. *Rep.* III.41, 1.31.
[13] Badian 1971, 397ff.: (H 124).   [14] Galsterer 1976, 168 and n. 36: (H 132).

evidence elsewhere, not to jeopardize the distinctive traditional structure of land-holding and society in these regions.[15]

These observations are clearly general and hence imprecise and should be verified as far as possible against the many different situations prevailing in the various regions of Italy. However, if nothing else, they serve to refute the doubtful and poorly documented theory that vast tracts of land were distributed to Roman citizens throughout the areas acquired in Italy after the Hannibalic War, thus leading to discontent among the allies.[16]

It is of course difficult to give a universally valid answer to the question of which lands were actually confiscated by Rome. In general it might have been expected that confiscation imposed on the rebel allied communities would have specifically indicated the lands expropriated, rather than defined them simply as a proportion of the entire territory of the community which was being punished; but it was probably the latter practice which was followed. The question of which land was confiscated is a serious one, as the answer to it would throw light on the true impact of the confiscations on the agricultural systems of Italy in the second century B.C. and hence on its economic, social and political structure, though to this question also there can be no universally applicable answer, as we shall see below.

It is generally thought that Rome confiscated the best arable land and that this was usually turned into pasture, thus contributing to the destruction of small and medium-sized farms.[17] There is undoubted evidence that this change of use did occur in certain specific areas, but it cannot be considered the norm, as the conditions and methods of farming in second-century Italy were extremely varied. Such a theory assumes that transhumant animal husbandry was adopted everywhere – and indeed it was certainly adopted more widely after the Hannibalic War. It would, on the theory under discussion, have been introduced in those fertile lowlands where small farms had previously been common and would thus have made possible the exploitation of the upland pastures of Italy. It is certainly true that the argument in favour of arable farming as opposed to stock-rearing had become a political issue as early as the Gracchan era, as seems to be illustrated by the tone of the pronouncements of Tiberius Gracchus against the use of slave labour and by the proud claim of the author of the Polla inscription, who vaunts himself on having turned pasture back into arable land.[18] The idea that this should be done must have had wide support among the rural plebs; but it is inconceivable that Gracchus allocated or intended to allocate

[15] Harris 1971, 147: (H 136).   [16] Nagle 1973, 367–78: (H 146).
[17] Toynbee 1965, II.286–95, 570–5: (A 37).   [18] Inscr. Italiae III.iii.1, no. 272.

pasture land or uncultivated land among his assignees; he wished to distribute cultivated and cultivable land, in other words good land.[19] Thus confiscated land in some areas must have continued to be used for arable purposes. Furthermore, archaeological evidence from some northern areas of the Tavoliere near Lucera, characterized in other periods by the practice of transhumant animal husbandry, reveals occasions during the second century B.C. of changes in land use, with traces of centuriation and of small farms cultivating olives and vines that seem to have given way to areas of pasture *or* extensive cereal cultivation.[20] Such changes are characteristic of Apulia, but it does not follow that they were universal in Italy.

If a general pattern is to be suggested for the Roman confiscations from the rebellious allies, it might well be supposed that for practical reasons they affected mainly the common lands of the allied states, both arable and pasture, rather than individual private estates, apart from those of the men primarily responsible for the rebellions. In the case of Apulia, the theory that arable land was turned into pasture would be quite acceptable.

The determining factor in this complex historical development is the fact that the Roman confiscations came at a time when agriculture in central and southern Italy had been seriously undermined by the long state of war. The decline of the Greek cities had already begun some time earlier. The actual devastation caused by the Hannibalic War was initially disastrous, although in practice it cannot have been continuous and was, in fact, limited.[21] Although the repercussions of the war on Italian agriculture were felt for a considerable time afterwards, this was not simply because of the devastations but partly also other, admittedly related, factors.[22] The enforced removal of the inhabitants from the fields (primarily to the cities), the subsequent difficulty in persuading them to return home and the fall in agricultural output, owing to a failure to sow seeds, a lack of seed or the seizure of produce by the belligerents, brought famine and misery that led to a decline in population in addition to that caused by the loss of human lives in the war; in other words, they prevented a growth in population for lack of the means of subsistence.

The depopulation of Italy, a recurrent theme throughout the century, first becomes evident in Latium itself as early as the end of the third century B.C. The deportation of the rebel Campanians defeated in 210 B.C., which may not have been carried out, would have meant their removal to the territories of Veii, Sutrium and Nepete on the right bank of the Tiber, where they would each have received up to 50 *iugera* of

---

[19] Tibiletti 1955, 257: (H 117).
[20] Toynbee 1965, II.342–4: (A 37); Gabba and Pasquinucci 1979, 41 n. 64: (H 93).
[21] Brunt 1971, 269ff.: (H 82).   [22] Brunt 1971, 278ff.: (H 82) (fundamental).

land.[23] The grant of the *trientabula* (public land within fifty miles of Rome) to private creditors of the state in the year 200 seems to indicate that this land was unoccupied.[24] The decline in the population of the Latin colonies had been the reason why twelve of them had declared that they were unable to contribute further to Rome's military forces in 209; this state of affairs was implicitly recognized in the punitive measures that the Roman government took against them in 204.[25] Large areas of the south, which may have been thinly populated in the first place, became utterly deserted as a result of the war. In 201–199 plots of land in Apulia and Samnium could be granted to the veterans of Scipio's campaigns in Spain and Africa, who numbered no fewer than 30–40,000.[26] It is difficult to believe that this action entailed the complete removal of the previous inhabitants. In 180 47,000 families from Liguria were moved to the territory of Beneventum, where they will have received arable land and common grazing rights.[27] The phenomenon of depopulation, particularly in Oscan areas, continued during the second century B.C. for various reasons and in various directions. This progressive decline in population in the centre and south is one of the underlying themes in any interpretation of the crisis of the pre-Gracchan and Gracchan period.[28] Such a depopulation must certainly have contributed, for better or worse, to the disappearance of many small farms, which had been abandoned or were on the point of abandonment because of the rent that in many cases had to be paid to the Roman government, and thus facilitated the emergence of the upper classes of Rome and Italy as large landowners. Where a population is sparse, an extensive form of agriculture naturally predominates and large areas of land remain uncultivated or easily fall into disuse. Circumstances of this kind provide a good explanation for the new scale of occupation of public land, legally or illegally, by rich Roman and Italian *possessores*, many of whom will indeed have converted arable land to pasture.

In describing the historical background to the agrarian law of Tiberius Gracchus, the historian Appian shows that he and his sources were aware of the profound impact of the vastly increased use of *ager publicus* on the social and economic climate of Italy and Rome.[29] (Poseidonius had also indicated the scale of the change that the dominance of Rome had brought about in Sicilian agriculture and in the Sicilian economy.[30]) The crucial changes and their often dramatic corollaries are presented as

[23] Livy xxvi.34.10; Tibiletti 1950, 189: (H 116).   [24] Livy xxxi.13.2–9.
[25] Tibiletti 1950, 189–91: (H 116).
[26] Livy xxxi.4.1–3, 49.5, xxxii.1.6; Gabba 1976, 39–40: (H 42).
[27] Livy xl.38.1–7, 41.3ff.; Tibiletti 1950, 205: (H 116).
[28] Livy xli.8.7; (Plut.) *Apophth. Scip.* 15; App. *B. Civ.* 1.7.28–30, 8.32, 9.35, 11.43 and 45.
[29] App. *B. Civ.* 1.7.26–8.34.
[30] Poseid. *FGrH* 87F108; Coarelli 1981, 1.8–14 with the notes: (1 6).

linked to the Roman conquest of Italy and the gradual but ever increasing appropriation of Italian territory by Rome. The latest step was the post-Hannibalic confiscation of land from the allied communities that had defected. Changes in farming and in Italian society are attributed primarily to the occupation of *ager publicus*, one of the effects of which had been the emergence of large estates in the place of the traditional Italian system of small peasant farms, with many of the previous owners being forced to emigrate or to become tenant farmers or hired farm-hands. This process of change had been made possible by a vast influx of capital, which had permitted the introduction of new crops, combined with the extension of grazing and the large-scale use of slaves instead of free labour. In short, a change in the use of *ager publicus* initiated the crisis for the small peasant farm.

The picture drawn with such clarity by Appian will obviously not apply equally to all regions. Nevertheless, it accurately captures the devastating significance of the exploitation of *ager publicus* during the second century B.C. both for 'industrial' crops and for grazing. Up to that time common lands had been an essential component in the prosperity and continued existence of the small peasant farm, and indeed in some areas their very structure was determined by the environment.

Against this background it is easy to understand the approval of a law *de modo agrorum* in the first third of the second century B.C., to regulate the occupation of public land by private individuals – involving a limit of 500 *iugera*; the restriction of grazing rights on public pastures (*ager scripturarius*, in other words land other than the 500 *iugera* mentioned above) to one hundred head of cattle and five hundred sheep, goats and pigs; and the compulsory use of free labour for supervision. The law, which is mentioned by Cato in 167 and quoted at length by Appian, forms part of the long history of Roman legislation concerning *ager publicus*;[31] it almost certainly dates from the post-Hannibalic period. Control of the use of *ager publicus* was the only means whereby the Roman state could oppose to some extent the structural changes that were occurring in the Italian countryside and the breakdown of traditional social and economic relationships, but the almost complete lack of any mechanism of control was bound to frustrate the implementation of the rules and thwart the intentions of the law. As far as the current situation is concerned, the law demonstrates above all that large areas of public land were available; its aim must have been to regulate competition for the use of such land at a time when the upper classes had discovered that the exploitation of *ager publicus* represented an excellent investment for the financial resources acquired as a result of the wars of conquest. The

[31] *ORF*⁴, Cato fr. 167; App. *B. Civ.* 1.8.33–4; Tibiletti 1948–9, 3–19: (H 115), 1950, 246–66: (H 116); Toynbee 1965, II.554–61: (A 37); Gabba 1979, 159–63: (H 160).

graziers on whom the aediles imposed heavy fines in 196 and 193 were probably owners of large herds grazed illegally on public land.[32] The theory that it was they who took up the leases when grazing rights were offered for rent cannot be verified, but there can be no doubt that the lease of such rights represents a further serious setback for the owners of small and medium-sized herds grazing *ager publicus*; in this light it becomes easier to understand the limits on grazing imposed by the law *de modo agrorum*.

To appreciate the speed with which the simultaneous availability of vast tracts of land ready for exploitation and of abundant financial resources could set in motion a process that was to change substantially the agrarian, social and economic structures of Italy in the second century B.C., it should be remembered that the prevailing situation favoured such a development. The moral and civic values, the behaviour and the ideals which had traditionally been associated with an archaic agrarian society – with C. Fabricius, M'. Curius and perhaps M. Atilius Regulus among its last exemplars – were already ceasing to be character-istic of the Roman upper classes during the second half of the third century B.C.[33] Although the turning-point had been the First Punic War, which had brought rich spoils from Sicily, the process had already begun between the fourth and third centuries, with a decline in ancient forms of dependent labour based on *clientela* and *nexum* (a decline which was partly due to the process of colonization) and with the decisive establishment of slavery. The actions of the Roman governing class and, presumably, those of the Italian upper classes were increasingly motivated by the desire for self-enrichment; the senatorial oligarchy first acquired wealth 'in a proper manner' (*bono modo*), by investing the spoils of war in land, and later, in defiance of prohibitions which were in fact largely inoper-ative, by engaging in commercial activities. Such attitudes and activities are illustrated, for example, in the funeral oration of L. Caecilius Metellus in 221 B.C.[34] and some decades later in the prologue of Cato's treatise *de agri cultura*.

If this treatise is considered for a moment in isolation from its context, it appears at first sight to offer a disconcerting contradiction. The large plantations it describes, which were the estates of careful but absent owners, required considerable investment; they were intended for grow-ing a small number of specialized crops; they produced for the market but also satisfied the needs of the owner and his workforce; they promised a high and secure income. The location of such estates in relation to urban markets was all-important. They were based mainly on

[32] Livy XXXIII.42.10, XXXV.10.11.
[33] Doubts expressed in Harris 1979, 66, 264–5: (A 21).
[34] *ORF*[4], p. 10; Gabba 1981, 541–58: (H 44).

the use of slave labour, some of it skilled, but they also needed free workers. The Catonian farm as thus depicted certainly appears to conflict with the ideology expressed in the prologue, which harks back to the model of the small, self-sufficient peasant farm cultivating several crops and complemented by the use of common land, and to the figure of the Roman citizen as a farmer-soldier.

In fact the contradiction is only apparent; it is resolved by the timocratic nature of Roman and Italian society, which was regarded, not without reason, as being entirely right and proper, and as consistent with the political order of Rome and the other Italian states. Minimal social differentiation was by now a thing of the past, and the governing class now laid increasing emphasis on its superior economic capacity, which derived from the rewards of the wars of conquest. In his treatise, Cato is addressing precisely these men of high social and political status and suggesting profitable ways of employing the capital at their disposal. There can be no doubt that Rome saw these wealthy classes and their predominance as the guarantee of social and political stability in the Italian states; the entire course of events from the Hannibalic War to the Social War demonstrates that the Roman government always sought to protect the social standing and pre-eminence of these classes. On the other hand, the social structure of the Roman and Italian citizen body was not upset, or rather should not have been upset, by the presence of wealthy elements. There was indeed a certain degree of social mobility, of which Cato himself could be an example, which ensured the social and, to a lesser extent, political advancement of suitable people. Hence the traditional small and medium-sized peasant farm, with its subsistence economy, still represented to a certain extent the foundation of society, a foundation that had to be defended, in as far as it was possible to do so with the rudimentary means available for non-violent intervention in social affairs. The recurrent eulogy of the small farm was matched by Rome's commitment to the policy of colonization and land assignation as a means of artificially reproducing the traditional Italian structure of the small farm supplemented by the use of common land. This is the only possible explanation for the very small parcels of land that were still being granted in the citizen colonies founded in southern Italy soon after the Hannibalic War, parcels which on their own would not have permitted the colonists to survive. It can be seen, however, that the size of these assignations meant that they fitted well into the situation that already existed in the areas colonized. The social and political order originally established in the Latin colonies was one in which distinctions were based on the ownership of land. The artificial creation of two or three distinct social strata, sometimes markedly distinct, each with a different amount of land, placed the upper classes *de facto* and *de iure* in an impregnable position of dominance, but at the same time demonstrated the intention and the possibility of having different forms of land use coexist without conflict or contradiction – medium-sized properties linked to a subsistence economy alongside considerably larger estates producing for the market.

The distinction also led to differences in forms of settlement. The upper class will have lived in the urban centre of the colony; most of the less wealthy colonists will have been settled not in the urban area but on their plots of land (where they will have had greater contact with the indigenous population), thus in this way too reproducing the traditional Italian way of life.[35]

The most typical case is that of the Latin colony of Aquileia of 181 B.C., in which the 3,000 *pedites* were allocated 50 *iugera*, the *centuriones* 100 *iugera* and the *equites* 140 *iugera*. A few years later the colony was strengthened by the arrival of 1,500 more families, most probably *pedites* (Livy XL.54.2, XLIII.17). There is evidence or good reason for supposing that the Latin colonies of Cremona and Placentia (218), Thurii (193), Vibo (192) and Bononia (189) had a number of census classes, usually two, distinguished by differences in the area of land allocated.[36] If the colony of Aquileia was typical, it may be deduced that the *centuriones* and *equites* constituted the ruling classes and that the magistrates were drawn from among their number. It is very probable that the three classes voted separately, as in the *comitia centuriata* in Rome. Archaeological evidence to support this theory may be found in the three separate voting areas that have been uncovered in the forum of Cosa (a Latin colony dating from 273 B.C.), which seem to correspond to three categories of citizens, that is to say three distinct census classes. The number of areas rises to five after the influx of new colonists in 197 B.C., which will have further diversified the composition of the civic assembly.[37]

It seems likely, as we shall see, that the role, size and composition of the ruling classes were precisely defined in the law setting up a colony. Here it suffices to observe that, although there will have been some scope for social mobility within a Latin colony, it will have been very difficult to rise from the *pedites* to the class of the *centuriones*, let alone to that of the *equites*, which was thus socially impregnable. Furthermore, the upper two census classes held farms that did not differ much in size from those described by Cato. It is therefore difficult to imagine that they worked them themselves; they must have had to employ native labour, in the case of Aquileia most probably drawn from among the Carni and Catali. It is also possible that they lived in the town and that it was from these very

[35] Tozzi 1972, 17, 22: (H 166); Frederiksen 1976, 342–7: (H 88).
[36] Tibiletti 1950, 219ff.: (H 116).
[37] Brown 1979, 24–5, 32–3: (H 231); Crawford 1981, 155: (H 129).

classes that there sprang the commercial class of Aquileia. On the other hand, the *pedites*, who held much smaller properties which they will have worked themselves with the help of their families or with some outside labour, will have been scattered around the territory of the colony. The question of the presence of native labour in Latin and citizen colonies is closely linked to the problem of the assimilation of the previous inhabitants within colonies established in inhabited regions and the question of the direct inclusion of outsiders in the number of settlers.

II. THE ROLE OF THE ITALIAN ALLIES

In 200 B.C. the consul P. Sulpicius Galba used a number of fundamental arguments to win over the *comitia centuriata*, which was reluctant to accept the Senate's proposal of war against Philip V of Macedonia: he argued that a conflict was inevitable and that it was therefore preferable that the war be fought in Macedonia rather than in Italy; moreover, should Philip land in Italy, it was to be feared that the Italian peoples who had earlier defected to the side of the Carthaginians would not remain loyal.[38] There must have been a very real danger of renewed defection among the Italian allies, who were at that very moment suffering from the punishment imposed by the Romans. It was not for nothing that the institution of the *tumultus italicus gallicusve* – an emergency summons to arms in the face of a sudden military threat – still applied in the second century B.C., whatever its origin and date, and that it was normally embodied in the laws establishing Latin colonies.[39] There is clear evidence that again in 193 B.C. some of the most astute members of the Roman governing class did not exclude the possibility of an invasion of Italy such as Hannibal had suggested to King Antiochus of Syria, based on the assumption that part of Italy would rise to support an enemy of Rome.[40] Contemporaries must have been fully aware of the uncertain and insecure nature of Rome's relations with a large proportion of its Italian allies, as had been revealed dramatically by the defections during the Hannibalic War, and must have known that Rome's victory and the punitive measures taken had achieved only an apparent stabilization of the situation. The military function of the eight citizen colonies established in southern Italy in 194 B.C. was probably not only to guard the coast but also to watch over the interior in insecure areas that were potentially hostile and rebellious.[41] The purpose they served was differ-

---

[38] Livy XXXI.6–8.

[39] Cic. *Phil.* VIII.2–3; Livy XXXI.2.6, XXXII.26.12, XXXIV.56.11, XXXV.2.7, XL.6.7–8; Ilari 1974, 18 n. 33: (H 140). Cf. *lex col. Genet.* lines 30–1: Ilari 1974, 31 n. 10.

[40] Livy XXXIV.6.3–6; Passerini 1933, 10–28: (E 157).

[41] Livy XXXII.29.3ff., XXXIV.45.1–5; Tibiletti 1950, 196–7: (H 116); Salmon 1970, 96ff.: (H 152).

ent from that of the assignations of land in Apulia and Samnium to
Scipio's veterans a few years earlier.

Hostility towards Rome, which had induced some Italian communities to side with Hannibal, derived from much older historic grudges and
complaints. Rome's military superiority had contained this hostility and
had kept the allies loyal even after the initial defeats inflicted by
Hannibal. Polybius rightly emphasized the remarkable ability of the
Roman state to inspire obedience and respect even in such difficult
times.[42] It took the defeat at Cannae to demonstrate how Roman power
might be overcome and to shatter in large part the practical and theoretical basis of the network of alliances which Rome had concluded with the
Italian communities. Polybius recognizes that it was not only the main
cities in Magna Graecia that defected: all the other Italian peoples now
turned their eyes towards the Carthaginians. Rome had lost its supremacy over Italy.[43] This was clear proof that the military and political
superiority of Rome had hitherto been the main reason for the cohesion
of Italy. Polybius accepted the legitimacy of the Romans' desire to
dominate Italy and treat it as their sphere of influence in their confrontation with the Gauls and the Carthaginians,[44] on the basis of a geo-
political concept which recognized the substantial unity of the Italian
peninsula. Indeed, it was the common danger presented by the Gauls that
at one point gave the Italian peoples a reason for uniting in the knowledge that the defence of Italy against the Gauls was not one of the
habitual wars waged simply to further Roman hegemony, but represented the salvation of everyone.[45] Of course, this awareness should not be
seen as the emergence of a unified Italian consciousness. Indeed, the
Hannibalic War demonstrated the fragility of this unifying force, which
was based on external factors. However, by her final victory over the
Carthaginians, Rome reasserted her absolute predominance in Italy,
which was confirmed by the punitive measures taken against disloyal
allies and in many cases by a strengthening of the conditions of subordination set out in the different treaties. The allies who had remained loyal
to Rome certainly shared in the spirit and benefits of victory and derived
from it a new incentive to loyalty and obedience.[46] The system of
alliances, which had been revived *de iure*, was completely altered *de facto*
by the new position Rome had acquired in the Mediterranean.

It must have been quite clear at least to the leaders of the Italian
communities, as it obviously was to the governing class in Rome, that the
victory over Carthage would not only reassert Roman domination over
Italy and Sicily, but would also open the way for a policy of imperial
expansion.[47] Hitherto the allied Italian states had been junior partners,

---

[42] III.90.13–14.   [43] III.118.3–5.   [44] I.6.6, 10.5–6, II.14.4–12.   [45] Polyb. II.23.13–14.
[46] Badian 1958, 144–5: (A 3).
[47] Polyb. v.104.3–4: speech delivered by Agelaus at Naupactus in 217 B.C.

but henceforth they were to be transformed increasingly into constituent parts of the Roman state that were necessary to its very existence and taken for granted socially and politically. From the end of the third century onwards, they became local units in a political system that was very different from that of the past, as it was now projected on an imperial scale. It is difficult to say when the treaties concluded by Rome first contained the clause stipulating the *maiestas populi romani*, 'the majesty of the Roman people', which the ally undertook to preserve;[48] nor is it by any means certain, although it is highly likely, that the clause appeared in treaties with Italian peoples. What is certain is that the concept of *maiestas populi romani* developed and crystallized after the Hannibalic War as a consequence of Roman expansionism.

Provided that the Italian allies accepted and complied with Rome's new imperial requirements – and in practice they were obliged to do so – they could share in some of the rewards. This was the main reason why the Italian upper classes sought gradual economic and social parity with the Roman upper classes and pursued a spontaneous policy of cultural and political assimilation and integration, and finally demanded direct participation in the exercise of power. In the latter half of the second century B.C. this demand was to collide with a stiffening of the traditional elitist attitude of the Roman governing class. On the political plane it would lead eventually, at least in the opinion of enlightened oligarchs, to obedience being imposed on the Italian allies by fear rather than being sought, as before, by conviction and respect; this seems to be the view which lies behind the reasoning of P. Scipio Nasica in the speech opposing the destruction of Carthage and of C. Laelius in Cicero's *de republica*.[49]

Rome used the traditional instruments at her disposal to organize her new relationship with her Italian allies; it is pointless to reproach Rome for failing completely to reorganize her network of alliances to suit her new political objectives. Certainly, after the Hannibalic War, the juridical concept of Italy, with its religious implications, was defined with increasing clarity, partly on the basis of geo-political theories of Greek origin.[50] From Rome's point of view, this concept of Italy is linked with the complex of political and military relations with her allies, the *socii italici*. It is only in relation to the predominant partner, that is to say Rome, that they are seen as a group and thus bear this title. Naturally this did not involve any desire on the part of Rome to standardize the position of her Italian allies on a political, legal or administrative plane; even less did it foreshadow the conscious creation of a national Romano-Italian state.

[48] Cic. *Balb.* 35–7. On this question: Sherwin-White 1973, 183–9: (H 113); De Martino 1972–5, 108–9: (A 13); Ilari 1974, 34–41: (H 140).   [49] Diod. Sic. XXXIV.33.5; Cic. *Rep.* III.4.
[50] Gabba 1978, 11–16: (H 131); Ilari 1974, 23: (H 140).

We should not be misled by the unitary view of Polybius, which may seem to conflict in some ways with what has been said here. For he was examining the Roman state from the point of view of the centre of power and was comparing it with the Hellenistic monarchies, which were regarded as single entities. Polybius was interested in the ways in which power was actually exercised. Convinced as he was of the solidity of the Roman state, he saw no need to analyse the bases of the political organization of Roman Italy or indeed the relations between Rome and her allies. Proof lies in his description of Roman military organization in terms of a single citizen militia. In this context, the allied contingents are depicted as integrated and homogeneous parts of the Roman army.[51]

The fact that from the second century B.C. onwards an ideology of Italy was emerging and developing, an ideology that was to reach its peak in the age of Augustus, does not mean either that Roman policy was directed towards forming any kind of Italian unity or that this was ever actually achieved in ancient times.

Italian history received particular attention, not in contrast to Roman history, but as part of it, in Cato's *Origines*; in books II and III, he deals with the foundations of cities and the origins of Italian peoples,[52] although it is not clear whether this constitutes a separate treatise on geography or forms part of the historical narrative. In any case, the work provides evidence of a more than passing interest in the history of the Italian peoples which had been absent from Roman historiography up to that time and which would be difficult to reconcile with Cato's supposedly hostile political attitude towards the allies.

As the century progressed, the Roman governing class certainly became increasingly conscious of the process of economic and social change through which both Rome and the Italian states were passing, if only because its more dramatic manifestations in the form of a decline in population and, in consequence, a military crisis were easily understood and immediately visible. Nevertheless, all this occurred in the midst of euphoria, immediate benefits and an obvious spread of prosperity as a result of the policy of conquest. At the same time, the means available to an ancient state for modifying any part of the structure of society were minimal, and it was not until the time of Tiberius Gracchus that an attempt was made to present a programme for the restoration of Romano-Italian society along traditional lines.

As we have seen, the Romanization of Italy was sought mainly by the Italian upper classes and not by Rome, which was interested in maintaining the predominant position of these classes and in defending their social and political identities, since they were the guarantors of stability

[51] Polyb. VI.21.4–5, 26.3–10.   [52] Nepos, *Cato* III.3–4; Kierdorf 1980: (H 200).

within their states and of the efficient operation of their institutions and indeed formed the link between Rome and the states in question. Some aspects of the new relationship that had developed between Rome and her Italian allies are difficult to understand and assess. For example, there is above all the question of whether and to what extent any changes in the constitutional arrangements of the allied states and the inevitable subordination of the activities of their governments to the aims of Rome caused tensions to develop throughout society between compliance with Roman policy and Roman interests on the one hand and local needs and local ways of thinking on the other hand; such tensions will have militated against participation in the internal affairs of the Italian communities. And, as we shall see, actual emigration from Italian communities may be seen as a dramatic form of expression of this decline in participation.

Roman support for the Italian oligarchies, which was much more consistent than in pre-Hannibalic days,[53] and their increasing espousal of Roman policy are two factors inextricably involved in the developments of the period; they emerge with great clarity from all aspects of the tradition. The roots are an underlying coincidence and indeed convergence of the political and economic interests of the Roman and Italian governing classes that would seem to be beyond doubt. Of course, this does not necessarily mean that the various aspects of Romano–Italian relations in the second century B.C. should be interpreted solely in terms of class conflict, even though social tensions are frequently apparent. Equally, the allies' support for Rome, which was to lead to a complex process of Romanization and assimilation, should not be understood as implying that a unified set of Italian ideals or sentiments existed among the allied elites. They were motivated by practical reasons of self-interest, so that it is possible to believe that while acting in this way they had no thought of renouncing their ancient local traditions and the identity of their states; indeed, the literature of the first century B.C. bears clear witness to the vitality of these traditions. This conclusion may be supported by evidence which is drawn from a later period and which therefore represents even better the situation pertaining in the second century B.C. Several decades after the Social War Cicero attempted to come to grips with the complex problems of the local community by postulating in *de legibus* (II.1–5) the concept of the existence of two '*patriae, unam naturae, alteram civitatis, . . . alteram loci, alteram iuris*' (two fatherlands, one by nature, the other by citizenship . . . one by place, the other by law), thus seeking to reconcile the still powerful local realities of Italian history with that of the politically united state, the true *patria*,

[53] Badian 1958, 147–8: (A 3).

which deserved the name of *res publica*. The Ciceronian theory indicates a means of overcoming the difficulties arising from provincial thinking and interests, which were deeply rooted in the mentality and behaviour of the Romano–Italian upper classes. Furthermore, at the time of the Social War itself, the oath that M. Livius Drusus extracted from his Italian followers, to whom he wished to grant Roman citizenship, obliged them to recognize Rome as their *patria* and therefore aimed to create a political and religious ideal that transcended local patriotism.[54] The conflicts within the narrow ruling elite of Arpinum at the close of the second century B.C. and the subsequent appeal to Rome show clearly the extent to which a municipal nobility was still wedded to local interests.[55]

III. MIGRATION AND URBANIZATION

Nevertheless, whatever the intentions and wishes of the Roman and Italian governing classes, Roman and Italian elements did occasionally coalesce, with repercussions on a scale that was hard to predict. This involved primarily Latin and Italian participation in the Roman government's colonization schemes.

In 197 B.C. the Latin colony of Cosa was granted permission to recruit 1,000 new colonists; those who had not been among the enemies of Rome after 218 B.C. were also eligible to participate. This is obviously a reference to Italian elements. Indeed, it is very probable that the new colonists, who would certainly have been enrolled in the lower census classes, included Etruscans.[56] This provision also seems to indicate some difficulty in finding colonists among Roman citizens and Latins. It is hard to say whether the new colonists who settled in Venusia in 200 and in Narnia in 199 were assembled in the same way.[57]

In 194 it was decided to found two Latin colonies in the territory of the Bruttii and in the *ager* of Thurii. The colony of Thurii was established in 193 with 3,000 *pedites* (20 *iugera*) and 300 *equites* (40 *iugera*);[58] that of Vibo Valentia, founded in 192, comprised 3,700 *pedites* (15 *iugera*) and 300 *equites* (30 *iugera*) and probably represented the resettlement of a colony established in 239 B.C.[59] In both cases the previous inhabitants will have been absorbed into the colony; this was normal practice, and was to be expected, especially in the case of Vibo. Nonetheless, the land available at Thurii, for example, would have been sufficient either to settle a larger

---

[54] Diod. Sic. xxxvii.11.   [55] Cic. *Leg.* iii.36.

[56] Livy xxxv.24.8–9; Tibiletti 1950, 193–4: (H 116); Brown 1979, 32–3, 45: (H 231).

[57] Livy xxxi.49.6, xxxii.2.6; Tibiletti 1950, 192: (H 116).

[58] Livy xxxiv.53.1–2; the colony of Thurii is probably identical with that of Castrum Frentinum: Livy xxxv.9.7–8.

[59] Livy xxxv.40.5–6; Vell. Pat. 1.14.8; Tibiletti 1950, 240–4: (H 116); Salmon 1970, 99–100: (H 152).

number of colonists or to make more generous grants of land; owing to a lack of men, the first of these options was probably held open to allow for a future expansion that seems never to have occurred. At the same time, Rome will have wished to avoid the disruption to the local economy that would have resulted from granting larger plots of land.

This phase of the policy of colonization had aims which were mainly defensive and thus differed from those of the assignations made to reward Scipio's veterans in Apulia and Samnium. It must have run up against the problem caused by the general decline in population as a result of the war and the lack of interest in colonization of the ravaged areas in the centre and south. This is confirmed by the admission of non-Roman colonists even in small citizen colonies comprising no more than 300 families.

In 195 B.C., some of the Hernici living in Ferentinum, who were by now assimilated to the Latins, enrolled themselves among the colonists of Puteoli, Salernum and Buxentum and, having been accepted, immediately passed themselves off as Roman *cives* without awaiting the first census in the colonies. It would appear that the Senate denied them the status of Roman *cives* in advance, but did not reject the right of Latins to enrol themselves as colonists;[60] whatever their origin, all colonists received equal parcels of land. The passage in Livy is far from clear, but it is hard to imagine that the Latins who enrolled as colonists remained legally subordinate.[61] What is certain is that within a few years Buxentum had already been abandoned.[62]

Roman citizens, Latins and probably also Italians[63] all received viritane assignments in 173 B.C. in the *ager Ligustinus et Gallicus*, but the area of land allotted differed, the citizens receiving 10 *iugera* and the rest 3 *iugera*. This substantial difference is open to a number of interpretations. It is unlikely that the non-Roman assignees would become *cives* merely by virtue of the assignation; in any case, the non-Romans, who were probably in the majority, were certainly integrated in the Roman government's colonization programme but they were deliberately given a separate status that was inferior for the purpose of the census. Furthermore, larger assignations might have had repercussions on the social and political order of the communities from which these colonists came.

At all events, these assignations should be considered in the context of the more general problem of the colonization of Cisalpine Gaul which progressed in line with the military reconquest of the area and which was

---

[60] Livy xxxiv.42.5–6. The interpretation is that of Smith 1954, 18–20: (H 114); for a different view see Luraschi 1979, 73–4 and n. 140: (H 143).

[61] Tibiletti 1950, 197: (H 116).   [62] Livy xxxix.23.3 (186 B.C.).

[63] Livy xlii.4.3–4 (and also xli.16.7–9). This interpretation of the expression *socii nominis Latini* follows Wegner 1969, 95–104: (H 156), which includes a discussion of the various theories.

responsible for the official settlement of more than 100,000 persons in the course of the century, to whom must be added spontaneous immigrants, who were certainly numerous. The historical writings of Cato and Polybius[64] faithfully echo the strong impression of richness and fertility that the Romans gained of the Po valley; this richness, fertility and populousness were admittedly due in large measure to the Roman colonization of the area, but initially they must have been the result of the natural state of the land and must have constituted the spur to colonization, which progressed all the more rapidly as living conditions in the region became more secure. It is worth emphasizing the pioneering spirit that must have inspired the Roman and Italian colonists of the region during this period, and the great difference between these men and the later Gracchan assignees who benefited from the 'organized assistance' of the state.[65]

At the same time, it may be assumed that the Roman ruling class took a generally favourable view of this largely spontaneous movement of the peasant masses towards the north (and towards the Iberian provinces) as it enhanced the availability of areas in the centre and south of the peninsula for the development of its own economic activities. Further preconditions were thus created, particularly in the south, for a profound change in the methods of working the land and hence a transformation of traditional agrarian society. The process of colonization was on such a scale that it must have affected Romans, Latins and Italians alike and must also have involved the local populations, albeit indirectly and as subordinates during the early stages. The latter were probably restricted to secondary settlements within the territory of the colonies and assignations, as some recent sophisticated topographical studies would seem to indicate.[66] In 172 B.C., however, the Ligurian communities of the Appennine regions, which had not committed any hostile acts since 179, were transferred to Gallia Transpadana and given land there.[67] The possibility cannot be ruled out that some indigenous social and economic relationships, such as clientage, as well as typically Celtic forms of dependence or forms of land tenure inherited from the Etruscan era may have survived long after the Roman conquest of these areas.[68]

In addition to the massive reinforcement of the Latin colonies of

---

[64] Heurgon 1974: (H 194); Tozzi 1976: (H 167).

[65] Tibiletti 1955, 268–9: (H 117). For the presence of Samnite elements in Cisalpine Gaul see Pais 1918, 415–57: (H 148); Robson 1934, 599–608: (H 165).

[66] Polybius' claim in II.35.4 that they were expelled cannot and should not be taken as true everywhere.

[67] Livy XLII.22.5–6; Pais 1918, 56off.: (A 29); an attempt to locate them in the area of Mantua in Luraschi 1981, 73–80: (H 144).

[68] Polyb. II.17.12; Heurgon 1967: (I 22). There is an obvious similarity with the situation indicated by the Sententia Minuciorum to have existed in Genoese territory.

Placentia and Cremona in 190,[69] there was the founding of the great Latin colony of Bononia in 189 B.C.[70] The citizen colonies of Mutina and Parma were established in 183; these were the first colonies of the citizen type to receive a large number of colonists (3,000) and to differ from the traditional maritime citizen colonies as far as aims and locations were concerned.[71] The same number of colonists was settled in the colony of Luna in 177.[72] The citizen colonies of Potentia and Pisaurum, which date from 184 B.C., were maritime colonies, however; at least some of the settlers came from southern Campania.[73] Another colony in Picenum was that of Auximum.[74] The colonies of Saturnia and Graviscae were founded in Etruria in 183 and 181, to be followed a few years later by that of Heba.[75]

The decision to establish a colony at Aquileia with the evident military purpose of protecting the point of easiest access to Italy was taken in 183 B.C., after a debate in the Senate on the question of whether it was to have citizen or Latin status.[76] The second option was adopted. It was probably argued successfully that Roman citizens sent so far away would have difficulty in exercising their civic rights. It should also be borne in mind, however, that it was easier to incorporate colonists from allied communities into a Latin colony and in fact it may be the case that Venetic elements were enrolled. Nonetheless, the clear demarcation of the first two census classes will have guaranteed that the control of local government rested with colonists of Roman or Latin origin.[77] The actual foundation took place in 181 and, as mentioned above, the colonists were allocated parcels of land enough to require the indigenous population to remain in the colony in a subordinate position. Aquileia is sometimes said to have been the last Latin colony, but it seems probable that one more was established, at Luca in 177 B.C., in order to stem the continual incursions of the Ligurians.[78]

It is worth recalling at this point that the great difference in size between the plots granted in Latin colonies and those of citizen colonies can be explained convincingly in terms of the staunchly upheld principle of avoiding radical changes in the structure of the Roman citizen body; large assignations of land in citizen colonies would have had just such an effect. The small plots of land granted as in outright ownership, which

[69] Livy XXXVII.46.9–47.2.   [70] Livy XXXVII.57.7–8; Vell. Pat. 1.15.2.

[71] Livy XXXIX.55.6.   [72] Livy XLI.13.4.   [73] Livy XXXIX.44.10; Lazzeroni 1962: (H 285).

[74] Perhaps prior to 174: Livy XLI.27.10–13; Harris 1971, 150 n. 6: (H 136). Dated to 157 by Vell. Pat. 1.15.3; moved to 128 by Salmon 1963, 10ff.: (H 150).

[75] Livy XXXIX.55.9, XL.29.1–2; Vell. Pat. 1.15.1. For Heba: Harris 1971, 150: (H 136) (between 167 and 157 B.C.).

[76] Livy XXXIX.55.5, XL.34.2; Vell. Pat. 1.15.2; De Sanctis 1907–64, IV.i.428: (A 14).

[77] For a different view see Bernardi 1973, 102–3: (H 126).

[78] Galsterer 1976, 63 n. 105: (H 132), contra the view that the references to Luca arise from confusion with Luna, certainly founded in 177.

were smaller than was needed for subsistence, were supplemented by the use of common land for arable farming and grazing. In Latin colonies, by contrast, it was necessary to create autonomous communities with their own social and political hierarchies.[79]

As Latin colonies had always served military ends, the main reason for the halt in the foundation of colonies of this kind is to be sought in the situation that was developing in Italy in the first three decades of the second century B.C.[80] If we consider that towards the end large numbers of Italians were being admitted to the citizen bodies of these colonies, it seems unlikely that the cause of their demise was the reluctance of Roman citizens to renounce their citizenship in order to acquire that of the colony. It is more probable that the halt in the foundation of new Latin colonies is to be explained in terms of the growing interest of the Roman and Italian upper classes in the exploitation of *ager publicus*; it may, however, also be seen as another step towards a more rational organization of Roman territory, similar to the gradual accession of *cives sine suffragio*, 'citizen communities without the right to vote', to full citizenship that took place during the first half of the second century B.C. In 188 the *ius suffragii*, 'the right to vote in Roman assemblies', was granted to Arpinum, Formiae and Fundi; other communities must have received it by 133 B.C.[81] In spite of this, Arpinum was able to preserve a body of public law different from that of Rome.[82] (It would be interesting to know whether it was before or after 188 that Arpinum obtained the territories in Cisalpine Gaul from which it was still receiving revenues at the time of Caesar.[83])

In fact, the entire process of colonization promoted by the Roman government began to slow down after the first three decades of the second century, not only for political reasons, but also because the urge that had driven Romans and Italians to seek new lands in the fertile area of Cisalpine Gaul or in Spain had waned. The policy of colonization provided a possible solution to the problem posed by the steady decline in the category of medium and small farmers in the centre and south, in that the colonists were mainly Romans and Italians from the lower social classes. It enabled them to regain, albeit in far-flung regions, the economic and social independence that had been seriously curtailed or even lost in their original communities. From the end of the second century B.C. onwards this independence was to be rediscovered in the army or as a result of army service. And it was therefore both a cause and an effect of

[79] Tibiletti 1950, 219–32: (H 116).
[80] Galsterer 1976, 64: (H 132). For a general treatment: Bernardi 1973, 101ff.: (H 126).
[81] Livy XXXVIII.36.7–9; Brunt 1965, 93: (H 127); Humbert 1978, 346–7: (H 139).
[82] Cic. *Leg.* III.36; Nicolet 1967: (H 75).
[83] Cic. *Fam.* XIII.11.1; Nicolet 1967, 302 n. 4: (H 75).

the acceleration in the transformation of agrarian society in the central and southern areas of the peninsula, which has been associated with emigration throughout the history of Italy.

Internal migration was also a powerful factor making for the assimilation of the different peoples of Italy. This mainly took the form of urbanization, Rome being naturally the main pole of attraction. Urbanization originally arose as a result of the hostilities during the Second Punic War and the wholesale abandonment of the areas most at risk. It was no easy task for the consuls of 206 B.C. to persuade refugee farmers to return to their devastated fields.[84] The phenomenon assumed larger proportions in the decades that followed, however, with the massive infiltration of Rome by Latins and Italians. In 198 B.C. as many as 12,000 who had been living in the city since 204 B.C. were sent back to their communities.[85] The problem continued to simmer, but in 177 it re-emerged in a more dramatic and complicated guise. The migration of Latins and allies to Rome led to the gradual abandonment of villages and lands and jeopardized the provision of soldiers.[86] Italian migrants were also settling in Latin colonies; for example, 4,000 Samnite and Paelignian families had moved to Fregellae, prompting complaints from their original communities, which were nonetheless obliged to supply the same military contingents. The colony of Fregellae was careful not to protest.[87] Fregellae will not have been the only such instance. As early as 199 the colony of Narnia had complained about infiltration by outsiders who behaved like colonists. An inscription in Aesernia dating probably from the second century B.C. attests the presence of *Samnites inquolae* within the Latin colony, who were duly organized in a corporate or collegiate association; it is not clear whether these were recent immigrants or the remnants of the population that had inhabited the region before the foundation of the colony in 263 B.C.[88]

It seems that one of the causes of migration to Rome was the opportunity offered initially perhaps only to Latin colonists, then to all Latins and finally also to Italian allies, to become Roman citizens if they moved to Rome and left male descendants in the town from which they came. This combination of rights and obligations, which was undoubtedly embodied in the laws establishing colonies and in treaties with the allies, was probably not a recent innovation, as has sometimes been supposed,[89] but abuse of it by more or less legal means was certainly a

---

[84] Livy xxviii.11.8–9.
[85] Livy xxxix.3.4–6; Tibiletti 1950, 204ff.: (H 116); Luraschi 1979, 63ff.: (H 143).
[86] Livy xli.8.6–7.   [87] Livy xli.8.8; Tibiletti 1950, 204, n. 3: (H 116).
[88] La Regina, *RIGS*, 327; Galsterer 1976, 54: (H 132); Humbert 1978, 346 n. 34: (H 139). For the *incolatus*: Laffi 1966, 193ff.: (H 102).
[89] Tibiletti 1950, 213 n. 4: (H 116); Badian 1958, 150: (A 3); Luraschi 1979, 91 and n. 209: (H 143); cf. McDonald 1944, 20–1: (H 145).

new development;[90] what must have been intended as an exceptional case
had now become widespread practice. In 177 the Roman government
took a series of measures – consular laws, consular edicts and *senatus
consulta* which were interlinked, though in what manner is far from clear[91]
– which in effect limited the capacity of Latins and allies to acquire
Roman citizenship through migration and the (Roman) census (*per
migrationem et censum*), obliged them to register in their own town of
origin and hence to return home, instituted enquiries to ascertain the
transgressors and established checks on the subterfuges used to circumvent the law. It is highly doubtful how far it was in practice possible to
apply these provisions; it is certain that in 173 a further consular edict
called upon *socii* to return home and be registered there.[92]

That such measures were prejudicial to the rights and interests of *socii*
who had moved to Rome is obvious and is explicitly stated by Cicero,[93]
although he is probably referring to the expulsion of Latins and allies in
the Gracchan and post-Gracchan period, which was motivated by entirely different political reasons. Furthermore, our sources leave no room
for doubt that the measures dating from the first half of the second
century B.C. were taken by the Roman government at the repeated
request of the governing classes of the allied states, which were concerned at the fall in the number of citizens in their communities and the
effect this had on the supply of the military contingents requested of
them by Rome. From a practical point of view, it must have been a matter
of indifference to the Romans whether these allies were registered in
their native communities or as citizens in Rome, but the latter option
threatened the political, social and economic stability of the allied states,
which Rome had to take steps to maintain. In a sense, the demographic
and military decline that the allied states were suffering prefigured the
social and economic transformation which was to affect Rome and Italy
as a whole and which, worsening as time went on, finally led to the
Gracchan attempt at restoration and reform in 133 B.C. From this point
of view it may be claimed that the measures taken by Rome favoured the
allies; equally, it cannot be ruled out that a certain elitism on the part of
the Romans played a small though not decisive role.

Two points require clarification: who were the immigrants and what
were their aims? In view of the scale of the phenomenon, it is easy to
conclude that in general they were allies belonging to the lower social
classes; it was their departure in large numbers from their native communities that threatened the latter's social and military capability, not the
absence of members of the aristocracy engaging in commerce, whether

90 Livy XLI.8.10–11.   91 Livy XLI.8.12, 9.9–12; Luraschi 1979, 64–6: (H 143).
92 Livy XLII.10.3.   93 Cic. *Sest.* 30; Luraschi 1979, 94 n. 222: (H 143).

they be few or many. It can be sensed that a profound change was thus beginning to occur in the relations within the allied cities between the lower classes and the governing classes, which were always more in-clined to identify themselves with the Roman governing class, its needs and its policies; for the more enterprising sections of the lower classes, emigration, that is to say non-participation in local affairs, increasingly meant mobility and freedom. The upper classes' traditional role as representatives of their societies and their interests gradually diminished in importance, although they continued to occupy positions of power owing to the support of Rome. In the Gracchan era the contrast was to intensify into social conflict. As far as aims are concerned, emigration was basically the result of economic factors and does not indicate any desire to obtain Roman citizenship. There were many factors that must have encouraged a move to Rome by the economically disadvantaged, who were now also in the process of becoming proletarianized: the decline of traditional agrarian society and the change in methods of farming, which Rome had unsuccessfully tried to curb with measures relating to the use of *ager publicus*; the awareness, brought about by overseas wars, of the possibility of a higher standard of living and of the vast spread of prosperity in the cities, particularly Rome; the profound change in needs, attitudes and behaviour (factors that bear some responsibility for the decline in the way of life that represented tra-ditional economic patterns); the new and varied opportunities offered by the capital city.

It is not difficult to suppose that this drift away from the land will have affected mainly areas which were not urbanized and where settlements were tribal in character. It seems that such areas only began to develop slowly towards forms of urban organization during the second century, although it is worth stressing that scattered forms of settlement never actually disappeared. At the same time, some small towns in the interior experienced a phase of decline during roughly the same period.[94]

It was certainly not Roman citizenship as such that attracted these emigrants; participation in the political life of the city would, by contrast, be demanded by allied groups belonging to the upper classes at the end of the century. It was the lure of the great city, which held out the chance of rehabilitation and social and economic recovery. This also explains the movement of population towards the Italian sea-ports which were more directly involved in the development of trade with the provinces. During the second century Ostia, Puteoli and also Pompeii grew as a result of the movement of population towards the towns.[95] After the arrival of the new colonists the city of Cosa also experienced an intensification of

---

[94] Crawford 1981, 158: (H 129).   [95] Gabba 1976, 316: (H 91).

building activity and exploitation of its territory that lasted nearly a century.[96] Registration in the Roman census, when that occurred, was simply an incidental consequence of migration which many will have avoided.

The desire for social and economic improvement also spurred the allies to volunteer in large numbers as colonists. The significance of this mobility should not be evaluated solely in socio-economic terms. It also had considerable cultural and religious consequences, in that it involved a rejection of narrow horizons and a receptiveness to new ways of life and thought. After the Hannibalic War, Rome had become the crossroads of the Mediterranean world. Urbanization had not involved simply an influx of Italian peasants from areas within the peninsula. People and ideas came from outside, and the latter found fertile ground in which to spread, not only among the lower classes. A new desire for alternative forms of religious experience can be observed in Roman and Italian society at the time of the Hannibalic War.[97] When this desire coincided with problems of public order, the Roman government was forced to intervene and suppress certain practices. The episode of the Bacchanalia in 186 revealed the penetration of Rome by people from southern Italy and Etruria and the introduction of alien cults. This penetration was regarded as a danger, threatening subversion of city, society and state, since it led to instances of *coniuratio*; eradication required the involvement of the whole of Italy.[98] Repression did not fail to arouse adverse reactions among Italian intellectuals. In 181 B.C., the destruction of the 'Books of Numa' represented the elimination of politically dangerous texts.[99] A similar incident occurred in 139 B.C., when the *praetor peregrinus* ordered the astrologers (Chaldeans), against whom Cato had already warned, to be expelled from Rome and Italy, made Jews not domiciled in Rome return to their homes in Italian towns, and cleared private altars from public places.[100] The political danger of alien cults, particularly oriental and mystical ones, lay mainly in the opportunity they gave their adherents to approach the deity direct without the mediation of the political authorities, as in the cults of the traditional religion of Rome.

In the second half of the second century B.C., there was a notable move to develop urban centres in areas of Roman and Italian territory outside Rome and many shrines were built or rebuilt.[101] Clearly the upper classes used the vast wealth accumulated as a result of war, imperial exploitation and trade to embellish and construct large sacred complexes both in their cities (such as the temple of Fortuna Primigenia in Praeneste and that of

---

[96] Brown 1979, 33: (H 231).   [97] McDonald 1944, 26ff.: (H 145).
[98] Cova 1974: (H 37).   [99] Livy XL.29.3ff.
[100] Val. Max. 1.3.3; Bickerman 1980, 329–35: (E 90).
[101] Cianfarani 1960: (H 232); also *Sannio*: (H 153). For a general treatment see Gros 1978: (H 242).

Hercules in Tibur) and in rural areas, the tribal sphere where ethnic shrines had always had an extremely important political and economic role in addition to their religious function. This blossoming of imposing buildings (such as the great theatre temple of Pietrabbondante in Pentrian Samnium, which was completed shortly before the Social War) certainly indicates the extent to which Greek culture had penetrated into Italian areas, but above all it proves the common political desire of the Roman and Italian upper classes, transcending autonomist tendencies and local pride, to redirect the religious needs of all social classes towards traditional cults and places of worship and thus stem dangerous experimentation with uncontrollable alien religions. The same aim later lies behind the Augustan reconstruction of the temples of Rome. In a sense, this period of intensive temple-building opens in the middle of the second century B.C. with Polybius' comment on the Romans' ability to control the masses by means of religious practices, and closes in the early years of the first century B.C. with the enquiries of the *pontifex* Q. Mucius Scaevola into the functions of religion for the people.[102]

IV. MILITARY OBLIGATIONS AND ECONOMIC INTERESTS

The lamentations of the Italian communities about the decline in population, which must undoubtedly have changed the numerical ratio between citizens and allies during the course of the second century B.C.,[103] dwell on the difficulties it caused in fulfilling their military obligations. The same problem lies at the heart of the Gracchan arguments at the time of the proposed agrarian law in 133 B.C., and there can be no doubt that it was capable of profoundly affecting the attitudes and decisions of the Roman government. Latin and Italian allies were obliged to meet Rome's requests for contingents of troops under the laws establishing colonies and under individual treaties, which will have laid down the two parties' reciprocal obligations to give military assistance and the services to be rendered by the allies; the treaties will also sometimes have given Rome the right to grant or recognize *vacationes*. Within the individual Italian states, with a rigidly timocratic system of government kept up to date by periodic censuses, military levies will have followed a procedure similar to that employed in Rome.[104] The common use of the census was an indirect spur to the political and administrative assimilation of Italian states. As far as Rome was concerned, the allied communities were entered in a kind of military register or roll, the so-called *formula togatorum*, which formed the basis of Rome's annual demands for the

[102] Polyb. VI.56.6–11; Aug. *Civ. D.* IV.27; Schiavone 1976, 5ff.: (H 111); cf. Cic. *Leg.* II.19, 25–6; Goar 1972, 22–8: (H 284).   [103] Badian 1958, 150: (A 3).   [104] Polyb. VI.21.5.

required allied contingents.[105] There was probably a system of alternation or rotation so that over a period of time the military burden fell evenly. Although the laws and treaties will have paid due regard to the diverse social and economic situations of the different allies, it is impossible to say whether they laid down the precise size of the contingents to be provided or indicated the criteria for setting the quotas according to the needs of the moment. It seems unlikely that no provision was made for changes in the size of the citizen bodies in the allied states.

The ratio of allied troops to Roman soldiery must have varied according to the occasion. The general proportions indicated in the ancient sources (an equal number of infantry but the allied cavalry three times the number of the Roman cavalry, according to Polybius; twice as many allies as Roman citizens at the time of the Hannibalic War according to Appian and at all times according to Velleius) appear to relate to different times in history if they are compared with the fairly reliable detailed figures that have come down to us.[106] There are many indications that the Roman government tended to place the greater part of the military burden on the allies immediately after the Hannibalic War and again in the second half of the second century B.C.[107] If this burden is to be evaluated correctly it should naturally be viewed in relation to the size of the populations of the allied communities, which we do not know. If the burden was heavier for the allies, this fact – along with the phenomenon of emigration – could explain why complaints about a decline in population were voiced primarily by the allies.

It must be assumed in any case that the entire system of allied military obligations was modified and updated over the years. For example, in 193 B.C. the enrolment of the allied contingents took account of the number of *juniores*, perhaps because the allied communities were unable, temporarily at least, to supply troops according to the *formula*.[108] Something that certainly underwent an almost complete transformation was the political and military significance of allied participation in Rome's wars after the Hannibalic War, a transformation which paralleled the shift in Roman policy from an Italian to a Mediterranean and imperial orientation. No more wars on a basis of equality or for mutual defence such as those against the Gauls; participation now meant involvement as subordinates in a policy of expansion. Undoubtedly the allies had by now been integrated into the Roman army,[109] but the political advantages of

[105] Polyb. vi.21.4; Ilari 1974: (H 140); Giuffrè 1975: (H 134). Brunt 1971, 545–8: (H 82), is fundamental.

[106] Polyb. iii.107.12, vi.26.7 and 30.2; App. *Hann.* 8.31; Vell. Pat. ii.15.2; Brunt 1971, 677–86: (H 82).   [107] Gabba 1976, 187 n. 61: (H 42).

[108] Livy xxxiv.56.6; McDonald 1944, 20: (H 145); Galsterer 1976, 160: (H 132); for a different view see Ilari 1974, 73–5: (H 140).

[109] Göhler 1939, 31: (H 135); Frank, *CAH*[1] viii.361. However, they were denied the benefits granted under the third *lex Porcia*, dating from about 150–135: McDonald 1944, 19–20: (H 145).

victory and conquest were reserved almost exclusively for Rome; some of the economic benefits did reach the allies, but certainly not in proportion to their war-effort. In this respect the disparity between Rome and the Italian states gradually widened, and the allies became increasingly aware that they had helped create an empire in which they enjoyed only part of the fruits and which was beyond their political control. It was primarily the Italian mercantile class which noticed this great disparity between what they gave and what they received through involvement in Roman policy, even though the members of this class had business links with their Roman equivalents and were certainly not in conflict with the generally Romanophile governing classes of their own communities, to which indeed they belonged. This does not necessarily mean that the allies were forced or coerced into participation in military operations, particularly in the early decades of the second century, or that it was for reasons of internal politics that they were sympathetic towards an expansionist policy which obliged them to send their sons to lands far from Italy. The attitudes to be found in allied communities were probably on balance the same as those encountered in Rome. In many cases both allies and Romans will have seen the overseas wars as providing an opportunity for enrichment, quite apart from the distribution of booty, which was usually shared equally among Roman and allied soldiers.[110] It was the pay and rewards received by allied troops that introduced Roman currency and an exchange economy to inland areas of the peninsula and brought with it corresponding forms of behaviour.[111] In this manner too, military activities may have served as a cement between Rome and her allies. Viewed in this light the expansionist policy of Rome may actually have prevented potential internal political conflicts from surfacing.[112]

It is more difficult to guess the position of the upper classes, probably torn between a generally pro-Roman attitude and the increasingly heavy responsibility of administering their communities. It was they who foresaw the consequences of the fall in population resulting from emigration. The problems will not have been confined to the levy itself; the financial burden on the allied communities deriving from their responsibility for the pay of their troops[113] will have fallen increasingly on the upper classes, because emigration drew away not only potential soldiers but also potential taxpayers. Although *tributum* was no longer levied in Rome after 167 B.C., the allied states undoubtedly continued to collect taxes from their citizens; this was not the least of their complaints

---

[110] Polyb. x.16.4; Livy XL.43.7, XLI.43.7. The discrepancy which occurred in 177, recorded in Livy XLI.12.7–8, is certainly an exception. For a general treatment see Brunt 1971, 394: (H 82); Harris 1979, 102–4: (A 21).   [111] Crawford 1983, 47–50: (B 88A).

[112] Momigliano 1974, 3 = 1980, 1.125–6: (B 20).   [113] Polyb. VI.21.5.

on the eve of the tribunate of Tiberius Gracchus.[114] It has to be said, however, that the Italian upper classes will have found some recompense for this fiscal burden in their participation in the exploitation of *ager publicus* and even more in the advantages that imperial expansion provided for their commercial activities.

During the second century B.C. the establishment and spread of Rome's political predominance in the Mediterranean basin brought with it growing commercial and economic expansion as well as the benefits that sprang directly from the military victories. As early as the middle of the third century B.C. a new set of ethics had begun to develop that was imbued with utilitarian principles; it cannot have failed to influence the process of expansion and it certainly helped to overcome the traces of a narrow 'peasant' mentality surviving in a significant section of the governing class. Economic change therefore had an important effect on attitudes and behaviour, a process in which the Italian upper classes were also directly involved.[115] The broad identity between merchants and landowners must have been even more obvious than at Rome. There is abundant evidence from as early as the third century B.C. that the mercantile classes of southern Italy, especially Campania but also elsewhere, had interests in the Greek East; during the second century these became still stronger and gave rise to measures by the Roman government to protect Roman and Italian traders.[116] Although there is at the moment a tendency to emphasize the prevalence of Roman *cives*, especially among the *negotiatores* in Delos, it remains a fact that much trade was in the hands of Italian *socii*. The designations 'Italians' and 'Rhomaioi' for merchants in the Greek world before 90 B.C. usually refer to Roman citizens and allies indifferently,[117] thus confirming the theory that the first signs of unity among inhabitants of the peninsula appeared abroad. The presence of Rhodian amphora stamps datable to the second century and part of the first in central Samnium (Monte Vairano, Larinum) seems to provide clear proof of the receptiveness of these regions to Greek cultural influences and also indirectly of the commercial enterprise of south Italian *negotiatores*.[118] The involvement of Italian elements in economic activity overseas led eventually to a demand for participation in the political management of the Roman state.

Collusion between Roman and Italian interest groups had a long history. The situation that led in 193 B.C. to approval of the *lex Sempronia de pecunia credita*, which arose out of the moneylenders' practice of

[114] App. *B. Civ.* 1.7.30, with commentary in Gabba 1958: (B 8); Gabba 1977, 22–3: (H 43); Nicolet 1978: (H 147).

[115] Gabba 1976, 75ff.: (H 42); Wilson 1966, 85ff.: (H 121); Brunt 1971, 209ff.: (H 82); Cassola 1971, 305–22: (H 128).   [116] Livy XXXVIII.44.4: 187, Ambracia; Harris 1979, 94: (A 21).

[117] Brunt 1971, 205ff.: (H 82); Ilari 1974, 3ff.: (H 140).

[118] *Sannio*, 342–8: (H 153); Bevilacqua 1980, 21–34: (H 226).

employing Latin and Italian agents to circumvent the prohibitions of the existing law, illustrates the close links between Romans and Italians in the financial field.[119] It would be reasonable to suggest that Cato's associates in his activities in the field of maritime loans were not all Roman citizens.[120] It seems natural to suppose that economic interests had a growing, if indirect influence on Rome's political decisions during the second century B.C., although that is not to say that they were determining factors. The sharing of interests between Romans and Italians suggests that even the latter were in a position to make their opinions known, in that their interests depended to a large extent on the credibility of Roman power.[121]

V. ROMAN INTERVENTION

So far we have indicated some of the main factors that led more or less indirectly and spontaneously to the increasing alignment of the Italian states with Rome during the second century B.C., in the sense that the main characteristics of autonomy and independence that each Italian state still possessed in theory were being slowly but inexorably eroded. Of course, this levelling process received some impetus from Rome's direct interventions in the internal affairs of the allied states. In modern scholarly work, the scale and character of such interventions provide the most important evidence for an evaluation of Roman policy towards the Italian *socii* during the second century and in the period leading up to the Social War. On this question the most interesting ancient source is Polybius VI.13.4–5, which forms part of the historian's reasoning on the position and competence of the Senate in the operation of the constitutional mechanisms of the Roman state.[122] 'Similarly, crimes committed in Italy, which require a public investigation, such as treason, conspiracy, poisoning and assassination, are under the jurisdiction of the Senate. Also if any private person or community in Italy is in need of arbitration or indeed claims damages or requires succour or protection, the Senate attends to all such matters.'

Polybius' text relates to a juridically defined territorial sphere much larger than the *ager Romanus* alone. It makes no distinction between administrative intervention and the criminal jurisdiction of the Roman state (magistrates acting on behalf of the Senate) in allied states, but it does separate criminal actions capable of jeopardizing the political,

[119] Livy xxxv.7.1–5; Göhler 1939, 53ff.: (H 135); McDonald 1944, 20: (H 145).
[120] Plut. *Cat. Mai.* 21.5–6; Gabba 1980, 92–4: (H 92).   [121] Harris 1979, 97–9: (A 21).
[122] Mommsen 1887–8, III.1197ff.: (A 25); Göhler 1939, 37–69: (H 135); Sherwin-White 1973, 119ff.: (H 113); McDonald 1944, 13ff.: (H 145); Walbank 1957–79, 1.679–80: (B 38); Badian 1958, 145ff.: (A 3).

military and social standing of the Italian states, and thus automatically necessitating Roman intervention to restore order, from other cases of much less importance in which Rome's intervention might be encouraged or requested by an allied city or one of its citizens. It goes without saying that in both types of case the need for and feasibility of Roman intervention must have been dealt with and provided for in treaties with the allies and in the laws establishing colonies. By their very legitimacy these forms of intervention differed sharply from the abuses of power that Roman magistrates could commit at the expense of allied states.

Instances of intervention requested by allied communities themselves are the best documented. They could take the form of arbitration by Roman magistrates to settle boundary disputes between two autonomous communities, such as those recorded in Latin inscriptions in the area of the Venetia,[123] or settlement of disputes within the same allied territory between the dominant community and a subordinate one, such as the celebrated case of the judgement delivered *ex senati consulto* by the brothers Q. and M. Minucii Rufi in 117 B.C. (documents of this kind were obviously expressed in Latin).[124] Direct intervention was also possible to subdue more or less violent political and social conflicts within allied cities – these were probably the cases in which Rome intervened at the request of individual citizens or groups of citizens, in other words elements in one of the factions in the struggle, and it is easy to imagine that the Roman government took the side of the upper classes. One example from the second century B.C. must suffice: the insurrection of Patavium in 175, for which the intervention of a consul was requested.[125] A century earlier, in 265 B.C., the Romans had responded to a call made under the terms of the relevant treaty by intervening in force to put down a seizure of power by the serfs in Volsinii.[126]

Other kinds of intervention prompted by non-Italian allied communities were designed to establish laws relating to the internal constitution of the cities, particularly the composition and recruitment of local senates. Their main aim was to maintain the dominant position of specifically identified elements within the citizen body of the cities. The settlements are of the greatest interest, as they will have been modelled on arrangements already tested in Italian areas, and probably also indicate the way in which in Latin colonies, for example, the pre-eminence of citizens registered in the highest census class was originally secured, especially where the citizen body was of varied and heterogeneous

---

[123] *CIL* 1².633 = *ILS* 5944a; *CIL* 1².634 = *ILS* 5944; *ILS* 2501 = *ILLRP* 176 (Patavium and Ateste), 142 or 116 B.C.; *CIL* 1².636 = *ILLRP* 477(Ateste and Vicetia), 135 B.C. Mazzarino 1979, 590–4: (B 53).   [124] *CIL* 1².584 = *ILS* 5946 = *ILLRP* 517 = Bruns, *Font.* 184.
[125] Livy XLI.17.3–4.   [126] Zon. VIII.7.8; Flor. 1.16; Harris 1971, 91–2: (H 136).

origin.[127] The examples from Sicily may indicate that similar Roman intervention occurred in Italian cities and hence that this was a further way of aligning Italian constitutions with that of Rome, even though it is probable that except in dangerous situations Rome did not often intervene in order to reform or reorganize the constitutions of allied cities. Finally, the obscure *senatus consultum* concerning Tibur in about 159 B.C. may give us an idea of the reprimand of an allied community by Rome.[128]

Instances of entirely legitimate intervention on the initiative of the Roman government itself were much more serious. The best known case is the *senatus consultum* of 186 B.C. to repress the Bacchic cult, whose manifestations were regarded as a form of *coniuratio* against the state.[129] Even though the *ager Teuranus* in Bruttium where the bronze tablet with the *senatus consultum* was discovered was probably *ager Romanus*,[130] there seems to be no reason to doubt that Roman repression directly or indirectly involved Roman and Latin territory and that of the Italian allies and the responsibilities of their respective magistrates.[131] Similar situations arose in the case of slave revolts and natural disasters requiring Roman intervention which it would have been difficult to limit strictly to the territory of the state of Rome.[132] Such interventions were exceptional and occasional in nature. Indeed, a further question is the Roman government's actual ability to control Italy, given the difficulty it had in knowing the state of affairs within its own territory.

If we accept the passage in Polybius and the other documentation that confirms and explains it, it seems obvious that we must reject as ill-founded the theory that Roman legislation was imposed upon the Italian allies.[133] Certainly many laws in the civil sphere proposed in Rome were spontaneously adopted by the Latins (and perhaps by allied communities) as they met the needs and requirements of these communities.[134] This acceptance of Roman legislation became increasingly common in the second half of the second century, which is probably one of the reasons why so many fragments of Roman laws of the Gracchan and post-Gracchan eras are found throughout Italy (the *leges de repetundis* published with Roman encouragement in many allied communities are obviously a case apart).[135] In only one case can it be said that a Roman law, the sumptuary *lex Fannia* of 161 B.C., was extended to the whole of Italy by means of another piece of legislation, the *lex Didia* of 143 B.C.[136]

---

[127] Cic. *Verr.* II.120–5. The instances quoted are: Agrigentum, probably 193; Heraclea, probably 132; Halaesa, 95; Gabba 1959: (I 11).

[128] *CIL* I².586 = *ILS* 19 = *ILLRP* 512 = Bruns, *Font.* 36.

[129] *CIL* I².581 = *ILS* 18 = *ILLRP* 511 = Bruns, *Font.* 36.

[130] Gelzer 1962–4, III.259 n. 15: (A 19); cf. Livy XXXIX.18.7.

[131] For a different view see Galsterer 1976, 169: (H 132).

[132] Livy XXXII.26.5–18, XXXIX.29.8ff., 41.6–7, XLII.10.7–8.

[133] Harris 1972: (H 137) has resolved the problem. [134] Cic. *Balb.* 20–1.

[135] Crawford 1981, 155–6: (H 129). [136] Macrob. *Satur.* III.17.6.

The explanation for this piece of Roman interference lies in a desire to protect the economic viability and hence the social and political standing of the governing class not only in Rome but also in the allied communities, where the upper classes were Rome's only contacts and the bases of her power.[137] As we shall see below, the Roman government was most probably authorized to take measures of this kind under the terms of treaties with the allies and of the laws establishing colonies, which safeguarded the position of the classes that actually held power.

There is no evidence for true amendment of the constitutions of the Italian states, but in view of all that has been said hitherto it is certain that the Italian states and Rome were steadily growing more alike during the second century B.C. As just remarked, the general cause lay in the shared interest of the Italian upper classes in the exploitation of the provinces, the integration of the middle and lower classes through the military institutions of the alliance, and Rome's interest in guaranteeing the position of the allied governing classes, all of which were consequences of the policy of expansion. One of the most significant aspects of this trend towards homogeneity concerns political institutions and magistracies.[138] It is attractive to suggest that the need for close and dependable co-operation with the Roman state might have provided the allied states with an incentive to bring the functions and titles of their magistrates more closely into line with those of Rome, first in the military sphere and then in civil affairs. This would be tantamount to saying that the cultural and linguistic assimilation sought by a large part of the Italian upper classes during the century, no doubt spontaneously but encouraged by repeated moments of contact with Rome, may have been mirrored in the institutional field; this may explain the adoption of new magistracies alongside traditional offices or the replacement of local titles by Roman ones, which always presupposes some internal constitutional development. The new magistracies were necessary as much for practical reasons of co-existence with Rome as because of the need for specialization and the greater complexity of political and administrative problems, especially as the ancient magistracies, such as the Oscan office of *meddix*, were losing the purpose and meaning they had enjoyed during the period of autonomy. For example, the prevalence of the censor (*censtur*, most probably borrowed from Latin, as it is not a native Italic form) as an eponymous magistrate in Oscan regions is difficult to separate from the implications which the census acquired in the second century B.C. in connection with the allies' duties and obligations towards

[137] Gabba 1981: (H 44). For a different view see Göhler 1939, 58–9: (H 135); Harris 1971, 112: (H 136); Galsterer 1976, 132–3: (H 132).

[138] Camporeale 1956: (H 278); Brunt 1965, 100–2: (H 127); Cristofani 1978: (H 279); Prosdocimi 1978, 29–74: (H 287); Campanile and Letta 1979: (H 277).

Rome. In some cases this adjustment to match Roman models is likely to have favoured a high degree of continuity in the structures of Italian magistracies before and after the Social War.

The upper classes of the allied communities derived significant indirect protection from another clause contained in some treaties. The *foedera* with the Cenomani, Insubres, Helvetii, Iapydes and other Gallic peoples expressly excluded any of them from being received into Roman citizenship – *nequis eorum a nobis civis recipiatur*.[139] These treaties date from the period between 197 and 104 B.C. Such a specific prohibition demonstrates the existence of its converse, namely that Rome usually reserved the right to make such grants of citizenship, as indeed is expressly attested. In the instances quoted by Cicero, the granting of Roman citizenship was evidently considered prejudicial to the interests of the other community. The clause in the *foedera* with the Cenomani etc. does not relate, as is generally supposed, to the possible granting of citizenship to members of the upper classes. On the contrary, its aim was to prevent members of the lower classes of these tribes from obtaining Roman citizenship and thus acquiring in their home state a position and rights that would harm the social and political structure peculiar to these communities; in other words, the granting of Roman citizenship would have automatically implied recognition of their equality with the ruling classes in economic and social terms also, as was to be demonstrated in 49 B.C. The possibility in principle that, but for the prohibition in the treaties, Rome might have made grants of citizenship to members of these tribes was linked to the duty of the tribes of Cisalpine Gaul to provide Rome with military contingents under the treaties; that they did so is well documented for the period up to the Social War.[140] For without the prohibition acts of valour would surely have been rewarded with Roman citizenship. A later case when this did happen is that of the Spanish cavalrymen of the *turma Salluitana* who were made citizens by the decree of Cn. Pompeius Strabo in 89 B.C.[141] The punitive significance of this action for the community, which saw members of its own subordinate classes made Roman citizens or freed from dependence on the city, can be sensed in the decree of L. Aemilius Paullus, who freed the slaves of the Hastenses in 190/89 and granted them not only the lands of the dominant city that they already occupied, which had become *ager publicus* of the Roman people with the conquest of the area, but also possession of the town.[142]

The social structure peculiar to Gallic communities and Rome's

[139] Cic. *Balb.* 32. The best commentary is in Luraschi 1979, 41ff.: (H 143).
[140] Livy XLI.1.8; 5.5, on which see Badian 1958, 276 n. 7: (A 3); App. *B. Civ.* 1.39.177, 42.188–9, 50.219–20; Plut. *Sert.* 4.1. Regarding Ligurian auxiliaries see Brunt 1971, 169 n. 3: (H 82).
[141] *CIL* I².709 = *ILS* 8888 = *ILLRP* 515.   [142] *CIL* I².614 = *ILS* 15 = *ILLRP* 514.

recognition of it may be compared with similar situations in Etruscan regions; here too Rome took care to leave the existing social and political situation undisturbed as far as possible.[143] More generally, the same objective was served by the provisions of treaties that granted the allies use of the *ager publicus populi Romani* within the territory of their communities.

The treaties between Rome and the different Italian peoples certainly contained many other clauses dealing with matters of common interest, which ultimately had the indirect effect of tying the allied states ever more closely to Rome. For example, provision was certainly made for the surrender of land for road-building.[144] As we know, extensive road-building was undertaken in the second century in parallel with territorial expansion, military conquest and the policy of colonization.[145] This policy of penetration, which cannot be separated from the economic aspect of the work that it generated, may have been viewed favourably by the allies in that it fostered trade and the movement of people and ideas, although we do not know the extent to which such movement, which altered the regional *status quo*, was welcomed or foreseen. Certainly the new network of Roman roads corresponded to needs and conceptions that were new even in relation to the most recent past.[146]

The political and social importance of the roads, which was recognized by contemporary writers, is confirmed by their role in the emergence of cities and in the participation of non-citizens in the political life of Rome.[147] Areas not reached by the roads naturally remained in isolation and benefited little from the circulation of men and ideas. It was the road network that carried most of the migrants within the peninsula. Against the background of the Roman policy of colonization, the roads always encouraged the appearance of settlements and often stimulated their growth into towns. Renovation of public and private buildings during the second century was a consequence of the general, if uneven, spread of prosperity across large areas of Italy. The main beneficiaries were the sea-ports, which profited from trade.

Against this background, the road-building projects and public works commissioned by the censors on *ager Romanus* (and, as far as the roads were concerned, in allied territory as well) must have acted as a powerful spur to development from both the political and the socio-economic points of view, but they were also a means of interference and control by the Roman government. Nevertheless, it seems that in the second half of the century the communities even on *ager Romanus* achieved greater

---

[143] Harris 1971, 114ff.: (H 136).
[144] Mommsen 1887–8, II.428 n. 4: (A 25); Wiseman 1970: (H 63).
[145] Toynbee 1965, II.654–81: (A 37).
[146] Regarding Etruria, Harris 1971, 161ff.: (H 136).   [147] Wiseman 1971, 28ff.: (H 64).

powers to commission public works financed with their own funds on their own territory.[148]

A contemporary phenomenon was the private donation of money for public building schemes, which may in general be ascribed to increasing prosperity among the Roman and Italian upper classes.[149] An awareness that far-reaching economic changes brought with them a serious and dangerous relaxation of ethical standards is shown by contemporary moralistic views on the decline in standards of behaviour, which indeed is simply a way of reacting to a new social and economic situation.

Historical and social factors such as Roman colonization, military recruitment, the adoption of Roman laws and magistracies, new roads, emigration and trade were ultimately also to have significant cultural repercussions; for the attainment of equality with the Roman ruling class by the Italian elites caused the gradual withering of indigenous cultures as a result of the adoption of Latin as an essential means of approaching and then entering the Roman world; paradoxically, the local elites did not actually intend to renounce their ancient local traditions. The elitist nature of Italian culture, especially Etruscan culture, seems undeniable; this may enable us to understand in general terms the decline of local cultures and their eventual disappearance in the first century B.C.[150] The longer survival of elements of the culture of Magna Graecia is the result of the deeper social roots of Greek culture, from which also sprang those intellectuals from Livius Andronicus to Ennius who settled in Rome and fostered the assimilation of Greek culture. Outside Magna Graecia Latinization was already well advanced in the second century, and was to develop further in the first with the granting of Roman citizenship. However, as has been said with regard to the disappearance of the Oscan language, 'the germ of this phenomenon is to be found rather in the receptive and passive attitude of Oscan speakers when confronted with a linguistic tradition that was so much more prestigious on the political and cultural plane'.[151] Confirmation can be found in the symbolic case of Cumae, which in 180 asked the Roman government for permission to use Latin for official purposes.[152] Until then this Campanian city, which had remained loyal during the Hannibalic War, had used Oscan, which it had probably obtained the right to retain, together with other characteristic elements of its previous autonomy, at the time of its incorporation into the Roman state with the granting of *civitas sine suffragio*.

Voluntary adaptation to Roman realities may also explain the decline of Etruscan between the second and first centuries B.C., although with

---

[148] Mommsen 1887–8, II³.429: (A 25) regarding Livy XLI.27.10–13 (174 B.C.); Gabba 1976, 316 n. 3 and 325: (H 91).   [149] Gabba 1976, 324–5: (H 91).   [150] Gabba 1978, 11–27: (H 131).

[151] Campanile 1976, 110: (H 276). See also Lejeune 1976: (H 286); De Simone 1980: (H 283); Prosdocimi 1978: (H 288).   [152] Livy XL.42.13; Sartori 1977, 156–7: (H 154).

important geographic differences – the Romanization of the southern regions preceded that of the northern regions of Etruria. In this instance there were special reasons inherent in the structure of Etruscan society, whose elites were to be among the first to integrate into the Roman state at the highest level in the first century B.C.

Turning our attention from the upper to the lower classes of Italian society, we find a similar process of assimilation and integration occurring, this time in the context of military organization. The proletarianization of the Romano-Italian military forces in the second half of the second century B.C. did not create class solidarity among the soldiers; but recruitment of men without property did represent the most obvious resolution of the crisis that had afflicted Romano-Italian society as a whole, as a result of the profound changes that had occurred in its traditional agrarian structure.

VI. THE TRANSFORMATION OF AGRICULTURE

The transformation of society and of the agrarian economy was but the final unfolding of a situation which had been developing since the third century. This situation now became more generalized and had a more serious impact because of the simultaneous emergence of new political factors – the expansionist policy of Rome – that made new resources available and favoured the development of new notions concerning the value and use of wealth.

Although the transformation of Italian social and economic structures varied from one region to another because of the different reactions it engendered, a number of common characteristics can be identified. Between the fourth and third centuries traditional forms of dependent labour had been declining as a result of the great wave of Roman colonization; this had brought with it the development of slavery, which partly replaced previous labour arrangements. Slave labour now became available in increasing quantity as a result of the wars in Sicily and against the Gauls. The decline in population and the abandonment of large areas in the centre and south caused by the Hannibalic War introduced a new element that grew more acute as the century progressed on account of the many factors indicated above: movements of population for reasons of colonization, prolonged military service far from Italy, urbanization and spontaneous emigration. The favourable and necessary conditions for a further expansion of slavery to fill the void were thus being created, particularly as the wars of conquest now provided the wealthy classes with slave labour on a much larger scale than hitherto.

At least as far as the first half of the second century is concerned, it cannot be said that the rich had a deliberate wish to drive free smallholders from the land, take over their farms and install a different form of agriculture based on slavery.[153] This rather simplistic view ignores the fact that the choice between free and slave labour in the Romano-Italian economy pre-dates this period and sprang not from a political decision based on economic considerations but from a concrete situation that had been developing for quite different reasons. The difference between the political and social value of the free peasant (a potential legionary) and that of the slave (exempt from military service) was expressed in terms of a stark choice by the polemics of the Gracchan era because they were considering and judging the outcome of a long and complex process that had undoubtedly *included* the expulsion of peasant landowners by the wealthy and their replacement by slaves. Of necessity, this view dwelt on one aspect of the crisis occasioned by social and economic change, namely the proletarianization of the rural middle and lower classes, which soon proved to be an extremely serious phenomenon, neither sought nor desired by the wealthy classes of Roman and Italian society.

The first consequence of the depopulation of the countryside was the predominance of an extensive form of agriculture, which simultaneously exploited the decline of the small peasant farm and helped undermine the typical structure of the economy in many areas of Italy, especially by the introduction of a new method of working public land that was more profitable for the rich and for the state. This is the main theme on which traditional sources dwelt in describing the crisis of society in the second century B.C. There seem to be two reasons for this preoccupation. First, *ager publicus* was traditionally seen as the only instrument available to the state if it wished to intervene in various ways in the solution of social and economic problems; the historiographical implications are well known. Secondly, the problem of the state lands now took on new characteristics as a result of the large-scale confiscations following the Hannibalic War; it was well known that the major speculative schemes of the wealthy revolved around *ager publicus*.

The transformation of the Italian agrarian economy followed various paths. It is uncertain whether truly political decisions were involved in particular phases or at least whether these were motivated by political requirements, for example in Campania or Sicily. Even in the cases that seem to be better documented, such as in Campania, it is not possible to identify precise phases of transition;[154] our knowledge of the outcome is better, but not good. There would have been different methods of working the soil, new forms of agriculture and of the agrarian economy. The change that was apparently most typical because it had greater

[153] Hopkins 1978, 4–5: (H 99).

political and military implications was that resulting from the reorganization of small farms producing for home consumption into larger plantations cultivated by slaves or part-time labourers or, in some cases, leased in individual plots to colonists. Some crops, particularly oil and wine, would therefore be 'industrialized', with production for market. In some areas in Campania and Apulia amalgamation of this kind may have favoured the expansion of cereal monoculture. In other cases the abundant supply of money and land permitted the rationalization of certain practices that already existed, such as transhumant stock-rearing, which must have come into more widespread use as part of the general trend towards the development of grazing owing to its more immediate profitability. The increase in pasture at the expense of arable land should be seen in the context of the depopulation of the mountain and hill regions of the Appennines, which had been brought under cultivation in earlier periods of history.

The Campanian and Samnite region may serve as a typical example, although the same also applies to many areas in the Appennines. The large walled strongholds that had been built on the hilltops in the Samnite era as refuges for the population scattered thinly on the floors of the valleys ceased to have a purpose in the middle of the third century. The desolation of these previously well-populated areas as a result of the Samnite Wars was accompanied by a change in the use of the land in the Roman era.[155]

These new forms of agriculture came to co-exist with other, archaic forms based on half-free labour that survived and would long continue to survive in some areas, either for local historical and social reasons or because of environmental conditions. It cannot be imagined that the system of small peasant farms with their economy based on self-sufficiency disappeared, even though the trend was in that direction; indeed, the policy of colonization and land assignation pursued by the Roman government in the first thirty years of the second century was designed to reproduce just such a system, particularly in Cisalpine Gaul. As has already been said, this does not indicate a contradiction; rather it confirms that the Roman ruling class, which would organize the conquests and take credit for the victories, did not have and could not have a colonist programme to govern the process of expansion, let alone a policy with regard to the change in social, economic and political relations in Italy. However, towards the 160s it became conscious of the changes that were taking place, a fact that is proved by the consideration given by the ruling class to the means of exercising power over its

---

[154] Unsatisfactory attempts to determine such phases in Frederiksen 1981, 1.267–87: (H 89); cf. also Carandini 1981, 11.250–5: (H 83), and Ghinatti 1977: (H 133).
[155] *Contra* Haller 1978: (H 237).

subjects. Not much later, namely in 133 B.C., the presentation of a systematic programme of reform by Tiberius Gracchus was accompanied by a substantial innovation: an attempt actually to analyse the causes of the crisis and establish links among social, economic, political and military factors. This socio-economic analysis led to a revival of the system of small peasant farms, by means of more effective large-scale state intervention on *ager publicus* than in the past; but the revived peasant farms were to exist alongside the new and different methods of working the land which had developed. Such an analysis and its practical consequences conflicted with economic reasoning,[156] which not only highlighted the value of the alternative, more modern trends towards industrialized and rationalized agriculture, but denied any validity to the socio-economic and ethical model of the farmer-soldier. This may have been the first time that such a thing had occurred in the political life of Rome; underlying the controversy were different models for the development of the economy and of society.

New elements had thus been introduced into the social and economic structure of Italian communities, which it is difficult not to consider as progressive factors at the time, in that they represented a better adaptation of Romano-Italian society to the demands of a new homogeneous state. In general, however, much continued as before, especially in the southern and central regions of the peninsula, so that the innovations often appear limited in extent; indeed, they were short-lived, mainly because they depended upon an availability and use of slave labour which could not last long. The unchanging aspects, by contrast, were determined by environmental, physical and geographic factors that ancient societies with the forms of intervention which they devised could not overcome or change except in a superficial way. Hence even changes in the method of working the land in the various periods of antiquity represented nothing more than repeated attempts to adapt a reality that survived unchanged in its constituent parts, in spite of the disruptions caused by political events.

The typical instrument of the 'industrial' phase of Italian agriculture in the second century B.C. was the country estate described by Cato in his treatise. It need hardly be said that this system, which introduced new agricultural techniques yielding large crops for the market (as well as sufficient produce for the owner and his labour force), had different characteristics and functions in the various areas of Italy in which archaeological evidence shows it to have been widespread. Such diversity was a product of the environment, the suitability of different crops for the locality and the differing demands of town markets in the vicinity.

---

[156] Dion. Hal. VIII.68–76; Gabba and Pasquinucci 1979, 64–73: (H 93).

The structure of the farms would have been fairly standard, however. Probably modelled on Greek farms in Magna Graecia and Sicily and on Carthaginian plantations, it must have been introduced in the Roman world in the second half of the third century and have spread in the first half of the second as the most rational system of agricultural exploitation.[157] Cato intended the description of this kind of farm to serve the particular social and political situation of a young landowner from the Roman political class investing his substantial wealth in estates of this kind to generate earnings that would then be used for socio-political ends. It is clear that in order to achieve these objectives and also by reason of the type of crops and the need of the landowner to exercise careful personal control, a farm of this type in the second century required the particular conditions to be found in southern Latium, Campania and perhaps some areas of southern Etruria but almost nowhere else in central Italy. Nor will it have been easy to transform and lay out vacant and available lands in accordance with Cato's suggestions. Elsewhere the organization of the country estate will have been adapted to suit local conditions, although the aim of achieving high profits by marketing the product remained the same. A farm described by two agronomists named Saserna (father and son; their work is known only at second-hand), which probably lay in the territory of the Bagienni in Cisalpine Gaul, may be quoted as an example from the end of the second century.[158] It should be noted that in parts of Cisalpine Gaul, especially the Transpadane area, that had not been colonized by the Romans, a system of land tenure and of farming which was closely bound up with the structure of local Celtic society continued to prevail in the second century and was still to be found in the first.

The agrarian structure of Etruria also long preserved features characteristic of the region's particular social organization, which Rome was careful not to destroy before the Social War. Thus in 196 B.C. the Roman army intervened to suppress a 'conspiracy of slaves' which seems to have been widespread.[159] The chief factor seems to have been the existence of large estates, belonging to noblemen, which were worked by 'serfs' and also by slaves. This kind of estate and method of farming was predominant in the coastal areas of Etruria and also, it seems, at Volaterrae, in the territory of which there is evidence of the presence of large consolidated estates throughout ancient times and in the early Middle Ages. Within such an estate there worked a large class of small, dependent farmers; archaeological research has succeeded in identifying such individuals,

[157] Gabba and Pasquinucci 1979, 30–2: (H 93); Maroti 1976: (H 103) (at the beginning of the second century). Frederiksen (n. 154) prefers to date its spread to the second half of the second century, at least in Campania.   [158] Kolendo 1973, 14–16: (H 202).
[159] Livy XXXIII.36.1–3.

but not in describing their true social status or their position with regard to ownership of the land.[160]

This problem is central to analysis of the structures of Etruscan society, especially in inland areas of the centre and north and in particular in Clusium. Archaeological evidence pointing to widely scattered rural settlement is often interpreted as a sign of the sub-division of agrarian property (with individual boundaries, among other things) as a result of a colonization scheme supposedly carried out by local nobles in the second century B.C. and the corresponding liberation of their 'serfs'.[161] This interpretation rests on an imaginative theory put forward by H. Rix on the basis of the forms of the names occurring in inscriptions from the area of Clusium and Perusia.[162] The *lautni* (who in the period before 90 B.C. are usually identified hypothetically with the 'serfs', the *penestai* of the Latin and Greek sources, although Rix considers them simply as slaves) are thought to have changed their system of nomenclature between the third and second centuries B.C. After the change onomastic formulae in three parts are found, where a *praenomen* served as the family name and a family name has the function of *cognomen*. It is claimed that the change testifies on the legal plane to a kind of liberation and on the social level to admission to 'citizenship' and ownership of the land. Leaving aside the doubts about the identification of *lautni* with 'serfs', the change in nomenclature may be explained more simply as the result of a reorganization of the Etruscan cities at the prompting of Rome for some purpose connected with the census. Even 'serfs' were obliged to serve in the military contingents Rome demanded of the Etruscan cities. Even if the Etruscan 'serfs' acquired some special status in relation to the land they tilled for their lords, the distinction between 'serf' and master remained unchanged until 91 B.C., as is shown by the Etruscan document known as the prophecy of Vegoia[163] and, perhaps, also by a comparison with Transpadane Gaul. Hence it is more likely that archaeological discoveries in the area in question reveal an internal organization of the large estate that differed from that practised in coastal areas on account of differences in the nature of the land.

In any case, the Etruscan evidence confirms the view that Cato's treatise cannot be considered typical of Italian agriculture in general, which varied considerably from one region to another. However, around the end of the second century and the beginning of the first century B.C., colonial allotments in the area of the Latin colony of Cosa

[160] Gabba and Pasquinucci 1979, 36 and n. 51: (H 93). With regard to the territories of Volaterrae and Clusium: Luchi 1981, 1.413ff.: (H 247).

[161] Gabba and Pasquinucci 1979, 37 n. 53: (H 93).

[162] Rix 1953, and 1977, 64–73, with discussion: (H 290 and 291).

[163] *Gromatici Veteres* 1.350 Lachman; Heurgon 1959: (I 21) and 1970: (H 97); *Gromatici Veteres* 1.423–4.

were replaced by vast 'industrialized' plantations similar to the Catonian estate; aided by ease of access to the sea, they displayed a strong trend towards producing for the market. It is noteworthy that similar transformations are usually found in those Etruscan areas that had previously been colonized by the Romans. This observation probably has more general application and may also hold true of other Italian areas where assignations had previously been made. In areas where there had been no direct Roman intervention the political, social and economic situation remained unchanged until the Social War, because, as mentioned above, Rome would for political reasons not wish to alter conditions that ensured the local predominance of the upper classes on which she relied.

In other regions Rome's intervention was massive, but it met its match in the form of environmental conditions that had always dictated particular methods of agriculture. This was true of Appennine and Subappennine areas, where forestry and grazing were the predominant activities and where there were also forms of collective land ownership.[164] Roman intervention was basically limited to rationalization of the existing economy by encouraging mercantilistic 'industrialization', particularly by means of extensive exploitation of state pastures. This does not mean that such intervention did not play a significant part in undermining the traditional structure in many localities. This applies to the rearing of large herds and flocks and to transhumance, for which we have good evidence in Roman sources for the second and first centuries B.C., particularly in Samnium, Lucania and Apulia, to name only the regions where it was most prevalent. Stock-rearing was certainly among the agricultural and pastoral activities of Italian peoples in very early times, including the movement of stock from mountain pasture to lowland grazing and *vice versa*. Although transhumant stock-rearing was thus a 'pre-political' activity and did not require a unitary political power to enable movements to take place over long distances,[165] it did undergo fresh expansion in the second century, with the large-scale investment of Roman and Italian capital and the ever increasing area of state land available for private occupation. Animal husbandry on a large scale naturally stimulated profitable related activities, the chief being the wool trade. Transhumance had now also to take place along lines laid down by this authority of the state; this fact was to continue to apply in the later history of the institution and it undoubtedly played a part in altering the context of stock-rearing and the utilization of large areas of Apulia. However, in this case too the archaeological and literary evidence is ambiguous and chronologically uncertain, so that it has been maintained

---

[164] Gabba and Pasquinucci 1979, 26ff.: (H 93); Giardina 1981, 1.87ff.: (H 95).
[165] Gabba and Pasquinucci 1979, 48ff.: (H 93).

with equal justification on the one hand that Roman domination coincided with a decline in the economic vitality of Apulia and, on the other, that in the second century Apulian agriculture was flourishing and that grazing became dominant in the middle of the first century B.C.[166] Both propositions are extreme, as it is a fact that transhumant grazing has never entailed the complete or even partial eradication of arable farming. Indeed, there is direct evidence of both the growing of cereals and the cultivation of vines and olives in various areas of Apulia, although it is difficult to ascertain the kind of farm in which these would have been grown.[167] Nor is it possible to determine the area of land reserved for stock-rearing. The presence of slaves, even though not a predominant element, is certainly characteristic of the region as it is linked to the practice of grazing; evidence of their presence in the second century is provided by the revolutionary movements among the shepherds mentioned above, which the Roman government hastened to suppress.

VII.   SOCIAL CONSEQUENCES AND ATTEMPTED SOLUTIONS

After 150 B.C., as a result of its political and military repercussions, the full gravity of this widespread transformation of Italian structures became apparent in its social consequences (rather than its economic consequences). Equally apparent was the Italian dimension of the phenomenon, as emerges clearly from the historiographical tradition reflected in the first book of Appian's *Civil Wars*.[168] Recruitment difficulties, the old argument used by Italian dignitaries in their complaints to Rome, became ever more common from the middle of the second century B.C. onwards, especially as a result of the incessant wars in Spain, and led to a succession of measures during the remainder of the century;[169] they eventually created the need for the new kind of levy introduced by Gaius Marius in 107 B.C.

It is highly likely that the second half of the second century saw a deterioration in Rome's relations with the allied communities, at least in Italy, and especially with the allied upper classes, which were subject to the ever more burdensome demands of imperial policy. In the face of her growing problems, Rome's hand had begun to press more heavily on the allies. There had been incidents involving the abuse of power previously, but those quoted by Gaius Gracchus[170] indicate arrogance towards the allies, who were treated as subjects. Even before 133 B.C. the idea may have been gaining ground in certain sections of the Italian upper classes that one way of at least alleviating the problem and raising themselves

---

[166] Discussion of the theories in Gabba and Pasquinucci 1979, 41 n. 64, 45 n. 74: (H 93).
[167] Grelle 1981, 1.192ff.: (H 240).   [168] Gabba 1956, 34ff.: (B 7).
[169] Gabba 1972, 777–8: (I 12).   [170] *ORF*⁴48 and 49 (Gell. *NA* x.3.3 and 5).

from their position of inferiority might be the acquisition of Roman citizenship. This is all the more likely as the spontaneous process of integration and assimilation must have been clear for all to see. Furthermore, Romans and Italians were on an equal footing in the provinces and in exploitation of the empire. On the other hand, these same ideas and attitudes may have caused a section of the Roman oligarchy to adopt a more rigidly exclusive stance than in the past.

Once the causes of the crisis and its Italian dimension were identified, the remedy proposed in 133 B.C. by the agrarian law of Tiberius Gracchus was bound also to have an Italian dimension,[171] in other words to affect the impoverished peasant classes of both Rome and the Italian states.[172] The historical tradition reflected in Appian clearly assumes that the distribution of small plots of *ager publicus* recovered by the state benefited Roman citizens and the poor among the allies, in keeping with the entire policy of assignation and colonization pursued by Rome during the second century B.C. This is the interpretation to be placed on the presence of Italian allies in Rome at the time of discussion of Gracchus' law.[173] It is fairly clear that the social conflict that existed within the civic body of Rome was now also present in the Italian communities. Similarly, the recovery of state lands held in excess of the limits permitted by the law also affected allied *possessores*, both Latins and Italians; it was those allies who had been harmed by the laws who appealed to Scipio Aemilianus in 130/29 B.C., even going to the length of invoking the treaties originally made with Rome.[174] From this dual point of view the problems resulting from the attempt to use *ager publicus* to resolve the social crisis in the Italian communities put in an entirely new light the relationship of the Italian allies to internal Roman policy before the Social War.

The connection between the social aspects of the agrarian problem and the overall question of the allies came into even sharper focus after 129 B.C. The strongest opposition to the application of the law now came from the allied *possessores*.[175] On the other hand, Italian interference in Rome was such that in 126 B.C. the tribune M. Junius Pennus proposed a further law for the expulsion of foreigners.[176] It was thought by the pro-Gracchan consul of 125, M. Fulvius Flaccus, that the hostility of the

---

[171] For subtle differences in the tenor of the accounts of Plutarch and Appian see Sordi 1978, 300–3: (H 57); Gabba 1956, 45–8: (B 7).

[172] An imaginative solution along these lines in Richardson 1980: (H 149).

[173] App. *B. Civ.* 1.10.41. Whether the allies benefited from Gracchus' law has been much debated and the view presented here is not unchallenged. For further discussion see Vol. IX.

[174] App. *B. Civ.* 1.19.78–81. It is difficult to determine whether the state lands affected by the recovery programme were principally those occupied by the allies or those in the hands of the Roman oligarchy. The epigraphic evidence which exists for the location of some Gracchan assignments is insufficient to decide this, especially as Roman state lands were scattered so widely in the Italian communities and their history between confiscation and 133 B.C. is untraceable.

[175] App. *B. Civ.* 1.21.86.   [176] Cic. *Off.* III.47; Fest. p. 388. Glossaria.

Italian holders of the land could be overcome or attenuated by granting them Roman citizenship so that 'out of gratitude for the greater favour, they might no longer quarrel about the land'.[177] Flaccus coaxed the Italians into wanting Roman citizenship in order to raise themselves from subject status to being partners in empire.[178] According to Appian, the allies would gladly have accepted the proposal, but it was defeated owing to the opposition of the Senate. The question was not as simple as this – the proposal contained an alternative whereby an ally who was not interested in Roman citizenship could receive the 'right of appeal', *ius provocationis*.[179] It may be deduced from this that the advantages of Roman citizen status were not universally evident at that time and that at least a section of the upper classes of the allied states preferred a guarantee against the abuse of power by Roman magistrates. Hence the desire to gain Roman citizenship was not yet generally felt, but it was already gaining ground.

The alternative proposal of the consul Fulvius Flaccus reappears in a more developed form in the *leges de repetundis* of the period as a recompense to non-Romans who had successfully upheld an accusation under these laws.[180] The first option – the granting of Roman citizenship – was applicable as a rule to all non-Romans, in other words Latins and Italians, and gave them and their descendants *civitas* with the right to vote (*suffragium*) and exemption from military service, *vacatio militiae*, which allowed new citizens to remain in their native city. According to the most logical interpretation of the fragmentary inscriptions which preserve the text of the laws, the second option was open to the same category of persons, in other words Latins and Italians; it gave them and their descendants *provocatio, vacatio militiae munerisque publici, immunitas* and the choice of going to court either at Rome or in their own city. This means that those who preferred this alternative were relieved of military duty, public functions and taxes; in effect they were thus brought close to the category of those who chose citizenship. The second option was not open, however, to those who had been magistrates in their own cities (dictator, praetor, aedile), in other words, in view of the timocratic structure of these communities, those who belonged to the highest census class. The reason for this exclusion was not that these groups already enjoyed such privileges or had Roman citizenship (which are not very sensible hypotheses) but that the Roman government wanted them to choose the first option, Roman citizenship, which did not carry with it *vacatio muneris*. In other words, the Roman government was concerned

---

[177] App. *B. Civ.* 1.21.86.

[178] App. *B. Civ.* 1.34.152; Göhler 1939, 132–5: (H 135); Gabba 1976, 70ff.: (H 42); for a different view see Galsterer 1976, 177ff.: (H 132).   [179] Val. Max. IX.5.1.

[180] *Lex repet.* (Bruns, *Font.*, 20; Girard, 16 = *FIRA* 7), 76–9 (123–2 B.C.); *Frag. Tarent.* (Girard, 9), 1ff.; cf. Cic. *Balb.* 54. Sherwin-White 1973, 215–16: (H 113); *id.* 1972, 94–6: (H 56); Galsterer 1976, 93ff.: (H 132); Venturini 1979, 31ff.: (H 61).

not to deprive the allied cities of their traditional ruling class and was thus at pains to maintain the identity of the latter, particularly in view of its possible intention to relinquish its position.

Indeed, it seems that another similar measure taken by the Roman government dates from this period (124 B.C.?), namely the granting of Roman citizenship to the magistrates of Latin colonies.[181] Although it was theoretically and legally impossible for a Roman citizen to have dual citizenship (a problem that is far from clear, however, and has been much discussed), in this case too it is obvious that Rome had no intention of decapitating the allied communities closest to home; she merely wished to meet a desire for Roman citizenship expressed by the Latin elites and assumed that these new citizens would remain in their cities and part of the local ruling classes. In fact, as far as we know, there are only rare instances of Roman senators originating from Latin or Italian cities before 90 B.C.[182] These Roman measures undoubtedly entail a high degree of inconsistency, which confirms the difficulty of reconciling conflicting interests and forces.

The question to be asked is rather how Rome could interfere so deeply in the internal affairs of allied communities to the extent of according an allied citizen exemption from military service, burdensome public duties and taxes within his own community. Such intervention must have been fully permitted by the tenor of the laws establishing colonies and the treaties with Italian communities, which, as mentioned above, gave the Roman government broad powers of interference and supervision as far as the composition of the allied ruling classes was concerned.

The rebellion of the Latin colony of Fregellae in 125 B.C. is also to be connected in some way with the rejection of the proposal of Fulvius Flaccus.[183] The situation in the city may have been particularly difficult after the immigration of 4,000 Paelignian and Samnite families,[184] which must have radically changed the composition of the assembly. Perhaps the Latin upper class aligned itself with Rome.[185] In any case, the rebellion illustrates a widespread sense of unease which C. Gracchus tried to assuage in 122 B.C. by means of his *rogatio de sociis*, which granted Roman citizenship to Latins and, it would appear, Latin rights to other allies, with voting rights in a tribe at Rome.[186] An edict of the consul C. Fannius expelled the *socii* from Rome in order that they could not take part in the voting.[187] The proposal was not passed.

The problems raised by the use of *ager publicus* thus accelerated the emergence of a situation that had been developing slowly throughout the

[181] Ascon. *Pis.* 3 Clark; Tibiletti 1953, 45–63: (H 155). Others believe that this privilege was not introduced until the first century B.C.   [182] Wiseman 1971, 17: (H 64).

[183] Plut. *C. Gracch.* 3.1; Aur. Vict. *De Vir. Ill.* 65.2.

[184] Livy XLI.8.8, in 177.   [185] Cic. *Fin.* v.62, *Phil.* III.17 (Q. Numitorius Pullus).

[186] App. *B. Civ.* 1.23.99, with commentary in Gabba 1958: (B 8); for a different view see Plut. *C. Gracch.* 8.3, 9.5; Vell. Pat. II.6.2.   [187] App. *B. Civ.* 1.23.100; Plut. *C. Gracch.* 12.2–4.

first half of the century. In 133 B.C. the spontaneous process of assimilation and integration that had been pursued in different ways by the upper and lower classes of the Italian states revealed the allies' position of inferiority even more starkly: they were the object of Rome's internal policy and its vicissitudes, not subjects with some power over decisions. The uncertainty of Roman political life, the sharp conflicts within its ruling class and the different opinions as to the course of imperial policy at the very moment when the economic and financial interests and implications that determined it were beginning to have a strong impact – these all showed the Italian allies the difficulty, not to say impossibility, of successfully influencing political decisions of historic importance that involved them directly.

The demand for Roman citizenship was gradually separated from the agrarian problem and was increasingly embodied in the clear desire to participate in government and in exploitation of the empire, but no longer as subjects; it was a desire for *consortium imperi civitatisque*.[188] The sacrifices made by the Italians in the creation of that empire had been far greater than those of the Romans themselves; as Velleius was to say, they had borne arms in its defence and could no longer be excluded and despised as foreigners.[189] And the process continued. By the end of the century German tribes had penetrated deep into Cisalpine Gaul and the sense of danger must have rekindled the spirit of unity that had emerged in the third century B.C. as a result of the Gallic wars. The sacrifices in terms of men that were demanded of the allies must have been enormous.[190] Gaius Marius did not hesitate to grant Roman citizenship to two cohorts of Camertes, thus ignoring the provisions of the treaty which probably precluded such a possibility.[191] The colonial law of L. Appuleius Saturninus, proposed in 100 B.C. for the benefit of Marius' soldiers, provided for the foundation of citizen colonies (rather than Latin ones) in which *socii* were also admitted, as in earlier instances.[192] The fear of a German invasion of Italy engendered at that time was still to dominate the view of Germany that Caesar expressed fifty years later in his *de bello gallico*. The common danger and common successful defence of Italy gave real substance to the argument of Velleius (cited above), which was undoubtedly a faithful echo of distant Italian complaints; and the events of these years must have caused even greater exasperation, particularly among the leaders, the *principes italicorum populorum*, who were thwarted in their demand for Roman citizenship. The failure of the policy of M. Livius Drusus in 91 B.C. was to be the final factor that would cause the cup of Italian exasperation to overflow and drive them to war.

[188] App. *B. Civ.* 1.34.152 and 35.155; Just. *Epit.* xxxviii.4.13; Gabba 1973, 347–60: (H 90).
[189] Vell. Pat. ii.15.2.   [190] Brunt 1971, 430–1: (H 82).
[191] Val. Max. v.2.8; Plut. *Mar.* 28.3; Cic. *Balb.* 46.
[192] App. *B. Civ.* 1.29.132 with commentary in Gabba 1958: (B 8); Cic. *Balb.* 48.

CHAPTER 8

ROME AGAINST PHILIP AND ANTIOCHUS

R. M. ERRINGTON

I. THE EAST AFTER THE PEACE OF PHOENICE

The Peace of Phoenice was intended to give Rome a free hand in Africa by closing the Balkan front. The peace terms seemed to secure the safety of the Straits of Otranto, therefore to protect Italy from Philip. Whether the Senate regarded this as a long-term settlement with Philip we cannot tell. It is quite possible that in 205 some senators would happily have returned to the *status quo* before 215. But events rapidly took another course, which enhanced the influence of those senators who wished to continue Roman intervention, and the new watchdog role established by the Peace lasted a mere five years – which sufficed, however, to defeat Carthage.

The Peace of Phoenice was in no sense a settlement of Balkan affairs; it regulated merely the relationship between the two principals. The traditional friendships and enmities of the Greek states among themselves were not fundamentally affected by several of them being *adscripti* to the treaty. Thus in the Peloponnese the border war between Philip's friend the Achaean League and Rome's friend Sparta continued sporadically even after the peace; thus Philip felt free to develop an aggressive policy in the Aegean (an area which was not mentioned in the treaty), a policy which affected the balance of power there, which Rome's friend Attalus of Pergamum, and also Rhodes and Egypt, wished to maintain. Nor were these the only new political developments in the Greek world during the five years. Antiochus III, who in less than twenty years had restored the Seleucid empire in Iran, Mesopotamia and in central Asia Minor, had thereby won himself a mighty military reputation, which he broadcast by taking the traditional Greek title for the Persian King, 'Great King' ($\beta\alpha\sigma\iota\lambda\epsilon\grave{\upsilon}\varsigma$ $\mu\acute{\epsilon}\gamma\alpha\varsigma$). In 204 or 203 he set out to recover western Asia Minor, which had for some years after the death of Lysimachus (281) been largely controlled by the Seleucids. Most affected by Antiochus' territorial ambitions were Rhodes and Egypt, both of which possessed territory in Asia Minor, and Attalus of Pergamum, whose kingdom had in effect been created at the expense of the Seleucids.

Western Greece and Illyria, which for the whole of Philip's reign had played a major part in his expansionist strategy, now ceased to be so important for Macedon. This did not mean that nothing at all happened nor that Philip or Rome were totally inactive here. In 203 Livy records the embassy of C. Terentius Varro (*cos.* 216), C. Mamilius (*pr.* 207) and M. Aurelius, who were sent to Philip in response to appeals by allied cities in Greece. These complained that they had failed to obtain satisfaction from Philip for his ravaging of their territories; they also reported that Philip had sent 4,000 soldiers to Africa to help Carthage.[1] The 4,000 Macedonian soldiers can only have been volunteers or mercenaries, since it is inconceivable that Philip should have chosen this of all times to send his first official support to Carthage. More interesting are the complaints of the cities. Livy does not name them, but Rome had very few *socii* in the Balkans who in 203 might have been recently attacked by Philip. It is also possible that a passage of Polybius might bear on the question.[2] In 198 Flamininus demanded that Philip hand over 'those places in Illyria which he had occupied since the Peace of Epirus'. *Prima facie* this shows that Philip had occupied territory in Illyria between 205 and 198; and it would therefore not be surprising if the complaints of the Roman *socii* in 203 referred to this. One of the three Roman envoys, M. Aurelius, remained in the Balkans and apparently raised some troops to protect these allies. He was still there in 201, when a Macedonian embassy to Rome, which requested the return of the Macedonians and their leader, Sopater, who had been captured at Zama, objected to his presence.[3] But the Roman reply was a practical one: to send out with a fleet the experienced ex-consul M. Valerius Laevinus, who had performed a similar function in and after 215, to relieve M. Aurelius and to observe Macedonian affairs.[4]

This complex of complaint and reaction has been regarded by many historians, rather subjectively, as the invention of later Roman annalists, who wished to paint as black as possible a picture of Philip's activities. The men involved, however, are real and the events themselves comprehensible enough, and should not be rejected. They indicate that the Senate not only retained an interest in trans-Adriatic affairs after the Peace of Phoenice, but was willing to send modest yet effective support to injured *socii*; and it seems likely that these *socii* are to be sought among the smaller communities of Illyria or north-western Greece – particularly if the record of an appeal of the Aetolians in 200 for help against Philip is authentic.[5]

However, Illyria was neither for Rome nor for Philip the first priority after Phoenice: Rome was occupied in Africa; Philip turned to the east

---

[1] Livy xxx.26.3–4. [2] Polyb. xviii.1.14. [3] Livy xxx.42.2. [4] Livy xxxi.3.3ff.
[5] Livy xxxi.29.4; cf. App. *Mac.* 4.2.

Map 11. Greece and Asia Minor.

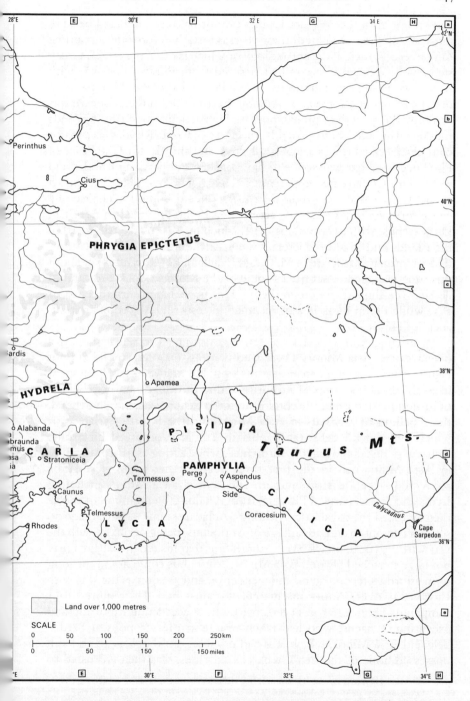

and above all to the Aegean. Events cannot be traced in detail because most of Polybius' account of these years is lost; therefore only an outline can be reconstructed, the chronology of which is often uncertain. Greek states with Aegean interests had suffered from Philip's first war with Rome, as the repeated attempts of Rhodes and Ptolemy Philopator to urge peace negotiations show. Among the grounds for their concern was certainly the growth of piracy, practised in particular by Rome's friends the Aetolians and Philip's friends, the cities of Crete. Rhodes, as a major commercial power, was severely affected; and shortly after the Peace of Phoenice a regular war seems to have broken out between Rhodes and some of the Cretan cities, apparently led by Hierapytna. This war, known as the 'Cretan War' (κρητικὸς πόλεμος),[6] offered Philip the chance of a cheap intervention. Diodorus records that Philip provided an Aetolian, Dicaearchus, with twenty ships, with which he was to take tribute from the islands and to aid the Cretans against Rhodes.[7] Polybius mentions that an intimate associate of Philip's, Heracleides of Tarentum, at about this time managed to set fire to some of the Rhodian dockyards and to destroy the ships that were in them.[8] This probably occurred in 204 or 203, while Philip himself was occupied in restoring Macedonian influence in Thrace.

Meanwhile Antiochus III was setting out to restore Seleucid control over western Asia Minor. There were various reasons why he did not begin until 204, after nineteen years as king. His first years had been spent in establishing his personal authority within the kingdom: the rebellion of Molon in Media and the condition of the eastern satrapies in general, the rebellion of Achaeus in Asia Minor and the Fourth Syrian War, which ended with defeat at Raphia in 217, had occupied him fully. Achaeus, a distant cousin of Antiochus', while acting as his commander in Asia Minor had in the first three years of his reign successfully recovered large areas of southern and central Asia Minor (including Lydia and at least parts of Phrygia) from Attalus of Pergamum. In 220 he then assumed the royal title. Although Achaeus seems to have made no serious attempt to take advantage of Antiochus' being occupied with the war with Egypt to attack Syria, suggesting that his territorial aims may not have stretched beyond Asia Minor, Antiochus could not in the long term afford to recognize his independence; and as soon as the war with Egypt was over, Antiochus marched against him. He required four campaigns (from 216 to 213 B.C) before he succeeded in capturing and executing Achaeus, who had taken refuge in the acropolis at Sardis. Seleucid Asia Minor, which still had no access to the Aegean and still possessed none of the rich Greek coastal cities, was then entrusted to

[6] *SIG* 567 (Hierapytna), 569 (Halasarna). See Holleaux 1938–68, IV, esp. 163ff.: (D 35).
[7] Diod. Sic. XXVIII.1; cf. Polyb. XVIII.54.8–12.   [8] Polyb. XIII.5.1–3; Polyaenus V.17.

Zeuxis, who took up residence in Sardis while Antiochus set out to repair
the damage to Seleucid possessions in the east caused by the relative
neglect of a generation and accentuated by the recent rebellion of
Molon.[9]

The 'Anabasis' of Antiochus, which occupied him from 212 to 205
B.C., restored Seleucid claims to authority over Armenia and Iran.[10] It
seems probable that Antiochus' aim was the restoration of the empire of
Seleucus I; but his achievements and the level of control which he was
able to impose fell in practice far short of this. He began in Armenia,
which he successfully reduced to vassal status (212);[11] in Media he seems
to have re-organized Seleucid administration and collected an army for
an attack on the Parthians. This resulted in a treaty of alliance with the
Parthian ruler Arsaces II, which opened up the land-route to the east.[12]
The Parthians nevertheless remained unbeaten and therefore a potential
danger. In Bactria (208–206 B.C.) Antiochus failed to re-establish
Seleucid authority by defeating Euthydemus, the current king. After a
long siege of Bactra, Antiochus was forced to compromise: he saved face
by taking Euthydemus' elephants and by making a treaty, the terms of
which are not known; but since he also recognized Euthydemus' title as
king and offered Euthydemus' son Demetrius one of his daughters in
marriage, the structure of the Bactrian kingdom was clearly not seriously
affected.[13] After crossing the Hindu Kush Antiochus made a treaty of
friendship with a local Indian ruler, Sophagasenus, which the court
historiography, followed by Polybius, depicted as renewing the friendship which Seleucus I had formed with Chandragupta. But apart from a
few more elephants, some provisions and some precious metal, the
Indian connection produced no more than a nostalgic reminiscence of
Alexander and Seleucus. For the rest, Antiochus returned through
Arachosia, Drangiane and Carmania – all Seleucid satrapies, the distance
of which from Syria had in the past given their governors great independence – into Persis. Here he seems to have encountered no difficulty,
and we may conclude that the personal presence of the king and his royal
army will have quickly restored an impression of eager loyalty in these
distant provinces.[14]

The results of the 'Anabasis' were for Antiochus certainly in many
ways disappointing. Neither Arsaces nor Euthydemus was crushed and
the consolidation of Seleucid power in eastern Iran was fairly superficial.
This was not admitted, however. On his return to the west Antiochus

[9] The fragmentary sources for the revolt of Achaeus are: Polyb. v.57–58.1, 72–78, 107.4,
VII.15–18, VIII.15–21. See also Schmitt 1964, 158ff.: (E 50); Will 1966–7, II.18ff.: (A 40).
[10] As a result of the loss of all but a few fragments of Polybius' account it is possible without
excessive speculation to trace these events only in outline: in general see Schmitt 1964, 85ff.: (E 50);
Will 1966–7, II.42ff.: (A 40). [11] Polyb. VIII.23; Strabo XI.14.15.
[12] Polyb. X.27–31; Justin XLI.5.7. [13] Polyb. X.49, XI.34.1–10. [14] Polyb. XI.34.11–14.

adopted the title Great King and Polybius comments, clearly influenced
by some official or semi-official source, that 'Antiochus made his kingdom secure by frightening his subjects by his courage and tireless energy;
as a result of this expedition he appeared worthy of the kingship, not only
to the Asiatics but also to the Europeans.'[15]

Immediately after his return from the east and relying on the reputation which his exaggeratedly successful deeds in distant lands in the steps
of Alexander and Seleucus had won for him among the Greeks, he set out
to restore Seleucid control over western Asia Minor. The details and
precise chronology of the early stages of this action in 204 and 203 are
uncertain; but Amyzon, an inland Ptolemaic possession in Caria, had
become Antiochus' by spring 203; and it would be reasonable to date his
recovery of neighbouring Alabanda, since the time of Antiochus II
known as 'Antioch of the Chrysaoreans', to the same time; Alinda had a
Seleucid garrison in 202/1; Tralles, if a badly damaged inscription
belongs to this time, will also have become Seleucid now; and a dossier
from Teos shows the presence of Antiochus personally at the Pergamene
harbour town probably in 204.[16] These are isolated details, but one thing
is certain. The same three friends of Rome who were most concerned
about Philip's Aegean activities were already directly or indirectly
affected by Antiochus' expansion. Rhodes had mainland possessions in
Caria ('the Rhodian Peraea'), which must have seemed to be threatened
by Antiochus; Egypt lost at least Amyzon at this time; and Pergamum
had to tolerate Antiochus' presence with an army at Teos. To rub salt
into the wounds of the losers, both Alabanda and Teos, following up an
initiative of their new protector Antiochus, took steps to have themselves widely recognized in the Greek world as 'holy and inviolate' (ἱερὰ
καὶ ἄσυλος); Antiochus also declared the inviolability of the sanctuary of
Artemis at Amyzon and insisted that his troops respect this; neighbouring Labraunda seems to have been treated similarly.[17] Antiochus clearly
wished to represent himself as friend and patron of the Greek cities and
thus win them over.

This activity in Asia Minor was interrupted after 203, however, when
Egyptian weakness resulting from the death of Ptolemy Philopator
seemed to offer Antiochus the chance of deciding in his favour the
century-old dispute between the two dynasties over the control of

[15] Polyb. xi.34.15–16.
[16] Amyzon and Alinda: Welles 1934, no. 38: (B 74); Robert 1983, nos. 9, 14–15: (B 193). Alabanda:
OGIS 234; Robert 1973, 448–64: (B 68). Tralles: Welles 1934, no. 41: (B 74). Teos: Herrmann 1965,
29ff.: (E 45); Giovannini 1983: (E 44); Allen 1983, 47–8: (E 52).
[17] Alabanda: OGIS 234, cf. Hesperia 1978, 49ff. Teos: GDI 5165–80; SIG 563–6. Amyzon: Welles
1934, no. 39: (B 74); Robert 1983, nos. 10–12: (B 193). Labraunda: Crampa 1972, no. 46: (B 46); cf.
Robert 1983, 139–40: (B 193).

Phoenicia and Coele Syria. The death of Philopator in summer 204,[18] at the age of about 35, was both sudden and premature, but the succession of his six-year-old son Ptolemy V Epiphanes need not in itself have produced a weak government in Alexandria. The weakness resulted rather from the conflict between the various groups of courtiers who aimed to control the child-king and in practice to exercise the real power in the state.[19] The first attempt was by the upstart family of Agathocles. Agathocles' sister Agathocleia had been the favourite concubine of Philopator and had used her private influence with the king to manoeuvre her brother into a position of such confidentiality with Philopator that he was immediately able to assume the regency for Epiphanes. He began reasonably efficiently by concealing Philopator's death until Epiphanes' mother Arsinoe could be assassinated, thus stifling her claim to the regency; by sending out influential rivals as ambassadors to Antiochus, to Philip and to Rome; and by recruiting fresh mercenaries in Aetolia. But he soon had to face increasing opposition, above all in the Alexandrian garrison and in traditional court circles. Probably late in 203 a movement led by Tlepolemus, the commander of the garrison at Pelusium, which enjoyed wide support in the army and the population of Alexandria, resulted in the fall of Agathocles' clique.

Tlepolemus was, it seems, a popular and competent military commander, but inexperienced in the central government, which he shared with a regency council of which the younger Sosibius was also a member. Moreover, serious differences of opinion soon upset the initial harmony of this council and it became clear that Tlepolemus would not quickly be in a position to introduce a firm government. It therefore seems possible that the decisive event which persuaded Antiochus to leave Asia Minor and to march into Coele Syria in 202 was precisely the collapse of the regime of Agathocles. His expectations were not disappointed. The Ptolemaic opposition was clearly very modest: only at Gaza in summer 201 did he meet with serious resistance, but even here a lengthy siege brought the fortress town into his possession. It was only after the fall of Gaza that the Egyptian government was able to react to the Seleucid attack, which in two campaigns had wrested Coele Syria, Phoenicia and Palestine from Ptolemaic rule. By then, however, it was already too late.

---

[18] This date has been much disputed, since there is a conflict between our documentary evidence, which dates the beginning of Epiphanes' second regnal year to October 204, and Polybius, who places Epiphanes' proclamation in 203/2. Since the documentary evidence can hardly be wrong, Polybius seems to have either made a mistake or to have departed from his 'annalistic' technique; given the fragmentary state of the text a final decision seems impossible: see in detail (also on the theory of Philopator's death having been concealed for more than a year) Schmitt 1964, 189–237: (E 50); Walbank 1957–79, II.434–7 and III.784–5: (B 38).

[19] The sources: Polyb. xv.25–34, xvi.21–2; Justin xxx.2.

The Aetolian mercenary general Scopas indeed won some initial successes. He seems to have briefly reconquered parts of Palestine; but in a battle at Panium, near the source of the Jordan, in spring or summer 200, Antiochus took his revenge for Raphia. The Ptolemaic army was defeated and forced to retreat. Antiochus spent the next two years re-organizing his new conquests, and it was 197 before he could again take up his plans for Asia Minor.[20]

After Antiochus' withdrawal from Asia Minor in 202 Philip showed that his Aegean ambitions were not exhausted in the profitable support of an Aetolian freebooter and modest help to his friends in Crete. By then his fleet was ready; and although in 202 he carefully avoided attacking towns which were directly under the control of another power and concentrated on conquering independent communities, his capture of Lysimacheia, Chalcedon and Cius which were allied to the Aetolians, of Perinthus which was closely attached to Byzantium, and of Thasos caused alarm. Moreover, his capture of the important trading cities of Cius and Thasos was marked by severe brutality which not only offended Greek opinion but in particular provoked the hostility of Rhodes. The Rhodians objected in principle to any military activity which threatened access to the Black Sea, and had tried to intervene diplomatically in favour of Cius: Polybius, probably reflecting a Rhodian source, writes that from this time they regarded themselves as being at war with Philip.[21]

Open hostilities were postponed, however, until 201. Early in 200, Philip possessed garrisons on the Cycladic islands of Andros, Paros and Cythnos, which prevented them from joining Rhodes.[22] When these islands became Macedonian, whether all at the same time or whether they were the only Cycladic islands which Philip took, is unclear; but in view of recent events it is probable that they were first occupied in 201 (though 202 is possible). In any case, they belonged to the group of independent states which, being without adequate protection, were the first to attract Philip's attention. This was not true for the Ptolemaic island of Samos, which Philip now took and garrisoned and where he captured more ships than he could man.[23]

During summer 201 two sea-battles took place. One developed out of Philip's siege of Chios, and was fought against the joint fleet of Rhodes, Pergamum and Byzantium in the straits between Chios and the Ionian peninsula. Philip suffered such large losses – larger than in any previous military operation, according to Polybius – that he refused to rejoin the

---

[20] The sources: Polyb. XVI.18–19, 22a, 39, XXIX.12.8; Josephus, *Ant. Jud.* XII.129ff.; St Jerome, *in Dan.* XI.13ff. On the chronology see Holleaux 1938–68, II.317–35: (D 35).

[21] Polyb. XV.23.6.   [22] Livy XXXI.15.8.

[23] Habicht 1957, 253ff. no. 64: (B 51); Polyb. XVI.2.9 (the ships).

battle the next day.[24] The other battle took place, against the Rhodians alone, off Lade, between Samos and Miletus. Here Philip defeated the Rhodians and immediately afterwards occupied Miletus, which, like Samos, until then had had a close relationship with the Ptolemies, though it was no longer garrisoned by them. Philip and his adviser Heracleides were voted wreaths by the Milesians, who, anticipating attack, tried to win favour by simulating enthusiasm.[25] A third event which belongs chronologically in the general context of the two sea-battles was an attack by Philip on Pergamum. According to Polybius he acted so violently that he even destroyed temples outside the walls (which he could not breach), especially the precinct of Athena Nicephorus, the 'Victory-Bringer' – which, if this were after the battle of Chios, would doubtless seem a particular provocation. He followed up this raid with an extensive march inland through Pergamene territory to Thyatira, the plain of Thebe on the Gulf of Adramyttium, and to Hiera Come.[26]

The order of these three events has been much disputed,[27] and although the order Chios, Pergamum, Lade seems marginally the most likely, it cannot be claimed that there is any conclusive argument in its favour. One thing, however, is certain. The events of spring and summer 201 showed that Philip was a serious danger to the balance of power in the Aegean and Asia Minor. Rhodes had already realized this in 202; and it was Rhodes which in 201 prodded Attalus to take the initiative in stopping Philip:[28] in 200 and again in 198 Philip claimed that they had attacked him first and he was not contradicted.[29] Formally this may have been correct. But his activities in Crete and among the independent states of the Aegean seaboard, and his capture of Samos from Egypt all pointed in the same direction. Philip had perhaps not originally planned to attack Pergamum but was provoked into it by Attalus' intervention in the siege of Chios. In favour of this is the fact that he did not follow up the attack, but subsequently concentrated on Caria where Rhodes had mainland interests, but where Philip also, around Mylasa and Euromus, had inherited influence and contacts which had still been active in the first years of his reign.[30] His activities in Caria in 201 are not wholly clear; but Iasus and Bargylia, probably Euromus and Pedasa and possibly Stratoniceia had fallen to him by the autumn; he had also unsuccessfully attacked Cnidus; but Prinassus, a small Rhodian town, and the Rhodian island of Nisyros fell to him.[31] An inscription indicates that before 197

[24] Polyb. XVI.2–9.   [25] Polyb. XVI.10.1, 15.   [26] Polyb. XVI.1.
[27] A sensible discussion of the chronological problems in Walbank 1957–79, II.497ff.: (B 38).
[28] Polyb. XVI.9.4.   [29] Polyb. XVI.34.5, XVIII.6.2.   [30] Crampa 1969, no. 7: (B 45).
[31] Iasus, Euromus, Pedasa, Bargylia: Polyb. XVI.12, 24.1, XVIII.44.4. Cnidus and Prinassus: Polyb. XVIII.11; Polyaenus IV.18. Stratoniceia: Livy XXXIII.18.22; Polyb. XXX.31.6, with Walbank 1957–79, III. ad loc.: (B 38); SIG 572.

Euromus had been renamed Philippi, and the most likely occasion for this honorific re-naming is the re-occupation in 201.[32] How many more Carian towns were directly affected by Philip's activities in 201 is uncertain; but during the following winter, while he was blockaded at Bargylia, he attacked Alabanda, Magnesia-on-the-Maeander and Mylasa in desperate attempts to obtain enough food for his men.[33]

The short-term threat to Rhodes and Attalus was thus already clear by autumn 201; long-term implications could be foreseen, if nothing were done. The battle of Lade had shown that neither partner without the other could hope to stop Philip; and Egypt, which had earlier played a stabilizing role in Aegean affairs, could not help since Philip had just taken Samos; Antiochus had already taken Amyzon and was now attacking Ptolemaic Phoenicia. Moreover, there were indications that Philip and Antiochus had some sort of agreement not to interfere with each others' activities in Asia Minor. Philip, indeed, seems to have taken the view that Zeuxis should help him with supplies (though he did not do so to any significant extent),[34] which suggests that they may even have envisaged some kind of co-operation, at least against Pergamum and Rhodes, the two major obstacles to their aspirations in Asia Minor. Later writers claimed to know that this agreement aimed to divide up Egyptian possessions,[35] which seems to have been an interpretation of the facts that Philip took Samos in 201, in 200 additionally Maronea and Aenus, while Antiochus was operating against Ptolemaic Syria. But in 201 what troubled the Rhodians and Attalus were Philip's concrete activities, not his modest co-operation with Antiochus, and above all his direct threat to Rhodian and Pergamene possessions. This sent them on the search for allies.

No potent ally was available among the Greek-speaking powers. The only hope lay in Rome, which had just successfully ended the war with Carthage. Attalus had fought alongside Rome in the First Macedonian War; Rhodes, along with other non-participants who were all basically friendly towards Rome, had helped to negotiate an end to the war. Formally a few Roman friends including Attalus were *adscripti* to the peace. But it is probable that informal assurances of continued Roman interest in Greek affairs had been given, the seriousness of which was evidenced by the recent intervention in favour of Rome's friends in western Greece or Illyria. It was thus almost inevitably to Rome that Rhodes and Attalus turned in the autumn of 201 when it seemed that

---

[32] Prof. Ümit Serdaroğlu and Mr R. P. Harper generously gave me advanced knowledge of this inscription. Text now published by Errington 1986: (B 50a).

[33] Polyb. XVI.24.6–8.   [34] Polyb. XVI.1.8–9.

[35] For sources and commentary see Walbank 1957–79, II.471ff.: (B 38). For this view Errington 1971, 336ff.: (D 24).

their own efforts could not cope with the crisis created by Rome's old enemy.[36]

We do not know in detail what the ambassadors of Rhodes and Attalus said in Rome, whether privately to those senators who were interested in eastern affairs or publicly in the Senate. They will doubtless have painted an unfavourable picture of Philip's activities in the Aegean and Asia Minor. In private they will above all have cultivated those senators who had participated in the First Macedonian War and who may well have been personally known to the envoys – if not, the envoys were badly chosen. And in this circle of 'eastern experts', perhaps headed by the ex-consul P. Sulpicius Galba, the possibilities of helping will have been discussed in detail. When the envoys from the east arrived at Rome the consular elections for 200 were imminent (perhaps December), and it may be in the light of their mission that Galba stood for election and was elected, with C. Aurelius, a relative of the M. Aurelius who was currently in the Balkans, as his colleague. The eastern experts were thus influential in Rome in late 201. Moreover, the Greeks also received diplomatic support: three *legati*, sufficiently highly placed to confront a king (or more than one, if necessary), were sent to the east, still during the winter and before the entry into office of Galba and Aurelius as consuls for 200 (the date of their entry into office, the Ides of March, fell perhaps in January by the Julian calendar in view of the technical dislocation of the official Roman calendar at this time). They were C. Claudius Nero (*cos.* 207), P. Sempronius Tuditanus (*cos.* 204, the peacemaker at Phoenice) and M. Aemilius Lepidus. Their instructions were to make clear to Philip in a personal interview the terms on which Rome was prepared to remain at peace with him. These were laid down in a *senatus consultum*: Rome demanded that Philip make war on none of the Greeks and that he give compensation, as determined by a fair tribunal, for his offences against Attalus; if he did this he might live in peace with Rome; should he be unwilling, the opposite would ensue.[37] The *legati* were then to go on to Egypt to announce the defeat of Carthage, to canvass support should war with Philip be necessary; and, in practice, to try to mediate between Antiochus and Ptolemy.[38]

This mission seems to have been conceived merely as an effort to bring immediate help to Attalus and Rhodes while avoiding upsetting established constitutional practice at Rome: that formal decisions to begin wars should be taken at the beginning of the consular year.[39] This means that the *senatus consultum* was formulated more for its propaganda effect among the Greeks than because it was expected that its demands might

---

[36] Livy XXXI.2.1–2.   [37] Polyb. XVI.27.2–3.
[38] Livy XXXI.2.3–4; Polyb. XVI.34.2.   [39] The view of Rich 1976: (H 20) is accepted here.

achieve more than a short-term effect with Philip. Negotiation was not intended: a few weeks later at most, long before any reply to the demands of the *senatus consultum* could have reached Rome, the new consuls entered office, Galba received Macedonia as his province, and was immediately instructed to present the *rogatio* to the *comitia centuriata* that war should be declared against Philip. It is impossible to believe that this grave decision was merely a result of the wishes of the envoys from Attalus and Rhodes, although it is likely enough that their complaints provided arguments for the eastern specialists, who wished to take up the war with Philip again. The root cause of their view, which the Senate clearly immediately accepted, lay fifteen years back, in the treaty which Philip had made with Hannibal in 215. As long as the Hannibalic War continued, it had been in practice impossible for the Senate to devote large forces to the war in the east, which had been run merely as a holding operation. This attitude had found its expression in the Aetolian treaty and in the Peace of Phoenice. But it would be a grave mistake to imagine (as Philip may have done) that the Peace of Phoenice had cancelled out the gratuitous provocation of 215. For many senators, particularly Scipio, who in 205 required all available forces for Africa, it is true that the First Macedonian War had never been more than a side-issue. But to those who had participated in it, who had fought that unsatisfactory war and who now composed the eastern lobby, it was more than that. Because of Hannibal's presence in Italy the Senate had not supported its men in the east as they might have hoped: triumphs were not won there, though triumphs had been won even in Illyria; and Macedonia certainly provided the potential for a triumph.

The importance of this aspect – at the precise time when Scipio's career re-emphasized with startling actuality the old truth that in Rome the influence of an individual within the state was directly related to his military successes – should not be underestimated. The willingness of many members of the Senate to make war because of the potential glory that was in it for them personally as commanders is a fact of Roman political life. Moreover, even after Phoenice, *legati* and small numbers of ships and troops had been sent to the Balkans when necessary, to maintain the peace and to demonstrate Roman interests. M. Valerius Laevinus was in eastern Adriatic waters with a small fleet at this very time. Also the smaller Greek states, which before Rome's intervention had merely accepted their inability to resist effectively the demands of the Great Powers, now found hope in Rome; and the wishes of the states currently damaged by Philip's activities fitted so well with the practical possibilities and with the wishes of the eastern lobby in the Senate for finishing the war with Philip that the Senate voted for war.

Once the Senate had decided a major issue of foreign policy it was not used to shows of independence by the *comitia centuriata*, such as took place at the beginning of 200. The first war *rogatio* of the new consul Sulpicius Galba was voted down in the assembly, after the tribune Q. Baebius had argued against it on grounds of general war-weariness. But it did not take long to get this decision reversed, once Galba had promised not to levy veterans from the African war for Macedonia. It may be that the final decision of the *comitia centuriata* to declare war was helped by the timely arrival of reports from Laevinus and by an embassy from Athens led by Cephisodorus, which complained of Philip's activities against Athens (though Livy places these before the rejected *rogatio*, and he may be right); but when the three *legati* were sent to Greece even before the new consuls had entered office, the decision for war had in principle already been taken in the Senate, which was not likely to be impressed by a tribune parading his conscience in public, even if this resulted in a temporary lack of senatorial control of the *comitia centuriata* and a certain delay. There is no trace of the Senate's reconsidering its opinion or doubting that it was correct. Probably by May at the latest the *comitia centuriata* voted for war.[40]

Philip seems to have had little idea of the peril which the end of Rome's war with Carthage brought for him. When Attalus and Rhodes sent envoys to Rome in autumn 201 he was still operating in Caria. As winter drew on, he found his fleet blockaded in the Gulf of Bargylia, and risked breaking out only when it became clear that the area could not provide enough food for his men,[41] though he retained Iasus, Euromus, Pedasa and Bargylia. The date of his escape from Bargylia is uncertain, but it may have been as late as February. Meanwhile events had not stood still on the Greek mainland. In the autumn Athens had given Macedon an excuse for hostility. At the Eleusinian Mysteries in late September 201 two uninitiated Acarnanians had strayed into the temple of Demeter, and on discovery had been put to death. Acarnania was an ally of Philip's and appealed to him; he sanctioned in due course a raid on Attica, in which Macedonian troops participated.[42] Precisely when this happened is uncertain; but it need not necessarily have been after Philip's return from Asia: he was by no means incommunicado in Caria, even though he thought it risky to try to get his whole fleet out of Bargylia. The Athenians reacted by abolishing the two tribes Antigonis and Demetrias and by sending envoys to all possible helpers: Cephisodorus apparently persuaded Attalus, Ptolemy, Rhodes, Aetolia and the Cretans to become Athenian allies; but when they did not send immediate help he personally travelled to Rome and probably arrived just before the first *rogatio* for

[40] Livy xxxi.5ff. The chronology is much disputed: I follow in general Rich 1976, 78ff.: (H 20).
[41] Polyb. xvi.6; Polyaenus iv.18.2.   [42] Livy xxxi.14.6–10.

war.[43] There may have also been an earlier Athenian embassy to Rome, possibly shortly after the Acarnanian attack; but whether this could have arrived in time to influence the Roman discussions about the war is doubtful, although Livy places its arrival even before the consular election and Appian, for what it is worth, supports this by making it contemporary with the Rhodian embassy.[44]

In the late winter the three Roman *legati* arrived in Greece, but made no effort to seek out Philip personally and to inform him of the terms of the *senatus consultum*. By the time they reached Athens the Romans had already visited Epirus, Amynander of Athamania and the Aetolian and Achaean Leagues, all of whom were currently friendly to or allied with Macedon. At each place they announced the terms of the *senatus consultum*.[45] This activity can only be seen as an attempt to frighten some of Philip's friends and to win their support or neutrality for the impending war. At the Piraeus the Romans conferred with Attalus – Tuditanus, the peacemaker of Phoenice, will have known him personally – and some Rhodians who had pursued Philip from Bargylia. They will doubtless have explained what the Senate meant by the *senatus consultum* and its practical implications (in terms of Roman expectations of help) for those who had appealed to Rome; moreover, they seem to have agreed on a common line of approach to the Athenians. They then all went up to Athens together and were greeted with great enthusiasm. Attalus in particular, the king who had been fighting Philip for a year and who, since his gaining possession of Aegina in 209, was Athens' most powerful neighbour, was received with splendid honours, the chief of which was the creation of a tribe Attalis which implied a cult and a priest – an honour which, only a few weeks earlier, had been cancelled for Philip's ancestors Antigonus and Demetrius. Rhodes had also been active against Philip, and the recent rescue of four Athenian ships was repaid with a crown of valour and *isopoliteia* (honorary citizenship)[46] for all Rhodians. The communications with the *ecclesia* were certainly influenced by the conversations with the *legati*. Both Attalus and the Rhodian speaker emphasized Roman readiness to make war on Philip and urged Athens to join them formally: the Athenians replied with a formal vote declaring war on Philip. Oddly enough, Polybius does not record that the Roman *legati* addressed the Athenian assembly, nor does Livy, who had the complete text of Polybius available.[47] They will have had sufficient opportunity to make the Roman position clear to the Athenian council, since they remained in Athens for some time.

[43] Paus. 1.36.5; Livy xxxi.5.6.
[44] Livy xxxi.1.10; App. *Mac.* 4.1–2. Habicht (1982), 153–4: (D 30), argues strongly against the historicity of the earlier embassy.   [45] Polyb. xvi.27.2–3.
[46] On the nature and function of grants of *isopoliteia* see Gawantka 1957: (I 13).
[47] Polyb. xvi.25–26; Livy xxxi.14.11–15.7.

Meanwhile the preparations for war continued. The Rhodian ships, returning home, took into alliance all the Cyclades except Andros, Paros and Cythnos, which were garrisoned by Philip.[48] This success was doubtless based on their impression of Roman readiness for war and willingness to protect those Greeks who were prepared to fight. While the *legati* were still in Athens, Philip's general Nicanor, perhaps as Philip's first reaction to the news of Athens' declaration of war, invaded Attica and penetrated as far as the Academy. The Romans reacted at once: Nicanor was not Philip, but they could hope to achieve two objects through an interview with him: they could persuade him to leave Attica with his army and thus relieve pressure on Athens, and they could expect him to inform Philip of the contents of the *senatus consultum*. Their *démarche* had the desired effect, and Nicanor withdrew at once from Attica.[49]

It is improbable that Philip did not already know the contents of the *senatus consultum* before its formal communication by the *legati* to Nicanor. Since their visit to the Epirotes, at the latest since their talks with the Achaeans at Aegium, news must have reached Pella of their propaganda activities. Philip neither reacted diplomatically nor did he allow the *senatus consultum* to change his plans. Livy records the devastation of Attica by Philocles with 2,000 infantry and 200 cavalry which, although the chronology is uncertain, seems to be a reply to Nicanor's formal communication of the *senatus consultum*.[50] Otherwise Philip threw all his efforts into a campaign in Thrace. This time he showed no interest in diplomatic considerations. The Ptolemaic possessions Maronea and Aenus fell to him just as the inland Thracian towns of Cypsela, Doriscus and Serrheum; in the Chersonese he occupied Elaeus, Alopeconnesus, Callipolis, Madytus, Sestus and a number of other smaller places. He then crossed the Hellespont and began to besiege Abydus which, together with Sestus, controlled the narrowest part of the Hellespont.[51] If he captured it, he would be in a position to control traffic through the Hellespont. Of immediate interest and particular importance was the summer traffic in grain from the grainlands of southern Russia to many Greek cities, not least to Athens. Whoever controlled the Hellespont at the time of the great summer grain-cargoes exerted a major influence on the fates of innumerable Greek cities.

We cannot hope to know finally why Philip chose to ignore the *senatus consultum* in such a provocative way. He seems to have been determined to obtain control of the whole north Aegean coast and the Hellespont, at whatever cost. Yet he knew that Rome had defeated Carthage and must have realized that this time the Senate would be able to send as many

48 Livy XXXI.15.8.   49 Polyb. XVI.27.   50 Livy XXXI.16.2.
51 Polyb. XVI.29–34; Livy XXXI.16.3–18.9.

troops and ships as necessary against him. The inescapable conclusion is
that Philip did not believe in the genuineness of the demands of the
senatus consultum, that he suspected, or even knew, that the Senate had
already decided on war, regardless of the results of any negotiations he
might begin, and that he was determined to improve his position as far as
possible in his current areas of interest before Roman troops arrived. The
dilatory behaviour of the *legati* and the fact that the nominal recipient of
their *senatus consultum* was among the last to receive formal notice of it
must have suggested this. It is indeed impossible to believe that the
Senate would have recommended cancelling the war-vote in the *comitia
centuriata* (which would have been quite unparalleled) that it had used all
its prestige to force through, even if Philip had reacted favourably to the
demands of the *legati*. We may be sure that, as indeed happened during
the war, further Roman demands would have followed, which in the end
would have been impossible for Philip to accept and would have made
the war 'necessary'. If Philip chose to regard the *legatio* and its *senatus
consultum* merely as a Roman attempt to win time and influence in Greece,
he was right; its demands were a fraud, and Philip seems to have
recognized them as such.

This becomes even clearer when we consider the last recorded activity
of the *legati* in the Aegean area. They showed no further inclination to
contact Philip until they arrived at Rhodes, where they learned that he
was besieging Abydus. They had doubtless, in the course of their
leisurely progress, communicated the *senatus consultum* to such islands as
they visited. But Philip himself was completely neglected. From Rhodes
M. Aemilius Lepidus, the youngest of the *legati*, travelled without his
colleagues to Abydus and at last formally instructed Philip in person of
the *senatus consultum*. By now demands had been added that he keep his
hands off Ptolemy's possessions and pay compensation to the Rhodians
for the damage he had caused them. The threat of war, if Philip did not
comply, remained. The interview ended abruptly when it developed into
a fruitless argument about who had started hostilities.[52] Philip was not
frightened off by Lepidus' threats and continued the siege; Abydus fell to
him shortly afterwards. Lepidus, it seems, had achieved nothing.

Philip thus paid as little attention to Lepidus' arrogant protestations at
Abydus as he had to the message of the *legati* sent via Nicanor from
Athens. Nor did the *legati* seem to think that he would. Their instructions
had been to confront Philip personally, but when it came to the point
only one of them travelled to Philip, and that the youngest and least
experienced, although Tuditanus, the Roman peace-maker at Phoenice,
was surely the man to confront Philip, if the implicit alleged aim of their

52 Polyb. XVI.34.

journey, to bring Philip to a peaceful settlement, were meant seriously. The only conclusion once again must be that the *legati* did not regard this part of their function as being very important, when measured against the propaganda value of the *senatus consultum* in the Greek cities as preparation for war. This being so, we should conclude that the purpose of Lepidus' visit to Philip at Abydus lay more in the immediate interests of the Greeks, above all of the Rhodians, the current hosts of the *legati*, who, as a trading state, always suspected military activity at the Hellespont. In 220 they had gone to war with Byzantium when it had tried to impose a transit toll on the Bosphorus; and Philip's capture of Cius in 202 was, according to Polybius, the last straw which had driven them to war. But Athens, as a large grain-importer, was also affected, and Attalus had sailed from Aegina to Tenedos on receiving news of the siege. Pressure from Greek allies, therefore, rather than fulfilment of senatorial instructions, seems likely to have been primarily responsible for the duty-visit of Lepidus to Philip at Abydus. He cannot have expected (or wished for) any success; but the Greek allies would again be given the impression that the Romans were doing all in their power to defend their interests. Until Galba's army arrived, it was all that could be done.

II. THE SECOND MACEDONIAN WAR

Despite the problems which the bargain with the tribune Q. Baebius caused – the undertaking had been given to levy none of the African veterans – Galba was ready by late summer 200;[53] and although he would be unable to undertake major military operations before the winter, he decided nevertheless to cross to Apollonia. This had the double advantage that the army, once assembled, would not immediately disperse for the winter in Italy; and it would show the Greeks that it was not lack of Roman commitment but merely winter conditions which hindered Roman activity. Presumably war was formally declared, as the fetial priests had explicitly allowed, at a Macedonian frontier-post. Philip learned of Galba's arrival shortly after the capitulation of Abydus, which seems also to have been the cue for the three *legati* to continue their journey to Antiochus and Ptolemy. The consul now represented Roman interests in the region.

Galba decided at once to seek winter quarters for his two legions in the friendly area around Apollonia. But since he also had some ships, he sent twenty triremes under the command of his *legatus* C. Claudius Centho to

---

[53] The main sources for the events of this section are: the fragments of Polyb. XVIII; Livy XXXI.22.4–47.3, XXXII.4.1–6.4, 9.6–25.12, 32–40, XXXIII.1–21.5, 24–5, 27–49.

Athens. Athenians had met him at Apollonia with the news that Athens was virtually under siege as a result of Macedonian attacks from Chalcis and Corinth. Energetic action by Centho, supported by three Rhodian quadriremes and three small Athenian boats, relieved the situation with an attack on Chalcis, where much war material was destroyed and plunder taken. The point of this raid was twofold: not just to damage Philip, but also to raise the morale of the Athenians (who had suffered Macedonian raids throughout the summer but received no effective Roman help) and of those who might be influenced by them. The war was thus from the beginning conceived and fought with two aims. One, which originated in Philip's stab in the back in 215 and which could only be achieved by military action, was the essentially destructive aim of making Philip acknowledge that he must act as Rome required; the other was the constructive aim of winning the 'hearts and minds' of the Greeks. This latter went back ultimately to the Illyrian wars, was firmly rooted in the alliances of the First Macedonian War and had gradually acquired conscious shape through the appeals of the Greeks since the Peace of Phoenice. In the pursuit of this constructive aim the primary methods were diplomatic and propagandist, but were supported by military action which was seen to be in the interests of Rome's Greek friends. The three *legati* had started the diplomatic and propaganda campaign by broadcasting Rome's demands that Philip stop attacking the Greeks. They had even tried to prevent specific Macedonian actions; but only after the arrival of the army and the fleet were the necessary concrete demonstrations of military support for the diplomatic aim possible. In the north-west, Galba made a similar demonstration of the Roman military presence. A *legatus*, L. Apustius, whom he sent with a detachment to attack Macedonian border districts, captured and destroyed Antipatreia and a number of minor towns and forts. The chief aim was doubtless to impress local states and dynasts, and it had some success. Immediately afterwards Pleuratus, Amynander of Athamania and Bato, king of the Dardanians, all arrived at the Roman camp and offered assistance.

Philip also saw the need to attend to his allies. The Achaean League had helped him against Rome in the first war, since when his interest in Peloponnesian affairs – except for his garrison on the Acrocorinth – had lapsed. In autumn 200 the Achaean assembly met to consult about raising a levy against their old enemy Nabis of Sparta. Philip came to the meeting and offered to fight the war for them, if the Achaeans gave him troops for his garrisons in Chalcis, Oreus and Corinth. They refused, since by his offer Philip clearly intended to commit the League to the new war with Rome. Despite the garrison on the Acrocorinth, the Achaeans were not prepared to follow him into the new war, or at least not immediately. For this he had only himself to blame. His Aegean commitments since 205 had not only led to his neglecting his old allies, in the meanwhile he had also offended many Greeks by excessive brutality, above all at Cius, Thasos and Abydus. Moreover, the Roman *legati* had visited Aegium in the spring, and will undoubtedly have assured the Achaeans that if they did not actively support Philip, Rome would not attack them. Under the circumstances, Philip now showed consummate tactlessness when he in effect demanded hostages to guarantee a commitment against Rome.

The pattern of the war was thus established immediately by P. Sulpicius Galba. After the winter he invaded western Macedonia unhindered. In Lyncestis he ravaged large areas, defeated part of Philip's army and took large quantities of plunder, but he did not press on into Lower Macedonia. In the autumn he returned to the coast, where he handed over his command to his successor P. Villius Tappulus, who for unknown reasons also arrived just in time to go into winter quarters. At the same time the Roman fleet continued to protect Athens while also raiding Macedonian possessions in the Aegean and on the coast of Macedonia. But since Sulpicius' army in Upper Macedonia could not support the fleet, no major success was gained; the capture of Andros, Oreus, Larisa Cremaste and Ptéleum were the naval achievements of the year.

Despite the indecisiveness of the events of the summer, the Aetolian League was impressed – above all, by the opportunities of plundering which its non-participation was costing it. Yet the decision not to participate had been taken formally, contrary to the urgings of Roman allies, at the Panaetolica, the spring meeting of the League. By late summer, however, opinion had changed; and after preliminary negotiations with L. Apustius (who, Livy says, 'promised everything'), the *strategos* Damocritus, who at the Panaetolica had opposed participation, now persuaded the Aetolians to join Rome, and immediately rushed out with the army, together with Amynander, into Thessaly. It was only thanks to Amynander that this careless operation did not turn into a full-scale disaster, when Philip suddenly attacked the Aetolians, who were conscientious only in collecting booty.

Rome on balance had had the advantage of the indecisive events of 199. P. Villius Tappulus, the new consular commander, made his winter base on Corcyra. In the spring he learned from a friendly Epirote, Charops, that Philip had occupied the Aous gorge, a major bottleneck on the main and most convenient invasion route into Macedonia. His aim was obviously to prevent a repetition of 199, when Sulpicius had invaded Upper Macedonia unhindered. Villius' immediate inclination was to fight, and he quickly brought his troops to a position only five miles from Philip's. But before he could engage, the Roman administrative system

intervened in the form of his successor, the consul of 198, T. Quinctius
Flamininus. Flamininus had taken advantage of the dislocation of the
Roman calendar, which placed his entry into office (nominally 15 March)
at the latest in January, to complete his official duties in Rome and to
cross the Adriatic in time to assume his command before the first
engagement of the year.

Roman policy had already been laid down by the Senate in 200. Philip
was the enemy, with those who supported him,[54] not the Greeks, who
were to be protected and (for the purposes of the war) won over for
action. Amynander and the Aetolians, some of the Epirotes, Athens,
Pergamum, Rhodes and the Cycladian islanders had already responded
favourably; the actions against Macedonia itself, and against Euboea and
Philip's other coastal possessions, spelled out clearly the dangers of
remaining a friend of Philip. This policy Flamininus, whose meteoric
career during the last years of the Hannibalic War had culminated in the
consulship before he was even thirty, had now to represent and develop.
Flamininus, like his two consular predecessors, had had experience in the
Greek world, in Magna Graecia, where he had learned Greek adequately
and experienced Greek ways of thought and aspirations. He differed
from them, however, in that he commanded a strong personal support in
the Senate which (he could hope) might in due course, given sufficient
evidence of his energy and progress, secure his prorogation and thus his
chance of personally supervising Roman interests in the Balkans for long
enough to be effective (whether or not he succeeded in defeating Philip
immediately).

From the beginning the Roman aim was to reduce Philip's power to
the point where he would normally act as Rome required without
argument or quibble. The war had begun without negotiations of any
kind having taken place; and dramatic results such as Flamininus required could not now be achieved by negotiations, as Philip found to his
cost. He immediately offered the new consul in effect to accept the terms
which Lepidus had stated at Abydus eighteen months before: that he
would evacuate places which he himself had captured and submit allegations of war damage to arbitration. But Flamininus' lack of interest in
serious negotiation became clear when he demanded the 'liberation' of
the Thessalians, who had belonged to Macedon for some 150 years, and
the talks ended as abruptly as they had begun. Flamininus' demand did
not mean any change in the basic Roman attitude to Philip. The demands
of the various Roman representatives were all so formulated that in the
given circumstances they were sure to be rejected by Philip. At the same
time they gave the Romans a propaganda advantage with the Greeks.

---

[54] Livy XXXI.6.1: the war was declared on *Philippo regi Macedonibusque qui sub regno eius essent.*

The difference is one of tactics and technique, and perhaps an indication that Flamininus might already be seeing the free and freed Greeks as a pillar of long-term Roman influence in the Balkans, after the immediate war-aims had been achieved. Thus, the change is not in attitude to Philip but in relation to the Greeks. For the first time (as far as we know) a Roman commander had committed himself to freeing specific Greek communities. Flamininus' demand that Philip evacuate Thessaly was not just the deliberate making of a demand that Philip must reject, but was a considered development of the propaganda programme and an indication of future policy. The principle was not new, but the application in detail was important.

Whether a comprehensive post-war policy towards the Greeks was already being consciously formulated is impossible to say. The Greeks were important for the war, particularly those, like the Thessalians, with close attachments to Macedon, and it is certain that winning the war was the single overriding objective of Roman activities in 198, as it had been in 199; events show that Thessaly had been chosen deliberately by Flamininus as one of the main areas of his military activity. After the break-up of the talks, Philip could not hold his apparently impregnable position at the Aous gorge, and his retreat to Thessaly cost some 2,000 men.[55] Expecting that Flamininus would follow at once, he followed a scorched-earth policy, inevitably at the cost of the Thessalians. Flamininus, however, did not follow immediately. His first priority was to secure his lines of communication to the west coast, which meant putting diplomatic pressure on Epirus, whose territory controlled the ˙ critical routes across the Pindus. Only then did he follow Philip into Thessaly.

The going was not easy. Philip had garrisoned the most important towns, and although the consul captured several smaller places, the larger towns caused him serious difficulty, above all Phaloria and Atrax. Phaloria, despite its 2,000-man-strong garrison, was eventually captured after a siege and the whole town burnt down; but Atrax held out for so long that Flamininus abandoned the siege. Time was running short – it was perhaps already September – and he required more central winter quarters with direct access for his transport ships than Epirus could provide. The northern shore of the Gulf of Corinth offered the best possibilities and here Phocis, with its adequate harbour of Anticyra, was friendly with Philip, which was a good reason for wintering there, since winter-quartering of troops always tended to strain relations with allies. Nor was Phocis likely to offer serious opposition, despite a Macedonian garrison at Elateia and perhaps some other places. And so it turned out.

---

[55] On the topography see Hammond 1966, 39ff.: (D 31).

Only Elateia required a siege before it too was occupied. The inhabitants, though the town was plundered, were declared free, as the Roman slogan demanded. The fleet also achieved some successes during the year. Commanded by the consul's brother L. Quinctius Flamininus, it captured Eretria and Carystus in Euboea, which left Philip with only his major fortress of Chalcis on the island.

These successes, above all the proof of Philip's inability to protect Euboea and Phocis, had political repercussions. The Achaean League, which a year before had refused to commit itself to the war with Rome, now inclined under its new *strategos* Aristaenus to take the major step of abandoning the nearly thirty-year-old alliance with Macedon and to join Rome – perhaps above all because of the operations of the Roman fleet in the Saronic Gulf and the operations which it was foreseeable that the Romans would undertake in the Corinthian, once they had established their base at Anticyra. The decision hung long in the balance at the meeting of the League held at Sicyon during the siege of Elateia, which was attended by representatives of Rome, Attalus, Athens and Rhodes. Finally Aristaenus won the critical vote and the League joined the alliance against Philip, though the allies proved too weak to expel Philip's garrison from the Acrocorinth and to restore Corinth to the League. A small consolation for Philip was that Argos, supported by Philocles' soldiers from Corinth, seceded from the League and remained loyal to Macedon.

Flamininus had set out with great consequence to 'free the Greeks'. He had not entered Macedonia, as Sulpicius Galba had done, but had concentrated on Macedonian possessions in Greece, removing them city by city from Macedonian control. In this way, without ever confronting Philip, he could hope to convince the Greeks that Philip was merely fighting to maintain his Greek empire, whereas Rome supported their fight for freedom. Under the circumstances Philip decided to try to gain precise information about the Roman price for peace. He accordingly suggested talks which took place around November 198 at Nicaea and Thronium, near Thermopylae. At this time Flamininus had not yet received news of his *prorogatio*, so that he did not know whether or not he would himself remain in command. For this reason he had no objection to talking to Philip – indeed, in case his command were not prorogued, he might even be able to negotiate terms which he could recommend to the Senate as being the effective achievement of Roman war-aims. If his command were renewed, as he hoped, it would not be difficult to feed the Senate suitable demands to guarantee the collapse of the negotiations. And even in the worst of all foreseeable events, if Flamininus were replaced and the Senate did not accept his negotiated terms, he would still not have lost anything by negotiating, since the positive effect on the

Greeks of accepting, apparently with serious intention, every negotiating offer which Philip made, was important for the Roman image.

The negotiations at Nicaea were therefore not a total charade, though demands within the framework of Roman propaganda, which would guarantee their failure, needed to be kept unmentioned in the background in case they should be required; these were the evacuation of Philip's three fortresses, which he called 'the Fetters of Greece' – Demetrias, Chalcis and the Acrocorinth. All Roman allies were represented. Flamininus demanded once again that Philip evacuate the whole of Greece; that he release all deserters and prisoners; that he evacuate the areas in Illyria which he had occupied since the Peace of Phoenice and that he restore all places taken from Ptolemy, that is Aenus, Maronea and Samos (if Ptolemy had not already recovered the latter).[56] The allies also registered their demands in detail, the Aetolians being particularly extreme; and the session ended with the presentation of the demands in writing. Philip replied the next day in closed session with Flamininus, who told the allies that his reply amounted to the partial satisfaction of their demands. The allies were not satisfied; but when Philip offered to send to the Senate to negotiate disputed points, Flamininus readily agreed, since his powerful backers in Rome would decide what to recommend to the Senate, depending on whether they succeeded in having his command prorogued or not. The talks therefore broke up after agreeing a two-months' truce; and representatives of all participants travelled to Rome.

Shortly after their arrival in Rome, but before the formal hearing, the Senate had decided that both consuls of 197 should remain in Italy, which implied that no new commander would be sent to Greece. The Greek allies had clearly been well primed by Flamininus, and now informed the Senate at length of the central importance of the 'Fetters'; they argued so cogently that the Senate refused to listen to the prepared statement of Philip's ambassadors, but merely asked if he were prepared to give up Chalcis, the Acrocorinth and Demetrias. When they confessed that they had no instructions on this issue the Senate voted to continue the war and that Flamininus should remain in command. Flamininus' scheme had thus succeeded admirably; he had obtained his command and the Senate's willingness to listen to the allies had convinced them of Rome's essential goodwill, as the propaganda had already indicated. The only one injured by this cynical business was Philip – but since he was the enemy, he did not matter.

By spring 197, Flamininus had won over the whole of central and southern Greece. In the Peloponnese Nabis, Rome's ally of the first war,

---

[56] This had occurred by 197 (Livy XXXIII.20.11–12), but we do not know precisely when.

joined the alliance, despite having just received Argos from Philip as the price for an alliance with him; in central Greece Boeotia, despite some internal difficulties, had also been won. Apart from the 'Fetters', Philip thus retained of his earlier sphere of influence in Greece only Phthiotis and Thessaly. It was therefore in this direction that Flamininus led his army. Initially his plan seems to have been to continue the laborious piecemeal town-by-town conquest of 198. He began at Phthiotic Thebes; but when he heard that Philip had entered Thessaly with a large army, the prospect of ending the war through a single decisive battle made him break off the siege and march to meet him. After some manoeuvring, Flamininus forced Philip to battle at Cynoscephalae. The armies were numerically about equal: against Philip's more than 25,000 men, Flamininus had the two Roman legions, supported in infantry by 6,000 Aetolians, 1,200 Athamanians, 500 Cretans from Gortyn and 300 Apolloniatae as well as 400 Aetolian cavalry. The uneven ground, however, suited the Romans and their allies so much better that the battle was a major success for Flamininus.[57] Philip's army was destroyed as a serious fighting force; and immediately after the battle he asked permission to send envoys to negotiate. The time had come for Flamininus to lay his cards on the table and say what he wanted. Philip had no immediate alternative to accepting what the Romans imposed.

From this time, we begin to get an idea of Rome's long-term conception for Greek affairs. There is, of course, a sense in which Rome was committed by the propaganda of the war years; but this had been cleverly kept in terms of demands on Philip and (as far as we can see) no formal commitment to any specific post-war general solution had been made. This did not mean that the allies did not have their own hopes and aspirations for the post-Macedonian era in Greece, nor their own views of what should happen to Philip and Macedon.

It became clear at once that Roman war-aims, as far as Macedon was concerned, had been achieved by decisively defeating Philip; Macedon was humbled, and what Philip retained was by the grace of Rome. He would, at least in the immediately foreseeable future, do what Rome wished. Flamininus, in granting Philip's request to open negotiations after the battle, also urged him to be cheerful, as a patron might treat a client fallen on hard times. This basically friendly attitude troubled the Aetolians, who hoped to exploit the demolition of Macedon; their demand that Philip be deposed was brusquely rejected by Flamininus. It would not have been easy to depose Philip; and in any case Rome had no interest in letting a power-vacuum in the Balkans come into existence,

---

[57] On questions relating to the battle see Walbank 1957–79, II.572ff.: (B 38); Pritchett 1969, 133–44: (I 30).

particularly in view of events in Asia Minor in 198 and 197, where Antiochus, after defeating Ptolemy and occupying Coele Syria, was rapidly re-occupying the coast. Moreover, it rapidly became clear that Greek hopes of freedom, which had been awakened by the Roman diplomatic campaign against Philip, could also be used to prevent the already unpopular Aetolians from capitalizing on the victory and replacing Philip in central Greece. This was just as little in the Roman interest as that Antiochus should replace Philip. Flamininus' aim was thus not so much a balance of power as a balance of weakness in the Balkans; and the war slogans could readily serve this purpose.

When the Aetolians re-joined Rome L. Apustius 'promised them everything'. Despite their separate peace treaty with Philip in 206, they had apparently received from Apustius the impression that the terms of the treaty of 212 would be valid also for this war – that is, that they would receive such places as were conquered in co-operation with the Romans. It was an impression which, however, was never confirmed in writing, for when, at the peace conference at Tempe which followed soon after the battle, their spokesman Phaeneas demanded the cession to Aetolia of Larisa Cremaste, Pharsalus, Phthiotic Thebes and Echinus, Philip's attitude was acquiescent; it was Flamininus who objected that they might only have Phthiotic Thebes, since it alone had resisted; the other towns, having surrendered, were under Roman protection. Against Phaeneas' argument that the treaty gave the towns to Aetolia, Flamininus replied brutally that the Romans had regarded the treaty as non-existent ever since the Aetolians had abandoned Rome and made peace with Philip in 206, and that it had in any case never applied to cities which surrendered voluntarily.[58]

The Aetolians' disappointment was enjoyed by the rest of the allies, who could now at least be sure that, whatever the final settlement turned out to be, they would not be delivered up to the overbearingly ambitious Aetolians. Philip offered the terms which had been demanded at Nicaea and at Rome, that he evacuate the whole of Greece, including the 'Fetters'. More was not now required of him, and Flamininus, after receiving hostages (including Philip's son Demetrius) and 200 talents, recommended that the Senate accept these terms. This it duly did, though the consul for 196, M. Claudius Marcellus, opposed the peace along with the Aetolians, in the hope of himself being able to continue the war.

[58] This latter assertion of Flamininus' seems to be possibly contradicted by the inscriptional text of the treaty which (lines 15–21) clearly deals with states who voluntarily come over to Rome or Aetolia and seems to allow their inclusion in the Aetolian League, perhaps under guarantee of their self-government. The stone is however broken just at the point where the conditions were detailed, a fact which makes it virtually impossible to judge whether Flamininus' assertion is correct: for discussion and literature see Walbank 1957–79, I.599f. and III.789: (B 38).

The Senate then appointed the usual ten-man commission to settle outstanding questions. At least four of the members were ex-consuls and included Flamininus' predecessors P. Sulpicius Galba and P. Villius Tappulus. When they arrived (late winter or spring 196) they brought a *senatus consultum*, of which Polybius reports what he says are 'the essentials': All the Greeks not subject to or garrisoned by Philip, whether in Asia or in Europe, shall be free and live according to their own laws; those subject to Philip and the cities garrisoned by him he shall hand over to the Romans before the Isthmian Games (June/July 196); Euromus, Pedasa, Bargylia and Iasus, also Abydus, Thasos, Myrina and Perinthus he shall leave free and withdraw his garrisons from them. Concerning the freedom of Cius, Flamininus shall write to Prusias according to the *senatus consultum*. All prisoners and deserters Philip shall restore to the Romans within the same time. He shall give up all his decked ships except for five and the 'sixteener'; he shall pay 1,000 talents, half immediately and half in ten annual instalments.[59]

The most important feature of the *senatus consultum* is the universal declaration of freedom for all Greeks, including explicitly those Greeks of Asia Minor who were not subject to and garrisoned by Philip and who therefore had had nothing directly to do with the war against Philip. This represents a clear and deliberate extension of Rome's declared sphere of interests into Asia Minor, a development which was in no way predestined by the circumstances of the war with Macedon. The reason for it was quite different, and lay in the activities of Antiochus III in Asia Minor during the war with Philip. The terms of the peace treaty with Philip and the settlement of the Greeks were thus not conditioned solely by Balkan events. Already the wider implications of the Romans' intervention in the Balkans were becoming apparent: they had defeated Philip by adopting an attitude of protecting the interests of the smaller Greek states against Macedon. This had so far been so successful that in its fully developed form of guaranteeing the freedom of each individual Greek state (even against other Greek states) it could, it seemed, also be used offensively – directly and immediately against the Aetolians in the Balkans, but also less immediately but perhaps more seriously in Asia Minor, as a warning to Antiochus.

Once more it had been Rome's allies Rhodes and Pergamum that first sounded the alarm. In 200 indeed the three Roman *legati* had gone on to Egypt and to Antiochus, from whom they doubtless received assurances that he had no intention of helping Philip. Nor did he. His aims, it turned out, were more ambitious. Already in 198 Attalus complained in Rome of an attack on his kingdom and asked the Senate for permission to pull

[59] Polyb. XVIII.44.

his forces out of the Macedonian war in order to deal with it. The Senate not only complied but sent out envoys who achieved the withdrawal of the Seleucid army from Pergamum. But they did not prevent the occupation of regions east of Pergamum, which had until recently been controlled by Attalus, nor the agreement whereby Prusias of Bithynia might occupy the part of Phrygia called Epictetus. Despite this, probably still in 198, Antiochus sent envoys to Rome, who were received honourably and amicably by the Senate.

In 197 Antiochus, starting in Cilicia, set out to recover the coastal territories of Asia Minor. He met little opposition. The Rhodians, fearing that he wished to join Philip, met him at Coracesium, but they gave up plans to oppose him when they heard about Cynoscephalae. They insisted, however, that Antiochus should not attack Ptolemaic possessions in their area and successfully preserved Caunus, Myndus, Halicarnassus and Samos. Otherwise Antiochus' forces, which took full advantage of the political weakness of Pergamum resulting from Attalus' suffering a stroke and from his subsequent death, achieved a steady stream of successes. By the autumn Antiochus possessed Ephesus and probably some towns of the Troad, Ilium and perhaps already Abydus. In autumn or early winter 197/6 Lampsacus appealed to Rome for help,[60] having decided to resist, as had Smyrna. But these were Antiochus' only problems. In Caria even Philip's erstwhile possessions had shrunk, probably by the end of 197, to Bargylia alone. The Rhodians re-occupied their Peraea, helped by Antiochus at Stratoniceia; Euromus had already in c. August 197 (Gorpiaios) sent envoys to Zeuxis, clearly immediately after receiving news of Cynoscephalae, and made a treaty of alliance with Antiochus;[61] neighbouring Pedasa had doubtless gone the same way, as had Iasus, to which Antiochus granted freedom and where, shortly afterwards a cult of Laodice was established.[62] Then in late winter or spring 196 Antiochus invested Smyrna and Lampsacus and sailed from Abydus to Europe, where he took control of the Chersonese and began to rebuild Lysimacheia.

During the three years of the war with Philip the political structure in the Aegean area had thus changed dramatically. The Romans and their allies had defeated Philip, but while they were doing it Antiochus had re-established Seleucid influence in coastal Asia Minor. It is possible that he regarded Rome as being irrelevant to Asia Minor, that he thought that Rome would not be concerned. He had treated the Rhodians, finally, as friends and had allowed them even to protect cities in their area which, according to them, still claimed loyalty to Ptolemy; even Pergamum, the

[60] *SIG* 591 with Holleaux 1938–68, v.141ff.: (D 35).
[61] Errington 1986, lines 8–11: (B50A).
[62] The inscriptions in Blümel 1985, nos. 3 and 4: (B44A).

old Seleucid enemy, he had spared after Roman intervention; he regarded himself, and at the most recent diplomatic contact had been treated as, an *amicus* of Rome. But that had been a year ago. Between lay a year of conquests and the defeat of Philip. By the time the *senatus consultum* which gave the ten *legati* their terms of reference was formulated, the Senate's attitude to Antiochus had clearly changed, and the reason is not difficult to find. Antiochus' conquests in Asia Minor, but above all his crossing to Europe, had made him seem a threat to the main strategic Roman achievement of the Macedonian War: the creation of a zone, in the Balkans, free from the immediate presence of another Great Power. Even if this threat were not immediate, Roman experience with the idea of freedom for Greek states nevertheless made the Senate take the initiative in Asia Minor. It is not necessary to believe that specific appeals from Greek states will have made this seem advisable, though Rhodes and Pergamum, now represented by Attalus' son and successor Eumenes II, will doubtless have stressed the danger. But, as with the intervention in the Balkans in 200, this can have been at most a convenient pretext. Greek was Greek, whether in Asia Minor or in the Balkans; to recognize this essential unity and to treat all Greeks of the Aegean area as being equally dear to Rome was a modest propagandist step, which might possibly give Antiochus pause for thought. At the same time the Senate resuscitated its interest in the conflict between Antiochus and Ptolemy and sent the consular L. Cornelius Lentulus to arbitrate – a further hint that, if cause were given, Rome might continue to show interest in Antiochus' affairs.

The activities of Flamininus and the ten *legati* in 196 were thus overshadowed by the actions of Antiochus. Of Philip's possessions which the *senatus consultum* explicitly declared free, four at least – Euromus, Iasus, Pedasa, Abydus – already counted as part of Antiochus' sphere of interest, though doubtless all were technically 'free and using their own laws'. Here, then, the *senatus consultum* seems to have been overtaken by events, though it is possible that the Senate already knew what had happened, at least to the Carian towns (Euromus was formally allied to Antiochus as early as August 197), when it formulated the *senatus consultum*, but maintained the fiction in order to preserve a recognized *locus standi* as the conqueror of Philip against Antiochus. On the other hand, the declaration of freedom explicitly for Asiatic Greeks had a programmatic character which might specifically help Smyrna and Lampsacus. But the apparent emphasis on Asia offered ammunition to the Aetolians, who saw fraud in the *senatus consultum* and broadcast their provocative view that the only really free cities would be those of Asia,

[63] Polyb. XVIII.45.10.

and that the Romans would keep for themselves key positions – above all, the 'Fetters', which they had told the Senate were so important – and thus ensure that the European Greeks merely changed masters.

The 'Fetters' indeed caused the *legati* difficulties, since some of them believed strongly that Rome should keep them as a precaution against Antiochus,[63] and a final decision was postponed; but the town of Corinth at least was restored to Achaea. The Isthmian Games in June/July was the date by which Philip should evacuate his garrisons and other Greek possessions. In order to counteract the Aetolian interpretation of the *senatus consultum* Flamininus determined on a *coup de théâtre* which should take place at the games. Excitement was already high, since an announcement was expected, when in the crowded stadium a herald made the following proclamation: 'The Roman Senate and the proconsul T. Quinctius Flamininus, having defeated King Philip and the Macedonians, leave the following peoples free, ungarrisoned, tribute-free and to live according to their own laws: the Corinthians, Phocians, Locrians, Euboeans, Phthiotic Achaeans, Magnesians, Thessalians and Perrhaebians.'[64] The enthusiasm was immediate and enormous; after such a public pronouncement at one of the great international games – which, by public demand, the herald repeated – there could be no doubting the immediate intentions of the Romans. The peoples named comprised all those who had recognized claims to independent existence and who had been part of Philip's Greek empire. The representatives of the freed communities were then invited to discuss details with the *legati*. The only serious dispute was raised by the Aetolians, who wished to receive Pharsalus and Leucas. The issue was referred to the Senate; otherwise they were allowed to accept Phocis and Locris into their League. The *legati* inclined to let Eumenes keep Oreus and Eretria, which had been captured by the joint fleet and left to Eumenes to look after, but Flamininus maintained that this would tear an enormous hole in the declaration of freedom – would, in effect, play into the Aetolians' hands – so these cities were also declared free. Two Illyrian border towns, Lychnidus and Parthus, were granted to Pleuratus; Amynander was quietly allowed to retain those border areas of Thessaly, including the important town of Gomphi, which he had acquired during the war. The *legati* then split up and visited the areas where further details needed to be regulated on the spot. We know that P. Cornelius Lentulus went to Bargylia, L. Stertinius to Lemnos, Thasos and the Thracian coast, Cn. Cornelius Lentulus to Philip and Aetolia. P. Villius Tappulus and L. Terentius Massaliota were sent to Antiochus at Lysimacheia. It would be

---

[64] Omitted from the list in Polyb. (XVIII.46.5) and Livy (XXXIII.32.5, from Polyb.) perhaps simply by Polybius' oversight, are the Orestae and Dolopes (Polyb. XVIII.47.6; Livy XXXIII.34.6).

reasonable to assume that the other *legati*, who are not mentioned explicitly by the sources in this context, did not sit idly at Corinth but also travelled, particularly in Thessaly and central Greece, where the greatest permanent changes were foreseen, meeting people and making arrangements.

That new organizations could not simply be created in a few weeks is obvious, and a reference in Livy to Flamininus' still carrying out re-organizations in Thessalian cities in 194 demonstrates this.[65] But the *legati* worked quickly; the newly organized Thessalian League elected its first *strategos* in early autumn 196,[66] and a decision that Magnesia should be organized as part of this federation also belongs to 196. This means that fundamental organizational decisions at the federal level – e.g. which communities were to belong to the league, what its function should be in relation to the federated communities, what system of voting should be applied, where the meetings should take place, who should attend them, how it should be financed – all belong to 196, between the Isthmia in June/July and the election of the first federal *strategos*, perhaps in September; and these decisions must all have been supervised by Flamininus and the *legati*. After the emotion of the Isthmia the *legati* who stayed in Greece thus spent the rest of their time in tedious administrative detail – a necessary consequence, if the 'freedom of the Greeks' was to be more than a slogan and take a concrete shape, which alone could achieve long-term stability in the Balkans.

III. ANTIOCHUS THE GREAT

When the ten *legati* separated to oversee the details of the settlement of Greece, two of them travelled to Antiochus. The importance of this mission was emphasized by the fact that in the end not only P. Villius Tappulus and L. Terentius Massaliota travelled to Lysimacheia, but that they were in due course joined by L. Stertinius and P. Cornelius Lentulus; and that L. Cornelius Lentulus, who had been sent by the Senate explicitly to talk to Ptolemy and Antiochus, arrived at the same time and became the Roman spokesman. The initiative which provoked the Roman *démarche* had come from Antiochus, who had sent Lysias and Hegesianax to Flamininus (but not, it seems, to Rome) at about the time of the Isthmia. Lysias and Hegesianax were interviewed immediately after the games, and they received a programmatic declaration: Antiochus was requested to leave autonomous cities of Asia Minor alone, to make war on none of them (this, above all, a reference to

---

[65] Livy XXXIV.51.4–6. See also Flamininus' letter to Chyretiae in Perrhaebia: Sherk, *Documents* 9, for an example of the type of decisions required.   [66] So Kramolisch 1978, 7ff.: (D 38).

Smyrna and Lampsacus), and to evacuate the cities which he had just taken from Ptolemy and from Philip. Additionally he was warned against crossing to Europe with an army, 'for none of the Greek cities was currently at war with or subject to anybody'.[67]

This was the point of departure of the Roman mission to Lysimacheia.[68] It soon became evident, however, that Antiochus was a much more polished diplomatic performer than Philip. The atmosphere of the meeting at the personal level was cordial until the main issues were discussed. L. Cornelius Lentulus reiterated the demands formulated at Corinth, that Antiochus should give up the cities which belonged to Ptolemy and which had belonged to Philip, 'since it was ludicrous that Antiochus should take the spoils of the Roman war against Philip'. He was asked to leave the autonomous cities unmolested, and finally – the main point of the exercise – he was asked why he was in Europe with large forces, and it was suggested to him that all thinking men would regard this an indication of an intention to attack the Romans. Antiochus was not impressed. He wondered at the Roman interest in Asia Minor, which had nothing to do with them, just as he did not concern himself with Italian affairs. He had crossed to Europe to take possession of the Chersonese and the Thracian cities, since he had the best rights to them: they had belonged to Lysimachus and had become Seleucid when Seleucus defeated Lysimachus;[69] Ptolemy and then Philip had occupied them at a time of troubles in his kingdom, and he was therefore not now exploiting Philip's misfortune, but asserting his own historic rights. In any case, he was scarcely offending Rome by restoring Lysimacheia, which had recently been destroyed by Thracians; this was intended as a residence for his son Seleucus, not as a base from which to attack the Romans. The autonomous cities of Asia did not enjoy freedom by virtue of a Roman decree but by his grace and favour. His dispute with Ptolemy would in any case soon be amicably settled, since he was planning a marriage alliance with him; in his dispute with Smyrna and Lampsacus – envoys from the cities were present – he would accept the arbitration not of Rome, but of Rhodes. The meeting ended inconclusively in a farce when a false rumour of Ptolemy's death arrived, which both parties pretended not to have heard, but which made both eager to investigate Egyptian affairs as soon as possible with the hope of influencing the succession.

The Romans were thoroughly discomfited by Antiochus' consummate performance. He had not only shown himself unimpressed by the Romans' assertion of Roman interests but had produced reasons for his

---

[67] Polyb. XVIII.49.3.   [68] Polyb. XVIII.50–53.

[69] At Corupedium in 281; the areas had never been properly occupied by the Seleucids.

presence in Europe at least as good as the Romans could produce for his not staying there. He had in effect developed a different world-political view, whereby he claimed Asia Minor for his sphere, as Italy was Rome's; between lay the buffer territory of the Aegean and the Balkans, where neither had exclusive rights. Since the defeat of Philip and for the present purpose, however, the Romans inclined to the view that *their* exclusive sphere of interests included the Balkans up to the Bosphorus and Hellespont, and that Asia Minor was a buffer area, where neither might claim exclusive rights. The conceptions were incompatible; the Roman, by hellenistic tradition, provocative. But since the Roman concept was still being developed when the meeting at Lysimacheia took place and since Antiochus' activities so far affected only a (for Rome) marginal area, talks could go on. Antiochus said he would send envoys to Flamininus, who arrived in spring 195. They tried to convince Flamininus that Antiochus planned no further conquests and represented an alliance. Flamininus was non-committal. The *legati* had by then returned to Italy; he therefore referred Antiochus' envoys to the Senate. But, presumably since they had no instructions about this, they did not go.[70]

That Flamininus and his army were still in Greece in 195 was related to uncertainty about Antiochus' ultimate aims, which the talks at Lysimacheia had exacerbated. If Flamininus knew his Macedonian history, he must have known that when Lysimachus was defeated by Seleucus he ruled not only Thrace but also Macedonia; thus Antiochus' historical argument could also justify a claim to Macedon. Whether or not this was a factor, Antiochus' self-righteous attitude and self-assertive activities were alarming; and although the credibility of the whole policy of 'Greek freedom' was endangered if Roman soldiers stayed in Greece and above all continued to occupy the 'Fetters', the Peloponnese offered good reason for their staying at least for 195. Nabis, though allied to Rome, had lost importance since his enemy the Achaean League had also joined Rome, and the violent behaviour of his regime at Argos – for thirty years, until 198, a member of the Achaean League – made him hated by most of the Greek states. A campaign against Nabis could accordingly be neatly dressed up in terms of the slogan of freedom: Argos should be freed from the tyrant. A *senatus consultum* gave Flamininus the right to act according to his own discretion.[71] He therefore summoned representatives of the allies to Corinth, and only when they had voted for war did he bring his troops out of winter quarters and begin the campaign. Although Nabis was defeated he was not destroyed, only weakened. The Laconian coastal towns were 'freed'

---

[70] Livy XXXIII.41.5, XXXIV.25.2.   [71] Livy XXXIII.45.3.

and put under the supervision (*'tutela'*) of the Achaean League, and Argos was reunited with the League.

Despite Antiochus' military activities in Thrace in 195 and despite Hannibal's successfully seeking refuge with him – which helped Scipio Africanus to his second consulship, for 194 – the Senate accepted Flamininus' policy of evacuation when it decided on the provinces for the year: the consuls should stay in Italy; the army should be withdrawn from Greece. It was now urgent, if Flamininus' policy, loudly proclaimed at the Isthmia in 196, were to remain credible and the accusations of the disappointed Aetolians be proved false, that something should finally be seen to be done. Only then could Rome hope to enjoy practical Greek goodwill, which was the ultimate aim of the policy. In spring 194, after he had spent the winter in deciding law suits and in political reorganization of cities which had been Philip's,[72] Flamininus summoned representatives of the Greeks to Corinth. They listened to a recapitulation of what the Romans and Flamininus had done for the Greeks and then heard that Demetrias and Chalcis would be evacuated within ten days and that Flamininus personally would give the Acrocorinth back to the Achaeans, 'so that all might know, whether it was the practice of the Romans or of the Aetolians to lie'.[73]

While the meeting was still in progress – a theatrical touch, typical of Flamininus – the first soldiers were seen leaving the Acrocorinth. Flamininus had great faith in the goodwill of the Greeks. Individual Greek states had in the past often enough shown themselves grateful to 'freedom-bringers' and other benefactors; indeed, a frequent causative clause of Hellenistic city decrees is precisely, 'that others might know that the city knows how to honour its benefactors'. But benefaction on such a massive scale and a policy so consistently based on it, carried beyond the stage where garrisons were 'temporarily' left and war-contributions 'temporarily' collected, was unique. There was inevitably risk involved, not so much that the value of the Roman benefaction in individual states would be unrecognized, as that the complex multi-state nature of the Greek world, left to itself, would produce political chaos out of the particularist 'freedom'. This might then give Antiochus precisely the excuse he needed (were he looking for one) to intervene. But the only practical alternative, of using Italian troops rather than Greek goodwill to maintain Greek friendship with Rome, offered even less prospect of success. Should it come to hostilities with Antiochus, then it was clearly better to fight with the support of Greeks, who could be expected to remember the practical sincerity of Rome's freedom policy, than to remain in occupation and inevitably cultivate mistrust and hate. Greeks always appreciated and honoured an extravagant gesture; this Flamininus had satisfactorily learned and practised.

Until his departure Flamininus continued his work of re-organizing, deciding disputes, exhorting common sense. Then he was gone. From the Greeks he took with him a collection of honorary decrees manifesting Greek goodwill, and the gold crowns that went with them; then there were some 2,000 Italians, who had been captured during the Hannibalic War and sold on the international slave markets, freed as a present from the Greek states to their freedom-bringer (though the gesture went back to a suggestion of Flamininus'). His three-day triumph over Philip and Nabis was spectacular. The booty from the Greek cities which had resisted was enormous: not only weapons and gold and silver coin and bullion, but works of art, bronze and marble statues and vases were displayed, together with the gold thanksgiving crowns from the Greek cities, the freed slaves, the captives and the eminent hostages from the defeated.[74]

Antiochus had not been idle since 196. In 195 a large army operated in Europe against the Thracians, and again in 194.[75] Then at the end of 194 or in spring 193 he sent Menippus and Hegesianax to Rome. At the start of the consular year 193 the Senate intended to deal with the details of the Greek settlement and in this connection large numbers of Greek states, including some from Asia Minor, had sent envoys to Rome. Their chief function seems to have been to provide the Senate with living evidence of the current depth of Greek goodwill and their presence had doubtless been engineered by Flamininus. The general atmosphere in which Antiochus' envoys found themselves was therefore one of self-satisfied patronage by the Romans and ostentatious goodwill towards Rome by the Greeks. It was not a favourable climate for Antiochus' men, whose instructions were to seek *amicitia* and negotiate an alliance (a direct repetition of Antiochus' alleged wishes in 195). The Senate, fearing complicated negotiations, referred Menippus and Hegesianax to a subcommittee consisting of its current eastern experts, Flamininus and the ten *legati*. The opportunity for straight speaking, which this interview behind closed doors allowed, was fully exploited by Flamininus. Confronted again with the question by what right Rome interested itself in Asiatic affairs, Flamininus played power politics. If Antiochus wanted friendship and alliance he must understand two things: first, if he wished Rome not to concern itself with Asia Minor then he must keep right out of Europe; secondly, if he did not restrict himself to Asia but crossed to Europe, then Rome would uphold its right to protect its friends in Asia and to acquire more.

[74] Livy xxxiv.52.4ff.   [75] Livy xxxiv.33.12; App. *Syr.* 6.21–22.

The next day Antiochus' envoys were received by the full Senate, and the other Greek envoys were also invited to be present. Menippus, it turned out, not only represented Antiochus but also Teos – since *c.* 203 part of Antiochus' kingdom – which had asked him to try to obtain Roman recognition of the *asylia* which Antiochus promoted as part of his public relations among the Greeks. We do not know the order of business, but in neither case can Menippus have been satisfied. The Senate granted his request for Teos, but added the unique proviso that the *asylia* should be valid only as long as Teos maintained its friendship with Rome; and since the only way in which little Teos would be likely to cease being friendly with Rome was if Rome fought a war with Antiochus, Antiochus was in effect being made responsible for preserving the *asylia*.[76] On the main issue Flamininus came straight to the point. He said nothing about the cynical ultimatum which he had stated in the sub-committee meeting, but urged the Greeks to report home that the Roman people would free them from Antiochus with the same good faith which it had shown in freeing them from Philip. If Antiochus left the Greeks in Asia autonomous and retired from Europe, he might continue to be a friend of Rome, if he wished. Since Antiochus' envoys had no instructions to negotiate on terms which implied a diminution of Antiochus' kingdom, they could merely plead for further talks. Antiochus had been publicly branded as a danger to Greek freedom before a large Greek audience and they had been unable to prevent it.[77]

Flamininus' cynical stage-managing had made good the diplomatic defeat of Lysimacheia. But whether it had also made peace more secure was less certain. The contradictory standpoints had not softened; and the more public diplomatic defeats were suffered, the more likely it was that one or other would decide that diplomacy was no longer adequate. Meanwhile the Senate, certain of its success, showed itself conciliatory and appointed three of the ten *legati* (P. Sulpicius Galba, P. Villius Tappulus and P. Aelius Paetus) to travel again to Antiochus. Their mission was dogged by misfortune. They first visited Eumenes, and while at Pergamum heard arguments for going to war with Antiochus, whose territory now surrounded Eumenes' kingdom. Moreover, P. Sulpicius fell ill and had to be left at Pergamum, while the others travelled on to Ephesus, only to find that Antiochus was in Pisidia; and although they were able to talk to Hannibal, they had to travel inland to Apamea, where Antiochus finally came to meet them. Neither side offered concessions, but before the talks ended the news of the death of the king's son

[76] The letter of the praetor M. Valerius Messala announcing this decision was found at Teos: Sherk, *Documents* 34. See Errington 1980: (E 42).

[77] Livy xxxiv.57–59; App. *Syr.* 6. This interpretation depends on rejecting the self-contradictory phrase *nisi decedat Europa* in Livy xxxiv.59.5, as argued by Badian 1964, 137 n. 70: (A 4).

Antiochus stopped the discussions. A later interview at Ephesus with Antiochus' adviser Minnio, who seems to have overestimated the strength of Antiochus' position, contributed nothing to a settlement. Nevertheless, on their return to Rome the *legati* reported calmly that they saw no immediate reason for war.[78] Even when Eumenes' brother Attalus personally travelled to Rome in spring 192 with the information that Antiochus had again crossed the Hellespont, the Senate made no change in its dispositions.[79] It seems clear that, if Antiochus restricted himself to the Chersonese and neighbouring districts of Thrace, the Senate would in practice, though under protest, accept this as the necessary price for peace. Only if he interfered further in the sphere which Rome now regarded as its protectorate would war follow.

Meanwhile the Roman peace was being shaken by the Aetolians. Probably in spring 193 they decided, in the absence of Roman troops, to try to upset the Roman settlement. It may be that they felt encouraged by a visit from Hegesianax and Menippus returning from Rome; Hegesianax visited Delphi, which was still controlled by the Aetolians, and received the grant of public honours appropriate to his status (*proxenia*).[80] Antiochus received a formal visit from the Aetolian Dicaearchus, brother of the *strategos* Thoas, who must have arrived before Minnio's talks with the Roman *legati* at Ephesus. He hoped to gain Antiochus' support for the planned uprising in Greece, but Antiochus remained cautious. Nor did Philip give the Aetolians any encouragement. Nabis, however, who also received an Aetolian envoy, immediately set out, contrary to his treaty with Rome, to regain control of the Laconian coastal cities, which precipitated both military and political reaction from the Achaeans: they sent reinforcements to Gytheum and an embassy to Rome. Since the three *legati*, returning from Ephesus, passed through Greece, they were able to recommend to the Senate action against Nabis. Accordingly, the praetor A. Atilius Serranus was sent with thirty quinqueremes to help the Achaeans. The Senate also reacted diplomatically to the news, and a new group of four *legati*, of which Flamininus and P. Villius Tappulus were members, went to talk to the Greeks and to remind them of Rome's continued interest in the settlement.[81]

Towards the end of 193 Thoas, after his year as *strategos*, had travelled to Ephesus. When he returned, Menippus came with him and at the spring meeting of the League (192) promised the Aetolians that Antiochus would restore the freedom of the Greeks. Flamininus had difficulty in obtaining permission to speak, and his suggestion to negoti-

[78] Livy xxxv.13.4–17.2; cf. App. *Syr.* 45–46; Livy xxxv.22.2.
[79] Livy xxxv.23.10–11.   [80] *SIG* 585, line 45.   [81] Livy xxxv.12–13.3, 22.2, 23.

ate in Rome rather than to involve Antiochus was answered by a decree, passed after he had withdrawn, inviting Antiochus to free Greece and to arbitrate between Rome and Aetolia. The Aetolian *strategos* Democritus was not satisfied with this. He provocatively refused to tell Flamininus its terms, but he would do so, he said, when he was camped on the banks of the Tiber. It was impossible not to conclude that the Aetolians had declared war, and that Antiochus' representatives had condoned this action (neither of which was true).[82]

Further events merely seemed to confirm this. The Aetolian delegate council, the *apocleti*, decided to try to seize Sparta, Chalcis and Demetrias. At Sparta they failed, after they had assassinated Nabis, thanks to rapid Achaean intervention; at Chalcis they also failed, because the Chalcidian government declared that, since Chalcis was already free, it did not need freeing, and took appropriately energetic action. At Demetrias, however, Flamininus had already had difficulty in convincing the people of the reality of their freedom. They had demanded a guarantee that Demetrias would not be restored to Philip, as the price for his remaining loyal to Rome; and Flamininus had hesitated to give this in public, since it would limit his chance of binding Philip with fraudulent hopes. Accordingly, the Aetolians were successful here. A subsequent visit by P. Villius confirmed that the Romans had lost credibility at Demetrias. It was a serious error of judgement.[83]

These Aetolian actions meant an open breach with Rome and would doubtless, even by themselves, have brought about Roman military intervention. They did not, however, necessarily imply war with Antiochus (though Eumenes doubtless did his best to persuade Flamininus that they did, when he met him on the Euripus during the crisis at Chalcis). Antiochus seems not to have expected that Aetolian action would follow so swiftly on Menippus' visit. He was involved with other projects: in Asia Minor with the still uncompleted conquest of Smyrna, Lampsacus and Alexandria Troas; and with Hannibal, to whom – although he had so far kept him at a discreet distance – he now intended to give a few ships and men, to see if he could cause a diversion in Africa. But immediately after the capture of Demetrias Thoas travelled again to Ephesus. According to Livy, he grossly exaggerated the enthusiasm for Antiochus in Greece, and false expectations seem indeed to be the only reasonable explanation for Antiochus' decision to cross to Demetrias in autumn 192. He could raise a mere 10,000 men, 500 cavalry and six elephants, all transported on sixty ships which he scraped together and which necessitated abandoning his support for Hannibal. There can be no question but that this was an emergency decision taken in order to consolidate what would otherwise be wasting assets: Demetrias, which Villius had already publicly threatened to recapture; and Aetolian enthusiasm, which could be expected to dissipate if he did nothing.

Antiochus' crossing to Demetrias, though provoked by events outside his control, was a deliberate assertion of his view that the Balkans were a no-man's land between Asia Minor and Italy, where he might legitimately have interests, although Roman representatives had repeatedly asserted the opposite view, that the Balkans were Rome's exclusive sphere of influence. But this had always been merely oral. Over Antiochus' possessions in Thrace and the Asiatic Greek cities, protests had continued for four years, but no action had followed. Indeed the Roman army had been withdrawn. It must therefore have been tempting to believe that the Senate's threats were without substance and that only a really major intervention would provoke Roman reaction. Moreover, Livy, echoing Polybius, suggests that at least one of Antiochus' advisers, Minnio, thought that, even if it should come to war, Antiochus would win; and Minnio was no mere trivial courtier but the minister who had conducted the final official interview with the last Roman *legati*. Under these circumstances Antiochus would doubtless tend to believe Thoas' assertions that many Greek states were just waiting for a favourable opportunity to rebel from Rome. A major bridgehead in central Greece, such as Aetolia could provide, would keep the Roman threat to his position in Asia Minor even more distant; and an armed conflict, if it came, would in the first instance occur in Greece, which was expendable, not in Asia Minor, which was now again an integral part of his kingdom. Antiochus' move to Demetrias thus seems to have been based on a fatal mixture of misleading information, false assessment and wishful thinking.

For the Senate Antiochus' crossing to Demetrias was the final confirmation of suspicions which it had harboured since at least 197, and which Antiochus' subsequent activities had done nothing to dissipate. Eumenes had taken every opportunity to nourish these suspicions and Antiochus seems to have seen this danger when he tried to prise him from his Roman friendship with the offer of a marriage alliance, which Eumenes had nonetheless turned down. In Greece the activities of the Aetolians, above all their recent contacts with Antiochus, suggested the possibility of a combination of interests, which diplomacy alone, however great the underlying Greek goodwill on which it could rely, could not hope to combat. The sending of the praetor Atilius Serranus to the Peloponnese in spring 192 with his fleet was the first indication that the Senate recognized this; moreover, the general underlying situation and rumours that Antiochus intended to send ships to Sicily had caused the Senate at the same time to take modest defensive measures for Italy and to foresee the necessity of sending legions to Greece again.[84] When the news of Antiochus' crossing reached Rome, the praetor M. Baebius Tamphilus was sent at once to Epirus with two legions, and one of the consuls, Flamininus' brother L. Quinctius Flamininus, levied additional troops so that when war was declared at the usual time at the beginning of the consular year the new consul could depart without his having to lose time in levying troops.

M'. Acilius Glabrio (*cos.* 191) received as his brief the conduct of the war 'against Antiochus and those in his empire' (*cum rege Antiocho quique sub imperio eius essent*). The praetor C. Livius Salinator became fleet commander; and as soon as weather conditions allowed, they crossed the Adriatic with all the immediately available forces.[85] When Glabrio arrived, Antiochus had already suffered severe disappointments. Except at Demetrias and by the Aetolians, he had been received everywhere coolly. His claim, based on the Aetolian view that Rome dominated the Greeks, that he had come to free Greece, fell on deaf ears since most Greek states since 196 had enjoyed greater practical independence than at any time since the middle of the fourth century, and the only states which Antiochus had managed to 'liberate' – Chalcis and a few Thessalian towns – he had had to do militarily, against the will of the local governments. The Achaean League had reacted to a diplomatic approach by declaring war and Philip, annoyed by Antiochus' clumsy support for a pretender to his throne – it was the brother-in-law of Amynander, who had returned to his Aetolian friendship – sent to Rome offering all help in the war. Baebius met Philip in Dassaretis during the winter and seems to have agreed, though probably only orally, that Philip might keep such places as he captured from the Aetolians and their allies;[86] the result was immediate activity, and Baebius was enabled to garrison the critically situated Larisa, just as Antiochus was preparing to storm it. Epirus tried to keep out of the conflict: Charops brought the message that, if Antiochus came in force he would be welcome; but if he could not guarantee protection, Epirus wished not to be involved. Even Boeotia, where Flamininus had had serious difficulties, hesitated, and a personal visit by Antiochus produced a decree which indeed indicated friendliness, but committed the Boeotians to no action. Only little Elis, isolated in the western Peloponnese and traditionally friendly to Aetolia, asked for a garrison, doubtless fearing the Achaeans. Antiochus finally found a more congenial occupation than this ungrateful diplomacy in spending

---

[84] Livy xxxv.23.

[85] The main narrative sources for the war with Antiochus and the Aetolians are: the fragments of Polyb. xx and xxi; Livy xxv.41–51, xxxvi.1–45, xxxvii.1–60, xxxviii.1–34, 37–41.

[86] Livy xxxvi.8.6, 10.10, xxxix.23.10.

the rest of the winter at Chalcis enjoying his recent marriage with a local girl.

In the spring events moved rapidly towards the resounding defeat of Antiochus at Thermopylae about the end of April. Even before the consul arrived, operations in Thessaly by Philip and Baebius had recovered most of the towns occupied by Amynander and the Aetolians a year before. Antiochus himself had apparently been persuaded by the Aetolians to help them achieve their old aim, of incorporating Acarnania in the League. He may indeed have hoped in this way to persuade the Romans to engage in western Greece, where it would be impossible for the Aetolians not to provide their full army to support him, since a defeat would mean the devastation of their own territory, but his failure in Acarnania and the devastatingly swift successes of Philip and Baebius in Thessaly prevented this. When Glabrio arrived in Thessaly about the beginning of April little was left to be done, and most of the remaining towns capitulated as soon as they realized that the consul had arrived. Antiochus, for unknown reasons, had received no substantial reinforcements since arriving at Demetrias, and was thus outnumbered two to one by the Romans, who had some 20,000 men and many allies from Illyria (to say nothing of the Macedonians who, after Glabrio's arrival and operating independently, occupied Athamania). He had the choice of retreating ingloriously to Asia or of choosing a place for battle where the Roman numerical superiority might not tell. His pride and reputation forbade the first alternative and he therefore chose to stand at Thermopylae. But his attempt was no more successful and considerably less glorious than that of the Greeks against the Persians 289 years before. The Aetolians provided only modest support, and the Romans inflicted such an overwhelming defeat that Antiochus evacuated Greece at once and returned to Ephesus. The whole Greek adventure had lasted little more than six months and ended in farce.

It had nevertheless shown the Senate the strength, but also the weakness of Flamininus' settlement of Greece. The conclusion was typical: not that the settlement was wrong in principle, but that the general conditions under which it had been implemented were too uncertain. Rome needed to ensure that no major threat to the peace existed, not merely in the Balkans, but in the whole Aegean area, including Asia Minor. Antiochus' campaign in Greece had demonstrated that the narrow lines of the Bosphorus and the Hellespont were wholly inadequate to define Roman strategic interests. It was necessary to redefine, but this time not just in terms of physical geography but in terms of geo-politics. The essential unity of the Aegean basin, of the Greek world of Asia and of Europe as a geo-political system, had been revealed with dazzling clarity.

There was never any doubt that the war would go on; the Senate made this clear when it gave L. Cornelius Scipio, consul for 190, as province Greece, with permission to cross to Asia if necessary. Scipio received as *legatus* his own brother Africanus, who was technically disqualified from holding a new consulship but whom the Senate expected to take a leading part in the campaign. Greece was the first priority after Thermopylae, since the Aetolians continued to resist; and despite major setbacks at the hands of Glabrio and Philip and despite negotiations both with Glabrio and in Rome, the siege of Naupactus, which Glabrio had begun in the autumn, still continued when the Scipios arrived.

Despite the formal priorities established by the Senate's formulation of the consul's province, there was no doubting that the Romans would cross to Asia. The Roman fleet under C. Livius had been operating with Eumenes' fleet in Asiatic waters since Thermopylae; and after a success at Corycus, in the strait between Chios and the Ionian peninsula, Livius spent the winter on Pergamene territory near Canae. The first action of the Scipios was therefore to arrange a six-month truce with the Aetolians, who were to use the time to negotiate in Rome, while the Scipios set out for Asia with their army on the land-route through Greece, Macedonia and Thrace. They doubtless chose this route because Antiochus' fleet, despite its setback at Corycus, was still very strong, and Antiochus had ordered reinforcements from Syria and had given Hannibal command of them. Until the allied fleet obtained supremacy it would have been desperately reckless to risk putting the army into ships and crossing direct to Pergamum. But the land-route, quite apart from its length (some 1,000 km from Naupactus to the Hellespont) was not without potential difficulties. Philip, whom the Senate had rewarded for his recent loyalty with the release of his son Demetrius, provided help with routes and negotiation with the Thracians. But two important coastal towns, Aenus and Maronea, freed by Rome in 196, were now garrisoned by Antiochus; and since 196 Lysimacheia had been built up into a fortress controlling access to the Chersonese, which, together with Abydus on the Asiatic shore, belonged to Antiochus. Nor was the attitude of Prusias of Bithynia on the Asiatic side of the Propontis necessarily friendly to Rome, or even neutral. If Antiochus had played his cards sensibly the Roman march into Asia could have been made into a nightmare.

In the event, however, it was merely the distance that created difficulties and cost time. It proved possible to circumvent Maronea and Aenus because the Thracians, sweetened by Philip, created no difficulties. The naval campaign in Asiatic waters in 190 had two decisive incidents: the first, when the Rhodians prevented Hannibal's reinforcements from joining Antiochus' admiral Polyxenidas at Ephesus; the second, a regular battle between the Roman fleet, now under L. Aemilius Regillus, and Antiochus' fleet off Myonnesus, in which Antiochus' fleet was so severely incapacitated that Antiochus panicked and withdrew not only his garrison but also the settlers in haste from Lysimacheia. However, since his haste allowed no time to remove the stores, the Romans, who arrived a few days later, actually chose Lysimacheia as the place where they could most suitably rest before crossing to Asia. Even the crossing of the Hellespont was in the end not contested by Antiochus. Abydus he simply gave up; and the Roman and Rhodian fleets, which after Myonnesus had sailed to the Hellespont, had no difficulty in ferrying the army over. Difficulties which the Romans had anticipated from Prusias were also easily avoided in the event through a diplomatic initiative.

By October 190 the Roman army was thus in Asia Minor and the allied fleet had obtained overwhelming superiority at sea. Antiochus had spent his time after returning from Europe in assembling army contingents from all parts of his empire; but despite the size of his army, which by the autumn had reached some 60,000 men, the Romans' arrival made him offer terms. The Romans, who since Antiochus' crossing to Greece regarded the Asiatic Greeks as their sphere of interest, were not impressed with his offer to cover half the Roman cost of the war and to abandon his claims to Smyrna, Lampsacus, Alexandria Troas and other towns which had joined Rome. The Scipios, reflecting the policy of the Senate, envisaged a fundamental change in the balance of influence in the Aegean area, and now that their army had safely landed in Asia they saw no reason not to use it to achieve their aims, the details of which had doubtless been constructed in consultation with Eumenes. These formed the basis of their reply: Antiochus must evacuate all Asia Minor north and west of the Taurus mountains and pay the whole costs of the war. These demands seemed so extreme that Antiochus broke off negotiations. Some time later, unusually late in the year for major military action (about mid-December), the decisive battle took place near Magnesia ad Sipylum. Antiochus, as at Thermopylae, though this time outnumbering the Romans and their allies at least by two to one, was routed.

There was not much to negotiate when Antiochus' representatives, Zeuxis and Antipater, arrived at Sardis, for many years Zeuxis' administrative capital, where the Romans had moved after the battle. The terms had been stated in the pre-battle talks and now merely acquired some precision: as before, Antiochus must evacuate all territory north and west of the Taurus. The war indemnity was made specific: Antiochus must pay 15,000 Euboeic talents – 500 immediately, 2,500 as soon as the terms were ratified in Rome, and the rest in twelve annual instalments; Eumenes should receive 400 talents and a quantity of grain, which Antiochus owed him by some treaty which Attalus had once made. Exiles and enemies of Rome were to be handed over: Hannibal, Thoas,

Mnasilochus the Acarnanian and the two Chalcidians Philon and Euboulidas; twenty hostages, including the king's youngest son Antiochus, were to be given as a pledge. Antiochus agreed, and embassies were prepared for the journey to Rome. The occasion was a turning-point in the history of Asia Minor, and not just Antiochus and the Scipios sent representatives, but almost all states and communities who felt themselves affected by the war sent envoys; for Eumenes it was so important that he travelled to Rome in person.

The Greeks did not wish to interfere with the terms of the peace treaty with Antiochus. This was a Roman matter, and the ratification of the preliminary terms with Antiochus created no difficulty. Final details and precise definitions, above all, of the 'Taurus line', were referred to a commission of ten *legati* who together with the new consul, Cn. Manlius Vulso (who was already in Asia), were to settle such problems on the spot and to take Antiochus' personal oath, but Zeuxis and Antipater were prepared to exchange oaths on the ratified terms. The Greeks' aim was to exert influence on the Senate over what was to happen to the areas which Antiochus must evacuate. The critical moment had come when it would emerge whether Rome would treat the Greeks of Asia Minor as it had treated the Balkan Greeks in 196 – and as its publicized programme for the war in Asia had announced – or whether the most influential friends, Eumenes and Rhodes, who under great strain had supported the Roman cause without wavering and made major contributions to its success, would now receive reward. There was, however, a pragmatic middle way, which the conditions of the war suggested and which the Senate steered. Eumenes and the Rhodian representatives both made long speeches. Eumenes maintained that the best solution would be for Rome to retain direct responsibility for the areas evacuated by Antiochus; but, failing this, he felt that there was no one more suitable for the job than himself. The Rhodians developed the view that the promised freedom for the Greek cities should be granted, and that there was plenty of non-Greek territory being vacated by Antiochus which could satisfy Eumenes' just wish for reward. The conflicts of interest were clear, since it was precisely the Greek cities which Eumenes – like Antiochus before him – coveted. For a Greek, they were the pearl in the crown of Asia Minor, with their developed Greek social institutions, their prosperity and complex economic structure and their interests and contacts throughout the Mediterranean. The representatives of the cities themselves all received the same reply: the ten *legati* would settle disputes on the spot. But the principles of the settlement were laid down in the instructions to the *legati*, which made it clear that, as in Greece (and as earlier in Africa), the Senate had no intention of maintaining a physical Roman presence in Asia Minor. The non-Greek territories vacated by Antiochus were divided into two categories: the Rhodians should receive Lycia and Caria south of the Maeander, with certain specific exceptions; Eumenes the rest. With the Greek cities the Senate established more differentiated principles, based on the attitude of each city to Rome during the war: those that had joined Rome before the battle of Magnesia were to be free; the rest were to go to Eumenes or Rhodes, depending on whether they were north or south of the Maeander.

Meanwhile Manlius (*cos.* 189), who, before the news of the winter battle of Magnesia had reached Rome, had been appointed to succeed L. Scipio and had been voted reinforcements to continue the war, had not been idle, though the war with Antiochus was over. He soon became expert on the affairs of Asia Minor by leading a major plundering expedition into central and southern Anatolia, primarily directed against the Gauls (Galatians), who had supported Antiochus, though he also passed through northern Caria, Lycia and Pisidia. His army killed large numbers of Gauls and seized exceptionally large amounts of booty, which the delicate political nature of the war with Antiochus had so far largely prevented. When he returned to Ephesus in late autumn representatives of the Asiatic Greek cities greeted him as the victor over the barbarians, and he received a constant stream of congratulatory visitors bearing expensive presents. Moreover, even in spring 188 he did not simply sit at Ephesus and wait for the *legati* to arrive, but marched to Pamphylia to receive the first major instalment of Antiochus' indemnity (2,500 talents). He interfered at Perge, where Antiochus still maintained a garrison, and had the garrison removed; and he was still here when he heard that the *legati* and Eumenes had arrived at Apamea, where he joined them.

Since the principles both of the treaty and of the settlement of the evacuated territories had already been laid down in Rome, it remained merely to stipulate such details as could best be done locally. For the treaty the main open question was the precise definition of the 'Taurus line', which had been the core of Roman demands ever since the first discussions in autumn 190. This was now fixed in two ways (though not without some ambiguity): by a coastal point (Cape Sarpedon) beyond which Antiochus might not sail, and a land-line, the River Tanais, which was probably the upper reaches of the Calycadnus (modern Göksu); the coastal provision was also strengthened by the restriction of Antiochus' navy to ten larger open ships, each of not more than thirty oars. In other respects the final treaty merely formulated (or brought up to date, as in the case of the indemnity, some of which had already been paid) what had already been agreed at Rome. The treaty was at once sworn by Manlius and shortly afterwards by Antiochus.[87]

The Senate had decided that the evacuated territories, apart from those

[87] For the treaty terms see McDonald 1967: (E 47); McDonald and Walbank 1969: (E 48).

cities which were defined as Rome's friends, should be divided between
Eumenes and Rhodes. What was now needed to be decided was into
which category the conduct during the war of each individual city placed
it and to settle disputes between cities. This was by no means as
wearisome and time-consuming as the equivalent settlements in mainland Greece had been in 196/5, since in Asia no new independent states
were created. By attributing to Rhodes and Pergamum all cities that had
opposed Rome or remained too long loyal to Antiochus, the Senate had
spared its *legati* much trouble. There were, however, certain exceptions
to the general principles, made for reasons we do not know. Eumenes
received Telmessus and its territory, as well as the Ptolemaic royal gift
estate of Ptolemy of Telmessus who had been closely associated with
Antiochus; in the upper Maeander region he also received the area
known as Caria Hydrela and the part of the *ager Hydrelitanus* which
bordered on Phrygia. The 'Taurus line', as defined in the treaty, opened
the possibility of a dispute about Pamphylia, but the Senate settled
inevitably in favour of Eumenes (except for the free cities of Side and
Aspendus). Antiochus' European possessions also were available for
distribution: Eumenes inevitably received the Chersonese, though
Aenus and Maronea – as recently as 196 freed by Rome from Philip –
were again declared free.

   The treaty of Apamea and the settlement of Asia Minor did not reduce
the Seleucids to a minor power, but it did restrict them to being an Asiatic
power, without the possibility of acquiring major influence in western
Asia Minor or in Europe. This still left them an enormous empire
stretching – with varying degrees of dependence – from the Taurus to
eastern Iran. The settlement of the vacated territories seems to confirm
the Roman strategic objectives of the war, of ensuring that the strategically important coastal areas of the Aegean basin were controlled by
friends of Rome. This was no more than the application to a new area of
the principle which had already been applied to the Balkans in 196 and
195, of insisting that areas in which the Senate recognized important
Roman interests were not only neutralized from outside influence but
were actively a preserve of Roman friends and Roman power. Eumenes,
Rhodes and the free Greek cities of Asia Minor had one thing in
common: they owed the advantages of the status which they received in
188 to Rome alone – and they knew it. Gratitude, according to
Flamininus' doctrine, which had survived the challenge of Antiochus in
Greece largely intact, was not only a cheap and easy substitute for
legions, but was also in the last resort and in the long term more effective.
Events in Asia Minor so far had given no reason to believe that
Flamininus' doctrine, suitably adapted to fit local conditions, would not
here also prove the most effective protection of Rome's position and
interests.

CHAPTER 9

ROME, THE FALL OF MACEDON AND THE SACK OF CORINTH

P. S. DEROW

I. ROME, PHILIP AND THE GREEKS AFTER APAMEA

It is only with the defeat of Antiochus and the Peace of Apamea (188) that the nature of the Roman settlement of Greece can begin to be discerned.[1] Roman troops did not leave Greece for two years after the Isthmian proclamation of 196, and it was two years after that that Antiochus sailed into Demetrias. Even in 196 the Aetolians had claimed that the Roman victory over Philip would bring the Greeks not liberation but only a change of master. This belief brought them to war. They lost and surrendered to the victors both their liberty and more money than their nation could afford. The Greeks had not believed their claim, and the Aetolians and their eastern ally were insufficient to the task. In a sense their claim was wrong. The Greeks found in Rome a master such as Philip had never come near to being, stronger and more deleterious.

[1] Far and away the most important sources for the relations between Rome and Greece from 188 to 146 are Polybius and Livy. The chronological arrangement of the relevant books of Polybius (which have mostly to do with Greece and the east) is as follows: Book XXII (188/7–185/4); XXIII (184/3–183/2); XXIV (182/1–181/80); XXV (180/79–177/6); XXVII (172/1–171/70); XXVIII (170/69); XXIX (169/8); XXX (168/7–165/4); XXXI (164/3–161/60); XXXII (160/59–157/6); XXXIII (156/5–153/2); XXXV (152/1–151/50); XXXVI (150/49–149/8); XXXVIII (147/6); XXXIX (146/5–145/4). For the internal economy of these books see Walbank 1957–79, III.56–61: (B 38). The Livian evidence is to be found in books XXXIX–XLV, especially in the following sections: XXXIX.23.5–29.3 (185), 33–37 (184), 46.6–50.11, 53 (183); XL.2.6–16.3 (182), 20.1–24.8 (181–180), 54–58 (180–179); XLI.19.4–11 (175), 22.2–25.8 (174), XLII.2.1–3, 4.5–6.4 (173), 10.11, 11.1–18.6, 19, 25–27 (172), 29–67 (171); XLIII.1 (171), 4–6.10, 7–8, 9.4–11.12 (170), 18–23 (169); XLIV.1–16.7 (169), 18.1–5, 20–46 (168); XLV.1–3 (168), 4.2–10.15, 17.34 (167). The *Periochae* of books XLVI–LII contain some bits and pieces relevant to the years 167–146. For the history of the Achaean League from 167 to 146 the independent account in Pausanias (VII.11–16) assumes an importance of its own, despite obvious difficulties. The narrative here follows Polybius and Livy (preferring the former) very closely, and running references will not normally be given along the way, save in cases of specific details (such as quotation) or controversy. Reference to Walbank 1957–79, III: (B 38) will for the most part go without saying; it must be consulted for points of interpretation of Polybius, for notices of other relevant evidence and for bibliography. A good deal of the important epigraphical evidence is collected in Sherk, *Documents*, and the two volumes of Moretti, *ISE*; virtually all of the most important texts will be found in *SIG*. A number of the basic ones are translated in Bagnall and Derow 1981: (B 210) and Austin 1981: (A 2). For the activities of Roman officials (including magistrates and ambassadors) the evidence is assembled under the year in question in *MRR*. For the state of the Roman calendar from 188 to 168 (always ahead of the seasonal year, but by a decreasing amount in the later years) and for a table of calendar equivalents see Derow 1973: (H 283). The equivalents there (and here) may be assumed to be correct to within a day or two: cf. Walbank 1957–79, III.vi: (B 38).

Troubles began in Achaea and Boeotia very early on and, in both cases, have their roots in the 190s. In 192 Sparta had joined the Achaean League, not by unanimous agreement. Late in 189, with others in power, Sparta sought to secede. The Spartans invoked the Romans but received from them no clear support, and in spring 188 Philopoemen brought them back into the League.[2] Some at Sparta, who disapproved of the Achaean settlement, complained to the Senate. This elicited a letter to the Achaeans from the consul of 187, M. Aemilius Lepidus, communicating the Roman judgement that the Spartan affair had not been correctly handled. No details were added, and the matter was not pressed. What is important is the fact that the Senate took cognizance of these Spartan *démarches* at all. Foreign affairs were properly the province of the League, not of individual cities.[3] In accepting an embassy from Sparta or some disgruntled Spartans, the Senate implicitly condoned a breach in the laws of the Achaean League. At the time of the first Spartan appeal to Rome the issue had been correctly drawn: Diophanes of Megalopolis desired to entrust settlement of the dispute entirely to Rome whilst Lycortas, following the precepts of Philopoemen, maintained that the Achaeans should be allowed to carry on their own affairs in accordance with their own laws and that the Romans, authors of their liberty, should support them in this.[4] The argument, in one form or another, went on for more than forty years.

In Boeotia occurred an analogous business, with the added ingredient that the policy of an individual and influential Roman was at issue. Flamininus had for some time been seeking to bring about the return to Boeotia of the exiled Zeuxippus (in whose interest he had earlier complied in the murder of Brachylles).[5] The Senate was persuaded to instruct the Boeotians to restore Zeuxippus. The Boeotians, fearful of effecting a rupture in their friendly relations with Macedon, declined and sent an embassy to Rome, where Zeuxippus represented himself. The Senate wrote to the Aetolians and Achaeans, complaining about the Boeotians and bidding them to see to the restoration of Zeuxippus. The Achaeans, eschewing force, tried to persuade the Boeotians to obey. The latter promised but did not carry through. There the issue was dropped. On Polybius' analysis, war would have broken out had the Senate then chosen to force the issue (XXII.4.16). Zeuxippus was not restored, but the Roman intervention was not without other effect. It tipped the balance (for the time at least) in favour of the wealthy in their conflict with the poor, and it showed Roman willingness to support their friends in

[2] For the background: Livy XXXV.37.1–2 (cf. Plut. *Philop.* 15.2; Paus. VIII.50.10f.), 38.30–33.
[3] Freeman 1893, 202–5: (I 10); Larsen 1968, 238–9: (D 41). [4] Livy XXXVIII.32.7–9.
[5] Brachylles' murder (197/6) and Flamininus' role in it: Polyb. XVIII.43.5–12. See Polyb. XX.4–7 on the continuing troubles in Boeotia down to 192/1.

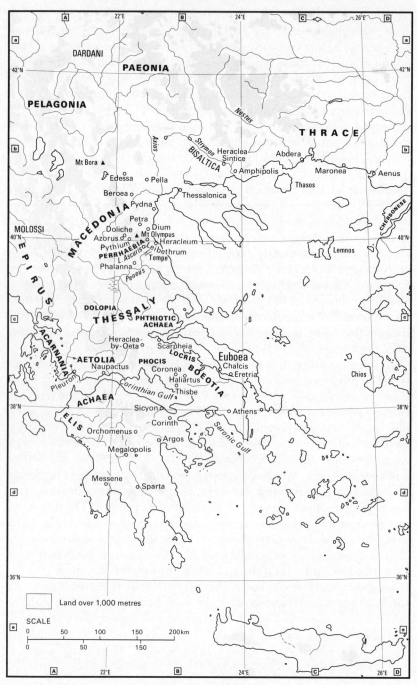

Map 12. Macedonia and Greece.

internal disputes.[6] The lines are visible here. There are Rome's friends, there are Macedon's friends; there are wealthy, there are poor. Two pairs, or is it one? Polybius does not say that the Senate aimed to support the wealthy; but that is the way it turned out.

The Spartans had shown the way, and it soon became clear that the Senate was interested in the affairs of Greece and was unlikely to turn a deaf ear to appeals or complaints laid before it. Philip of Macedon had joined Rome as an ally in the war against Antiochus, partly because it had been made clear that there was no other course for him to follow, and partly because he saw therein the possibility of tangible extension of his influence in the north.[7] During the war he had taken control of towns in Thrace, Thessaly, Perrhaebia and Athamania. Clearly he felt entitled to do so. To just what extent he had been encouraged in this belief by the Roman generals in the field (as the Aetolians evidently had been early in the war against Philip) is not easy to say,[8] but whatever the case, the reception of appeals at Rome left no doubt that he was mistaken. These came from the peoples directly involved and from King Eumenes of Pergamum.

In the Thracian cities at least there was factional strife, one side favouring (and being favoured by) Philip, the other Eumenes. The latter's supporters had appealed to him, and it was his envoys who laid their case before the Senate. Philip himself sent ambassadors to Rome to defend himself against his accusers. The scene was one that would repeat itself many times over, with these and other characters, and so was the Senate's response. After lengthy discussions in 185 a commission, led by Q. Caecilius Metellus, was sent to investigate 'and to provide safe conduct to those who wished to state their case in person and to accuse the king' (Polyb. XXII.6.5). The role played here by the king of Pergamum and the invited accusers looks back as well: to the meeting between the Romans and Antiochus at Lysimacheia in 196. The non-Thracian cases were heard at Tempe, with Metellus and the Roman envoys sitting as arbitrators between accusers and accused (Livy XXXIX.25.1). Philip was ordered to withdraw from all the cities in question: his kingdom was to be reduced to the ancient boundaries of Macedonia (Livy XXXIX.26.14). Metellus went on to Thessalonica where the question of the Thracian cities, above all Aenus and Maronea, was considered. Eumenes' envoys said the cities should either be completely free or, if

---

[6] Polyb. XXII.3.3 for the εὔποροι, and the κακέκται who outnumbered them; cf. XX.6.2–3; also XX.7.3 for the alienation of 'the many' from Rome attributed to the murder of Brachylles. On the connection between Roman conduct and class conflict in Greece throughout this period see above all de Ste Croix 1981, ch. 5.iii and Appendix 4 (esp. 523–9) with notes (659–60): (A 35).

[7] See above, Ch. 8.

[8] That he did receive some such encouragement is beyond doubt: cf. Livy XXXIX.23.10 and Walbank 1957–79, III.104 (on XXI.11.9): (B 38).

given to anyone, then to him. Philip's claim was that they belonged to him as prizes of an ally in the war. Here the Roman envoys could not decide: if the ten commissioners settling Asia had assigned them to Eumenes, then that would hold; if Philip had captured them in war then he should hold them as the prize of victory; if neither of these was true, decision should be reserved to the Senate, Philip in the meanwhile withdrawing his garrisons. Envoys from Philip and Eumenes, as well as the exiles from Aenus and Maronea, went to Rome and put before the Senate the same arguments they had put before Caecilius. The Senate evinced neither doubt nor hesitation. Not only was Philip to withdraw from the cities in Thessaly, Perrhaebia and Athamania, he was also to withdraw from Aenus and Maronea and in general to quit all forts, territories and cities on the coast of Thrace. Such scruples as Metellus and his colleagues had had were overridden, and Philip's loss was complete. A new commission, led by Appius Claudius,[9] was despatched in 184 to check on Philip's compliance with Metellus' directive and to convey the new orders formally. Philip heard of these first when his own envoys returned from Rome. The evacuation of Aenus and Maronea was begun straightaway and was accompanied by a massacre of Philip's opponents at Maronea. Before Appius Claudius, he sought to blame this upon the factional split at Maronea, but the Senate's envoys would hear no defence. They left after condemning the king for his behaviour towards Maronea and, more significantly, for his 'estrangement' towards the Romans.[10]

There is little doubt that the massacre at Maronea was Philip's doing. There is equally little doubt that all the Roman decisions went against him not because of the justice of the opposing cases, but out of a desire to reduce the extent of his control and influence by ordering him to step back. So it had been with Carthage and Antiochus. So it had been with Philip himself a scant decade and a half before. Philip reacted strongly, but not openly. He wished to put himself in a position from which he could resist Roman orders. This required preparation and time. To gain it he sent to Rome as his advocate and defender his son Demetrius, who had won friends, favour and a kind of influence whilst serving as a hostage of his father's good behaviour during the war against Antiochus. This part of Philip's plan was to misfire disastrously.

---

[9] Probably, but not certainly, the consul of 185, Ap. Claudius Ap.f. P.n. Pulcher, but possibly Ap. Claudius Nero, praetor 195; cf. Walbank 1957–79, III on XXII.11.4: (B 38).

[10] Ἡ πρὸς τοὺς Ῥωμαίους ἀλλοτριότης, Polyb. XXII.14.6; cf. XXIII.8.2. This is the first appearance of this uncomfortably open-ended charge. Wielded by Romans to begin with, it will be taken over by Rome's friends in the Greek states for use against their political rivals: the Epirote Charops, after Rome's defeat of Perseus, can sentence his opponents to death on the charge of 'thinking otherwise than the Romans' (ἀλλότρια φρονοῦντες Ῥωμαίων, Polyb. XXXII.6.2). Cf. Sherk, Documents 43 (SIG 684), and 16 for an appearance of the notion in a more formal context (letter of Q. Fabius Maximus to Dyme, probably of 115 B.C.).

Such, at least, was Philip's ultimate aim according to Polybius, who saw Philip's desire to defend himself against such treatment by Rome as leading directly to preparations for war, a war conceived and discussed by the king in secret colloquy with his friends and advisers on the morrow of Appius Claudius' visit.[11] This war that Philip planned was, again on Polybius' view (XXII.18.10), the war that Perseus undertook. It will be seen later that Rome's war against Perseus has its own explanation, but this does not affect anything Polybius says about Rome's treatment of Philip or about Philip's reaction to that treatment. For the moment, Philip achieved the respite he wanted, and in 183 a Roman embassy led by Q. Marcius Philippus saw the king withdraw from all his Thracian holdings. There had been further complaints, but they did not lead to further Roman orders. For this Demetrius was at least in part responsible. His success, however, owed itself far less to his diplomatic ability than to the fact that Flamininus and others saw in him a congenial successor to the Macedonian throne, a role in which Demetrius was not unwilling to see himself cast. The young prince's part in bringing about an improvement in Roman–Macedonian relations was accordingly exaggerated and great favour shown him. The effect of this upon Perseus, the heir apparent, and upon Philip himself was inevitable. Demetrius returned to Macedon in 183, and his evident popularity at Rome brought him a kind of popularity at home. All this immediately aroused fears in Perseus about the succession and concern in Philip that Demetrius was thinking too much about his Roman connections. Suspicion, fuelled by Perseus, continued unabated, and in 180 Philip finally arranged the murder of what he was convinced was, actually or potentially, a dangerously disloyal son. That he was right about Demetrius seems clear.[12] It is, however, hard to say whether there were those at Rome who believed that the succession of Demetrius (and supersession of Perseus) could actually be secured, or whether by showing such favour to him they sought to create dissension and the weakness to which this would give rise.

Rome's handling of affairs in the Peloponnese during these years was less overbearing, but handling it none the less was, and not without similarity to what was being done in Macedon. All the Roman envoys to

[11] Polyb. XXII.14.7–12. That Polybius' aetiology of the war against Perseus took this line is indicated by the run of the narrative implied in the 'table of contents' of book XXII at XXII.1.5 (cf. Derow 1979, 12 n. 36: (D 21)), as well as by the language of, especially, XXII.14.8–10 which is very much that of III.6.7.

[12] In Livy's account (XL.54–56) Philip realized shortly before his own death that Demetrius had been wrongly condemned and determined that Perseus should not succeed him. This is not credible, however genuine Philip's remorse may have been: see Walbank 1940, 238–53, esp. 252–3: (D 54). On Demetrius (ibid.): 'Vain and ambitious, he had lent himself to clumsy manoeuvring by Flamininus and his circle, and had himself to thank for his untimely end; Philip could not afford to let him live on as a Roman pretender.'

Philip visited the Achaeans also. The question of Sparta's position *vis-à-vis* the Achaean League appeared to have been left in the hands of the Achaeans after the caution administered through the consul Lepidus in the winter of 188/7. But in the summer of 185, Q. Caecilius, returning from his mission to Philip, arrived at Argos where the Nemean festival was being celebrated. Aristaenus, then general, called the magistrates of the League together, and Metellus castigated the Achaeans for their harsh treatment of the Spartans. How Metellus came to be there is a question of some importance. There is no record that his brief included anything other than Macedonian affairs. According to the account in Pausanias (VII.8.6, 9.1), he had been approached by some disaffected Spartans and persuaded by them to intervene. Polybius (XXII.10.14) reports the suspicion in Achaea that Aristaenus and Diophanes were responsible for his presence. The two accounts are not incompatible with one another. They are, however, incompatible with the view that Metellus had been formally instructed to discuss the Spartan question with the Achaeans. In the event, Aristaenus did not defend the League's conduct, thereby indicating, as Polybius saw it (XXII.10.3), his agreement with Metellus. Diophanes went a step further and suggested to Metellus that the Achaeans were guilty of mismanagement not only in the case of Sparta but in that of Messene as well. Lycortas and Archon defended the *status quo*, and after discussion this view was adopted by the magistrates and communicated to Metellus. The latter, having sensed support, was not satisfied with this and requested that a meeting of the League assembly be summoned. He was asked to produce his instructions from the Senate on the matter, but had none, and his request was accordingly refused.[13] Metellus, in turn, thoroughly vexed at having had nothing granted to him, refused to receive formally the reply of the magistrates and went back to Rome without one.

He was followed there by a delegation from the Spartan dissidents, led by Areus and Alcibiades (former exiles who had been restored to Sparta by the Achaeans), and by one from the Achaean League, sent to offer a defence against Metellus' hostile report. The Spartan question was

[13] Polyb. XXII.10.11–12: 'They refused to summon the assembly, for the laws did not allow it unless someone brought a written communication from the Senate concerning the business for which it desired the assembly to be summoned.' This is made more precise by the Achaean envoys at Rome later in the same year (XXII.12.6): 'For it is the law of the Achaeans not to call together the many [μὴ συγκαλεῖν τοὺς πολλούς, i.e., not to summon a *synkletos*], unless a resolution about alliance or war needs to be considered or unless someone brings a letter from the Senate.' This (and the converse provision that questions of alliance and war were reserved for specially summoned meetings, *synkletoi*) represents second-century Achaean practice. How early it became so is not known, but the element involving the Senate seems likely to date from the time of the League's alliance with Rome (on which see next note). On Achaean *synkletoi* and *syndodoi* (regular meetings of federal council and assembly, of which there were most likely four a year) see Walbank 1957–79, III.406–14: (B 38).

referred to the embassy led by Ap. Claudius, to be dealt with after their visit to Macedonia and Thrace, and the Achaeans were in the meanwhile urged to treat Roman envoys with the same attention and respect accorded to Achaean envoys in Rome. The Achaeans forbore to say that this was what they had done.

At Cleitor in Arcadia in 184 Ap. Claudius sat as judge between the Achaean League and the dissident Spartans. Lycortas, as general, defended Achaean conduct eloquently (perhaps too eloquently in Livy's fine version of his speech at XXXIX.37.9–18) and pleaded the sanctity of the League's formal resolutions. Ap. Claudius 'advised the Achaeans to come to terms while it was still possible to do so of their own free will, lest presently they be forced to take the same action against their will and under compulsion' (XXXIX.37.19). Lycortas then asked that the Romans change what they would have changed and not require the Achaeans to abrogate laws they had sworn to uphold.

On this note the outstanding questions were referred to the Senate for decision. In the winter of 184/3 no fewer than four groups of contending Spartans appeared in Rome. The Senate appointed a commission of three to untangle the disputes and reach decisions agreeable to all. These were Flamininus, Q. Caecilius Metellus and Ap. Claudius. A large measure of agreement was reached between the Romans and the dissident Spartans, and seals were set to the decisions that Lycortas had asked the Romans to take. Achaean envoys had been sent to Rome at the time, not to participate in these discussions (in which, consistent with League policy, they indeed took no part), but to renew the League's alliance with Rome and to watch the outcome of the various Spartan demands. Flamininus invited them to sign the agreement that had been reached. They hesitated, for it involved the repeal of some Achaean sentences of exile and death. In the end they signed, pleased that it was specified that Sparta was to remain in the League. A great deal had been at stake. The Peloponnese was added to the Macedonian and Thracian itinerary of Q. Marcius Philippus and his embassy of 183 with, presumably, instructions to communicate formally the Senate's decisions to the Achaean League and to see to their implementation.

In the meanwhile the discontent in Messene which Diophanes had brought to the attention of Q. Metellus was quickening. Amongst those who wished to detach Messene from the Achaean League was Deinocrates. In the winter of 184/3 he was in Rome seeking, by what means it is not clear, to bring about a change in the situation of Messene. When he learned that Flamininus, whom he had come to know well during the war against Nabis, had been appointed as an ambassador to King Prusias of Bithynia, he immediately reckoned that a Peloponnesian intervention by Flamininus would do best to guarantee his success.

Flamininus attempted to oblige. He stopped at Naupactus on his journey east in 183 and wrote to the Achaean magistrates, ordering them to summon a meeting of the assembly. They replied by asking what precisely were his instructions on the matter. He had more sense than to press the attempt any further, and Deinocrates' hopes were dashed. Yet the Messenians cannot but have inferred that there was sympathy for their cause at Rome, feeling against the Achaeans, and they would not have been mistaken.

Messene had probably seceded from the Achaean League by the time of Flamininus' *démarche*, or it may be that the revolt began in earnest after his failure. It was round the time of Q. Marcius Philippus' arrival in the Peloponnese that the Achaeans formally declared war against Messene. Philippus' behaviour in these circumstances is not known in any detail, but it can safely be inferred that he tried to persuade the Achaeans to refer the matter to Rome rather than deal with it themselves. That is certainly the direction of his message to the Senate at the conclusion of his embassy (Polyb. XXIII.9.8). At the time he reported, there was an Achaean embassy in Rome seeking Roman support against the rebels in accordance with the treaty of alliance that bound Rome and Achaea.[14] Philippus favoured a different sort of policy, and his was adopted. Clear in its intent, it was not in the spirit (or even the letter) of the alliance. Philippus 'had reported that as the Achaeans did not wish to refer anything to the Senate, but had a great opinion of themselves and were attempting to manage everything on their own, if the Senate paid no attention to their request for the moment and expressed their displeasure in moderate terms, Sparta and Messene would soon see eye to eye, upon which (he said) the Achaeans would be only too glad to come running for help to the Romans' (Polyb. XXIII.9.8–11). Sparta, not yet fully settled, was kept that way. To the Spartan envoy in Rome the Senate replied, 'as they wished the city to remain in suspense, that they had done all in their power for the Spartans, but at present they did not think that the matter concerned them' (XXIII.9.11). To the Achaeans' request that the terms of the alliance be observed the Senate answered 'that not even if the people of Sparta, Corinth or Argos revolted from the League should the Achaeans be surprised if the Senate did not think it concerned them. And publicizing this reply, which was a sort of proclamation to those who wished to secede from the League that they could do so so far as the

---

[14] The treaty was concluded between 197 (Polyb. XVIII.42.6–8) and 184 (Livy XXXIX.37.9–10), and the best case yet put forward, Badian 1952: (D 5), is for a date between November 192 and spring 191; cf. Walbank 1957–79, III on XXIII.4.12 and XXXIX.3.8: (B 38). The form of the Achaean request in 183 ('that no one from Italy should import either arms or corn' (μήθ' ὅπλα μήτε σῖτον) into Messenia) implies that the treaty was of what appears to have been a standard form, the best example of which is the alliance between Rome and Maronea, probably of the 160s; for the text see Triantofyllos, *Arch. Delt.* 28 (1973) [1977] Chron., plate 418; cf. Derow 1984, 234: (B 6).

Romans were concerned, they continued to detain the envoys, waiting to see how the Achaeans would get on with Messene' (xxiii.9.13–14).

The Achaeans, contrary to the hopes of at least some Romans, got on well in their handling of the revolt. The war cost them Philopoemen, but Lycortas carried through to victory and in 182 Messene was restored to its original position in the League. Upon hearing of this, the Senate, 'entirely ignoring their previous answer, gave another reply to the same envoys, informing them that they had seen to it that no one should import arms and corn from Italy to Messene' (Polyb. xxiii.17.3). No doubt the Senate had maintained the letter of the alliance while trying at the same time seriously to weaken the Achaeans. The implication of their conduct, however, is clear, and it was not lost on Polybius. 'This', he writes, 'made it entirely clear to everyone that so far from shirking and not caring about the less important items of foreign affairs, they were displeased if all matters were not referred to them and if everything was not done in accordance with their decision' (xxiii.17.4). Philippus' ploy achieved some success in that Sparta does seem to have seceded from the Achaean League while Messene was in revolt. There too, however, the Achaean cause prevailed, more peacefully by the look of it. Pro-Achaeans gained control and the Achaeans, taking Rome's expression of lack of interest seriously (or at least making use of it) admitted Sparta back into the League. An embassy from the Achaeans went to Rome to inform the Senate about Messene and Sparta. Those in Sparta who would have had things otherwise also sent envoys, as did the exiles who had not been taken back and whose part had been taken by Diophanes and some others. Once again official and unofficial legations were received alike.

About Messene the Senate expressed no displeasure. The Spartan exiles, however, brought back with them a letter in which the Senate showed itself in favour of their restoration. The Achaean envoy who had been in Rome explained that the Senate had written on behalf of the exiles not out of genuine concern but because of the insistence of the exiles in presenting their case. It was decided to believe this, and no action was taken. There the matter might have stood, but when Hyperbatus became general (for 181/80), he raised the question of how the Senate's letter should be dealt with. Lycortas advised no action, arguing that the Romans would understand the importance of not violating laws and oaths. The opposite viewpoint was advocated by Hyperbatus and Callicrates. It was a strong line. They urged the Achaeans to obey the written order and not to reckon law, stele or anything else more important than this obedience. A majority evidently favoured the policy of Lycortas, and an embassy was sent to Rome to put his case before the Senate. The envoys were Callicrates, Lydiadas and the young Aratus. On Polybius' account (and there is no other), Callicrates no sooner entered

the Senate-house than he began to accuse his political opponents and
give the Senate a lecture on Greek politics (xxiv.8.9–9.15). He explained
that in all the democratic states there were two parties. One counselled
adherence to the written requests of Rome at the expense of laws, *stelai*
and everything else. The other maintained that these latter things ought
not lightly to be violated. In Achaea the second group was the more
popular with the multitude. The partisans of Rome reaped contempt and
slander from the mob, their opponents favour and support. But, he said,
let the Senate give indication of their displeasure at this state of affairs and
the men of politics will go over to their side and the mob will follow out
of fear. Let the Senate fail to do this and the policy now more popular will
become yet more so. The advice was easily summarized: if the Romans
wanted their orders obeyed, they should see to it that they supported
those who promised obedience. They should show their displeasure at
such conduct as the recent Achaean leadership had undertaken in resisting Q. Philippus' efforts to have the Messenian question referred to
Rome (and insisting on dealing with it themselves) and in not restoring
the former exiles.

Callicrates was taken seriously, and 'now for the first time the Senate
adopted the aim of weakening those members of the several states who
worked for the best, and of strengthening those who, rightly or wrongly,
appealed to its authority' (xxiv.10.4). The consequence, Polybius judges,
'was that gradually, as time went on, the Romans had plenty of flatterers
but few true friends'. This is, in some measure, a tendentious judgement,
but its validity in general is not in doubt.[15] And there is no question at all
about the determination of the Senate on this occasion to put its weight
solidly behind Callicrates and his policy. 'They actually went so far on the
present occasion as to write not only to the Achaeans about the return of
the exiles, bidding them to contribute to strengthening the position of
these men, but also to the Aetolians, Epirotes, Athenians, Boeotians and
Acarnanians, calling them all to witness for the purpose of crushing the
Achaeans. Speaking of Callicrates alone, with no mention of the other
envoys, they wrote in their official answer that there ought to be more
men in the several states like Callicrates' (xxiv.10.6–7). Now able to use
the threat of Rome's displeasure against his opponents, Callicrates
returned home. The exiles were restored, and Callicrates was elected to
the *strategia*, 'unaware that he had been the initiator of great evils for all
the Greeks and most of all for the Achaeans'.[16]

---

[15] See Derow 1970: (D 19), but note that the connection between Callicrates' *démarche* at Rome and
Perseus' accession to the Macedonian throne needs very much to be borne in mind; cf. below, pp.
302–3. Other views of Callicrates have been taken: cf. Walbank 1957–79, III on xxiv.10.8: (B 38).

[16] Polyb. xxiv.10.8, 14–15. The generalship was most likely that for 180/79 (and not 179/8), but
see Walbank 1957–79, III on xxiv.10.14: (B 38).

This was not the first time that Rome had set about supporting those favourable to her in states she controlled or wished to control. She had been doing so for centuries. But it was the first time that it had been done so openly as a matter of public policy, and the first time that being favourable to Rome was openly equated with absolute readiness to obey Rome's orders. This was indeed imperialism in a strict and very Roman sense.[17] In Achaea from the time of the League's earliest dealings with Rome there had been a debate between those, like Philopoemen and Lycortas, who wished insofar as possible to deal with Rome on a basis of equality, and those, like Aristaenus and Diophanes, who believed that obedience to Roman orders must take precedence over everything.[18] Callicrates' mission in 180 and the Senate's response did not decide the question once and for all. It did give a great deal of momentum to the latter group. More important, it changed the nature of the debate by putting the threat of Roman displeasure as a weapon into the hands of those who styled themselves pro-Romans. The rules of politics were thereby altered, surely for ill. So it was for the Achaean League, and so, we may believe Polybius, it was for the other states of Greece.

The year 180, then, marks a turning-point, but there is a question whether the 'evils for all the Greeks and most of all for the Achaeans' that followed would have done so, or done so with the same speed and acerbity, had there not been another turning-point at almost the same time. In 179 Philip V died, and Perseus succeeded to the throne of Macedon. Both personality and policy brought him early popularity. After renewing the Macedonian alliance with Rome at the very outset of his reign, he recalled under amnesty fugitive debtors and those who had been driven into exile by sentence of courts or for crimes against the throne. Publicity of a high order was given to these steps: lists of those thus to be welcomed back were posted at the sanctuaries of Apollo at Delos and Delphi and Itonian Athena in Thessaly. In Macedonia itself he remitted all royal debts and freed those who had been imprisoned for offences against the crown. *Ellenokopein* is Polybius' word for his early policy (xxv.3.1): 'to play the Greek' or 'to court the favour of the Greeks'? Something of both. The effect, certainly, and the aim possibly, was to turn Greek eyes towards himself. For those who wished not to look towards Rome, or not to have to look only there, there was to be another focus available. Evidence of both the direction of his policy and of its success comes from a decree of the Delphic amphictyony of

---

[17] For Roman orders, and their obedience by others, as the basic element in Polybius' conception (an informed and correct one, I believe) of Roman imperialism (i.e., the expansion of Roman *imperium*), see Derow 1979, 1–15, esp. 4–6: (D 21).

[18] For Lycortas and Diophanes cf. above, pp. 296–7; for Philopoemen and Aristaenus see esp. Polyb. xxiv.11–13.

summer 178. After the liberation of Delphi from Aetolian control by the Romans in 191–188 the amphictyony was reconstituted as a distinctly pro-Roman body.[19] But in 178 there are listed among the *hieromnemones* two 'from King Perseus' (*SIG* 636): an achievement of note for the young king and clear indication of the rapidity with which the good repute and the influence of the kingdom of Macedon was being resuscitated. It indicates also the readiness of the Greeks to forget Philip's recent bloody doings in Thrace and his violence towards Athens and Rhodes at the end of the previous century. Philip's popularity had waned considerably after his early years on the throne, and with it that of Macedon. There was much to retrieve, and this Perseus managed with remarkable efficiency. One cannot but ask whether Roman policy in Greece, in the later 180s and as defined and enunciated in 180, made that easier. One must ask also how this Macedonian renaissance was remarked at Rome, and to this question at least there is a clear answer.

Late in the summer of 178 there arrived at Rome an embassy from the Lycians which had been sent to complain to the Senate about the domineering behaviour of the Rhodians towards Lycia. The Rhodians believed that, and behaved as if, Lycia had been given over to them as a gift by the Roman settlement of Asia Minor in 188. The Lycians disagreed. Their embassy in 178 bore the desired fruit, as the Senate decided to inform the Rhodians that inspection of the records had revealed that the Lycians had been given to them not as a gift, but rather as friends and allies. So they claimed, but the claim was manifestly false.[20] The reasons for this duplicity are not far to seek and were indeed recognized at the time. 'The Romans seemed to be setting themselves up as arbiters in the matter of the Rhodians and the Lycians with the object of exhausting the stores and treasure of the Rhodians, having heard of their recent escorting of the bride of Perseus and of the refitting of their ships' (Polyb. xxv.4.7–8). The bride they had brought home to Perseus was the Seleucid princess Laodice, and in return they had received a great quantity of wood for shipbuilding. The Senate's decision about Lycia signalled Rome's displeasure with Rhodes, and with Perseus, whose diplomatic successes are thus seen to extend beyond Greece itself to the Aegean and the eastern Mediterranean.

From the beginning of his reign Perseus attracted the notice and the concern of Rome, and he attracted supporters in the various states of Greece. The two things operated together. There were Rome's friends and their opponents in Greece, and there was coming into being a group favouring closer, or at least improved, relations with Macedon. More

---

[19] On the reconstituted amphictyony cf. Giovannini 1970: (D 29).
[20] Compare Polyb. xxv.4.5 (the decision in 178) with Polyb. xxi.46.8, xxii.5.4 (the disposition made by the Roman commissioners in 188).

and more the latter two categories converged and came to be identified (not necessarily the same thing), developments which took place against the background of increasing Roman suspicion of Perseus, evinced early on and fostered by more than a few of Rome's friends. In this is to be seen the reason for the pernicious exacerbation of the division portrayed by Callicrates, for in the atmosphere of growing hostility between the two powers failure to follow Rome implicitly became tantamount to treason. Perseus threatened to provide an alternative focus for Greek politics. In another world this might have led to constructive tension, but in that world it led instead to a situation in which one side must perish and fall prey to the one which sided with victory. Viewed from the other side, this same set of developments contains the most basic element of the explanation of Rome's war against Perseus. The reassertion of Macedon's position in Greece was quite simply incompatible with Roman supremacy there – with, that is, the supremacy of Roman orders and the closely related desire, displayed clearly by the Senate in the 180s, that all matters of contention should be referred to Rome. There could not be two arbiters. As Perseus became more and more an alternative focus, the possibility grew apace that there would be two. As had been the case with Antiochus from 197, Roman control of affairs was felt to be at risk. The answer would be the same. This time, however, the opposition was not concentrated in one people of Greece, as it had largely been with the Aetolians before, but was there (whether as genuine opposition to Rome and Roman control, or as opposition to Rome's friends, or as positive feeling towards Perseus and his kingdom) inside most, if not indeed all, of the states of Greece. Therein lies the reason for much that happened in the years after 180/79 and therein the tragedy.

II. PERSEUS

It is as early as 175 that Livy can say 'anxiety about the Macedonian war beset them' (XLI.19.4). In the previous year embassies had arrived at Rome from the Dardani complaining of attacks by the Bastarnae and claiming that Perseus was behind these and in league with the Bastarnae. Something was clearly afoot (a Thessalian embassy confirmed the report) and had been since Philip V's death in 179, but in assessing the charges one must bear in mind the long-standing antipathy of the Dardanians towards Macedon and its kings (Livy XL.57.6). A legation, led by A. Postumius Albinus (*cos.* 180), was sent to investigate. This mission returned to Rome in 175, along with a team of envoys from Perseus, who came to defend the king against the charge of inciting the Bastarnae. The Senate, significantly, left the question open. 'They neither absolved Perseus of the charge nor pressed it' (Livy XLI.19.6). They did, however, remember it later when it proved useful to do so. For the moment they warned him 'to take the greatest care that he be seen to hold sacred his treaty with Rome' (*ibid.*). The pace of activity on both sides soon accelerated. In 174 Roman envoys returned from Carthage and reported that the Carthaginian senate had received by night an embassy from Perseus. A team of very senior legates was sent to Macedon to conduct more investigations, C. Laelius (*cos.* 190), M. Valerius Messalla (*cos.* 188), and Sex. Digitius (*pr.* 194). The precise purpose of their mission is not stated. They returned to Rome early in 173 and announced that they had not been able to see the king, being given instead stories about his being ill or being away (both versions they reckoned to be lies). They were, however, in no doubt that preparations for war were being made and that Perseus would not long delay recourse to arms. A Macedonian war was openly anticipated, and prodigies were accordingly attended to.

In fact, Perseus had been away from Macedon during part of 174. The Dolopians had been proving recalcitrant to Macedonian control, and there was a move there to refer some matters of dispute to the Senate instead of to the king of Macedon. Perseus acted quickly, arrived with an army and re-established firm Macedonian control. This claim of jurisdiction was consistent with the status of the Dolopians under Philip (at least for a time), but whether or not it was consistent with the Roman order to Philip in 185 that Macedon was to be confined within its ancient boundaries is quite another question. A measure of challenge to Rome must be seen in Perseus' actions here. From Dolopia he proceeded with his army to the oracle at Delphi and thence homeward through Phthiotic Achaea and Thessaly. This was at once a show of force and a show of restraint and friendship. Initial alarm at his presence in central Greece was quieted when he made his passage in peace. As a mission of goodwill it was not without effect.

About the same time, Perseus made a concerted effort to re-establish relations with the Achaean League. All dealings had been broken off during the war against Philip and had never been renewed. Support for this within the League came both from those who genuinely wished closer ties with Macedon and from those who, in a spirit of moderation, desired simply that normal relations should exist with Macedon as they existed with the other independent states of Greece. Callicrates argued that any move in this direction would be the same as an attack upon Achaea's alliance with Rome and accused his opponents of speaking against Rome. The question was deferred, pending the arrival of a formal embassy from Perseus (whose approach so far had necessarily been by letter), but those 'who feared that this would cause offence amongst the Romans' (Livy XLI.24.20) saw to it that the embassy was not received. It soon became clear that their reading of the Senate's mind was correct.

The middle and later 170s were years of ferment in a number of parts of Greece. By 174 a civil war had broken out in Aetolia. At the root of the conflict was debt, but little more is known. News of this had been brought to Rome by C. Laelius, who had led the embassy to Perseus in 174. The Senate's response was quick, and the size and composition of the embassy that went to Aetolia is indicative of the seriousness of the problem. It was led by C. Valerius Laevinus (*cos.* 176), grandson of the Laevinus who negotiated the Aetolian treaty of 211, and included Ap. Claudius, the ambassador of 184, and three others. They made little progress. More was achieved in the following year, when a commission led by M. Claudius Marcellus (probably the consul of 183) brought about a cessation of open hostilities. The same year saw Ap. Claudius back in Greece, this time in Thessaly and Perrhaebia where he had been sent in response to a report that the Thessalians were in arms. He calmed the situation by the abolition of illegal interest and the imposition of a schedule for the repayment of just debts. In Crete also, civil disturbances flared up and were temporarily quelled by the arrival of a Roman envoy, Q. Minucius, with ten ships. The arguments between the Lycians and the Rhodians continued with increasing intensity, and to judge from Livy's comment in that context (XLI.25.8) there was a great deal more going on besides.

Why so much boiled over in so many places at just this time we do not know, but part of the answer (and much of the importance of it) lies in the fact that it did so against the backdrop of increasing hostility between Perseus and Rome. Power in Thessaly had been put in the hands of the well-to-do by Flamininus twenty years before,[21] and it was the oppressive conduct of the creditors that lay behind the present difficulties there. The Aetolians had been hard put to pay the indemnity imposed upon them after their war with Rome, and, Polybius would add, their usual recourse to brigandage was not thereafter available to them. What can be safely said is that in none of these cases are the warring factions described as pro- or anti-Roman (or Macedonian), and that in no case is Perseus said to have been implicated in the troubles. That claim is made only later. The question of Perseus was not, however, beyond the brief of the Roman ambassadors who went to Greece in these years. In 173 M. Marcellus went also to the Peloponnese, where, equipped with explicit instructions from the Senate (one assumes), he addressed a specially summoned meeting of the Achaean League. The message he bore was twofold: to praise the Achaeans for their rejection of Perseus' overtures, and to make very clear the hostility which the Romans felt towards the Macedonian king. Whether Perseus' activities in these years are to be

---

[21] Livy XXXIV.51.6 (194 B.C.), and see above, Ch. 8.

construed as actually directed against Rome is at least a question. About the direction of Roman propaganda there is no room for doubt. Their line was firmly against Perseus, increasingly so, and their friends were expected to follow it.

One of those who followed the Roman line with the most vigour – for it had long been his own – was Eumenes of Pergamum. Rewarded by the Romans at Apamea with control over much of western Asia Minor, he had been Philip's rival over the possession of the cities in Thrace. He was Perseus' rival for goodwill and influence among the Greeks at large. His generosity in pursuit of this was in keeping with the open-handedness of his line,[22] as he tried to bind both states and individuals to himself. He had some success, but more people favoured Perseus. Why? Livy (here probably reflecting Polybius) offers possible reasons (XLII.5.6): 'whether because the states were predisposed, on account of the reputation and dignity of the Macedonian kings, to despise the origins of a kingdom newly formed, or because they were desirous of a change in their condition, or because they did not wish everything to become completely subject to the Romans'. One may doubt that there were many in the first category, but not that there were large numbers in the latter two groups. At Rome, by contrast, Eumenes was held in high esteem, and this mattered more.

Events were moving faster. A five-man commission, led by the consular C. Valerius Laevinus, was despatched in 173 to observe Macedonian activities and then to proceed to Alexandria to renew Rome's friendship with Ptolemy VI, and early in the next consular year both the consuls of 172 tried to have Macedonia allocated as a province. At this juncture Eumenes came to Rome himself and sought to quicken the pace even more. So far the Senate had not levelled specific charges against Perseus. Eumenes brought with him a prepared list of charges (Livy XLII.11–13). His general contention was the same as Polybius', namely that Philip had been planning a war and Perseus was about to execute it. His kingdom and his army were strong, his diplomacy preternaturally successful. (Eumenes, tactfully and insidiously, raised the possibility that it was ill-will towards the Romans that was winning so many over to the Macedonian cause.) He had married a daughter of Seleucus and given his sister in marriage to Prusias of Bithynia. He secured a formal alliance with the Boeotian confederacy and had very nearly succeeded in gaining access to Achaea. He had been appealed to by the Aetolians during their civil strife. Money, troops and weapons were his in unprecedented amounts. The most famous states of Greece and Asia were looking towards him increasingly by the day. Abrupolis, friend and ally of the

---

[22] See Robert 1937, 84–7: (E 162).

Romans, had been driven from his kingdom. Outspoken pro-Romans, one in Illyria and two in Boeotia, had been murdered. Aid had been sent to the Byzantines, contrary to Perseus' treaty with Rome. He had made war on the Dolopians. He had crossed through Doris and Thessaly with his army in order to aid the worse cause against the better in their civil war. He had caused confusion and turmoil in Thessaly and Perrhaebia by offering the hope of a cancellation of debts, the aim being to bring about the overthrow of the nobility through the agency of the debtors. And throughout all this Rome's inactivity had been read as acquiescence. Whether Eumenes described these events as he did because he saw them so or because he reckoned that such an account would be needed to produce the desired effect is not clear. Some of what he related appears here for the first time. Some does not, and it will be recalled that the earlier reports of events in Aetolia, Thessaly and Perrhaebia, as well as of Perseus' march through central Greece, did not tell against Perseus at all.

Eumenes' interpretations, however, were both useful and timely. If they were not all believed at Rome, they were at least adopted as official Roman propaganda.[23] Pretexts had been lacking. Sometime, probably not long, after Eumenes left Rome, the embassy led by C. Valerius Laevinus returned. Their report agreed with that of Eumenes, and they had more to tell. They brought with them one Rammius of Brundisium, with whom Roman envoys and generals had been accustomed to lodge when passing through, who alleged that Perseus had attempted to suborn him to poison his visitors. Also came Praxo of Delphi. Eumenes, after leaving Rome, had travelled to Delphi, where, it was claimed, an attempt was made to assassinate him. Praxo had given lodging to the alleged assassins, and Perseus was said to have been behind the plot. All that was enough to go on. No time was lost in declaring Perseus a *hostis*. The conduct of the war was to be entrusted to the consuls of 171, but preparations were begun immediately. Diplomatic preparations for the war were also set in train, with embassies sent to the states and kingdoms of Greece and Asia. Their aim was both to secure support for the coming war and to see what inroads Perseus had managed to make against Roman domination. Of those thus investigated only the Rhodians were seriously suspect in their loyalty. Dealt with more directly was King Genthius of Illyria, who was reported by the ever-loyal Issaeans to be joining in Perseus' preparations for war against the Romans and attacking their own territory. The Senate despatched ambassadors to complain

---

[23] Sherk, *Documents* 40 (*SIG* 643), is (almost certainly) an official Roman communication to the Delphic Amphictyony, belonging presumably to the eve of Rome's war against Perseus. Not enough survives to permit anything like complete restoration, but the charges against Perseus that it clearly does contain are strikingly similar to those brought by Eumenes in Livy's account (XLII.11–13); and cf. below, pp. 308–9, on Q. Marcius Philippus' meeting with Perseus in the winter of 172/1.

to Genthius about his actions and, no doubt, to bid him watch his step. What effect this had in driving Genthius into Perseus' camp in fact one can only guess.

By this time (into the summer of 172) preparations were well under way. A fleet of fifty ships was being assembled along with two legions of allied infantry and cavalry. A. Atilius Serranus (*pr.* 173) was to collect the force at Brundisium and send it across to Apollonia. The army, with which Cn. Sicinius (*pr.* 172) was to cross to Greece and hold the fort pending the arrival of one of the consuls of 171, was ordered to assemble at Brundisium on the Ides of February (Roman, i.e. 28 October 172 B.C.). All this proceeded as directed, and when the consular elections were held on 18 February (Roman, i.e. 2 November 172 B.C.), the forces under Sicinius must have been on their way to Apollonia. The consuls of 171 entered office on the Ides of March (i.e. 27 November 172 B.C.), and the war that had already been set in motion was duly declared by the centuriate assembly.[24]

Rome's efficiency in preparations and in getting a serious force across the Adriatic before the onset of winter was notable and an improvement even on their advance action in 192. But it was not altogether enough. Perseus' activity was at least as efficient, and the Roman embassy sent to Greece under the leadership of Q. Marcius Philippus to secure support for Rome found the Macedonian preparations to be in advance of their own.[25] Philippus and his team were ruthlessly effective in dealing with what confronted them, both tactically and politically.

At Corcyra the envoys decided which of the Greek states each of them would approach; virtually every one was to be visited. Before they set off on their several missions a letter arrived from Perseus enquiring, understandably, what reason the Romans had for sending troops into Greece or for garrisoning cities. No written answer was given, but the king's messenger was told that the Romans were acting for the protection of the cities themselves. While two of the legates went to Cephallenia and the western Peloponnese and a third to King Genthius, Q. Marcius and A. Atilius (*pr.* 192 and 173) set off on the most important part of the exercise, travelling first through Epirus, Acarnania and Thessaly. The pro-Romans were most in evidence, and their ascendancy was further fostered. After a friendly meeting with the Thessalians, the Roman

---

[24] The chronology of, and a certain amount else surrounding, the immediate background of Rome's declaration of war against Perseus does not always emerge with complete clarity from Livy and Polybius. See Rich 1976, 88–99: (H 20), and, especially on points of chronology and the narrative in Livy, book XLII, Warrior 1981: (B 42).

[25] This embassy left Rome as Cn. Sicinius prepared to cross to Apollonia, thus probably at some point in November 172, and returned to Rome in January/February 171: see Warrior 1981, 12–13: (B 42); cf. Walbank 1957–79, III.290–1: (B 38) (but the date for Philippus' departure given there is somewhat too early).

envoys met Perseus himself. Philippus read out the charges – a list very close to that brought to Rome by Eumenes and publicized by the Romans themselves at Delphi. Perseus defended himself, without much hope that his words would have any effect. Philippus suggested that Perseus send an embassy to the Senate, offering the hope of settlement. Perseus took the bait. Philippus appeared to assent grudgingly to the truce[26] this would require. He had in fact achieved his aim with remarkable ease: 'the request for a truce was clearly essential and Marcius was eager for it and was seeking for nothing else at the conference' (Livy XLII.43.2). His success was made easy by Perseus' desire to avoid war with Rome and (apparently) his belief that negotiation with Rome was possible. His conduct here gives perhaps the best indication that throughout the decade the aim of all his activity, both military and diplomatic, had been to make Macedon such that the Romans would be 'more cautious about giving unjust and severe orders to the Macedonians', as Polybius (XXVII.8.3) puts it in an analogous context in the next year. To Philippus and the Romans Perseus' willingness to treat gave the time that was needed. His tactical initiative was blunted. Philippus went immediately to Boeotia, assisted the Boeotian in repenting of their federal alliance with Perseus, and, as he had hoped, persuaded them to abandon their federation altogether. The pro-Romans in Thebes and elsewhere agreed to go to Rome and to surrender their cities individually to the faith of the Roman people. Perseus was thereby deprived of an important ally, and Philippus achieved in Boeotia what he had been unable to achieve in Achaea a dozen years before. The Achaeans themselves were approached next and approached just as were all the others, without any mark of favour to recognize their previous loyalty. This occasioned resentment (Livy XLII.37.8), but it cannot have occasioned much surprise. The Achaean magistrates agreed to despatch a thousand troops to garrison Chalcis for the Romans.

Philippus and his team repaired to Rome, pleased chiefly with the duping of Perseus – 'with the time consumed by the truce the war would be waged on even terms' (Livy XLII.47.3) – and with the dismemberment of the Boeotian League. Most of the Senate approved, but there were those, 'older men and mindful of old custom', who 'said they did not recognize Roman ways in the conduct of that embassy'.[27] All the same, when Perseus' envoys arrived they were ordered to leave Rome within

---

[26] *Indutiae* in Livy (XLII.43.2), ἀνοχαί in Polybius (XXVII.5.7), which must imply (against Walbank 1957–79: (B 38) *ad loc.*) that by the time Philippus met Perseus the war had been declared at Rome; cf. Warrior 1981, 13 with notes: (B 42). The embassy left Rome no long time (if indeed at all?) before the declaration.

[27] Livy XLII.47.4; cf. Diod. Sic. XXX.7.1 (indicating a Polybian original for the report). On the '*nova sapientia*' here complained about and its implications for Roman policy during these years see Briscoe 1964: (D 8).

thirty days after a perfunctory hearing in the Senate. The issue here was, of course, one of means and not one of ends. There was no question that something had to be done about Perseus and no question about what that was. Yet it remains an indication that new attitudes were developing at Rome, new feelings about how people who were (or might be) hostile to Rome, or who simply were not Romans, might be treated. This is seen here. It is seen in the infringement upon the rights of Rome's Latin allies administered through one of the consuls of 177 (Livy XLI.9.9). It is seen in the conduct of M. Popillius Laenas in Liguria in 173 and 172, where the inability of the Senate to control a consul (and his friends) augured trouble to come (Livy XLII.7–10, 21–22). It is there in the high-handed treatment by M. Popillius' colleague as consul in 173, L. Postumius Albinus, of Rome's allies at Praeneste (Livy XLII.1.7–12), and essentially the same thing may be judged to be at issue in the attempt by one of the censors of 169 (supported, it seems, by much of the Senate) to disenfranchise freedmen at Rome (Livy XLV.15.1–7). Roman conduct during the war against Perseus and immediately after it tells the same story.

The war in Macedonia fell to P. Licinius Crassus, who crossed to Apollonia and took over the area and the troops held by Cn. Sicinius. C. Cassius Longinus, Licinius' colleague, was unwilling to be outdone. He set off with his army and the intention of entering the Greek theatre by land from the north-west. Reports from Aquileia of his presence there and the direction of his march alerted the Senate to what was afoot, and he was eventually restrained. Licinius, in the meanwhile, advanced through Epirus into Thessaly and was drawn into a cavalry engagement at Callicinus. The Macedonian horse prevailed, with two immediate results. Perseus sued for peace, hoping that this taste of Macedonian bravery might make the Romans 'more cautious about delivering harsh and unjust orders to the Macedonians' (Polyb. XXVIII.7.3). He would have done better to lose the battle, for defeat, as ever, rendered the Romans intransigent, and angry. They were not altogether without *Romanae artes*, and peace then would have left Perseus and his kingdom intact.

The other immediate result of Rome's defeat in the field came when the news of it spread about Greece: 'the attachment of the many to Perseus, theretofore for the most part concealed, burst forth like fire' (Polyb. XXVII.9.1). Polybius apologizes for this (XXVII.9–10), likening it to the thoughtless reaction of a crowd at an athletic contest to an underdog, and reckons that a word reminding people of what evils they had received at the hands of Macedon and what goods at the hands of Rome would have put an end to their sentimentality. This may be doubted: there were pro-Romans about the place to remind them of the beneficence of Rome. The question to be asked about Polybius' comment is what he means by 'the many'. Is the word being used neutrally: 'a great many people felt sympathy for Perseus'? Or is it being used, as is usually the case, pejoratively, the reference being to 'the mob', and implying that it was above all the lower classes who were tending towards Perseus, glad of the discomfiture of Rome and of the 'friends' of the Romans in the various states? It is, of course, the same 'many' who were said by Callicrates in 180 to be favourable to the nationalists and hostile to those who supported Rome as he did himself. The question is quite the same as that about the poor and wealthy of Boeotia early in the 180s. The answer is also the same. In a word, leading men – Polybius' *politeuomenoi*, Livy's *principes*, all of them men of substance – were divided on these issues. The sympathy of the majority of the population, which is to say the lower classes, was, as Callicrates said, with the nationalists. Rome was for the pro-Romans and for small and reliable governments, for the wealthy, that is. Democracies were tolerated as long as they were reliable, but it must ever be remembered that when the choice of government lay with Rome, as in Thessaly after the war against Philip and as in most of Greece after the war against the Achaeans, it was not democracy that was chosen. Nor did 'the many' ever take the lead. The real question is whom did they follow. The answers – Brachylles, Philopoemen, Lycortas, later Andriscus even, Diaeus and Critolaus, amongst others – are consistent in their implication.

Licinius' defeat at Callicinus was less important in its military consequences. In this respect it was matched by the success he achieved at Phalanna before going into winter quarters. Somewhat more tangible success was gained in the opening year of the war by the praetor C. Lucretius Gallus. He captured the recalcitrant town of Haliartus in Boeotia, enslaved its population, and after that received the surrender of Thisbe, where the pro-Romans were put into power and had their position confirmed by decree of the Senate.[28] But what distinguished the commands of both Licinius and Lucretius was the rapacity and cruelty with which they conducted the campaign in Greece. In 170 Licinius was succeeded by the consul A. Hostilius Mancinus and Lucretius by the praetor L. Hortensius. The consul achieved nothing, the praetor notoriety. He put into Thracian Abdera and immediately demanded 100,000 *denarii* and 50,000 *modii* of corn. The Abderitans sought time to consult the consul and the Senate, whereupon Hortensius turned upon the city, executed the leading citizens and sold the rest into slavery. Abderitan emissaries reported this to the Senate, which sent envoys to restore the Abderitans to freedom and to inform the consul and the erring praetor that the war against Abdera had not been justly undertaken.

[28] Sherk, *Documents* 2 (*SIG* 646) with commentary; see *ibid.* 3 for the similar and contemporary situation at Boeotian Coronea (and *n.b.* Livy XLIII.4.11 and the treatment by Robert cited by Sherk).

Similar, if on the whole less striking, reports came in with increasing frequency. Few dared actually to complain: they rather decided to inform the Senate of the behaviour and exactions of the Roman commanders and to hope for the best. From outside the Greek theatre such messages were received from peoples whose territory had been traversed, and mishandled, by C. Cassius in his private journey to the war in 171. The plaintiffs were invited to deliver accusations in Cassius' presence. Whether they would have done this is not known, as Cassius was taken on, and thus away from this threat, by the consul Hostilius as a military tribune. From Greece itself came envoys from Athens. Their entire fleet and army had been put at the disposal of Licinius and Lucretius. This offer had been declined, but these commanders had requisitioned 100,000 *modii* of corn. From Chalcis came reports of plundering and enslavement by Lucretius and year-round billeting of sailors reckless of their conduct by Hortensius. The Senate pleaded ignorance, expressed regret, and wrote to Hortensius with instructions to set things right. Two tribunes instituted a prosecution against Lucretius. He was condemned unanimously. It all added up to two years of warfare without any success worth mentioning and with support in Greece being seriously eroded by the behaviour of Roman commanders.

Measures were taken. The Greek allies were informed that only requests for assistance accompanied by a *senatus consultum* should be honoured. A commission of two was sent to investigate the lack of success in Macedonia. The consular elections were arranged for January (Roman, i.e. 19 September–17 October 170 B.C.), and all senators were recalled to Rome and required to stay within a mile of the capital. Q. Marcius Philippus was elected to the consulship with Cn. Servilius Caepio. The commission returned at the end of February (Roman, i.e. mid-November 169 B.C.) and reported concern amongst the allies and a general laxity of discipline within the Roman army. When their report was discussed upon the entry of the new consuls into office, reinforcements of Roman and Latin troops were agreed and the decision was taken that the new legions formed should have their military tribunes elected by the people and not appointed by the consuls.

Macedonia fell to Q. Marcius Philippus, as must have been intended. He had had experience in Greece, which his predecessors in the command had not, and it would appear that the primary aim in entrusting the province to him was more diplomatic than military. That had been the nature of his experience there, and his previous consulship (in 186 B.C.) had been spent not on the battlefield but in dealing with what was seen as evidence of serious disaffection in Italy, the 'Bacchanalian conspiracy'.[29] Diplomacy was certainly the order for the winter. On instructions from

[29] See pp. 186 and 227.

the Senate Hostilius sent envoys to the Achaeans, Aetolians and Acarnanians. The envoys were C. Popillius Laenas (*cos.* 172) and Cn. Octavius. The purpose was twofold. In the Peloponnese they attempted to persuade people of the 'gentleness and kindness' of the Senate (Polyb. xxviii.3.3), particularly, it seems, by reporting the Senate's decision that orders for material support by Roman generals must be accompanied by *senatus consulta*. They also made it clear that they knew who had been forthcoming in their support for Rome and who, on the other hand, had been withdrawing from public affairs. The latter, they said, evoked Rome's displeasure as much as did Rome's enemies. Polybius, not uninvolved, comments: 'In consequence they created a general state of anxiety and doubt as to how one ought to act or to speak so as to make oneself agreeable under the present circumstances. It was said that, when the Achaean assembly met, Popillius and his colleagues had decided to accuse Lycortas, Archon and Polybius before it and to prove that they were estranged from Rome's policy and were keeping quiet at present, not because they were naturally disposed to do so, but because they were watching the progress of events and waiting for a favourable opportunity to act' (Polyb. xxviii.3.6–8). But lack of plausible pretext for this prevented them from so acting, and the Achaeans were given no more than a brief and cordial message. It was time for moderation; that was clear enough.

   In Aetolia the message was one of encouragement and kindness but included a request that the Aetolians give hostages to the Romans. This was supported by the pro-Roman Lyciscus, but opposed by others with the backing of the 'mob'. Another notorious pro-Roman was stoned in the assembly by the angry people. Popillius delivered a brief rebuke for this but said nothing further about hostages, and left Aetolia full of mutual suspicion and utter disorder. The pro-Romans in Acarnania took the initiative of asking for the installation of Roman garrisons: many, they said, were falling away towards Perseus and Macedonia. This was opposed, and the pro-Romans were accused of blackening their rivals and seeking the garrisons in order to establish their own absolute domination. The Roman envoys, 'seeing that the idea of garrisons was displeasing to the "mob" and wishing to act in accordance with the policy of the Senate' (Polyb. xxviii.5.6), decided against the garrisons and, with a word of thanks and encouragement, departed. The need for moderation was clear everywhere. The polarization of the 170s was well on the way to becoming complete, and the moderates in all the states needed to be shown that they, as well as the strident pro-Romans, could look forward with hope to a Roman victory. Such sensibilities had for the moment to be looked after; recriminations and accusations could wait upon the victory.

The diplomacy of the consul was true to character. With the Achaeans he dealt with apparent generosity. They had thought it expedient to offer him full military support, but the offer, presented by Polybius in person, was declined. The Romans were not going to put themselves under any such obligations. The consul also sought, according to Polybius, to prevent the Achaeans from acceding to the request of Ap. Claudius Centho, then operating in Epirus, for five thousand troops. Polybius professes uncertainty as to whether Philippus wished to spare the Achaeans the expense of this (more than 120 talents) or to keep Centho idle (xxviii.13.8). As the request was not accompanied by the required *senatus consultum* Polybius was able to have the matter referred to the consul without divulging anything of Philippus' message. Doubtless it was not intended by Philippus, but Polybius' conduct of this affair 'furnished those who wished to accuse him to Appius with a good pretext in having thus put a stop to his plan of procuring assistance' (xxviii.13.14). In dealing with the Rhodians Philippus achieved a great success. Strife between pro-Romans and pro-Macedonians was possibly keener there than anywhere else. In 169 the Rhodians sent friendly and, it was hoped, disarming embassies to the Senate and to the consul. Both were received kindly, as the circumstances clearly demanded. Philippus added in a private way a suggestion that the Rhodians should adopt the role of mediators in Rome's war with Perseus. This advice was read by the anti-Romans at Rhodes as a sign of Roman weakness. This was a mistake. It was also taken seriously and led to an attempt by the Rhodians at such mediation. This was a disastrous mistake. Polybius inclines towards the view that Philippus was seeking to make the Rhodians act in such a way as 'to give the Romans a plausible pretext for treating them in any way they saw fit'.[30] Hindsight, he admits, but that is the way it turned out.

Philippus' prosecution of the war itself was also more energetic and more successful than that of either of his predecessors. From a position in Perrhaebia between Azorus and Doliche south and west of the Olympus massif he determined to force an entry into Macedonia. The more obvious routes were held by Perseus' garrisons, but Philippus found another over the eastern shoulder of Olympus not far from the Macedonian garrison by Lake Ascuris. The descent over steep and pathless ground to the plain between Leibethrum and Heracleum was not easy, and once there the consul could, on Livy's reckoning (xliv.6.4–17), have been stranded. But Perseus, either in panic (so Livy, *ibid.*) or realizing that a Roman army could now be supplied and reinforced by sea in

---

[30] Polyb. xxviii.17.8. That Philippus was counselling mediation in Rome's war with Perseus and not in the Syrian war between Antiochus IV and Ptolemy VI is required by Polybius' remarks in xxviii.17.7–9: see Walbank 1957–79, iii, on xxviii.17.4: (b 38).

Macedon, abandoned most of his southerly positions, including Tempe and Dium. Philippus proceeded to occupy Dium and began a drive towards the north, but lack of supplies forced him back.[31] The year ended with the opposing armies separated only by the River Elpeus and southern Macedonia open to the Romans by both land and sea.

In western Greece as well the situation had by this time altered perceptibly. A rift within Epirus had been growing, with the Thesprotian Charops taking an increasingly strident pro-Roman line and forcing his chief opponent, the Molossian Cephalus, steadily from a position of neutrality towards outright alliance with Perseus.[32] In 170 two Molossians masterminded a plot to seize the consul Hostilius, a clear attempt to commit Epirus to the Macedonian cause. The plot failed, but in the course of 169 the rift became complete. Epirus split, the Molossians openly supporting Perseus and the Chaonians and Thesprotians Rome. It was to deal with this situation that Appius Claudius Centho had sought Achaean help. If the Molossians were not by themselves a serious threat, the Illyrian king Genthius was, or might have been. Perseus had been trying to entice him into open alliance, but Genthius held out for money which Perseus was unwilling to let him have. An Illyrian campaign by Perseus in the winter of 170/69 had failed to bring Genthius into the war, but by the latter part of 169 the two had come to terms. In the light of Roman success on the Macedonian front in 169, the importance to Perseus of Genthius' adherence is easy to see. The motivation of Genthius, suspect indeed in Roman eyes but so far not openly disloyal, is much less obvious. Against the inadequate forces of Claudius Centho late in the year he was not in serious danger, but the winter of 169/8 could be counted upon to produce new plans and preparations at Rome.

The consuls elected for 168 were L. Aemilius Paullus (*cos.* 182) and C. Licinius Crassus. Lots were cast for provinces soon after the election, and Macedonia fell to Paullus. Envoys were immediately despatched to Greece to ascertain the situations of the Roman armies in Macedonia and Illyria. They returned to Rome shortly after the new consuls entered office on the Ides of March (Roman, i.e. 4 January 168), and the arrangements for the coming campaign were decided on the basis of their report. Aemilius Paullus would take substantial reinforcements to Macedonia, and the praetor Cn. Octavius would leave with him to take command of a strengthened Aegean fleet. In response to the changed situation in Illyria it was decided to send the praetor L. Anicius Gallus (previously allotted the peregrine jurisdiction), again with reinforce-

---

[31] For a brief discussion, with essential bibliography, of Philippus' entry into Macedonia see Walbank 1957–79, III.341–2: (B 38).

[32] On Charops and Cephalus see Walbank 1957–79, III on XXVII.15: (B 38); cf. also Polyb. XXX.7.2.

ments, to succeed Ap. Claudius Centho in the command against Genthius. The Latin Games were held early to facilitate early departure by the new commanders.[33] They arrived in their provinces at the beginning of spring.

Most of the details of the Illyrian campaign are lost, but there is no doubt that it was brief. Ap. Claudius Centho began operations early, and Anicius Gallus came up from Apollonia to take over command at the Genusus. Within a month of this the war was over. After defeats on sea and land Genthius shut himself up in Scodra where he soon surrendered. 'The war was unique in that its conclusion was reported at Rome before its beginning' (Livy XLIV.32.5).

The Macedonian campaign did not last much longer. Over the winter Perseus had strengthened his position on the Elpeus and sent strong garrisons to Petra and Pythium to prevent himself from being taken in the rear by a force coming round Olympus. Paullus decided against a direct assault across the Elpeus and opted instead for a clandestine attempt on Pythium that would start off disguised as a naval move against the coastal areas of Macedon. Cn. Octavius was ordered to bring the fleet and supplies up to Heracleum, and on 17 June a picked force led by P. Cornelius Scipio Nasica marched there from the Elpeus. Provisioned by the fleet, which then sailed north, he set off inland under cover of night and after three nights' marches reached Pythium. An attack in the early morning of 20 June drove the Macedonian garrison out. Perseus was thus forced to abandon the Elpeus and fell back towards Pydna to a position between the Aeson (modern Pelikas) and Leucus (modern Mavroneri) rivers. On 21 June Paullus and the rest of the army joined up with Nasica's force but elected to postpone battle. The Romans fortified their camp across the Leucus from the Macedonians. That night the moon went into portentous eclipse, and on the next day occurred the battle of Pydna. It began as a skirmish across the Leucus but soon turned into a rout. Twenty thousand Macedonians are said to have been killed; six thousand who had fled to Pydna were captured there and another five thousand taken prisoner along the way (Livy XLIV.42.7).[34] Perseus retreated to his capital at Pella. He had the presence of mind to burn the royal records but time for no more than that before he fled from there, ultimately to Samothrace where he surrendered. With that the war was over. With that the need for moderation was over, and the axe fell.

In the twelve months after Pydna Greece was very much altered.

---

[33] At XLIV.19.4 Livy reports that the Latin Games were to be held *pr. id. Apr.* (i.e. 2 February 168) and at XLIV.22.16 that they took place *pr. kal. Apr.* (i.e. 20 January 168). Whether Ides or Kalends is correct must be an open question, but the slightly later date seems on balance more likely.

[34] For discussion of Paullus' campaign (including Nasica's march) and the battle itself, along with essential bibliography, see Walbank 1957-79, III.378-90: (B 38).

During the year before the battle the Achaeans and Aetolians had been treated with circumspection and a measure of indulgence. During the year following it Roman ambassadors visited the Achaeans again. This time they informed them that one thousand individuals (among them Polybius), whose loyalty had become suspect, were to be deported to Italy. This list was drawn up by Callicrates and those of his party. This was harsh, but gentle when compared to the handling of Aetolia, where 550 leading men were murdered while Roman soldiers surrounded the council-chamber and others driven into exile (Livy XLV.28.7). A fate even more special was reserved for Epirus, particularly for the Molossians, who had taken the side of Perseus in the war and from among whom had originated the plot to kidnap the consul Hostilius in 170. After the laxity of the earlier years of the war the Roman army had had discipline imposed upon it. The patience of the soldiers was rewarded when Aemilius Paullus led them home in 167. In accordance with a decree of the Senate seventy towns of Epirus (mostly Molossian) were given them to plunder. One hundred and fifty thousand people were said to have been sold into slavery as a result of Paullus' march to the sea (Polyb. XXX.15). The domination of the Epirote Charops, who had learned his Latin in Rome and had learned the force of Rome's displeasure as a political weapon earlier and better than most, was more than assured.

In these and the other states of mainland Greece the ascendancy of the pro-Romans was assured by deportations, bloodbaths and fear. For the moment, however, the states remained intact. The kingdoms of Illyria and Macedon were eradicated. The policy was decided at Rome and implemented in Illyria by Anicius Gallus with the aid of a senatorial commission of five and in Macedon by Aemilius Paullus and a commission of ten. The Illyrians were to be free and without Roman garrison and their land divided into three parts. The first of these was the region of Pista, the second comprised all the Labeatae, the third the Agravonitae and the areas round Rhizon and Olcinium. How these divisions were to function is not specified, but it may be permissible to draw an analogy with the Macedonian republics created at the same time. Except for some (as the Issaeans) who had taken the Roman side from the beginning or who defected to Rome during the war, all were to pay to Rome as tribute half the taxes they had paid to the king. This tribute, which the Macedonian republics also paid, must be seen in part as a replacement for the indemnity that the kings would have paid, had they remained. At the same time, it cannot but suggest something of a continuing subject status for those who paid it. The Macedonians were similarly to be free and to render to Rome half the taxes that had gone to Perseus.

Four republics were established from Perseus' kingdom. The first, with its capital at Amphipolis, comprised mainly the areas between the Rivers Strymon and Nessus, with some additions to the east of the Nessus (but excluding Aenus, Maronea and Abdera) and to the west of the Strymon (Basaltica with Heraclea Sintice). The second had Thessalonica as its capital and ran (with the aforementioned exceptions) from the Strymon to the Axius, taking in eastern Paeonia and all Chalcidice. The third was based upon Pella and stretched from the Axius to the Peneus, incorporating Edessa, Beroea and western Paeonia. The fourth took in the wilder region across Mt Bora to the borders of Epirus and Illyria; its capital is given by Livy as Pelagonia (XLV.29.9). The four republics were to be firmly separate entities. Intermarriage across boundaries was not permitted, and ownership of land and buildings in more than one of the parts was prohibited. Only the Dardanians were allowed to import salt. The third district was disarmed, but the other three were permitted to maintain armed garrisons on their barbarian frontiers. No Macedonian timber was to be cut by anyone for ships, and while the iron and copper mines continued in operation, those of gold and silver were closed.[35] Politically, the four republics were to govern themselves separately, each with its own body of elected representatives, or *synedroi*; their constitutional arrangements were laid down by Aemilius Paullus.[36] A province, but not quite. One may see here an attempt on the part of Rome to avoid taking over direct control while establishing a system that would make indirect control as easy as possible. The arrangement sought to ensure reliability and certainly guaranteed weakness. In less than twenty years the pretender Andriscus would show how fragile a conception it was and, perhaps, how little it was wanted by the Macedonians themselves.

Reprisals came to Rhodes, too. The attempt at mediation that Q. Marcius Philippus had elicited led almost to a declaration of war against the hapless Rhodians and all the way to the creation of Delos as a free port very much more attractive therefore than Rhodes for Aegean traffic. The state as a whole suffered in time. The leading anti-Romans there were mostly left to find their own deaths. Even Eumenes of Pergamum fell under 'baleful suspicion', and by 164 a Roman embassy in Asia Minor

---

[35] On Livy's account the aim was to deny the *publicani* a field of operation: see XLV.18.4, 'they (the mines) could not be run without the *publicani*, and whenever there was a *publicanus* either the rights of the people was a nonentity or the freedom of the allies destroyed'; cf. Hill 1952, 90: (H 49); Badian 1968,18: (A 5). It may be relevant that there had been trouble between Senate and *publicani* during the censorship of 184, 179 and 169. At the same time, it may be that the Senate felt unsure that these mines could be operated without the maintenance of some kind of military presence. Whatever the reason for closing them in 167, they were re-opened without incident in 158 (Cassiodorus, *Chron.*, under 158 B.C.).

[36] On the Macedonian and Illyrian republics cf. Larsen 1968, 295–300: (D 41), and Larsen in *ESAR* IV.298–9, 300.

THE END OF GREEK FREEDOM

was openly inviting accusations against the king of Pergamum, placing him thus in the position formerly occupied by Antiochus III in 196 and Philip V in 185. The futures of Eumenes and Rhodes are part of another story[37] but serve to indicate that Rome's will to *imperium* went on very much as before. Still, the victory over Perseus did mark the achievement of an objective, as is indicated by the Senate's dealings with the Odrysian king Cotys in 166. He sent an embassy to Rome to ask that his son, sent as a hostage to Perseus and captured along with the children of that monarch by the Romans, be returned to him, and also to explain his co-operation with Perseus. 'The Romans, thinking that they had attained their purpose now that the war against Perseus had ended in their favour, and that it served no purpose to prolong their difference with Cotys, allowed him to take back his son' (Polyb. xxx.17.2). There were times when there was point in maintaining such differences, but now was not one of them. Things were, for once, in order, and a far-ranging ambassa-dorial tour of Greece and the east in 165, led by Ti. Sempronius Gracchus (*cos.* 177, 163; *cens.* 169), brought back favourable reports about everyone.

III. THE END OF GREEK FREEDOM

With the loss of Livy's continuous narrative after 167 B.C. and the increasingly fragmentary state of Polybius' *Histories*, it becomes imposs-ible to construct an account that can be full enough to be wholly satisfying. How far the indications that there are may be extrapolated and how far silence is to be construed as evidence of anything are questions that can only be borne in mind as one proceeds. Even about the Achaean League evidence is patchy, particularly before 147. On five occasions between 165 and 150 the Achaeans are known to have sent embassies to Rome seeking the return of the detainees or at least that they should have the charges and suspicions against them put to the test of a proper trial. On the first four of these occasions the Senate declined, reckoning that Roman interests were best served by maintaining Callicrates and his friends in power, and that the continued detention of the Achaeans, on charges still open, best served this aim. They relented in 150 and allowed those still alive (fewer than 300) to return, to be buried at home instead of in Italy, as Cato put it.[38] The atmosphere in Achaea was throughout these

---

[37] The embassy was led by C. Sulpicius Galus (*cos.* 166); for the invitation to traducers of Eumenes: Polyb. xxxi.6.1–2. The 'baleful suspicion' (ὑποψία μοχθηρά) appears in a letter of Attalus III of Pergamum of 156 B.C. (Welles, *RC* 61.14) which contains also an appreciation of Rome's foreign policy very like that expressed by Polybius in xxiii.17.3 (for which see above, pp. 299–300).

[38] Earlier attempts: Polyb. xxx.30.1, 32.1–12 (164); xxxii.2.14–17 (159); xxxiii.1.3–8 (155); xxxiii.14 (154/3). Their release in 150 and Cato's quip: Plut. *Cat. Maj.* 9, also printed as Polyb. xxxv.6; cf. Walbank 1957–79, III *ad loc*: (в 38).

years one of tension tinged with the bitterness and hatred felt towards
Callicrates by the majority.

That the situation was the same elsewhere is the view of Polybius, and
there is no evidence pointing in any other direction. The work of
Callicrates in Achaea was being done in Aetolia by Lyciscus, in Boeotia
by Mnasippus, in Acarnania by Chremas, in Epirus by Charops. Polybius
saw the deaths of the last four, in quick succession in the early 150s, as 'a
sort of purification of Greece' (XXXII.5.3), followed by improvement of
relations in the states concerned. Whether a backlash of any magnitude
also followed their deaths one can only guess, but the extent of hostility
towards the Romans in Greece a decade or so later suggests something of
the kind. At the same time the Senate retained its desire to be informed of
all that was going on, and other embassies besides that of Gracchus in 165
made tours of inspection in Greece and the east. The Senate's desire was
recognized, and disputes, of more or less local kinds, continued to be
referred to Rome. The Senate might decide about these itself, send an
embassy to investigate, or refer the matter to other Greeks for arbitration. In 164 a territorial dispute had arisen between Sparta and
Megalopolis, and the decision on this was entrusted to the embassy led by
C. Sulpicius Galus, which was to observe the state of affairs in Greece
generally on its way to Asia Minor. The details of his activity in Greece,
known only from Pausanias (VII.11.1–3), reveal much. In the territorial
dispute he declined to decide and entrusted the decision instead to
Callicrates. While in Greece he was approached by some Aetolians from
Pleuron who wished to detach their city from the Achaean League. He
allowed them to send an embassy of their own to Rome. The Senate
authorized their secession and sent additional instructions to Galus,
bidding him sever as many cities from the League as he might be able.
There is bias and error in some parts of Pausanias' narrative of these years
but also a strong basis of fact. If his account here is anything like correct,
it emerges that the Romans were not content to have their friends in
power and that they were desiring to reduce the Achaean League more
than fifteen years before this requirement was officially imposed.

If there was tension within the states of Greece during these years, at
least peace mostly prevailed. The first exception came in the Adriatic,
where in 156 Rome fought a brief war against the Dalmatians. Polybius'
account of the outbreak of this war is of more than passing interest. In
response to complaints, chiefly from Issa, about Dalmatian piracy, the
Senate sent an embassy to the Dalmatians. The ambassadors were not
properly received and reported as well that violence would have been
done to them had they not made an early and quiet departure. The Senate
heard of this in a mood of great indignation at the awkwardness and
disobedience of the Dalmatians. 'But their chief motive for action was

that for several reasons they thought the time a suitable one for making war on the Dalmatians. For to begin with they had never once set foot in those parts of Illyria since they had expelled Demetrius of Pharos, and next they did not at all wish the men of Italy to be utterly undone by the long peace, it now being twelve years since the war with Perseus and their campaigns in Macedonia. They therefore resolved by undertaking a war against the Dalmatians both to recreate, as it were, the spirit and zeal of their own troops and by striking terror into the Illyrians to compel them to obey their orders. These, then, were the reasons why the Romans went to war against the Dalmatians, but to the world at large they gave out that they had decided on war owing to the insult to their ambassadors' (XXXII.13.4–9).[39] Obedience was still the thing and the readiness to enforce it evidently greater than it had been before.

Serious trouble lay a few years ahead. The surviving Achaean detainees returned to find what must have been a painfully and alarmingly familiar situation in the Peloponnese. Sparta was at odds with the rest of the Achaean League, and while secessionist feelings were on the increase in Sparta suppressionist ones were growing apace within the League at large. In winter of 150/49 embassies went to Rome from both. The Achaean mission was led by Callicrates who died on the way. The Senate declined to judge the matter just then and promised to send an embassy to arbitrate. How this dispute would have played itself out had it been allowed to do so on its own can only be guessed, but Roman determination in forcing her will upon the Dalmatians must suggest the answer. It was, however, not allowed to, for once again, as in 180/79, an event in Macedonia coincided influentially with the affairs of the Peloponnese, this time fatally. In the north a pretender to the Macedonian throne had arisen, or 'fallen from the sky' as Polybius put it (XXXVI.10.2). Andriscus easily overcame the slight resistance offered by the Macedonian republics and quickly amassed a large following there. In 149 a Roman army was sent under the command of the praetor P. Iuventius Thalna. He met Andriscus in the field and lost the battle and his life. More forces were sent in 148 under the praetor Q. Caecilius Metellus, a man without connections in the area.[40] By the end of the year he had defeated and captured Andriscus and restored quiet in Macedonia. Having done this he remained there ominously with his army.

During these two years the Senate refrained from sending its embassy to the Peloponnese, a delay which can occasion no surprise. It was always the Roman way to deal with one thing at a time in so far as possible, and that was very much the way of these years of Andriscus, Carthage and the

---

[39] Preferring the manuscripts at 13.6 (ἀπόλλυσθαι) to Reiske's misogynistic emendation (ἀποθηλύνεσθαι).

[40] The connection goes back at least as far as the ambassador of 185.

Achaeans. As the Senate delayed, the Achaeans, under the highly popular leadership of Diaeus and Critolaus, carried on in dealing with Sparta, as others before them had once carried on in dealing with Messenia. They did not heed advice from Metellus to wait for word from Rome and had brought the dispute within sight of settlement when the Roman envoys, led by L. Aurelius Orestes (cos. 157), arrived in the summer of 147. Whether the Senate's message would have been the same had the rising in Macedon not intervened cannot be known. Evidence of unrest and hostility towards Rome in Greece cannot have been without effect, and it was now clear, as it had not been in 149, what an Achaea without Callicrates would look like. In the event, the message was both clear and harsh. Orestes summoned the magistrates of the League cities and Diaeus the federal general and informed them that the Senate had decided that neither Sparta nor yet Corinth were to belong to the League and that Argos, Heraclea-by-Oeta and Arcadian Orchomenus were also to be detached. Orestes (and no doubt the Senate) had clearly been unwilling to communicate this directly to an Achaean assembly, but the Achaeans he had summoned rushed from the meeting and did this themselves. There was a furious reaction, and rage was vented upon everything that looked like a Spartan. Violence was nearly done to the Romans' place of lodging where some Spartans had sought refuge. Upon hearing of this the Senate despatched another embassy, led by Sex. Iulius Caesar (cos. 157). They attempted mollification, but the orders for the removal of the aforementioned cities stood. The Romans did not wish completely to destroy the League, and obedience was still possible. It sounds like an ultimatum and may indeed have been one in fact. Caesar arranged a meeting at Tegea between Spartan and Achaean representatives, but Critolaus prevented anything from being accomplished, pleading that no decisions could be taken before the Achaean assembly next met, in six months' time. Caesar and his colleagues departed, and with this formal communication between Rome and the Achaean League was at an end. When the Romans declared war, sometime early in 146, the reason alleged was the treatment of L. Aurelius Orestes and his fellow-ambassadors at Corinth.

The winter of 147/6 was spent by the Achaeans in preparation for a war against Sparta with every likelihood that this would mean war with Rome. Support throughout the Achaean cities was great, and there was support elsewhere in Greece.[41] For the Achaeans it was a simple question: adherence to Roman orders and substantial reduction of the League or war. They chose to defend their confederacy. Others elsewhere had come to see clearly the direction that Roman policy and Roman rule were

[41] For the evidence of the widespread popular support for the war see above all Fuks 1970: (D 27).

taking. In the spring of 146 the assembly of the Achaean League met at Corinth. Polybius comments disparagingly on the predominance there of manual labourers and artisans (xxxviii.12.5). Evidently feelings for democracy and nationalism were especially strong amongst these, but there were very few dissenters. War was declared, 'nominally against Sparta but in reality against Rome' (Polyb. xxxviii.13.6). An embassy from Metellus arrived fortuitously at the time of this meeting, offering the Achaeans a last chance to acquiesce peacefully to Rome's orders. He must have known by then that L. Mummius, consul of 146, was on his way to Greece with an army and that the fleet lately at Carthage was to be sent there.[42] Metellus wished to add the credit for settling this affair to that already gained for his handling of Macedonia. It did not matter how the settlement was achieved: when he sent his envoys to offer the hope of peace he was already starting his march south. The Achaean army under Critolaus went to lay siege to the rebellious Heraclea, whether because they thought they had the leisure to deal with this secession or out of some hope that action there might make it possible to block Metellus' passage at Thermopylae. There was time for neither, and Critolaus was killed and his army defeated at Scarpheia in Locris. Advancing Achaean reinforcements were soon after cut to pieces by Metellus as he swept towards the Isthmus. There Mummius took over command and routed the remaining Achaean forces under Diaeus. 'Corinth opened its gates, most of its inhabitants fled, the remainder suffered the rigour of a Roman sack.'[43] More was to come. The Senate decreed that Corinth was to be burnt and everything in it sold or carried off to Rome.

A senatorial commission of ten was despatched to assist L. Mummius in the settlement of Greece. Macedonia became a Roman province, henceforth to receive a Roman governor. His brief would include southern Greece, not for a long time a separate province itself. In Greece confederacies were dissolved and democracy ceased to be the normal form of government, although some mitigation of these penalties occurred before too long.[44] Greece had been much altered in the aftermath of the Roman victory of 168. Following the victory of 146 the alteration was more extensive, more complete, and it was permanent.

---

[42] See Paus. vii.15.1–2 and cf. Polyb. xxxviii.12.1; on the likelihood of a lacuna before the latter, cf. Walbank 1957–79, iii *ad loc.*: (B 38). On the fleet see Polyb. xxxviii.16.3.

[43] Benecke, *CAH*[1] viii.304.

[44] Paus. vii.16.9–10; cf. Larsen in *ESAR* iv.306–11, and, on Achaea in and after 146, cf. Schwertfeger 1974, 18–78: (D 51).

CHAPTER 10

THE SELEUCIDS AND THEIR RIVALS

C. HABICHT

I. ASIA MINOR, 188–158 B.C.

The war between Antiochus III and the Romans had been decided in Asia Minor and it was in Asia Minor, almost exclusively, that territory changed hands. Antiochus had to cede all his possessions west of the Taurus mountains to Rome; these amounted to more than one third of the vast Anatolian block. Rome imposed this condition, like all others, unilaterally on the king and settled affairs without allowing her allies to participate. The Senate decided; the allies waited upon its pleasure. The Greek cities that had sided with the Romans before the decisive battle were declared free; the Rhodians were given Caria south of the River Maeander and Lycia. The rest of the territory that had belonged to Antiochus was incorporated into the kingdom of Eumenes II of Pergamum.[1] It was the lion's share.

The territories Eumenes and Rhodes received were unequivocally a gift,[2] a gift from Rome, which implied an expectation that both powers would act as guarantors of the new order and that both would prevent any development disturbing to Rome. The Rhodian acquisitions, situated on the southern margin of Anatolia, were not so crucial in this respect as those of Eumenes; he therefore held the key to the preservation of the *status quo*. His newly enlarged realm bordered on three of the four remaining major powers, that is, on the kingdoms of Bithynia and Cappadocia and, between them, on the Celtic tribes in Galatia. Eumenes did not share a border with the kingdom of Pontus in the north, but the other three powers who were his neighbours all were neighbours of Pontus.

(a) The Attalid monarchy at its peak

During the war Bithynia and Pontus had remained neutral, whereas the Galatians and the king of Cappadocia had fought for Antiochus. The

---

[1] Bickerman 1937: (E 5) on the superiority of the annalistic tradition (Livy XXXVII.56.1–6) over Polybius (XXI.24.6–9, 46.2–12). The fate of several cities remains disputed: Bernhardt 1971, 54–71: (D 7). However, most cases can be settled through the coinage: Seyrig 1963: (B 134).

[2] Schmitt 1957, 93–128: (E 77).

Galatians were punished with a plundering expedition led by the consul of 189, Cn. Manlius Vulso, who was supported by Pergamene forces. Ariarathes IV of Cappadocia fared better. He arranged the engagement of his daughter Stratonice to Eumenes and thereby won the latter's protection and the indulgence of the Senate.[3]

Having the neighbour-state Cappadocia as an ally did add considerably to Eumenes' strength, but his other neighbours, the Galatians and King Prusias I of Bithynia, were his enemies and almost as soon as the oaths for the treaty of Apamea were sworn, Eumenes found himself at war with both of them. The causes were intimately connected with a clause in the peace treaty. Earlier, when the Roman army was on its way to the Hellespont, Prusias had been inclined to respond to Antiochus' call and join forces with him. A letter from the brothers Scipio, assuring him that Rome would respect the integrity of his realm, caused him to remain neutral. He had, however, already seized part of Phrygia, the so-called Phrygia Epictetus that had belonged to Attalus I of Pergamum. Attalus' son Eumenes, in his dealings with the Senate in 189, had convinced the *patres* that the disputed area rightfully belonged to him. The treaty of Apamea stipulated that it be restored.[4] It is strange indeed that such a clause was incorporated in the treaty with Antiochus. By remaining neutral, Prusias had served Roman interests and for this service had been recognized as a 'friend of the Roman people'. Nevertheless Rome now acted against his interests. Naturally enough, Prusias refused to comply. War was inevitable; it became the first major test for the new state of affairs in Asia Minor.

Hostilities began *c.* 187 and lasted into 183. Prusias found allies among those enemies of Eumenes who were also enemies of Rome. He won support from Philip V of Macedonia, who was then engaged in a bitter dispute with Eumenes over the Thracian cities Aenus and Maronea; he probably received aid from the Pontic king Pharnaces; and, most important, he received aid from the Galatians, who were led by the chieftain of the Tolistobogian tribe, Ortiagon, who had recently become king of all three tribes. Furthermore, Prusias counted among his generals none other than Hannibal, who, after his escape from Antiochus' court, had reached Bithynia via Armenia and Crete.[5]

<hr>

[3] Vulso: Stähelin 1907, 50–66: (E 169); Pagnon 1982: (E 49). The dates of Stratonice's birth and marriage are disputed: Hopp 1977, 27–9: (E 60); Allen 1983, 200–6: (E 52). Inscription of her statue erected by the people of Pergamum: *IvP*, III, pl. 2.

[4] Habicht 1956, 90–100: (E 56); *id. PW*, 'Prusias', 1097–1105; Schmitt 1964, 276–7: (E 50). The most important document is *AE* 1940, 44. Restoration to Eumenes: Livy XXXVIII.39.15 (the corresponding passage, Polyb. XXI.46.10, is corrupt).

[5] At the time of the events in Polyb. XXII.8.5 (Errington 1969, 257–63: (D 23): late summer 187; but see n. 49) war was at least imminent. Hannibal is said to have founded Artaxata in Armenia and Prusias ad Olympum (modern Prusa).

Map 13. Asia Minor and Syria.

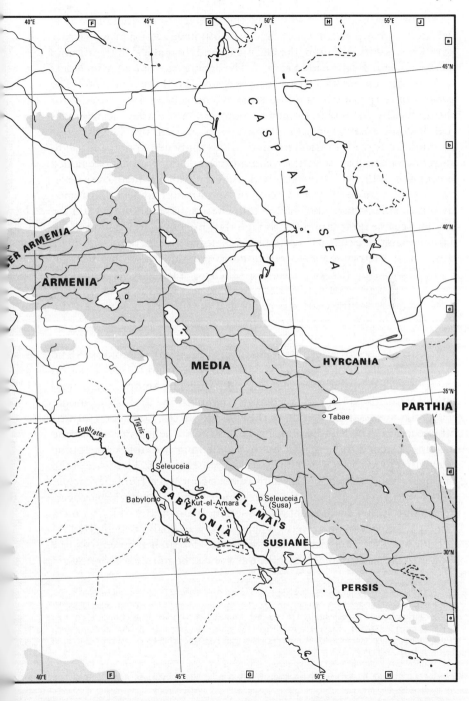

Almost nothing is known about the military operations: Hannibal defeated Eumenes in a naval engagement; Eumenes won a major victory over Prusias and Ortiagon, the Galatians 'and their allies' in the autumn of 184.[6] Finally Rome had to step in. The Senate had long remained deaf to Eumenes' complaints that Prusias resisted the Roman demand. The *patres* obviously were caught in the dilemma they had created for themselves by yielding to Eumenes' claim, but in 183, after the Scipiones had lost all their power, a Roman embassy led by T. Quinctius Flamininus forced Prusias to give in to Eumenes and to agree to surrender Hannibal, who then committed suicide. Eumenes regained possession of Phrygia Epictetus and also established control over Galatia. For almost a century the Greeks of Asia Minor had been threatened by the Galatians; now they hailed Eumenes as 'Saviour' (*Soter*) and the epithet became quite common, though the king never styled himself so. To commemorate the victory Eumenes enlarged the sanctuary of Athena 'Bringer of Victory' (*Nikephoros*) in Pergamum and raised her festival, founded by his father long ago, to panhellenic rank. In 182 numerous Greek cities were invited to participate. The new festival, henceforward to be held every fifth year, was celebrated for the first time in 181;[7] by then the king was involved again in a major war.

This war, fought against Pharnaces I of Pontus and his allies, arose, our sources say, as a result of Pharnaces' aggressive ambition.[8] The Pontic rulers had long wanted to control the flourishing Greek cities on the south coast of the Black Sea and, in particular, Sinope. Pharnaces' father, Mithridates III, had failed in an attempt in 220 to subdue Sinope, mainly because of Rhodian aid to the city. Pharnaces, however, stormed Sinope in 183. The Rhodians protested in Rome. The Senate, at the same meeting, listened to Eumenes' envoys – the king had differences of his own with Pharnaces – and to Pharnaces' representatives. The cause of the dispute is not specified, but it seems to have concerned Eumenes' newly won control over Galatia, through which he had become Pharnaces' neighbour. In any event Galatia was soon the main theatre of action and a principal subject of the treaty, when peace was finally concluded.

Following its standard policy, the Senate despatched an embassy to look into the situation. Meanwhile, the war had begun and other powers

[6] *Riv. Fil.* 60 (1932) 446ff.
[7] Hannibal's death: Habicht 1956, 96–100: (E 56). Flamininus went on to see King Seleucus IV. Incorporation of Galatia: Stähelin 1907, 61: (E 169). Eumenes as 'Saviour': Robert 1934, 284 n. 1: (B 63); *id.* 1937, 73 n. 1: (E 162). Sanctuary of Athena: Ohlemutz 1940, 38: (E 63); the festival: Jones 1974: (E 61), superseding previous work. For silver tetradrachms of Athena Nikephoros from these years: LeRider 1973: (B 111).
[8] Main sources: Polyb. XXIII.9.1–3, XXIV.1.1–3, 5, 14–15, XXV.2, XXVII.7.5, fr. 112; Diod. Sic. XXIX.22–24; Livy XLII.2.6; Just. *Epit.* XXXVIII.6.2. Recent bibliography: Hopp 1977, 44–8: (E 60); Burstein 1980: (E 12).

had become involved: for Eumenes, the king of Bithynia, Prusias II, who had just succeeded his father, and Ariarathes of Cappadocia;[9] for Pharnaces, some Galatian chieftains and Mithridates, satrap of Armenia. King Seleucus IV of Syria almost joined the Pontic king, but in the end refrained, to avoid violating the treaty with Rome (p. 339). For some time the initiative lay with Pharnaces. He captured the Greek city of Tieium in Bithynia and seems to have invaded Galatia. The Roman ambassadors, who reported back to the Senate, supported Eumenes and a second embassy was sent out to urge Pharnaces to end hostilities. In 181 there was a truce, soon violated by the Pontic king, who continued to ravage Galatia during the winter of 181/80. Eumenes' three brothers now urged the Senate to punish the aggressor, but the Conscript Fathers confined themselves to sending out a third embassy with instructions to end the war by any means.[10]

This embassy arrived in the spring of 180, just in time to halt a major counter-attack by Eumenes and Ariarathes which had already advanced well into Pontic territory. Peace negotiations were held in Pergamum in the presence of the Romans. The Pontic delegation played for time, the Romans returned home in frustration, and the war continued. Eumenes, just recovered from an illness, now exerted himself to put an end to the war without Roman support. He greatly enlarged his army and blockaded the Hellespont in an attempt to weaken Pharnaces, but pressure from Rhodes forced him to withdraw.[11] In the autumn of 180 or spring of 179, he took the field with his allies, and Pharnaces indicated at last that he was ready for peace.

The peace treaty is described in some detail by Polybius.[12] Pharnaces had to renounce all his ambitions in Galatia, which thus remained firmly under Eumenes' control; he had to restore Tieium to Eumenes (who then gave it to Prusias of Bithynia); he also had to return whatever he had taken from Ariarathes and from Morzius, the dynast of Gangra in Paphlagonia. Ariarathes was to receive 300 talents from Mithridates of Armenia as an indemnity. Pharnaces, however, kept Sinope; Eumenes, it appears, now that his relations with Rhodes were strained, was indifferent to the fate of a city which had close ties with the Rhodians.

Included in the treaty are several other powers that are not mentioned as participants in the war: Artaxias, the ruler of Greater Armenia,

---

[9] A decree of Cos at this time praises Ariarathes and his queen Antiochis: Segre and Pugliese-Carratelli 1972: (E 164); Piejko 1983: (E 158).

[10] Of three Roman embassies during the war, the first was 'to look into the matter of the Sinopeans and into the differences between the kings', the second 'to look more closely into the differences of the aforementioned', the third 'to end the war by any means'.

[11] Eumenes exploited perhaps more fully the treaty of 183 with 33 cities of Crete: IC iv.179; Dunst 1956: (E 54). A fragmentary treaty of his with Lato is dated c. 180: SEG xvi.524.

[12] Polyb. xxv.2; Walbank 1957–79, iii.271–4: (B 38).

Acusilochus (unknown); in Europe, the Sarmatian chieftain Gatalos, and a number of Greek cities, viz. Heraclea on the Black Sea, Cyzicus on the Propontis (Sea of Marmara), Mesambria (Mesebâr) on the west coast of the Black Sea and Chersonesus (Sevastopol) in the Crimea. Whether all of these had participated in the war is disputed.[13] The peace may have come about partly because the Romans had begun to put pressure on Pharnaces at the very end of the war.[14]

Eumenes had been victorious in two major wars. The confidence that Rome had placed in him seemed fully justified, and yet in both wars peace had come only when the Senate finally exerted pressure. Eumenes, though he had won the alliance of Cappadocia and had established control over Galatia, though under the treaty of Apamea he was secured against an attack by a Seleucid king, nevertheless faced Celts, who resented the loss of their freedom; the kings of Pontus and Bithynia, who, momentarily weakened, continued to be or again became his enemies;[15] Macedonia, which remained an enemy; and Rhodes, which had turned hostile. The situation in Asia Minor was delicate and dependent on continued Roman support for the Pergamene king.

Nonetheless, the kingdom of Eumenes was now the dominant power. The 170s witnessed the height of the monarchy and of Pergamene art. In the capital magnificent buildings were erected, new festivals created, and the royal residence finally transformed into a place of splendour.[16] Strabo calls attention to the sanctuary of Athena Nikephoros (p. 328), to prestigious votives and to the foundation of libraries. A new festival was instituted in honour of Asclepius, who now rose to prominence, and of Heracles; the king's own brothers were the first to preside over the games that formed part of the festival. The city was considerably enlarged and was fortified with new walls. The most famous enterprises, however, were on the acropolis: the enlargement of the sanctuary of Athena and, above all, the erection of the Great Altar to Zeus. The major frieze, displaying the gigantomachy, appears to have been begun soon after the battle of Magnesia and completed by 170, followed by work on

[13] Bickerman 1932: (E 124) argues that non-participants in the war could be included in the treaty. Against this view: Dahlheim 1968, 213ff.: (H 86). Both opinions have supporters. This writer tends to agree with the latter.

[14] This, however, cannot be inferred from Pharnaces' treaty with Chersonesus (*IPE* 1².402, 3–5, 26–8), traditionally dated to 179, since its true date is *c.* 155 B.C.: Burstein 1980: (E 12).

[15] Prusias II, an ally of Eumenes against Pharnaces, soon rejoined his enemies (as reflected by his marriage to Apame, the sister of Perseus, *c.* 177).

[16] The fundamental publications are the volumes of *Altertümer von Pergamon* (since 1885); see details in Hansen 1971, 485–6: (E 57) (and vols. XI.2–XI.4 (1975–84), XII (1978), XIII (1981)). Reports on current work: *MDAI(A)* 1899, 1902, 1904, 1907, 1908, 1910, 1912; *Abh. Akad. Berlin* 1928 no. 3; 1932 no. 5; *Arch. Anz.* 1966, 1970, 1973–83. General survey and detailed bibliography in Hansen 1971: (E 57); Allen 1983, 76–135: (E 52).

the smaller frieze, that of the royal ancestor Telephus, which had not yet been completed in 158 when Eumenes died.[17]

The increased importance of the kingdom caused an expansion and intensification of its foreign relations. Attalid ambassadors appear in new areas, such as Thessaly, where common enmity towards Macedonia seems to have prompted the contact.[18] Increased wealth allowed the king to give, or at least to offer, money to a large number of Greek states. Eumenes donated buildings, grain and other goods. To Athens, for instance, he sent an architect and also, it seems, a foreman to build the stoa that bears his name, the Stoa of Eumenes, for the benefit of the spectators in the theatre.[19] He did, however, suffer a few setbacks when Pergamene diplomacy was tactless; for instance, when the king offered to pay the Council of the Achaean League and was rebuffed, or when he was too eager to gain what the Senate had not assigned him; in Thrace his envoys tried to persuade the Roman commissioners that the cities of Aenus and Maronea, also claimed by Philip V, were, in fact, an 'appendage' to the gift of the Thracian Chersonese. In the end, the Senate refused to let either party have them.[20]

A visible and important change within the kingdom of Eumenes was the introduction of a new royal silver coinage, the 'basketbearers' (*cistophori*). The basket, depicted on the obverse, is associated with Dionysus, a favourite god of the Attalids. The new coinage was supposed to replace the old silver pieces bearing the portrait of Philetaerus, the founder of the dynasty. Its circulation was confined to the realm of the Attalids – the coins are almost never found elsewhere – and within the limits of the kingdom it was the only lawful coinage. Scholars now

---

[17] Strabo XIII, p. 624; *IvP* III no. 3: Prince Athenaeus *agonothetes* of the second celebration. For the cult of Asclepius in Pergamum: Ohlemutz 1940, 123–73: (E 63), and *IvP* III, pp. 1–20. The Great Altar: Schrammen 1906: (B 197); Kähler 1948: (B 175); Schober 1951: (B 196); Rohde 1982: (E 64). A head recently found is probably from a statue of Asclepius, perhaps the one by Phyromachus (Simon 1975, 19–20: (I 33), and see p. 360). On the frieze of Telephus, 'a kind of *Aeneid* of the Attalids' (Gruben 1966, 408: (I 16)), see Stähler 1966: (B 201). Whether the work began early or late in the 180s is disputed. It is almost unanimously agreed, however, that the larger frieze was completed by *c*. 170, to be followed by work on the smaller frieze. It is, however, argued by Callaghan 1981 and 1982: (B 153 and 155) that both friezes were begun simultaneously and only after 166 B.C. Christians considered the altar (to pagans one of the seven wonders of the world) 'Satan's throne' (Apoc. John. 3.13, if this is the altar and not the temple of Roma and Augustus or, possibly, of Asclepius).

[18] *IG* IX.2.512 from Larissa. One ambassador honoured is a well-known kinsman of Eumenes; another, Demetrius, also honoured at Delos (*IG* XI.765–6) and later at Ephesus (*JÖAI* 50 (1976) *Beibl*. 12 no. 4), had charge of Eumenes' seal. Common interests of Eumenes and the Thessalians: Polyb. XXII.6.

[19] Eumenes' relations with Greek states: Polyb. XXXII.8.5; Livy XLII.5.3. References in Robert 1937, 84–5: (E 162); and also, for Athens: Ferguson 1911, 299 (D 26); for Delphi: Daux 1936, 497–511 (D 15); for Miletus: Herrmann 1965: (E 142); for Cos: Sherwin-White 1978, 132–3: (E 168). Stoa of Eumenes in Athens: Vitr. *De Arch.* V.9.1. Bibliography in Hansen 1971, 295 n. 181: (E 57); add Thompson 1953, 256–9 (D 53).

[20] Achaea: Polyb. XXII.1.6, 7–9; Diod. Sic. XXIX.17. Thrace: Werner 1977, 167ff.: (D 55).

generally agree that the new coins were not minted before 188 and that they were royal money, despite the fact that the pieces lack the portraits as well as the names of the kings, and that they were struck in various cities. Recently, the view that the cistophoric coinage began immediately after the peace of 188 has won wide acceptance, though there are strong arguments in favour of putting the beginning even later, in either *c.* 175 or *c.* 166 when King Eumenes had already fallen out with Rome.[21]

Late in 175 Eumenes seized an opportunity to befriend a traditional enemy; he helped the Seleucid prince Antiochus, youngest son of Antiochus the Great, to win the throne after the assassination of his brother, King Seleucus IV (p. 341). It was a masterly move and one that earned him Antiochus' gratitude. Relations between the two kingdoms, traditionally hostile, immediately became cordial and remained so as long as Antiochus lived.[22] On the other hand, his aid to Antiochus had alienated Seleucus' legitimate heirs; this was to have consequences later, when they regained their inheritance (p. 357).

(b) Rome's rebuff to Eumenes

Now at the height of his fortunes, Eumenes gambled once too often. As he had been instrumental in preparing Rome to go to war with Antiochus III, so again he was instrumental in causing the Senate to decide to wage war against Perseus of Macedonia. When Eumenes addressed the Senate in 172, he accused the king of violating the treaty and preparing war against Rome; later he accused him of plotting the attempt on his life at Delphi on his way home that had left him near death. Rome declared war on Perseus, and Eumenes, once again, seemed to have won, but he failed to foresee that his very success would render superfluous the role which, for thirty years, he had been allowed to play. Once the Macedonian monarchy was annihilated, the Senate rebuked and humiliated Eumenes and gave encouragement to his enemies, the Galatians and King Prusias.[23] The Senate concealed the political issue in a personal attack on Eumenes; it voiced allegations of treachery; for treason, it was insinuated, had been committed by Eumenes in secret negotiations with Perseus.[24] The Senate courted the king's brother Attalus, and even made him a secret offer of the crown or at least a realm

[21] Kienast 1961: (B 102); Seyrig 1963: (B 135); Boehringer 1972, 44–6: (B 82); Kleiner and Noe 1976: (B 105); Mørkholm 1979: (B 116). Kleiner and Noe date its introduction to *c.* 166, Mørkholm prefers *c.* 175. See further Waggoner 1979: (B 145); Kleiner 1980: (B 104); Mørkholm 1982: (B 119).

[22] The theory of Rostovtzeff, 1941, 656–9: (A 31), that a period of close co-operation in economic affairs followed rests on erroneous assumptions and has to be abandoned: Seyrig 1963, 26–8: (B 135). There is now, however, more documentary evidence for the friendship between Eumenes and Antiochus: Herrmann 1965, 82–7: (E 142).

[23] Habicht, *PW*, 'Prusias', 1113–15. Gruen 1984, 569ff.: (A 20), denies that there was such encouragement.   [24] Schleussner 1973: (D 50).

of his own.[25] The allegations were probably not true.[26] Eumenes had participated in the war from beginning to end and his brothers Attalus and Athenaeus had fought at Pydna with a considerable part of his army.[27]

The king himself was convinced that he could easily prove his loyalty before the Senate and a majority of the senators must have known they had no valid reason for suspecting him, but they did not want this issue resolved, so, just after they had heard King Prusias address them and knowing that Eumenes was then in Italy on his way to Rome, they voted not to allow kings to speak before them. Eumenes, therefore, under strict rules of fair play between allies, had a good reason to complain of his treatment by Rome, though that was the only one, because the situation had changed since 193. Eumenes then had actually been threatened by Antiochus' aggressive expansion, whereas in 172 there was no threat whatsoever from Perseus. Likewise, Rome in 193 may have had a legitimate grievance against Antiochus, whereas it did not have any against Perseus in 172. The two states had been partners in an unscrupulous war and after the victory Rome continued to be unscrupulous. Eumenes made the mistake of expecting loyalty from a Senate which, after the defeat of Perseus and the compliance of Antiochus IV (pp. 344–5), no longer needed him.

In 168, apparently encouraged by the absence of part of the Pergamene forces in Macedonia, the Galatians rebelled. Eumenes, after two years of heavy fighting during which he once came close to being captured by the enemy, finally won a decisive victory, somewhere in Phrygia, and suppressed the insurrection. It was a hollow victory; before it, Roman commissioners had secretly encouraged the Galatians; after it, the Senate, openly hostile, declared his Celtic subjects free.[28] Eumenes, however, did not entirely comply and his tenacity, in turn, gave Prusias ammunition for years of denunciations before the Senate of Pergamene activities in Galatia.[29] Eumenes had fought four times for the possession of Galatia; for its loss there was but one compensation: contrary to

---

[25] Polyb. xxx.1–3; Livy xlv.19–20. They promised him the Thracian cities Aenus and Maronea as a gift, but when he remained loyal to his brother, declared them free (suppressed in Livy) and concluded a treaty with Maronea: *Arch. Delt.* 28 (1973), pl. 418. Gruen 1984, 574–5: (A 20), is sceptical of the tradition. [26] Most scholars agree, despite minor differences of opinion.

[27] Eumenes and the Thessalian cavalry by and large had kept an engagement in 171 from becoming a Roman disaster: Livy xlii.59–60. The Thessalians founded a festival to commemorate the occasion: *Arch. Delt.* 16 (1960) 185; *Bull. épigr.* 1964, 227; Kramolisch 1978, 135–6: (D 38).

[28] Main sources: Polyb. xxix.22, xxx.1.2, 2.8, 3.7–9, 19.12; Diod. Sic. xxxi.12.–14; Polyaenus, *Strat.* iv.8.1; Welles, *RC* 52.8–14; Swoboda, Keil and Knoll 1935, 32 nos. 74–5 (Amlada): (B 202). *FD* iii.3.241–2 (Sardis), discussed by Daux 1932: (D 14). Robert 1934: (B 63) (Tralles). For the victory in Phrygia see *IvP* 165, augmented by *MDAI(A)* 27 (1902) 90 no. 74. The date of *IvP* 167 is not 165, but 149 (no connection with this war): Jones 1974, 186–9: (E 61). Stähelin 1907, 66–72: (E 169), remains the best modern account. For the freedom of Galatia: Polyb. xxxi.2.

[29] Prusias' allegations (n. 134) are in part confirmed by the secret correspondence of Eumenes and Attalus with the priest Attis of Pessinus (pp. 373–4).

Roman expectations, their own conduct and Eumenes' courageous stand against the barbarians caused a wave of goodwill and genuine sympathy for him to spread throughout the Greek states of Asia Minor and the Aegean world. He was also reconciled with Rhodes, another of the Senate's victims.[30]

The shift in Roman policy after 168 is significant. Eumenes and Rhodes, Rome's oldest and firmest allies, dropped completely from favour and Antiochus IV of Syria, who had been more than loyal (pp. 344-5), became an object of suspicion, while their enemies – Prusias II, the Galatians, some cities in Asia Minor that had differences with Eumenes, like Selge in Pisidia, or were opposed to Rhodian domination, and the Jewish rebels in Antiochus' kingdom – all found an open ear in the *curia* for their ambassadors' assertions that Eumenes, Ariarathes and Antiochus had formed a block with common interests that, if something less than a formal alliance, was still prepared for common action and was therefore dangerous to Rome.[31] The Senate, well aware that it had treated two of these kings badly, found it necessary to watch them closely through repeated inspections. Nor was that all; the Roman commissioner C. Sulpicius Galus publicly invited accusations against Eumenes. For ten days in 164 in Sardis, one of Eumenes' most important cities, Galus listened to the meanest slanders against a king who was still Rome's 'friend and ally'.[32] The conduct of Cn. Octavius in Syria (p. 354) was similar. Under these cloudy skies Eumenes received another blow: in 164 his two friends Ariarathes and Antiochus both died.

During his last years the Pergamene ruler once more made major benefactions to several Greek states.[33] In 160/59, his health failing, he appointed his brother Attalus co-ruler. Eumenes died some time later, apparently in 158.[34]

(c) Rhodes, 189–164 B.C.[35]

After the war against Antiochus the republic of Rhodes was amply rewarded by Rome for what it had contributed to the Roman victory.

[30] Polyb. xxxi.6.6. Welles, *RC* 52.8–14, and the documents from Sardis and Tralles (n. 28); see Holleaux 1924, 323–6: (E 59). Rhodes: Polyb. xxxi.31; Diod. Sic. xxxi.36.

[31] *Koinopragia* ('concerted action') is used repeatedly (Polyb. xxx.30.4, xxxi.9.8).

[32] Details in *MRR* 438–44. Chronology: Walbank 1957–79, iii.33ff.: (B 38).

[33] Such as Delphi: *FD* iii.3.237–9, all of 160/59; Miletus: Herrmann 1965: (E 142); Rhodes: see n. 30.

[34] Appointment of Attalus: Hopp 1977, 3–15: (E 60). Eumenes' death is generally dated to 159, since it is assumed that he died in his 38th or 39th regnal year. A new inscription, mentioning his 40th year, suggests the date must be 158: Petzl 1978, 263, no. 12: (B 59).

[35] Main sources: excerpts from Polybius, books xxi–xxx, with Walbank 1957–79, iii: (B 38). Also many passages in books xxxvii–xlv of Livy; most of them are Livy's adaptations of Polybius' narrative, others are derived from Roman sources, a few outright annalistic falsifications, for which

The gift of Caria south of the Maeander and of Lycia added greatly to the Rhodian realm in Asia Minor, the so-called *Peraea*. Special clauses in the peace treaty served Rhodian interests. One imposed an interdiction on Antiochus against making war on 'the islands', others upheld the rights and privileges of Rhodian property-owners and merchants within his empire.[36] The Senate was even prepared to grant the city's demand that the town of Soli in Cilicia be declared free, despite the fact, duly stressed by Antiochus' envoys, that the preliminary treaty had left Cilicia under the king's rule. And the Aetolians owed the peace they were granted in the same year, 189, at least in part to the good offices of the ambassadors from Rhodes and from Athens who spoke in their favour before the consul in Greece and before the Senate.[37]

In Asia Minor Rhodes had to fill part of the vacuum created by the retreat of Antiochus and to defend the new state of affairs created by Rome in the south, just as King Eumenes had to defend it north of the Maeander. Caria as a whole, where the Rhodians had had a small dominion for some time, seems not to have opposed directly Rhodian rule, but some cities did not welcome it. Alabanda managed to obtain a decree from the Senate declaring the city free, that is to say, exempt from Rhodian domination.[38] An inscription from Apollonia in the Salbace Mountains suggests that Rhodian domination was less troublesome to the native inhabitants of the countryside than to the larger cities, who were afraid of losing their grip on the territories surrounding them.[39] It is, however, difficult to say whether these instances permit generalization. Strong Rhodian influence was felt even north of the Maeander, where several free cities attached themselves to Rhodes rather than to Eumenes. In a treaty concluded during the 180s Miletus and Heraclea-on-Latmus agreed not to act contrary to the interests of Rhodes, their dominant ally.[40]

In Lycia, on the other hand, Rhodes encountered stiff resistance. The Lycians had fought for Antiochus and resented becoming subjects of Rhodes. In 189 they had envoys from Ilium plead their case before the

see Schmitt 1957, 140 n. 4, 150 n. 1, 212–15: (E 77). Also Diod. Sic. XXIX.11, XXX.24, XXXI.5; Livy, *Per.* XLVI; Dio. Cass. frs. 66.2, 68.1–3; Zon. IX.23.3; App. *Mac.* 11.2–3, 17. Fragments of Cato's speech for the Rhodians in Gell. *NA* VI.3; Calboli 1978: (H 34). Several inscriptions give details on the beginning and end of Rhodian domination in Caria and Lycia. For modern work see the exhaustive discussion of Schmitt 1957, 81–172: (E 77), and the survey of Gruen 1975: (E 76); for the Rhodian dominions in Asia Minor: Fraser and Bean 1954: (E 75).

[36] Schmitt 1957, 85: (E 77); Gruen 1975, 65: (E 76).
[37] One of the Rhodian delegates may have been Timarchus, honoured by the Aetolians sometime before 169 (*ILindos* 195).
[38] *REG* 11 (1898) 258ff. Bibliography in Schmitt 1957, 97 n. 1: (E 77). The city had assumed the name Antioch before 250, but returned c. 190 to its old name: Robert 1973, 453–66: (B 68).
[39] Robert 1954, 303–12 no. 167: (E 163).
[40] *IMilet* 150, 35; for the date see *Arch. Anz.* 1977, 95; Robert 1978, 509–10: (B 69).

Senate, whose polite reply encouraged such high hopes in Lycia that the Confederacy voted to establish a cult of 'Rome the Goddess Manifest'. Soon, however, they learned that the Rhodian claim had been upheld;[41] nothing was left for the Lycians except recourse to arms. They fought for many years against the Rhodians. Finally, in 177, when Rhodes seemed to be prevailing, a Lycian delegate obtained a decree from the Senate that the Lycians had not been given to Rhodes as a gift, but as friends and allies. Encouraged by this decree, the Lycians at once resumed hostilities and the war continued until, in the end, Rhodes and Rome fell out and the Lycians won.

From the beginning Rhodian relations with King Eumenes were delicate. On the one hand, the republic and the king had been rivals for the spoils of the victory over Antiochus; on the other, both were bound together by their common interest in the stability of the new order in Asia Minor. It was for this reason that Eumenes supported the Rhodians in 181 against the rebellious Lycians. Soon, however, after the Rhodians had forced the king to abandon his attempt to blockade the Hellespont during his war with Pharnaces (p. 329), relations became hostile. The king thereafter lent clandestine support to the Lycians and denounced Rhodian policy before the Senate, while Rhodes refused to admit his envoys to an international festival[42] and two Rhodians, who were asked by the Achaean League to investigate whether honours granted earlier to Eumenes by the Achaeans had been legal, exceeded their instructions and convinced the Achaeans to cancel them all, thereby creating new disputes.[43]

The two sides, however, had more to worry about than their mutual quarrels once the war between Rome and King Perseus began. Both rallied to the Romans. The Rhodians, in fact, had no choice. They had no complaints against Perseus and had nothing to gain from war; on the other hand, they could not afford to disappoint the expectations of the Senate. For this reason they turned down the Macedonian ambassadors who had come to ask Rhodes to mediate. They also obeyed the Roman demands for military aid, slight as these seem to have been. They were active against Perseus: once a Rhodian fleet captured a Macedonian envoy on his way to King Antiochus IV, then campaigning in Egypt. But the longer the war dragged on, the more the Rhodians felt its adverse effects on their economy. Once they had to ask the Senate's permission to

[41] Polyb. XXII.5.3–6; cult of Roma: *JHS* 68 (1948) 46ff.; bibliography in Mellor 1975, 37 n. 56: (I 25), and Robert 1978, 288 n. 57: (B 70); Sherwin-White 1984, 49–50: (A 34).
[42] Polyb. XXVII.7.5–7; Livy XLII.14.8; App. *Mac.* 11.2–3. Commerce between the former allies suddenly all but ended in the 170s: Schmitt 1957, 135: (E 77).
[43] Polyb. XXVII.18.3, XXVIII.7.3–15, with Holleaux 1938–68, I.441–3: (D 35). As Livy XLII.17.7 shows, these honours had been cancelled before 172.

import grain from Sicily. And the situation grew even worse when Egypt and Syria also went to war. The interests of Rhodes demanded that peace be established on both fronts, and the earlier the better. In 169 Rhodian ambassadors went to Alexandria to mediate between the two kings, but mediation of the Macedonian war was a much more delicate question. The consul of 169, Marcius Philippus, who was then campaigning without much success against Perseus, seems to have suggested such an initiative to a Rhodian ambassador in a private conversation.[44] When the Rhodians decided to attempt mediation in 168, they obviously thought that the recent alliance between Perseus and the Illyrian king Gentius would have inclined the Senate towards peace. Just the opposite happened. The Senate was more determined than ever to dispose of the Macedonian kingdom. The Rhodians failed to understand what the election of Aemilius Paullus to a second consulship and his appointment as general in Macedonia had meant. When their envoys arrived at Paullus' headquarters at Pydna, they were given a frosty reception. Only a few days later the consul destroyed the royal army on the battlefield. Other envoys from Rhodes, who had been sent to Rome and had been kept waiting there, were introduced to the Senate-house only after the news of the victory had arrived. They had come to mediate a war the Romans had won. Now they could only offer their congratulations. The Senate chose to interpret their mission as motivated entirely by the interests of Perseus and, for that reason, as a hostile act towards Rome. The ambassadors were told that with this action the friendship between Rome and Rhodes had come to an end.

The intimidated Rhodians at once sentenced to death the politicians responsible for the attempt at mediation and made every effort to conciliate the Romans. It was in vain. In 167, the Senate formally decreed that Caria and Lycia, given to Rhodes in 188, were to be free. Moreover, the Carian towns Caunus and Stratoniceia, which had been Rhodian long before 188 and which had revolted after Pydna and been subdued, also were granted their freedom by the Senate. These two cities alone had brought the Rhodians an annual income of 120 talents and their loss was a severe blow to the Rhodian economy. Still worse, however, was the Romans' gift of the island of Delos to Athens on condition that Delos be a free port. Traffic shifted from Rhodes to Delos, and Rhodes lost some 140 talents in annual harbour dues. The republic also lost its hegemony over the League of Islanders, and for a while there was even talk of a Roman war against Rhodes, promoted by an ambitious praetor, but

---

[44] Polyb. XXVIII.17; App. *Mac.* 17. It remains disputed whether Philippus meant mediation in the Syrian war, as Gruen 1975, 71–4: (E 76) or in the Macedonian war, as Walbank 1957–79, III.350–1: (B 38). The latter view seems correct.

finally prevented (if the threat was, in fact, intended to be taken seriously) by a famous speech of Cato.[45]

With the Rhodians ousted from Asia Minor[46] and from their hegemony over the islands, with their economy profoundly shaken and their pride shattered, the Senate had fulfilled its purpose 'to make an example of Rhodes'.[47] Eventually, in 164, it paid heed to what the Rhodians had been requesting over the last few years and granted them a treaty. Friendship was restored, but not, as before, on the basis of equal partnership.

II. THE SELEUCID MONARCHY, 187–162 B.C.

(a) Seleucus IV

Within the short span of only seven years Roman armies had defeated the Hellenistic world's two most powerful kings, Philip V and Antiochus III. While defeat was followed in both cases by a substantial loss of territory and other severe conditions, Rome had made no effort to replace either monarch on the throne or to destroy the monarchy. The fate of the two rulers, however, was different. Philip lived on for eighteen years and was able to recoup his strength, whereas Antiochus lost his life in an attempt to raise money from a native temple in Elymais only a year after the settlement with Rome. His eldest son, Antiochus, had died six years earlier. The second, Seleucus, had been co-ruler since 189 and was now about thirty years old. He succeeded his father as Seleucus IV. Our sources are unanimous in depicting him as inactive and weak. Only one piece of personal evidence survives from his twelve-year reign, a letter written in May 186 to the city of Seleuceia in northern Syria to request a grant of citizenship for a courtier who had served his father and himself well.[48]

Seleucus was able through diplomacy to regain lost ground. At the very beginning of his reign he won a reconciliation with two former enemies in Greece, Achaea and Athens. Political and personal reasons alike caused him to make an effort in Achaea, since in 190 one thousand Achaeans had come to the aid of King Eumenes and had fought brilliantly against Seleucus when he was besieging Pergamum. Late in

[45] Schmitt 1957, 151ff.: (E 77); Gruen 1975, 77ff.: (E 76); for Cato's role: Astin 1978, 137ff., 273ff.: (H 68). Rhodian campaigns in Asia Minor between 168 and 164: Polyb. xxx.5.11–16, 21.2–5, 23.2, 31.4–8; *ILindos* 200–2.
[46] The Lycian Confederacy expressed its gratitude by a dedication to Jupiter Capitolinus and the Roman people: *CIL* I².725; Mellor 1978, 321 n. 14: (B 54). The Carian city of Amyzon began a new era (of liberty) in 167: Robert 1954, 309: (E 163); while another, Antioch-on-Maeander, praised the Romans as the 'common benefactors of the Greeks' and instituted a cult of Roma: Habicht 1957, 242 no. 65: (B 51).   [47] Polyb. xxix.19.5.
[48] Seleucus: Stähelin, *PW*, 'Seleucus IV'. The letter: Welles, *RC* 45, with Holleaux 1933: (B 52).

the summer of 187, at the request of his envoys, the Achaean assembly renewed their former friendship, although they politely declined 'for the moment' the king's offer of a gift of ten warships.[49] Only a few months later, in April 186, the Athenians, who had supported Rome in the war, honoured a Seleucid ambassador. The voting of honours implies that normal relations had been re-established.[50]

Seleucus did not fight a single war and came close only once, in *c.* 182, when Eumenes was fighting against King Pharnaces of Pontus (p. 329) and Pharnaces offered 500 talents if Seleucus would help him. Seleucus had already moved his army so that he could intervene, when 'it occurred to him' that the treaty of Apamea forbade his crossing the Taurus Mountains.[51] His original intention shows that Seleucus had no desire to come to terms with the ruler of Pergamum, whose predecessors had been subordinate to the Seleucid kings and who had acquired most of what the Seleucids had recently lost.

Instead, the king sought out Eumenes' enemies. Perseus, the Macedonian king, was one and Rhodes was no longer Eumenes' friend (p. 336). Seleucus saw his chance. He offered his daughter Laodice to Perseus to be his queen and Perseus accepted. Since the treaty of Apamea prohibited Seleucid vessels from sailing west of Cilicia, Seleucus asked the Rhodians to escort the bride to Macedonia, to which they agreed and used the occasion to parade their naval strength. The wedding ceremony, in 177, was an international event. It seems to be reflected in a dedicatory inscription to the young queen from Delos and a hoard of one hundred magnificent mint-fresh silver coins bearing the portrait of Perseus, to be dated before 174, found in Mersin in Cilicia; the coins had obviously been given to one of the courtiers who accompanied the princess.[52] The Senate was extremely suspicious of the harmony shown by the three powers involved in this wedding and the one that was soon to follow between King Prusias II of Bithynia and Perseus' sister Apame.[53] The Rhodians later felt the *patres'* anger (p. 337).

Perhaps the most significant feature of Seleucus' reign is his avoidance of any closer contact with Rome. If this impression is not caused merely

[49] This number is the maximum allowed to the Seleucids by the treaty of Apamea, Polyb. XXI.43.13. For the date: Errington 1969, 257–63: (D 23); the conventional date, 185, is defended by Walbank 1957–79, III.9–10: (B 38).

[50] Pritchett and Meritt 1940, 117–18: (B 215); cf. Ferguson 1911, 283–6: (D 26).

[51] Polyb. fr. 96; Niese 1910, 75–6: (D 46); Diod. Sic. XXIX.24; Bevan 1902, 123–4: (E 4).

[52] Inscription: *IG* XI.1074; coin hoard: Seyrig 1973, 47–8: (B 219). The dedication in Delos for the king by a courtier in 178 may be connected with this event: *IDélos* 1450A43 (text) and 443B71 (date).

[53] Seibert 1967, 43–4: (I 32). An indication that Seleucus in 186 wanted the friendship of Macedon is the naming of his son Demetrius, whose mother may have been an Antigonid princess: Mørkholm 1966, 34: (E 33); Helliesen 1981: (E 22). The political significance of the royal weddings, generally acknowledged, seems to be underestimated by Giovannini 1969, 855: (D 28), and Gruen 1975, 66–7: (E 76).

by the deficiency of our sources, the fact is remarkable: by then an almost constant stream of yearly embassies from eastern courts was pouring into Rome; in this period at least seven are attested for Macedonia, at least five for Pergamum. The Seleucid ruler did send envoys to Rome: he had to deliver an instalment of the war indemnity every year and he must have had some contact with the Senate before the Romans accepted the prince Demetrius as a hostage in exchange for the king's brother Antiochus, but, except for these unavoidable and rather technical missions, there were apparently few, if any, of political importance. The king may well have realized that he had little to gain from closer connections with Rome and that he would be wiser to avoid her as best he could.

Seleucus may have been a quiet person, but there is no indication that he lacked authority within his own realm. As a result of the war against Rome, some client kings became more or less independent, as, for instance, Armenia (p. 329); in other cases it is impossible to determine the circumstances. Seleucus had also inherited a cash problem and he was careful with his expenditures. The scarcity of silver is reflected in the small quantity of coins minted during his reign and in other numismatic features.[54] He soon fell behind schedule in paying the indemnity to Rome. On the other hand, the resources of the kingdom were in no way exhausted, as his successor would soon prove. Perhaps he was not concerned with glory, but he did care, as his relations with Rome suggest, about his dignity and he may well have cared about his subjects' welfare; under his rule they enjoyed twelve years of uninterrupted peace.

A pious Jew, the author of II *Maccabees*, records that in Seleucus' time the holy city enjoyed peace and lawful government and the king himself paid for the liturgical needs of the holy temple. Paradoxically, it was this very temple which is somehow connected with Seleucus' downfall; the same author goes on to tell the story of the king's chancellor Heliodorus, who was sent to raise money from the temple. For one reason or another, which later Jewish legend has obscured, the mission failed. Whether Heliodorus had been bribed or not, it was this failure rather than a plot with the Ptolemaic court, that prompted him, on 3 September 175, to have the king assassinated.[55] He proclaimed his victim's son Antiochus, then a boy of four or five, king and the dowager queen Laodice regent.

At the time of the murder the dead king's brother Antiochus happened to be in Athens, on his way back from Rome, where he had been a hostage but was replaced in 178 at the latest by his nephew Demetrius, a

---

[54] Seyrig 1958, 194–6: (B 132): Mørkholm 1966, 31–2: (E 33); Boehringer 1972, 96: (B 82).

[55] II *Macc.* 3.4–40; Bickerman 1939–44: (E 88). Habicht 1976, 209–14: (B 10). In 178 Heliodorus made dedications to Apollo at Delos: Durrbach 1921, 95–6: (B 50); and he received there at least three statues, one of them from Seleucus himself with strong words of the king's affection (*IG* XI.1112–14). Heliodorus is occasionally assumed to have been part of a conspiracy formed in Alexandria: Plöger 1955, 79: (E 107); Bunge 1974, 58 n. 4: (E 9).

son of Seleucus. He thought the boy Antiochus was unfit to rule, so he decided to take matters into his own hands. When he arrived in Asia Minor, he was met by Eumenes, solemnly crowned, and then escorted by Pergamene armed forces to the frontier of the Seleucid kingdom.[56] He soon overcame his opponents and was proclaimed King Antiochus IV. As a result of a deal he apparently concluded with the opposing party, he married his brother's widow, adopted her son Antiochus, and tolerated him as his co-ruler for several years.[57]

(b) The early years of Antiochus IV

The events that brought Antiochus to the throne moved so quickly that scholars have often assumed part or all of them, including the assassination of Seleucus, had been arranged by Rome and Eumenes, perhaps with Heliodorus the pawn.[58] No such explanation is required. On the other hand, the Senate may have welcomed an usurpation which would bring discord to the dynasty and would likely weaken the kingdom. The Conscript Fathers must also have realized that their hostage, the legitimate heir Prince Demetrius, was a weapon that could, if necessary, be used to discipline Antiochus. Swift as the seizure of royal power had been, it cannot have been completed, as the cuneiform king-list has it, 'the same month' Seleucus was murdered, that is, before 22 September 175. No doubt the new king antedated his accession to make his reign appear strictly consecutive with his brother's and therefore legitimate.

Antiochus was in his late thirties when he seized power. He had a stronger personality than his brother; our sources agree that he was high-spirited, capable, energetic and self-confident; he was also ambitious. He assumed divine epithets, which no other Hellenistic king had done, such as 'God Manifest' (*Theos Epiphanes*) and, after his defeat of Egypt, 'The Victorious' (*Nikephoros*).[59] The sources, in particular Polybius, also speak of often eccentric behaviour, capricious actions, and even insanity – Antiochus Epiphanes, they say, was nicknamed *Epimanes*, the 'madman'. Opinions differ on the value of these statements. They could easily be unfounded gossip, promulgated by the king's enemies, Deme-

---

[56] App. *Syr.* 45.233–4, confirmed and illustrated by the Athenian decree for Eumenes and his family (*OGIS* 248) who are praised for the assistance given to Antiochus. A copy sent to Eumenes was found in Pergamum. It was at first believed to be a decree of Antioch, the Seleucid capital, but recognized to be Athenian by Holleaux 1900: (E 46). See also n. 65.

[57] Mørkholm 1963, 63–76: (B 112), and 1966, 36, 41–58: (E 33), whose main conclusions have been generally accepted.

[58] Bouché-Leclercq 1913, 241: (E 8); Will 1982, 304–5: (A 40). Just scepticism in Errington 1971, 273: (D 24), and Hopp 1977, 35 n. 6: (E 60).

[59] Mørkholm 1963: (B 112): *Theos Epiphanes* from 173/2 on; *Theos Epiphanes Nikephoros* since 169/8. The use of *Theos* was restricted; it appears on royal coins, but is never used by the chancery of the king. A remarkable portrait of Antiochus: Kyrieleis 1980: (B 176).

trius (his nephew and a friend of Polybius) and King Ptolemy VIII Euergetes II (also a nephew, on his mother's side).[60] Antiochus' policy certainly displays no symptoms of capriciousness or insanity, quite the contrary: it is steady and prudent. Antiochus proved to the world that his kingdom was still a power to be reckoned with and that his army was second only to Rome's. He had a lasting impact on his subjects, favourable in most cases, disastrous for the Jews (p. 346).

First of all, Antiochus was more successful than Seleucus in breaking out of the political isolation that the war against Rome had caused. His accession transformed the traditional enmity towards the Attalids into a cordial relationship and wooed Cappadocia, which had been close to Eumenes for some time, to his side. Antiochus gained further ground through sumptuous gifts to many Greek states. Benefactions are attested for Athens, Rhodes, Miletus, Cyzicus, Megalopolis and Tegea, for the Boeotian and Achaean Leagues, and for the sanctuaries in Olympia and Delos.[61] The king paid off the last instalment of the indemnity due to Rome in 173; from that time onwards the Seleucids minted substantially more coinage than they had in the previous fifteen years.[62] The king had considerable resources.

His active diplomacy is reflected in the number of extant decrees voted by Greek states. One of Antiochus' agents, Eudemus of Seleuceia in Cilicia, was voted honours by at least seven different states – Argos, the Boeotian League, Rhodes, Byzantium, Cyzicus, Chalcedon and Lampsacus – and by some more than once. He received these honours between 174 and 171, the first years of the king's reign.[63] Many more such decrees, now lost, must have existed. King Perseus of Macedonia, too, though slightly earlier, had tried to win the goodwill of Greece, but with a smaller effort. Many states sent embassies to Antiochus. In 168/7 an embassy from Delphi came to the court and was assisted by two brothers in Antiochus' entourage, Dicaearchus and Philonides from Laodicea in Syria, of whom the latter was a well-known philosopher.[64]

[60] Tarn 1951, 183: (F 152); Kiechle 1963, 159: (E 28); Mørkholm 1966, 181–8: (E 33). For a different view: Welwei 1963, 62ff.: (B 44). Ptolemy VIII as a source: Ath. x.438D.

[61] Mørkholm 1966, 54–5: (E 33) (Cappadocia). For the Greek states, general statements in Polyb. XXVI.1.10–11 and Livy XLI.20.5–10. Details in Mørkholm 1966, 55–63: (E 33). The assumption that the king contributed to the building of the temple of Zeus at Lebadea in Boeotia has been refuted by Etienne and Knoepfler 1976, 342 n. 300: (D 25).

[62] Indemnity: Livy XLII.6.7; Mørkholm 1966, 65: (E 33). II Macc. 8.10 is therefore erroneous. Volume of coinage: Boehringer 1972, 86: (B 82).

[63] Heberdey and Wilhelm 1896, 108–17: (E 140) (SIG 644–5); for the document from Lampsacus, I.Lampsakos 6.

[64] OGIS 241 with Daux 1936, 511–13: (D 15). Since Dicaearchus and his sons are here appointed thearodoci, the entry of the two brothers in the list of Delphian thearodoci must be later (BCH 45 (1921) 24 col. IV, lines 78–80 and pp. 37, 41); G. J. Toomer, GRBS 13 (1972) 187 n. 45. For Philonides see n. 138; for a new inscription from Laodicea, dated 174: ISyrie 1261.

Athens, however, from the beginning was the city that had the closest ties with the king and profited most from his liberality. Antiochus had lived there for several years after his release from Rome and had come from there to win the crown. The Athenians rejoiced at his success and heaped praises on King Eumenes and his brothers for the aid they provided. Several statues of the Seleucid king stood in the agora; three Athenian decrees honouring high-ranking friends of his, and a fourth decree, voted by the noble clans of the Eumolpids and Ceryces, in honour of the elder Philonides of Laodicea, still survive. Two Athenian citizens dedicated statues of Antiochus in the sanctuary of Apollo at Delos.[65] The king's most lavish gift to the city was the work he commissioned, under the direction of his royal architect, the Roman D. Cossutius, to fulfil his promise to complete the magnificent temple of Olympian Zeus, left unfinished by the Pisistratids.[66] Construction was still underway when the king died in 164; the temple was not completed for another three hundred years.

(c) The war with Egypt

Antiochus' first major test was a war with Egypt, begun by Egypt to recover southern Syria and Palestine, which had been lost to Antiochus III in 200. This so-called 'Sixth Syrian War' had long been in the making. Ptolemy V Epiphanes would have renewed hostilities had he not been assassinated in 180. His widow Cleopatra – Antiochus' sister – acted as regent for her son, Ptolemy VI, and kept him from war, but when she died in 176 the new government, led by the king's guardians Eulaeus and Lenaeus, prepared for war. They justified it with the claim that the disputed lands had been promised to Egypt as Cleopatra's dowry when she married Ptolemy V in 194/3.[67] Their intentions were so poorly concealed that Antiochus was very early informed what to expect by a representative he had sent to the court of Alexandria. When the enemy

---

[65] Antiochus in Athens in the fall of 178 B.C.: *Hesperia* 51 (1982) 60 no. 3. Athenian decree for Eumenes: *OGIS* 248 (the statues of Antiochus in lines 55–6). *IG* II².982 for the Milesian Menestheus; for his family: Habicht 1976, 214: (B 10). Robert 1969: (B 67) for Menodorus. Moretti, *ISE* 34 for Arridaeus. *IG* II².1236 (Eumolpids and Ceryces) with the restorations of Robert 1960, 109 n. 3: (B 64). *IDélos* 1540–1 (Athenians).

[66] Vitr. *De Arch. praef.* v.14.17; Polyb. XXVI.1.11; Livy XLI.20.8; Strabo IX, p. 396; Wycherley 1978, 155ff.: (B 207). Close to the Olympieum was found the Greek inscription of *D. Cossutius P. f. cives Romanus*, probably the architect (*IG* II².4099). The Latin graffito of *Cossutius*, from Antioch (*ISyrie* 825), probably refers to a later member of this family which was one of the Republic's most active in marble trade and marble work; cf. Rawson 1975: (H 211), who, however, is inclined to accept identification with the architect.

[67] Diod. Sic. XXIX.29; Porph. *FGrH* 260F 48; Shore and Smith 1959, 55: (B 220) (death of Cleopatra). On Eulaeus and Lenaeus: Mørkholm 1961, 32–43: (E 154); Robert 1963, 71–6: (B 65).

finally attacked in the fall of 170 or the early part of 169 he was ready.[68] He counter-attacked and won a decisive victory near Pelusium.

The war was fought while the Romans were fighting Perseus; the participants, despite their diplomatic efforts in Rome and despite the attempts of several Greek states to mediate, were left to themselves. Antiochus won control of almost all of Egypt except for the capital. He could have had himself proclaimed king and pharaoh and many scholars believed that this is what he did, but the view prevailing now is that he rather tried to establish a protectorate of sorts in the name of Ptolemy VI Philometor, his nephew, with himself as guardian.[69] Antiochus had a pretext for this in 169 when the young king was in his hands, but the new government in Alexandria under Comanus and Cineas had the other two children of Ptolemy V, Ptolemy VIII Euergetes II and Cleopatra, proclaimed king and queen. Philometor, when he was left behind in Antiochus' withdrawal, joined them in Alexandria. Antiochus returned with his army in 168 and laid siege to the capital. Under the circumstances he could no longer claim that he was acting as Philometor's protector, but his ultimate plans are unknown, because suddenly the war became a mere episode. On 22 June 168 the Romans defeated Perseus. Immediately afterwards the Roman ambassador, C. Popillius Laenas, appeared before Antiochus in a suburb of Alexandria and delivered an ultimatum to the king to withdraw all his forces from Egypt and Cyprus, which he had just occupied. Antiochus complied immediately and avoided war with Rome. His compliance, painful as it must have been, shows wisdom and restraint and effectively disproves the allegations that he was unbalanced.

Since the king was under no obligation to respect the integrity of Egypt, it has rightly been said that the Roman demand in 168 added 'a new clause' to the treaty of 188.[70] Popillius' treatment of Antiochus, an acknowledged 'friend of the Roman people' and a king of flawless loyalty to Rome, is much the same as the Senate then chose to administer to its two main allies, Eumenes and Rhodes (pp. 332, 337). Not only was it

[68] II *Macc.* 4.21. Habicht 1976, 219: (B 10) (preparations in Egypt). On the eve of the war, Antiochus, whose son (the future Antiochus V) had been born a few years earlier, had his nephew and co-ruler killed (August 170) through his minister Andronicus, who in turn was executed a little later; Habicht *op. cit.* 222. Outbreak of the war: for the earlier date Skeat 1961: (B 222), followed by Mørkholm 1966, 69 n. 21: (E 33). There are difficulties; early spring 169 may be correct: Walbank 1957–79, III.321ff.: (B 38). On the course of the war: Otto 1934, 1–66: (E 156); Bickerman 1952: (E 7); Volkmann *PW*, 'Ptolemaios', 1705–10; Walbank *op. cit.* 321ff., 352ff., 402ff.; Will 1982, 313–20: (A 40).

[69] For the former view: Otto 1934, 51ff.: (E 156), followed with modifications by Pédech 1964, 151: (B 26); Fraser 1972, II.211–12: (E 137). For the latter view: Bickerman 1952, 402: (E 7); Aymard 1952, 85ff.: (D 3); Mørkholm 1966, 80ff.: (E 33); Walbank 1957–79, III.358: (B 38); Mooren 1979, 78ff.: (E 31). See also Will 1982, 319: (A 40).

[70] The sources are collected and discussed in Walbank 1957–79, III.401–4: (B 38). Antiochus' restraint: Tarn 1951, 192: (F 152). The 'new clause': Will 1982, 322: (A 40).

extremely harsh, not only did it lack the tact previously observed by the Senate in foreign relations, but none of the three powers had done anything to deserve it. The Senate simply no longer bothered to conceal the fact that Rome now had the power to dictate her will. The Roman aristocracy, it is true, seldom favoured annexation, but their attitude, often regarded as self-restriction, that is to say, a virtue,[71] included a moral deficiency: unwillingness to assume the responsibility for the conditions they had created.[72] Roman policy at this time was imperialistic; it did not allow for meaningful negotiations, for mutual acknowledgement of legitimate political goals, for compromise; there were demands on one side and obedience on the other.[73]

It has been argued that the ultimatum presented by Popillius broke Antiochus' spirit and that his subsequent actions became erratic. The known facts, however, do not sustain this theory and it has rightly been rejected by subsequent historians.[74] Antiochus accepted what was unavoidable and turned his energies to the eastern frontier of his kingdom, where Roman interference was less likely than in the Mediterranean. Whether this had been his intention before he was drawn into the struggle with Egypt cannot be known. In 166, before he set out, he organized a magnificent spectacle, a festival in Daphne, the charming suburb of the capital, Antioch, in honour of Apollo, whose temple there was renowned. In addition to the solemn procession and usual agonistic features, which attracted large numbers of athletes and artists from far away, there was a splendid military parade, similar in some ways to a Roman triumph. Only a year before Aemilius Paullus, the victor of Pydna, had held comparable festivities in Amphipolis; Antiochus' festival was obviously, at least in part, an answer to the Roman celebration, perhaps an attempt to outdo it. The parade of the victorious army from Egypt was both a demonstration of strength and an opportunity for Antiochus to review the forces he would use in his eastern campaign.[75]

[71] This, at least, is the impression created by Badian 1968: (A 5); more strongly Werner 1972, 557: (A 39): 'Selbstbändigung und freiwillige Beschränkung seiner tatsächlichen Herrschaftsmöglichkeiten.'

[72] Bleicken 1964, 183: (I 2): 'Antinomie von tatsächlicher Herrschaft und Mangel an Willen zum Regieren.' 'Aber der ganze Jammer des Ostens war, dass die Römer diese Sehnsucht nach Übernahme moralischer Herrscherpflichten nicht erfüllten.'

[73] On Roman imperialism: Badian 1968: (A 5); Werner 1972: (A 39); Veyne 1975: (A 38); Musti 1978: (B 22); Harris 1979: (A 21); Richardson 1979: (A 30); Sherwin-White 1980: (A 33); North 1981: (A 28); Gruen 1984: (A 20).

[74] The theory is Otto's (1934, 8off.: (E 156)), followed by Bengtson 1977, 493: (A 9), but duly criticized by Pédech 1964, 152 n. 278: (B 26); Mørkholm 1966, 96: (E 33); Briscoe 1969, 51: (D 9). Cf. Will 1982, 345: (A 40).

[75] Polyb. xxx.25–6. Diod. Sic. xxxi.16.2. See Mørkholm 1966, 97–100: (E 33), and Walbank 1957–79, III.448–54: (B 38). The far-reaching theory of Tarn 1951, 192–5: (F 152), that what Antiochus celebrated was in fact the victory of Eucratidas (according to Tarn, his cousin as well as his general) over Demetrius of Bactria, has been refuted by Altheim 1947–8, II.20ff.: (E 122), and Narain 1957, 53ff.: (F 103). Different, but equally hazardous, speculations in Bunge 1976: (E 11).

This was just the sort of event to make the Senate again suspicious of Antiochus. Two Roman embassies, the first in 166, the second in 164, were sent to explore his state of mind and his intentions. The Romans, it seems, realized the danger that could arise from co-operation between Antiochus and Eumenes, both victims of the Senate's change in foreign policy, and they were afraid that such a union might attract other powers, such as Ariarathes of Cappadocia. The first embassy, however, led by Ti. Sempronius Gracchus (the father of the famous tribunes), was disarmed by the king's charm and satisfied by his assurances; the second embassy arrived in Syria about the time the king met his fate in Iran.[76]

It is not for this chapter to describe Antiochus' administration or evaluate his foundation of cities, but one part of his internal policy must be discussed: the conflict with his Jewish subjects.

(d) Antiochus and the Jews[77]

The Jews came to regard Antiochus as the archetypal oppressor, 'the wicked root', so wicked that Christians would call him the Antichrist.[78] Their condemnation derived from his desecration of the holy temple and his persecution of Jews for their religion; the condemnation implies that the king bears all the responsibility for these acts and that he alone is to blame for them. The Jewish version has prevailed for centuries; the true story, however, is different, much more complex and the result of special circumstances. The king, certainly, had he understood the Jews, could have avoided the conflict, but nevertheless was not the one who provoked it. The Jewish side took the initiative in the events leading to persecution and martyrdom and consequently must share the responsibility.

---

[76] Sources in *MRR* I. 438 and 439–40 (where, however, the first embassy is erroneously dated to 165); Walbank 1957–79, III.33; 454: (B 38). On Cappadocia: Mørkholm 1966, 100–1: (E 33). For Gracchus: Gelzer 1962–4, III.166–7: (A 19); for the chronology of the second embassy see II *Macc.* 11.34–8.

[77] The principal sources: I *Macc.* (from which Jos. *AJ* XII.137–361 is almost exclusively derived), a Greek translation of an Aramaic original, first century B.C.; II *Macc.*, in original Greek, composed of (i) the account of Judas' deeds, written by Jason of Cyrene in five books shortly before 152; (ii) an abridgement of this with the addition of 1.1–10a, 2.19–32 and 15.37–9, published in 124 B.C.; (iii) a revision of this, adding 1.10b–2.18 and changing the order of events here and there, to be dated before A.D. 70. Habicht 1976, 169–77: (B 10). The book of Daniel (esp. ch. 11) repeatedly alludes to the events; its author witnessed the profanation of the temple in December 168, but did not live to see the temple rededicated in December 165; he also witnessed the persecution of 167, but not its end early in 163 nor Antiochus' death late in 164. The book, therefore, was published *c.* 165. Bickerman 1937, 143–4: (E 86). A couple of documents, besides those inserted in *Maccabees*, are preserved in Jos. *AJ* XII.258–264, discussed by Bickerman 1937, 188ff.: (E 87). Recent studies: Schürer 1973, 125ff.: (E 112); Habicht 1974: (E 100) and 1976: (B 10 and E 101); Vidal-Naquet 1978: (E 118); Bringmann 1980 and 1983: (E 91 and 92) (all with copious bibliography).

[78] I *Macc.* 1.10. Cyprian, *ad Fortunatum* XI.115: *immo in Antiocho antichristus expressus.*

Since their return from exile centuries before, under the Achaemenids, Ptolemies and, from the year 200, Seleucids, Jews had been free to live in accordance with their own law and religion. When Antiochus III conquered Palestine, he solemnly granted them the right to their own way of life;[79] the Jewish subjects of his successor, Seleucus IV, appreciated the peace and prosperity they enjoyed (p. 340). Antiochus IV changed this idyllic picture when he revoked the privileges and prohibited the practice of the Jewish religion. What caused such a dramatic change?

Earlier scholarship explained it as Antiochus' alleged desire to strengthen hellenism throughout the kingdom at the expense of traditional native cultures and customs. His motive was said to have been the conviction that hellenism meant unification and that unification would give the monarchy greater strength.[80] The primary basis for this theory was I *Macc.* 1.41–3:

> Moreover King Antiochus wrote to his whole kingdom, that all should be one people, and everyone should leave his laws: so all the heathen agreed according to the commandment of the king. Yea, many also of the Israelites consented to his religion, and sacrificed unto idols, and profaned the sabbath (tr. the King James Version).

More recent research has refuted this view. Such a policy, even if it had not been unworkable, was simply alien to the way of thinking and acting of Hellenistic kings and especially to the traditions of the Seleucids, who (like the Achaemenids before them) had to deal with a great number of native cultures, for which they had always shown the greatest respect. Moreover, the theory that such a policy existed is not compatible with the sources. The statement from I *Maccabees* quoted above is not just 'a manifest exaggeration',[81] it is false in general and specifically for Judaea, since the king was not the one who initiated the plan to hellenize the Jews, but Jews themselves had put this demand before him. When Antiochus granted their demand, he was unaware of what the consequences of his concession could be.

The Jews themselves took the initiative to adapt their nation to a Greek way of life. This fact is unequivocally attested in both I and II *Maccabees* and their testimony deserves credence, since both are hostile to Antiochus.[82] The story, in short, is this. In 174 Jason, the brother of the

---

[79] See the documents issued by him, Jos. *AJ* XII.138–144 and 145–146, both discussed by Bickerman, the former in 1935: (E 85), the latter in 1946–8: (E 89).

[80] This has long been the dominant theory, held by historians such as Bevan, Wilcken, Meyer, more recently Otto 1934, 85: (E 156); Tarn 1951, 186: (F 152); Kiechle 1963, 167–8: (E 28). For a fair evaluation and decisive criticism see Tcherikover 1961, 175–86: (E 115); Bringmann 1983, 99ff.: (E 92).

[81] So Mørkholm 1966, 132 n. 53: (E 33); similarly Tcherikover 1961, 183–4: (E 115); Hengel 1973, 516ff.: (E 102).   [82] II *Macc.* 4.4–15, with which I *Macc.* 1.11–15 agrees in all essential points.

conservative high-priest Onias, appeared before the king. Jason was the spokesman for those Jews who had been advocating hellenization. He offered Antiochus a substantial sum of money if the king would appoint him to his brother's place, and he promised more if Antiochus would permit him to transform Jerusalem into a Greek city, name it Antioch, build a gymnasium, and institute a corps of youths as Greeks did, an ephebate. The king granted all his requests and put Jason in charge of the enrolment of citizens for the city of Antioch.[83] The new high-priest swiftly carried out his plans; his 'hellenistic reform' was met by enthusiasm as well as resentment among the Jews.

Nothing indicates that it was Jason's intention to change the Jewish faith, but his opponents felt that his reforms affected Jewish religion as well as their traditional way of life. The policy of segregation from the outer world had, for centuries, facilitated (or rather made possible) the preservation of that religion. To open up the gates to Hellenistic manners was therefore considered a danger, perhaps even a mortal danger, to the ancestral faith. In addition, there were other reasons for divisiveness, the struggle for power between the different factions, the inclination of some families towards the Ptolemies, of others towards the ruling royal house,[84] and the contrasts between rich and poor, city and country, priests and laymen. The men selected by Jason to be citizens of Antioch on the soil of Jerusalem would become a new privileged class within the nation.

Tension was already running high when, after a few years, Jason was outmanoeuvred by a certain Menelaus, who offered the king a higher bid for Jason's post and secured it. As a consequence more radical reformers seized power. Menelaus' followers and their opponents clashed, and the king had to intervene. The climax came when a rumour spread that Antiochus, then campaigning in Egypt, had been killed in battle. Jason seized his opportunity and invaded the country with an army recruited from Nabataean Arabs, amongst whom he had lived while in exile. He forced an entry into Jerusalem and tried to regain control of the city, but finally, after heavy fighting, he was expelled.[85]

Antiochus was returning from Egypt when he heard of these events. He thought there was a rebellion and the Jews were using his preoccupa-

[83] For the interpretation of II *Macc.* 4.9 and 19 see Bickerman 1937, 59–65: (E 86), and, with different conclusions, Tcherikover 1961, 161–9, 404–9: (E 115), followed by most scholars since; Habicht 1976, 216–17: (B 10); Bringmann 1983, 83–4: (E 92).

[84] The only factions in the sources are the Tobiads and the Oniads; bibliography in Habicht 1976, 211: (B 10). There must have been others. The Tobiad Hyrcanus, who feuded with his older brothers and took his life after the accession of Antiochus IV, may have supported the house of Seleucus IV or the Ptolemies.

[85] II *Macc.* 4.23–9, 43–50. Menelaus also had Jason's predecessor Onias killed through the same royal minister who was held responsible for the murder of Antiochus' nephew and co-ruler in 170 (n. 68). The battle in Jerusalem: II *Macc.* 5.5–7.

tion with a major war to stab him in the back.[86] He attempted to suppress
the insurrection with punitive measures. He removed part of the treasure
of the temple, garrisoned Jerusalem and Mount Gerizim, the religious
centre of the Samaritans, and, shortly thereafter, by royal decree in the
autumn of 168, prohibited the practice of the Jewish religion and
demanded the worship of pagan gods. The temple was transformed into
a sanctuary of Zeus.[87] The great majority of Jews, it seems, obeyed the
king's orders. Some who did not suffered death, among them several
who refused even to simulate compliance, when the opportunity was
offered by the authorities. There were martyrdoms, but the surviving
stories, however edifying and famous, are legendary.[88]

Open resistance to the oppression came from two sides, from the
group of the 'Pious' (*Hassidim*), and from people living in the countryside. The Hassidim, apparently influenced by intellectuals, were so pious
that they even refrained, in the beginning, from defending themselves on
a Sabbath. The resistance from the countryside was more pragmatic. The
men around Mattathias and his sons from Modein realized that, if the
Jewish faith was to have a chance to survive, religious scruples had to be
subordinated to the needs of the day. Led by Mattathias' son Judas
Maccabaeus, they began a guerrilla war. Progress was slow but steady.[89]
The Jewish rebels defeated royal troops in more than one skirmish, and
late in 165 even recaptured Jerusalem and the area of the temple. The
king's garrison kept control of the citadel only, where the high-priest
Menelaus and all the Jews who were loyal to him and to the king took
refuge.

The royal government had taken the insurrection lightly in the
beginning, but now felt the need to change its policy. The king realized
that the persecution of Judaism, a measure he took against the supposed
insurrection, had in fact caused insurrection. Consequently, he took the
first step and withdrew the oppressive order. In a letter directed to
Menelaus he declared an amnesty for all Jews who put down their arms
before an appointed day. He also reaffirmed the principle that Jews
should be free to live in accordance with their own law.[90] The formula
included freedom of religion. It is clear that the king hoped to end
hostilities by this act. Judas and his followers, however, continued the

[86] II *Macc.* 5.11.
[87] I *Macc.* 1.20ff.; II *Macc.* 5.11ff. Bringmann 1980 and 1983: (E 91 and 92) argues that Menelaus
suggested these measures to the king, for purely political reasons.
[88] II *Macc.* 6.18–31, 7.1–42. For the late origin of ch. 7: Habicht 1976, 171: (B 10); for the
martyrdom of Eleazar (ch. 6) *ibid.* 173.
[89] Sabbath: I *Macc.* 2.32–8, 41; II *Macc.* 6.11. The story of Mattathias (I *Macc.* 2) is suppressed in II
Macc., which is cool towards the Maccabean or Hasmonean family. Etymology and meaning of
Judas' surname remain disputed: Schürer 1973, 158 n. 49: (E 112).
[90] The king's letter is preserved in II *Macc.* 11.27–32, discussed in Habicht 1976, 7–18: (E 101), and
Bringmann 1983, 40ff.: (E 92).

war, because the king still backed the hated Menelaus. A large army, led by the chancellor Lysias, marched towards Jerusalem in the summer of 164 to crush the rebellion. Judas soon had to negotiate and to accept most of Lysias' conditions. A few details were left to the discretion of the king, but Antiochus died at this very moment and the decision passed to his son, Antiochus, who succeeded him at the end of 164; the new king, however, was only nine years old, so the decision was actually made by Lysias, his guardian. This time, at the beginning of 163, the government unconditionally and solemnly granted the Jews religious freedom and the right to live as their ancestors had.[91] The relationship between the crown and the nation that had existed from 200 to 168 was restored. In order to show how serious its intentions were, the new government sacrificed Menelaus. He was executed and replaced by Alcimus, who was expected to be acceptable to orthodox Jews and, in fact, the Hassidim did make their peace with him and with the king. The war for the God of Israel was over.

(e) Antiochus in the east[92]

In the spring of 165 King Antiochus began the campaign in the east from which he was not to return. Before leaving he appointed his son Antiochus co-ruler and the chancellor Lysias guardian of the boy. Sources for the campaign are extremely meagre and modern theories on the causes and aims of the expedition are therefore contradictory. There is, however, agreement on one essential fact: some of the eastern satrapies needed to be reinforced, some that had been lost needed to be recovered. Forty years before, the king's father, Antiochus III, had made a strong and successful effort to consolidate his authority throughout his eastern dominions. His defeat at the hands of the Romans, however, had undercut his power and shaken his prestige; it undoubtedly caused repercussions in the east and encouraged those who wished to throw off Seleucid rule.

That this is what actually happened can be at least partially corroborated from the scanty evidence. Iranian troops, numerous in the royal army at Raphia in 217 and at Magnesia in 190, are absent at Daphne in 166. The satraps of Greater and Lesser Armenia, Artaxias and Zariadres, who had been appointed by Antiochus III, both assumed the title king

---

[91] The document, II *Macc.* 11.22–6, refers to the death of the king as a very recent event.

[92] Sources: Polyb. XXI.9; Diod. Sic. XXXI.17a; App. *Syr.* 46.236, 66.349 and 352; Tac. *Hist.* V.8.4–5; Porphyr. *FGrH* 260F 38, 53, 56; I *Macc.* 6.1–16; II *Macc.* 1.10–16, 9; Jos. *AJ* XII.354–361. Modern works: Meyer 1921, 216–23: (I 26); Altheim 1947–8, II.35–50: (E 122); Tarn 1951, 213ff.: (F 152); Narain 1957, 53ff.: (F 103); LeRider 1965, 311–21: (E 149); Mørkholm 1966, 166–80: (E 33); Will 1982, 348–55: (A 40).

after 188 and henceforward acted as independent rulers.[93] The case of Bactria is similar. King Euthydemus I had been forced to bow before Antiochus III, who had then reinstated him. After 190, however, there is no sign that any Bactrian ruler was a dependent of the Seleucid king. Bactria and the adjacent satrapies, Sogdiana, Aria and Margiane, were definitely lost to the Seleucids. The new realm was also safe from any immediate Seleucid attack, since the Parthians had occupied land between the two.[94] Farther to the south, in Persia, the homeland of the Achaemenids, a local dynasty of priests and princes had risen to power. By the first years of the reign of Antiochus IV at the latest, these so-called *fratadara* had won their independence from royal authority and the control of at least part of Persis around Persepolis and Istakhr.[95] More to the west, in the land of the Elamites, Antiochus the Great had encountered stiff resistance, which led him to his death in 187; his misfortune caused (or strengthened) the drive for independence in Elymais.[96]

Antiochus' expedition has to be viewed against the background of a disintegrating empire. What his ultimate goals were is hard to say and a matter of controversy. Tarn's opinion that the king intended to restore Alexander's empire by recovering Parthia, Bactria and India has been refuted by subsequent scholars as excessive and utopian.[97] Closer to the truth seems to be the view that he wanted to protect western Iran, endangered by the Parthians and by local uprisings, and to recover lost territory where he could,[98] but a definite answer, if at all possible, can only come from an assessment of the king's actions before his premature death.

First, he invaded Greater Armenia and defeated Artaxias, who was left on the throne as a vassal king.[99] Several passages of the elder Pliny, though difficult to interpret, seem to show that Antiochus also campaigned in the area of the Persian Gulf, where he refounded a colony of

---

[93] Strabo XI. pp. 528, 531; Polyb. XXV.2.12, XXXI.16; Diod. Sic. XXXI.17a, 27a; Plut. *Luc.* 31.3–4. It may be more than coincidence that the name of Artaxias' father was Zariadres (Zariatr), as revealed by two Aramaic inscriptions: Dupont-Sommer 1946–8: (B 49). Artaxias naming his capital Artaxata shows his self-esteem. Some recently found Greek inscriptions show that Hellenistic influence in Armenia was already considerable around 200: Habicht 1953: (E 139); Trever 1953, 113–46: (E 172) (which I have not seen).

[94] For Bactria in this period see, besides the major works of Tarn 1951: (F 152) and Narain 1957: (F 103); Simonetta 1958, 154ff.: (F 144); Will 1982, 350–2: (A 40). For the Parthian kingdom: Debevoise 1938: (E 132); Junge, *PW* 'Parthia'; for the sequence and genealogy of the earlier kings: Wolski 1962: (E 178). See further LeRider 1965, 311ff.: (E 149).

[95] Stiehl 1959: (E 170); Schmitt 1964, 46–50: (E 50).

[96] Stiehl 1956, 13ff., and 1959, 375, 379: (E 114 and 170); LeRider 1965, 349ff.: (E 149); Will 1982, 355: (A 40).   [97] See n. 75.

[98] So Stiehl 1959, 375ff.: (E 170), and Mørkholm 1966, 166ff.: (B 33), both emphasize the attempt to strengthen royal authority in Elymais and Persis. More generally: Will 1982, 352: (A 40), 'réaffirmer la présence séleucide' (in Iran).

[99] The fate of Zariadres was probably similar; Meyer 1921, 217: (I 26).

Alexander under the name Antioch on the site of the later Spasinu Charax. The victories of Numenius over the Persians, recorded by the same writer, may well belong to the same or another, perhaps simultaneous, expedition.[100] The king's presence, probably in 164, in Ecbatana in Media can be inferred from the renaming of the city 'Epiphania' in his honour; one source, in fact, does report that he marched from Persepolis to Ecbatana. It is also attested that he attempted to raise money from the temple of Nanaia in Elymais, but had to retreat before the opposition of the natives. Soon afterwards, the king fell ill and died in the autumn of 164 in Tabae in Paraetacene.[101]

The facts so far related show that Antiochus regained control of Armenia and that he attempted to regain lost territories in Persis and Elymais. The key question, however, is whether he planned to invade Parthia or not. Many historians have assumed that Parthia was his target; their assumption is based on the king's itinerary and a passage in Tacitus; others disagree.[102] His itinerary seems not to furnish any clues, at least as long as Tabae has not been located. The answer, therefore, must be sought in the following passage of Tacitus:

After the Macedonians gained supremacy, King Antiochus endeavoured to abolish Jewish superstition and to introduce Greek civilization; the war with the Parthians, however, prevented his improving this basest of all peoples; for it was exactly at that time that Arsaces had revolted. Later on, since the power of Macedon had waned, the Parthians were not yet come to their strength, and the Romans were far away, the Jews selected their own kings (*Hist.* v.8.4–5, tr. C. H. Moore).

Some scholars identify this Antiochus as Antiochus VII, who captured Jerusalem in 134 and lost his life during a campaign against the Parthians in 129; some, though they concede that the sentence about Jewish superstition and Greek civilization can fit only Antiochus IV, maintain that the allusion to a Parthian war fits only Antiochus VII; but the king in question, it is clear, is one and the same throughout, that is,

[100] Plin. *HN* VI.138–139, 147: Antioch, for the coinage of which see Mørkholm 1970: (B 114). Numenius: Plin. *HN* VI.152. Opinion is divided whether he served Antiochus III or Antiochus IV; several scholars are undecided: LeRider 1965, 303, 310: (E 149).

[101] Mørkholm 1966, 117, 171–2 n. 22: (E 33) (Epiphania). Ecbatana: II *Macc.* 9.2–3. The account is not too reliable, and ch. 9, in fact, invents a fictitious letter of the king: Habicht 1976, 3–7: (E 101); but the accuracy of the reported itinerary need not be doubted. Temple of Nanaia: Polyb. XXXI.9.1–2; Porph. *FGrH* 260 F 53. Different accounts of other writers are discussed by Holleaux 1916: (E 23). See also Mendels 1981: (E 30). Tabae has not been located, but cannot have been far from Gabae (modern Ispahan): Weissbach, *PW*, 'Tabai'; Treidler, *PW*, 'Paraitakene'.

[102] Most scholars agree that Parthia was his target. Mørkholm 1966, 176–7: (E 33), however, argues that Parthian aggression began only later (which is true for Media). Antiochus could have had other reasons than Parthian aggression for waging war (see below).

Antiochus IV.[103] The Tacitus passage derives ultimately from either Polybius or Poseidonius;[104] it attests to a war between Antiochus IV and the Parthians – Antiochus, therefore, may be assumed to have intended to invade Parthia.

In support of this view it has been pointed out that what is known about his campaign closely resembles the famous 'Anabasis' of his father, who had succeeded in regaining the Parthian king's formal recognition of his supremacy.[105] The Parthian king Mithridates I (Arsaces V), who succeeded his brother Phraates I (Arsaces IV) c. 171, was the first Parthian monarch to strike coins and the coins bore his own portrait,[106] which proves that he considered himself a sovereign ruler and therefore implies the cancellation of the treaty that his father had concluded with Antiochus III. This, then, may well be the 'revolt' of which Tacitus is speaking and which would have prompted Antiochus Epiphanes' reaction. Antiochus' ultimate goal, it seems, was the subjugation of the Parthians, but he died before hostilities began and his army was soon led home.

The king died in his prime. He could not accomplish what he intended and it is idle to speculate how he would have fared against the Parthians, had he lived longer. It is, however, worth noting that the Parthians, so far as is known, did not attack Seleucid territory (p. 363) for more than fifteen years to come, and it need not be doubted that – Parthia aside – the presence of the king and his army in the eastern satrapies encouraged those loyal to the dynasty. Antiochus, on the whole, was an able monarch, committed to his duties. His only serious mistake had been his misjudgement of the situation in Judaea, but as soon as he realized that his policy was a failure, he changed it. The Romans denied him a major success in the south; death prevented him from trying his strength in the east.

(f) Antiochus V

The king was succeeded by his son Antiochus V Eupator, who was under the tutelage of the chancellor Lysias. Epiphanes is said to have changed this arrangement shortly before he died by substituting a certain

[103] As argued by Kolbe 1935, 56–7: (E 103) (followed by Jacoby ad FGrH 260 F 55–7); Altheim 1947–8, II.36: (E 122); LeRider 1965, 312: (E 149); and Will 1982, 354: (A 40). Antiochus VII, on the other hand, was able to impose his conditions on the Jews, and several years before his Parthian campaign.

[104] Meyer 1921, 268 n. 3: (I 26). Jacoby, loc. cit. (n. 103). See also Jacoby's remarks on Poseidonius, FGrH 87 F 69 and 109.

[105] Altheim 1947–8, II.36ff.: (E 122). For Antiochus III see Holleaux 1930, 138–43: (D 34); Herzfeld 1932, 37–8: (B 171).   [106] LeRider 1965, 311–23: (E 149).

Philippus, who was with him in the east, for Lysias. Most scholars have accepted the story of this substitution, though some have doubted it; for good reasons, since the young Antiochus was in Lysias' hands. Philippus probably advanced the claim as a pretext for seizing power.[107] The news about Philippus reached Lysias when he seemed to be on the verge of wiping out the Jewish rebels. It forced him to compromise and the high-priest Menelaus was made the scapegoat (p. 350). Lysias then took the field against Philippus, defeated him, and had him executed.[108] King and guardian seemed safe.

Trouble, however, lay ahead for both of them, first from the still malignant Roman Senate, and second from the king's cousin Demetrius, who had been deprived of the throne by Antiochus' usurpation in 175. A Roman embassy had come to see Epiphanes (p. 346) when he was in the east. On the way to Antioch the ambassadors contacted the Maccabean party that was negotiating with Lysias in the autumn of 164, wrote them a short letter, and promised them their advice. Moreover, they 'agreed' to some concessions Lysias had already made,[109] which was tantamount to supporting rebellious subjects of a king who was an 'ally and friend' of Rome. Strange as their conduct was, it is not unique; that same year C. Sulpicius in Sardis invited accusations against King Eumenes, another 'ally and friend' of Rome.[110] About a year later another Roman embassy, headed by Cn. Octavius, arrived at Antioch to inspect matters under the new regime. When Octavius discovered that the king, in violation of the treaty of Apamea, possessed a fleet and elephants, he had the ships burnt and the animals hamstrung. The Romans must have known about these violations all along and they had not cared, so it is hard to say what caused the Senate to enforce the letter of the old treaty at this time. Anyway, these actions caused an uproar in the city of Laodicea and Octavius was murdered by a certain Leptines (early 162).[111]

The murder put Lysias in a difficult position with Rome; his relations

[107] I *Macc.* 6.14, 55; Jos. *AJ* XII.360. Accepted by Meyer 1921, 221: (I 26); Mørkholm 1966, 172: (E 33); Schürer 1973, 166: (E 112) and Will 1982, 353: (A 40). Disputed by Niese 1910, 218 n. 6: (D 46); Bevan 1930, 514: (E 83); Habicht 1976, 248–9: (B 10); and Gruen 1976, 79–80: (E 20): Antiochus IV 'would not likely give incentive for chaos after his death'.

[108] I *Macc.* 6.63; II *Macc.* 9.29; Jos. *AJ* XII.386. I *Macc.* is silent about Philippus' fate; the second says he escaped to Egypt; Josephus has him executed. Josephus is probably correct and the statement of II *Macc.* erroneous, owing to a confusion between Philippus and Onias, the son of the Jewish high-priest Onias III: Bouché-Leclerq 1913, 310 n. 2: (E 8); Habicht 1976, 249: (B 10).

[109] II *Macc.* 11.34–7; Habicht 1976, 7ff.: (E 101), where earlier opinions are cited, including those which dismiss the letter as a forgery; Paltiel 1982, 252: (E 37); Bringmann 1983, 47ff.: (E 92).

[110] Above p. 334. The present writer cannot agree with the attempt of Gruen 1976, 78: (E 20), and 1984, 581: (A 20), to belittle the importance of this and to deny, in general, that Roman policy at this time was often malignant.

[111] The career and embassy of Octavius: Münzer, *PW*, 'Octavius' 1810–14. See further the decree of Argos in his honour, *BCH* 81 (1957) 181–202, and, for the incident in question, *P. Herc.* 1044, col. 9 1ff., as discussed by I. Gallo, *Frammenti Biografici da Papiri* (Rome 1980) 115–17.

with the new king of Cappadocia, Ariarathes V, were tense because Lysias had executed Ariarathes' mother, a Seleucid princess, and sister. The chancellor did what he could to conciliate both Rome and Ariarathes. He sent an embassy to Rome to offer apologies and returned the bones of Antiochis and her daughter to Cappadocia, but he was unpopular in Syria[112] and his position remained shaky. As soon as a strong pretender appeared, Lysias and his protégé, the boy-king Antiochus, were helpless.

Late in 162 a pretender arrived. Demetrius, the son of Seleucus IV, had spent at least sixteen years as a hostage in Rome. It is significant that he had been kept in Rome long after the indemnity demanded by the treaty of 188 had been paid off (in 173, p. 342), and it is easy to speculate that the Senate had kept him partly in connivance with Antiochus, who had seized the throne that rightfully belonged to Demetrius, partly as a weapon that could be used against Antiochus, should he fail to satisfy the wishes of Rome.[113] After Antiochus' death Demetrius approached the Senate, argued that it was absurd to hold him hostage for Antiochus' children, and demanded his restoration to the throne of his father. The Senate refused, as Polybius states, because they assumed that it would be easier to deal with an under-aged king and his guardian than with a full-grown king. Cn. Octavius was sent out to enforce the treaty of 188. After his murder, Demetrius, now twenty-three years old, approached the Senate once more, against the advice of Polybius, this time only with the request that he be released, but was rebuked again.[114] Shortly thereafter, he escaped with the help of paternal friends, of Polybius and an ambassador of Ptolemy VI, perhaps also with the tacit approval of influential Romans. By the time his escape was discovered it was too late for pursuit. The Senate confined itself to sending another embassy to the east, headed by Ti. Gracchus, to look into conditions in Greece, Asia, and especially Syria.[115]

On his way home Demetrius seems to have avoided the territory of Eumenes. From a port belonging to the Lycian Confederacy, which had become independent in 167, he sent a message to Rome saying that his

[112] Polyb. xxxi.7.2–4. The circumstances under which the ladies left Cappadocia are not known, but may have been connected with the death of Ariarathes IV: Breglia Pulci Doria 1978, 121–2: (E 128). For Queen Antiochis see n. 9. Lysias: Polyb. xxxi.8.6, 12.4.

[113] Will 1982, 322: (A 40), suggests that the ultimatum transmitted by Popillius in 168 may have contained an allusion to Demetrius and his rights.

[114] Polyb. xxxi.2 with Walbank 1957–79, iii.465–6: (B 38); App. *Syr.* 46.238 (first attempt); Polyb. xxxi.11; App. *Syr.* 47.241–2; Just. *Epit.* xxxiv.3.8. Polybius advised him 'not to stumble twice on the same stone'.

[115] Polyb. xxxi.11–15, eyewitness and personal friend of several key persons involved; Gelzer 1962–4, iii.161–4: (A 19). It has often been suggested that the Scipios, perhaps also the Aemilii, favoured, or tolerated, Demetrius' escape; for instance Badian 1958, 108: (A 3). Sceptical is Gruen 1984, 665 n. 246: (A 20). Embassy of Gracchus: Polyb. xxxi.23.

target was not his cousin, King Antiochus V, but the chancellor Lysias, who had failed to avenge the murder of Octavius. That fooled no one and, in fact, as soon as Demetrius had landed in Syrian Tripolis, he proclaimed himself king, seized Apamea, the military capital of the kingdom, and marched on Antioch. Lysias and Antiochus were captured. Demetrius had them executed; before the end of 162 he was acknowledged as king throughout the empire.[116]

III. THE DECLINE OF THE SELEUCIDS, 162–129 B.C.

(a) Demetrius I[117]

From the day of his accession Demetrius faced tremendous problems. Within his realm were men loyal to the house of Antiochus or men who at least used such a pretext to further their ambitions. The most powerful was the Milesian Timarchus, satrap of Media and perhaps of Babylonia as well; he was aided by his brother Heraclides, once director of the king's finances.[118] Timarchus wasted no time in proclaiming himself, on his coins, 'Timarchus the Great King'. He annexed adjacent territories and concluded an alliance with Artaxias of Armenia, who now reappears as an independent ruler.[119] Timarchus and his brother had been sent to Rome more than once as ambassadors and had the support of many Roman senators, gained, reputedly, through bribery.[120] Timarchus, or

---

[116] Zon. IX.25.6–8; I Macc. 7.1–4; II Macc. 14.1–2; App. Syr. 47.242. Chronology: Volkmann 1925, 389: (B 143); Schürer 1973, 129–30: (E 112).

[117] Principal sources: Polyb. III.5.2–3, XXXI.33, XXXII.2–3, 10–11, XXXIII.6, 18–19; Diod. Sic. XXXI.19.19a, 27a, 28–30, 32.32a, 36.40a. The only coherent narratives surviving come from Jewish authors and focus on Syria and Palestine: I Macc. 7–10; II Macc. 14–15 (ending with Nicanor's defeat in 161); Jos. AJ XII.389–XIII.62. References to their works will only be given in special cases. Josephus from book XIII on, close as he remains to I Macc., has also consulted another well-informed source, either Nicolaus or Strabo, that ultimately derives from Poseidonius; Schürer 1973, 21–2, with bibliography: (E 112). The other literary sources consist of scattered references, mainly App. Syr. 47.243–244, 67.354–355, 70.367; Livy, Per. XLVI–XLVIII; Strabo XIII, p. 624; Porph. FGrH 260 F 32.14; Just. Epit. XXXIV.1–2, XXXV.1–2; Zon. IX.24.8–9, 25.8.

[118] Timarchus: Olshausen 1974, 216–17: (I 29). Heraclides: ibid. 212–13. In Miletus the brothers dedicated the bouleuterion (meeting place of the Council) to King Antiochus IV: Milet I.2, nos. 1–2; Tuchelt 1975: (B 204). Some 250 years later, a Milesian claimed descendancy from 'King Timarchus': Hommel 1976: (E 144). The Milesian Eirenias also had influence with Antiochus IV: Herrmann 1965: (E 142). On the other hand, the party of Demetrius in Miletus is represented by Apollonius and by his sons Menestheus, Meleager and Apollonius, who are called generals of Demetrius in an epigram from Miletus (Peek, GVI 1286). All four appear repeatedly in Polybius; Menestheus was honoured by the Athenians (n. 65). Apollonius was governor of Coele Syria under Demetrius II (I Macc. 10.69).

[119] Timarchus' coins, including a gold stater, are rare; most of them were melted down by Demetrius. Timarchus seems to have minted coins in Ecbatana and Seleuceia on the Tigris: Jenkins 1951, 1ff.: (B 99); LeRider 1965, 332–4: (E 149); Houghton 1979: (E 25). For military operations: Diod. Sic. XXXI.27a; for Artaxias, p. 351.

[120] Harris 1979, 90: (A 21), observes that this is the first attested instance of large-scale bribery of senators.

an Elamite dynast by the name of Hycnapses, may have controlled Susa for a part of 162/1.[121] Ptolemy, satrap of Commagene beyond the Euphrates, defected at the same time[122] and the Maccabees, now striving for the independence of Judaea, took up arms against all who were loyal to the high-priest and the king.

In addition, there were enormous external difficulties, the greatest of which was the hostility Demetrius had provoked in Rome by escaping and by pretending in the east that he had the Senate's approval. The Senate's hostility, once it became known, strengthened all forces that were opposed or disloyal to Demetrius. The king himself immediately felt isolated. The situation was worse than when Seleucus IV became king. Demetrius could not hope for any help from Eumenes, who had been active in placing Antiochus on the throne Demetrius had now reclaimed, nor from Cappadocia, which had been close to Eumenes for twenty-five years.

Demetrius worked hard to overcome these difficulties. He tried to placate the Senate; through Menochares he contacted first Ti. Gracchus, then the Senate, but the results were not reassuring.[123] He offered the hand of his sister Laodice, the widow of King Perseus, to his neighbour and cousin, the newly crowned Ariarathes V of Cappadocia, in an attempt to win his friendship. Ariarathes must have been flattered, but the Romans on the spot pressured him to decline and he then added insult to injury by making the affair public in Rome.[124] Demetrius did succeed with another project: he married off Nysa, daughter of Antiochus IV, to King Pharnaces of Pontus, but Pharnaces, himself isolated and rather weak after his defeat in 179 (p. 329), was little help.[125]

Demetrius had more success within his kingdom. In Judaea his troops, previously defeated, were finally victorious and seemed about to suppress the rebellion.[126] Much more important, however, was his swift recovery of the eastern satrapies. Timarchus had obtained a decree from

[121] Suggested by LeRider 1965, 86 nos. 65, 346–7: (E 149), because of a coin with the legend 'King Hycnapses', minted in Susa. The alternative date c. 150 is perhaps more likely.

[122] Diod. Sic. xxxi.19a. More generally xxxi.27a: 'some of his own satraps became disloyal'.

[123] Polyb. xxxi.33. He won the personal support of Ti. Gracchus. Demetrius' gift of grain to Rhodes (Diod. Sic. xxxi.36), where Menochares and Gracchus met, may have been promised or delivered on this occasion. On the embassy to Rome, p. 358.

[124] Diod. Sic. xxxi.28 attests that it was pressure by, or regard for, Rome that made Ariarathes turn down the offer; Just. Epit. xxxv.1.2. Gruen 1976: (E 20) unconvincingly argues that there was no pressure. The negotiations belong to winter 161/60, since Ariarathes' embassy was in Rome before autumn 160.

[125] The marriage is mentioned, as a fairly recent event, in the Athenian decree, IDélos 1497 bis, of 160/59, now firmly dated: bibliography in Hopp 1977, 4 n. 8: (E 60). The context makes it clear that Nysa was the daughter of Antiochus IV, not of Antiochus III or his eldest son, Antiochus: Mørkholm 1966, 60: (E 33).

[126] Judas defeated Nicanor in the battle of Adasa, but soon he lost a battle and his life against Bacchides (autumn 161): Meyer 1921, 236–52: (I 26); Schürer 1973, 168–73: (E 112).

the Senate that he was king as far as the Romans were concerned.[127] Although this was far from official recognition, it was tantamount to an assertion that Rome did not recognize Demetrius and was, therefore, injurious to his cause. Encouraged by this, Timarchus invaded Mesopotamia with a large army and reached Seleuceia-Zeugma, where he planned to cross the Euphrates and invade Syria, but he was defeated and killed by Demetrius, in 161 or 160. This victory enabled the king to recover the upper satrapies. In Babylonia he was hailed as 'Saviour' (*Soter*) and the epithet became part of his royal title.[128]

Demetrius' main concern remained the unsettled relations with Rome. He had approached the Roman ambassadors through Menochares and had been encouraged by Gracchus' reaction,[129] so he now sent Menochares to Rome. Menochares was admitted to the Senate chamber early in 159, some time after Ariarathes' envoys had been praised there for announcing the king's rebuttal of Demetrius. Menochares offered Rome a crown of 10,000 gold staters, said to be a token of gratitude for the hospitality shown Demetrius while he was there. He had also brought those responsible for the murder of Octavius. The senators were divided on how to respond; in the end they accepted the gift, though not the men extradited by the king, and decreed that the king would find Rome amenable if he complied with the Senate's wishes (these, however, were not specified).[130] Whether this response implied the formal recognition of Demetrius as king has been debated, but this is not the crucial issue, since Demetrius did not need Roman recognition to be king. The Senate, for this reason, did not commit itself; instead, it announced that Demetrius would be tolerated as long as he was obedient. This was all but a declaration that Rome considered itself Demetrius' master; moreover, insofar as the decree seemed to confer some sort of recognition, it was dishonest, because a short time before, in 161, at the request of envoys from Judas Maccabaeus, the Senate had granted an alliance to Demetrius'

[127] Diod. Sic. XXXI.27a, where the wording is slightly corrupt but the meaning not in doubt. Gruen 1976, 85: (E 20), whose view, however, that the decree 'was no more than a polite formality' – or an 'innocuous statement', 1984, 45: (A 20) – seems unrealistic. The text has Timarchus coming to Rome in person, certainly a mistake: Meyer 1921, 240 n. 3: (I 26). Perhaps Heraclides approached the Senate on his behalf: Will 1982, 368: (A 40).

[128] A cuneiform tablet from Babylon, dated 14 May 161, mentions Demetrius as king and seems to presuppose his victory: Parker and Dubberstein 1956, 23: (B 214). For coins minted after the victory see Küthmann 1954, 4–5: (B 109). Demetrius as 'Saviour': App. *Syr.* 47.242.

[129] Polyb. XXXI.33.2–4. Menochares seems to be the man who received a statue in Delos as one of the 'first friends' of King Demetrius in charge of his correspondence, *IDélos* 1543. He seems also to be mentioned in *PHerc.* 1044, fr. 10.2–3, where Crönert restored [συ]|νεχάρην. This violates the syllabic division, and the second letter is, in fact, *omicron*: Capasso 1976, 55: (I 3). Since King Demetrius himself appears in line 1, the restoration [Μη]|νοχάρην is compelling.

[130] Polyb. XXXII.2–3; Diod. Sic. XXXI.29.30; App. *Syr.* 47.243; Zon. IX.25.8. Both Polybius and Diodorus quote the main sentence as τεύξεται τῶν φιλανθρώπων Δημήτριος, ἐὰν τὸ ἱκανὸν ποιῇ τῇ συγκλήτῳ κατὰ τὴν τῆς ἀρχῆς ἐξουσίαν.

Jewish subjects. This act, whatever its actual or potential effects, was incompatible with normal relations between Rome and the Seleucid kingdom.[131]

Demetrius now knew that he could expect no support from Rome, but Cappadocia soon seemed to present an opportunity to improve his position and take vengeance on Ariarathes. King Ariarathes IV had been married to Antiochis. The queen is said to have believed she was barren and so had faked the birth of two boys, Ariarathes and Orophernes; later, however, she did give birth to Mithridates. When he was born she revealed the truth, the false princes were sent abroad, Mithridates took the dynastic name Ariarathes, and in 163 succeeded his father. The supposedly false prince Ariarathes disappears from history, but his brother Orophernes claimed the throne. The truth behind this sensational story cannot be known, but Orophernes may well have been, in fact, a genuine son of the former king. It was undisputed that he was born before Ariarathes V.[132] In any case Demetrius stepped in and supported him. In 159/8 Ariarathes was driven out of the country.[133]

In the summer of 158 he went to Rome and asked for help. He was kept waiting for a long time, during which he courted individual senators, as did, and with greater success, the envoys of Orophernes and Demetrius. Eventually, in 157, the Senate decreed that Cappadocia be divided between the two rivals. Orophernes, it seems, refused to comply, but Ariarathes now received active support from Attalus, the new king of Pergamum, and in 156 Orophernes, already unpopular at home, was defeated and Ariarathes reinstated by Pergamene forces. Demetrius, apparently, had not protected Orophernes, though he did give him asylum in his capital.

It is perhaps more than coincidence that just at that time (156) the territory of Attalus was invaded by another of his enemies, King Prusias

---

[131] I *Macc.* 8.17–30; Jos. *AJ* XII.415–419 (a different text), XIV.233 (letter of C. Fannius, *cos.* 161, on behalf of the Jewish envoys); II *Macc.* 4.11; Just. *Epit.* XXXVI.3.39. See Meyer 1921, 246–7: (I 26); recently Giovannini and Müller 1971, 166–71: (E 98); Fischer 1974: (E 94); Timpe 1974: (E 116); Gauger 1977, 153–328: (B 9); Vidal-Naquet 1978, 859–60: (E 118); Gruen 1984, 748ff.: (A 20). Problems abound, but the fact that a treaty was concluded in 161 is beyond doubt; Gauger's criticism of the sources is excessive.

[132] Diod. Sic. XXXI.19.6–8 (a shorter and slightly different version in Zon. IX.24.8), discussed by Breglia Pulcia Doria 1978: (E 128). It is obvious that the story reflects what Ariarathes V wanted known.

[133] Demetrius was promised 1,000 talents for his aid by Orophernes (App. *Syr.* 47.244, with whom Diod. Sic. XXXI.32 is in agreement) and received at once 600 and a crown of 70 talents. Orophernes set aside a sum of 400 talents as a cash reserve in the temple of Athena in Priene. While chronology is uncertain, Demetrius would hardly have taken any serious action before his envoys returned from Rome; 160, therefore, as advocated by Hansen 1971, 125: (E 57), is unsuitable. On the other hand, it was Attalus who counteracted the expulsion of Ariarathes, Diod. Sic. XXXI.32a, where the name Eumenes is a mistake; see Hopp 1977, 79 n. 110: (E 60). Since Eumenes died in 158 (n. 34), Demetrius' invasion of Cappadocia may be dated to 158.

II of Bithynia. The causes of the war are unknown, but for years Prusias had been complaining to Rome that Eumenes and Attalus were trying to regain some control of Galatia, despite the Senate's declaration in 166 that Galatia was to be free. Nor is the reason Prusias took up arms at that particular moment known. It could have been the opportunity presented by the involvement of Pergamene forces in Cappadocia; it could have been a bribe offered by Demetrius. In any event, a battle was fought, Attalus' forces were defeated, and a war began that lasted for two years.[134] Both sides presented their case before the Senate, which, in turn, intervened with no less than four embassies. In 155, after a treacherous assault that violated a truce and affected Roman envoys as well as Attalus, Prusias succeeded in driving his enemy into the capital, but was unable to take Pergamum. He ravaged the sanctuaries outside the city: of Athena Nikephoros, a memorial of his father's defeat in 183 (p. 328), and Asclepius, from which he looted the famous statue of the god, a work of the Athenian Phyromachus (n. 17), and other objects.

Having been repelled from the harbour-town of Elaea by Attalus' kinsman Sosander, he turned homeward and ravaged the territory of Attalus and the cities under his protection. During the following winter Attalus prepared for a major counter-attack; reinforcements came from Ariarathes V and from the Pontic king Mithridates IV who, sometime after 159, had succeeded his brother Pharnaces.[135] Roman intervention prevented the resumption of hostilities in the spring of 154, but Prusias' intransigence caused the Romans to terminate their friendship with him. Prusias, now influenced by Roman pressure and the threat from a large fleet, to which Rhodes, Cyzicus and others had contributed, finally yielded. No territory changed hands, but Prusias had to turn over twenty battleships, restore whatever he had taken, and pay indemnities to Attalus and a number of Greek cities. In many ways the war resembles the earlier one between Eumenes and Pharnaces (p. 328): the reaction of the Senate was slow and reserved, a major counter-attack against the aggressor was curtailed by Rome, and the aggressor only minimally punished. Rome had no intention of weakening the Attalids' rival.

There was a sequel to this war which had its origins in the quarrel in Cappadocia. Orophernes had deposited 400 talents in Priene (n. 133), but after he had been expelled, Ariarathes claimed the money as a possession of the kingdom. The Prienians refused. Orophernes, it seems, had lived in Priene when he was in exile from the court, and later rewarded the city,

[134] Prusias' complaints: Habicht 1957, PW, 'Prusias', 1113–15. Sources for the war: *ibid.* 1115ff. Recent bibliography: Vitucci 1953, 75–82: (E 176); Habicht 1956, 101–10: (E 56): Polyb. XXXII.15 belongs to book XXXIII, between chs. 1 and 7. Hopp 1977, 74–9: (E 60). The route of Prusias' retreat has been reconstructed by Robert 1937, 111–18: (E 162).

[135] Mithridates made a dedication on the Capitol in Rome (*CIL* I².730); Mellor 1978, 325–7 no. 5: (B 54). For the date (not earlier than 160/59) see n. 125.

which in turn endured hardship out of loyalty to him.[136] Priene was attacked, its territory ravaged by the forces of both Ariarathes and Attalus, who bore a personal grudge against the city. Priene sought help from Rhodes, to no avail, and then from Rome. Enough is preserved of a decree of the Senate, inscribed on the temple of Athena in Priene, to show that Rome did intervene; the magistrate-in-charge was instructed to write to both kings and the Prienians were finally able to return the money to Orophernes, their benefactor.[137]

The events of 157–154 in Cappadocia and Asia undoubtedly diminished the prestige of Demetrius; moreover, his personality showed more and more characteristics that made him unpopular. He did not, as Antiochus IV had done, reach out to his subjects or include them in royal spectacles; he preferred seclusion and was reputed to be a drunkard. How serious his interest in Epicurean philosophy was, is hard to say, but it certainly did nothing for his image among his subjects.[138] The people of Antioch hated the king for his harshness. Orophernes was able to stir them into a major uprising, in an attempt to win the throne of his cousin for himself. Demetrius suppressed the rebellion with measures which made him look even worse in the eyes of many and did not prevent the Antiochenes from rebelling again.[139] Worst of all, he made a serious political mistake. With Rome already hostile and Attalus and Ariarathes his enemies, he now antagonized Ptolemy Philometor. In 155/4 Demetrius bribed Archias, the Ptolemaic governor of Cyprus, to betray the island, for which the Seleucids had always had an appetite. Archias, however, was caught and tried; during the trial he hanged himself.[140] Ptolemy was infuriated. He joined Attalus and Ariarathes and the

[136] Orophernes had been sent to Ionia, probably to Priene (Diod. Sic. xxxi.19.7; Polyb. xxxii.11.10). He dedicated the cult statue of Athena Polias, in whose bases have been found the only existing coins of the king: Regling 1927, 8ff., 44ff.: (B 127); Kleiner, *PW*, 'Priene', 1195. He also donated a statue of the Demos, if the letter to the city (Welles, *RC* 63) is in fact his. He almost certainly made these gifts while king, between 158 and 156. Priene participated in a festival held by Demetrius I, before or after Orophernes had found refuge with him (*IPriene* 108, lines 152–5).

[137] The main source is Polyb. xxxiii.6 (see also Diod. Sic. xxxi.32), with two fragmentary documents, the second being part of the Senate's decree (Sherk, *Documents* 6). From the order of excerpts from Polybius the episode belongs to one of the years 155/4–153/2: Walbank 1957–79, iii.61–2: (B 38). The most likely date is 154, shortly before or after the peace between Attalus and Prusias, when Pergamene and Cappadocian forces were united in Asia.

[138] On the king's relations with Philonides from Laodicea in northern Syria see *PHerc.* 1044, with Gallo (n. 111), fr. 27, pp. 152–3. The fragmentary state of the papyrus presents many problems; nevertheless it seems that Philonides had been Demetrius' teacher before 175, that he participated in efforts to spare Laodicea punishment after the murder of Octavius, and that he was the head of a school in the capital that was visited by the king himself.

[139] Just. *Epit.* xxxv.1.3–4. Orophernes was imprisoned in Seleuceia in northern Syria. Antioch's hostility endangered Demetrius again in the affair of Andriscus.

[140] Antiochus III attempted to take Cyprus by surprise in 197. Antiochus IV took it in 168, but the Romans forced his immediate withdrawal. Demetrius' move: Polyb. xxxiii.5; for the chronology: Walbank 1957–79, iii.41–2, 546: (B 38), who rightly rejects the dates 158/7 (Otto 1934, 112 n. 6: (E 156) and 151/50 (Volkmann 1924, 53–4: (B 142)).

three kings, as Polybius says, 'converged on Demetrius'.[141] Attalus had prepared the instrument years before, when he was reacting to the overthrow of Ariarathes. A young man by the name of Balas lived in Smyrna; he claimed to be the son of Antiochus IV, to whom he bore a striking resemblance. Attalus had him conducted to Pergamum, invested him, as he had done with Antiochus IV in 175, with the diadem and the royal purple, and called him by the dynastic name Alexander. He settled him close to the Seleucid border under the protection of the Cilician dynast Zenophanes, whom Attalus had supported in a quarrel with Demetrius, and he had the rumour spread through Syria that Alexander would soon come to claim his father's throne.[142] In 153 the time seemed ripe for a move. Under the guidance of the Milesian Heraclides, who had once been in charge of Antiochus' finances (p. 356), Alexander Balas, with Antiochus' daughter Laodice at his side, appeared in Rome; in 152 he obtained a decree from the Senate that granted him permission to claim 'the throne of his ancestors' and even promised Roman support.[143]

This was a signal that Rome wanted Demetrius overthrown. There was no need for material aid. Heraclides gathered an army in Ephesus with the help of Attalus. Before October 152 Alexander made a landing, perhaps with ships supplied by Ptolemy, in Ptolemais, where the garrison betrayed the city to him. The Maccabean party under Judas' brother Jonathan, courted by both king and pretender, finally chose the latter, who appointed the Hasmonean rebel high-priest. At first Demetrius was victorious, but eventually, though he fought courageously, he lost a battle, the kingdom, and his life in the summer of 150.[144]

(b) Kings and usurpers[145]

Perhaps it was inevitable that the new king, Alexander, should execute his predecessor's son Antigonus, his wife Laodice, and a number of his

---

[141] Polyb. III.5.3: συστραφέντων ἐπ᾽ αὐτὸν τῶν ἄλλων βασιλέων.

[142] Diod. Sic. XXXI.32a. Zenophanes was perhaps the dynast of Olba, as suggested by Hopp 1977, 80 n. 119: (E 60). On the role of the Pergamene king see Ritter 1965, 137–8: (131). Most pagan sources call Balas an imposter (App. *Syr*. 67.354, 70.367; Trogus, *Prol*. XXXV; Just. *Epit*. XXXV.1.6–7; Ath. v.211A; Livy, *Per*. LII). This is undoubtedly what Polybius, the friend of Demetrius, wrote. On the other hand, the Jewish tradition, obliged to Balas for privileges, presents him as a genuine son of Antiochus (I *Macc*. 10.1; Jos. *AJ* XIII.35). So is he regarded by Strabo XIII, p. 624, and, of course, by the decree of the Senate (n. 143).

[143] Polyb. XXXIII.18.12; Gruen 1976, 91–3: (E 20). Shortly before, the Senate had received Demetrius' son coolly.

[144] Alexander seems to have become master of Tyre and Sidon in 152: Küthmann 1954, 8: (B 109). Jonathan: Tcherikover 1961, 232ff.: (E 115). The latest date for Demetrius is at present 1 June 151 (or a date sometime between 6 April 151 and 26 March 150). The earliest date for Alexander is 21 October 150: Parker and Dubberstein 1956, 23: (B 214). It remains a puzzle, for whom the bronze coin with 'King Antiochus' and the date 151/50 was minted, apparently in Antioch: Heichelheim 1944: (B 95); Bellinger 1945: (B 79).

[145] Jewish sources: I *Macc*. 10–15; Jos. *BJ* 1.48–50, *AJ* XIII.35–224. In addition, besides those quoted in the notes, App. *Syr*. 67–8, 355–358; Livy, *Per*. p. 145, 213 Rossbach; Just. *Epit*. XXXV.1–2, XXXVI.1; Charax, *FGrH* 103 F 29.

friends, but Alexander was not by nature a cruel man. Twenty-three years of age when he became king, more affable than Demetrius had been, he was popular at first, the more so because he cultivated the memory of Antiochus IV, whose son he pretended to be. He wore the radiate crown in tribute to him; he assumed the title 'Son of God' (*Theopator*) and had his bronze coins struck with the epithets *Epiphanes*, *Nikephoros* and *Eupator*, all characteristic of Antiochus IV and Antiochus V.[146] He also restored certain privileges, once granted by Epiphanes, but cancelled by Demetrius, to some Syrian cities.[147] In reality, however, Alexander was a creature of foreign kings and the puppet of Ptolemy Philometor. Although his prestige may have been given a boost by his marriage to the Egyptian king's daughter Cleopatra, that memorable event, which took place in Ptolemais, was not so much a pledge of continued Egyptian support as a symptom of mounting Ptolemaic influence in Seleucid affairs.[148]

It soon became apparent that Alexander, despite some familiarity with Stoic philosophy, cared little for duty. Much of the daily business he left to favourites, in particular to his minister Ammonius. While the king himself mostly resided in Ptolemais, two other men, Hierax and Diodotus, governed the capital. He had so little control over his realm that two cities in Syria, Aradus and Marathus, fought each other in a war caused by the corruption of Ammonius. Alexander made no attempt to restore royal authority over Judaea, where Jonathan had risen from rather despicable beginnings as a rebel to the dignity of high-priest. His elevation into the circle of the king's favourites – he was an honoured guest at the royal wedding – marks the level to which the kingdom of Seleucus I had fallen.[149]

Worst of all, Alexander remained apathetic even after he had lost two important satrapies, Media and Susiane, in 148/7 (or soon thereafter). No wonder, then, that at the first challenge to his rule he found himself deserted by the very men who had once helped him win the throne: Attalus and Ariarathes did not lift a finger in his support, and Ptolemy, his father-in-law, even joined the side of the pretender. The challenge came from the quarter where it might have been expected, from the sons

[146] For *Theopator* see Maricq 1958, 378–82: (B 180); for the rest: Volkmann 1924, 61ff.: (B 142). Portraits of Alexander: Charbonneaux and Laumonier 1955: (E 13); Mørkholm 1981: (B 118).
[147] El-Zein 1972, 164–5: (E 17), for the autonomous coins of Apamea. For coins of Antioch and Seleuceia with the legend 'of the brother peoples' ('Ἀδελφῶν Δήμων), sometimes thought to illustrate the erosion of royal authority, see Rigsby 1980, 242–8: (E 39).
[148] The coins minted for the occasion have Cleopatra in the foreground, Alexander behind her: Küthmann 1954, 9–10: (B 109). Ptolemaic influence is revealed by the royal mints in Syria changing from the traditional Attic standard of Seleucid coins to the Phoenician standard of the Ptolemies.
[149] Diod. Sic. XXXII.9c, XXXIII.3 and Livy, *Per.* L, call Alexander downright incompetent. His connection with philosophers, hardly more than superficial familiarity: Ath. V.211A–D. The war of the cities: Diod. Sic. XXXIII.5; Rey-Coquais 1974, 131: (E 159): Mørkholm 1975–6: (B 115). Jonathan: Meyer 1921, 253–6: (I 26).

of Demetrius I, Demetrius and Antiochus, who had been sent to Asia
Minor by their father before he made his last stand. Demetrius the son,
when he was hardly more than thirteen years old, undertook an expedition to avenge his father. Determined to do away with the man whom he
regarded as an imposter, he landed in Phoenicia in 147 with an army of
mercenaries collected mainly from Crete and the Greek islands. For some
time his moves seem to reflect the dominant influence of a Cretan by the
name of Lasthenes.[150]

Although some of the sources imply that Alexander was almost
immediately overthrown, the decisive battle did not take place until two
years later, in the summer of 145. Not much is known about those two
years, except that the Jews under Jonathan fought successfully against
Apollonius, whom Demetrius had appointed satrap of Coele Syria.[151]
Eventually Ptolemy Philometor intervened and decided the struggle. He
brought an army into Palestine on the pretence that he was coming to
support his son-in-law. He accepted the welcome of numerous cities, but
put his own garrisons into them and suddenly turned against Alexander,
according to some authors because he had come to despise his conduct,
according to others because Alexander refused to extradite his minister
Ammonius, whom Ptolemy accused of being responsible for an attempt
on his life.[152]

The change of face occurred in Ptolemais in the presence of
Alexander's queen. Ptolemy promised her to Demetrius with whom he
concluded an alliance. Alexander was forced to leave the capital; he went
to Cilicia to muster an army. Meanwhile Antioch was in an uproar; the
mob killed the hated Ammonius, but they did not support Demetrius,
for fear that he might seek revenge for their treatment of his father. They
received Ptolemy with enthusiasm, and applauded the attempt of
Alexander's former ministers Diodotus and Hierax to crown him with
the diadem of the Seleucids. The king declined. He might have feared
Rome's reaction and seems to have been satisfied with Demetrius'
promise to cede Coele Syria and Palestine, which the Ptolemies had lost
fifty-five years before.[153] Ptolemy managed to reconcile the city and

---

[150] Jos. *AJ* XIII.86, 126–7; cf. I *Macc.* 10.67, 11.31–2; Just. *Epit.* XXXV.2.2. Lasthenes may well be
Lasthenes, son of Eunomos, from Cnossus who was honoured as *proxenos*, some time after 168, by an
Epirote tribe in Butrinto: Cabanes 1974, 130 no. 10: (D 11). There are only two other individuals of
that name attested in Crete, but from a different time: Masson, *BCH* 107 (1983) 396–7.

[151] Schürer 1973, 181: (E 112); Bar-Kochva 1976: (E 2).

[152] Diod. Sic. XXXII.9c; I *Macc.* 11.10; Jos. *AJ* XIII.106–107. According to I *Macc.*, Ptolemy really
wanted to establish himself on the throne of the Seleucids, and the attempt, real or fictitious, was
only a pretext for changing his alliance. Different is Josephus' story that the crown was forced upon
him. Josephus, however, is as partial to him as I *Macc.* is to Alexander. Ptolemy's conduct in Antioch
(below) seems to disprove the accusation that he wanted to be king of Asia.

[153] Diod. Sic. XXXIII.9c; Livy, *Per.* LII; I *Macc.* 11.12–13; Jos. *AJ* XIII.109–116. According to
Josephus, the marriage between Demetrius and Cleopatra was concluded before Alexander died.
Regarding Ptolemy's refusal, Josephus aptly remarks that he was afraid of Rome's reaction. A
dedication by Demetrius in honour of Ptolemy has been found in Paphos, *SEG* XIII.585.

Demetrius; Demetrius was acknowledged as his father's heir to the throne.

Alexander arrived with an army, was defeated in a battle fought near Antioch, at the River Oenoparas, but escaped and fled for refuge to an Arab dynast, who, a few days later, had him murdered. His head was brought to Ptolemy, but Ptolemy himself had been severely wounded and soon died. Demetrius was the sole winner and he acted in cold blood. He could not stop Ptolemy's field army from retreating to Egypt, but he seized his elephants and had his garrisons in the coastal cities slaughtered. No more was heard about the ceding of Palestine. Demetrius also stopped Jonathan's attempts to storm the citadel of Jerusalem, still occupied by a Seleucid garrison and Jewish hellenizers. Jonathan paid homage to the king in Ptolemais and extorted some major concessions from him.[154]

Demetrius II, now called 'The Victorious' (*Nikator*) like the founder of the dynasty, seemed safe on the throne of his ancestors, but a grave mistake soon jeopardized his position. With the exception of the mercenaries with whom he had come, he dismissed his forces, that is to say, the regular Seleucid army. They became restless and bitter and created serious difficulties. In Antioch the unemployed soldiers and the general population, harassed by Demetrius after their protector, King Ptolemy, had disappeared, rallied to attack the palace. The king had only Jonathan to call upon. Jonathan responded; three thousand Jewish soldiers came to the king's rescue and got the upper hand in a vicious battle fought in the streets of Antioch.[155] In Apamea, the main arsenal of the kingdom, a citizen named Diodotus – he called himself Tryphon, was perhaps of Macedonian origin and probably the same man who, together with Hierax, had administered the capital and proclaimed Philometor king – collected the jobless and unruly soldiers and took possession of the elephants and all the armour stored in the city. He then persuaded an Arab dynast, perhaps the emir of Emesa (Homs), to hand over Alexander's son Antiochus, a boy two years old, and proclaimed him King Antiochus VI in late summer of 145.[156]

Demetrius, at first contemptuous of Tryphon, was soon forced to send

---

[154] The battlefield: Strabo XVI, p. 751; for the identification Honigmann, *PW*, 'Οἰνοπάρας', 2253. For main events: Polyb. XXXIX.7; Diod. Sic. XXXII.9d and 10.1; App. *Syr.* 67.355; Trogus, *Prol.* XXXV; Just. *Epit.* XXXV.2.4; Livy, *Per.* LII; I *Macc.* 11.14–19; Jos. *AJ* XIII.116–119; Porph. *FGrH* 260 F 32.15. The latest date for Ptolemy, 15 July 145, even if posthumous, approximately dates the battle: Skeat 1955, 34: (B 221). Demetrius and Jonathan after the battle: Schürer 1973, 182: (E 112).

[155] Demetrius' cruelty in Antioch: Diod. Sic. XXXIII.4; Just. *Epit.* XXXVI.1.1; Livy, *Per.* LII, ascribed by Diodorus to the influence of his chancellor, probably Lasthenes. The war in Antioch: I *Macc.* 11.42–51; Jos. *AJ* XIII.134–142.

[156] On Tryphon see Hoffmann, *PW*, 'Tryphon', 715–22; Schürer 1973, 183–97: (E 112). Since there are coins of Antiochus VI from year 167 of the Seleucid era which ended in October 145, all these events must have followed each other in rapid succession. It is significant that Antiochus took the epithet *Dionysus Epiphanes* and that he (Tryphon) had posthumous coins of Antiochus IV

an army against him. The usurper defeated it and grew in strength. He won Chalcis on the edge of the desert and in 145/4 forced Demetrius to abandon Antioch and to retreat to the adjacent coastal town of Seleuceia.[157] Tryphon then made generous offers in Antiochus' name to Jonathan, who was embittered because Demetrius had used his people to extricate himself in Antioch and then had revoked his earlier concessions. An alliance was concluded that guaranteed Jonathan his position as high-priest, confirmed all earlier privileges and appointed Jonathan's brother Simon to be Antiochus' satrap of the coastal region between Egypt and Tyre. The treaty created an opportunity for the Jews to attack the cities which remained loyal to Demetrius in that region, to seize them in the name of Antiochus and, should the new king fail, to annex them. Jonathan, in fact, captured Ascalon and Gaza. He also fought successfully in Galilee against the forces of Demetrius, while his brother Simon captured the fortress of Beth-sur in southern Judaea itself.[158]

Meanwhile there was fighting in northern Syria. Despite some setbacks, Tryphon kept gaining ground, until he controlled, besides Antioch and most of its hinterland, the coastal cities of Aradus, Orthosia, Byblus, Berytus, Ptolemais and Dora; Demetrius held on to Seleuceia, Laodicea, Sidon and Tyre. Tryphon also occupied Coracesium, a stronghold in western Cilicia, and encouraged Cilician pirates to raid the territory controlled by Demetrius; the internal struggle for control of the Seleucid empire contributed much to the rapid spread of Cilician piracy.[159]

Once he had gained the upper hand in the struggle, Tryphon became more concerned about his ally Jonathan than about his royal foe, and with good reason, for Jonathan had had success after success; he had captured (through Simon) Joppa and fortified Jerusalem. It must now have been obvious that he was striving for an independent Jewish state, especially if he had indeed sent ambassadors to Rome and received

---

Epiphanes minted, whose grandson he pretended to be: Küthmann 1954, 17: (B 109); Mørkholm 1963, 71: (B 112), and 1966, 185: (E 33) (who wants Alexander to be the one who minted these); El-Zein 1972, 153–4, 210 n. 29: (E 17).

[157] Diod. Sic. xxxiii.4a. Retreat of Demetrius to Seleuceia: Livy, *Per.* lii (Cilicia according to Jos. *AJ* xiii.145). In 145/4 Antioch minted first for Demetrius (*IGCH* no. 1593), then for Antiochus VI: the change dates these events. Antiochus' pieces of 146/5 must therefore have been struck somewhere else, probably in Apamea: El-Zein 1972, 231 n. 45: (E 17). The letters *TP Y* on his coins show Tryphon's prominence.

[158] Schürer 1973, 183–6: (E 112).

[159] A paradoxical victory of Demetrius' general Sarpedon over an army of Tryphon is recorded by Poseidonius, *FGrH* 87 F 29, a later victory of Demetrius over Antiochus, dated to 140/39, by Porph. *FGrH* 260 F 32.16. Ptolemais began to coin for Antiochus in 144/3. Not Berytus, said to have been destroyed by Tryphon (Strabo xvi, p. 756), but Byblus minted for him: Seyrig 1950, 9–12: (B 131). On the other hand, Tyre and Sidon minted continuously for Demetrius II. For Coracesium: Strabo xiv, p. 668.

encouragement from the Senate.[160] Before the winter of 143/2, Tryphon turned against him.[161] After some manoeuvring, he took Jonathan prisoner in Ptolemais and moved on Judaea, but the Jews did not yield as he had expected; they elected Simon to his brother's place and defended themselves. Tryphon tried to take Jerusalem with a surprise assault and failed when a heavy snowfall prevented his cavalry from attacking; he returned to Ptolemais and had Jonathan killed.[162] Soon thereafter, he had his ward murdered and himself proclaimed king, with the additional title of *Autokrator*. For the first time there was a king who did not even pretend to have a connection with the royal house, and in fact made it quite clear that he wanted to do away with all tradition.[163]

It was a natural consequence of these events that Simon now approached Demetrius and concluded an alliance with him. The king granted him all his former privileges (over which he had no control anyway) and only a few months later, in June 142, Simon, who had taken the city of Gazara (Gezer), finally forced the garrison in the citadel of Jerusalem to surrender: 'The yoke of the Gentile was taken from

[160] As reported by I *Macc.* 12.1–4 and Jos. *AJ* xiii.163–165. Opinions are divided whether there was in fact such an embassy: so Fischer 1970, 96ff.: (E 18); Gauger 1977, 278–83: (B 9); or whether the report is only a doublet of Simon's embassy a little later: so Momigliano 1930, 148–9: (E 105); Giovannini and Müller 1971, 170 n. 53: (E 98), with whom the present writer agrees. The question remains open in Schürer 1973, 184: (E 112) and Gruen 1984, 748: (A 20).

[161] The Jewish writers give as Tryphon's reason his desire to become king and his fear that Jonathan might not let him have his way. As to the chronology, winter 143/2 was the time of great distress for the Jews, after Jonathan had been killed (I *Macc.* 12.52–4; Jos. *AJ* xiii.194–196). The year must therefore be Jonathan's last and Simon's first. Simon's first year is equated with Sel. 170 in I *Macc.* 13.41–2, but the same events are equated with Sel. 169 in II *Macc.* 1.7. The use of θλῖψις depicting the Jewish situation in both I *Macc.* 13.5 and II *Macc.* 1.7 proves that these are the same events. It follows that the date in I *Macc.* reckons from the era in spring 312, the date in II *Macc.* from that in spring 311. See Bickermann 1933, 239–41: (E 84); but also Bringmann 1983, 21ff. and his entire ch. 1: (E 92).

[162] Schürer 1973, 186–8: (E 112), with bibliography, n. 42, on the identification of Jonathan with the 'Wicked Priest' of the Qumran texts.

[163] Tryphon's assumption of the title *Autokrator*, his dating, not by the Seleucid era but by his own regnal years, and the symbols he chose for his coins show his break with Seleucid tradition: Seyrig 1950, 12.34: (B 131). A marble head of Tryphon with the diadem is said to have been found in Syrian Chalcis, one of Tryphon's strongholds, and intentionally damaged after his fall: Fischer 1971: (B 166). The chronology of Tryphon's accession and Antiochus' murder is vexed; Hoffmann, *PW*, 'Tryphon', 720–1. Most of the ancient authors date these events to 139, but I *Macc.* 13.31 clearly indicates spring 141, and this is corroborated by the fact that Antiochus' last coins are dated 142/1, the earliest of Antiochus VII 139/8. Since this king seems to have disposed of Tryphon swiftly, Tryphon can hardly have lived until 136/5. His coins bear numbers of years 2, 3 and 4 and should be dated 141/40, 140/39 and 139/8. The attempt of Baldus (1970: (E 1)) to show that Tryphon proclaimed himself king in 142/1, but kept Antiochus as his (dependent) co-ruler until 139/8, is open to serious objections: Fischer 1972: (E 19). It follows that the assertion of the authors that Tryphon became king in 139/8 must be abandoned: Seyrig 1950, 12–17: (B 131); Schürer 1973, 131, 189 n. 2: (E 112). Tryphon may, however, not have killed Antiochus VI until 139/8, when he learnt that Demetrius was in Parthian captivity. The following equations have to be made: Sel. 171 (142/1) is Antiochus VI's last and Tryphon's first year; Sel. 174 (139/8) is Antiochus VII's first and Tryphon's last (fourth) year (and Simon's fifth year).

Israel.'[164] From then on, the Jews counted the years of their own leader, 'year one of Simon', an obvious manifestation of their belief that they were independent and of their determination to remain independent. In September 141 an assembly of the Jews, held in Jerusalem, praised Simon in a long decree, intended mainly to confirm by their own free will the honours the king had bestowed upon him, the high-priesthood and the leadership of the nation. At the same time, an embassy that Simon had sent to Rome returned with a decree of the Senate that guaranteed, as far as Rome was concerned, the integrity of Jewish territory.[165] For the second time in history, there was an independent Jewish state.

The alliance between Demetrius and the Jews did not so much strengthen the king as weaken Tryphon. In 142/1 Demetrius, Tryphon and Simon, each controlling parts of Syria and Palestine, were almost deadlocked. Tryphon asked for Roman support to improve his position and was rebuked in a peculiar manner: the Senate accepted his gifts, but had them inscribed with the name of Antiochus VI, the king Tryphon had murdered.[166] Eventually Demetrius began a major effort to change things to his advantage. In the course of the year which began in autumn 141/40 he left Seleuceia and went to Mesopotamia, which had remained loyal. He intended to push back the Parthians, who had taken advantage of the struggle within the Seleucid realm to invade Seleucid territory. Demetrius hoped to enhance his prestige with a victory and create an army strong enough to crush Tryphon. He was defeated and taken prisoner, sometime in 140/39 (p. 371).

When his younger brother Antiochus, who was in Rhodes, learned of this, he decided to take over. He had difficulty entering the kingdom, however, since Tryphon controlled most of the coast. Several ports closed their harbours, but Cleopatra, his brother's wife, besieged by Tryphon in Seleuceia, not only received him but also accepted him as her husband (she had already heard that Demetrius had married a daughter of the Parthian king). The forces of Demetrius that still operated in that region must have joined Antiochus also, and in 139/8 he was proclaimed King Antiochus VII. He soon concluded an alliance with Simon. Tryphon was defeated in northern Syria and besieged in Dora in Phoeni-

[164] Schürer 1973, 191–2: (E 112), where the surrender of the citadel of Jerusalem is dated June 141; 142 has to be preferred (see n. 161).
[165] The document for Simon: I Macc. 14.27–45; Schürer 1973, 193–4: (E 112). Despatch of the embassy: I Macc. 14.24; its return: ibid. 14.40. The return also appears in I Macc. 15.15, under the year 139/8 (beginning in autumn 139), which has created great difficulties (Schürer, op. cit. 195–6 nn. 16–17). It has, however, been shown that I Macc. 15.15–24 is not only inserted in the wrong place, but is a forgery: Giovannini and Müller 1971: (E 98). The decree of the Senate is perhaps the one transmitted by Jos. AJ xiv.145–148, used as the basis on which to fabricate the forged document (see, however, n. 170). The embassy should have been in Rome in 142: Schürer, op. cit. 194–7, with bibliography, esp. Giovannini and Müller; in addition, Fischer 1974, 90–1: (E 94); Gauger 1977, 261–310: (B 9); Gruen 1984, 749: (A 20).   [166] Diod. Sic. xxxiii.28a.

cia. He escaped to Apamea, his home town. There, unable to defend himself any longer, he took his own life.[167]

(c) The catastrophe of hellenism[168]

Once Tryphon was dead, Antiochus VII gained swift recognition throughout the Seleucid empire. Antiochus Sidetes – the nickname comes from the city of Side in southern Asia Minor, where he had been brought up – was a young man, twenty years of age, able and gallant. On his coins from 135/4 onwards he is 'King Antiochus', with the addition of 'Benefactor' (*Euergetes*) and, during his last year, 'The Great' (*Megas*).

After Antiochus had established himself firmly on the throne, he had to deal at once with two major problems: his Jewish subjects, who were developing an independent state within his realm, and the Parthians, who had taken advantage of the internal struggles in Syria to occupy large parts of the kingdom. The Parthians, who also held his older brother Demetrius in captivity, posed the more important and the more difficult problem, but logic demanded that the Jewish question be resolved first. The king had already shown his intentions. When he was besieging Tryphon in Dora, the Jewish leader Simon sent 2,000 picked troops to assist him. The king, with victory well in hand, refused their service and thereby signalled that he regarded the treaty with Simon as void. He demanded the recognition of his sovereignty and the restitution of several towns recently seized by the Jews; when he learned that Simon was prepared to make only minimal concessions, he resorted to force. For a while Simon's sons, who now led the army, seem to have held their ground against the king's general Cendebaeus. The king had to take matters into his own hands; in 135 he invaded Judaea.

By then Simon was dead. A few months earlier he and two of his sons had fallen victim to a plot conceived by his son-in-law Ptolemy, who

---

[167] I *Macc.* curiously does not record his end. Most of Tryphon's coins were melted down by Antiochus VII, but in Orthosia 33 pieces, all in mint condition, have been found. Thirteen are dated, all to Tryphon's last year. Orthosia was the place he stopped last before meeting his destiny: Seyrig 1950, 1–23: (B 131). By coincidence, Frontin. *Strat.* II.13.2 says that Tryphon had coins scattered to slow down the pursuing horsemen.

[168] The literary sources survive only in scattered pieces. The fragments of Poseidonius in *FGrH* 87. See also Diod. Sic. XXXIV.1, 15–19, 21; I *Macc.* 15.10–16.24; Jos. *AJ* XIII.224–259 (partly following Nicolaus of Damascus, *FGrH* 90) and *BJ* 1.51–63; Trogus, *Prol.* (and Just. *Epit.* XXXVI, XXXVIII, XXXIX, XLII); App. *Syr.* 68.358–360; Livy, *Per.* LVII–LIX; Jul. Obseq. *ad a.* 130; Oros. V.10.8; Euseb. *Chron.* I, pp. 255–6 Schoene. Valuable precision can be derived from the coinage of Antiochus VII, Phraates II, Camniscires and other rulers: LeRider 1965, 361–86: (E 149); Strauss 1971: (B 139); and from Babylonian cuneiform tablets: Olmstead 1937: (B 213) and Parker and Dubberstein 1956: (B 214). A dedication from Ptolemais/Akko which was thought to refer to Antiochus VII is for his son Antiochus IX: Fischer 1970, 102–9: (E 18). Modern accounts: Meyer 1921, 265–73: (I 26); DeSanctis 1907–64, IV.195–206: (A 14); Schürer 1973, 198–207: (E 112); Will 1982, 410–16: (A 40). For Antiochus' eastern campaign: Fischer *op. cit.*

wanted to seize power for himself (*c.* March 135), with or without the king's knowledge. John, however, another son, happened to be in Jerusalem at the time of the murder; he secured his father's position for himself and drove Ptolemy out of the country.[169] Almost immediately he had to face the attack of the royal army and soon found himself besieged in Jerusalem. The siege went on for a year. Hostilities were interrupted once by a truce to allow the Jews to celebrate the Feast of Tabernacles, to which the king himself contributed gifts, but, soon after, famine forced John to ask for terms. Antiochus' counsellors advised him to exterminate the Jewish nation or at least enforce radical changes in their way of life, but the king granted peace with moderate conditions and dismantled the fortifications of the city (*c.* October 134).[170] About the same time he sent rich gifts to P. Cornelius Scipio Aemilianus, who had visited the east in 139 and now had assumed command in Spain.[171]

Seleucid authority over the Jewish nation had been restored, but not for long. A few years later, when Antiochus' efforts to resolve the Parthian question had ended in disaster, royal authority vanished from Judaea. An ancient writer observed that Antiochus VII was the last of the Seleucids to rule over the Jews.[172]

Nothing is known about Antiochus' activities from the time of his success in Judaea until he began his eastern campaign in 131.[173] He was probably engaged in preparations for the expedition which, as he must have anticipated, would be a serious task, for the situation in the east had deteriorated since Alexander's rule.

The Seleucid princes, because of their internal feuds, had neglected the dangerous growth of Parthian power far too long. They had remained lethargic in the face of severe losses.[174] In the early 160s, it seems, the Parthian king Mithridates I struck coins with his own portrait, which implied that he no longer acknowledged Seleucid suzerainty. Antiochus IV made plans to invade, but died before he could carry them out (p. 352). Scholars once believed that Parthian aggression began shortly

---

[169] Schürer 1973, 197–202: (E 112). I *Macc.* ends its narrative with John's accession, thereby avoiding mentioning his surrender in 134.

[170] Poseidonius, *FGrH* 87F109 (Diod. Sic. xxxiv.1); Jos. *AJ* xiii.236–247; *BJ* 1.61; Just. *Epit.* xxxvi.1.10; Plut. *Mor.* 184EF. Coins of Antiochus VII were minted in Jerusalem. The decree of the Roman Senate in favour of the Jews, preserved in Jos. *AJ* xiv.145–148, may date from December 134, i.e. from the time immediately after the city's surrender; *MRR* 1.491 n. 2, admitted as a possibility by Giovannini and Müller 1971, 165: (E 98), who, however, argue for 142; see also n. 165, furthermore Rajak 1981: (E 110).

[171] Livy, *Per.* lvii, discussed by Astin 1967, 127 and 138–9: (H 67).

[172] Just. *Epit.* xxxvi.1.10.

[173] Speculations on 'many wars against neighbours' (Just. *Epit.* xxxviii.10.11) in Bouché-Leclerq 1913, 370: (E 8).

[174] The fundamental study on the eastern satrapies of the Seleucids, based largely on the study of the coinage, is LeRider 1965, 361–80: (E 149). References that can easily be found there are given only in special cases.

after the death of Antiochus IV and that they conquered Media as early as *c*. 160. It has since become clear that Demetrius I continued to strike coins in Ecbatana, the capital of Media, and that his successor Alexander also had coins minted there. In addition, a dedication from Bisutun in Media, dated to the summer of 148, proves that a Seleucid governor-general was in charge of the 'upper satrapies'. Mithridates occupied Media only in *c*. 147.[175] Camniscires, the ruler of Elymais, seized Susa and the satrapy of Susiane about the same time.[176] Alexander Balas apparently did not react to the simultaneous loss of two major provinces. The Parthian king now followed the example of the rulers of Bactria and of the usurper Timarchus (p. 356) and styled himself 'The Great King'.

The next blow fell in 141. Mithridates invaded and occupied southern Mesopotamia. Cuneiform tablets attest to his rule in Babylon and in Seleuceia on the Tigris in July 141 and, before October of the same year, in Uruk.[177] Demetrius II, then involved in his struggle with Tryphon, nonetheless responded to the call of his eastern subjects. In the spring of 140 he marched on Parthia. Persis, Elymais and Bactria gave him substantial support and he was successful at first, but in Media one of Mithridates' generals defeated him and took him prisoner (139).[178] The Parthian king now assumed the title 'King of Kings' and had his prisoner displayed in the regions Demetrius had reconquered or come to reconquer. He then assigned him a residence in Hyrcania and married off one of his daughters to him. Mithridates was also victorious in a battle fought, probably in 140, against the Elamites at Kut-el-Amara, where the Schatt-al-hai joins the Tigris; he took Susa and Susiane away from them, but he did not hold them long: coins show that Susa and the satrapy Susiane were under the control of an independent ruler, Tigraios, perhaps the successor of Camniscires, for several years, *c*. 138–132.

Mithridates, the architect of Parthian greatness, died in 138 and his son and successor Phraates II had to face the challenge of Antiochus' expedition in 131.[179] Antiochus' army, including a strong contingent of Jewish soldiers commanded by the high-priest John in person, was larger than any Seleucid army had been for at least forty years. The Seleucid king was victorious in three successive battles, one of them fought against the Parthian satrap Indates on the River Lycus (Zabu êlû) between Gaugamela and Arbela. He reconquered Babylonia; when he entered Babylon, he assumed the title 'The Great King'.[180] He soon

---

[175] The lower chronology has now generally been adopted. The dedication from Bisutun: Robert 1963, 76: (B 65).   [176] LeRider 1965, 349–54: (E 149); Strauss 1971, 109–40: (B 139).

[177] Olmstead 1937, 12–13: (B 213); LeRider 1965, 363–4: (E 149).

[178] Diod. Sic. XXXIII.8, XXXIV.15; App. *Syr.* 69.363–364; Porph. *FGrH* 260F32.16; Just. *Epit.* XXXVI.1.2ff.; I *Macc.* 14.1–3; Jos. *AJ* XIII.184–186.

[179] The sources are transcribed in full in Fischer 1970, 29–35: (E 18).

[180] Just. *Epit.* XXXVIII.10.6. *IDélos* 1547–8.

372 THE SELEUCIDS AND THEIR RIVALS

recovered Seleuceia on the Tigris, Susa and Susiane, and he invaded Media, where the final scene was played. Phraates was concerned enough to open negotiations, but he refused Antiochus' demand for his subordination and released Demetrius, who twice had escaped and twice been caught; he hoped that concern for his crown might move Antiochus to retreat.

When the winter of 130/29 came, the large Seleucid army and the enormous number of camp-followers had to be distributed in groups throughout the country. The native population, who suffered from the mere presence of so many foreigners and who also were harassed by them, turned hostile towards the army they had welcomed a few months before. A large number of them, obeying Phraates' orders, attacked all the camps on a given day. When Antiochus left his own encampment to go to the rescue of one of the posts, he encountered the Parthian army, which far outnumbered his own force. His staff suggested retreat to the hills, where he would be safe from the enemy's cavalry. The king, however, refused. He fought bravely, but several of his high-ranking officers and part of his army deserted and he lost the battle and his life (spring 129). Phraates is said to have remarked, 'Your drunken audacity has tripped you up, Antiochus, for you expected to gulp down the kingdom of Arsaces in big wine-cups.'[181] He ordered the king's remains to be sent back to Syria. He also tried, in vain, to recapture Demetrius, who escaped to Syria.

The victory, however, was decisive. Parthia kept Media and recovered Babylonia and Susiane. For a year or so, a local dynast, who had been a satrap of the Seleucids, Hyspaosines of Charax, seized power in Babylon and Seleuceia, but this was a mere episode (128/7).[182] Parthian control over both places was re-established by 126/5. Phraates intended to invade Syria after this victory, but he was forced to deal with unexpected trouble. He had hired 'Scythians', probably Tocharians, for the war against Antiochus; they arrived after the battle, but still demanded to be paid. When the king refused, they invaded Hyrcania. Phraates fought them and was defeated and killed in a battle in which the remnants of Antiochus' army, pressed into Parthian service, deserted to the enemy, thereby avenging their king (c. 128).

The defeat and death of Antiochus VII has rightly been called 'the catastrophe of hellenism in continental Asia and at the same time of the Seleucid empire'.[183] The casualties were enormous; there was not a single household in the capital of Antioch, it was said, that did not mourn the death of one of its members. Never again did a Seleucid king dare to take

Ath. x.439DE, tr. A. S. Bradford.   [182] LeRider 1965, 368: (E 149).
[183] Meyer 1921, 272: (I 26), and 1925, 67: (E 152).

the field against the Parthians. The eastern satrapies beyond the Euphrates were lost forever. The kingdom, once by far the largest of all Hellenistic monarchies, was now reduced to Cilicia and northern Syria. The Jewish high-priest John Hyrcanus[184] extricated himself unharmed from the disaster in Media and swiftly regained his independence from the Seleucid princes who followed Antiochus VII. These princes were not much more than *condottieri*, fighting against their cousins, against the growing and increasingly aggressive power of the Jews, against the Nabataean and Ituraean Arabs, the Greek cities in Syria and Phoenicia, and the local dynasts. The final agony of the Seleucids had begun.

IV. ASIA MINOR, 158–129 B.C.

(a) The last Attalids and the origin of Roman Asia

When Eumenes II died in 158, his son Attalus was too young to rule.[185] The kingdom passed to Eumenes' brother Attalus, whom Eumenes had already made his co-ruler, undoubtedly with the understanding that his son was to succeed him. Attalus had always been loyal, even when his loyalty incurred the Senate's disapproval (p. 332). An expression of this loyalty was Attalus' formal epithet *Philadelphos* ('the one who loves his brother⟨s⟩'). Attalus made it clear from the beginning that his brother's son was to be his heir. He also married his brother's widow Stratonice.

With the accession of Attalus II relations with Rome improved, since the Senate harboured no grudge against him as it had against Eumenes. The change, however, was only superficial; there was no change in the Roman policy that had penalized the kingdom by setting Galatia free (p. 333), and Roman suspicion about Pergamene activities was kept alive by the repeated charges of enemies, especially Prusias II and the Galatians. Eumenes and Attalus were accused of secret activities in Galatia (p. 334); the accusations were not without foundation. Soon after his accession Attalus considered using force to regain some control of Galatia, and all his advisers but one shared his view. A unique document, a secret letter written by Attalus *c.* 158 to the priest of Pessinus in Galatia (published much later), gives a valuable insight into the matter.

---

[184] For the surname and its origin: Schürer 1973, 201 n. 2: (E 112).

[185] A birth-date in the sixties seems to follow from Polyb. xxxiii.18.2. For the vexed question who were the parents of Attalus III: Hansen 1971, 471–4: (E 57); Hopp 1977, 16–26: (E 60); Walbank 1957–79, iii.417–18: (B 38); Allen 1983, 189–94: (E 52). On balance, the view seems preferable that he was the son of Eumenes and Stratonice, not to be easily reconciled with Polyb. xxx.9.6 (an oddly phrased addition to the text after 138 B.C.). The alternative seems to be that he was Eumenes' son by a concubine. There are decisive arguments against the view once widely held, that he was born in 171 as the son of Attalus (II) and Stratonice, and there is little to recommend the opinion of Vatin and Hopp that he was borne by Stratonice to an anonymous natural father; against: Polyb. xviii.41, not discussed by Hopp or Walbank.

When we came to Pergamum and I assembled not only Athenaeus and Sosander and Menogenes but many others also of my 'relatives', and when I laid before them what we discussed in Apamea and told them our decision, there was a very long discussion, and at first all inclined to the same opinion with us, but Chlorus vehemently held forth the Roman power and counselled us in no way to do anything without them. In this at first few concurred, but afterwards, as day after day we kept considering, it appealed more and more, and to launch an undertaking without their participation began to seem fraught with great danger; if we were successful the attempt promised to bring us envy and detraction and baneful suspicion – that which they felt also toward my brother – while if we failed we should meet certain destruction. For they would not, it seemed to us, regard our disaster with sympathy but would rather be delighted to see it, because we had undertaken such projects without them. . . . I decided, therefore, to send to Rome on every occasion men to make constant report of cases where we are in doubt. . . .[186]

Nothing shows more clearly than this document how the Senate's message after the Third Macedonian War to its former allies came to be understood at the court of the Attalids: they were to have no independent policy. Action in pursuit of policy was restricted to cases where it served Roman interests (as in the support given to Ariarathes in 157, p. 359, or to the Syrian pretender Alexander, p. 362), or where no Roman interest was at stake. Self-defence, of course, was still tolerated, as in 156, when Prusias attacked Attalus (p. 359), but the Senate intervened, when, in the aftermath of that war, Attalus and Ariarathes took punitive action against the city of Priene (p. 361). The Senate's concern in Asia Minor then was to preserve the *status quo*. Little room was left for Attalid policy.

It is, therefore, somewhat surprising that the Senate did not react sooner and more strongly than it actually did to Attalus' one display of adventurous spirit: in 149 Attalus was instrumental in having his old foe Prusias of Bithynia overthrown. Prusias had sent his son Nicomedes to Rome to petition the Senate for an exemption from the payment of the rest of the indemnity which he owed to Attalus under the treaty of 154. He is also said to have instructed Menas, should the mission fail, to have the prince assassinated, since he wanted to leave the throne to another son. When the matter was discussed in the Senate, Attalus' ambassador Andronicus easily won the day by demonstrating that the indemnity did not cover the amount of damage done. Menas revealed his instructions to the prince, the two contacted Andronicus, and the Pergamene promised Attalus' support if Nicomedes would rise against his father. In a town in north-western Greece on their way home Nicomedes was proclaimed king in the presence of Andronicus, some Pergamene and some

---

[186] Welles, *RC* 61. The traditional interpretation of this document, attacked by Sherwin-White 1984, 39–40: (A 34), seems to be correct. See also Gruen 1984, 591 n. 87: (A 20).

Bithynian troops. Attalus received him in his capital and demanded from Prusias the cession of part of his kingdom to Nicomedes. When this was rejected, he invaded Bithynia. Prusias informed the Senate, convinced that Rome would not tolerate such a flagrant breach of the peace. In fact, Roman intervention was so slow and so hesitant that the Senate's partiality became obvious, much to the anger of Cato. Prusias was abandoned by his subjects, his troops, and the Romans; he was killed by his son's soldiers in Nicomedia in the temple of Zeus where he had sought refuge (149). Attalus had helped Nicomedes II to the Bithynian throne.[187]

There was a sequel to this war. Prusias' last resort had been five hundred Thracian soldiers, sent at his request by his kinsman Diegylis, the king of the Thracian Caeni who dwelt in the hinterland of Byzantium. Diegylis is described as utterly vicious and cruel; he harassed the Greek cities, particularly those in the Thracian Chersonese, the Gallipoli peninsula, which had become Attalid territory after the war against Antiochus. He seized and burned down Lysimacheia. Attalus declared war and defeated and killed Diegylis in or shortly before 145. The city of Elaeus (Gallipoli) praised him as 'Saviour and Benefactor'. After some time, however, the Thracian raids began again, and when the Attalid dynasty ended and there was no Attalid governor in charge of the Chersonese and the Thracian lands, Thracian pressure on the Greek cities seems to have increased.[188]

During this time Attalus twice showed his loyalty to Rome by supporting Roman armies: in 148 in Macedonia against Andriscus with his fleet, in 146 against the Achaeans with a detachment of soldiers under the command of his general Philopoemen, who also had charge of the king's seal as is shown by a dedication erected in his honour in the Heraeum of Samos by Attalus himself. Several works of art from the rich booty of Corinth found their way to Pergamum and some were still there to be seen by Pausanias in the later second century A.D.[189]

---

[187] Habicht, *PW*, 'Prusias', 1120–4. Walbank 1957–79, III.673: (B 38), suggests that Prusias' order to assassinate the prince may have been invented to justify the conspiracy of Menas and Nicomedes. For Cato's role: Astin 1978, 125: (H 68). The Numidian king Massinissa also seems to have given support to Nicomedes (*IDélos* 1577). Attalus II, in a dedication in Pergamum after the victory, unabashedly and falsely stated that Prusias had violated the treaty of 154, concluded under the auspices of Rome (*OGIS* 327)! See also *OGIS* 299, with Jones 1974, 188: (E 61).

[188] For Diegylis see Diod. Sic. XXXIII.14–15, XXXIV.12 (his son Zibelmius); Strabo XIII, p. 624; App. *Mithr.* 6; Trogus, *Prol.* XXXVI. Attalus in Gallipoli: *CRAI* 1917, 25–8; *CQ* 11 (1917) 1–2. See also the dedications from Panium, *OGIS* 303–4. For the date of the expedition see *OGIS* 330, with Robert 1928, 439–41: (B 62), and 1935, 76–8: (E 161); Jones 1974, 189: (E 61). For the renewal of Thracian incursions, *OGIS* 339, 12–16 and 55. In general: Hopp 1977, 96–8: (E 60).

[189] War against Andriscus: Strabo XIII, p. 624; Zon. IX.28; Hopp 1977, 93–6: (E 60). Achaean War: Paus. VIII.16.1, 8; Pliny, *HN* VII.126. For Philopoemen: Paus. *loc. cit.*; *MDAI(A)* 44 (1919) 30 no. 16; Plut. *Mor.* 792A. He must have been the successor of Demetrius (n. 18).

In the capital Attalus completed the smaller frieze of the Great Altar (n. 17) and built and dedicated the temple of Hera 'the Queen' (*Basilis*) in the vicinity of the upper gymnasium. In conformity with the tradition of the royal house he made rich donations to various Greek cities and sanctuaries outside the kingdom, the most lavish of which was the erection of a magnificent stoa in the agora of Athens.[190] Within his realm Attalus founded or refounded a number of cities, among which were Philadelphia in Lydia and Attaleia in Pamphylia that still bears his name today.[191]

When the Roman ambassadors to the east, led by Scipio Aemilianus, visited Pergamum in 139 they found a well-organized and stable kingdom.[192] The king, by now over eighty years of age, had done much to strengthen it. He was on good terms with his Cappadocian neighbour and had contributed to the decline of Seleucid power. Bithynia, formerly a country hostile to the Pergamenes, was now ruled by a king indebted to Attalus. The old monarch had not only repelled Thracian aggression against his European territories, but also succeeded in expanding his kingdom there. In 139 it could hardly have been foreseen that a few years later the monarchy of the Attalids would disappear.

Attalus died in 138 and was succeeded by his nephew Attalus III *Philometor* ('who loves his mother').[193] A letter from Attalus to Ephesus, the home of one of young Attalus' teachers, shows how seriously the king had taken the responsibility of preparing the crown prince to govern. Other inscriptions show that Philometor had been given some royal functions to perform several years before his uncle died.[194] It was

[190] For the temple of Hera: *MDAI(A)* 37 (1912) 283 no. 6. For the Stoa of Attalus and its dedicatory inscription: Thompson and Wycherley 1972, 103–8: (B 203). Attalus and Ariarathes V as princes were thought to have dedicated in Athens a statue of the philosopher Carneades, as their teacher (*IG* II².3781). The dedicants, however, could be Athenian citizens named after the kings: so Mattingly 1971, 29–32: (D 43). For donations in Miletus see Herrmann 1965, 96–7: (E 142); Müller 1976, 53 n. 99: (E 155); Hopp 1977, 6–13: (E 60). A gift to Iulius on Ceus: *IG* XII.5.625. A royal delegation paid respect to the sanctuary of the Cabiri in Samothrace (*IG* XII.8.170, 79).

[191] Hansen 1971, 177ff.: (E 57); Hopp 1977, 102–4: (E 60). Attaleia: Strabo XIII, p. 667.

[192] Astin 1959: (E 123); Knibbe 1960: (E 146).

[193] Strabo XIII, p. 624, gives Attalus twenty-one years. Cistophoric coins show that year 21 was his last and Attalus III's first year: Kleiner 1972, 18–23: (B 103). This must then be 139/8, since Eumenes' last year (year 40) can only have been 159/8 and this was also Attalus' first year. Consequently, the fourth year of Attalus III that appears in two of his letters (Welles, *RC* 66.19, 67.17) was 136/5 and not, as is usually assumed, 135/4.

[194] Letter of Attalus: *JÖAI* 47 (1964–5) 2 no. 1, with emendations listed in Rigsby 1979, 45 n. 26: (E 160). Participation in the government: Welles, *RC* 65 line 14, 66 line 9; Swoboda, Keil and Knoll 1935, 33–4 no. 75: (B 202). For the sequence and chronology of the three letters published there see also Magie 1950, 774: (E 150), and Hopp 1977, 70–4: (E 60). There is a dedication of 146/5 from the gymnasium in Pergamum by the new ephebes, in honour of Prince Attalus (*MDAI(A)* 29 (1904) 170 no. 14); it tells nothing about the age of Attalus (*pace* Hopp, p. 25). Apollonius, son of Demetrius (col. II.48), may be the son of the former minister of Eumenes' seal (n. 18), and Dionysius, son of Asclepiades (col. I.47), will be the eponymous magistrate of Pergamum in 105, as attested in the document Jos. *AJ* XIV.149; he therefore held office at the age of *c.* 58 years.

not the latter's fault that the nephew did not live up to people's expectations. Attalus III, Diodorus says, was 'unlike his predecessors'.[195] He is charged with cruelty, disregard for his responsibilities, and a preference for the study of various sciences. Except for the last, it is extremely difficult to assess the validity of these charges. The king is accused of having many of his predecessor's counsellors and their families slaughtered in the royal palace by the most brutal barbarians in his service. No names or other details are given, except that the king is said to have suspected some of his victims of having been implicated in the death of his mother (who was still alive in October 136) and his bride Berenice, others of plotting. The few surviving documents issued by Attalus III give no indication that he did in fact neglect his duties, but neither do they prove that he did not.[196] In the autumn of 133 the Roman Senate formally decreed that all of Attalus' acts, down to the day before he died, should remain valid (p. 378). This shows the Roman opinion, at least, that whatever the king's qualities, the administrative routine was carried out more or less normally.

The sources also say that Attalus III was hated by his subjects and that they longed for his overthrow. The charge, however, may have been invented in order to make the Roman takeover look desirable. Decrees praising Attalus survive and honours were bestowed upon him. On the other hand, official documents of this kind do not prove that he was, in fact, popular.[197] Attalus was an active investigator of a variety of sciences and some art techniques: pharmacology, botany, zoology, medicine, agriculture and metalwork. He planted, cultivated and tested drugs, and apparently wrote works on a variety of such topics. The ancient scholars Varro, Columella, the elder Pliny and especially Galen speak of his achievements seriously and with respect.[198] Such interests and activities, however, were not regarded as befitting a king and this eccentricity may well have been the origin of the accusation that Attalus neglected his duties.

Because of the extreme deficiency (and obvious hostility) of our sources, Attalus III will always remain an enigmatic figure, but the sources do bear out the fact that he was 'unlike his predecessors'. Apart from internal affairs, his reign seems to have been uneventful. Chance alone preserves the information that the king once fought a successful

[195] Diod. Sic. xxxiv.3. For his rule see Magie 1950, 30–2: (E 150); Hansen 1971, 142–7: (E 57); Hopp 1977, 107–20: (E 60). References have been kept to a minimum. That it was Attalus who had the grammarian Daphitas executed for stinging verses about the royal house is far from certain, although Fontenrose 1960: (E 55) has convinced several scholars including Hopp 1977, 119 n. 66: (E 60). See Braund 1982, 354–7: (E 125).   [196] Welles, RC 66–7, perhaps also 68–9.

[197] OGIS 332; MDAI(A) 32 (1907) 311 no. 33; ibid. 33 (1908) 375 no. 1. See also n. 194. Nicander of Colophon (or rather Nicander II) dedicated a hymn, the beginning of which survives, to the king: Gow and Schofield 1953, 7–8: (I 14).   [198] References in Hansen 1971, 144–5: (E 57).

campaign and was granted extravagant honours by the people of Pergamum on his return. Whom he fought, where and when he fought is not known.[199] Even less illuminating is the information that in 134/3 he sent (as did Antiochus VII of Syria) splendid gifts to Scipio Aemilianus who was campaigning in Spain – he must have met him more than once and certainly did so in the capital in 139.[200]

The one truly memorable event of Attalus' reign is his bequest to Rome: before he died in the spring of 133, without family or heir, he willed whatever was his to the Roman people.[201] The king's testament took the Romans by surprise. The first to react was the tribune Tiberius Gracchus; he introduced a bill with a provision that the bequest be used to help finance his agrarian programme. He also declared that the Senate had no right whatsoever to deal with something bequeathed to the Roman people.[202] Only after Gracchus' death was the Senate free to act. As already mentioned, a decree was passed that all measures taken by the deceased king down to the day before he died should remain valid and not be changed by the Roman representatives who were to be sent to Asia. Acceptance of the bequest is clearly implied,[203] and, in fact, before the end of the year, a committee of five Roman *legati*, headed by the *pontifex maximus* Scipio Nasica (who, as the murderer of Gracchus, had become highly unpopular), went out to settle affairs. The committee ran into difficulties. Not only did Scipio die soon after his arrival in Pergamum, but a pretender to the throne challenged Rome.[204]

Soon after Attalus' death, Aristonicus, who claimed to be and may have been an illegitimate son of King Eumenes II, had himself proclaimed King Eumenes III, as coins with the abbreviated title and name show.[205] At first he had considerable success, partly owing to the fact that the Romans were involved in internal feuding, the last stages of the

[199] OGIS 332; see IvP III, p. 3, and Hopp 1977, 111–12: (E 60).   [200] Cic. Deiot. 19.

[201] Main sources in Greenidge and Clay 1960, 11–12: (B 212).

[202] Plut. Ti. Gracch. 14; Badian 1972, 712–14: (H 32). The statement seems to have referred specifically to the cities in Attalus' kingdom. The bill may never have been passed.

[203] OGIS 435 (Sherk, Documents 11) with the comments of Drew-Bear 1972: (E 134), superseding all previous work. As Drew-Bear has shown, OGIS 436 lines 1–5 (Sherk no. 13) is from another copy of the same decree. Gruen 1984, 603–4: (A 20), dates these documents to 129 B.C.

[204] The bilingual funerary inscription of Scipio has been found in Pergamum: MDAI(A) 35 (1910) 483 no. 77; Tuchelt MDAI (I) 29 (1979) 309–16.

[205] Demonstrated by Robinson 1954: (B 129) from cistophoric tetradrachms, dated to years 2, 3 and 4, and minted in Thyatira, Apollonis and Stratoniceia-on-Caicus. Another from Synnada with the legend BA AP has been interpreted Βα(σιλέως) Ἀρ(ιστονίκου), 'King Aristonicus', most recently by Hopp 1977, 121ff.: (E 60), who theorizes from this that Aristonicus' usurpation occurred during Attalus' lifetime, that the usurper took the title 'King Aristonicus' and changed it, after Attalus' death, to 'King Eumenes'. If correct, this would shed new light on Attalus' motives for the bequest, but such a change is extremely unlikely, and the absence of a date year I would then be very hard to explain. The theory collapses, in any event, since this coin is considerably earlier: Kleiner and Noe 1976, 81: (B 105); perhaps referring to King Ariarathes IV: Mørkholm 1979, 52–4: (B 116). See further Adams 1980: (B 76) with Gruen 1984, 595 n. 101: (A 20).

Spanish War, and a slave revolt in Sicily and so were slow to decide upon the bequest and slow to react to the usurpation. Most of the major cities seem to have opposed Aristonicus; some, if not most, had been declared free in Attalus' will. For Pergamum this was the confirmation of an already existing state of affairs, but for others, like Ephesus, a new grant.[206] Pergamum immediately reacted to Aristonicus' move with a decree designed to strengthen the citizen body; this was passed before it was known whether Rome would accept the bequest.[207] Among the Greek cities only Phocaea is known to have joined Aristonicus spontaneously. Others like Samos, Colophon and Myndus (in Ionia and Caria) had to be taken by force.

Aristonicus has sometimes been regarded as the leading spirit of a social movement. He is said to have mobilized the slaves and the rural poor against the free and the wealthy in the cities. The evidence does not bear this out. Aristonicus, it is true, after he had suffered some setbacks, appealed to poor people and to slaves. It is also true that he called his followers 'citizens of Sun-city' (*Heliopolitai*) and that the Stoic philosopher Blossius of Cumae joined him after the death of Tiberius Gracchus, to whom he had been close. These facts, however, prove only that Aristonicus was eventually forced to look for support where he could find it. Nothing suggests that he began as a social reformer or that he was transformed into one. His goal most likely was political: to establish himself as the successor of the kings. An appeal to the lower strata of society in emergencies was common in antiquity. Most of the usurper's support during the war will have come from those who had political and national reasons rather than the desire to change the conditions under which they lived.

The war must have begun in 133.[208] Aristonicus was opposed by much of the urban population as well as other inhabitants of the former kingdom, by the kings of Asia Minor allied with Rome, Nicomedes II of Bithynia, Mithridates V of Pontus, Ariarathes V of Cappadocia, and

[206] That Attalus in his will reaffirmed the freedom of Pergamum is attested in the Pergamene decree cited n. 207, line 5. Rigsby 1979: (E 160) has shown that the 'era of the province of Asia' from 134/3 is, in fact, a municipal era of Ephesus – so, independently, Adams 1980 311–14: (B 76) – probably motivated by a grant of freedom to the city in Attalus' will.

[207] *OGIS* 338; Hopp 1977, 131–5: (E 60).

[208] The principal modern works are Vavřinek 1957: (E 69); Dumont 1966: (E 135); Carrata-Thomes 1968: (E 130); Hansen 1971, 150–9: (E 57); Rubinsohn 1973: (B 30); Vavřinek 1975: (E 70); Hopp 1977, 131–47: (E 60); Delplace 1978: (E 133); Adams 1980: (B 76); Collins 1981: (E 131); Braund 1983, 21–3, 49ff.: (E 126); Gruen 1984, 592ff.: (A 20); Sherwin-White 1984, 84–8: (A 34). Inscriptions referring to the war (besides those cited in other notes): *IGRom* IV.131 (Cyzicus); *JÖAI* 11 (1908) 69 no. 6, perhaps also *LW* 504 (Halicarnassus); Holleaux 1919: (E 24) from Bargylia with Jones 1974, 191–2: (E 61), and Herrmann 1974, 257–8: (E 143); Herrmann 1962, 5 no. 2: (E 141) (Maeonia); *Epigraphica Anatolica* 3 (1984) 157 (Gordos). General allusions to the war are to be found in Robert 1937, 459–67: (E 162), from Bargylia; *OGIS* 339.16–24 from Sestos; *IG* XII *Suppl.* 116 from Methymna; *IvP* 14 from Pergamum.

Pylaemenes of Paphlagonia, and by Byzantium and other cities abroad. A
Roman army under the consul and *pontifex maximus* Publius Licinius
Crassus finally arrived in 131, but Crassus was soon defeated and killed in
a battle near Pergamum; Ariarathes was another casualty. Crassus'
successor, the consul Marcus Perperna, defeated Aristonicus in 130 and
took him prisoner in Stratoniceia-on-Caicus, but Perperna died while the
victory celebrations, to be held in Pergamum, were being prepared.[209] So
the consul of 129, Manius Aquillius, assumed command, had the last
strongholds of Aristonicus' followers stormed, and brought the war to
an end. With the assistance of ten senatorial envoys he transformed the
kingdom of the Attalids into the Roman province of Asia.[210]

(b) Rhodes after 164 B.C.[211]

Once the Senate had capped the humiliation of the Rhodians in 164 by
granting them the treaty they had long been petitioning for, Rome could
indulge in a more generous attitude. The Senate agreed to allow Rhodes
to acquire the Carian city of Calynda, whose inhabitants preferred
Rhodian rule to the domination of Caunus. The Rhodians, to show their
gratitude, voted to erect a colossal figure of the people of Rome. In Caria,
at least, Rhodes remained attractive to a number of smaller towns,
especially to those that had uneasy relations with larger cities; Ceramus
for one, it seems, at her own initiative, was granted a treaty by Rhodes
c. 163.[212]

Since the Rhodian economy had been hard hit by the Roman punitive
measures, Rhodes was quite prepared to accept royal donations – and
what they implied – from such men as Eumenes II in 161/60 and

[209] The identity of this Stratoniceia (as opposed to Carian Stratoniceia) has been argued by
Broughton 1934: (E 129), and established when the coins minted there were recognized as coins of
Aristonicus (n. 205). For the victory of Perperna and the festival to be held in Pergamum see *IPriene*
108.223–32, 109.91–5; for the victories of both Perperna and Aquillius see *OGIS* 695.89 with n. 17.
Perperna granted a privilege to the sanctuary of the Persian Artemis, Anaitis, in Hieracome in Lydia:
Tac. *Ann.* IV.62.2; Robert 1948, 37–8: (B 61).
[210] Strabo XIV, p. 646; Sherk, *Documents* 25.15. Gruen 1984, 605–8: (A 20), argues that transformation into a Roman province came considerably later. For several years Aquillius was occupied with
the building of roads and several milestones survive: *CIL* I².646–51; Magie 1950, 157–8, 1048–9: (E
150); he returned to celebrate a triumph in 126. Pergamum established a cult of Aquillius, which still
existed two generations later: Jones 1974, 197–8: (E 61).
[211] The principal sources are Polyb. XXXI.4–5, XXXI.31; Diod. Sic. XXXI.36; for the Cretan war:
Polyb. XXXIII.4 (Diod. Sic. XXXI.37), XXXIII.13.2, 15.3–17; Diod. Sic. XXXI.38, 43–45; Trogus, *Prol.*
XXXV; *ILindos* p. 1009, and perhaps also *SIG* 673. The date is disputed: Robert, in Holleaux 1938–68,
IV.i.173 n. 2: (D 35). For the Rhodian squadron in the Third Punic War see App. *Lib.* 112.534. A
Rhodian delegation in the sanctuary of the Cabiri in Samothrace, c. 130: *IG* XII.8.171, 65. In general:
Schmitt 1957, 171–80: (E 77); Sherwin-White 1984, 30–6: (A 34); for the cult of Roma: Mellor 1975,
27–36: (I 25).
[212] Michel, *Recueil* 458, with Robert 1935, 60–1: (E 161). For later Rhodian activities in Caria, c.
130, see Holleaux 1919, 16–19: (E 24); Robert 1937, 463: (E 162).

Demetrius I at about the same time.[213] It seems significant that the donors were kings whose relations with Rome were rather delicate. Part of what Eumenes promised was left for Attalus II to pay after Eumenes died in 158. Perhaps these gifts influenced the Rhodians to lend Attalus naval support in his war against Prusias (n. 134) and, in that same year, to decline a request from Priene to intervene when Attalus and Ariarathes were ravaging Prienian territory (n. 137). In any event, they had their hands full with a war of their own against Cretan cities (155–153) and it was not going well at all. The cause of the war may be connected with Rhodian attempts to suppress Cretan piracy. Allusions in Polybius and Diodorus make it clear that the Rhodians suffered unexpected defeats and that the Cretans were on the attack in several places, such as Carpathos, where they were finally repelled, and Siphnos, which they seized through treachery and brutally sacked before they were forced to retreat and were destroyed. Both sides appealed to the Achaean League in 154/3 for military assistance, but the Achaeans kept out of the struggle. At last, prompted by a Rhodian embassy, Roman envoys seem to have laid the war to rest.

A Rhodian squadron participated in the last Roman war against Carthage in 147, but the destruction of Carthage may not have been welcomed in Rhodes; it certainly meant the disappearance of a competitor, but probably also the loss of a partner in international trade.[214] The destruction of Carthage was witnessed not only by Polybius, but apparently by the most famous Rhodian of his time, the Stoic philosopher Panaetius, who was a friend of Scipio Aemilianus and who appeared again in his entourage during the latter's famous mission to the east in 140/39.[215] After Rhodes had been reduced to a second-rate power, men such as Panaetius and his pupil Poseidonius made the island a famous cultural centre that rivalled Athens and surpassed Pergamum. Its philosophical school, throughout the later second and the entire first century, attracted eminent Romans. Their respect for Rhodians such as Panaetius may well lie behind the phrase in a decree of the Senate, passed in 135, upholding an earlier decision made by Rhodian arbitrators in a quarrel between Priene and Samos: 'It is no easy matter for us to change what the people of Rhodes, on whose arbitration both sides had agreed, have ruled.'[216]

---

[213] For Eumenes: Diod. Sic. xxxi.36; for Demetrius, n. 123. Polybius scorns the Rhodians for the acceptance of Eumenes' gift, probably because his fellow-Achaeans had shown greater pride rejecting an earlier offer by the king: n. 20. See Walbank 1957–79, III.515: (B 38).

[214] Schmitt 1957, 278: (E 77).

[215] See Blinkenberg in *ILindos*, pp. 501–2; for the Roman embassy of 140/39: Astin 1959: (E 123); Knibbe 1960: (E 146). [216] Sherk, *Documents* 10, B 10–11.

V. EPILOGUE: ROMAN POLICY IN THE EAST, 189–129 B.C.

It can be argued and has in fact been argued that Roman policy in the east during the third century was defensive, reacting only to developments that seemed to endanger Rome's security. Roman policy in the second century, on the contrary, was aggressive, often treacherous, unpredictable, cruel and immoral. These verdicts are mainly based on the account of the contemporary historian Polybius. He was Greek, to be sure, but he cannot be accused of anti-Roman bias. Being himself a victim of an arbitrary Roman action, he had, in his misfortune, the good luck of being well treated by the members of a powerful Roman family. During the many years he spent in Rome he came to admire the efficiency of the Roman state and some of the ideals of the nobility. Above all, he was fascinated by the unfailing instinct for power displayed, individually and collectively, by Roman senators. And he was overwhelmed by the dimensions of Rome's growing empire. Rome's arm already reached out to the whole of Italy and Sicily, to Africa, Spain, Greece, Asia Minor, the Near East and Egypt. For Polybius this was the universe. He never ceased to be a Greek and a patriotic Achaean, but he eventually persuaded himself that the conquest of the world by the Romans was not only a great and memorable achievement, but that it was also beneficial for those conquered.

Nevertheless it is this admirer of Rome who reports many of the actions which made Roman policy in the east unique and awful. It has been observed, rightly I think, that his standards were different from ours, that he was more inclined than modern historians to tolerate acts of questionable morality, if a worthwhile political gain resulted.[217] It is, however, fairly obvious that Polybius must have gone through some pain before he arrived, on balance, at a favourable verdict of Rome's rise to world power. A good many passages in his work suggest at least that he felt some uneasiness, that he had reservations about Roman actions. However, the deficiencies of the Greek states and the Greek society from which he came and the respect and honour paid to him personally by some of the most eminent Romans undoubtedly made him more inclined to stress the glorious rather than the dark features of Roman expansion.[218]

Be that as it may, it is not so much Polybius' judgement that is relevant here as that of those who read him in order to form an opinion on Rome's rise to world power. They cannot fail to notice that, from the end of the third century onwards, Roman policy was aggressive. In 200, for instance, the Romans had reasons for going to war with Philip (mainly the

[217] Walbank 1972, 171–3: (B 39).   [218] Walbank 1972, 166–73, 178, 181: (B 39).

indecisive peace of 205), but hardly a sufficient cause. They had no obligation whatsoever towards Athens, Aetolia or Rhodes, and a very slight one, at best, towards Attalus. Some of Philip's actions, however, caused concern. But the Romans made no serious attempt to settle the disputed questions through negotiations. Instead, they presented Philip with flat demands that made war unavoidable.

No sooner was Philip defeated than the Senate proclaimed that all the Greeks of Asia should be free. This was a statement unwarranted by the events, unacceptable to Antiochus and therefore hazardous to the peace. It was, moreover, altogether needless, unless it was meant to provide some basis for future Roman intervention. It is therefore significant that this doctrine was promptly abandoned as no longer useful after Antiochus' defeat: it had served its purpose. True enough, Antiochus himself had played into the Romans' hands when he tied himself to the Aetolians and made the fatal mistake of invading Greece. Nonetheless, the conflict originated from unwarranted and provocative declarations on the part of Rome. Twenty years later, when the Romans declared war on King Perseus, they had no cause at all. Perseus was willing to avoid war by almost all means, but was not given a chance. The fate of the Carthaginians in 149 was similar. It cannot be denied that Roman policy had become aggressive by the end of the Hannibalic War and that after the victories over Philip and Antiochus the veil dropped from Rome's aggressive character.

Macedon and Carthage had been enemies, Antiochus neither enemy nor friend. It was for the allies and friends to experience the treacherous character of Roman policy. The assurances given to Prusias of Bithynia in order to keep him away from Antiochus' camp were withdrawn as soon as Antiochus was defeated, and part of Prusias' realm was given to his foe Eumenes (p. 325). Rome's oldest and firmest allies in the east, Pergamum and Rhodes, fared even worse, once Macedon was extinguished (pp. 332, 337). It was utterly dishonest of the Senate to play the prince Demetrius against his father, King Philip, or Attalus against his brother, King Eumenes (p. 332), or the Galatians against the latter (p. 333). The same class of nobles that had assured Demetrius I that he would find Rome amenable if he satisfied Roman expectations soon thereafter gave its support to an obscure pretender, although Demetrius had done no harm to Rome (pp. 357–8).

Roman policy was also unpredictable, since wherever the Senate concluded that a situation could be exploited to Rome's advantage, it did so without much regard for legal claims. In 189 the Senate gave away large parts of Asia Minor as a gift. Twelve years later the Rhodians were formally told that the gift had not been a gift, and eventually it was taken away from both Rhodes and Eumenes (pp. 336–7, 333). Likewise, there was nothing in the treaty with Antiochus III preventing the Seleucid king from making war against Egypt. But in 168 Rome threatened Antiochus IV (who had not been the aggressor) with war, if he did not withdraw from Egypt and Cyprus (p. 344). This was tantamount to adding a clause unilaterally to the treaty. Nor did Rome hesitate to violate that treaty to a degree that made it obsolete. When it was concluded the parties had established peace and friendship between themselves. Loyalty was to be expected and was in fact observed by the Seleucids. Rome, on the contrary, contacted and encouraged rebellious subjects of Antiochus Epiphanes and even accepted them as allies (pp. 354, 358–9). Roman policy, it may be said, was determined by political considerations; to these, questions of law and morality were subordinated. Philip V was the first to complain openly about this, when he realized that the peace he had concluded with Rome went contrary to his expectations; it was not only the end of hostilities, but also the beginning of Roman interference in his affairs.[219] Philip recognized what soon became more and more apparent: that Rome did not intend to negotiate but to give orders.

If indeed the Senate considered itself to be the final arbiter of world affairs, then the notorious arrogance of Roman representatives in the east is easily explained. Aemilius Lepidus displayed such arrogance in his encounter with Philip as early as 200, Cornelius Lentulus in his dealings with Antiochus III in 196, the consul Acilius in 189 *vis-à-vis* the Aetolian ambassadors. Similar was the conduct of Popillius Laenas towards Antiochus in 168 (p. 344), of Sulpicius Galus towards Eumenes in 164 (p. 334) and of Octavius in Syria (p. 354). Even cases of outright criminality were taken lightly by the Senate: nothing suggests that T. Flamininus was censured for having acquiesced in the murder of the *boeotarch* Brachylles, and the treacherous conduct of Marcius Philippus' dealings with Perseus, although criticized by some senators, was approved by the majority of the House.[220]

There is no need to elaborate on Roman cruelty, since the phenomenon is well known. The treatment of Epirus in 167 may be cited as just one example, inflicted on the unlucky country by a man who was considered by many to be a model of Roman virtue, L. Aemilius Paullus. The ways in which the second-century Senate handled international affairs and conducted its foreign policy show that it was fully aware of Rome's superior power. This superiority was recognized early and far beyond the frontiers of Rome. About 180 B.C. the Achaean Callicrates formulated his political doctrine that the Achaeans, while being allies of

---

[219] Polyb. XXIII.2.7; Livy XXXIX.26, 28.
[220] Flamininus: Polyb. XVIII.43. 'Pilate's role', Walbank 1957–79, III.180: (B 38). Philippus: Briscoe 1964: (D 8).

Rome, could do nothing better than to regard Roman requests as orders to be obeyed, superior even to the laws and the treaties of the Achaeans themselves.[221] It is therefore no surprise to find the same Callicrates later stating that the Achaeans without Roman authorization should not make war with anybody nor give military support to anybody.[222] By that time King Attalus of Pergamum too had been forced to admit that he had better avoid any move that could be viewed by the Romans as a sign of an independent policy (p. 374). If there had still been doubts about the superior power of Rome or the Senate's determination to exploit it even in areas that seemed of no immediate concern to Rome, they were dispelled by the fate of Macedon, the retreat of Antiochus from Egypt and the punishment inflicted upon Eumenes and Rhodes. This is clear from the facts and is also explicitly stated by Polybius, who says that thereafter 'it was universally accepted as a necessary fact that all must submit to the Romans and obey their orders'.[223] This feeling was so general that when the free city of Athens in the later part of the century granted the guild of artists some privileges, it was found desirable to add 'provided that nothing in this is found contrary to the Romans'.[224]

When Polybius announces that he decided to continue his narrative beyond the year 168 which capped the rise of Rome to supremacy and when he adds that this would also enable his readers to see how those subject to Roman domination reacted to it, he thought this period an important one for forming a judgement about Roman domination by both contemporaries and posterity.[225] Rather surprisingly, he nowhere discusses the problem thoroughly. Only a partial answer is given in a long chapter (XXXVI.9), where he quotes anonymous Greek voices either condemning or defending Roman policy and Roman domination. There are parallels for such a method in ancient historiography, which allows the historian to discuss controversial issues without openly committing himself.[226] There has been much discussion as to whether Polybius himself sides with the attacking or the defending opinions.[227] His opinion may lie between, but what matters more is that to those who judge Roman policy from a distance in time the attackers seem to have by far the stronger case.

It is perhaps the most significant feature of Roman policy that the Senate was not prepared to regard a settlement with another major power – even if it was made after a decisive victory and therefore advantageous to Rome – to be final. As Philip learned in 200 and again in 185 and Perseus somewhat later, peace with Rome as far as the Senate was

---

[221] Polyb. XXIV.8–13; Errington 1969, 200ff.: (D 23).   [222] Polyb. XXXIII.16.7–8.

[223] Polyb. III.4.3, tr. W. R. Paton.   [224] FD III.2.68, 60.   [225] Polyb. III.4.6–7.

[226] Compare the anonymous Athenians judging Alcibiades on his return to Athens in 408 (Xen. Hell. 1.4.13–17) or the famous discussion about Augustus in Tac. Ann. 1.9–10.

[227] Discussion and bibliography in Walbank 1957–79, III.663ff.: (B 38).

concerned was only an intermediate stage. So was the peace with Antiochus of 189, as his son, Antiochus IV, came to realize in 168, and so was the peace of 201 with Carthage. For republican states of lesser strength, there were other means to secure their obedience: the treaty between Rome and the Aetolians obliged the Aetolians to respect the *maiestas* of the Roman people; the treaty granted to Rhodes in 164 may have carried a similar clause. The Achaeans, however, who had been allied with Rome from the early years of the century, paid for their first firm opposition to an arbitrary Roman act with the destruction of Corinth and the dismemberment of their League.

No doubt, second-century Rome was driven to extend its power, whether deliberately, as Polybius asserts,[228] or by instinct. The result was that all major Hellenistic states, whether monarchies or republics, were either eliminated, reduced to the role of satellites of Rome, or henceforth entirely negligible. Whereas Hellenistic culture survived and proved strong enough to conquer even Rome, political domination shifted to other powers, to the Romans, the Parthians, the Jews. It now was for them to decide whether to protect Hellenistic culture, as the Parthians tried to do from the beginning and the Romans learned to do, or whether to attack it, as seemed natural for the Jews (although the Hasmonean dynasty adopted a good many Hellenistic features). There can be no doubt that Roman policy in the second century played into the hands of native, non-Greek people in Egypt and in the Near East. Roman policy thereby contributed at least to the rise of the Hasmoneans and to the expansion of the Parthians. By adding to the difficulties of the Seleucids, Roman policy made it easier for the Parthians to reach the Euphrates; in an indirect way the Romans put self-imposed limits on the possible growth of their empire. When they supported the Jews against their Seleucid masters, the Romans created major problems for their own descendants. There was, however, a long time to come before the Romans, in the days of Pompey, themselves took over Syria and Palestine, and still more time before they annexed Egypt. On the other hand, Macedon, Greece and a large part of Asia Minor were their direct responsibility by 129. It may safely be doubted that Roman domination improved conditions of life for those who inhabited Macedon and Greece. For Roman Asia, on the other hand, it is beyond doubt that life became much harder when the Romans took over from the kings. The hardships brought about by the methods of exploitation used by the *publicani* are well known. They led to violent reaction in 88, when, on the instigation of King Mithridates Eupator, the Romans and Italians throughout the province were slaughtered. After that, Asia had to suffer

---

[228] Derow 1979: (D 21).

for two more generations: from the punishment inflicted by Sulla, from the last Mithridatic War, the civil wars between Pompey and Caesar, between the murderers and the heirs of Caesar and finally between Antony and Octavian. A time of respite came only after Octavian's final victory. A century had gone by since the establishment of the Roman province. In its turn Asia had experienced more oppression and violence, more poverty and injustice than under its previous masters, the Persians, Alexander, the Seleucids or the Attalids. Roman rule in the east during the Republic enriched many Romans; for those subject to it, it was anything but beneficial.[229]

---

[229] This chapter was delivered in 1984.

CHAPTER 11

THE GREEKS OF BACTRIA AND INDIA

A. K. NARAIN

I. INTRODUCTION

No history of the Greeks can be considered complete without an account of their shared experience in the ancient east. In the Achaemenid period, when the Persian empire extended from Greece to Gandhara, a meeting between the east and the west had taken place. Indian soldiers in the Persian army fought on Greek soil, and Greeks such as Scylax made explorations in India for the Persians. Babylonian documents record that in the fifth century B.C. there was an Indian settlement in Nippur and its inhabitants were warriors who had served in the army and had received land; they could lease their plots but had to pay state taxes and perform state duties.[1] An Indian woman, Busasa, kept a tavern in the town of Kish.[2] There were also some Greeks settled in the far eastern parts of the Persian empire: some had been allowed to dwell there as a reward for their assistance to the Achaemenids, while others were exiled as a punishment for their recalcitrance.[3] Because the Ionians were either the first or the most dominant group among the Greeks with whom people in the east came in contact, the Persians called all of them *Yauna*, and the Indians used *Yona* and *Yavana* for them.[4] Pāṇini of Gandhara, in the fifth

---

[1] Dandamayev 1972, 35ff.: (F 41); Bongard-Levin 1985, 63–4: (F 31). In relation to this chapter as a whole see also *CAH Pls. to Vol. VII. 1*, pp. 25–32.

[2] Olmstead 1948, 148: (F 117).

[3] Rawlinson 1912, 32: (F 129); Narain 1957–80, 2–3: (F 103); Cozzoli 1958, 273 n. 6: (F 37); Will *CAH²* VII.i.30; Holt 1984, ch. 5: (F 69). Apart from the definite reference in Herodotus VI.9 there are other references in Herodotus and later sources which provide circumstantial evidence for the presence of Greeks in the far eastern parts of the Achaemenid empire before Alexander's arrival there; cf. Herodotus IV.204; Diod. Sic. XVII.110.4–5, also the contents list of book xvii; Arrian V.1–4; Curtius VII.5.28–35. Cf. Hegyi 1966: (F 64), who draws attention to Herodotus IV.142 that the Ionians 'did not regard the Persian rule as an intolerable slavery. . . . The serving of the Persian king and loyalty to him brought for the Greeks not only reward but at the same time also the appreciation and respect of their compatriots.'

[4] Narain 1957–80, 165–9: (F 103); Töttössy 1977, 129–35: (F 153A). But here I am using the terms 'Greeks' and 'Yavanas' not only as equivalents but also in a very broad sense to include the Macedonians from Yugoslavia as well as the Libyans from Barca in Cyrene, along with the Greeks from various cities in Asia Minor and the mainland Greece, who came to the east before, during and after the time of Alexander.

century B.C., knew their script as *Yavanānī*.[5] The imperial money economy of the Persians showed mixed circulation of their own darics and sigloi with the Athenian Owls and the Indian Bent-Bar coins.[6] Doubtless the settlers must have earned their living by craft and commerce, and participated in the exchange of goods, services and ideas taking place in the Persian empire.

In the course of his campaign in the eastern parts of what remained of the Persian empire Alexander had met with some of these first settlers. They 'had not ceased to follow the customs of their native land, but they were already bilingual, having gradually degenerated from their original language through the influence of a foreign tongue'.[7] Alexander is recorded as having massacred some for the crimes their ancestors had allegedly committed and fraternized with others because of their association with Dionysus.[8] But Alexander brought with him a new wave of settlers and he is believed to have founded several cities in the east. Although conclusive evidence of the identity and location of their material existence still remains to be discovered, and it is difficult to determine whether true *poleis*, 'cities' in the political sense, or only *katoikiai*, military foundations, were meant,[9] there is sufficient circumstantial evidence to assume clusters of peoples from various Greek cities, and of the Macedonians and others, settling in Bactria and other regions

---

[5] *Ashṭādhyāyī* IV.1.49. Pāṇini also associated the Yavanas with the Kambojas, cf. his *Gaṇapāṭha* 178 on II.1.72.   [6] Narain 1957–80, 3–5: (F 103).

[7] Diod. Sic. XVII.110.4–5; Curtius VII.5.29.

[8] E.g. massacre of the Branchidae (Strabo XI.11.4, XIV.1.5; Plutarch, *Moralia* 557 B; Curtius VII.5.28–35) and fraternization with the Nysaeans of Kohi-i-Mor (Arrian V.1–2, VI.2–3). Some scholars refuse to believe in the massacre of the Branchidae, for hardly any satisfactory reason. Tarn 1948, 67: (F 151), calls it a 'clumsy fabrication'; Bernard 1985, 123–5: (F 24). Holt 1984, 174 n. 36: (F 69), who accepts the existence of pre-Alexander Greeks in Bactria, considers it 'unnecessary' to postulate a large population of them. He thinks that the Barcaeans were 'apparently no longer there by the time of Alexander's arrival' and that the Branchidae 'were all destroyed'. But if Holt is right (and not Tarn) on the issue of the wholesale annihilation of the Branchidae, and the evidence of Diod. Sic. XVII.99.5 and XVIII.7.2–9 about the mass killing of the Greek colonists of Alexander in Bactria must be considered, Tarn's dilemma (p. 72) of accounting for the large number of Greeks in Bactria remains unsolved; his postulation that the Seleucids must have encouraged settlements in the area on a large scale is hard to substantiate in light of the available evidence and their political fortune there. On the other hand 'it is hardly necessary to think of large scale importation by Seleucids', as Dani 1957, 198–9: (F 42), points out, with a reminder about the British in India. Exception has been taken to my earlier statement that the Greeks of Bactria were *mostly* descendants of earlier settlers, e.g. Walbank 1958, 126: (F 157); Holt 1984, 174: (F 69); but see also others, e.g. Klima 1958, 173: (F 77), who consider my supposition 'very plausible'. It is true that the documentation is not so full as one would like it to be, but that is so for the entire history of the Greeks of Bactria and India. The question here is not so much about the number as about the character and composition of the Greek population involved in the creation of a new state in Bactria and India. It is not to deny the role of the post-Alexander Greeks, even though most of them were not very happy to be in the area and were eager to return home, but to establish a balance in the dynamics of the then prevailing historical forces there by including the role and interests of the pre-Alexander Greeks and their Indo-Iranian relations, which provided a *locus standi* as well as support, in the rationale of their success.

[9] Koshelenko 1972, 59–78: (F 79); *id.* 1979, chs. 4 and 5, esp. 212–21: (F 80); Holt 1986: (F 66); Musti 1984, 189–90: (F 101A), discusses the matter in the context of the Seleucids.

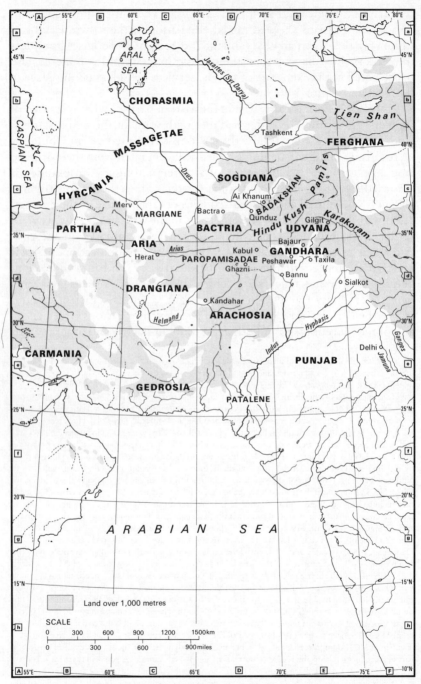

Map 14. The Greek lands of central and southern Asia.

of eastern and southern Afghanistan, either voluntarily or on orders of Alexander according to his plan. It is possible that some of his garrisons and military outposts established as part of the logistics of his campaign survived to develop into 'cities' after his death and were named after him.

Be that as it may, Greek settlements of this second phase were more mixed in composition than the first ones. These Greeks who cherished their individuality and freedom, and considered the Macedonians as barbarians, were never a cohesive group in their original homes; nor did they form such a group in their new homes in the east. If Alexander's victory had kindled hopes and aspirations among the first settlers and their subdued elements had burst forth to revive their old traditions, the mixed responses they received from Alexander and the Macedonians created rivalries and hostilities among their restive elements which could be contained only with difficulty and by force. They would rise in revolt not only after Alexander was dead but even before, at the rumour of his death.[10] The Greeks in the east seem never to have liked the Macedonians; the appointment of Stasanor, a Greek and not a Macedonian, as satrap to administer Bactria in 320, and his virtually independent behaviour are significant facts. Perhaps the Greek elements, because of older roots in Bactria, were able to muster local support in their favour from the Iranian nobility, who not only owned vast tracts of land but had also shown their mettle in warfare.[11] Because of the non-military role of those among them who lived by commerce and crafts, they were active participants in the local society and economy. The existence of pseudo-Athenian coins and other imitations and mintings of local origin in Afghanistan suggests that some of the settlers involved in trading and a money economy had established workshops for striking coins when they found a disruption in the flow of money from the west during the last days of the Persian empire. Mintings from these workshops, along with those of some of the ambitious local satraps, are known to have been circulating in Afghanistan during the confused period of the invasion, and probably in the days of transition, before Alexandrian and early Seleucid issues could become available to bring stability into the system.[12]

[10] Diod. Sic. XVII.99.5; XVIII.7.1; Curtius IX.7.1–3. Note the example of Athenodorus and the role of the native Bactrians. It is surprising that some scholars play down the animosity between the Greeks and the Macedonians. It is not simply a question of their desire to return home being no different from that of the Greeks (Briant 1973, 63: (F 103)), this matter needs to be discussed at length. Will, *CAH*² VII.i.30, concedes that, 'There is a problem here. . . . But the fact remains that there were large numbers of Greeks in Bactria, that they revolted in 325 and then again in 323, that they survived despite their defeat and the accompanying massacres, and that once calm was restored the satrap appointed to Bactria was a Greek (the Cypriot Stasanor) and not a Macedonian.' See also Koshelenko 1979, 182ff.: (F 80).

[11] Narain 1957–80, 5–6: (F 103); Musti 1984, 212–13: (F 101A).

[12] Narain 1957–80, 3–4: (F 103); Head 1906, 1ff.: (F 63); Schlumberger and Curiel 1953, 3ff.: (F 138); but see Bernard 1985, 26–35: (F 24); cf. Mitchiner 1975, 1.1–27: (F 101).

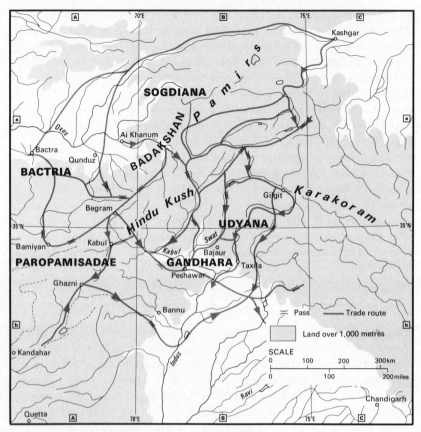

Map 15. Bactria and North-western India.

When Seleucus regained Babylon and Antigonus yielded the eastern
domains to him, Seleucus became Alexander's successor in the east only
de jure. To claim his inheritance he had to mount a campaign in that area
once he was free from his western involvements. But it was already too
late. Chandragupta Maurya had overthrown the Nandas, whose might
had deterred Alexander's army from crossing the River Hyphasis (Beas).
As a result of his confrontation with Chandragupta, Seleucus had to cede
most of Afghanistan south of the Hindu Kush as well as Baluchistan to
the Mauryas.[13] The two families entered into a matrimonial alliance, and
Chandragupta gave five hundred elephants to Seleucus which the latter
found useful in his combats in the west. North of the Hindu Kush, in

<hr/>

[13] Some scholars do not include Aria in the list of provinces ceded to Chandragupta Maurya by
Seleucus.

Bactria and adjoining areas, the anti-Macedonian Greek elements, who probably also had some local support, as well as some satraps of eastern origins, had become unco-operative and, wherever possible, independent for all practical purposes. There is no clear information about Seleucus' own movements in the north. But it is generally assumed that the appointment of his son Antiochus I as a co-ruler or viceroy, and the campaigns of Demodamus beyond the Syr Darya, as well as the minting and circulation of some coins in the region, constitute sufficient evidence for the acceptance of Seleucid jurisdiction over Bactria. However, the return of Antiochus I to his western affairs in 281 seems to have provided an opportunity to the restive Greeks to rise again. The last definite reference to Antiochus' control of Bactria is in a Babylonian record of the years 276–274. It refers to twenty elephants which the governor of Bactria, whose name is not given, had sent to the king.[14] But the classical sources and the numismatic evidence indicate that the Seleucid jurisdiction over Bactria continued until at least a couple of years after the death of Antiochus I in 261.

According to Justin, Diodotus (Theodotus), 'governor of the thousand cities of Bactria, revolted and assumed the title of king, and above all the other people of the east, influenced by his example, fell away from the Macedonians'.[15] The Greek–Macedonian dichotomy in eastern affairs is also reflected in Apollodorus, the author of the *Parthica*, when he refers to 'the Greeks who caused Bactriana to revolt from the Syrian kings who succeeded Seleucus Nicator', and states that 'those kings subdued more of India than the Macedonians'.[16] Unfortunately the work of Apollodorus is lost but, in spite of the doubts expressed by Strabo, the fragmentary quotations preserved by the latter provide both insights and reasons for caution. An example is Strabo's statement, following Apollodorus, about these Greeks of Bactria that 'more tribes were subdued by them than by Alexander – mostly by Menander (*at least if he actually crossed the Hypanis towards the east and advanced as far as the Imaus*), for some were subdued by him personally and others by Demetrius, the son of Euthydemus the king of the Bactrians; and they took possession not only of Patalene but also, on the rest of the coast, of what is called the kingdom of Saraostus and Sigerdis. In short, Apollodorus says that Bactriana is the ornament of Ariana as a whole; and more than that, they extended their empire even as far as the Seres and the Phryni.'[17]

Similarly there are other statements in Strabo based on Apollodorus, e.g. 'when those kings [i.e. the Greeks who caused Bactriana to revolt] had grown in power they also attacked India', and '. . . any parts beyond

---

[14] Austin 1981, 240: (A 2).   [15] Justin XLI.4.
[16] Strabo XV.1.3. Burstein 1985, 51–2: (A 10A), has drawn attention to the insistence on the *Greekness* of those who revolted.   [17] Strabo XI.11.1.

the Hypanis of which an account has been added by those who, after
Alexander, advanced beyond the Hypanis, as far as the Ganges and
Palibothra'.[18] Now, these Greeks of Bactria have left no history of their
own, and the classical sources, both in the west and in the east, do not
have more than a few jumbled statements made only when they are found
to be of some relevance to the subjects which constitute their own
interests. Ignored by ancient historians in both areas, they have been
squeezed out between the two and attract our attention largely on
account of their beautiful coinage, which has become the main source for
their history.

It is interesting that both the western and the Indian classical sources
refer to only eight or nine kings of the Bactrian Greeks.[19] But their coins
bear at least thirty-one names of kings and two of queens. However,
numismatists and historians have concluded, on justifiable grounds, that
some of these names represent more than one king, thus increasing the
number of kings to forty or more.[20] Between them they cover a time-span
of about two hundred years and territories extending, at one time or
another, from Sogdiana to the Punjab, making forays even farther in
both directions. The only way the time and space involved in their
history can be rationalized is by assuming the simultaneous rule of more
than one king, not always belonging to the same family, sharing roles of
power. Any attempt to arrange them in linear succession or assign them
to only one or two dynastic families is next to impossible in the present
state of our knowledge.

II. THE EARLY RULERS

Whether the Greeks of Bactria under Diodotus gained their independence from the Seleucids as a result of open revolt or through a gradual
transition to power is a topic that the present author has discussed
elsewhere. He still believes that Diodotus broke away to freedom in
c. 256 B.C.[21] Before the Parthians celebrated their freedom from the

[18] Ibid. xv.1.3, 27–8.

[19] The kings named in the western classical sources are: Diodotus (Theodotus) and his son of the same name (Strabo, Trogus and Justin); Euthydemus I (Polybius and Strabo); Demetrius I, son of Euthydemus I (Polybius and Strabo); Eucratides I (Strabo, Justin and Aelian); Menander (Strabo, Trogus, Justin, Plutarch and Periplus); Apollodotus (Trogus and Periplus). To these may be added Demetrius II rex Indorum, a contemporary of Eucratides I, and the unnamed son of the latter who murdered him (Justin). The Indian Puranas speak of eight Yavana kings but do not give their names, cf. Pargiter 1913, 44ff.: (F 119).

[20] Compare lists in Narain 1955–76: (F 102); Lahiri 1965: (F 83); Mitchiner 1975: (F 101); also see older catalogues of coins in the British Museum (Gardner 1898–1966: (F 53)), Lahore Museum (Whitehead 1914: (F 160)), Indian Museum, Calcutta (Smith 1906: (F 148)).

[21] Narain 1957–80, 12–16: (F 103). Some prefer a round number 250 and others date the event still later. See Wolski 1947, 13–70: (F 165A); id. 1956–7, 35–52: (F 166); id. 1982, 131–46: (F 167); Will 1979, 1.301–8: (A 40); Musti 1984, 213–16, 219ff.: (F 101A), notes the 'high' and 'low' chronology of Bactria's secession; see Bikerman 1944: (F 25) and Newell 1938, 245: (F 114) for 'high' chronology.

Seleucids in 248/7 B.C., Diodotus, king of Bactria, had already been succeeded by his son of the same name. Both the father and son struck coins in gold and silver with their canting badge of Zeus hurling a thunderbolt;[22] Athena, Artemis and Hermes appeared on their copper. The coin portraits of Diodotus I show him with an older face and a double chin; those of Diodotus II, on the other hand, show him as a younger man with a sharp angular face.[23] In fact the older face of the former shows that he had already been a satrap for a time before he became king, and the absence of mature features for the latter is in keeping with the information that the reign of Diodotus II was cut short by his untimely death at the hands of Euthydemus.[24] For reasons of monetary expedience and commercial advantage the Diodoti issued some coins with the name of Antiochus as well, a practice the elder Diodotus had begun as a satrap.[25] Diodotus I considered himself a saviour of the Greeks in Bactria; some of his coins include the title of *Soter*.[26]

Doubtless the coins of the Diodoti were struck in Bactria, as were also some of the early Seleucid coins, before Diodotus I became king, which were meant for circulation in the east. Newell assigns most of them to the mint of Bactra because 'this city represents the nearest large commercial and political centre to the spot where the Oxus Treasure was unearthed'; and what constitutes for him finally the determining factor is that the particular group of Seleucid issues which he assigns to Bactra 'leads directly into the immediately following issues of the Bactrian kings Diodotus and Euthydemus I, whose coins would have been struck in Bactria only – never in Parthia or in the lands south of the Hindu Kush. The only logical location for a large and active royal mint would be at Bactra.'[27] But the findspot of the Oxus Treasure has never been certain. Convincing claims have now been made in favour of locating it north of the Oxus.[28] Moreover, the relevant group of control marks (⊛⊛◭⊛◭⊕⇲) have nothing in them to suggest the name of Bactra or its other name, Zariaspa, nor can they represent the name of Diodotus.[29] Percy Gardner, the first to discuss the problem, thought that these coins were struck at Dionysopolis, which he equated with Nysa, 'a city of the Paropamisus identified by General Cunningham with the modern Begram, near Cabul'.[30] Sir Henry Howorth equated it with Nissa in

[22] Narain 1955–76, 3–4: (F 102); Mitchiner 1975, 1.39–44: (F 101). Trevor 1940, 115: (F 154), thought that the coin-type suited the name Diodotus, 'the gift of Zeus'.
[23] Cp. illustrations in Mitchiner 1975, 1.40, 42: (F 101). Also *Pls. to Vol. VII. 1*, pl. 28.
[24] Polyb. XI.39.   [25] Narain 1957–80, 16–17: (F 103); Mitchiner 1975, 1.36, 39–40: (F 101).
[26] Narain 1957–80, 17: (F 103); Mitchiner 1975, 1.41: (F 101); Macdonald 1922, 440: (F 89), and Tarn 1951–84, 201: (F 152), regard these issues as commemorative medals struck by Agathocles; cf. also Holt 1984, 69–91 (F 69).   [27] Newell 1938, 229: (F 114).
[28] Litvinsky and Pichikiyan 1981, 133–67: (F 88).
[29] Narain 1957–80, 14–15: (F 103).   [30] Gardner 1879, 12: (F 52).

Parthia.[31] Newell rightly rejected the location of the mint in Paropamisus or Parthia in favour of Bactria; and, since he did not find a Dionysopolis or Nysa listed in Bactria, he proposed Bactra on the basis of the circumstantial evidence available to him.[32] But now the discovery of the Graeco-Bactrian city at Ai Khanum provides a welcome solution. One of the control marks listed above (◎) – the first in the group because it was used on the earliest series of the joint coinage of Seleucus and Antiochus – has been found stamped on the exceptionally large brick covering a sarcophagus belonging to the earliest chronological phase of habitation in Ai Khanum so far known.[33] Bernard has noted the presence of this monogram on the brick but finds the mirage of Bactra too attractive to abandon and still follows Newell.[34] This is strange because he has even found evidence for the existence of a mint at Ai Khanum.[35] The commercial importance of Badakshan in antiquity, because of lapis lazuli, is generally recognized. If this monogram can be resolved to read Dionysopolis as Gardner and Howorth thought it did, in spite of their differences, not only does the mint stand identified but also the ancient name of Ai Khanum. The proximity of Ai Khanum to Takht-i Sangin, the recently suggested location of the Oxus Treasure, adds further support to our view. The geographical situation of Ai Khanum in the remote eastern parts of Bactria and the commercial viability of Badakshan are in themselves cogent reasons to assume an early Greek settlement there. Ai Khanum lies a little too far to the east of the route followed by Alexander from Bactria to Paropamisadae to be one of the Alexandrias.[36] On the other hand, its geographical position might very well be the reason why Diodotus, a governor of an eastern province of Bactria, found it safe to raise a rebellion. Only future discoveries can settle whether or not the city was renamed later as Diodoteia or Diodotopolis. Even if the control mark (◎) is not taken as indicative of a city name, or that of a governor, but that of a moneyer, it cannot be denied at any rate that the coins bearing this monogram, and at least some of the others belonging to this group,[37] were minted in the workshops at

[31] Howorth 1888, 295: (F 71).   [32] Newell 1938, 228ff.: (F 114).

[33] Bernard 1973, 9, pl. 97: (F 11).

[34] Bernard 1985, 39ff.: (F 24); also Bernard and Guillaume 1980, 9ff.: (F 19).

[35] Bernard 1985, 35ff.: (F 24). Attention may also be drawn to the observation made by Alexander Grant, in Gardner 1879, 1: (F 52), about the place of discovery of the Oxus Treasure that it was 'eight marches beyond the Oxus at an old fort, on the tongue of land formed by two joining rivers'. Could not Ai Khanum itself be considered a suitable alternative to the site of Takht-i Sangin for the 'Oxus Treasure'?   [36] Engels 1978, 97, map. 12: (F 46).

[37] According to Newell 1938, 246: (F 114), this group includes monograms which have the Greek letter *delta* as the principal element. Some of these, e.g. Δ Δ , which are found on many Seleucid coins including those of Seleucus I and Antiochus III, were probably minted in other workshops: Narain 1957–80, 15: (F 103). But see Bernard and Guillaume 1980, 18–19: (F 19); Bernard 1985, 35ff.: (F 24).

Ai Khanum and not in Bactra. Later, if and when the Diodoti moved their capital to the city of Bactra, they probably used other workshops, too, in Bactra as well as elsewhere in their kingdom, known to have had many cities.

Not much is known about the career and achievements of the Diodoti. It is agreed that they ruled over Sogdiana, and possibly in Margiane too, which bordered on Parthia.[38] It is therefore not surprising that the Parthians feared the might of Diodotus I and that no sooner had he died than they made alliance with his son Diodotus II,[39] which provided security and strength to both the new states and frustrated Seleucus II's attempts to reassert Seleucid hegemony in the upper satrapies. According to Strabo, when the Greeks took possession of the country of Bactriana they divided it into satrapies, but he does not give their names and it is not easy to identify them or their satraps.[40]

Perhaps one of the satraps was Euthydemus, a native of Magnesia.[41] According to Polybius he took possession of the throne of Bactria by destroying the descendants of those who had revolted against the Seleucids. Although this statement is not specific it is believed that Euthydemus came to power after killing Diodotus II.[42] Grousset and de la Vallée-Poussin thought that he was a satrap of Sogdiana, but Cunningham put him in charge of Aria and Margiane.[43] Since the first encounter of Antiochus III with Euthydemus in 208 B.C. took place on the banks of the River Arius, the latter was then definitely in possession of it. But since we have no evidence for including Aria in the kingdom of the Diodoti, and since it was included in the list of four satrapies ceded to Chandragupta by Seleucus, it is most likely that Euthydemus started his career as a satrap of the outlying satrapy of Margiane, close to Parthia, and it was only *after* he occupied the Bactrian throne and possibly when the Mauryan empire was in the process of disintegration after the death of Asoka that he took possession of Aria as well.[44] Probably it was this expansion of the Bactrian kingdom westwards that alerted Antiochus III and prompted him to march against Euthydemus, not only to restrain him from having further designs and punish him, but also thereby to try

[38] Narain 1957–80, 17: (F 103). [39] Justin XLI.4.

[40] Strabo XI.516. Tarn 1951–84, 113–14: (F 152), thought that these satrapies were the Seleucid eparchies and that 'the Greek kings of Bactria were in fact the originators of what became the almost universal organisation of Asia in the first century B.C.', and that this 'might date from Diodotus'.

[41] This was the Lydian city of Magnesia ad Sipylum: Macdonald 1922, 440: (F 89); Newell 1941, 274: (F 115).

[42] Polyb. XI.39; Narain 1957–80, 18: (F 103); Walbank 1957–79, II.264–5 and 312–13: (B 38).

[43] Grousset 1929, 53: (F 55); de la Vallée-Poussin 1930, 233: (F 44).

[44] Out of the four satrapies ceded to Chandragupta by Seleucus, it appears that Aria being the farthest to the west was the first to be lost after the death of Asoka, c. 232 B.C. It was not lost to the Seleucids but to the Greeks of Bactria, and the time coincides with the rise of Euthydemus.

once more to recover as much as possible of the east lost by Seleucus.[45]

The consolidation of Graeco-Bactrian power was largely thanks to the achievements of Euthydemus and his successors. Polybius gives an account of Antiochus III's expedition against Euthydemus and how it concluded, after the latter had withstood a two-year siege of Bactra, through the help of a mediator, Teleas. Having recognized Euthydemus' status and promised to marry his daughter to Demetrius, a son of Euthydemus, and having received in return some elephants, Antiochus III crossed the Hindu Kush and returned to his own kingdom by way of Paropamisadae, Arachosia, Drangiana and Carmania. No details of his engagements and successes or failures, if any, are given by Polybius except that he renewed his family alliance with Sophagasenus, 'the king of the Indians', who added some more elephants to his force.[46]

Polybius reveals an important fact, which was conveyed to Antiochus by Euthydemus, that there was an imminent danger of hordes of nomads approaching from the north and of Bactria relapsing into barbarism. Therefore, after Antiochus III's departure from Bactria, it appears that Euthydemus directed his attention to the north. He used his resources to consolidate his holdings in Sogdiana and probably succeeded in pushing his frontiers towards Chinese Turkestan. Strabo's statement that the Greeks of Bactria extended 'their empire even as far as the Seres and Phryni' seems relevant.[47] This is evident also from the provenance, and barbaric imitations, of the coins of Euthydemus and Demetrius on the one hand and the striking of some nickel coins by a Euthydemus II, who could be another son of Euthydemus, on the other.[48] Survival of some Greek numismatic terms like *satera* for stater, and *trakhme* for drachm, in the Kharosthi documents of Chinese Turkestan adds further strength to this view.[49] Having succeeded in containing the danger from the north, Euthydemus looked in other directions. Tarn thought that Euthydemus occupied the Parthian satrapies of Astauene and Apavarktikene and perhaps part of Parthyene, which became the Bactrian satrapies of Tapuria and Traxiane.[50] Tarn may be right in postulating activities of Euthydemus in the westerly direction because of his earlier possessions in Margiane and Aria and their proximity to Parthia.

Written sources know only of Demetrius as the son of Euthydemus, but numismatic evidence strongly suggests at least one more son, who bore the same name as his father. Perhaps Demetrius was the elder and Euthydemus II was the younger of the two. Both issued coins with their

---

[45] Seleucus II had failed to achieve success in the east. Antiochus III succeeded at least in containing the rising power of the Bactrian Greeks. Successors of Euthydemus did not look westward for expansion in central and western Iran but southward and eastward in Afghanistan and Pakistan.   [46] Polyb. XI.39.   [47] Strabo XI.11.1–2.   [48] Narain 1957–80, 27: (F 103).

[49] *Ibid.* 25–7.   [50] Tarn 1951–84, 88: (F 152).

realistic portraits on the obverse and Heracles on the reverse, now standing and crowning himself, and not seated as on the coins of their father. Since the coins of Euthydemus II always portray him as youthful without any variation, and are not copious in number, it appears that he was a joint or sub-king in charge of affairs in the north, who either predeceased his father while still young or had only a brief tenure during the reign of his brother Demetrius, who succeeded his father.

But the classical sources appear to have mixed up Demetrius I, son of Euthydemus I, who was old enough in 206 B.C. to have been offered a Seleucid princess in marriage by Antiochus III, and Demetrius II, the *rex Indorum*, who was a contemporary of Eucratides I. Demetrius I issued coins on the Attic standard with unilingual legends only. On his main type he is shown wearing an elephant scalp on the obverse and the reverse has a standing Heracles. Demetrius II, on the other hand, with an altogether different face, is shown either bareheaded or wearing a flat kausia on the obverse of his main types, and with either Zeus or his daughter Athena on the reverse. He issued coins with both unilingual and bilingual legends on the Attic and Indian weight systems respectively.[51] Demetrius I, taking advantage of the disintegrating Mauryan empire in its outlying western parts and of the death of Antiochus III in 187, appears to have extended the Graeco-Bactrian kingdom to Arachosia, which explains the listing of a Demetrias-in-Arachosia by Isidore of Charax,[52] as well as the use of the coin-types of both Euthydemus and Demetrius I by the early Scytho-Parthians in Arachosia.[53] About Carmania there is no evidence, and the possibility of Drangiana and parts of Gedrosia being included in his kingdom remains to be clearly determined.[54] Paropamisadae and Gandhara were the last regions of the Mauryan empire in the west, ruled by Sophagasenus and Virasena or their successors, respectively, to be lost to the Yavanas. The task of conquest was left to Demetrius II. But before we return to him we must notice how history repeats itself once again. Just as Euthydemus came to power after overthrowing the Diodotids there were others, too, who had followed his example.[55] Of these the earliest were Antimachus Theos, who preceded Demetrius II, and Eucratides Megas, whose time overlapped with both of them.

Antimachus Theos has been overlooked by ancient historians, but his

[51] For coins see Narain 1955–76, 4–5 (Demetrius I), 6–7 (Demetrius II): (F 102). Also see Mitchiner 1975, 1.55–61: (F 101), who lists their coins without separating the two series; Lahiri 1965, 106–10, pl. 12 and 13: (F 83), distinguishes two Demetrii but his classification of types is different from Narain.

[52] For Demetrias-in-Arachosia see Isidore of Charax, *Parthian Stations*, p. 9 (ed. Schoff, 1976); Tarn 1951–84, 94: (F 152).

[53] For both 'standing Heracles' and 'seated Heracles' were adopted by the Scytho-Parthian kings; Narain 1957–80, 24, 160: (F 103). [54] *Ibid.* 24–5. [55] Strabo XI.9.2.

coins leave no doubt about his powerful and very individual personality among the early group of Graeco-Bactrian kings. While his relationship to either the Diodoti or to Euthydemus may be debated,[56] it is known that he issued some commemorative medals in the names of both Diodotus I and Euthydemus I.[57] He was probably a satrap in charge of a province in the northern or north-eastern region of the kingdom of Euthydemus. When Demetrius I became busy in expanding the Euthydemid power in the south, Antimachus carved out his independence. To legitimize his position he issued commemorative medals and adopted the title of *Theos*. His main coin-type showing on the obverse his realistic portrait with a mysterious smile has attracted much attention.[58] Like other early kings, he issued unilingual coins of Attic weight and his favourite deity was Poseidon. But he was the first among them to strike the Indian type of square or rectangular copper coins with the figure of an elephant on one side and with a thunderbolt, the attribute of Zeus, on the other.[59] Probably he crossed the Hindu Kush and found it necessary to match the Indian money circulating in the region for local needs. It was left to Demetrius II to strike bilingual coins to mark the actual occupation of territories in Paropamisadae and western parts of Gandhara.

The coins of Demetrius II link him with Antimachus Theos, and indirectly more with the Diodotids than with the Euthydemids.[60] He was no doubt later than both Antimachus I and Demetrius I, but a contemporary of Eucratides I. He was the first king to issue silver money on the reduced Indian weight standard with legends in both Greek and Indian Prakrit; he also issued some square copper bilinguals on the Indian model. His favourite deities were Zeus and Athena. For his copper he used the thunderbolt and the trident, attributes of Zeus and Poseidon respectively; he used other devices related to the earlier issues of the Diodotids and of Antimachus I. He wears the same headdress as Antimachus with whom it is tempting to see a resemblance, rather than to Demetrius I. It is significant that the monogram used on the bilingual copper of Demetrius II is the same as on the square copper of Antimachus I.[61]

Demetrius II adopted the epithet of *Aniketos* and he was the first Graeco-Bactrian king to translate his epithet into an Indian language.[62] With Kabul and western Gandhara in his hands he could cross the Indus and occupy Taxila, but there is hardly any evidence that he did so in the

[56] Smith 1906, 5: (F 148); Rawlinson 1912, 62: (F 129).
[57] Narain 1955–76, 5–6: (F 102); Mitchiner 1975, I.73–4: (F 101).
[58] Tarn 1951–84, 92: (F 152); Trever 1940, 7: (F 154); but see Holt 1981, 20 n. 5: (F 65).
[59] Narain 1955–76, 6: (F 102); Mitchiner 1975, I.75: (F 101).
[60] For a discussion see Narain 1957–80, 29–31, 34–7, 50–3: (F 103).   [61] *Ibid.* 52.

material remains of the city.[63] Perhaps his ambition was cut short by the defeat he suffered at the hands of Eucratides. At any rate Taxila did not become part of the Yavana domain before Agathocles, and success farther east was to wait for Menander. Possible references to a Demetrius in the Indian sources are extremely dubious.[64]

It is not clear whether Eucratides was a satrap of one of the northern provinces of the Graeco-Bactrian kingdom or was a soldier of fortune. There is hardly any evidence to establish his ties with the families of Diodotus, Euthydemus or Antimachus. Nor is there any satisfactory reason to associate him with the Seleucid Antiochus IV.[65] If the commemorative medal struck by him depicts the jugate busts of his father and mother, who is shown wearing a diadem, we may assume a royal link, which probably provided him a *locus standi* among the Graeco-Bactrians.[66] Justin states explicitly that he rose to power in Bactria, 'almost at the same time that Mithridates ascended the throne among the Parthians'.[67] Later, Aelian also remembered him as a ruler of Bactria when a certain Soras was ruling over a city, Perimula, inhabited by fish-eaters, in South India.[68] Since nothing is known about Soras, Aelian's information is of no use. But the synchronism established by Justin dates the rise of Eucratides *c.* 171 B.C., which seems correct since Timarchus in 162 is known to have imitated the well-known Dioscuri coin-type of Eucratides I, with the title of Megas, which the latter could have adopted only after some remarkable success and not in the first years of his reign.[69] According to Justin, Eucratides fought various wars and in spite of his losses he withstood a five-month siege by his contemporary *rex Indorum* Demetrius II and, having repulsed him by continual sallies with a garrison of only three hundred soldiers, he escaped and 'reduced India under his power. But as he was returning from the country, he was killed

[62] *Apadihata* is a rarely used Prakrit word to translate the Greek word *Aniketos*.

[63] Narain 1957–80, 53: (F 103). Only one coin was found in the Taxila excavations: Marshall 1951, II.798: (F 98). [64] Narain 1957–80, 39–44, 174–9: (F 103).

[65] *Ibid.* 56–7. Tarn 1951–84, 197: (F 152), thought that Laodice, probably the mother of Eucratides, was a sister of Antiochus III. Holt 1981, 41: (F 65), thinks that Laodice was a Euthydemid princess.

[66] But the possibility that the Heliocles-Laodice coin was not in commemoration of the parents of Eucratides but the marriage of his son has also been considered: von Sallet 1879, 23ff., 103: (F 156).

[67] Justin XLI.6.1.

[68] Aelian, *On the Characteristics of Animals* XV.8 (cf. translation by Schofield (1958) III.218–19). This source refers to Eucratides only in passing as a ruler of Bactria when a city in South India, Perimula, was ruled by a certain Soras; it does not yield any new information. Moreover, the Indian king and his date are not identified.

[69] It is generally accepted that Mithridates I came to power in 171. Timarchus became king in 162 or 161: Bellinger 1945, 40–4: (B 79), and Houghton 1979, 213–17: (E 25). Eucratides I issued coins first without any epithet, and they show him bareheaded on the obverse and mounted Dioscuri on the reverse; Narain 1955–76, 9–10: (F 102). Mitchiner 1975, I.88–9: (F 101), attributes the issuance of this coin-type to what he calls the 'Middle period' and dates it in 165–160. He puts the Apollo type of Eucratides II in the 'Early period' of Eucratides I. But cf. Narain 1957–80, 71, 107: (F 103).

on his march by his son, with whom he had shared his throne, and who was so far from concealing the murder, that as if he had killed an enemy, and not his father, he drove his chariot through his blood, and ordered his body to be cast out unburied.'[70] We may speculate on the name of the killer son, but that he could be someone else's son is unlikely, for why should Eucratides make anyone else's son his *socius regni*? A Heliocles was definitely his son but if Plato was another, it was probable that the former, who took the title of *Dikaios*, was a loyal son; and the latter, who adopted arrogantly the epithet *Epiphanes* and flamboyantly issued coins with Helios driving a quadriga, could be the parricide, who was soon superseded by Heliocles.[71] This tragic end of Eucratides at the peak of his success at the hands of a parricide, so vividly described by Justin, leaves no scope for a longer reign and further expansion of domain by him.

Most probably Eucratides was able to usurp power in the north when Demetrius II Aniketos was busy occupying new lands in the south, in the Paropamisadae and western Gandhara. His success against Demetrius II and the consequent possibility of a brief presence in 'India' were no doubt the final features of the career cut short by his son. Justin's reference to the several wars Eucratides fought makes good sense on the supposition that they took place before his engagement with Demetrius II. For he must have consolidated his control over considerable parts of the Graeco-Bactrian kingdom before taking on Demetrius II. One cannot help having the impression from Justin that the entire career of Eucratides was spent fighting wars. And if Justin's comparative assessment in favour of the Parthians against the Bactrians combined with Strabo's reference to Bactria losing two satrapies to Parthia is related to Eucratides,[72] one wonders if his assumption of the title *Megas* was more an expression of ambition on the part of an usurper than a statement of unmixed achievements. His unique twenty-stater piece[73] is more an example of flamboyance and a competitive role against his contemporary rivals like Agathocles than of any monetary or political significance. In fact the way Eucratides is depicted on his main coin-type and the representation of the Dioscuri as charging vigorously on the reverse of his coins complement the character as known from Justin. Doubtless Eucratides was a brave warrior and one of the notable rulers among the Graeco-Bactrians, who could be emulated by other ambitious rebels of his time like Timarchus.[74]

[70] Justin XLI.6.
[71] Tarn 1951–84, 219–20: (F 152); Bivar 1950, 9–12: (F 26); Narain 1957–80, 70–3: (F 103).
[72] Strabo XV.1.3, XI.11.2; Tarn 1951–84, 219: (F 152).
[73] S. Narain 1956, 217–18: (F 113); Mitchiner 1975, 1.91: (F 101).
[74] Tarn 1951–84, 218: (F 152); Bellinger 1950, 314: (F 6); Houghton 1979, 213–17: (E 25). All coins of Timarchus bear the title *Basileus Megalou*, and the assumption is that he adopted Eucratides' type and title by virtue of his alliance. If Timarchus would not be considered a 'Great' king because of the title *Megalou* he adopted, why should Eucratides be so considered on *this* ground?

Nevertheless recent attempts to represent him as greater than the evidence actually requires, and to extend his tenure to twenty-five years or more, are hardly convincing.[75] To relate the beginning of an era from the accession of Eucratides[76] requires more imagination than one can justify at present. There is nothing of substance in Aelian which would support any special claim to greatness.[77] So also there is hardly anything in the text of the inscription found on an ostracon at Ai Khanum to support the theory that the figure 24 there is the regnal year of Eucratides.[78] Similarly, in order to associate the end of Ai Khanum with that of the reign of Eucratides, and not later, we need more substantial evidence than is presently available, particularly when the work at the site is still incomplete.[79] There are reasons not only to doubt even the inclusion of Badakshan in the domain of Eucratides but also to think of a destruction of the site in 145 B.C., which is the later date suggested for the end of the reign of Eucratides.[80] It has been shown that the Yuezhi were still north of the Oxus in 128 B.C. and that the incursions of the Scythians from the north, on account of the Yuezhi pressure, could not have taken place much earlier and that they were taking place in westerly directions affecting the Parthians and causing the deaths of two of their kings.[81] There do not seem to be grounds to revise the chronology of Eucratides: he ruled from c. 171 to 155 B.C. Much of the problem appears to be largely the result of a failure to recognize that all the coins which bear the name

[75] Mitchiner 1975, 1.65–72: (F 101), dates him c. 171–135 B.C. Simonetta 1958, 173: (F 144), and Bernard 1980, 442–4: (F 17); id. 1980, 24–7: (F 19); id. 1985, 97ff.: (F 24), date him 170–145 B.C. See also Fussman 1980, 36–7: (F 51); Holt 1981, 41–2: (F 65); Rapin 1983, 369–70: (F 127). But see Tarn, 1951–84, 219: (F 152), and Bellinger 1950, 314: (F 6), who believe Eucratides died in 159/8 B.C.

[76] Bernard 1980, 442: (F 17); id. 1985, 102: (F 18), but he does not identify the Soras mentioned by Aelian, although the synchronism with Soras is central to his argument. Nilkanta Sastri 1972, 61: (F 116), who knew Aelian's source for Soras, only suggested that the word is derived from Tamil Sola, perhaps standing for Cola, one of the early ruling clans or dynasties of southern India which, though known from the time of Asoka, came to prominence during 9th–12th centuries A.D. It is not clear whether the Soras of Aelian was the personal name of a king or the name of the clan or dynasty. Even if it was a personal name we have no means of knowing his identity or date. To find a date for Eucratides on the basis of this synchronism is arguing in a circle.

[77] It is nothing more than a very casual reference to 'the time when Eucratides was ruler of Bactria'. Aelian does not add anything about Eucratides' date or his achievements. It is asking too much to agree with Bernard's statement: 'Le synchronisme dont il fait état montre que le règne d'Eucratides dut servir à des historiographes de l'Asie Centrale, des Grecs sans doute, comme point de repère chronologique pour des événements extérieurs au domaine propre de la colonisation grecque. On mesure en même temps par là le retentissement qu'eut dans les régions voisines de l'empire grec ce règne qui put ainsi servir de référence à celui d'un potentat de la côte méridionale de l'Inde.' It may be noted that Aelian was not a historiographer of Central Asia, and also that the city of Perimula in extreme South India cannot be regarded as a region bordering the so-called Greek empire.

[78] There is no mention of Eucratides before or after the number 24. The missing part following the number is supposed to contain references to month and day. This is somewhat unusual; one may compare this with the examples of inscriptions which refer to reckoning systems related to the names of Menander, Azes and Kanishka.

[79] The excavations at the site had to be discontinued for reasons beyond the control of the excavators. [80] Bernard 1985, 97ff.: (F 24). [81] Narain 1957–80, 128–42: (F 103).

of Eucratides are not the issues of a single king. This has led to a merging
of the career and coinage of at least two kings of the same name,
Eucratides I Megas and Eucratides II Soter.[82] That there were at least
two of them was first suggested as early as 1738 and since then it has been
supported by many, including the present author.[83] Whether the second
was a son or a grandson of the first may be argued, but that there was
more than one king who issued all the coins bearing the name of
Eucratides seems beyond question.[84]

Among the notable early Graeco-Bactrian kings, Pantaleon and
Agathocles are generally considered as brothers and as ruling around the
same time as Eucratides I. A recent discovery of an Agathocles coin
commemorating Pantaleon supports the theory that, of the two,
Pantaleon was the elder brother who probably ruled and died before
Agathocles.[85] This commemorative coin is the last of a series issued by
Agathocles which included commemoration of Alexander, Antiochus,
Diodotus, Euthydemus and Demetrius. Probably the two brothers
started as joint or sub-kings and Agathocles took over after a brief reign
by Pantaleon. It is more than likely that, when Eucratides I Megas was
usurping power in Bactria and Demetrius II was heading towards
Paropamisadae and the Indus, these two brothers were harassing
Eucratides in the several wars mentioned by Justin and holding forts in
north-eastern and eastern Bactria against Eucratides I.[86] The commemorative medals issued by Agathocles were probably meant to strengthen
the legitimation of his position in Bactria as against Eucratides I the
usurper.[87]

[82] It is difficult to believe that a usurper who was killed by his own son ruled over Bactria and
India for 36 years (Mitchiner) or even 25 or 26 years (Bernard, Holt) at a stretch in the history of a
large group of kings (about forty) belonging to several families and torn by relatives and in-fighting
within the limited span of about two hundred years. In view of the very realistic old age portraits of
Euthydemus I among the early kings and of Strato among the later ones it is hard to accept that if
Eucratides had actually ruled for such a long period his mints did not find any reason to strike at least
some coins showing his old age, even towards the close of his reign. Bernard's theory identifying the
year 24 in one of the ostraca inscriptions found in the 'Treasury' of Ai Khanum as belonging to the
reign of Eucratides is a speculation which neither this text, nor for that matter any of the inscriptions
of the 'Treasury', supports. Contrast for example the case of the Bajaur casket inscription of
Menander where the name of the king is mentioned, after the year.

[83] Narain 1957–80, 71: (F 103); Bayer 1738, xxxix, 95: (F 5). Bernard 1985, 97: (F 24), mentions
Bayer's date for the end of Eucratides approvingly but does not refer to the latter's division of coins
between Eucratides I and II. While some recent writers (Mitchiner 1975, 1.65–72: (F 101); Holt 1981:
(F 65)) have assumed, without convincing reasons, that the coins bearing the name of Eucratides
belong to only one king, the classification by Bayer has been widely accepted.

[84] Narain 1957–80, 123–4: (F 103). In view of the murder of Eucratides while returning from
'India' and of his name being remembered more as a king of Bactria, and not of India, it is not
unreasonable to postulate that most of the square copper coins listed under his name were actually
posthumous mintings. Round bilinguals in silver and copper with the Dioscuri (Mitchiner 1975,
1.96–7: (F 101)), on the other hand, were no doubt his issues.

[85] Narain 1957–80, 59–60: (F 103). For Agathocles commemorating Pantaleon see Francfort
1975, 19–22: (F 48).   [86] Justin xli.6; Narain 1957–80, 58ff.: (F 103).

[87] Tarn 1951–84, 201, 263, 439–40, 446–51: (F 152); Narain 1957–80, 60–1: (F 103).

So far nothing is known about Pantaleon and Agathocles from the literary sources. But numismatic and archaeological evidence shows that their activities were mostly confined more to eastern rather than to western parts of Bactria. Perhaps Eucratides I was able to control the western and even central parts of it, as well as some territories north of the Oxus. Discoveries at Ai Khanum seem to favour the Euthydemids and/or the rivals of Eucratides in eastern Bactria, for it is their coinage which overwhelmingly predominates there.[88] On the other hand, coins of Pantaleon and Agathocles are rare in the western parts of Bactria. Their unilingual tetradrachms, and the commemorative medals issued by Agathocles, were struck on the Attic standard. Their favourite deity, Zeus, associates them with the Diodoti and Demetrius II. Significantly their round copper and nickel coins which are unilingual – as against the square, rectangular or triangular ones which are bilingual – depict on the obverse a young Dionysus wearing an ivy wreath, with thyrsus over his shoulder, and a panther on the reverse. These coins, which have been found at Ai Khanum,[89] are certainly important if the depiction of Dionysus could be an allusion to Dionysopolis, probably the ancient name of Ai Khanum.[90] Moreover, the occurrence of this type also on nickel indicates that these coins were meant for circulation, like those of Euthydemus II, in the north-eastern parts of the kingdom which obviously included Badakshan and probably extended even towards Chinese Turkestan, if Strabo's reference to Greek extensions in the direction of Seres and Phryni is correct.[91] While both the brothers struck some copper bilinguals with an Indian Yakshi goddess and maneless lion, Agathocles also issued coins with additional types.[92] The most significant of them are not only those which use the Buddhist motif of Chaitya and devices found on the local coins of Taxila,[93] but the rectangular silver bilinguals which represent for the first time the hero-gods Vāsudeva and Samkarshaṇa[94] of the Brahmanical Bhāgavat cult to which later Heliodorus, the envoy of Antialcidas of Taxila to Bhāgabhadra of Vidishā (near Bhopal), was devoutly affiliated.[95] It is not without significance that the two brothers are the only ones among the Bactrian Greeks who introduced on their coins the Indian Brahmi script in addition to Kharosthi, which was normally used in the Indo-Greek bilingual coin-

[88] Only ten coins bearing the name of Eucratides have been noticed in the two hoards found at Ai Khanum as against 112 bearing the name of Euthydemus (if two kings of the name of Euthydemus and Eucratides are not to be distinguished).
[89] Cf. Bernard 1985, 65: (F 24).   [90] Narain 1986: (F 112); see above pp. 396–7.
[91] Strabo XI.11.1; Narain 1957–80, 25–7: (F 103).   [92] Mitchiner 1975, I.81–4: (F 101).
[93] Ibid. I.81–3. For local Taxila coins see Allan 1934: (F 1).
[94] For the Agathocles coins showing the Indian deities see Bernard 1971, 441: (F 8); Narain 1973, 73–7: (F 107), the coins which are of silver were mistakenly mentioned as of copper by me; Filliozat 1973, 123: (F 47); Audouin and Bernard 1974, 8–21, pl. 1: (F 2); Mitchiner 1975, I.80: (F 101).
[95] For Heliodorus' affiliation to Bhagavat cult see Narain 1957–80, 118–19: (F 103).

age.[96] In fact the six coins of Agathocles with the legend in Brahmi script which have been found at Ai Khanum are among the earliest examples of this script found outside the Indo-Pakistan sub-continent.[97] Agathocles was the first Yavana king to possess Taxila and initiate a forward policy of extending patronage to Indian religions and cults, both Buddhist and Brahmanical. He probably opened, or used, more northerly passes and routes than the usually frequented ones in the south to reach Taxila, and thus made commercial and cultural contacts easier between north-eastern and eastern Afghanistan on the one hand and north-western Pakistan on the other.[98] This was probably because Eucratides I, or his family, was controlling most of the southerly passes and routes for a while, which would not allow their use easily to his rivals and their associates.

III. MENANDER

The policy initiated by Agathocles was followed by Menander. It is generally accepted that Menander was married to Agathocleia, probably a sister or daughter of Agathocles.[99] Menander is the only Graeco-Bactrian king whose name has survived in Indian classical sources.[100] He is the first, and one of the only two definite names out of possibly three or four of the Graeco-Bactrian kings, known from inscriptions found in South Asia.[101] He was surely the most famous of the Yavana kings,

[96] Narain 1955–76, 7–8: (F 102); Mitchiner 1975, I.81, 84: (F 101).

[97] It is difficult to date any Brahmi inscription in South Asia before the time of Asoka. Even he used Kharosthi for his inscriptions found in the north-western parts of the Indian sub-continent. The only pre-Greek use of this script may be noted on some local coins of Taxila and adjoining regions, and they are rare. In the light of this not only the use of Brahmi by Pantaleon and Agathocles is significant but more so the discovery of some of these coins at Ai Khanum. Of added importance is the discovery of large bricks with the stamp of a Brahmi letter juxtaposed with a Greek monogram: Narain 1986, 797–801: (F 110).

[98] This is indicated not only by the presence of punch-marked coins but also by reference to Karshapanas in the ostraca inscriptions of the 'Treasury' at Ai Khanum. Archaeological discoveries show that the Badakshan region was in communication with Gandhara through the northern routes and Swat valley. [99] Tarn 1951–84, 78, 225: (F 152); Narain 1957–80, 75: (F 103).

[100] Cf. *Milindapañha*, the Pali Buddhist text, edited by Trenckner 1928: (F 100) and translated into English by Rhys Davids 1890, 1894: (F 100). For the Chinese version of this work cf. Demivielle 1924–5, 168: (F 45); Pelliot 1914, 413–19: (F 121); Levi 1936, 126: (F 87). See also Abhayanandi's commentary *Mahāvritti* on Jainendra's *Vyākaraṇa*, edited by Lazarus 1918, 286: (F 84), where the name of Menander is Indianized as Mahendra: Narain 1957–80, 83: (F 103). There is also a reference to King Minara of Tukharas in Taranath's *History of Buddhism* (in Tibetan), identified with Menander by Lassen, cf. Narain 1957–80, 98: (F 103).

[101] The other is Antialcidas referred to in the Besnager pillar inscription of Heliodorus, cf. *Memoirs of the Archaeological Survey of India*, No. 5; Narain 1957–80. pl. 6: (F 103), for text and illustration; Burstein 1985, 53: (A 10A). The Bajaur casket inscription in Kharosthi is still the only inscription which gives the name of Menander and possibly his regnal year: Narain 1957–80, pl. 6: (F 103), for text and illustration. A recent publication, Sharma 1980: (F 142), claiming to have found an inscription in Brahmi characters with the name of Menander, is very misleading, for not only is the

remembered as Milinda in the Buddhist tradition. According to the Pali Buddhist work *Milindapañha* (*Questions of King Milinda*), he was born in a village called Kalasi, not far from Alasanda, probably an Alexandria, which was about 200 *yojana* from Sāgala.[102] Probably he was assigned to govern the satrapy of either Arachosia or Paropamisadae, his home area, because of his matrimonial links, and he rose to kingship about the time that Eucratides I died, *c.* 155 B.C.[103] His marriage to a royal princess, Agathocleia, must have contributed to the legitimation of his rule. In any case it is clear from the dialogue he had with Buddhist monk Nagasena that Menander came from a family of kings.[104]

The variety and the wide provenance of his coinage affirm the importance and extent of his power. His appearance is vividly rendered on his Attic tetradrachm by 'a fine portrait in very high relief which is of exceptional quality even among the masterpieces executed by other artists on Bactrian coins'.[105] It has been well observed that 'the owner of the austere and intellectual features on this unique Greek tetradrachm could well have engaged in debate with a Buddhist sage'.[106] The favourite deity of his coinage is Athena which might or might not have been copied from the archaising statue of Athena Alkidemos at Pella but which surely associates Menander with Diodotus and Demetrius II.[107] Some gold staters bearing the bust of Athena and an owl but with no legends are usually attributed to Menander.[108] The striking of bilingual silver tetradrachms, though first started by Demetrius II, became a

---

name not at all there to read but also it is palaeographically much later in time than Menander: see Verma 1981, 77–80: (F 155); Gupta 1985, 200–1: (F 59). I too have personally examined it and find no basis to support Sharma.

One may wonder if names like those of Strato, Philiskos (= Philoxenos), Hermaios in the Greek inscriptions found at Ai Khanum could be of those who became kings later. In the absence of royal titles and other indications this may be nothing more than wishful thinking. There is the example of Theodamus whose Kharosthi inscription has been noticed by Konow 1929, 6: (F 78); but no coin of Theodamus has been found.

[102] Tarn 1951–84, 41, 420: (F 152); for the identity of Sāgala see Narain 1957–80, 172–3: (F 103). But I do not rule out its identity now with Sanghol near Chandigarh, which will extend the actual control of the Yavanas further east than Ravi, a limit I had suggested earlier. The site which is now being excavated has already yielded rich material for the Saka phase; the Greek phase still remains to be excavated.

[103] Narain 1957–80, 77: (F 103). Most scholars accept this date with a plus/minus of five years.

[104] *Milindapañha*, ed. Trenckner 1928, 329: (F 100); Narain 1957–80, 74: (F 103).

[105] Jenkins 1968, 109: (F 75).   [106] Kraay 1973, 161, see esp. fig. 167: (F 81).

[107] Jenkins and Kraay (*opp. citt.*) see in this type a Macedonian descent of Menander. But note the specific information about Menander's birthplace in the *Milindapañha* and cf. Tarn 1951–84, 99, 310, 420–2, 432–3: (F 152); Narain, 1957–80, 74–5: (F 103). Also note Tarn, *op. cit.* 269, who thinks that adoption of Athena goes against Menander being a Buddhist, and he plays down his adoption of the Buddhist symbol, the *Dharma-chakra* = 'wheel of law', on his copper.

[108] Whitehead 1940, 105–6: (F 162); Narain 1957–80, 99: (F 103). Almost all specimens with any indication of provenance seem to have come from Charsadda, cf. Haughton 1958, 66: (F 62). If the isolated Greek letter *alpha* on these staters represent the regnal year of Menander, they were perhaps struck in the very first year of his reign: Bivar 1970, 126: (F 30).

normal practice from the time of Menander.[109] But it is the copper coinage in various denominations which provides the large variety of types used by Menander.[110] He adopted two epithets, *Soter* and *Dikaios*, on his money.[111] Often his coins bear single Greek letters in addition to the monograms, and it has been argued that they represent either the regnal years of the king or marks of value.[112]

The Shinkot (or Bajaur) Buddhist casket inscription,[113] which mentions Menander's name and one of his regnal years, probably marks the introduction of an era that continued to be used even by the Saka kings who followed the Yavanas in the upper Indus valley for a system of dating using Greek month-names for their records in Kharosthi.[114] Numismatic, epigraphic and archaeological evidence agree that Menander ruled over much of Afghanistan and Pakistan, and his kingdom certainly included Kabul, Ghazni, Kandahar, Quetta, Bannu, Peshawar, Taxila, Swat and Sialkot.[115] With much of Afghanistan and Pakistan under him, Menander was well placed to expand either to areas north of of the Hindu Kush at the cost of the successors of Eucratides I, or eastward at the cost of the fragmentary successor states of the Mauryan empire. So far, the numismatic evidence for his activities north of the Hindu Kush is tenuous.[116] On the other hand, Heliocles I is more likely to have ruled over much of Bactria in the north and he was probably the last among those whose domain included territories even north of the Oxus.[117] The coins of Heliocles I constitute one third of the entire Qunduz hoard, and they were also the latest Graeco-Bactrian types imitated by the Yuezhi and possibly by some of the other nomadic chiefs

[109] Bivar is incorrect in stating that the bilingual tetradrachms were 'unknown before the time of Menander': Bivar 1970, 134: (F 30).

[110] Narain 1957–80, 99: (F 103). So far 18 varieties have been listed in Narain 1955–76, 14–15: (F 102), 20 in Lahiri 1965, 153–62: (F 83), and 24 in Mitchiner 1975, II. 130–9: (F 101). Also *Pls. to Vol. VII. 1*, pl. 36.

[111] Narain 1957–8, 99–100: (F 103). Some scholars have seen in the two epithets two kings of the name of Menander: Lahiri 1965, 160: (F 83).

[112] Bivar 1970, 123ff.: (F 30), *contra* MacDowall 1975, 39ff.: (F 91).

[113] Majumdar 1937–8, 1–10: (F 96); Narain 1957–80, pl. 6.1: (F 103).

[114] This era has also been named as the Old Saka Era. Thomas 1952, 111–12: (F 153), was perhaps the first to suggest that the Sakas used an era of Greek origin. The use of Macedonian month-names such as Apellaios (Hadda, year 28), Artemisios (Wardak, year 51), Audunaios (Kurram, year 20), Daisios (Sui Vihar, year 11), Panemos (Taxila, year 78) in the Kharosthi inscriptions of the later Saka-Pahlava kings supports the hypothesis. Its association with Menander was suggested by Narain 1957–80, 142–4: (F 103); see also Wheeler 1962, 125: (F 159); Smith 1958, 178: (F 146), *id.* 1977–8, 330–1: (F 147), where he states 158 as the starting date; Bivar 1970, 126: (F 3).

[115] Narain 1957–80, 97: (F 103).

[116] This is mainly based on the Attic tetradrachm of Menander. Now there are two specimens, cf. Mitchiner 1975, II. 120: (F 101); Narain 1957–80, 97: (F 103); Jenkins 1968, 109: (F 75). Plutarch called Menander a Bactrian king.

[117] Narain 1957–80, 70–2, 104–6: (F 103); *id.* 1955–76, 12–13: (F 102).

in the Oxus valley.[118] But the Attic tetradrachms of Menander and his gold staters,[119] along with the references in Apollodorus and Plutarch, may indicate as well his impact in some parts of Bactria proper even if not north of the Oxus.

There is certainly some truth in Apollodorus and Strabo when they attribute to Menander the advances made by the Greeks of Bactria beyond the Hypanis (modern Gharra, a tributary of the Indus) and even as far as the Ganges and Palibothra.[120] There is hardly any reason to doubt the subjugation of territories up to the Hypanis by Menander. That the Yavanas advanced even beyond in the east, in the Ganges–Jamuna valley, about the middle of the second century B.C. is supported by the cumulative evidence provided in the Indian sources. *Yugapurāṇa* records their attack over Saket (Ayodhya) and their reaching as far as Kusumadhvaja (Pâtaliputra), but returning home post-haste because of their internal dissensions.[121] Patañjali's grammatical treatise refers to the Yavanas besieging the cities of Saket and Madhyamikā (near Chittor).[122] Kalidasa alludes to the defeat of an advancing Yavana unit at the hands of Vasumitra, the grandson of Pushymitra who had overthrown the Mauryas, on the banks of the River Kali Sindhu in north-central India.[123] Since all these accounts are generally datable *c.* 150 B.C. or a little later, they fit in very well with Menander's time and his role as known from coins and from the western classical sources. But the Yavanas were not able to make territorial gains in the Ganges–Jamuna valley.[124] Whitehead believes that the Indo-Greeks could have done no more than conduct cold-weather campaigns or make long-distance raids.[125] While this may be so, we must also look for deeper causes for the failure of the Indo-Greeks to find a foothold in the Ganges–Jamuna valley.[126]

To enable Menander to conduct his campaigns in various directions and to maintain firm control of his domain a well-planned administrative system and able joint or sub-kings and military commanders were as necessary as local co-operation. 'Strategoi' and 'Meridarchs' are known

---

[118] Out of 627 coins recorded from the Qunduz hoard 221 are of Heliocles I: Curiel and Fussman 1965, 13: (F 39); earlier information about number of coins in Bivar 1955, 2: (F 27), and Narain 1957–80, 106: (F 103), is incorrect. Also the exact site of the discovery is known as Khist Tepe on the River Oxus (Amu Darya) near Qunduz.   [119] Mitchiner 1975, II.120: (F 101).

[120] Strabo XI.11.1–2, XV.1.27–8.

[121] See for reference and discussion on the relevant text Narain 1957–80, 84–5, 174–9: (F 103).

[122] Patañjali's *Mahābhāshya* II.118–19 Kielhorn (F 120). An echo of the Yavanas besieging the city of Mathura has been noted also in a later grammatical work, Abhayanandi's *Mahāvritti* on Jainendra's *Vyākaraṇa*, 286 Lazarus: (F 84); cf. Narain 1957–80, 83 n. 6: (F 103).

[123] Kalidasa's *Mālavikāgnimitra* 227–8 Misra: (F 76). For the identity of the river see Narain 1957–80, 82: (F 103).   [124] *Ibid.* 82–90.

[125] Whitehead 1940, 92: (F 162); but cf. Marshall 1951, 1.32 n. 4: (F 98).

[126] Narain 1957–80, 90–5: (F 103).

from inscriptions.[127] Apollodotus, if there was an earlier one,[128] could have been a joint king, and as we have suggested elsewhere, Antimachus II, Polyxenus and Epander were probably his sub-kings.[129] Menander is also known to have appointed Indians to high administrative positions; one name which has survived is that of Viyakamitra, the governor of Swat valley (Udyāna).[130]

Of the joint kings and sub-kings of Menander suggested above, Apollodotus alone is mentioned in the western classical sources. Out of the two references available,[131] the present author had raised questions about one of them, and argued that both the literary and the numismatic evidence indicate the existence of only one Apollodotus, who flourished later than Menander and could be one of his sons.[132] Tarn had thought that both Menander and Apollodotus were lieutenants of Demetrius I and were responsible for spearheading his military campaigns in India.[133] With the revised opinion about Demetrius I and Menander, this theory is out of the question. Moreover, the recent discovery of a unilingual Attic tetradrachm in the name of Apollodotus[134] resolves the problem in favour of having two kings of the same name, one earlier and another later. But it is still difficult to place Apollodotus I before Eucratides I in Kapisa.[135] The kausia headdress of Apollodotus on the obverse and Athena on the reverse of the Attic tetradrachm link him with Antimachus Theos on the one hand and Demetrius II and Menander on the other. Apollodotus I may now be counted as a junior contemporary of Menander, probably a brother and a joint king.[136] It is possible that he staked his claim after the death of Menander, during the regency of Agathocleia when Strato I was a minor, and was able to wrest power during a gap in the long reign of Strato I.[137] Apollodotus II then would be a son not of Menander, as I thought earlier, but of Apollodotus I. In

---

[127] Narain 1957–80, 95: (F 103). For the texts of the inscriptions see Konow 1929: (F 78).

[128] For a discussion of the problem: Narain 1957–80, 64ff.: (F 103); *id.* 1957, 121ff.: (F 104); Guépin 1956, 1ff.: (F 56); Jenkins 1959, 20ff.: (F 73); MacDowall and Wilson 1960, 221ff.: (F 90). With the recent discovery of an Attic tetradrachm with the portrait of an Apollodotus different from those on the bilingual coins, the question now appears solved in favour of two kings of the same name: Bernard 1974, 307: (F 13).   [129] Narain 1957–80, 95–6: (F 103).

[130] Viyakamitra of the Shinkot (Bajaur) casket inscription of Menander's reign, cf. Narain 1957–80, 79–80, 95: (F 103).

[131] Trogus' *Prologue* XLI and *The Periplus of the Erythraean Sea* 47 Schoff.

[132] Narain 1957–80, 64–9, 122–7: (F 103). *Contra* Jenkins 1959, 20ff.: (F 73); MacDowall and Wilson 1960, 221ff.: (F 90).   [133] Tarn 1951–84, 141–56: (F 152).

[134] Petitot-Biehler 1975, 37–9, pl. 5.50: (F 122).   [135] Narain 1957–80, 64, 122–4: (F 103).

[136] I have shown the weakness of the theory which dates Apollodotus I before Eucratides I: Narain 1957–80, 64–9, 122–9: (F 103). In view of the new tetradrachm, if we must have two Apollodoti the earlier one can only be about the time of Menander. Tarn may be partially right about treating him as a contemporary of Menander, though I do not agree with the whole scenario presented by him regarding the role and relationship of Apollodotus I: Tarn 1951–84, 14ff.: (F 152).

[137] Narain 1957–80, 146–8: (F 103).

any case the coins bearing the name of Apollodotus are abundant and are often found in association with those of Menander. Among those attributed to Apollodotus I, besides the new tetradrachm, the most remarkable ones are the silver square coins with the device of an elephant and a bull, and bearing a bilingual legend.[138] Menander appears on his coins both as a youth and as well advanced in middle age; it is most likely that he ruled for about twenty-five years and died c. 130 B.C. According to the Buddhist sources he handed over his kingdom to his son and retired from the world, but Plutarch reports that he died in a camp.[139] Be that as it may, it is generally agreed that his son and successor, Strato, was not of age, and therefore Menander's queen, Agathocleia, ruled as a regent and became the first woman among the Graeco-Bactrians to mint coins.[140]

If Menander's name has survived in Indian sources it is because of his affiliation to Buddhism and patronage of that religion. His dialogue with the Buddhist monk Nagasena as recorded in the *Questions of King Milinda* is a lucid exposition of early Buddhist doctrine.[141] One of his copper coin-types depicts the Buddhist *Dharma-chakra*, the Wheel of Law.[142] The fact of his conversion to Buddhism finds an echo in Plutarch's statement that at Menander's death 'the cities celebrated his funeral as usual in other respects, but in respect of his remains, they put forth rival claims and only with difficulty came to terms, agreeing that they should divide the ashes equally and go away and should erect monuments to him in all their cities'.[143] For this is unmistakably Buddhist and recalls the similar situation at the time of the Buddha's passing away. Menander's connection with Buddhism is preserved also in the Chinese, Indo-Chinese and Tibetan Buddhist traditions of later times, and like Asoka and Kanishka, he became a legendary figure.[144] We do not believe with Tarn that Menander adopted the faith only nominally and as a matter of policy against the Brahmanical leadership of the post-Mauryan kings with whom he fought.[145]

Menander's achievements and period show Graeco-Indian power at its apogee. He certainly ruled from Kabul in the west to Chandigarh in the east, and from Swat in the north to Kandahar in the south. Extension of his authority in Bactria, even if not as far as the Oxus or beyond it, may not be out of the question. Thus if the impact of Yavana power was felt in

---

[138] Narain 1955–76, 26–7: (F 102); Mitchiner 1975, II.116–17: (F 101).

[139] Plutarch, *Moralia* 821 D–F.   [140] Narain 1957–80, 110–11: (F 103).

[141] Early Buddhist philosophy is explained in the text in the form of questions and answers. But see Tarn 1951–84, 414–36: (F 152), for an excursus on 'The Milindapañha and Pseudo-Aristeas'.

[142] Narain 1955–76, 15: (F 102); Mitchiner 1975, II.134: (F 101); see also above, n. 107.

[143] Plutarch, *Moralia* 821 D–F.

[144] This is clear from the various versions of the *Milindapañha* and the survival of Menander's name in Tibetan tradition: Narain 1957–80, 98: (F103).

[145] *Ibid.* 97–9; Tarn 1951–84, 175: (F 152).

the Ganges–Jamuna valley as well as in western India,[146] and if it manifested itself in trade and commerce, art and religion from the latter half of the second century B.C. onwards, the credit goes to Menander. His extensive coinage and its predominance over those of other Graeco-Bactrian and Graeco-Indian kings, the expansive kingdom and above all the survival of his name both in the western and eastern sources surely make him the greatest of the Yavana kings.

IV. SUCCESSORS OF MENANDER

After Menander there began the process of decline and fall of the Graeco-Bactrian and Graeco-Indian kings. During the century that followed Menander more than twenty rulers are known to have struck coins.[147] While their names are yet to be discovered in any literary source of the west or of the east, already a new king, Thrason, has been added to our list from a recent discovery of one of his silver drachms.[148] The possibility of another king, Theodamus, is so far known only from an inscription on a seal found at Bajaur.[149] In the absence of even the slender clues which have been available hitherto from the literary sources, the task of historical reconstruction of this later phase is frustrating indeed. While some numismatic conclusions can be made to indicate probabilities, any historical arrangement is bound to be very hypothetical and open to more criticism than can be levelled against the arrangement for the earlier period. At any rate it is clear that these kings, after Heliocles I in the north and Menander in the south, cannot be put in a linear succession, ruling on an average not more than five or six years. It is evident that they belonged to several families and more likely than not some of them were striking coins as joint or sub-kings concurrently with the ruling sovereigns. Monograms, irrespective of their interpretation, and the provenance of their coinage, in spite of imperfect records, indicate a waxing and waning of territories, whether for external or internal reasons. The present author has divided these later rulers and their territorial holdings on the basis of the predominating type of their coins and their consistent

---

[146] Narain 1957–80, 94–5: (F 103). The evidence of the *Periplus* may also be recalled here.

[147] Narain 1957–80: (F 103); chapters 5 and 6 deal with them: see p. 104 for their names, and for their coin-types. See Narain 1955–76, 15–37: (F 102).

[148] So far only one specimen of this coin is known, in a private collection in Bombay. It has on the obverse the bust of the king and on the reverse Athena hurling a thunderbolt. The Greek inscription on the coin reads *Basileus Megalou Thrasonos* and the Kharosthi reads *Maharajasa Mahatasa Thrasasa*. I have seen the photograph of the coin and it is reported by Robert C. Senior in his Sale List 4 of January 1983:(F 141). The coin is said to have been found with Menander drachms.

[149] Konow 1929, 6: (F 78). On palaeographical grounds Konow dates the seal in the 'first half of the first century of the Christian era', and that he could be a king depends upon the interpretation of the prefix *su* (= Saka *shau* = king) before the name. If the date suggested is true, Theodamus could be a satrap under the Saka-Pahlava rule.

geographical distribution.[150] It has rightly been observed that 'we get an impression of the simultaneous rule of more than one king, of mutual antagonism, confusion, and of civil war. The Yavanas seem to have been their own worst enemies.'[151]

Heliocles I was probably the last Graeco-Bactrian to rule on both sides of the River Oxus until about 140, when he was succeeded by his son Eucratides II. Sometime during the reign of the latter the Yuezhi from Chinese Central Asia had arrived in the region north of the Oxus. Pushed by them, some of the Scythians from the north crossed the Oxus at points near its central bend and, moving westward, harassed the Parthians during the period c. 138–124 B.C. Phraates II and Artabanus II perished in their battles against them. But, finally quelled by Mithridates II, they were obliged to move southward through Merv and Herat to Seistan (Drangiana) where they found a new home.[152] We do not know if, and to what extent, the Bactrian Greeks suffered from their movement southward at this time; their passage through Parthia might have been disturbing, if at all, only marginally in the west; at least none of the Bactrian Greeks is known to have suffered the fate of the Parthian kings. It is only later, after several generations, when these Scythians move northward from Seistan, that the Bactrian Greeks suffer from their activities.[153]

While Eucratides II (140–130 B.C.), represented by 130 coins in the Qunduz hoard, no doubt ruled in central and western Bactria, and Archebius (130–120), Heliocles II (120–115) and Antialcidas (115–100) filled the succession roster in his group,[154] things were not so smooth in the eastern and southern parts of the Graeco-Bactrian and Graeco-Indian domains after Menander's death. This was more because of internal reasons than external. Menander's son was a minor, so that for the first time a woman took charge of the state. She was Menander's queen Agathocleia, who acted as regent for some time before his young son Strato I could rule on his own. She struck some coins with her own portrait, and on others she is shown jointly with Strato. Her portrait has a very 'Indian' look about it as regards features, hairstyle and even in what

[150] Narain 1957–80, 101–5: (F 103).   [151] Whitehead 1923, 308: (F 161).
[152] Strabo XI.9.2 probably refers to this period. Mithridates II dislodged these Scythians from western parts of Bactria: Narain 1957–80, 134, 140–1: (F 103).
[153] The evidence of the Qunduz hoard indicates that the Greeks were still in control of central parts of Bactria; if they suffered at all it must have been in the western parts closer to Parthia. The Scytho-Parthians (Pahlavas) came to power in Seistan after or about the time of Mithridates II's death and the independence of Gotarzes in Babylonia, c. 88 B.C. It is a generation later that Azes I is known to have overstruck the coins of Apollodotus II and Hippostratus: Narain 1957–80, 140–2: (F 103).
[154] In the Qunduz hoard, out of 627 there were 144 coins of Eucratides, 221 of Heliocles I and 130 of Eucratides II; there were only 3 of Antialcidas: Curiel and Fussman 1965: (F 39).

is visible of the dress.[155] She adopted the title *Basilisses Theotropou*.[156] Apollodotus I, who may have been a joint or sub-king during the time of Menander, probably did not like the regency of Agathocleia and encouraged defections in the Menander group. Along with him, or following soon after, others such as Antimachus II and Zoilus I, in whose group Lysias was included, founded their own establishments wherever they could.[157]

This provided an opportunity for Antialcidas, a member of the Eucratides group, to extend his power in Gandhara and become a king of Taxila, while Antimachus II was in possession of the Swat valley.[158] Lysias, one of the Menander group and a contemporary rival of Antialcidas, fought with him in the remaining portions of Afghanistan; if one of his coins was indeed found in the Ai Khanum hoard, against none of Antialcidas, Lysias could have been holding briefly the remote northeastern part of the Bactrian Greek kingdom before the Yuezhi crossed the Oxus and forced Lysias and his group to contend with Antialcidas in the southern regions of Afghanistan.[159]

Antialcidas, surely one of the better known of the later kings, is known to have sent an envoy from Taxila, Heliodorus, to the court of Bhāgabhadra, an Indian king of central India. By the time Antialcidas' rule ended in Gandhara c. 100 B.C. the Yuezhi had crossed the Oxus and occupied Bactria proper, bringing to an end the Bactrian Greek holdings there, confining them in regions south of the Hindu Kush and in the enclaves of the Indo-Afghan borderlands and in the upper Indus and Swat valleys. But from these regions, too, they were squeezed out in the next few decades by the Sakas, coming from the north through the Pamir passes, and by the Scytho-Parthians, known as Pahlavas to Indian sources, moving upwards from Sacastene (Seistan) to Ghazni and then to Gandhara.[160]

Among the last kings of the various groups, some are known to have minted more coins than others. Though almost all of them struck a few unilingual coins in the Attic system, the main bulk of their coinage remained bilingual in the Indian system of weight. If quantitatively Strato I and II, Apollodotus II, Diomedes, Nicias, Hippostratus and Hermaeus appear to dominate the period, it is Amyntas who steals the

---

[155] Haughton 1948, 134–41: (F 61); Narain 1957–80, 110: (F 103).
[156] *Ibid.*; Whitehead 1970, 216: (F 164).   [157] Narain 1957–80, 112–14: (F 103).
[158] *Ibid.*
[159] A hoard of coins found by farmers during 1973–4 at Ai Khanum, but not from the excavations, contained at least 141 and possibly more coins; the other hoard found in the stratified excavations in October 1973, on the other hand, contained only 63. One coin of Lysias is included in the reconstructed inventory of the hoard but is considered as an 'intrusion' by Holt 1981, 9–10: (F 65). I do not see any reason to agree, not only in view of the incomplete evidence but also because five coins of Lysias as against one of Antialcidas were included in the Qunduz hoard.
[160] Narain 1957–80, 132–8: (F 103).

show by minting the largest silver coins and by adopting the title of *Nikator*.[161] Hermaeus was the last king.[162] By marrying Calliope, probably a regnant queen belonging to another family,[163] he made the last bid to unify the Greeks of Bactria and India. But it was too late: by the middle of the first century B.C. the three-pronged movement of the Yuezhi-Kushan, Saka and Pahlava ethnic groups had already divided the kingdom between themselves.[164]

V. CONCLUSION

The Bactrian Greek state did not arise out of a conquest as did the Achaemenid empire or that of Alexander in the east; it was also not an immediate successor-state of Alexander like those of the Seleucids and Ptolemies. On the contrary, it arose out of a revolt and it lived with a series of them: Diodotus revolted against the Seleucids, Euthydemus against the Diodoti and Eucratides against the Euthydemids. It was not a monolithic dynastic state like those of the Seleucids or Ptolemies, but one in which related and unrelated families, legitimate successors as well as usurpers, ever feuding, somehow adjusted for their existence as a composite state. They survived through a story of recurring conflicts and changing authorities and loyalties. At no time in its life of about two hundred years did any one king, or any one of the dynastic groups, rule over the entire kingdom, consisting of those regions in the east where Alexander had to deal with high resistance not only from the Iranians and Indians but also from the Greek settlers, and where he had both experienced the toughest of his battles and also ordered more massacres than in the west. In spite of the in-fighting and the condition of flux, this composite state was able to maintain its identity and survive for a long period. Above all, military force combined with economic control provided security as well as prosperity and enabled the state to last as long as it did. While the military strategy and administration were fought out by the rulers within their own fold, the economic and political structure of the state was shared with the local elites with such social relations and acceptance of religious systems as to reduce the gap between the ruler and the ruled so that finally they became one.

It is not possible to affirm that this entire state was ruled from one capital city throughout its existence. In the beginning it could have been Bactra or Zariaspa, or most probably, as the evidence now emerges, it was the city at the site of Ai Khanum, perhaps named Dionysopolis (or

---

[161] Curiel and Fussman 1965, 46, pls. 52–3: (F 39); Mitchiner 1975, II.219: (F 101).
[162] Narain 1957–80, 157–64: (F 103).
[163] *Ibid.* 161–2. For illustration of the joint coin see Mitchiner 1975, II.226: (F 101).
[164] Narain 1957–80, ch. 5 *passim*: (F 103).

Diodoteia) until it was moved by Euthydemus to Bactra.[165] No doubt, however, by the second century B.C. there was already more than one city from which the government was administered.[166] If there was any satrapal division of the state at the outset, as may be inferred from Strabo and others,[167] it was soon found to be redundant because of revolts and resultant fragmentation which made such large territorial jurisdictions out of place. At any rate it is agreed that it did not have the triple Seleucid division of satrapy, eparchy and hyparchy.[168] Probably the institution of satrapal office yielded to that of the joint kings and sub-kings, *socius regni*, the office mentioned by Justin in the case of Eucratides I.[169] They were supposed to assist the king in the administration with more freedom and power than a satrap. Coins also indicate that at times a queen could be a regent for a minor son, or even a co-ruler as in the example of Hermaeus and Calliope. The only name of an administrative position which has survived in inscriptions is that of Meridarch,[170] an institution not heard of in the Seleucid system.[171] Perhaps the Bactrian Greeks believed in having only lower or smaller units of administration, consisting of a district or a division rather than large provinces, and these were put probably under the direct control of the king or his joint or sub-kings. Assuming that the Sakas and Pahlavas followed the Bactrian Greeks and adopted aspects of their administration and nomenclature, one may infer from their inscriptions that some *strategoi* were probably also appointed; they represented the coercive element of the state.[172] In the case of the Sakas, the *strategoi* do not appear to have been in full charge of the satrapies because they had also the Kshatrapas and Mahakshatrapas in their administration. But if the latter were the equivalents of sub-kings and joint-kings of the Bactrian Greek state, the *strategoi* may have been in charge of the frontier or strategic military settlements. Or perhaps a system of dual administration dividing the 'civil' and 'military' roles was

[165] While there is no doubt that Bactra/Zariaspa was the capital of the state under Euthydemus (as is clear from Polybius, for it was there that Euthydemus had withdrawn and held out against Antiochus III), there is no specific evidence whether it was the capital of Diodotus from the very start; in view of the Ai Khanum evidence it seems more likely that his capital was in the remote north-eastern part of Bactria before it was moved to Bactra, whether or not by Diodotus himself.

[166] Besides the one at Ai Khanum and Bactra we may visualize a chief city at each of the following locations (in some cases perhaps more than one): in the Qunduz valley, Begram, Charsada, Taxila Sāgala and the Swat valley.

[167] Strabo XI.11.2; also indirectly in Justin XLI.6. Based on Ptolemy's evidence, Tarn envisages as many as nine province-names east of the Paropamisadae during the time of Menander in addition to several others in other regions of the Bactrian Greek kingdom (1951–84, 240: (F 152)).

[168] *Ibid.* 242.   [169] Justin XLI.6.

[170] Konow 1929, 1–5: (F 78). Two Meridarchs are known from inscriptions, Theodorus in the Swat valley and one whose name cannot be read at Taxila.

[171] Tarn 1951–84, 242: (F 152).

[172] *Ibid.* 241. But there is no actual reference to the office or to a name of an incumbent during the period of the Bactrian and Indian Greeks (if the indirect evidence about Viyakamitra is not accepted). *Strategoi* are known only from later Scytho-Parthian coins.

in operation. One may even postulate that the *strategoi* were the links between the king and the Meridarchs. The *Milindapañha* refers to the *amacca*, a Pali word (*amātya* in Sanskrit) which may be translated as 'ministers' or 'councillors', who were always available to advise Menander; the text mentions the names of Anantakāya (Antiochus), Devamantiya (Diomedes ?), Sabbadinna or Dinna (Dion) and Maṅkura (a non-Greek?) as Menander's *amacca*.[173] Could they be taken as equivalents of the 'Friends' (*philoi*) of the Seleucid system?[174] While no specific information is available on their inter-state diplomatic relations with kings or kingdoms to their west, there is evidence for the despatch of an envoy, Heliodorus, from Taxila by one of the Indo-Greek kings, Antialcidas, to the court of Bhāgabhadra, an Indian king in Central India.[175] This envoy, said to be a son of Dion, could be a son of Dinna, an *amacca* of Menander.[176]

No doubt the Greeks of Bactria and India presided over a flourishing economy. This is clearly indicated by their coinage and the monetary exchange they had established with other currencies. But again there is not much to enlighten us about their fiscal administration and monetary management. We are still in the dark as to whether the monograms on their coins stand for mints or moneyers, or both. But we do know from the recent discovery of ink inscriptions on vases at Ai Khanum that there were functionaries involved in the accounting and storage of money and goods received.[177] Whether these accumulations were items of tribute or revenue receipts, or the wealth of a business magnate resulting from trade and commerce, may be questioned. But from such names as Oxeboakes, Oxubazes, Aryandes in these documents, the participatory roles of the Indo-Iranians in their management are evident. The occurrence of Kharosthi letters with Greek monograms on the coins, as well as of Brahmi along with Greek on an important funerary monument, tells the same story.[178]

The affluence and the scramble for wealth and power, which must have been a major reason for the in-fighting and political fragmentation of the state, in turn also sapped the military strength of the population and made them more a nation of shopkeepers than of energetic soldiers.

[173] *Milindapañha* II, *The Questions of King Milinda* Part 1, 47ff.: (F 100).

[174] See Walbank, *CAH*[2] VII.i.68–71. He notes, 'kings, Friends and army are often mentioned together as three focal points of importance in a Hellenistic kingdom' (n. 25).

[175] It is likely that Antialcidas sought the friendship of this king from Vidisha (Bhopal) in Central India to strengthen his hold over Taxila because the Indo-Greeks under Menander had suffered a reverse in that area: Narain 1957–80, 82: (F 103).

[176] Since Antialcidas came to occupy Taxila soon after the death of Menander it is not unlikely that the former wisely chose a son of one of the 'ministers' of Menander for the post of an envoy.

[177] Rapin 1983: (F 127).

[178] Tarn 1951–84, 356: (F 152), for Kharosthi letters, and Narain 1986: (F 110) for Brahmi.

The observation of Zhang Qian, the Chinese envoy to the Yuezhi, about Bactria in 129/8 B.C. seems appropriate:[179]

The Daxia, situated in the south of the Oxus river . . . have walled cities and houses. . . . They have had no great kings or chiefs. Some cities and towns had small chiefs. Their soldiers were weak and feared fighting. They were skilful in trade. When the Da Yuezhi migrated westward, they attacked and defeated them and subjugated all the Daxia.

A long period of interaction with the peoples and cultures of the region made the Greeks of Bactria and India part of the local milieu. They had kept their identity as long as they could before they were absorbed in the melting pot of south Asia. They were socially integrated into the caste system of India, they became Buddhists and Hindus, master craftsmen and architects, adopted Indian names and titles, and wrote in Indian script and languages. In this process they not only internalized many ideas and institutions of Iranian and Indian origin but also made abiding contributions to various aspects of the life and culture of south Asia, for example in art and iconography, literature and drama, astronomy and the calendrical system.

While the literary sources, both Indian and western, yield little infor-mation, material remains have proved comparatively more rewarding, particularly those from the recent but still incomplete excavations at Ai Khanum. A brief glimpse of how the east and the west interacted there may be apt here.[180] Of the public structures at Ai Khanum, while there are such typically Greek items as a gymnasium and a theatre, albeit with an 'oriental' touch, the builders had turned to Persian models for their concept and execution of the palace construction, though Graeco-Bactrian elements may be discerned in the architectural embellishments. If the plan of private apartments and the flat roofs of the buildings were characteristically eastern and of non-hellenic inspiration, the use of an ornamental edging of terracotta lines gave them a Greek look, as did the decor of cylindrical stone columns and rectangular stone pilasters. But the importance the inhabitants gave to their luxurious bathrooms was not Greek. Although the gymnasium was protected in the Greek tra-dition by Hermes and Heracles and the presiding deities on the coins generally belong to the Greek pantheon, the three temples discovered at Ai Khanum are not Greek at all: their massive structure standing on a high three-stepped podium and other details were borrowed from Iranian or Central Asian tradition; one of them, a large stepped platform

---

[179] *Shiji* ch. 123, translation of the passage by Kajuo Enoki in Narain 1957–80, 139: (F 103).
[180] See a splendid summary of the result of work at Ai Khanum in Bernard 1982: (F 23). The account that follows is based essentially on this report. See also *Pls. to Vol. VII. 1*, pp. 25–7 with pls. 26 and 27.

at the south-west corner of the acropolis, could belong even to Indian tradition. The Greeks followed their own custom of burial, but the rites they performed in the temples were not hellenic. Similarly, while Greek inscriptions on stone and imprints from papyrus manuscripts have survived to indicate their links to Delphi and the elite's love for Greek poetry and philosophy, and while there are Greek inscriptions on the vases found in the so-called 'Treasury', the use of Aramaic, Brahmi and Kharosthi scripts may also be noted.[181] If among the settlers and func- tionaries of the city there were Greeks of various origins as well as Macedonians, there were also, as mentioned above, people of Iranian and other backgrounds. In the arts, too, examples of Greek tradition as well as those belonging to Iranian, Indian and Central Asian traditions abound. While iconographic elements of their deities remained mostly Greek in their execution, artists were aware not only of local canons and practices but they also introduced innovations in technique that were rarely seen in Greece. These are particularly noticeable in the depiction of cult figures and in making monumental statues and mural bas-reliefs. Bernard has observed that the taste of these people 'remained tradition- ally Greek, even to the point of perpetuating an outdated Classical style'.[182] This is well taken; it underscores the pre-Alexander elements in the east, the 'hellenic' as against the 'Hellenistic'. Tarn observed that 'it must be emphasised that Greeks were not in India for the purpose of Hellenising Indians, and there is no sign that they ever attempted to do so; they had come to India for a definite purpose, which had failed, and they stayed there to rule what they could because there was nothing else they could do'.[183] When the Greeks of Bactria and India lost their kingdom they were not all killed, nor did they return to Greece. They merged with the people of the area and worked for the new masters;[184] contributing considerably to the culture and civilization in southern and central Asia, they became part of its history. I still believe 'they came, they saw, but India conquered'.[185]

---

[181] For Aramaic see Grenet 1983, 373–81: (F 54).

[182] Bernard 1982, 158: (F 23).

[183] Tarn 1951–84, 375–6: (F 152).

[184] Besides those who must have been absorbed in administrative positions or in army there is also the example of the slave Agesilas, one of the architects in the time of Kanishka.

[185] Narain 1957–80, 11: (F 103). About thirty years ago when I wrote this line, most of about fifty reviews (in eight languages) which I saw took this as my *leitmotif*; some agreed with me and others did not. But as I said in the preface of my book, it is not easy to settle matters conclusively. In response to a recent remark that my assessment, as counterpart to that of Tarn, 'is no less ethnocentric' (Holt in his Introduction to the latest reprint edition of Tarn's book, p. v), I only refer to another statement: 'it must not be thought, however, that Dr Narain writes from a narrowly nationalistic viewpoint – far from it: he has gone fully into the evidence on both sides and is scrupulously fair in his treatment of it': Jenkins in his *Review* in the *Journal of the Royal Central Asian Society* 1957: (F 72).

APPENDIX I: THE GRAECO-BACTRIAN AND THE INDO-GREEK KINGS IN CHRONOLOGICAL AND GENEALOGICAL GROUP ARRANGEMENTS

256–248			Diodotus I	
248–235			Diodotus II	
235–200	Euthydemus I			
200–185	Demetrius I			
200–190	Euthydemus II			
195–185			Antimachus I	
185–180	Pantaleon			
185–175			Demetrius II	
180–165	Agathocles			
171–155				Eucratides I
155–130	Agathocleia =		= Menander	
155–153				Plato
140–125			Apollodotus I	Heliocles I
140–130				Eucratides II
130–125	Zoilus I	Antimachus II		
130–120				Archebius
130–120			Agathocleia & Strato I	
125–120			Polyxenus	
125–115		Philoxenus		Heliocles II
120–95			Strato I	
120–110	Lysias			
115–100				Antialcidas
115–110	Thrasos	Epander		
110–95			Apollodotus II	
100–95	Theophilus	Nicias		Diomedes
95–90	Artemidorus	Peucolaus	Strato I & II	
95–80	Telephus	Hippostratus		Amyntas
85–75		Dionysius	Strato II	
80–75			Apollophanes	
75–55		Calliope =		= Hermaeus

Note: The dates given above, which are by no means absolute because of the very nature of the evidence, are revised estimates from earlier conclusions (Narain 1957–80, 181: (F 103)). So also the genealogical group arrangements of the kings are not strictly genealogical but indicate direct or indirect kinship in an extended family sense either by descent or by marriage. Those listed in the first three groups cumulatively appear to form one internal group succeeding the Diodoti. The fourth group may be treated as external started by an usurper, Eucratides I.

APPENDIX II: TERRITORIAL JURISDICTIONS OF THE GRAECO-BACTRIAN AND INDO-GREEK KINGS

The territorial assignments indicated below are based on conclusions of earlier work (Narain 1957–80: (F 103)) and some revisions made in the text above. Just as the chronology of the kings and joint/sub-kings are often overlapping, their territorial jurisdictions also often overlap. The political geography has been divided into eleven territorial areas based on numismatic distribution and other evidence. They are numbered as follows:

(1) Bactria (western and central). (2) Bactria (eastern or Badakshan). (3) Sogdiana (or northern Bactria, north of Oxus). (4) Aria. (5) Arachosia (northern or Ghazni area). (6) Arachosia (southern or Seistan/Drangiana). (7) Paropamisadae (Kabul valley). (8) Gandhara (western or west of Indus). (9) Gandhara (eastern or Taxila region). (10) Udyana (Swat valley). (11) Eastern Punjab.

Name of king	Territories										
	1	2	3	4	5	6	7	8	9	10	11
Diodotus I	×	×									
Diodotus II	×	×	×								
Euthydemus I	×	×	×	×							
Demetrius I	×	×	×	×	×						
Euthydemus II	×	×	×								
Antimachus I	×	×									
Demetrius II	×	×	×	×	×	×	×				
Eucratides I	×		×	×	×			×			
Pantaleon	×	×					×	×	×		
Agathocles	×	×					×	×	×	×	
Menander	×			×	×	×	×	×	×	×	×
Heliocles I	×	×	×	×							
Eucratides II	×	×	×	×							
Apollodotus I	×				×		×	×	×		
Antimachus II					×					×	
Polyxenus					×			×			
Epander							×				
Strato I & Agathocleia					×			×	×		×
Archebius	×				×		×				
Zoilus I					×					×	
Heliocles II							×				
Lysias	×	×			×		×	×			
Antialcidas	×				×		×	×	×		
Philoxenus	×				×		×	×	×		
Diomedes								×			
Peucolaus							×				
Thrasos											?
Artemidorus								×			
Theophilus	×							×			
Nicias								×			
Hippostratus								×	×		
Telephus								×			
Apollodotus II								×	×	×	×
Amyntas	×						×	×			
Strato II											×
Zoilus II											×
Dionysius											×
Apollophanes											×
Hermaeus & Calliope	×						×	×	×		

CHAPTER 12

ROMAN TRADITION AND THE GREEK
WORLD

ELIZABETH RAWSON

I. THE ROMAN TRADITION

It is difficult to look directly at the Rome of the late third century and isolate her characteristics and traditions; too little contemporary evidence survives. Perhaps we may do best to attempt to see her first through the eyes of two contrasted writers, Polybius and Fabius Pictor. Polybius wrote in the middle of the second century, but tried to describe the Romans in his first book as they were at the time of the First Punic War, while his extended account in book VI of their institutions is meant to be a picture of these as they were at their best, near the start of the struggle against Hannibal.

That 'best' should give us pause, and of course Polybius' sources were primarily aristocratic Romans looking back to an idealized past. But Polybius is not entirely uncritical. His Romans are also more unlike his own familiar Greeks than is sometimes supposed.[1] Above all, they are soldiers: immensely courageous, partly because subject to a strict and indeed terrifying discipline,[2] though also spurred on by praise and rewards; persistent to the point of obstinacy – they think that force can control even the weather, and thus, impressive as their rapid and determined building of a fleet against the Carthaginians was, they have frequently met disaster at sea.[3] Their haughtiness, especially in defeat, is imposing, but sometimes impractical. At a later point Polybius notes their thoroughness when sacking a town – they even dismember the dogs. In book VI he shows a great admiration not only for the structure and weapons of the legion, so different from those of the Greek phalanx, but for the whole way in which a campaign is organized, following it from the first enlistment of the men to the measuring of the camp. King Pyrrhus of Epirus is supposed to have wondered if a people so well organized in military affairs could be called barbarian; Polybius certainly does not call the Romans so – it is their Gallic enemies whom he regards as typical barbarians, brave but often disorganized and so not really

---

[1] As by Momigliano 1975, 22: (I 27).   [2] Polyb. 1.17.11.
[3] Polyb. 1.20.11–13, 37.7–10, XXVII.8.8.

formidable. But some of his Greek characters do call the Romans barbarians, and indeed at the start of the second century the playwright Plautus was still ready to apply the word to them and their language, if primarily just to mean non-Greek[4] (he also identifies them as porridge-eaters, *pultiphagi*[5]); while Cato was to complain that the Greeks called the Romans *Opici*, assimilating them to rough Italic tribes of southern Italy against which the Greek colonial cities had long struggled.[6]

The other fact that Polybius stresses is the sheer size of the Roman military and naval effort. The manpower resources of Rome and her Italian allies were, in the eyes of a Greek from the Peloponnese, enormous; her navies in particular larger than anything a Greek power could produce.[7] In general, he regarded the Romans even of the third century as wealthy, though simple in their way of life. He notoriously admired Roman piety and the role given to religion in public life,[8] for he held that this contributed to the obedience of the lower, and the traditional integrity of the upper, class (he believed that none of the latter took bribes until shortly before the period in which he was writing). He is thinking of the fear of divine punishment in this and a future life, a fear which in fact Greek and Etruscan influence were probably largely responsible for imposing on the Romans. There were still primitive aspects to Roman religion; in times of crisis, says Polybius, when he reaches the disasters of the first years of the Hannibalic War, the Romans think nothing unworthy of them in their effort to placate the gods.[9] This is perhaps a veiled reference to the sacrifice involving the burial of a Gallic and a Greek couple (though it was the Sibylline books that advised this, a collection of oracles in Greek supposedly originating at archaic Cumae but acquired at an early date by the Roman state). Polybius describes openly the more harmless, if uncivilized, custom of the women, who sweep out the shrines with their hair in such emergencies.

He also admires the Roman political system; but here it is true that he does, with some violence, assimilate it to the Greek pattern of the 'mixed' constitution, or rather, in his case, a 'balanced' constitution.[10] In rough outline, however, there were similarities between Greek and Roman institutions, if Rome is regarded simply as a city-state; and Polybius, at least in the surviving parts of his work, gives us little idea of the way in which Rome had already gone beyond this conception, especially through bestowing the status of *civitas sine suffragio* and *Latinitas*, and how by colonization and alliance she had come to dominate Italy. (As early as 215, however, her ability to colonize widely, caused as he

4 Plaut. *Asin.* 11, *Most.* 828, etc.   5 Plaut. *Mostell.* 828, *Poen.* 54.
6 Pliny, *HN* XXIX.14.   7 Polyb. 1.26.8–9, 11.24.   8 Polyb. VI.56.
9 Polyb. III.112.9.   10 Polyb. VI.11.11.

thought by the generous granting of full citizenship to freedmen, had struck Philip V of Macedon.[11])

If it is always complained that Polybius, in book VI, draws his horizontal divisions – consuls, senate, popular assembly – without counterpointing them with the vital vertical divisions resulting from the *clientelae* of the great nobles, he does note, for his own time, how an aristocrat is expected to spend his days in the Forum, collecting supporters by defending clients in the courts; and also the narrowly legalistic outlook that led most Romans religiously to fulfil their pecuniary obligations, but never to go an inch beyond them.[12] And the materialistic attitude which regarded the acquisition of wealth, so long as it was done in acceptable ways, as one of the most important things in life, comes over clearly; as it does in a genuine late third-century document, the eulogy of L. Metellus, given at his funeral in 221, and also praising his military achievements, prominence in the Senate, and many children.[13] Opportunities for the acquisition of wealth (except by gaining booty) must, however, have been limited at this time, when Rome's economy was largely agricultural; it is Cato, not Polybius, who looks back to this tradition, saying that our ancestors, if they wished to praise a man, praised him as a good farmer and cultivator.[14] The *lex Claudia* of 218 limited the extent to which a Roman senator or his son might engage in trade (and thus incidentally barred one route to foreign contacts, while it was probably also forbidden, by this or another law, to senators to own land abroad); but foreign trade at least was still restricted in volume. Opportunities for conspicuous consumption were also limited: Cicero thinks C. Duilius, who had won a victory in the First Punic War, and who liked in his old age to be accompanied of an evening by a torchbearer and a flute-player, on the Greek model, was absolutely unexampled.[15]

Polybius perhaps also underestimates the strength of aristocratic family feeling, in spite of his well-known description of a great man's funeral, with masked figures representing all his prominent ancestors;[16] which he regarded as admirably calculated to inspire youthful members of the family to seek the fame that rewards valour. He notes too that young Scipio Aemilianus was under intense pressure to live up to the traditions of his house, and we can well believe that this was so when we read the surviving epitaphs of third- and second-century members of the family – though one, dating from as early as the late third century, pauses to note that its subject's beauty, *forma*, was equal to his *virtus*, a sign probably of Greek influence, perhaps primarily Homeric.[17]

---

[11] *SIG* 543.   [12] Polyb. XXXI.23.11, cf. 26.9–28.9.   [13] Pliny, *HN* VII.139.40.
[14] Cato, *Agr. praef.*
[15] Cic. *Sen.* 44 (another version has it that they were privileges officially granted).
[16] Polyb. VI.53–4.   [17] *ILLRP* 309.

Polybius has nothing to say about the arts or intellectual activities at Rome in the third century, perhaps because they did not seem to him worth talking of, though he criticizes Greek states that lack education and the arts. Cicero tells us, however, that the only complaint he had of Roman institutions was that no public provision was made for education; it is a pity that this passage is lost.[18]

What Polybius does is to show us what aspects of Rome's tradition a Greek could believe to be the cause of her great achievements, even believe to be better than their Greek equivalents. The Romans, partly because of their inbuilt reverence for ancestral tradition, partly perhaps in response to Greek admiration, were slow to modify these aspects. In spite of the famous tag from Horace, the conqueror was never taken wholly captive; the vitality of the Roman tradition was greater than that of almost any other area that came under the influence of Greek civilization, in part of course because the Romans were in fact the conquering and not the conquered or colonized partner.

It was possible to stress the connections, not the differences, between Greeks and Romans. The senator Fabius Pictor, who wrote a history of Rome in the Greek language, perhaps shortly after rather than during the Hannibalic War, attempted to prove not only that her policy in her recent wars had been eminently just, but that she was to all intents a Greek city. He was trying, no doubt, to redress the balance against the pro-Carthaginian historians from Sicily and Magna Graecia, in an unprecedented attempt to influence Greek opinion.[19] He accepted, of course, the story of Aeneas' coming to Latium, which had been current for a long time, and which fitted Rome nicely into Greek legendary history, though it did not make her Greek. But we now know that he had Hercules' visit to Italy,[20] and perhaps to the site of Rome, and he almost certainly had the tale of the Arcadian Evander's settlement on the Palatine. (He also had accounts of legendary connections between Sicily and Latium, which fell out of the tradition when Sicily lost all political importance.) For the actual foundation of Rome by Romulus and Remus he seems to have followed a Greek writer, Diocles of Peparethus (though Diocles may have been building on a genuinely Roman version),[21] and it is hard to doubt that he knew Timaeus' great history dealing extensively with the western Mediterranean, though Roman historians seem to have made a point of differing from Timaeus wherever possible.

Fabius also had an account of an old festival, the *Ludi Romani*, probably designed to show how Greek Rome was.[22] His naiveté is shown

---

[18] Cic. *Rep.* IV.3.   [19] Gelzer 1962–4, III.51: (A 19); Momigliano 1966, 55: (B 18).
[20] Alföldi 1974, 389: (H 275).   [21] Peter, *HRRel.* frs. 5a–b.
[22] *Ibid.* fr. 16. The thesis was perhaps not first introduced into the passage by Dionysius, who is our direct source.

by his belief that the games, and their cost, had not changed since their foundation in the early fifth century B.C., but in spite of his desire to prove a thesis, his description is perhaps reasonably accurate for his own time. He apparently began with an account of the Greek customs involved in the preliminaries to the games which the Augustan Dionysius of Halicarnassus, our immediate source, has passed over. Dionysius does describe the procession, the sacrifice and the games themselves, quoting from Homer (as possibly Fabius had not done) to prove that early Greek customs lay behind the Roman ones. The chariot-races, the musical instruments, the dancers in armour or dressed as satyrs all recall Greece; the images of the gods are carried in 'showing the same likenesses as those made by the Greeks, with the same dress and symbols as they have in Greece'. Victorious athletes are rewarded 'in the most Greek of ways', with wreaths. The passage provides a number of puzzles, but it is probably true that some of the customs mentioned were archaic, and ultimately of Greek origin, perhaps (though not necessarily) filtered through Etruria; while others were doubtless comparatively recent imports, either from Magna Graecia or Sicily, from both of which Rome received much influence, from the late fourth century; or even from Greece itself, with which Rome was in direct if occasional touch.

Fabius will hardly have seemed to his readers to prove more than the 'faint traces of a common origin' which Plutarch says that the Greeks admitted at the time of Flamininus' first passage to Greece in 198 B.C. (as indeed they must have done when they allowed the Romans to compete in the Isthmian Games in 228).[23] By that time the pace of hellenization had quickened dramatically. But the term is often used in altogether too undefined and undifferentiated a fashion. We must distinguish many elements in it, and many sources of origin, establishing which aspects of it the Romans were at different stages able to admire or absorb, and which they would only very slowly come to appreciate or would even positively reject.

II. THE HANNIBALIC WAR

During the first years of the Hannibalic War Rome was too hard-pressed to look much beyond her immediate problems in the west, except that the Senate turned in its anxiety to whatever religious means could be found for obtaining the gods' favour; and this meant turning not only to such traditional Italic institutions as the *ver sacrum*, but also to the Greek ones recommended by the Sibylline books, which as we saw were or purported to be an archaic collection of Greek oracles. Thus in 217 a *lecti-*

---

[23] Plut. *Flam.* 11.4; Zon. VIII.19.7.

sternium, a Greek rite not in itself new at Rome, by which the images of the gods were placed on couches and offered feasts, was held to the twelve Great Gods, chosen and paired according to Greek conceptions.[24] In the next year Fabius Pictor, later the historian, was sent to the oracle at Delphi. The Romans had probably dedicated gifts, and consulted the oracle, occasionally from early times. They were to turn to it again some ten years after Fabius' visit.[25] The Sibylline books also recommended the vowing of a temple to Venus Erycina, whose cult in Sicily showed Greek as well as Punic influences.[26] Games to Apollo, who was probably still felt to be a Greek god (his temple was outside the *pomerium* or city boundary and he was worshipped *Graeco ritu*) were instituted in 212 and paid for by public collection (a Greek custom which, introduced in this time of financial stringency, became common); they were made regular in 208 – all this on the advice both of the Sibylline books and the native prophecies of Marcius. In 208 a Roman envoy was told to attend the Olympic Games while in Greece (though for political purposes).[27] In 205 Rome even sent to her most distant ally, Attalus of Pergamum, to help her import the rites of the Great Mother from Phrygia, as Delphi and the Sibylline oracles had commanded.[28] Both Venus Erycina and the Great Mother were actually given temples within the *pomerium*; perhaps the connections of both cults with the Aeneas story made them seem not wholly foreign, but it is noteworthy that both were firmly adapted to their new context. Venus of Eryx did not bring her temple prostitutes with her, and was regarded as a goddess of victory rather than love, and the orgiastic elements in the worship of the Mother were strictly controlled, her eunuch priests being restricted in number and activity, and the post strictly confined to foreigners. The traditional structure of Roman religion was never, in our period, to be broken down.

The Senate does not seem to have had very much prejudice against foreign rites in themselves, in spite of its action in 213 in repressing what Livy calls foreign superstitions. It acted through a praetor to destroy a mass of written prophecies, prayers and books on sacrifice, which were leading to irregular practices even in the Forum and on the Capitol, especially by women, and to the financial exploitation of the rural plebs gathered in the city during the war. It was then primarily a police measure, rather than an attempt to extirpate foreign influence as such.[29]

---

[24] Livy XXII.10.9: cf. *SIG* 589, a *lectisternium* to the 12 Olympian gods at Magnesia.
[25] Livy XXII.57, XXIII.11, XXVIII.45.12.   [26] Livy XXII.9.7, 10.10, XXIII.30.13, 31.9.
[27] Livy XXV.12.15, XXVI.23.2, XXVII.11.6, 23.5, 35.3–4.
[28] Livy XXIX. 10.4–11.8. It is perhaps unlikely that the Roman envoys went themselves to Pessinus to fetch the sacred stone as Livy reports; it may have come from the Megalesion at Pergamum, as Varro, *Ling.* VI.15, supposes.   [29] Livy XXV.1.6–12.

Both the *Ludi Apollinares* and, when they came to be set up shortly after the War, the *Megalesia* of the Great Mother, were *ludi scaenici*, at which plays were produced. The first production of a real Latin play was believed to have come in 240 with Livius Andronicus' first adaptation from a Greek original; this is the better of two ancient chronologies, but is not quite universally accepted. Livius was a freedman, traditionally from Tarentum, and possibly enslaved on its fall in 272. It is not inconceivable that plays in Latin were already known in the Latin-speaking towns on the borders of theatrically-minded Campania, and companies of Greek actors from the Greek city of Neapolis there may even have reached Rome.[30] It is clear, from late red-figure vases and other evidence, that both Magna Graecia and Campania were familiar with performances of Attic tragedy, especially Euripides, and of New Comedy, as well as of their own burlesque dramas in Greek, which in Campania at least had led to imitations in the Oscan language, though perhaps these did not take written form. It was from flourishing Oscan-speaking Capua, near Neapolis, that Naevius, Rome's second play-wright, came; he wrote both comedies and tragedies on Greek models (Livius too wrote both, in unGreek fashion: there was clearly a shortage of authors). Sicily also had theatrical traditions, and it is often thought that many Romans developed a taste for drama there in the First Punic War. It has been objected that armies are 'almost perfect non-conductors of culture'; but many Englishmen did come to Italian opera when fighting in Italy in the Second World War.

Even if its beginnings are slightly earlier, it seems to have been in the last two decades of the third century that Roman drama gained its real hold and arrived at some kind of maturity; the *Ludi Plebei*, set up about 220, were or soon became *scaenici* as well. Naevius was active till near the end of the Hannibalic war; by then, Plautus had begun to write comedy. The Romans seem to have ignored plays by Sicilian or Italiote authors, perhaps because of their growing contempt for these areas and increasing interest in 'real' Greece, even if this still had to be largely mediated through the west. Of many of the plays produced by the Roman poets we have only the titles. Those of the tragedies suggest, as is often pointed out, that the Romans were (not surprisingly) interested in the legends of the Trojan War, and also that they were not averse from stories about Dionysus and Dionysiac religion, which had made its way into Italy and was thus not unfamiliar; but that, perhaps, they avoided the hostile portraits of Odysseus that were to be found in a number of later fifth-century tragedies, since he was much honoured in the western areas he was thought to have visited. If Roman taste could really be reflected in

---

[30] Fraenkel 1960, 439: (H 180).

this way, the poets must have had an extensive repertory of models from which to choose.

The plays may have been known originally as much by the Greek author's name and title as by those of the Latin adapter, or so some passages of Plautus would suggest.[31] Dress and setting remained strictly Greek, but the adaptations were in many respects remarkably Roman. Livius and Naevius probably established many of the traditions of the Roman stage: for tragedy, in particular, the elevated language, exploiting the native love of alliteration, assonance and play on words; and, for both tragedy and comedy, the remarkable expansion of the parts of the accompanying flautist and the actors as singers. Whether this was done under the influence of Hellenistic Greek, or native Italian, semi-dramatic forms is still disputed; it is also possible that trained choruses were hard to obtain in Rome (some tragedies at least do seem to have had a chorus, though comedies do not), and that the musical element had therefore to be transferred to the actors.

Possibly under the stimulus of the Hannibalic War and the national feeling it provoked came the first creation of a literature based on Greek forms, but Roman in content. All Naevius' *praetextae*, plays based on Roman history, may date from this period (the *Clastidium* certainly does); they were perhaps all, like that, produced for such special occasions as the triumphs or funerals of great men. There is no good evidence that Naevius set any comedies in Italy. But we have Cicero's warrant for regarding his historical epic concerning the First Punic War as a work of his old age and so of this period.[32] Though the plays had been written in metres adapted from the Greek, the *Bellum Punicum* was still in the to us somewhat mysterious 'Saturnian' verse, which Livius Andronicus had employed for his adaptation of Homer's *Odyssey*. How far Naevius was influenced in his choice of subject by Greek historical epics, which he may or may not have known, and how far by the strong feeling of the Romans for their less as well as their more distant past, we cannot tell.

According to a notice in Livy, in 207 Livius Andronicus (by now surely very elderly) composed for the state a hymn to Juno, to be sung by a chorus of virgins[33] – in other words a *partheneion*, probably new in its kind at Rome, though old-fangled in Greece by now. There is a slight possibility that Livy's source here was accepting the lower and less reliable chronology for the poet, and that the hymn was really written some time earlier. According to the Augustan scholar Verrius Flaccus (accepting the later date), Livius' hymn led to permission being given for a guild of 'scribes and actors' (supposedly linked because Livius both wrote and acted; the guild was conceivably already in some sort of

[31] Plaut. *Poen.* 1 in particular: Aristarchus' *Achilles*.
[32] Cic. *Sen.* 50.   [33] Livy XXVII.37.3, cf. XXXI.12.9.

existence) to meet and make dedications in the temple of Minerva on the Aventine.[34] If poets were associated thus with government or other clerks, *scribae* proper, this shows us how unused to creative writers Rome still was. The history of this institution is obscure; what, for example, was its relation to the society of *parasiti Apollinis*, who were actors of some kind, possibly the less well-regarded mimes? This body, according to another passage of Verrius (often, however, disbelieved) existed during the Hannibalic War,[35] having perhaps been founded with the new games to Apollo. At all events it is interesting that actors in Rome were under the protection of Minerva or Apollo, or both; they were not, as in Greece, associated with Dionysus, and organized into companies of artists bearing his name. There may have been some precedent in Sicily for linking Apollo with the theatre,[36] but it may be that, as with Venus Erycina and the Magna Mater, the Romans were trying to avoid the emotional and extravagant.

Greek medicine, like Greek drama, was percolating into the city at this time. We happen to know that a Greek from the Peloponnese, who specialized in wounds, set himself up in Rome with state assistance just before the war, and was remembered later as the first representative of Greek medicine in the city.[37] Since we can hardly doubt that doctors from Magna Graecia or Sicily, in both of which there were strong if now perhaps old-fashioned medical traditions, had reached Rome before this, the notice is further evidence of the Romans' growing disregard for the Greeks of the west. But Greek medicine did not altogether 'take' at Rome yet, as we shall see; the Peloponnesian was regarded as a butcher, and few or no Romans took up the profession; none tried to translate Greek medical literature into Latin.

As the war went on, armies were again committed to Greek-speaking areas, in Magna Graecia and Sicily, and the attempted intervention of Philip V of Macedon in support of Hannibal led to the first formal alliance of Rome with a state of old Greece – the Aetolian League, unfortunately a predatory and comparatively unsophisticated people later to prove a liability. The terms of the treaty, which included one by which Rome was to have all the moveable booty in any Greek town taken by the allies, including the enslaved population, do not suggest that she was eager to recommend herself to Greek public opinion, though on one occasion a general, professing favour to the Greeks, did permit ransom, noting it as a non-Roman custom.[38] One or two other alliances followed, however, including those with (probably) Athens, with Sparta and with

[34] Festus, *Gloss. Lat.* 446 L.   [35] Festus, *Gloss. Lat.* 436, cf. 438.
[36] Webster 1964, 257: (H 219) – if not Apollo, at least the Muses.
[37] Peter, *HRRel.* Cassius Hemina fr. 26.   [38] Livy XXVI.24.11; Polyb. IX.42.

King Attalus of Pergamum. But Rome's naval superiority prevented Philip from invading Italy, and the Romans pulled out of Greece entirely on the conclusion of the Peace of Phoenice in 205. There had been considerable diplomatic activity, however, and the Senate doubtless found itself better informed about affairs in Greece than it had ever been. Meanwhile, as Polybius says, the eyes of the Greeks were turned onto the great struggle playing itself out in the west, and several Greek historians, mainly westerners, took Hannibal as a hero, a bias that Fabius Pictor was probably to try to redress. Another Roman senator, Cincius Alimentus, who had actually been taken captive by Hannibal, also wrote a history of Rome in Greek. Between them they established the position that historiography, with its military and political slant, was a respectable activity for a Roman senator, at least in old age, revolutionary as this might appear.

How far, at this time, had the hellenization of the dominant political elite, or of some members of it, progressed? The answer is probably 'not very far', though we know too little about education in Rome at this period to be sure – and it should be remembered that Greek civilization was felt to be dependent on, or even identical with, Greek *paideia*, education. There is some evidence that in the upper classes Roman boys were taught mainly within the family, until they were entrusted to a distinguished public figure to gain experience of the courts and politics under his wing; military service from the age of seventeen (earlier in crises) would cut short such training, at least as a full-time occupation. There was one theory later that the first school for learning one's letters was set up by a freedman of Sp. Carvilius, supposedly the first man in Rome to divorce his wife, perhaps about 230 B.C. 'Letters and Law' were to Plautus the staple of education, and Cicero as a boy still learnt by heart the archaic code of the Twelve Tables.[39] Literature, to the Greeks the basis of real education, was first taught according to Suetonius by Livius Andronicus *domi forisque*, in his house and elsewhere – perhaps in his master's house and those of other nobles, rather than in a real school.[40] His Latin *Odysseia* may have been produced primarily for teaching purposes, but Suetonius, who may have had no evidence, thought he also taught Greek literature – primarily no doubt Homer in the original. Many Romans of various classes will have known some Greek, though they may often have spoken it with a Sicilian or Italiote accent: a number of nobles bore Greek cognomina, presumably nick-names in origin, and one was actually called Atticus – had he been to Athens, or did he just speak unusually pure Greek? – while at the start of the century an ambassador had attempted, disastrously, to address the Tarentines in

---

[39] Plut. *Quaest. Rom.* 59, cf. 54; Plaut. *Mostell.* 126; Cic. *Leg.* II.59.   [40] Suet. *Gram.* 1.2.

Greek. Some Romans may have read a certain amount in Greek too (the priestly *decemviri* who were responsible for consulting the Sibylline books must always have been able to read oracular Greek verse). Given the Roman regard for the past, and the fact that historiography was to be the first prose genre produced in the city, one suspects that Timaeus and other western historians were among the best known authors. A reading public for Latin can hardly have existed; Latin plays seem long only to have been known from performance, though Greek plays were always much read in Athens and elsewhere.

Fortunately Plutarch was interested in the question of Greek culture as it affected the subjects of several of his biographies, and there are scraps of other evidence concerning the same figures. None of these famous men need be typical even of their own class, but their cases may be suggestive.

Fabius Maximus, the great Cunctator, was to be written up as the traditionalist opponent of the hellenizing Scipio Africanus. But two Fabii had been envoys to Alexandria in the third century, and it was as we saw a Fabius who was sent to Delphi (as a much earlier ancestor was supposed to have been) and was later to take the great step of writing a book in Greek. Cicero says (and historical statements in his dialogues usually have some basis) that Fabius Maximus had read much 'for a Roman', and knew the history of foreign wars as well as of Rome's.[41] He might have read some Greek, probably Sicilian, historians. He brought back one statue from the capture of Tarentum in 209, the giant Hercules of Lysippus; but statues were traditional booty, and the Fabii claimed special devotion to Hercules, who, though Greek in origin, had long been naturalized in Rome and Italy.[42] Fabius is not recorded as taking any other advantage of his opportunities at Tarentum. The famous M. Marcellus, the 'sword of Rome' while Fabius was her shield, went a step further. Plutarch says that he admired the Greek culture that he had not had time to acquire (in fact, opportunities had doubtless been restricted in his youth); even after his Gallic campaigns in the 220s he sent spoils as a gift to Delphi, and also to King Hiero of Syracuse (perhaps his family already had ties with Sicily, as others certainly did, here or in Greek-speaking areas of southern Italy). At the sack of Syracuse in 211 Marcellus tried to save the great scientist Archimedes; it was as a military engineer that he had impressed the Romans, but Marcellus brought back to Rome Archimedes' celestial globes, keeping one for himself, though nothing else according to Cicero,[43] and dedicating the other in a temple where all could see it. We hear nothing of his annexing books, but he

---

[41] Cic. *Sen.* 12 (but *bella* is often excised on the grounds that *domestica bella* means civil wars, which the Romans had not had; *domestica et externa* could mean simply 'native and foreign history').
[42] Pliny, *HN* XXXIV.40; Plut. *Fab.* 1.   [43] Cic. *Rep.* 1.21.

carried off many works of art, boasting even to the Greeks, according to Plutarch, that he had taught the Romans to admire Greek art.[44] It is paradoxical, but also fateful for their attitudes to Greece, that the visual arts, which on the whole they despised, were one of the elements of Greek civilization that the Romans accepted most easily; but their local art was ultimately Greek-influenced, and indeed minor Greek artists had worked in Rome and elsewhere in central Italy, so that the contrast with Greek art proper was not too shocking. Marcellus, who naturally became patron of the city he had taken, also dedicated gifts from the booty at distant Samothrace, with which Rome felt a link through Aeneas, and at Rhodes, with which naval state she had probably long had some sort of connection. He also erected a gymnasium for the people of Catana in Sicily, which perhaps suggests some sympathy with the Greek way of life, though hardly a desire that Romans should take to exercising naked.[45] Marcellus had also spared the general population of Syracuse, though Fabius may have enslaved that of Tarentum, and Valerius Laevinus certainly did that of Agrigentum (though he had made the treaty with the Aetolians, and was now no doubt their patron, as his son was to be). Their possession of Greek slaves was also to be significant for Roman attitudes, and the tension in these between admiration and contempt.

Even leading members of the generation that emerged in the later part of the Hannibalic War, who were later to have a great deal to do with the Greek world, probably had little formal Greek education. Cato, who claimed to have spent his youth labouring on Sabine hillsides, clearly had none, though if it is true that, just at the end of the war, he met the hellenized South Italian Ennius and studied Greek literature with him, he was anxious to remedy the omission, to some extent at least.[46] Scipio Africanus is a difficult case to evaluate, since Polybius has probably made him over in the likeness of a Hellenistic statesman, and attributed to him characteristics, such as scepticism in religion, perhaps implausible in a Roman of this period: while our annalistic sources have worked him up as a contrast to the traditionalist Fabius Maximus. But it is probably true that, possibly already as aedile in 213 and then subsequently in his command in Spain, he showed an awareness of the traditions of Hellenistic kingship, as aedile distributing oil to the plebs, and later telling the Spaniards that they might regard him as kingly, though he could not take the title; while he showed a courtesy and restraint to a captive lady that was surely modelled on Alexander's (if not on that of Alexander's own model, Xenophon's Cyrus).[47] He may even have been responsible for equating the idea of a Roman consul with that of a king, by using the

[44] Plut. *Marc.* 21.5.   [45] Plut. *Marc.* 30.4–5.   [46] See n. 116.   [47] Polyb. x.38 and 40.

symbols of Roman office as presents for a foreign monarch. He sent gifts to Delphi from Spain.[48] In Sicily, before his invasion of Africa, he is supposed to have adopted Greek dress and spent his time in the theatre, palaestra and baths, shocking his quaestor Cato and provoking an official investigation: but the story, only in Plutarch, is often thought a throwback from the later quarrels of Cato and Scipio.[49] And it should be noted that Scipio's heroes, according to Polybius, were the Sicilians Dionysius and Agathocles, who might be seen as a rather old-fashioned choice (or perhaps only a personal one – they had fought Carthage);[50] while Cicero says of Scipio's son that he united his father's greatness of soul with richer learning.[51]

It is likely that T. Quinctius Flamininus, the conqueror of Philip V and 'Liberator' of Greece, also acquired little *doctrina* in his earlier years. We know that he spoke Greek fluently and got on well with Greeks;[52] but this would seem to be the fruit of the time he spent at Tarentum in the Hannibalic War, and there is no evidence that he had a real Greek education. An ability to speak colloquial Greek, or even to understand the more flowery language of formal orations, does not, it should be remembered, imply an ability to cope with the language of Homer or of fifth-century Attic authors, let alone other dialects. And it is dubious to what extent Flamininus took up Greek ways; a coin with his image struck in Greece shows him bearded in traditional Roman fashion (though Scipio appears, on Spanish coins thought to represent him, as cleanshaven).[53] But to both Scipio and Flamininus we shall have to return.

III. CONTACTS WITH THE GREEK WORLD IN THE EARLY SECOND CENTURY

The Second Macedonian War (200–197) brought Rome into direct contact with the Greek world and initiated a period of unprecedently rapid social and cultural change. Relationships of many different kinds between the two peoples began to be formed. The armies that campaigned in Macedon and Greece against Philip, and a few years later in Asia Minor as a result of the declaration of war against Antiochus of Syria, returned home with few losses, enriched by booty and often perhaps with new ideas of refinement and luxury (as later moralizing historians supposed – engraved plate, elegant stuffs and inlaid furniture are picked out, with music-girls and other luxurious accompaniments to

---

[48] Livy xxx.15.11–12; App. *Pun.* 32.137 – sometimes disbelieved. Delphi: Livy xxviii.45.12.
[49] Plut. *Cat. Mai.* 3.7; Astin 1978, 14: (H 68).
[50] Polyb. xv.35. [51] Cic. *Sen.* 35. [52] Plut. *Flam.* 5.5.
[53] Scullard 1970, 41, 248: (H 77). Gell. *NA* iii.4 shows that middle-aged men generally shaved in the mid-second century.

feasts, and the regarding of cooking for the first time as an art); one modern estimate suggests that over half the adult male population fought at some time in the army, though of course not all of it in the east.[54] Some Romans, mostly captured in the Hannibalic War rather than later, actually served as slaves in Greek parts – 1,200 in Greece according to Plutarch, whose figure perhaps does not include Latins and Italians; these the Achaeans ransomed, and Rome probably exerted pressure to recover those in other areas.[55] Such men, many no doubt humble countrymen, would have brought home a peculiarly intimate knowledge of Greek domestic manners – or of Greek agriculture; ordinary soldiers, however, were often billeted on the local population.

There were some Romans along with the Campanian and other south Italian traders and businessmen (also some Latins, especially from Praeneste) who began to be more prominently visible in Greece and the Aegean, though not yet in the numbers typical of the second half of the century. They might turn out to be long-term settlers, who put their sons through the local schools or even their adopted city's *ephebeia* (an organization giving young men a period of now only tenuously military service, with a little intellectual education sometimes thrown in), held local priesthoods or were initiates at Samothrace or Eleusis, and took a prominent part in local life, being rewarded with proxenyships and other honours. But it cannot be doubted that they were often in touch with family or friends in Italy, and that some at least retired in old age to their original homes, bringing with them a certain knowledge of Greek language and life; a few had probably even been patrons of literature and the arts.

More temporary were the visits to the east of Roman senators, a good few of whom were, increasingly, sent out on fact-finding or arbitrational embassies. Some came from families developing, in the traditional manner, *clientelae* in areas newly come under Roman influence. Such, for example, were the patrician Claudii, who had long had links in Campania, Sicily and Magna Graecia. Two at least now served under Flamininus, one was on the commission sent out to advise Vulso in Asia; subsequently Claudii went as envoys to Macedon, the Achaean League, Sparta and even Syria – but hardly ever to Africa or the west. On these embassies they will have stayed with local magnates, or in the special guest-houses for Roman visitors attested in more than one Greek centre; they will have given and received gifts and political advice. But it is interesting that there is no evidence for any of the Claudii being interested in Greek art or literature; it is unlikely that many Roman aristocrats

[54] Peter, *HRRel.* Piso fr. 34; Livy xxxix.6.7–9; Hopkins 1978, 35: (H 99).
[55] Plut. *Flam.* 13.4–5. Livy xxxvii.60.2: 4,000 Romans and Italians restored by the Cretans (number from the unreliable Valerius Antias). Victims of piracy, in part?

really were. They probably took to Greek manners and luxury, however; Cato delivered a speech against the *mores* of one Ap. Claudius Nero, a sure sign.

At the same time, there were now many more Greeks in Rome, as in central Italy in general. There clearly came to be many humbler Greek or Greek-speaking settlers; though traders and sailors maybe did not always get beyond Puteoli in Campania or at most Ostia, whence small boats perhaps under local masters took wares up the Tiber to the port of Rome (to which additions and improvements were made between 193 and 174), yet for Plautus the language of business and shipping is largely Greek. When war with Perseus of Macedon broke out in 171 there were Macedonian residents, as well as envoys, who were told to leave the city and Italy.[56] Above all, of course, there was the influx of Greek-speaking, or at least partly hellenized, slaves into Italy; many were put to agricultural tasks in the country, helping, in certain areas, to transform the nature of agriculture, but not all entirely insulated from the surviving free peasants; some, including the well-educated, of whom there were clearly a number, worked in the swelling households of the rich, especially at Rome. If they were freed, some might be given small properties by their masters, like (no doubt) the model smallholder C. Furius Cresimus held up to admiration by a later second-century historian;[57] others engaged either on their own behalf or that of a patron on business ventures of many kinds.

Rome took foreign hostages, for example, Philip's son Demetrius and other Macedonians, then rotating hostages from the Syrian court – though not all stayed in Rome, some being farmed out to country towns. We know that the Syrian prince Demetrius at least, who came to Rome as a child, mixed on familiar terms with young Roman aristocrats.[58] A few notables, such as the younger Charops from Epirus,[59] came (like most of the hostages, with a suite) to be educated in Rome. There were also perpetual queues of Greek envoys, leading citizens come from various states to appeal to the Senate and to treat it to displays of elaborate Greek oratory which, though interpreters were used, most members may have been increasingly able to follow. The speeches doubtless included *exempla* from Greek history, the examples or illustrations thought so necessary by rhetoricians, and also compliments to Rome, perhaps as having a mixed constitution on the approved model, or as the successor to the great empires of the past, especially Persia and Macedon. (One Roman, a certain Aemilius Sura, seems to have taken up this last idea in

56 Polyb. xxvii.6.3.   57 Peter, *HRRel*. Piso fr. 33. *MRR* puts the occasion *c.* 191.
58 Polyb. xxxi.2.5.   59 Polyb. xxvii.15.4 – perhaps in the 170s?

some sort of book.[60]) Even kings came – Amynander of Athamania was expected to make a great impression in 198, on account of his title, but after the repeated visits of Pergamene and other royalty, such a petty Balkan kinglet would have cut little ice.[61] Sometimes envoys were forced to stay for a considerable period of time; there was bad congestion in 184 owing to a great influx of embassies with complaints against Philip. And a Greek inscription shows one group of ambassadors, perhaps around 170, who had attended each morning at the receptions of great Romans to gain their favour, and worked on the patrons of the city they were representing by visiting them in their homes.[62]

The two races met, then, at all levels; they did not actually mingle much, except in so far as freed slaves became for most purposes full Roman citizens, and their sons wholly so. But legal intermarriage between Romans and foreigners, *peregrini*, was not allowed, and what has often been a fertile source of cultural influence was thus not available to the Romans.

One way of measuring the impact of the new relationship is by study of the comedies of Plautus. Most cannot be precisely dated, or even securely attributed to a single man, whose very name poses problems; but they certainly run from the closing years of the Hannibalic War through the succeeding period into the 180s. The stage, for the historian, has the advantage of addressing, and needing to please, a wide if unfortunately not precisely definable audience, of whose tastes something can be said. This audience included all classes – special seats for senators were established in 195.[63] Women and probably slaves were present. The shows were free; to some of them many country people may have been at leisure to come in, either because the games fell at slack times of year or also because, as some argue, where subsistence agriculture prevails peasants tend to be underemployed. In fact, Plautus' comedies, though clearly written for Rome, may also have been seen in the country towns of the *ager Romanus* and Latium, for a manager or *dominus gregis* would wish to keep his actors, who were often his slaves, in fairly continual employment, and besides this there can be no doubt that especially in southern Latium and the now increasingly Latin-speaking parts of northern Campania there was a lively theatrical life, probably partly independent of Rome. It was indeed primarily through the stage that Greek culture impinged on the poorer classes (and through the visual arts, always especially important to the illiterate, and from which,

---

[60] Swain 1940: (1 34) for the date of this work; he suggests that Ennius knew the idea too, though it was not yet taken up generally in Rome. But Mendels 1981: (E 30) dates Sura much later.

[61] Polyb. XVIII.10.7.

[62] Polyb. XXIII.1; *SIG* 656 (with new readings by P. Herrmann. *ZPE* 7 (1971) 72–7).

[63] Livy XXXIV.54.4.

especially with the aid of an *aedituus* or verger in a temple, many may have learnt something of Greek mythology as well as Roman history).

Though the *palliata*, as the name implies (it refers to the Greek *pallium* or cloak), deals with Greek characters, and indeed is closely based on Greek originals, it becomes more and more possible, as our knowledge of Greek New Comedy advances, to identify Roman changes and additions. Both what is Greek and what is Roman in these plays is informative.

The recent tendency has been to abandon the low estimate of Plautus' audience that used to be common. This audience clearly has some knowledge of the theatrical traditions that now went back over a generation, and can pick up references and parodies. It sometimes likes to know who wrote the original play. It prefers comedies to be set in 'Athens of Attica', as 'more Greek'; though in fact various cities of *germana Graecia*, 'real Greece', do appear, it is necessary to be defensive about a play that takes place in Syracuse, and a character offers a girl as dowry 'a thousand good Attic *logi* (stories or plots?) without a Sicilian one among them'.[64] The audience also has a basic knowledge of Greek myth (though only basic, and Plautus himself, who as Fraenkel shows inserts many of the mythological references, occasionally makes mistakes), just as it has heard of some figures of Greek history (Alexander and the great Sicilians, primarily), the sages Thales and Solon, and even the artists Apelles and Zeuxis, though these are only names; it does not know the philosophers, apart from Socrates (and there are two general references to the poverty of the Cynics)[65] – in contrast to the audiences of the first century, who are expected to relish jokes about Democritus and Epicurus. Rhetors, obviously not yet known in Rome, are not mocked, though there is a general jeer at Greeks who walk about with books under their arms but also create drunken disturbances.[66] The Greeks indeed are regarded as dissipated, as the word *pergraecari* suggests, and their slaves are undisciplined. Plautus takes his spectators into what must be for them to some extent an amoral, fantasy world, peopled by idle young men and their courtesan mistresses, cunning slaves and greedy parasites; but his specifically Roman references, often legal or military, bring them back to the real one, where his standards tend to be conservative and traditional.

The audience also knows, and probably itself employs, a good many Greek words, clearly considered vulgar, since the middle-class characters rarely use them. Some can be shown to be South Italian or Sicilian; opinions differ on whether they were mostly picked up by soldiers on

---

[64] Plaut. *Men.* Prol.7ff., *Pers.* 394.

[65] Plaut. *Mostell.* 775, *Pseud.* 532, *Men.* 409, *Poen.* 1271, *Epid.* 626; Cynics: *Pers.* 123, *Stich.* 704; Socrates: *Pseud.* 465; Thales: *Rud.* 1003, *Bacch.* 122, *Capt.* 274.   [66] Plaut. *Curc.* 288.

campaign or introduced to Rome by slaves, traders and others. One also suspects that some of the female spectators wear the fashionable articles of apparel with Greek names that are the subject of complaint;[67] perhaps many respectable matrons still avoided these, but the terms of the *lex Oppia* of 215 show that already matrons had abandoned the traditional toga for 'multicoloured dresses'.[68]

It is true that this audience prefers low to high comedy – Plautus greatly elaborates the role of the slaves, and sometimes that of the parasite, cutting down on the more serious middle-class characters – and it is fond of descriptions of horrific punishments inflicted on slaves. But it does not want, or does not get, much direct presentation of violence or obscenity. In fact, though the plot is rarely uplifting – sometimes the reverse – Plautus keeps much of the sententiousness that marked Greek New Comedy, even expands it; we know that later at least Roman audiences greatly enjoyed the moralizing they heard on both the comic and the tragic stage (and anthologies were made from it). This, for Plautus, is 'philosophizing', and seen as learned and Greek. In the absence of many other sources of moral advice, it may be that ordinary Romans articulated many of their moral perceptions by what they experienced in the theatre.

Plautus also assumes a certain level of literacy in most of his spectators; words are described as differing by a single letter, slaves read and write. Fraenkel contrasts Plautus' work with the anonymous German travesties of Shakespeare's plays given in seventeenth-century Germany by the 'English Comedians', to the great advantage of both the Roman dramatist and his audience.[69] Indeed, though the Roman stage never produced a Shakespeare, the Roman public was perhaps not much inferior to that on the Bankside.

Naturally, some members of the oligarchy, who were becoming deeply involved in Greek affairs, were more profoundly influenced by Greek ideas than the average spectator in the theatre. But the old idea that Flamininus or the Scipiones were influenced in policy by sentimental, basically literary, philhellenism is not plausible. As we have seen, they had probably not read much Greek literature; and if Rome intervened to protect the Greeks against Philip, it was doubtless largely to punish the latter for his 'stab in the back' during the Hannibalic War, and his later rupture of the Peace of Phoenice, and also in response to the inherent pressures of the militaristic society of Rome.[70] If the Greeks were subsequently declared free, this was to weaken Macedon while not committing Rome to garrisoning or administering a large new territory; when the principle was not convenient to her she abandoned it, reward-

---

[67] Plaut. *Epid.* 223ff. [68] Livy XXXIV.1.3.
[69] Fraenkel 1960 387: (H 180). [70] Harris 1979, 212: (A 21).

ing for example her friend the king of Pergamum with territory. But favour to Greece was expressed more than once, and we need not doubt that the Romans' feelings towards the Greeks were different from those they held towards Gauls, Spaniards or Carthaginians. Flamininus (who had probably not scrupled to enslave any Greeks proper, perhaps chiefly Thessalians, who had fought in Philip's army at Cynoscephalae) professes amity and high moral sentiments in his surviving letter to the Chyretians.[71] It is worth noting that the letter is not in very good Greek, whoever actually wrote it, and indeed those responsible for translating Latin documents were for a long time varyingly inept, sometimes incapable even of coping with the definite article that Greek has but Latin lacks; though a technical vocabulary of Greek terms for Roman institutions did rapidly emerge, and where letters are concerned, the basic framework of the Hellenistic chancery style may have been adopted even before 200 B.C. But even generals in the east would not seem to have used Greek secretaries, who were certainly not employed by the state at Rome, where the *scribae* of the Treasury seem to have translated decrees of the Senate that needed to be communicated to the Greeks into a language that must have struck the latter as barbarous. If the Romans wrote to the Greeks in Greek of a kind, they seem usually to have spoken to them in Latin, which an interpreter translated.

To return to Flamininus, Plutarch probably does not mean to imply that he himself composed the Greek elegiacs placed on his dedications at Delphi, and indeed this is barely conceivable.[72] No other patronage by him of Greek (or Roman) writers is recorded, though he naturally carried sculptures to Rome as booty.[73] It was probably his Greek clients who set up a statue of him at Rome with a Greek inscription.[74] And much of his subsequent favour to Greeks will be thanks to the fact that he regarded himself as their patron, though being their patron may also have led him to feel sympathy for them; he certainly cared exceedingly for praise and honours from them.

Scipio Africanus, of course, was to treat on equal terms with Hellenistic monarchs, visit and correspond with them; he became personally friendly with Philip, and (it was thought, too much so) with Antiochus. In letters he and his brother Lucius assert benevolence to all Greeks, or that the Romans are not opposed to kings as such, as is widely believed.[75] Both made dedications at Delos, and Lucius at least was represented in a statue at Rome wearing Greek dress.[76] But Lucius' choice of the bastard title Asiagenus (rather than Asiaticus) suggests an indeed rather surprising ignorance of Greek. Africanus himself lived in modern splendour

[71] Sherk, *Documents* 33.   [72] Plut. *Flam.* 12.6–7.
[73] Livy XXXIV 52.4; also precious vessels in huge quantity.   [74] Plut. *Flam.* 1.
[75] Sherk, *Documents* 35; Polyb. XXI.11.   [76] Cic. *Rab. Post.* 27.

(his wife assisted at religious ceremonies in great state[77]); he clearly gave his son, who was to write a history in Greek and whose superior *doctrina* we have seen Cicero note, something of a Greek education – more remarkably, perhaps his daughter too, for she was later a patroness of learned men.

Scipio was perhaps regarded during his own lifetime as almost super-human, and in direct touch with Jupiter in a way that was not traditional at Rome. Certainly after his death it would seem that Ennius, the Italian from near Tarentum who had become a Roman poet, and who had praised Scipio in a special work bearing his name, suggested in an epitaph that his great deeds had opened to him the gates of heaven.[78] Heroization such as this implies was not really a Roman conception, but, as has been pointed out, Ennius was not a Roman.[79] Certainly no actual cult was set up to Scipio in Rome, though by the time of his death generals in the east, above all Flamininus, had even been hailed there as saviour-gods in the Hellenistic fashion. Scipio and the other great generals often made dedications at Greek shrines, but Greek deities are not predominant among the gods of all kinds, traditional and less traditional, to whom they set up temples in Rome as a result of vows made on campaign. True, a second temple of Venus Erycina was built in 181 B.C., this one outside the *pomerium*, and at least a place where prostitutes made offerings, though there were still no temple prostitutes proper;[80] one or two other new cults might be mentioned. And a few old ones seem to have changed their nature; the goddess Salus, who to Plautus still typifies Safety in political or military contexts, by the time of Terence has become, sometimes at least, Health, the Greek Hygeia.[81]

The rather younger Fulvius Nobilior probably had more interest in Greek art and literature than Scipio. In a fashion that was to be a portent for the future, it led him in fact to ill-treat the Greeks; he enslaved the inhabitants of Same, and it was doubtful if he should have sacked Ambracia in 189, as the city had not been stormed. It had been Pyrrhus' capital, and its fall will have impressed Roman opinion; it was full of works of art, all of which Fulvius carried off (except the sculptures of terracotta, though some of these were by Zeuxis; Fulvius was obviously still unable to judge work at its true value, and associated terracotta with the despised Italian tradition[82]). His opponents, who included M. Aemilius Lepidus and Cato, got the Senate to vote that the Ambracians should get their objects back. It is doubtful if they did; at all events the statues of the Muses that remained in Fulvius' temple of Hercules

---

[77] Polyb. xxxi.26. [78] Vahlen 1928, 216: (B 37A).
[79] Walbank, *PCPS* 13 (1967) 57. [80] Livy XL.34.4, Ov. *Fast.* IV.865ff.
[81] Ter. *Hec.* 338. [82] Pliny, *HN* xxxv.9.66.

Musarum came from Ambracia.[83] We do not know whether there had been an odd cult of Hercules and the Muses there, or whether it was Fulvius who associated them, perhaps as symbols of the union of warlike valour and poetic fame; at all events, Ennius had accompanied Fulvius to Greece, as Greek poets had accompanied Alexander and later kings on campaign, and he celebrated his patron's deeds in the *Ambracia*, perhaps a play, as well as in his epic *Annales*. Poetry, if now under the protection of the Muses, did not deny its earlier roots; an ancient shrine of the Camenae was moved to Fulvius' temple, and Ennius, who unlike Naevius did not directly invoke these Italian goddesses, may possibly have asserted their identity with the Muses. The new precinct was no Museum in the Alexandrian sense – for example we hear nothing of a library – but we do have evidence for poets later giving readings there, and some sort of *collegium poetarum* meeting, while the tragic poet Accius was to dedicate a statue of himself in the temple.[84] Perhaps the poets, or some of them, with Fulvius' approval, now detached themselves from scribes and/or actors and the low and mercenary associations of Minerva, goddess of crafts, and met henceforth in this temple. If so, it was a mark of their increasing status. Fulvius probably set up an inscribed calendar in the temple (rather than depositing a book in it, though the Latin of our source is ambiguous), which also contained would-be learned notes, such as naive etymologies of the names of the Roman months;[85] he, or whoever compiled it for him, must have had some knowledge of Greek antiquarian scholarship, possibly only as it appeared in so many Greek historians, and perhaps also some knowledge of astronomy. It has been argued that the probably Pythagorean statement that studying the heavens increases devotion to the ineffable god, attributed by a late source to a Fulvius, also goes back to this work (here conceived as a book), and that the Muses stand for a Pythagorean harmony.[86] It is at least true that Pythagorean views, as we shall see, would not be out of place in a Roman of this generation. More certainly, Fulvius celebrated with splendour, and with the aid of artists collected from Greece, the games that he had vowed on campaign.[87] There were athletic contests for the first time, says Livy, no doubt meaning contests strictly on the Greek model, but a troupe of 'artists of Dionysus' was probably also imported to give plays in Greek. It is likely that others followed Fulvius' lead in this.[88]

Fulvius' campaign marked the break with Rome by her earliest Greek

---

[83] Cic. *Arch.* 11.27.   [84] Val. Max. iii.7.11; Pliny, *HN* xxxiv.19.

[85] *Gramm. Rom. Frag.* 15.   [86] Boyancé 1955: (H 172); Martina 1981: (H 209).

[87] Livy xxxix.22.2.

[88] Livy xxxix.22.10, from the unreliable Valerius Antias again, says that in this very year L. Scipio imported artists from Asia for his games.

allies, the Aetolians. One by one, her relations with other Greek states began to turn sour; the Greeks did not always realize that the gift of freedom was, in Roman eyes, a *beneficium* which implied a corresponding sense of *officium*, or obligation, on the part of the beneficiary, and the Romans often behaved in a disingenuous and brutal fashion, while themselves being shocked at the intrigue and corruption endemic among the factious Greeks. In the 170s in particular, a period of unease and disputes among the Roman aristocracy, and of the build-up to and start of the war with Perseus of Macedon, Macedonians and Greeks were shockingly treated at the hands of Machiavellian diplomats like Q. Marcius Philippus, and greedy and savage commanders like the praetors Lucretius, Hortensius, Octavius and others. The idea that the Greeks needed to be terrorized into submission had been put into the heads of such Romans by the sort of Greek politician loathed by Polybius. There was a reaction against this *nova sapientia*, new-style wisdom, among the older Romans, says Livy, who felt that it was a betrayal of 'ancient custom',[89] and there was some attempt to check and punish abuses both in the east and the west. These dubious new figures seem to have been, in several cases at least, hellenizers – at least to the extent of desiring Greek objects of art and luxury with which they could make a figure at Rome (including no doubt slaves: they were quick to enslave Greek populations, though indeed even the best Romans only had occasional qualms about this). Marcius Philippus stressed his Greek *cognomen* and links with the royal house of Macedon. But the clearest case is Cn. Octavius, who had a Greek doctor in his suite, could translate a Latin speech by Aemilius Paullus into Greek off the cuff, made a dedication at Delos and was honoured at Olympia and elsewhere, and was finally murdered in Syria – actually while anointing himself in the gymnasium – for his Roman arrogance, by anti-Roman elements.[90] Little better, it seems, was Sulpicius Galus, who studied Greek literature more deeply than any other noble of his time, says Cicero, and was particularly interested in astronomy, being able to explain eclipses to the Roman army (though *pace* Livy probably not to predict them): we are told of his 'many arrogant words and deeds towards the Greek race', especially to the famous states of Sparta and Argos, and then to Eumenes of Pergamum (it appears that in most of this he was carrying out the orders of the Senate, and Polybius may be somewhat biased).[91] But this takes us into a slightly later period.

The peak of serious hellenization in Rome in the earlier part of the second century is represented, without a doubt, by Ennius. He was not only the greatest poet but in many ways also the most significant cultural

---

[89] Livy XLII.47.4–9, Diod. Sic. XXX.7.1.   [90] *PW* XVII.2.1810.
[91] Cic. *Brut.* 20.78, *Rep.* I. 14.21–3, *Sen.* 14.49; Paus. VII.11.1–2, Polyb. XXXI.6.

influence of his time, a figure of impressive scope and considerable sophistication, but clearly not a typical Roman, though he ended as a Roman citizen. His case should remind us that much Greek influence doubtless reached Rome indirectly, via immigrants from parts of the peninsula that were in some ways more thoroughly hellenized than Rome, either because they lay close to surviving Greek colonies, or because they were now sending at least proportionately larger numbers of *negotiatores* to the east. There was money, from the profits of these men or from booty, in many Latin and Italian states, as the monumental building schemes from before the mid-second century, and later, show; in several places in Campania, Samnium and Latium such schemes included permanent theatres based on Greek models, which were probably sometimes used, as in Greece, not only for plays but for poetic recitations, lectures and rhetorical encomia and displays in Greek or sometimes Latin (and perhaps Oscan). This is perhaps reflected in the flattering tales of Greek legendary founders so many towns had by Cato's day (though some may be much older). Cicero tells us that in his boyhood 'Italy was devoted to the arts of Greece', and that the Latin cities pursued literary studies more energetically than did Rome[92] – possibly in part because of the demands of war and politics on the Roman upper class. What he says probably applies to a rather earlier period as well.

Ennius himself was born at Rudiae in the heel of Italy, a Messapian town but so hellenized that Strabo was to call it a Greek city, and he may have had a fully Greek education there or at Tarentum – a rather old-fashioned education perhaps, probably with some kind of rhetoric as well as *grammatice*, but not the main-stream Greek philosophy centred on Athens. He tells us he spoke Oscan, however, as well as Greek and Latin[93] (he may have learnt the last young – his sister married in the nearby Latin colony of Brundisium – or else when serving in the army during the Hannibalic War); and he perhaps also knew the ancient Messapian language. He did visit Greece proper, but it is not known how extensively, with Fulvius Nobilior, whose campaigns did not take him far from the Adriatic. If Ennius was a man of much greater genius than Livius Andronicus, he could also surely do much more because Rome was now more receptive. His works are more Greek than those of Livius, but also more Roman; Ennius, genuinely at the same time a Greek, an Italian and a Roman, seems to have felt no conflict between those roles (which is not evidence that a Roman aristocrat might not have felt some), but only great pride when a relative, perhaps the son, of his patron Fulvius Nobilior obtained Roman citizenship for him in 184.[94] He died in 169, at the age of seventy.

[92] Cic. *De Or.* 3.43: *Arch.* 5. Wiseman 1983: (H 66).   [93] Gell. *NA* XVII.17.1.
[94] *Annals* 525 Sk.; Cic. *Brut.* 20.79.

He naturalized in Latin (a slower and heavier language) various Greek metres, but above all the heroic hexameter, which he could wield with great power, if sometimes still awkwardly.[95] The ancient Saturnians persisted for a time, but mainly in the traditional contexts of triumphal or funerary inscriptions, and there is some slight evidence that a hexameter version of Livius Andronicus' *Odyssey* was soon found necessary, perhaps for educational purposes (Horace was still brought up on Livius, in what version we do not know).[96] At any event Ennius considered the Saturnian verse of Livius and Naevius rustic and primitive; he himself was a *poeta*, a 'maker' or craftsman, he wrote *poemata*, not *carmina* (the latter word evoked all sorts of antique spells and formulae).[97] He was the first man in Rome, he claimed, to be *dicti studiosus*, which has been thought to translate the Greek *philologos*, and imply a newly serious study of language and literature.[98] But the basis of his claim to be, by the *Annales*, a new Homer, or rather, according to Pythagorean principles, the actual re-incarnation of Homer, was a celebration of the Roman historical tradition that Cicero was still to find satisfying; and it was he who formulated the line that stamped itself on the Roman consciousness (perhaps it originally referred primarily to military discipline) about Rome's dependence on the customs of ancient days and men of ancient mark:

moribus antiquis res stat Romana virisque.[99]

His view of *virtus*, too, is the Roman view of Plautus and the Scipionic *elogia*, the sustaining of family honour, especially in war – though he tends to put *sapientia*, wisdom, at least as high as *vis*, force.

Ennius perhaps began his career in Rome by writing for the stage; his comedies were of no moment, but his tragedies developed the specifically Latin metrical patterns and diction of his predecessors. Though he bases many of his plays on Euripides, perhaps shows some traces of Greek rhetoric, and more than once didactically explains a Greek term, in a semi-philosophical digression, yet his plays have a Roman grandeur (or sometimes bombast) and he wrote a couple of *praetextae*, on themes from Roman history. In his dramatic works too, if less than in the *Annals*, values tend to be Roman rather than Greek, let alone truly Euripidean; for example he stresses social rather than moral distinctions or equates the two. We can compare the opening of his *Medea* with that of Euripides'

---

[95] Conceivably the prophetic Carmina Marciana, circulating at the time of the Hannibalic War, were in hexameters, the metre used in Greek for oracles; and, from some date, the *sortes* issued at various oracular shrines.   [96] *FPL* Bu. frs. 37–40; Hor. *Epist.* ii.1.69.
[97] The Greek word *poeta* had, however, already been used by Naevius and Plautus.
[98] *Annals* 209Sk.   [99] *Annals* 156Sk.

play; here he has left out the obscurer geographical references, doubtless beyond his Roman audience.

His knowledge of other Greek authors seems to have been wide, if odd by later standards, and he produced translations or adaptations of various kinds. He was alert to the Pythagorean traditions of his South Italian homeland, of which the Romans had probably long had some superficial awareness, and which seem to have been still acceptable to them, in spite of not coming directly from 'real Greece'. Though the Pythagorean philosophic circles in Magna Graecia had been broken up and scattered long before, some memory of them and their beliefs persisted (and the Romans could read of the history of the sect in Timaeus' work). One should note that the astronomy of Sulpicius Galus seems to have been strongly Pythagorizing; his neatly schematic distances for moon, sun and stars from the earth are certainly so and, at this stage in the history of Greek science, are markedly naive and old-fashioned.[100] Apart from allowing Homer, in the dream at the start of the *Annals*, to lecture him on Pythagorean cosmology, Ennius seems in his *Epicharmus* to have expounded natural philosophy as put forward in a popular poem falsely attributed to this early fifth-century Sicilian poet, who was regarded as a Pythagorean. He based his *Hedyphagetica* on another Sicilian work, the gastronomic poem of the fourth-century Archestratus of Gela. The Romans were becoming interested in fine cookery, as Cato complains (there is no evidence that the work was a moralizing parody). But one observes that Ennius did not try to introduce them to Sicilian pastoral verse.

He also made known some of the Hellenistic literature of which there had been little awareness yet in Rome. His *Euhemerus* recounted that – again Sicilian – author's imaginary voyage, which was intended to show that most of the gods, even Zeus, were in origin only great men, a view which, perhaps surprisingly, was to find some favour in Rome. This work was perhaps in prose, of a notably primitive and simple kind; as in many societies, poetry had been earlier in developing its expressive powers. But possibly our quotations are from a prose paraphrase of verse. The *Sota* was probably based on the light-hearted iambics of the third-century poet Sotades, who worked in Alexandria; if so, this is the first sign of literary influence from that great cultural centre, in spite of its long-standing diplomatic contacts with Rome. The mixed verse of the *Saturae* included fables and moralizing; though the name perhaps harks back to Roman semi-dramatic traditions, the influence of the Greek diatribe and of Menippean Satire have been suggested in the work itself. And Ennius is explicitly said to have introduced elegiac metre to

[100] Pliny, *HN* 11.83.

Rome,[101] perhaps by means of the epigram; his epitaph for Scipio was in this form. The elegiac epigram, though ancient by origin, was of course a dominant Hellenistic genre. It is interesting, however, that when the Romans gave up using Saturnians for epitaphs, as they now began to do, they often, as inscriptions show, used iambic metre, familiar from the stage, not elegiacs; this is very unGreek.

Ennius' *Protrepticus* perhaps recommended the study of philosophy. But Ennius' philosophy, as far as we can see, only deserves the title by courtesy, consisting as it does of semi-religious, semi-scientific speculation, such as the identification of different gods with natural phenomena. There is no certain influence from any of the great schools of the Hellenistic period. Though he puts it into the mouth of a character in a play, Ennius may have approved of the claim that one should philosophize to a certain extent only; this was undoubtedly a usual Roman standpoint at a later period. In ours, there was obviously much suspicion of the activity. Cicero suggests that Sulpicius Galus, even though he combined his scientific interests with a full political career, could be criticized by a leading figure of the previous generation for spending too much time on useless studies.

Scholars have recently stressed, perhaps over-stressed, Ennius' position as a member of the fraternity of Hellenistic learned poets; they have tried to trace an awareness of scholiastic interpretations in his knowledge of Greek poets, and found Hellenistic patterns in his work, arguing for example that the dream that opens the *Annals*, in which Ennius meets Homer, looks back not only to Pythagoras and Hesiod, but to Callimachus' dream at the beginning of the *Aitia*, and is even an answer to Callimachus' argument that no one can write epic now: Ennius, as Homer himself *redivivus*, is exempt from the ban.[102] If so, surely few of Ennius' readers will have appreciated this fine point. He is also sometimes thought to have had great influence on the language, like a true Alexandrian scholar-poet, introducing for example double consonants in spelling; but the first century B.C. was uncertain if technical grammatical works were not by a younger figure of the same name, and Suetonius certainly thought true *grammatice* was only expounded in Latin after his time.[103] But Ennius did divide his *Annals*, as Naevius had not done his *Bellum Punicum*, into books of the length normal in the Greek book-trade, which suggests that he looked to some form of publication, rather than simply to reading his own verse to friends or pupils.

Certainly Suetonius believed that Ennius did teach, both his own poems and Greek literature. One Roman scholar also saw some kind of

[101] Isid. *Etym.* 1.39.14–15.
[102] Skutsch 1967 esp. 119ff.: (B 35), 1985, 147ff.: (B 35A); Wülfing-von Martitz 1972: (H 221) (and others *ibid.*).   [103] Suet. *Gram.* 1.

self-portrait in the faithful friend of lower rank to whom a Roman general turns in the *Annals*, whose secrecy and reliability are combined with learning, especially concerning the manners and laws of the past.[104] Here too Hellenistic models have been adduced, but the possibility of at least imagining such a figure in a Roman context points to a significant social development, and though self-portraiture may not have been in Ennius' mind one suspects that such indeed was his relation to the nobles, sometimes perhaps his pupils, whom Cicero pictures calling informally at the poet's humble ménage, or walking with him in Rome.[105] The story that on his death he was commemorated by a statue in the tomb of the Scipios is probably untrue – Cicero does not assert it as a fact[106] – but it may be fairly early, and we may take it to indicate the remarkable position that a poet had now been able to make for himself in Rome.

IV. REACTION AND ACCEPTANCE

The transformation of Roman society under the impact of new wealth and new customs, mostly from the Greek world (though trade and mining in the west, like booty, especially slaves, from it, contributed to prosperity) can hardly be exaggerated. It has often been believed that in certain quarters there was violent rejection of Greek influence in favour of the old ways; but it has also been argued that the Romans, intellect- ually unsophisticated as they were, in spite of lamenting the decline of *mores antiqui* as they had doubtless always done, did not realize how far it was Greek influence that was transforming their society, and did not take up conscious attitudes towards this influence as something to be wel- comed or resisted. According to this view, not only was there no simple clash between a definable philhellene party on the one hand, inspired by love for Greek art and literature as well as aping Greek ways of life, and favourable on a political level to the Greeks, and on the other a hellenophobe one, desirous of keeping out of political and miltary entanglements in the east as well as of preserving Roman traditions (few would in fact now argue for so simple a conflict); but Greek ways seeped into Rome without much of an issue being made of them – some slight prejudice in some minds against some Greek customs has to be admitted.

It has also been suggested that if a few members of the intensely competitive Roman oligarchy took up Greek luxury and culture ostenta- tiously, the rest were forced to do the same through fear of being left behind in the race for influence. Certainly Greece could suggest profit-

---

[104] *Annals* 268ff.Sk.   [105] Cic. *De or.* II.68.276, *Acad.* II.16.51.
[106] Cic. *Arch.* 9.22; cf. Livy xxxviii.56.4.

able new methods of stressing individual or family achievements – poetic tributes, sculptural or other monuments, new ways of suggesting divine favour or even the blurring of the line between human and divine. But if it is true that the Roman upper class was, as has been stressed of late, innovative and flexible (Polybius observes Rome's willingness to learn and borrow from other nations[107]), yet there were strong pressures for conservatism as well, largely rooted in the reverence for the ancestors, the *maiores*, which had its religious as well as social aspects. For some at least, moral authority, which was important in Roman public life, might seem to lie in preserving the old ways; and might the ruling class as a whole not have some sense of its role as the guardian of national tradition, especially in religion, where neglect of accustomed cults could anger the gods?

It is certainly not easy to document conscious awareness of and debate about the clash of traditions in the earlier part of the second century. Many of the arguments used in the past are too weak to support the superstructure erected on them. For example, it is far from clear how seriously the Senate really opposed foreign, including Greek, religion as such. In 186, when the Bacchic mysteries were strictly regulated throughout Italy, it seems to have been not the long-established devotion itself, but the strong organization that congregations were developing, with lay officials, private funds and so on, which provoked action (perhaps also a somewhat hysterical belief in the vices and scandals attributed to these as to so many secret religious groups throughout history). If Livy is to be trusted, however, some prejudice could be raised by pointing out that magistrates had often been told to prevent *sacra externa*.[108] In 181 the 'Books of Numa', supposedly recently found in the king's grave, were also suppressed by the civil authorities – there is no mention of the priestly colleges – but in this case it is unclear whether there was anything felt to be really alien, as opposed to dangerously unofficial, about their content, described by our earliest sources as Pythagorean and as destroyed because they were philosophical (speculation has been active; possibly rationalizing explanations of Numaic rites were given).[109] On the other hand Etruscan divination, which was still felt as foreign, was encouraged, at some time probably in our period, though it was put under the control of the college of *decemviri*, who also dealt with Greek cults.[110] Astrology, an art of oriental origin but given a Greek dress, was beginning to be known; Ennius perhaps made an attack on it in his *Iphigeneia*, doubtless thinking this more likely to be received

[107] Polyb. VI.25.11. Cf. North 1976, 12: (H 107); Crawford 1978, 84: (A 12).
[108] XXXIX.16.8–9.   [109] Pliny, *HN* XIII.84ff.; Livy XL.29.
[110] Torelli, *Elogia Tarquiniensia* (Florence 1975) 108.

with favour than Euripides' assault on conventional divination,[111] and Cato forbade his bailiff to have anything to do with 'Chaldaei'. But astrology was probably still mainly confined to foreigners, especially slaves, like the Graeco-Egyptian cult of Isis, which Ennius may perhaps also have found occasion to mention.[112] The Senate was not to take steps against either Chaldaei or the Egyptian rites till after our period, and then perhaps largely, again, because they were unofficial and socially disturbing. It allowed generals to vow temples to whatever gods they pleased; some ancient deities such as Vejovis received new shrines in this manner, but we cannot tell if they were set up as a demonstration of traditional attitudes, and other such divinities seem to decline in importance.

There is no actual evidence of alarm at the sceptical or unorthodox religious views sometimes put forward on the stage, or in some of Ennius' works, though it is hard to suppose that traditionalists approved of them. It had probably always been legitimate, however, to make fun of the gods (on certain occasions); and it was the traditionalist Cato who said that a *haruspex* ought to laugh when he saw another *haruspex*. There seems to be little consciousness in the second century of a great religious crisis as postulated by modern scholars. However, there is nothing to parallel the procession of Greek divinities introduced to Rome on the command of the Sibylline books in the third century, and it is interesting that we know of no official delegation to question the Delphic oracle; while favour was shown to the town, and the free status conferred on it by Acilius Glabrio was ratified, the oracle's decline is thought to have been hastened by Rome's preference for her own, or Etruscan, methods of divination.[113] It does look, then, as if the Senate was at least now cautious about the official introduction or patronage of foreign rites.

There was little Greek influence on Roman political institutions (or legal ones, unless the setting up, perhaps in our period, of the court of the *centumviri* reflects the Greek custom of empanelling very large juries). However, we may observe the rumpus over restricting the vote of freedmen to the four urban tribes, out of the full thirty-five. There must have been more freedmen now than ever before – there were simply more slaves, and especially more skilled and educated slaves for whose services freedom might seem a proper reward. Should such men, however, wield the considerable political power that enrolment in any tribe where they had property might give them? In 174 (and probably earlier) freedmen

---

[111] *Iph.* xcv, Jocelyn 1967: (H 196) – but *astrologi* may be astronomers. Africanus' arch with seven gilt statues (Livy xxxvii.3.7, 190 B.C.) has been thought to honour the seven planetary gods, but is perhaps a little early for this to be likely: G. Spano, *MAL* 8, iii (1951) 173–205.

[112] If Cic. *Div.* 1.132 is quoting him: Salem 1938: (B 31).

[113] De Sanctis 1907–64, IV.ii.361ff.: (A 14); Latte 1967, 223–4 (decline of old Roman religion, 264ff.): (H 205). Guesthouse for Romans at Delphi, *SIG* 609 with commentary (= Sherk, *Documents*, 37); cf. for Sparta, E. Ziebarth, *Rh. Mus.* 64 (1909) 335.

with a son or with substantial property were allowed to register in whatever tribe they wished; in 169 this was reversed for the first category, and Ti. Gracchus, father of the tribunes and later regarded as a severe character, tried unsuccessfully to disenfranchize entirely all freedmen except those in the top property class, whose existence is worth noting. (It is also worth noting that Gracchus was one of the Senate's experts on eastern affairs, and was willing to report favourably on the situation there; he left a speech in Greek that he had delivered to the Rhodians.[114] As usual, simple philhellenism or its opposite is not in question.) But there is no evidence that prejudice against Greeks, rather than against foreigners in general, including pretty uncivilized ones, or against those who had gone through the debasing experience of slavery, was involved, and indeed the power which great men, their patrons, might exercise through their freedmen may have been part of the question at issue.

It seems less easy to deny that there may have been some conscious rejection of Greek influence in matters of morality and education. Argument here has to centre on the elder Cato, the one figure of the time of whose ideas we can really know something, since extensive fragments of his speeches and other writings survive, with the whole of his treatise on agriculture. He was a man whose opinions clearly impressed his contemporaries – even the Greek Polybius finds them worth quoting. If the possessor of the most forceful and versatile mind of any Roman of his time did not reach out to general judgements on the changes of his epoch, few others are likely to have done so.

Scholars have presented us with many Catos. The representative of opposition by peasants, or at least rural landowners, to the hellenized ruling aristocracy appears less often nowadays; the spokesman of the aristocracy into which he had made his way, intent as such on curbing the threat posed to it by great individuals who saw themselves as Hellenistic rulers or even kings, is still to be found. The idea that Cato was a simple, comprehensive hellenophobe cannot survive a glance at his fragments; the belief that he was deeply opposed to many aspects of Greek influence, but felt that it was necessary to learn from Greece in building up a sound educational literature in Latin, is more tenacious, and may go with a belief that Cato shows in his historical work, the *Origines*, a special value for Italian traditions and perhaps for peoples of the western Mediterranean in general. But recently he has been presented merely as a *novus homo*, who inevitably as such came at times into conflict with members of the aristocracy, though he had no lasting or principled hostility to the hellenizing Scipio Africanus or Fulvius Nobilior; as a man who cared (as

---

[114] Treggiari 1969, 45: (H 118). Greek speech: Cic. *Brut.* 20.79.

he clearly did) primarily for law, service to the state, and thrift – one should increase not dissipate one's property, but not make money out of public office; one should devote one's efforts to agriculture and warfare – and whose literary works, written to some extent for amusement, involved at times vigorous and lively overstatement, but were too naive and chaotic seriously to put forward any general views.[115] It is, however, probably better to think that Cato did have some real convictions about the dangers to the Romans in Greek civilization, but was ready to make some use of some sides of it, though without being quite the far-seeing eclectic with great literary and educational schemes that he has some-times been assumed to be.

His long career spanned almost the whole of our period, from the Hannibalic War to the fall of Carthage, for which last event he was partly responsible. Some of the apparent contradictions in this career perhaps stem from its length. As we saw, he had little formal education in youth, but he perhaps learnt Greek, or some Greek, on service in Sicily and (probably) at Tarentum during the war. Cicero's statement that he lodged at Tarentum with a pro-Roman Greek named Nearchus may rest, as so much else in the *De Senectute* does, on Cato's own statements, and in reporting the Pythagorean doctrines that Cato supposedly learnt from Nearchus, Cicero was probably at least building on signs of Pythagorean influence in Cato's works (we can still see, in the *De Agricultura*, a Pythagorean regard for cabbage).[116] It is unnecessary to reject the story that he later brought Ennius to Rome, and studied Greek literature with him, though it is disquieting that Cicero does not mention it.[117] A later break between the two men may have been caused as much by Ennius' readiness to celebrate other patrons, notably Scipio and Fulvius Nobilior, whom Cato disliked (and in verse too – Cato had no opinion of verse) as by his transmitting to Rome aspects of Greek thought and literature of which Cato will certainly have disapproved.

Cato reached Greece proper with the Roman army in 191. He played a part in the battle of Thermopylae which suggests that he and his commander knew the course of events in 480, though they may have been told of them on the spot. And he passed some time at Athens, which he claimed to have spent discovering what Greek culture was about.[118] He must have continued thereafter to study Greek literature, as indeed Nepos' biography states, though it is not likely that the educated slave, Chilo, whom he kept in Rome in the 180s, helped his master, as so many educated slaves did in the first century, for he is described as a *grammatistes* or elementary teacher.[119] But acquaintance with Homer,

[115] Astin 1978: (H 68).   [116] Cic. *Sen.* 41; Cato, *Agr.* 157.   [117] Badian 1972: (H 70).
[118] Pliny, *HN* XXIX. 13.   [119] Nep. *Cato* 3.2; Plut. *Cat. Mai.* 20.3.

Demosthenes and probably Xenophon, with leading figures of Greek history and famous Greek institutions, can be traced in Cato's fragments or is attested in anecdotes, not all from his last years. Xenophon was to become popular at Rome;[120] one wonders if his easy Greek, as well as his practical outlook, had something to do with this. On the other hand, though Plutarch says that Cato took some things from Thucydides, as well as much from Demosthenes,[121] it seems unlikely that he was able to come to real grips with either the language or the thought of the great historian at least.

Cato had made his mark politically by soldiering and by pleading in court, in the traditional Roman fashion. In 195 he was consul, with his old patron L. Valerius Flaccus, and his views on luxury were revealed by his unsuccessful opposition to the repeal of the *lex Oppia*, a sumptuary measure of war-time origin; to try as he and others were doing to retain such controls in peace was significant. Now or earlier, as praetor, he passed a law limiting a provincial governor's expenditure. He himself governed Spain, and fought there, vowing a temple to Victoria Virgo, whom he perhaps did not feel to be a Greek divinity, though Greek and Roman elements combine in the conception of Victoria. He insisted that he had lived in Spain in strict simplicity, without causing the state expense.[122] Returning, he began his career of prosecuting officials for peculation, extortion from provincials and other crimes supposedly hitherto strange to public life. In particular, he had some part in the attacks on Scipio and his brother, in the 180s, which seem to have turned on accountability for public money, though the course of events is irrecoverable. But his greatest moment was his censorship in 184, with Flaccus; he revised the rolls of the Senate and cavalry with extreme strictness, in particular excluding from the former T. Flamininus' brother, whom he accused of murdering a Gallic prisoner to gratify the whim of a catamite. He registered, as censors had to do, the property of all citizens, inventing an ingenious way to tax luxury items, and punishing those who neglected their fields.

It is true that the iniquitous practices that Cato combated are not actually stated in our wretched fragments of his speeches to be Greek (though they are in the speech that Livy puts into his mouth *à propos* of the *lex Oppia*),[123] but simplicity of life is repeatedly associated with 'our ancestors', and it is paradoxical to suppose that the other term of the contrast was not sometimes present in Cato's mind, whether he was inveighing against the erection of statues to effeminate cooks, or to women in the provinces (this apparently in an attack on Fulvius

[120] Münscher 1920, 70ff.: (B 21).   [121] Plut. *Cat. Mai.* 2.4.
[122] *ORF*[4] Cato frs. 51, 53, 54.   [123] Livy xxxiv.4.

Nobilior), or the placing of images of the gods in private houses 'as if they were furniture', or taking poets on campaign (Fulvius again), or indeed of reciting Greek verses as well as indulging in other undignified actions. Cato did not stand entirely alone; Pliny tells us that the censors of 189 forbade the import of foreign perfumes; Plautus' *Trinummus*, which may date from the eighties, reflects anxiety about *mali mores*[124] and the non-observance of laws, and a statue of Cato was set up in the temple of Salus praising him for saving Rome from decline (though possibly Plutarch is wrong to suppose the statue and censorship contemporary[125]).

But Cato's censorship could not escape the paradoxicality to which he was always condemned, or the Greek influence of which he had to admit a certain measure. The heavy spending on useful public building works (1,000 talents on the sewage system) helped to turn Rome into something more like a Hellenistic city. In particular the Basilica Porcia introduced a Greek architectural form, under a Greek name (and his own), for a building designed for legal and commercial activities. Nevertheless, some years later, after more building had taken place, anti-Roman Macedonians could still poke fun at the unpretentious and old-fashioned public and private edifices in the city (as well as at individual leading citizens and, comprehensively, Roman customs, institutions and history).[126]

The most significant achievement of Cato's later life was to be in literary work, though he continued to be litigious in the extreme and a watchdog of official behaviour. Here above all he was inevitably to a considerable extent dependent on the Greeks. His first objective seems to have been the proper education of his delicate but talented son by his aristocratic first wife; the boy will have been about ten in the late 180s. The Greek slave Chilo was allowed to teach a large class of other boys (whether freeborn or more likely the slaves Cato encouraged other servants of his to train for sale);[127] young Cato was his father's care. We know that a Roman history in specially large letters was produced for the boy;[128] this was perhaps the first history in Latin of any kind (though the date of a Latin version of Pictor's history is problematic), but though it may be the genesis of, it cannot be identical with, the *Origines*, on which Cato was at work in the last years of his life. It was perhaps Roman rather than Greek to give the history of one's country so central a part in elementary education. Possibly a few years later than this first work came the *libri ad Marcum filium*, of which we know too little, for example whether they were in any sense 'published' by Cato. Rather than a proper

---

[124] Pliny, *HN* XIII.24; Plaut. *Trin.* 28ff.   [125] Plut. *Cat. Mai.* 19.3.
[126] Livy XL.5.7.   [127] Plut. *Cat. Mai.* 20.3, 21.7.   [128] Plut. *Cat. Mai.* 20.5.

Greek-style encyclopaedia reflecting a more practical and Roman version of the Greek liberal education (*enkyklios paideia*), with separate books on different subjects, they may have been a rather disorganized collection of advice of different kinds.[129] They certainly forbade Marcus to have anything to do with Greek doctors, to whom Cato pronounced himself unambiguously hostile, on the grounds that they were sworn to do away with every barbarian they treated, and for pay at that.[130] Plutarch supposes that this shows that Cato knew the story of Hippocrates' refusal to treat the Persian King, and it appears from Pliny that Greek doctors at Rome in the second century had acquired a bad reputation for savage and dangerous remedies.[131] It was, besides, traditionally the duty of the *pater familias* to look after his household (Cato had a notebook with a collection of prescriptions for this purpose),[132] and the idea of healing for pay was alien. Nonetheless, it is clear that there were numerous Greek doctors in Rome by now.

In the same (somewhat ill-organized) passage Cato told his son that he would explain *suo loco*, in its right place, that the import of Greek literature to Rome would prove the city's ruin; Marcus might look into this, though not study it thoroughly. Cato clearly means Greek literature in general, not medical literature only; and we have no right to say that he did not mean these words seriously, or the sweeping condemnation of the Greeks as *nequissimum et indocile genus*, a completely worthless and unruly race. We do not know whether he in fact dealt with the whole subject *suo loco*, but the promise reveals that he took the matter to be an important one.

Cato also taught his son about the laws of his country, the old staple of Roman upper-class education. He may have written on the subject, either in the *libri ad Marcum filium* or separately, but he may have felt that it was already in safe hands. The first Roman legal work we know of is the *Tripertita* of Sex. Aelius Catus, perhaps of about 200 B.C.; the three parts consisted of the Twelve Tables, a commentary on its archaic language, and a collection of legal formulae or procedures.[133] If one enquires as to the results of Cato's intensive education of his son, one finds that the latter continued to evoke his father's approval; he was noted for courage, and became a well-regarded writer on the subject of law.[134]

All Cato's treatises were doubtless basically didactic; Cicero comments on his passion for teaching as well as learning. He doubtless took the view that public men at least must write only for serious purposes (the introduction to the *De Agricultura*, possibly inspired by Xenophon, says that one must give account of one's leisure, as well as one's active hours).

---

[129] Astin 1978, 332: (H 68).　　[130] Pliny, *HN* xxix.13.
[131] Plut. *Cat. Mai.* xxiii.3; Pliny xxvi.12–20.　　[132] Plut. *Cat. Mai.* 23.4.
[133] Pompon. *Dig.* 1.2.2.38.　　[134] Gell. *NA* xiii.20.9.

But the *De Re Militari*, for example, was presumably not written for his son, as it addressed the supreme commander in the second person singular.[135] Perhaps it was designed in the first instance for a specific person or persons; but Cato envisages it becoming more widely known, and as a result unfairly criticized.[136] Probably there was no proper publication or sale of books, but manuscripts inevitably circulated and were copied. If the subject of this work was Roman enough, to write about it was of course Greek. In particular it was to follow in the footsteps of King Pyrrhus and his adviser Cineas, whose works may well have been already familiar to the Romans, who were interested in their authors. Little is known of Cato's work, which was used, but much mangled, by the late author Vegetius; changes in organization and equipment probably made it rapidly out of date.

The *De Agricultura*, of uncertain date, survives to us and is of interest both for what it does and does not do. What it does do is to accept without discussion that its subject is a form of modern agriculture: it is addressed to the owner (in a few passages apparently to the slave bailiff or *vilicus*) of a fair-sized estate run mainly by slaves and selling its surplus of specialized produce, wine or oil, on the market. There is no hankering, except in the rather irrelevant preface, after the old-fashioned small peasant farm; though neither does it deal with the great ranches probably already to be found in parts of southern Italy, in spite of the fact that on one occasion Cato claimed that pasture was far and away the most profitable type of land;[137] nor with the fulling establishments, pitchworks and other forms of real estate which Plutarch says in his old age Cato found more lucrative than agricultural property.[138]

The book opens with a formal preface very much on the Greek literary model (though the *maiores* and military prowess add a Roman note). But though it attempts to go through the process of acquiring and developing a farm in due order – one notes that this farm is not thought of as inherited – it soon degenerates into a hodge-podge of maxims, charms, recipes, prescriptions and Best Buys, the confusion of which is unlikely to be entirely the result of a lack of final polish, or textual corruption or interpolation. In spite of Cato's dislike of Greek doctors, a good deal of Greek druggists' terminology appears,[139] along with popular medicine, not all of it unmixed with superstition. Acquaintance with the procedures of Greek technical literature is also sporadically betrayed – 'there are three kinds of cabbage, and I will show their nature and effect' – but only sporadically.

A Greek treatise on almost any subject, a *techne* or, as the Romans were

[135] Fr. 13 Jordan.   [136] Pliny, *HN* xxx *praef.*   [137] Cic. *Off.* II.89.
[138] Plut. *Cat. Mai.* 21.5.   [139] Boscherini 1970: (H 170).

to say, an *ars* (as both subject and treatise were known) first defines its subject, and then subdivides it, going on to deal separately and in order with the various parts, kinds or aspects. This is a method that goes back through the great philosophers to the sophists, who first taught the Greeks to think and speak in an orderly fashion. In the first century B.C. at Rome Varro treated agriculture on this model, criticizing all his predecessors, including Cato, for not starting with an accurate definition of the subject and for including irrelevant material. In fact, it seems pretty clear that it was only from the start of the first century that Greek method was used by the Romans for organizing treatises on any subject – rhetoric, grammar and the rest.[140] Cato's failure shows how unsophisticated Rome still was; the prose writings of many comparatively primitive peoples show a similar tendency to hodge-podge. The early Romans also found it hard to generalize; Cato's farm is clearly in southern Latium or northern Campania (he is certainly not writing of the Sabine or Alban hills where his original estates were), and particular craftsmen in that area are recommended for brooms, tools and the like. Similarly, till even later, Roman legal writers often seem to have found it hard to do other than record or comment on particular cases. And the lack of a clear sense of form is visible in other contexts as well; Plautus, in comparison with his originals, thinks in terms of separate scenes, not of the play as a whole, and the *sc. de Bacchanalibus* at least ends chaotically.

Parallel to an inability to organize material clearly in a treatise is the inability, in a society still only superficially influenced by Greek grammar and rhetoric, to organize a speech coherently, or to produce a clear narrative line with proper logical and syntactical subordination of secondary elements. Cicero thought that all the oratorical virtues except polish and rhythm, but including good examples of tropes and figures, were to be found in Cato's speeches,[141] and Plutarch believed that all his work showed Greek influence. But Cicero also says that Cato was not yet *doctus* or *eruditus* and lacked 'foreign and imported art'.[142] As it happens, Cicero's freedman Tiro wrote a long criticism of Cato's speech 'For the Rhodians' of 167, and this is partly preserved to us by A. Gellius.[143] Since Tiro is criticizing a speech made in the Senate (and so by Greek classification deliberative in genre) as though it were a forensic one, most of his technical criticisms seem misconceived, though Gellius, writing in the archaizing period, springs too readily to Cato's support. Gellius does, however, twice suggest that Cato's arguments were not well organized, and this rings true. But the reflections on justice, honour and expediency recall the stock heads of Greek deliberative oratory, the tendency to

140 Rawson 1978: (H 213).   141 Cic. *Brut.* 69.
142 Cic. *De or.* III.135.   143 Gell. *NA* VI.3.

argument rather than pathos or abuse has been seen as Greek, like the stress on the idea of arrogance and the frank recognition that states act from self-interest. Most of the figures of speech, however, especially alliteration and repetition, seem native to the earliest Latin we know, that of prayers and religious formulae, and indeed some of them were positively discouraged by Greek teachers. A general awareness of Greek oratory, read and heard, but not formal teaching in rhetoric, would explain Cato's style in his speeches, much more elevated than that of the *De Agricultura*, often vigorous, amusing or cutting. A substantial fragment of another speech represents Cato as working on it seriously beforehand, with a secretary and an earlier speech of his own to help him, and is a sustained and amusing example of the figure of *praeteritio*, perhaps a conscious one.[144] Cato obviously kept his speeches carefully; we do not know if he published any, except those that he included in his historical work.

In fact some rhetorical training may have been available in Rome by the eighties or seventies of the second century; Ennius speaks of those who practise rhetoric (though not necessarily in a Roman context)[145] and Suetonius says the early *grammatici* also taught rhetoric (though he may be thinking of a slightly later date).[146] Cicero, however, in the *Brutus* only sees real signs of Greek training in the speeches of public men active in the second half of the century,[147] and the Epicurean Philodemus is probably quoting a mid second-century source when he says that the Spartans and Romans carry on their political life successfully without any use of rhetoric.[148] Cato noted how brief his own speech to the Athenians in 191 was, compared with what the interpreter made of it,[149] and indeed all his speeches were short by Greek or later standards (so were what Cicero calls the *oratiunculae* of some at least of his contemporaries) and all began piously with invocations to the gods.[150] Cato also said that the words of the Greeks came from their lips, but those of the Romans from their hearts,[151] and laughed at the lengthy training of Isocrates' pupils, fully prepared to speak by the time they came before Minos the judge of Hades.[152] He probably did not write a separate work on rhetoric, but in the *libri ad filium* or elsewhere gave his well-known advice to stick to the subject as the words would follow, *rem tene verba sequentur*,[153] and defined the orator as 'a good man skilled in speaking', *vir bonus dicendi peritus*.[154] Whether this last owes anything to Greek works in defence of rhetoric against those philosophers who attacked it as immoral, or not, it helped

---

[144] *ORF*⁴ fr. 173.   [145] Vahlen 1928, 217: (B 37 A).   [146] Suet. *Gram.* 4.6.
[147] Cic. *Brut.* 96ff.; Galba, Scipio and Laelius *docti*, Cato only *studiosus*: *Tusc.* 1.3.1.
[148] Phld. *Rhet.* 1.14, 11.65 and 85 Sudhaus.   [149] Plut. *Cat. Mai.* 12.5.
[150] Cic. *Brut.* 63.   [151] Plut. *Cat. Mai.* 12.5.   [152] Plut. *Cat. Mai.* 23.2.
[153] Fr. 15 Jordan.   [154] Fr. 14 Jordan.

point the way for Cicero's conception of the orator as a true statesman. But Cato himself, where rhetoric was concerned, probably followed his own advice to look into, but not study in detail, Greek literature.

How efficiently Fabius Pictor and the other Roman senators who wrote histories in Greek articulated their narratives in that language we do not know (and they may have had help from Greek slaves or freedmen). Cato's late work, the *Origines*, was perhaps the first real historical work in Latin, for the brief notices preserved for each year on whitened boards by the *pontifices*, and elaborated later, do not deserve the title. Slight as the fragments of Cato's work are, we can see the heavy, redundant, paratactic sentence structure; and the overall plan of the work, though interesting, was inelegant. The first book dealt, conventionally enough by Greek standards, with the prehistory and early history of Rome; but Cato, who was not himself a *Romano di Roma*, went on to shatter the traditional historiographical model. Books II and III turned to the foundation and origins of all other Italian states and tribes, even the Gauls of the northern plains which had perhaps been regarded as part of Italy since the late third century and had been extensively colonized by Rome. It has been suggested that Cato was simply influenced by Timaeus, who began his history with much ethnography of the peoples of the western Mediterranean; but it may be significant that Cato noted that some cities were older than Rome, and praised various peoples for their warlike qualities, and perhaps in general lauded the Italian way of life, *Italiae disciplinam et vitam*.[155] It is interesting that we know by chance that when in Greece Cato particularly trusted and favoured the troops of the Latin colony of Firmum.[156] He may even have felt that Rome did not always reward her allies as she should; one fragment laments that only the leader of a Tusculan force that saved Rome from a Sabine *coup* in the fifth century had been rewarded with the citizenship,[157] though this may mainly reflect his belief that it was armies not generals who won victories, and the variety of languages and cultures still surviving in Italy makes it unlikely that he thought of a wide extension of citizenship. Some pro-Italian feeling there must be; even those who cannot organize their thoughts well may have strongly held convictions.

But in spite of this regard for Italy, the early history of many of her communities had to mean the Greek legends that they, or the Greeks for them, had produced to explain their institutions or for cultural respectability. Cato seems to have had no hesitation in chronicling tales which made half the population of Italy – including the Sabines, supposed to be Spartans by origin – descended from Greeks. (It is perhaps chance that no fragments deal with Hercules or Evander in Latium, though a

155 Peter, *HRRel.* frs. 73, 76, cf. 21.   156 Plut. *Cat. Mai.* 13.5.
157 Peter, *HRRel.* fr. 25.

number involve Aeneas; but for Cato the Romans certainly inherit Greek blood through the Aborigines and the Sabines.) In fact Cato is contemptuous of the ignorance of a tribe that cannot produce a story of this kind.[158] Whether he tried to reconcile his views by contrasting warlike and moral ancient Greeks with their decadent modern successors, as some later Roman writers do, we do not know. His research must have been quite extensive; his sources were probably both written and oral. Among the former Italiote and Siceliote historians will have bulked large. There is some evidence that he even looked out for inscriptions, which he could have learnt to do from Timaeus.[159] He uses the Greek scholarly weapons of etymology and aetiology, and though on the whole avoiding the miraculous, reports natural wonders, what the Greeks call *paradoxa*. In this last field his biographer Nepos noted his *diligentia*, but denied him *doctrina*, perhaps Greek scientific learning.[160] Cato has an eye here for agricultural and legal points of interest,[161] however, that perhaps betray the Roman behind the at least superficially hellenizing scholar.

Passing quickly, it seems, over the early Republic though perhaps not omitting it entirely, Cato then recounted the great wars in which Rome (and her Italian allies – their part may have been stressed) conquered the Mediterranean world. If he seems to have been brief on the wars in the east, it has been rightly observed that Polybius, who was specially interested in them, and Livy, who used Polybius, have biased us; though Cato may well have had a particular interest in Spain, and certainly retailed his own campaigns there. He stressed the role of the legions as a whole, and omitted the very names of individual generals, referring to them, at least usually, simply by their official rank;[162] this perhaps had roots in archaic Latin usage, but must have been purposely extended. It is perhaps illegitimate, however, to transfer the attitude to the internal political life of Rome, and argue that Cato was consciously aware that the rule of the oligarchy was threatened by the emergence of over-great individuals, usually generals and usually hellenizing. He did note, however, that the Roman constitution was not the work of a single lawgiver (as so many Greek ones of course were), but of long ages.[163] On the other hand, his belief that Roman history provided *exempla* superior to the most renowned episodes in Greek history becomes explicit in his account of the military tribune Caedicius, author of a greater exploit than that of Leonidas at Thermopylae, but meeting with less eloquent praise.[164] Here an individual (though not a general) did step forth.

---

[158] Peter, *HRRel.* fr. 31.
[159] Peter, *HRRel.* fr. 58 is often thought to rest on an archaic inscription; cf. Cic. *Sen.* 21.
[160] Nep. *Cato* 3.4.   [161] Peter, *HRRel.* frs. 39, 43, 57, 61.
[162] Nep. *Cato* 3.4; Pliny, *HN* VIII.11.   [163] Cic. *Rep.* II.1.2.
[164] Peter, *HRRel.* fr. 83. It is conceivable that Cato did not give even this name, as it appears differently in other sources.

Further formal incongruity will have been caused by Cato's insertion of some of his own speeches, apparently *in extenso*, into the last books of the *Origines*.[165] Short by later standards, they were probably still too long for their place. Cato presumably knew that speeches were a feature of Greek historiography, but had not grasped their proper function.

Cato is at his most Greek in the *Origines*, but it was perhaps at the same time, late in his life, that he rejected Greek philosophy uncompromisingly; it was only at this period that it was really becoming known in Rome. It seemed to him *mera mortualia*, probably 'mere funeral-dirges', which were proverbially near-nonsense.[166] He is said by Plutarch to have declared that Socrates' teaching (of which he may have known something from Xenophon's *Memorabilia*) was destructive of his country's laws and that the man's only recommendation was that he was a patient husband and father.[167] With some untechnical political philosophy he was acquainted; he knew the idea that Carthage, if not Rome too, was an example of the mixed or at least a tripartite constitution.[168] But if two Epicurean philosophers were really expelled from Rome as early as 173, for 'teaching the young pleasures', Cato no doubt approved, as he will have done for the expulsion of philosophers and rhetors in 161 – indeed Pliny says that he thought all Greeks should be expelled from Italy, though this can hardly be serious.[169] In 155 he strongly deprecated the upsetting effect on the young of the 'philosophic embassy' from Athens (see below). Let the young men of Rome return to listening to the laws and the magistrates, he said, and let the philosophers give their immoral lectures to the youth of Greece.[170] He was still concerned with education, and his views on it were still largely traditional.

It remains to deal with Cato's foreign policy, if he had one. It certainly seems uncertain whether he steadily advocated any sort of disengagement from the Greek East, which was in reality hardly practicable. He is not said to have disapproved of Rome's earlier campaigns, or even (for certain) of the war against Perseus, though we can be sure he disliked the rush to enlist for that war in hopes of personal enrichment. He did thereafter approve of the 'freeing' of Macedon, on the grounds that it could not be protected by Rome,[171] and he opposed the attempt to declare war on Rhodes for sympathizing with Perseus, and for tactlessly trying to arbitrate between him and Rome. Here he put forward a whole collection of reasons, but he was perhaps greatly influenced by the fact that once again the proponents of war were much moved by thoughts of

[165] Peter, *HRRel.* frs. 95, 106.   [166] Gell. *NA* xviii.7.3.
[167] Plut. *Cat. Mai.* 23.1.   [168] Peter, *HRRel.* fr. 80.
[169] Ath. xii.547a – now or, perhaps more likely, in 154 (an L. Postumius was consul in both years): Pliny, *HN* vii.113.   [170] Plut. *Cat. Mai.* 22.5.   [171] *ORF*⁴ fr. 162.

gain.[172] These two cases are not enough for us to build far-reaching theories upon; and on both occasions Cato had a majority in the Senate. He expressed on several occasions a Roman and republican distaste for kings, but he could also praise an eastern monarch if need be.[173] It is worth noting, however, that in spite of his early experience of both war and diplomacy in Greece, he never went back as an ambassador in later years (as he did to Africa), and that there is no sign that he had any sort of *clientela* in the area (as he did in Spain). He must have been regarded as unusually unsympathetic to Greeks, and unwilling to have more to do with them than he must.

Cato stands, to some extent, nonetheless, for a synthesis of Greek and Roman elements. Aemilius Paullus, the conqueror of Perseus, represents another synthesis, with stronger Greek elements, which was perhaps more significant for the future. Born about 230 B.C., he was doubtless brought up, as we would expect in that period, largely in the Roman tradition. He remained till his death an exceedingly conscientious augur, and a strict disciplinarian to his army at a time when (says Plutarch) most generals were trying to win the favour of their men as a step to a further command.[174] But he was, unlike Cato, anxious that his sons should have both a traditional and a Greek education. They were provided with Greek grammarians, 'sophists' (probably philosophers), rhetoricians, sculptors, painters and huntsmen. Some of these were perhaps only recruited after the defeat of Perseus and when the two elder sons were already grown up; we know that Paullus' son Scipio Aemilianus was introduced to hunting in Macedonia, and it was when Paullus was in Athens that he boldly asked the Athenians for a philosopher and a painter. The Athenians combined the two in the person of one Metrodorus, and though Paullus thought he had a great catch, the Athenians probably did not consider sending anyone of eminence. Metrodorus' philosophical school is not recorded; Paullus had apparently not specified what he wanted.[175]

We are told that Paullus attended his sons' lessons when he could, and he must at least have read some Homer, if he was able when at Olympia to comment that Pheidias' Zeus there was the Zeus of Homer;[176] he somehow got hold of an Athena by Pheidias to dedicate at Rome. Otherwise, what struck him on his sightseeing tour of Greece seem to have been mainly strategic possibilities.

[172] *ORF*[4] frs. 163–71. Cf. Sall. *Cat.* 51.5.

[173] Plut. *Cat. Mai.* 8.8; *ORF*[4] frs. 58, 180. Note that it was after a speech by Eumenes that Cato said that kings were carnivorous animals: perhaps when Eumenes had urged war with Perseus? Possibly, in backing Ptolemy Euergetes' claim to Cyprus, Cato was showing disapproval also of intervening in the affairs of Egypt (*ORF*[4] frs. 177ff.).

[174] Plut. *Aem.* 3–4. The main source for this life is probably Polybius.

[175] Plut. *Aem.* 6.4–5.   [176] Polyb. xxx.10.6.

After his Macedonian victory, he discoursed on the power of Fortune, the Greek Tyche, and Perseus' punishment by Nemesis – Greek ideas, if popular and superficial ones.[177] He behaved in many ways as a Hellenistic king victorious over a rival might be expected to behave; he set up his own statue on the pillar that Perseus had prepared for himself at Delphi, and sailed up the Tiber on the royal galley.[178] The claim that the Aemilii were descended from Pythagoras perhaps dates from this period (as other bogus genealogies of great Roman families, usually involving figures of Greek mythology, may do). But Paullus showed a Roman severity too. He rebuked Sulpicius Galus for lax discipline, though a friend of this student of Greek science;[179] perhaps from him he learned to understand eclipses, but he sacrificed piously when one occurred. He threw deserters to wild beasts, enslaved the whole population of Epirus (though on the Senate's orders and perhaps unwillingly), claimed that it was military experience that allowed him to organize games in Greece efficiently, and died a martyr to his augural duties.[180] His funeral was celebrated with the performance of plays by Terence and Pacuvius; and by the savage gladiatorial games, probably of Etruscan origin, that were becoming increasingly popular.

Faute de mieux, perhaps, Cato approved of Paullus, marrying his beloved son to the latter's daughter. And he was to look with favour on Paullus' son, Scipio Aemilianus (adopted by Scipio), who was much influenced by his father and whose combination of Greek and Roman traditions probably owed much to him.

V. FROM THE BATTLE OF PYDNA TO THE FALL OF CORINTH

The end of the Third Macedonian War brought a new flood of educated Greeks to Rome and Italy. The whole Macedonian court was deported (Perseus' son Alexander was kept in Rome, learnt metal-work and Latin, and became a *scriba* – he at least should have been able to translate legal Latin into decent Greek).[181] So were the thousand hostages from Achaea, of whom Polybius was one; he too, exceptionally, was allowed to remain in Rome. King Genthius of Illyria, with all his family, was confined in Umbria.[182]

Events had altered the pattern of Rome's relationships in the Greek world; Macedon was eliminated, Rhodes weakened, and compensatory favour to Athens, which led to a revival of prosperity there, may have helped cause the movement towards classicism, in the visual arts at least, discernible a little later in Italy. If this favour was mainly owing to

[177] Plut. *Aem.* 26.5–27.4.   [178] Plut. *Aem.* 28.2, 30.1.   [179] Livy XLV.28.9.
[180] Plut. *Aem.* 39.2.   [181] Plut. *Aem.* 37.3.   [182] Livy XLV.43.9.

Athens' loyalty to Rome, it may be that the Romans' respect for her great past did play some part. To Delos, now a free port under Athenian control, Roman and Italian businessmen began to flock in numbers unknown before; it became a great entrepôt for the slave trade. The flood of embassies to Rome from Greek states continued (it was to decline, though not disappear, when, later, Roman governors were on the spot). It is scarcely possible to exaggerate the extent to which Greek states felt unable to take any action without getting Rome's approval: even King Attalus of Pergamum, favoured and distant, was persuaded by a councillor that it would be wise 'to send at all times to Rome to make continual report' about his military and political problems with the Galatians, in order to avoid Roman jealousy and suspicion.[183]

The war also brought to Rome the books of the Macedonian royal library, given by Aemilius Paullus to his sons, Scipio and Fabius Aemilianus,[184] but probably made freely available by them to other readers, as the great libraries of Lucullus and others were in the next century. It has been suggested that the library was not very up-to-date, and this might be one reason for the Roman tendency to look to Greek literature of the classical rather than the Hellenistic period. Certainly Perseus and his immediate predecessors had not had literary tastes, but the library may have had a nucleus going back to Archelaus, the patron of Euripides and other Greek poets, and then reflecting the links of the court in the fourth century with the Academy and with Aristotle. It is not known if it was in this library that young Scipio found Xenophon's *Cyropaedeia*, certainly known to Alexander the Great; it may have reached Italy earlier, but at all events Scipio became devoted to it[185] (indeed the only authors that Scipio is recorded as praising or quoting are the in a sense elementary Homer and Xenophon, though his reading will not have been restricted to these). We may guess with some plausibility that the Macedonian library also possessed the works of Antigonus Gonatas' Stoic protégé Persaeus (we know he wrote on kingship and the Spartan constitution) and the other Stoics admired by Antigonus, like Cynics such as Bion; though Cynicism was too subversive to have much influence on the Romans, the arrival of the library may have paved the way for the coming impact of philosophy, and especially of a more up-to-date Stoicism. Another visitor to the court of Macedon had been the astronomical poet Aratus, and Cicero suggests that his work was or could have been known to Scipio and his friends, and even to Sulpicius Galus; it was certainly later much read in Rome.

For this period it is certain, from Polybius, what was only highly

---

[183] *IGRom*. III.222; Welles 1934, no. 61: (B 74); cf. Polyb XXIII.17.4 agreeing that the Romans wanted everything submitted to them.   [184] Plut. *Aem*. 28.6.
[185] Cic. *QFr*. I.1.23, *Tusc*. II.62; *Sen*. 59 includes Scipio's friend Laelius.

probable in the preceding one, that there was much consciousness of the
difference between 'the Greek way of life' and 'the Roman way of life' –
Polybius uses the word *hairesis*. He describes A. Postumius Albinus, a
young man of distinguished family who first appears as a junior officer in
the war with Perseus, as one whose enthusiasm from boyhood for Greek
studies, the Greek language and the less worthy aspects of Greek culture
– love of pleasure and hatred of toil – turned the older and more
distinguished Romans against Greek ways.[186] Cato may be among
these, for Polybius shows him rebuking Albinus for apologizing in case
the style and organization of his history in Greek were faulty; there was
no need to write one at all. (Albinus even wrote a poem in Greek as well.)
Polybius also looked back to the fall of Syracuse and regretted that the
Romans had carried off its spoils, especially the works of art. To imitate
the habits of the conquered had been an error, and hatred had been
created among the subject population.[187] Young Scipio Aemilianus, who
spent his time in study and hunting, instead of pleading in the Forum,
was unhappy at being regarded as unRoman, though he did not indulge
in the 'Greek laxity' that Polybius says infected Roman youths during the
war with Macedon, and ran riot with the transference of Macedonian
wealth to Rome[188] – affairs with boys and courtesans, concerts and stage
performances (*acroamata*), drinking parties: 'many paid a talent for a
catamite or three hundred drachmas for a jar of caviare'. Here Polybius is
using a speech of Cato's which contrasted such spending with that on
agricultural land. Polybius' views are in fact probably much influenced
by those of his Roman friends, and perhaps even by Cato's. He strongly
approves of those who were disgusted by the flattery of King Prusias of
Bithynia on his visit to Rome,[189] and those, notably M. Aemilius
Lepidus, *pontifex maximus* and *princeps senatus* (later to insist on a simple
funeral), and Aemilius Paullus, who closed their doors to the murderous
Charops of Epirus.[190] It may be that the occasional aping of Roman
habits by foreign potentates – Prusias was not the only example – helped
the Romans to be conscious of their own way of life.

   In 161, as we saw, philosophers and rhetors were actually expelled
from Rome, though it has been doubted whether the measure was strictly
enforced against those living with a patron, and one observes that the
grammatici, who taught the language and some literature, seem to have
been exempted (people did have to learn Greek).[191] In the same year a

---

[186] Polyb. xxxix.1.   [187] Polyb. ix.10.
[188] Polyb. xxxi.25.4. If it is true that commercial bakers only became known at the time of the war
with Perseus (Pliny, *HN* xviii.197) this is another index of changing ways; Plautus has the word
artopta, *Aul.* 400, but does not use *pistor* in the sense of baker.
[189] Polyb. xxx.18; Braund (1982): (E 125) on Prusias' pose as a Roman freedman.
[190] Polyb. xxxii.6.5.   [191] Suet. *Gram.* 25.

sumptuary law regulating expense at dinners was introduced. On the other hand, in 164 the Romans acquired an accurate public sundial from the censor Marcius Philippus; in the third century they had ignorantly supposed that one carried off from Sicily would work in Rome too. A few years later Scipio Nasica set up a public water-clock. Civilization was advancing.

The period after Pydna would have been called, till a few years back, by anyone writing on the cultural and intellectual traditions of the time, the age of the Scipionic Circle. But the concept has recently become discredited, as largely a creation of Cicero, who, in a desire for dramatic concentration, gathered together most of the intellectuals of this or rather a slightly later period in his *De Republica*, of which Scipio is the central figure. It is true, however, that the period between Pydna and the fall of Carthage is that of Scipio's younger manhood, and that he and his friends Laelius and Furius Philus are among the most interesting figures of their time. They, and particularly Scipio, may be seen as the heirs of Aemilius Paullus, who had found it possible to combine what he saw as best in both Greek and Roman traditions. Polybius in fact does not find it paradoxical that Scipio should ask a Greek to help him become more worthy of his ancestors. Indeed Polybius 'believed that there was no one more suitable than he was himself to do this', there being as he pointed out plenty of teachers of mere school subjects flooding into Rome at this time.[192] Polybius encouraged Scipio to seek a reputation for temperance (the idea if not the practice was Greek), financial generosity (unRoman) and courage (with preparation in the hunting field, where the Romans did not usually seek it).[193] The young man's qualities were seen in 151, when it was impossible to recruit for the Spanish War, owing to an unexampled panic that shocked the older generation; he volunteered to serve, and then distinguished himself in single combat.[194] He was later to show himself a strict disciplinarian in the field, like his father, and at Rome a positively Catonian scourge of lax morals – as well as a friend of learned Greeks.

Whether, as ancient tradition has it, Scipio, Furius and Laelius were in their youth friends and patrons of Terence, whose brief career was traditionally run in the 160s, is uncertain. The nobles whom Terence tells us were accused of helping to write his comedies must, it was already thought by a scholar of the first century B.C., have been older, as they were described as having been made use of by the people in war and in peace.[195] This may imply some advance in the *cursus honorum*, though Scipio had fought bravely, young as he was, against Perseus. The scholar concerned suggested the names of Q. Fabius Labeo and M. Popillius,

192 Polyb. xxxi.24.5–6.   193 Polyb. xxxi.25.2, 29.
194 Polyb. xxxv.4.8, 5.1–2.   195 Ter. *Ad.* 15ff.; *Gramm. Rom. Frag.* 387.

both consulars, and, as he reveals, poets; or else that of Sulpicius Galus, who did perhaps have an interest in the stage, for several plays are recorded as produced in his magistracies. However, some connection on Terence's part with Paullus' family is suggested by the choice of one of his comedies for representation at Paullus' funeral.

At any rate, what is significant is that it is now conceivable that Roman nobles might be secretly writing verse, and that Terence does not feel it necessary, from loyalty to them, flatly to deny the rumour; and also that Terence, though a slave by origin, should frequent aristocratic circles simply on the basis of his talent. His art, so much more refined than that of Plautus, or indeed than that of Plautus' successor Caecilius, recently dead, perhaps partly reflects the growing sophistication of taste of his patrons. But his lack of popular success, with most of his plays, suggests that audiences had not changed much since Plautus' time; though Terence must have thought that they would sit through prologues (rather rhetorical in style and organization) about literary disputes and the nature of translation. This was a subject for which the Romans could not find assistance among the basically monoglot Greeks, though they may have been influenced by Greek ideas of 'imitation' of an earlier work. But to say that *bene vertere* is *male scribere*, good translating is bad writing, can only be a Roman formulation.[196] Whether any earlier playwrights had used the prologue for such discussions we do not know; the prologue to the *Hecyra* suggests theatrical quarrels in which Caecilius was involved.

Compared with Plautus, Terence seems at first sight to be far more Greek. He keeps Greek titles for his plays (as Caecilius often did), though the Romans did not worry about the accurate transliteration of Greek names until, at the end of the century, some of the newly self-conscious Roman *grammatici* demanded it. He does not despise philosophy, indeed represents it as – in moderation – a proper activity for a young man, in Greece at least. The lyrical element in his plays is smaller and the farcical additions and the exuberant play with the Latin language are reduced, though not wholly done away with: Terence's diction is still richer than Menander's elegantly transparent Greek, and, as was to be so often the case in Roman poetry, pathos and emotion are brought out, at the expense, in this case, of gnomic detachment. There is some desire, it seems, for a measure of realism – the language is more colloquial (educatedly colloquial) than that of Plautus, offering ellipses, interjections, and so on, while Terence avoids breaking theatrical illusion by patently Roman insertions, by direct addresses to the audience, of which there were many in Greek New Comedy, and by the formal prologues,

[196] Ter. *Eun.* 7.

favoured by the Athenian dramatists, that explain the plot beforehand. Scholars have recently stressed his comparative individuality as an artist. By free use and combination of models he enlivens plot and action (his beloved Menander might sometimes seem rather slight); more interestingly, he minimizes Greek local colour, thus giving his characters a universal humanity, if also some lack of individuality. It might be wrong to deduce too much about Roman culture in his time from this universality, for Terence was an ex-slave, probably from Africa, and will have had neither a strong Roman patriotism nor roots in the Italian theatrical tradition. But it may be that he and his patrons could take Greek details for granted now, and he possibly foreshadows the acceptance, in some quarters at Rome, of cosmopolitan Stoicism. He is said, however, to have died on a study-tour of Greece, the first that we know of a Roman writer taking.[197]

There has recently been much disagreement whether his *Adelphoe* reflects contemporary interest in Rome in the proper education of young men. Some find a Roman preference for severity in the final unexpected condemnation of the hitherto sympathetically liberal old Micio, and think that this, or at least Demea's speech justifying a father's right to correct extravagant and inexperienced youth, is a Terentian addition. This is disputed; certainly attempts to identify Demea with Cato, and so on, are misconceived.[198] But it is possible that Terence's endings do tend to be more serious and moral than those of his models; and even that his plays are apt to be concerned with relations between fathers and sons, which must often have been difficult in Rome in this period. And if it is true that Terence lays less stress than his Greek models on the weakness of man, and more on his worth and dignity, this perhaps has something to do with Roman self-confidence and *gravitas*, and adumbrates a real humanism that is inconceivable without the civilizing influence of Greece, but is not itself purely Greek.

With the other comic poets of the time we suffer from miserable fragments and uncertain chronology. Titinius, who introduced the *togata*, still based on New Comedy but set in the country towns of south Latium or (probably) Rome, was at one time seen as representing a post-Terentian reaction against the Greek atmosphere of the *palliata*, but in fact his date is probably considerably earlier in the century[199] and his work influenced by traditions and tastes in southern Latium, where he may have been born and his plays may conceivably have been first produced, rather than by attitudes in Rome itself. It is interesting that characters from these towns seem to be laughed at for aping Greek ways. In the *togata* free women were more prominently represented than in the

197 Suet. *Vit. Ter.* 5.   198 Büchner 1974, 412ff.: (H 174).
199 Weinstock, *PW* 2.VI.2.1540.

palliata, in accordance with the comparative freedom they enjoyed in Italy, and we are told that slaves were not allowed to appear cleverer than their masters, as they so often did in the latter.[200] The prologue to the *Casina* of Plautus reveals that, perhaps in or soon after Terence's time, there was a demand for the revival of earlier plays; the *Casina* is one of Plautus' most lively and indecent comedies, and we may suspect that the tastes of the educated and the uneducated were now drawing apart. The next prominent composer of *palliatae*, Turpilius, was probably to write more in the Plautine than the Terentian tradition.

Polybius speaks with crushing contempt of Roman audiences even in this period. At the time of L. Anicius' games celebrating his victory over Genthius some time in the mid sixties, several distinguished Greek flute-players brought over for the occasion were put all together onto the great stage that had been built in the circus, together with a chorus, and to liven things up were made to lead mock fights between various groups. There was great applause. Two dancers, their accompanists, and four boxers, with buglers and trumpeters, joined in. 'As for the tragic actors', says Polybius, 'whatever I said of them I would seem to be making fun of my readers.'[201] What on earth happened we are left to wonder; perhaps the audience expected a larger musical element in the dialogue, and doubtless few could follow fifth-century tragic language. (Plays in Greek, which continued to be produced in Rome, were never a great success, implies Cicero.[202]) One recalls Terence's audience, which preferred to watch boxers, gladiators or rope-dancers.[203]

And yet tragedy in Latin, though Polybius does not deign to mention it, was still successful. This is the age of Ennius' nephew Pacuvius (though he may have begun producing somewhat earlier). He was born in the Latin colony of Brundisium, but retired at the end of his long life to nearby Greek Tarentum;[204] he may, like Ennius, have had a Greek education. Cicero, perhaps embroidering, notes a friendship with Laelius.[205] With the art of tragedy, Pacuvius practised that of painting, a reminder perhaps of the incomplete specialization still obtaining in Rome. He was perhaps the earliest poet to be regarded in the classical period as *doctus*, though Horace and Quintilian, reporting the judgement, reject it.[206] Various explanations of the term have been offered – the semi-philosophical disquisitions, such as that on *terra* and *aether*, based on Euripides, in his *Chryses*, or the possibility that some of his plays were based on relatively unknown post-Euripidean models. The choice of obscure legends of a romantic or pathetic kind has been seen as Hellenistic. Pacuvius' style is more elaborate than his uncle's, though it is

[200] Donat. *ap.* Ter. *Eun.* 57.   [201] Polyb. xxx.22.   [202] Cic. *Att.* xvi.5.1.
[203] Ter. *Hec. prol.* 1.4, 11.33.   [204] Hieron. *Chron.* 142 H; Gell. *NA* xiii.2.2.
[205] Cic. *Amic.* 24.   [206] Hor. *Epist.* ii.1.55; Quint. *Inst.* x.1.97.

hard to decide to what extent he is attempting effects based on the Greek; with his heavy compound adjectives he must be doing so. But early first-century rhetorical writers complained that his argumentative passages were incoherent and did not follow rhetorical rules.[207] And Cicero observes that he cut down the lamentation that Sophocles had given the wounded Odysseus in his *Niptra*;[208] this was doubtless in deference to Roman taste. It would be useful to know more of his *Antiope*, based on Euripides, where Amphion defends a life of study against his brother's preference for action; how far did Pacuvius feel he could go? There is elsewhere an attack on divination as such, which is probably bolder than Ennius' assault on unofficial *vates* and *harioli*, and marks a movement of opinion in Rome, though the play may have shown the speaker as mistaken.

In 154 the censors apparently began to build a permanent stone theatre, the first in Rome. The Senate was persuaded shortly thereafter by Scipio Nasica Corculum to have it destroyed and all seating at the games was forbidden for a time, though seats at plays had, it is quite clear, been usual. This seems to have been a *cause célèbre*, and it is often suggested that conservatives feared that a permanent theatre might be used, as theatres often were in Greek cities, for political assemblies. There were no seats in the Roman *comitium*, or in its imitations elsewhere in Italy, and this must have helped to cut meetings short; might not a comfortably seated populace demand a larger political role? The evidence suggests, however, that the opposition saw the idea of seats at any sort of *ludi* as soft and unmilitary; if Augustine is right, Scipio Corculum argued that *Graeca luxuria* was ruining manly ancestral practices.[209] Cicero's *Brutus* suggests that no speech of Corculum survived, and Augustine's wording may be influenced by a later historian, but anxiety about a decline in Rome's military standards was clearly prevalent in the years after the fall of Macedon.

Feeling against the Senate was developing, over the levy in particular. It is just possible that politicians of what one may call a proto-*popularis* tendency looked back not only to the Struggle of the Orders in Rome, but found support in Greek political traditions, even those of a somewhat democratic kind. Cicero's *De Republica* suggests that by 129 there was an interest in the moderate democracy of Rhodes,[210] and the Gracchi may have been affected by the reformist ideas of the Spartan kings, Agis and Cleomenes, while they were compared, perhaps already in their own day (but with hostile intent?) to Athenian democratic

---

[207] *Rhet. Her.* II.27.43; cf. Cic. *Inv.* 1.94.   [208] Cic. *Tusc.* II.21.48.

[209] Livy, *Per.* XLVIII; Cic. *Brut.* 79; August. *Civ.D.* 1.31. Taylor 1966, 29ff.: (H 30).

[210] Cic. *Rep.* 1.47, III.48.

politicians and orators. This takes us outside our period, but there may have been debates within it that we cannot reconstruct.

The great debate that we do know of, that about the declaration of war with Carthage, may have taken place in somewhat Greek terms, if the theory that fear of an external enemy is necessary to keep a state from luxury and decay was really put forward by Scipio Nasica.[211] Certainly the effect that the war would have on foreign, no doubt primarily Greek, opinion was, says Polybius, seriously taken into account.[212] Something of political and intellectual interest may also be extracted from the tiny fragments of a historian of this time. Cassius Hemina, who seems to have composed at least part of his history (in Latin) before the Third Punic War, wrote with brevity, but with a more complex sentence-structure than Cato's *Origines*, or indeed some later historical works, can boast.[213] He could produce commonplaces of Greek philosophy, quoted Greek phrases, and may have criticized a merely literary historian, without practical experience, in a way that recalls Polybius on Timaeus.[214] To write in Latin was surely not a polemical act for him, as it may have been for Cato. But in spite of Greek influences he was one of the first Roman historians to subordinate the origin-stories and the recent wars to the reconstruction, of interest only to Romans, of the internal history of the early Republic. However, he deployed the traditional weapons of Greek antiquarianism, etymology and aetiology, with unsophisticated enthusiasm (the Latin towns Crustumerium and Aricia were founded by 'Sicels' called Clytemnestra and Archilochus[215]). He rationalized and euhemerized the early legends; he gave a cool explanation, possibly under Stoic or Cynic influence, of the ill-fame attaching to suicide;[216] at the same time he shows an interest in Greek mystery religions and, still, Pythagoreanism – he was not yet aware that it was chronologically impossible that King Numa should have been a pupil of Pythagoras,[217] and in fact the Romans had no convenient instruments for comparing dates of Greek and Latin history till the mid first century.

Cassius combines naiveté with some sophisticated Greek influences. Rome had been having some distinguished visitors of late, though they came primarily as envoys rather than to teach (some intellectuals had done so earlier, like Antiochus' ambassador Hegesianax in the 190s, but there is no evidence that the Romans took anything from them). Perhaps in 168, or possibly some years later,[218] the great *grammaticus* Crates of Mallos arrived. It was only because he broke his leg in an open drain that he stayed to give lectures, which Suetonius thought introduced true

---

[211] Gelzer 1962–4, II.39: (A 19).   [212] Polyb. XXXVI.2.   [213] Leeman 1963, 72: (H 207).
[214] Peter, *HRRel.* fr. 28.   [215] Peter, *HRRel.* frs. 2 and 3.   [216] Peter, *HRRel.* fr. 15.
[217] Peter, *HRRel.* fr. 37.   [218] Suet. *Gram.* 2.2 is confused.

grammatical learning into Rome; before that the *poetae* and *semi-Graeci* Livius Andronicus and Ennius had simply read Greek poetry, and their own, with their pupils (Suetonius cannot be literally accurate). Crates perhaps lectured both on what we would call grammatical theory and on Homer, on whom he wrote extensively. Cassius may have been influenced by Crates' Stoic faith in etymology.

Suetonius tells us that it was owing to Crates' influence that certain Romans began to bring forward Latin poems 'by their friends or others', which had not been widely circulated, and to lecture on them, reading and commenting.[219] It may be that at least C. Octavius Lampadio, whom Suetonius seems to regard as definitely the first of the true Roman *grammatici*, did this for Naevius' *Bellum Punicum* very soon after Crates' visit: he also divided the work into seven books, in other words producing an edition, which copyists could use. (One would like to see him as a freedman of the hellenizing senator Octavius, but he does not bear the same *praenomen*, as one would expect in that case; but a freedman, probably of Greek background, he almost certainly is.) Crates is said by a late source to have advised the export of parchment to Italy from Pergamum (whence the material derived its name);[220] though papyrus was no doubt normally used for writing, Crates may have seen that there was scope for developing the book-trade now in Rome. It is also remarkable that Crates' visit to Rome seems to be the first sign of Rome receiving any intellectual or cultural influence from Pergamum, with which there had so long been friendly political relations, though the kings of Pergamum were great patrons of philosophy and learning. In fact certain Pergamene scholars seem markedly to ignore Rome, like Polemon of Ilium, who wrote about the foundation legends of Greek towns in southern Italy, or to be unsympathetic to her, like Demetrius of Scepsis, who denied that Aeneas ever left Asia. Nor is there any clear evidence yet of cultural influence from Rhodes, another considerable centre for things of the mind, though with her again Rome had long been associated.

In 155 the famous philosophic embassy arrived in Rome from Athens (the point at issue was the fine imposed on Athens for destroying the border-town of Oropus). In sending the heads of the main philosophic schools (Epicurus' Garden significantly excepted), the Athenians must have thought that they would now carry weight in Rome. They all gave public lectures. Their different styles of eloquence made a vast impression, and Plutarch says that many young men ran wild for philosophy, and many older men were happy to see this.[221] The praetor C. Acilius (author of a history in Greek) begged to interpret for the

---

219 Suet. *Gram.* 2.3–4.   220 Lydus, *Mens.* 14.11 W.   221 Plut. *Cat. Mai.* 22.

ambassadors, and essayed a philosophic joke in which he perhaps confused Academic Scepticism and Stoic paradox. But the great Sceptic Carneades caused a furore by arguing one day for the importance of justice in politics, and the next for that of injustice.[222] If the Romans were truly just, they would give up all their conquests and return to shepherds' huts. The Romans were shocked; they always tried to persuade themselves and others that all their wars were just, undertaken in defence of themselves or their allies. Cato, as we saw, recommended the Senate to conclude the envoys' business as soon as possible.

Whether Carneades started the Romans looking consciously for a moral justification of Empire (and whether this was to be given them by the later philosophers Panaetius or Poseidonius) is uncertain. More permanent effect was perhaps produced by the Stoic Diogenes of Babylon (Critolaus the Peripatetic seems to have had less impact; the school was not very vital at the time). We know that Laelius and others became to some extent genuine disciples, presumably getting further than the superficial acquaintance with a few leading doctrines that may have been becoming reasonably common, and gaining some knowledge of the way in which philosophers actually argue. But it is only on a few members of the next generation – such as Q. Tubero and Rutilius Rufus – that Stoicism had a serious practical effect. Even so, the works which Greek philosophers began to dedicate to their aristocratic Roman pupils seem markedly untechnical, while the *Index Stoicorum* lists no Romans (though two obscure Samnites) as professional philosophers at this time. Laelius was to be most famous as a conscientious augur, and his speech on the religion of Numa in 145 was archaizing in language and highly conservative in tendency.[223]

Scipio Aemilianus almost certainly listened to the philosophers. Some time in the forties the Stoic Panaetius was to come to Rome, and on repeated visits spent much time with Scipio and his friends. It is unlikely that he arrived before 148, and so it is not our task to decide whether he, or other prominent Athenians, shocked by Rome's destruction of Corinth and Carthage, felt that a conscious effort must be made to civilize her leading men – perhaps it is not very probable; nor whether Panaetius' modified Stoic doctrine, humane and shorn of paradox, was produced for Roman consumption, or, as is more likely, developed in answer to attacks on Stoicism by the Sceptics, especially Carneades. The main Greek influence on Scipio in the years before 148 was probably still that of Polybius, no great intellectual, indeed opposed to the Sceptics, rather an intelligent, soldierly, not unbookish man from a political family. The relationship between them, and the position gained by Polybius at Rome,

[222] Lactant. *Div. Inst.* v.14.3–5.   [223] Cic. *Brut.* 21.83.

was significant for the future, however. Polybius seems to be the first Greek public man to be really trusted in Rome and, having partially detached himself from his background, to have been used as an adviser and assistant by great Romans. He was with Scipio at Carthage, primarily perhaps as a technical expert in military matters; he was with Mummius in Greece, helping to re-organize the country politically after her final disaster.

On the fall of Carthage, Scipio, conscious like his father of the power of Tyche, and aware of the Greek belief that all empires pass away, shed tears and quoted Homer[224] (in the first century famous Romans seem more inclined to quote Greek drama in moments of stress). But he also accompanied the capture of the city with traditional Roman rites, including perhaps the resurrection of the rite of *evocatio*, by which Punic Tanit or Juno was summoned to leave the city which had been hers, as Camillus had summoned Juno of Veii long before. Scipio's friend Furius Philus, doubtless another pupil of the philosophic embassy, was probably the author of a handbook on this ancient rite,[225] and may thus have opened the era of the antiquarian monograph in Rome. Laelius' famous speech on Numaic religion, and some evidence from a rather later period, do suggest that Scipio and his friends were interested in the revival of traditional Roman rites that had decayed.

Mummius, the destroyer of Corinth, was a man who, says Cicero, used a simple and old-fashioned style in his speeches, and he was to set up a record of his victories in the now archaic Saturnian metre;[226] but, though stories circulated of his ignorance of the value of the masterworks of art taken in the sack of Corinth, neither he nor his brother (who loathed rhetors and democracy, but had studied Stoicism, which may partly account for the dislike of rhetors, and wrote verse epistles from Greece to his friends[227]) was totally hostile to the Greeks and Greek ways; the hellenomaniac Albinus was on his staff. Plutarch has a story of Mummius weeping when a boy in the stricken city quoted Homer to him;[228] Tacitus has a mysterious reference to the introduction of new *theatrales artes*, by which he may mean citharoedic contests, a wholly Greek event, at Mummius' triumphal games.[229] It was then not only Scipio and his friends who were now able to take what they wanted, without strain, from both the Roman and Greek traditions. It is an over-simplification to say that in war, politics and religion they remained largely Roman, and filled their *otium*, their leisure, with Greek studies and amusements,

---

[224] Polyb. xxxviii.22. [225] Macrob. *Satur.* iii.9.6. Rawson 1973, 168: (H 289).
[226] Cic. *Brut.* 94; *ILLRP* 122 – irregular, even for Saturnians; if this is what they are meant to be, perhaps few now knew how to write them.
[227] Cic. *Brut.* 94, *Att.* xiii.6a, *Rep.* iii.34.46–7, v.9.11.
[228] Plut. *Quaest. conv.* ix.737a. [229] Tac. *Ann.* xiv.21.

though there is some truth in it; in fact rhetoric and philosophy were beginning to have a real effect on public life. There were, perhaps, as many different syntheses of Greek and Roman traditions as there were intelligent and educated Romans.

VI. CONCLUSION

The distance which Rome had travelled in less than a century was enormous. But there was still a long way to go. In 148 probably no Roman, of the upper class at least, had thought to pay an extended visit to Athens or Rhodes for serious study with the best Greek masters of rhetoric or philosophy, or, unless he happened to be there already on public business, had gone sightseeing in Greece. Exiles withdrew to the cities of Latium or Etruria, not to the Greek East. It was barely respectable for a noble to write verse, certainly not for him to abandon public ambitions altogether for a life of study, as a few men of prominent family did in the first century. If philosophy was beginning to be known, Academic Scepticism, Epicureanism and Cynicism were probably still all distrusted. In 146, when political developments disrupted the Museum at Alexandria, it seems that none of the scholars who had worked there fled to Rome, though we are told that 'Greece and the islands' were filled with refugee intellectuals of every kind[230] (it is true that there was an Alexandrian painter in Rome somewhat earlier[231]). It was not till the first century that, as Philodemus shows, a visit to Rome became the normal ambition of a Greek teacher,[232] partly owing to the extinction of the various royal courts that had offered patronage, and to the impoverishment of many Greek cities, partly perhaps to the fact that by now so many famous Greek libraries had come to Rome, mainly as spoils of war, that scholarly activity could be carried on there as well as anywhere else, and Rome and Alexandria could be spoken of in the same breath as intellectual centres.

It was only in the first century, too, that Cicero and others began consciously to measure Roman against Greek literary and intellectual achievements, in the attempt, that no longer seemed ridiculous, to equal or outdo them. It was only then that Latin verse, in spite of its already long history, reached the ease and elegance of maturity; it was certainly only then that prose became supple and expressive, and indeed that *grammatici* and practising writers forced some consistency and regularity on the language. Historical works uniting moral and political analysis

---

[230] Ath. iv.184b–c (from Andron of Alexandria and Menecles of Barca).

[231] Diod. Sic. xxxi.18; cf. Val. Max. v.i – a *topographos*, either a scene-painter or one who painted the pictures of cities etc. carried in triumphs.   [232] Phld. *Rhet.* ii.145 Sudhaus.

with literary polish began to appear; treatises on almost every subject started to use the procedures of Greek logical organization, forging also a language in which to discuss rhetoric and 'grammar', and ultimately in the hands of Cicero and others, for philosophy too (though not, as Cicero points out, for mathematics). Medicine was not naturalized, but much of the prejudice against Greek doctors gave way. In religion, the forms of divination and the cults that the Greeks had adapted from the east proved, in this adapted form, irresistible even to many members of the upper class; on the other hand, many of this class now turned to Epicureanism, which rejected divination and all divine intervention. In politics, almost every great man with interests in the east now had an entourage of Greek advisers and assistants.

But the earlier period, as we have seen, had laid the foundations for most of these developments. Above all, it had on the one hand provided the basis for a real civilization that should be something more than a pale copy of a Greek model, but should preserve and develop much that was genuinely Roman or Italian. And, on the other, though it ultimately distanced the educated or wealthy Roman from his humbler fellow-countrymen (not that all of these were completely untouched by any sort of Greek influence), it allowed and initiated that possibility of understanding and co-operation between the Latin- and Greek-speaking elites, which was to be one of the most important factors in the long survival of the Roman Empire.

CHAPTER 13

THE TRANSFORMATION OF ITALY,
300 – 133 B.C.
THE EVIDENCE OF ARCHAEOLOGY

JEAN-PAUL MOREL

The central issue in the development of Italy during the third and second centuries B.C. is without doubt that of its hellenization; nevertheless it would be a mistake to relate everything to this factor. In the first place, hellenization, particularly in Rome, had been in progress since the early years of the city and it continued after the period now under consideration. It assumed numerous aspects, the variants among which must be noted, but was not in itself enough to be entirely responsible for the character of the period. Secondly, the process of hellenization encountered obstacles, was halted by boundaries and provoked reactions. Lastly, certain of the phenomena which are to be analysed – and those not the least important – clearly lay outside the problematical area of hellenization. Prominent among such phenomena are those relating to the production of goods for domestic consumption and for trade. Indeed, an enquiry confined to art and architecture would be unacceptable in the light of the approach taken recently by archaeology: 'antiquarianism' and 'material culture' have also, thanks to the progress of research, acquired an importance which must be taken into account.

The subject is not without its difficulties. The period in question is one which has inspired the least concerted study, in contrast with archaic and 'mid-Republican' Rome on the one hand and Rome after the Gracchi on the other. Moreover, many of the works of art or groups of objects on which the present observations must be based are still very insecurely dated and highly conjectural in their attributions (though remarkable advances have been made in this direction).

The orderly presentation of the subject requires that within the overall period several distinct 'sub-periods' be identified. Although in fact these correspond with the main lines of development, the necessarily somewhat artificial nature of such a subdivision into periods has to be acknowledged, with its inherent risk of giving prominence to disruption at the expense of the elements of continuity. Inevitably wars, and particularly the Second Punic War, appear, not only *a priori* but also on examination, as essential landmarks: in all the fields under discussion they were a period of standstill, it is true, but also of new opportunities and new incentives, in short, of fundamental changes.

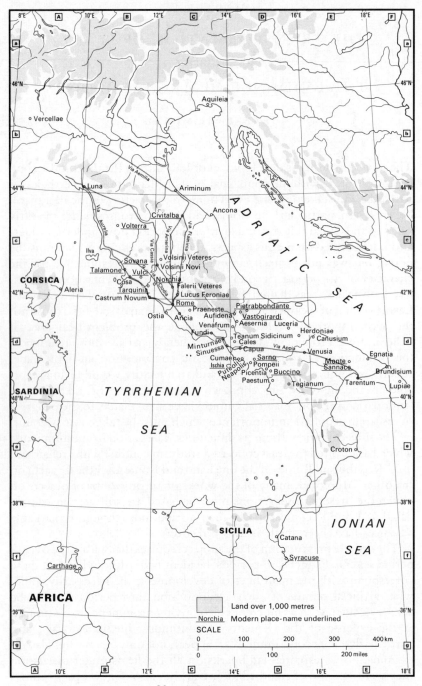

Map 16. Italy and Sicily.

I. BEFORE THE SECOND PUNIC WAR

a. The first quarter of the third century

(i) Introduction

The evidence leaves no doubt that the beginning of the third century and even the end of the fourth century constituted an intensely creative period in Italy. Less obvious, perhaps, is the concept of the central part played at this time by Rome, which was long believed to have developed its artistic and economic powers of production rather later. As a corollary, it would seem necessary to reduce to more realistic proportions the vitality, at least in commercial matters, attributed to other regions of Italy, especially Magna Graecia. In short, at the turn of the fourth century and the beginning of the third century, Rome was in no way behind the rest of Italy in production and in art, and was at the same time taking a more vigorous initiative than the remainder of the peninsula in marking out the first outlines of an economic expansionism which was to be consolidated in the second century.

At first sight, however, the predominant impression is of an Italian *koiné* with a certain uniformity in the nature and standard of its artistic expression and production of artifacts. Models circulated in large numbers and were adopted without reserve. There appears at that time to have been no radical difference in quality or concept of either artistic or material culture between Southern Italy and Central Italy or between Magna Graecia and the Italian 'natives', from Lucania to Rome and Etruria. This unity makes the disruptive effects of the Pyrrhic War and of the surrender of Tarentum in 272 appear all the more striking: what followed was an interruption in the flood of civilizing influences which had been spreading from the south of Italy and the creation of disparities between the various regions. It was to be the end of the close dependence of Central Italy on Magna Graecia in the sphere of cultural development.

(ii) Production and trade

During the first part of the third century the production of artifacts in all the regions of Central and Southern Italy is impressive both for its range and for its quality – a quality which calls for many of their bronzes, ceramics and terracottas to be regarded as works of art, and as such they will be discussed later. In this context pottery was a particularly sensitive barometer, requiring as it did only raw materials which were widely available and technical skills which had already been exercised in peninsular Italy for a long time; moreover, pottery served a host of different needs that made it a basic necessity. The variations which occur over and above these constant factors are therefore very significant. In fact, the ceramic products of Italy at the beginning of the third century are characterized by their very high average quality, both of technique and of decoration, compared with those of the preceding and the succeeding periods.[1] Such pottery as that of Gnathia in Apulia, of Capua and Teano in Northern Campania and of Malacena in Northern Etruria is remarkable for its originality of design and its meticulous craftsmanship. Ideas which caught on widely did not, however, reappear as slavish imitations: each region, each workshop even, preserved its own individuality, in which both local trends and ethnic traditions were amply represented. Thus in the pottery of Malacena, produced in the neighbourhood of Volterra, shapes borrowed from the Greek repertoire were given details of form and relief decoration derived from Etruscan tradition. Similarly the *pocola* of Rome and of Southern Etruria combined shapes which were typically regional with painted decoration taken directly from Tarentine models.

It is important to emphasize one fact which runs counter to accepted opinion, particularly in relation to Magna Graecia: Southern Italy at the beginning of the Hellenistic period has been credited with having had tremendous vitality, not only in respect of arts and crafts but also in the commercial sphere, which would presumably have been reflected in large quantities of exports. There is, however, no such evidence, at least so far as pottery is concerned.[2] Despite their originality and their quality, the products of this period were distributed over a range of only a few kilometres, or a few dozen kilometres in the case of the most successful.

There was nevertheless one important exception, namely the products of Rome and, in particular, the black-glazed vessels from the '*atelier des petites estampilles*'.[3] These vessels, admittedly carefully made but by no means remarkable for their artistic qualities, were widely distributed over Central Italy, from the Garigliano to the Adriatic and to Northern Etruria, an area centred on Rome. They were, moreover, exported overseas to Aleria in Corsica, throughout the coastal region extending from Liguria to Catalonia and in the territories dominated by Carthage (Africa, Western Sicily and Sardinia). Modest as they are, they bear witness to the growing commercial ambitions of Rome, which were exceptional in Italy at that time and which are confirmed by other indications such as the renewal of the treaty between Rome and Carthage and the development of the port of Ostia. From that era can be traced the formation of the Rome–Marseille–Carthage commercial triangle, which was to be strengthened, but with a quite different impetus, at the beginning of the second century.

---

[1] Characteristic examples in Forti 1965: (B 167); Montagna Pasquinucci 1972: (H 253); Morel, Torelli and Coarelli 1973: (B 186).   [2] Morel 1980: (B 184).   [3] Morel 1969: (H 254).

(iii) Art and architecture

Models and ideas spread more vigorously in the field of art than in that of ordinary craft products, which Central Italy had no great need to import. In art and at the highest levels of craft production (not easily distinguishable from art at the time) Rome in particular took part, perhaps especially actively, in a Central Italian *koiné* which had numerous links with Southern Italy and Sicily. Reference has already been made to the *pocola*, which were vessels bearing the name of a divinity in Latin, often combined with a graceful and imaginative painted decoration – decoration which was also found, but with no accompanying inscription, on other vessels which must be classified under the same heading.[4] Like the vases of Malacena, *pocola* combined a Central Italian basis (as regards shape) with unmistakably Greek influence (as regards painted decoration, which was similar to that on Gnathian ware and was probably the work of Tarentine artists). This phenomenon occurs in numerous examples of artistic or decorative work of this same period from Latium and Etruria, such as ornamental painting (in Etruria, black-glazed vessels of the Hesse group, or mural decoration like that of the Tomba dei Festoni at Tarquinia), or even, at the opposite extreme, 'triumphal' painting. This last type, of which only the most meagre traces remain, was probably very important in the tradition of Etruria (the François tomb), of Samnium (tombs at Paestum) and of Rome. In Rome it has survived only in one fragment found in a tomb on the Esquiline,[5] but a splendidly revealing example. The features which were always to typify Roman commemorative art (such as continuous narrative, the size of the figures proportionate to their rank, concern for detail and a didactic purpose expressed in this instance by written captions) are here combined with a high standard of execution which shows familiarity with the most recent advances in major Greek painting, such as the use of 'lights'.

Every aspect of art and artistic craftsmanship was involved in this renaissance, which took over the mastery of form and sometimes the moral purpose of Greek art. The small terracotta altars (*arulae*) often borrowed their iconographical and stylistic models from Southern Italy.[6] At the very time when the Athenians, in 280/79, erected in their agora a statue of Demosthenes as a symbol of intellectual conviction dedicated to the service of a great political cause, the Romans set up in their Forum statues of Alcibiades and of Pythagoras, respectively 'the bravest and the wisest of the Greeks'.[7] Numerous other statues, of great variety, reveal a high artistic standard and often similar influences, from the famous

[4] Morel, Torelli and Coarelli 1973, 57–69: (B 186).
[5] Coarelli, *RMR*, 200–8; *id.* 1976: (B 159).
[6] Ricciotti, *RMR*, 72–5.   [7] Pliny, *HN* XXXIV.26. See also Balty 1978: (H 224).

'Brutus' – difficult to interpret because so unusual but which it is tempting, despite controversy,[8] to attribute to this period – to the thousands of terracotta heads excavated from dozens of votive deposits thereabout Central Italy. These terracottas are particularly interesting, inasmuch as they were modelled by local artists with a freedom permitted by a complete mastery of their material, but also often with a fairly strong desire to emulate examples of Greek art of high quality. They thus reflect the diversity of the Italian reaction to these models. It remains none the less true that almost all of them indicate a facility, a solidity of construction and a care for detail which were not to be lost until the end of the third century, when they gave way to a degeneracy of style that revealed unmistakable signs of the gulf which was then opening up between 'great' and 'popular' art. Some of these votive offerings, temple decorations and portrait heads are of a quality which does indeed bring them very close to contemporary Greek art: among them the Fortnum head in Rome – 'one of the first examples, and perhaps the most indicative, of the close contact between Rome and non-colonial Greek culture';[9] the large and ambitious terracotta busts in the style of Praxiteles found at Ariccia, where the influence of Sicily and of Magna Graecia is clearly visible;[10] or again the pediment decoration of the great temple of the Scasato at Falerii Veteres, with the eclectic features typical of art in outlying areas.[11]

Also by the early third century Roman coinage included series of silver coins distinguishable from Greek coinage only by the legend, ROMANO, so hellenic was their style at that date, though it was soon to develop into something more truly 'Roman'.[12]

Greek influence is less apparent in architecture, where plans, elevations, decoration and materials remained very traditional. Marble, for example, continued to be totally unknown in the architecture of Central Italy. Rome at this time distinguished itself more by utilitarian achievements, such as roads and aqueducts, in which her genius was to continue to be outstanding. In 312 Appius Claudius Caecus marked out the Appian Way and constructed the first Roman aqueduct, the Aqua Appia, to be followed in 272 by the Anio Vetus.

The Greek style of architectural decoration, however, adapted to the local tufa, made a tentative and marginal appearance in a notable monument: the sarcophagus of Lucius Cornelius Scipio Barbatus (Fig. 1), which demonstrates an evident desire among the ruling class for a break with the Central Italian tradition. Such a break applied not only to decoration, in which there is obvious hellenic – and especially Syracusan

[8] Gross, *HIM*, 11.564–75: (H 192), with Torelli, *ibid.* 575–7.
[9] La Rocca, *RMR*, 197–9.   [10] Zevi Gallina, *RMR*, 321–4.   [11] La Rocca, *RMR*, 330–2.
[12] Crawford 1974, 1.44, and 11.745: (B 88).

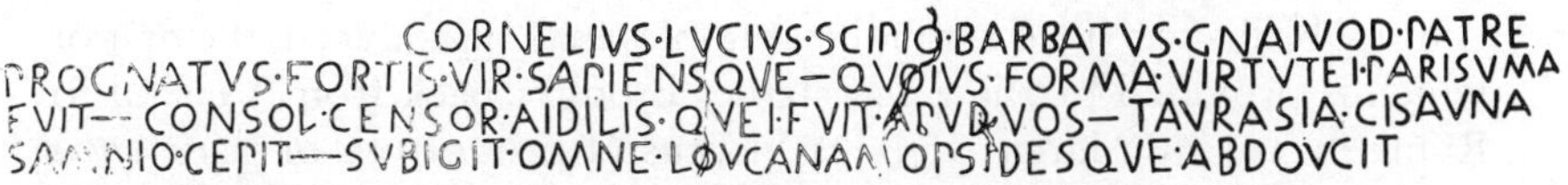

CORNELIVS·LVCIVS·SCIPIO·BARBATVS·GNAIVOD·PATRE
PROGNATVS·FORTIS·VIR·SAPIENSQVE—QVOIVS·FORMA·VIRTVTEI·PARISVMA
FVIT——CONSOL·CENSOR·AIDILIS·QVEI·FVIT·APVD·VOS—TAVRASIA·CISAVNA
SAMNIO·CEPIT——SVBIGIT·OMNE·LOVCANAM·OPSIDESQVE·ABDOVCIT

Fig. 1. The inscription on the sarcophagus of L. Cornelius Scipio Barbatus. (After F.
Coarelli, *Il sepolcro degli Scipioni* (Rome, 1972), 9. fig. 1.)

– inspiration, but also to the concept of the tomb itself as analogous to an
altar, and no longer to a house, which brought it into line with the Greek
Heroa. (In fact rock-tombs were no longer to be the rule, even in Etruria,
after the third century.) Similarly the *elogium* which was later inscribed on
this sarcophagus was consistent with the typically Greek idea of the
physical beauty of the person honoured, 'whose good looks were equal
to his valour': *quoius forma virtutei parisuma fuit.*[13]

b. *From the surrender of Tarentum to the beginning of the Second Punic War, 272–218 B.C.*

The surrender of Tarentum in 272, following closely on the ravages
caused in Southern Italy by the Pyrrhic War, is not merely a symbolic
date. Whatever may have been the fate of the city itself afterwards (a
much debated point, but it seems hard to deny that it experienced a
fundamental decline), its fall coincided with the end of the supremacy of
the culture of Magna Graecia, which during the preceding decades had
spread its influence across Central Italy. Subsequently, by contrast, each
Italian region tended rather to fall back on itself, either because it had
been hard hit, as in the case of the South, or because, generally speaking,
competition with Magna Graecia was less of a factor. At the same time,
however, another model was not slow to emerge – that of Rome. In this
connection, one year earlier, the date 273 marks a turning-point as
important as that of 272, for it was the year when the two Latin colonies
of Paestum and Cosa were founded, which were to set the imprint of
Rome on a Magna Graecia and on an Etruria both equally in decline.
From this time forward it must be noted that *Roman* models were being
implanted throughout Italy, especially in the sphere of town planning
and of architecture. These models did not necessarily have a wide impact,
but they already proclaimed, on these carefully chosen sites, a new type of
supremacy. A concomitant movement was the convergence on Rome,
and only on Rome, to a much greater extent than before, of the contributions of the most highly cultivated centres – no longer solely or even
principally through the medium of ideas or artists or craftsmen, but in
the form of objects or works of art plundered or taken from cities of

---

[13] *CIL* 1².7 = vi.1285. On the sarcophagus: Zevi, *RMR*, 236–9.

cultural brilliance. Two symbolic examples may be adduced, the first of which is provided by the 2,000 statues brought back from Volsinii to Rome in 264 by Marcus Fulvius Flaccus (a proportion of these *signa Tuscanica* was to adorn the *donaria* erected on the *area sacra* of S. Omobono in Rome, traces of which have been recovered[14]). This was the first of a long series of spoils which, during the third century, were progressively to empty Italy and Sicily of their substance, before it became the turn of Greece and of Asia Minor in the following century. The second example, which is perhaps even more symbolic of the desire of Rome at that time to appropriate the emblems of an artistic and scientific culture superior to her own although not yet capable of assimilating it, is the sundial brought in 263 from Catana by the consul Manius Valerius Messalla, who set it up on the Comitium without, however, adjusting it to the new latitude.[15]

The increasing hold of Rome on Italy can be observed in the network of new roads scoring the countryside and disturbing the established features of human geography (Map 16). The series had been inaugurated with the Via Appia in 312, to be followed by the Aurelia in 241, the Amerina at about the same time, the Flaminia and perhaps the Clodia in about 220 and others still to come – the Aemilia and the Cassia, the dates of which are controversial.[16] Designed to serve the needs of Rome's expansion, the movements of its army and the communications with its colonies, these roads often bypassed ancient cities, which thenceforward fell into decay.

It is easy to gain the impression that Italy at this period was sealed off into restricted areas between which there was little circulation of products or models. (This same applies, in a more general way, to the whole of the western basin of the Mediterranean at this same time, including Punic Africa and the Massaliote world.) It is an impression which rests, as will be seen, on valid evidence, but it must not obscure another process, at least equally important, which was then getting under way – the Romanization of Italy.

(i) Production and trade

Black-glazed pottery[17] once more provides a guideline, for reasons already mentioned. Compared with the preceding and subsequent periods, the years now under consideration are typified by more marked regional differences in Italy. Not only was Italy importing less than ever from Greece, but there was practically no trade even between one region

---

[14] Pliny, *HN* XXXIV.34. On the *donaria* see Mercando 1963–4: (H 251); Torelli 1968: (H 267).
[15] Varro *ap.* Pliny, *HN* VII.214; cf. Poccetti 1979, 77: (B 60).
[16] So Harris 1971, *passim*: (H 136), who tends to bring forward many generally accepted dates.
[17] Morel 1980, 94–9: (H 258); see also Morel, Torelli and Coarelli 1973, 49–50: (B 186).

and another. This state of affairs, too often forgotten, was the one which normally obtained with regard to pottery in Republican Italy. It had, however, been modified in earlier times and was to be modified still further in the next period by striking exceptions (mention has already been made of the '*atelier des petites estampilles*'). Between the first two Punic Wars, by contrast, there was no sign of any real exception. It is true that pottery decorated in relief known as 'Cales ware' is to be found on sites quite widely dispersed throughout Italy, chiefly in Northern Campania and in Etruria, and also on several sites overseas, but this was a type of pottery of exceptional technical and aesthetic qualities and even in this case the quantities recorded are insignificant. In other words, it is an exception which is of practically no account.

The regional differentiation of types of pottery makes a study of the products of this period very difficult, and they are probably among the least well known. However, this apparent differentiation must be qualified by certain observations. Pottery like the Cales ware mentioned above, manufactured at least to a large extent in Northern Campania, clearly took its inspiration from Etruscan traditions. On the other hand there is a common fund of styles to be noted among the local products of sites like Rome, Rimini, Cosa or Minturnae – a sign, among others, of the influence which Rome was then beginning to exercise in this field also.

The break with Greece proper and with Magna Graecia seems henceforward to have been complete. One archaic feature persisted, however, which brought Italy closer to Greek 'ceramic' culture: it was the survival of categories of terracotta vessels of a votive or ritual character. Thus there are the *phialai mesomphaloi* of Cales, certain vessels of Rome on which a painted 'H' denotes a dedication to Hercules, the 'Heraklesschalen' of Latium referring to the same god, and inscribed vessels from Rimini evoking various deities. Nevertheless, although these series reveal a dignity which pottery was to lose completely in the next century, each of them comprised only a negligible number of vessels and was frequently of no economic importance.

The pottery of the last three-quarters of the third century often presents another interesting aspect: quite a large number of black-glazed vessels (and, more seldom, ordinary vases or even objects of bronze) bear makers' marks (Fig. 2).[18] This phenomenon occurs regularly at all periods on amphoras and bricks, perhaps because these products of the *opus doliare*, being regarded as a sort of adjunct to agricultural production, were not demeaning to those who made them. It seems to have been otherwise with the semi-fine pottery, which, under the Republic, was hardly ever marked. The relative abundance of exceptions in the period

[18] Morel 1983, 22–4: (H 260).

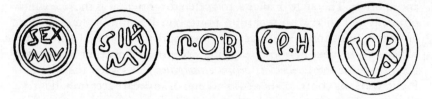

Fig. 2. Potters' marks from Cales, third century B.C. (After C. L. Woolley, *JRS* 1 (1911) 2, p. 203, fig. 39.)

under consideration is thus all the more striking. These signatures, whoever they designate (owners of workshops, managers, foremen, workers, or any of these as the case might be), throw some light on the working conditions of the time. In particular they reveal or confirm: (i) a certain pride or an attachment to their work on the part of the craftsmen, who were not yet reduced to the status of anonymous cog-wheels; (ii) a considerable partitioning of production (in one group of 159 marked fragments found at Cales there were 34 different marks with 17 different names – moreover, it is quite the exception to find a mark which is characteristic of pottery of one site on another site, however close at hand); (iii) the inclusion among these craftsmen of free men alongside slaves and perhaps freedmen. Thus the relief-ware from Cales was signed alike by a *L(ucius) Canoleius L(ucii) f(ilius) T(iti) n(epos)* and by a *K(aeso) Serponius V(ibii) s(ervus)* (Fig. 3). In short, it was a system of small workshops with slaves forming only a part of the workforce, which is consistent with the state of affairs in agriculture at the same period, where the peasant smallholding predominated and where slavery contributed only subsidiary or complementary labour. A fact which must be noted also, although not easy to interpret, is that the use of marks remained confined to that same region – Tyrrhenian Central Italy – where methods of production by slave labour were to flourish during the following century.

Towards the end of this period there are some signs of a resumption, still very tentative, of the export of Italian artifacts, including the Cales ware already mentioned and perhaps also the archaic Campanian A ware (a product of Naples) which is to be found still in remarkably small quantities in the Marseille area.

Exports of agricultural produce are more obvious and show that in certain areas of Italy a more vigorous system of agriculture was being instituted, especially in the cultivation of vines. It is possible to learn something about these exports from the so-called 'Graeco-Italic' amphoras,[19] spindle-shaped receptacles which were still very hellenic in

[19] Hesnard and Lemoine 1981, 243–8, 255, 257: (B 172); Manacorda 1981, 22–4: (H 248).

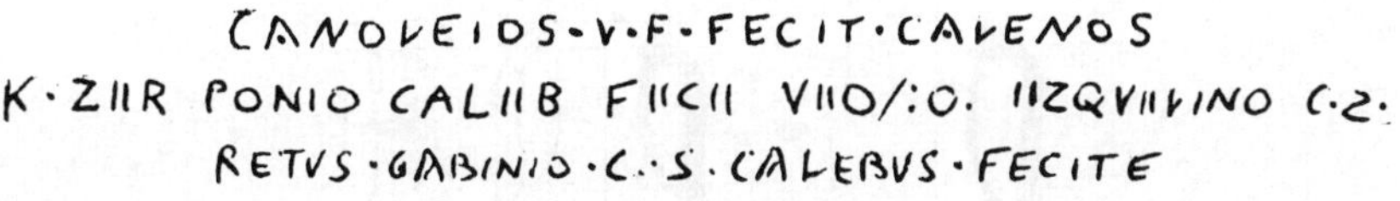

CANOVEIOS·V·F·FECIT·CAVENOS
K·ZIIR PONIO CALIIB FIICII VIIO/:O. IIZQVIIVINO C.Z.
RETVS·GABINIO·C.·S. CALEBVS·FECITE

Fig. 3. Potters' marks on relief-ware from Cales.

their general shape (Fig. 4). Some of them unquestionably go back to the third century, and a whole series of workshops has been located on the borders of Campania and Latium, in the plain of Fondi and in the neighbourhood of Sinuessa, near Cosa, mostly on coastal sites, which fits with what is known from other sources about the maritime export of these containers. Apart from their distribution within Tyrrhenian Italy, they were exported in the third century to localities and regions as various as the Adriatic coast, Vercelli (probably *via* Liguria) and Pech Maho in the Languedoc.[20] They provide evidence of the first export trading in agricultural produce from Italy of which there is tangible proof since the Etruscan wine amphoras of the seventh and sixth centuries. The fact that overseas trade had begun at this time to present an economic and political problem and was the basis of rivalry between factions is confirmed by the vote, at the very end of the period under consideration, of the Claudian plebiscite of 220/19. This vote restricted the capacity of ships owned by senators and their sons to '300 amphoras' – amphoras most probably of the Graeco-Italian type.

(ii) Architecture and town planning

From this time it was particularly Rome which dominated the interplay of loans and influences in central Italy. In the realms of commerce and politics, the *Urbs* endowed itself with new facilities. The first market conceived as such (*macellum*) in Rome probably dates from this period. At the beginning of the First Punic War a complete reconstruction of the Comitium gave it the appearance which it was to retain, essentially, until the end of the Republic: that of a circular place of assembly, with tiers on the inside, in imitation of the Greek and perhaps more specifically the Sicilian *ekklesiasteria*. (It was from Catana, as has been noted, that Manius Valerius Messalla took the sundial which he set up in the Comitium.) New techniques for decoration and for comfort were borrowed from the worlds of Greece and Carthage, such as the *opus signinum*, a kind of mosaic flooring which was in use in Rome and in Ostia from the middle of the third century at latest.[21] But when it was a question of refurbishing buildings of a ritualistic or religious character, such as the Regia (in 240),

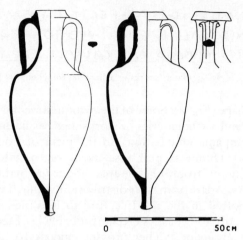

Fig. 4. Profiles of 'Greco-Italic' amphoras. (After Morel 1976, 477, fig. 5: (H 256).)

there was a tendency to respect the traditional designs. Tufa, with the addition of travertine, still continued to be the standard material when the *area sacra* of S. Omobono was rebuilt in 264 (it was then that Marcus Fulvius Flaccus erected an *ex-voto* adorned with statues taken from Volsinii), as it was for the temples erected during the First Punic War in the Forum Olitorium by Gaius Duilius or Aulus Atilius Calatinus.

The Latin colonies founded at this time (of which Cosa and Paestum are the best examples) received at the outset *fora* containing copies of models provided by Rome: temples of Jupiter, circular *comitia* and *tabernae* (Fig. 5). This was a particularly striking innovation in a city already as ancient and as well laid out as Paestum, where the planning of a forum with a square measuring 157 m by 57 m could be achieved only by cutting deep into the existing urban fabric, to the detriment of part of the sanctuary of Hera. The hypothesis cannot be excluded that the celebrated ground-plan of this city, as revealed by excavation and by aerial photography, may date from this period. As for Cosa, it represents an exception in Central–Southern Etruria and extends northward the expansion-zone of the great architectural innovations from Latium and Campania. In Roman colonies, too, such as Minturnae and Ostia, the *fora* reflected the 'will to power' of Rome and her unifying influence.[22]

Other towns, although not colonies, likewise bear witness to the hold which Rome had on Italy and the standstill brought about in the development of local cultures. A very significant instance is the transplantation of the ancient Etruscan and Faliscan centres of Volsinii and Falerii to the new sites of Volsinii Novi and Falerii Novi, selected in

[22] Drerup, *HIM*, II.401–4: (B 163). Paestum: Greco and Theodorescu 1980, 10 and 22: (B 168). Cosa: Brown 1979: (H 231).

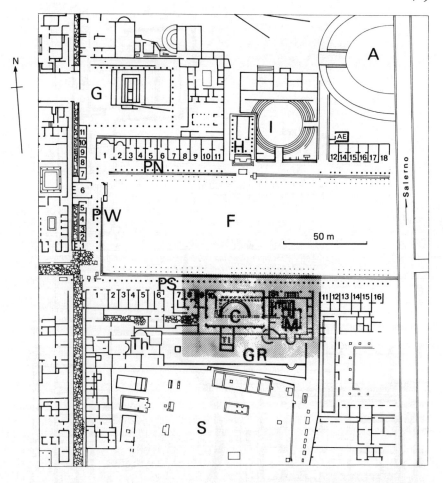

Fig. 5. Plan of the forum of Paestum. (After Greco and Theodorescu 1980, 48, fig. 2: (B 168).)
KEY: A: amphitheatre; AE: aerarium (public treasury); C: *curia*; F: forum; G: gymnasium; GR: 'Roman garden'; H: *capitolium*; I: *comitium*; M: *macellum*; PS, PW, PN: porticoes (south, west, north); S: Heraeum (sanctuary of Hera); St: stoa; Th; thermal baths; TG: Greek temple; TI: Italic temple; 1–18 *tabernae* (shops).

compliance with the interests of Rome – interests shortly to be consolidated by the planning of the new Roman roads, the Via Amerina to Falerii Novi and the Via Cassia to Volsinii Novi. It may be said of Falerii Novi in particular, built as it was on virgin ground to be the new centre of the region, that it constituted 'an impressive symbol of *Romanitas*'.[23]

Apart from towns which were so to speak the show-case of Roman

[23] Potter 1979, 99: (B 188).

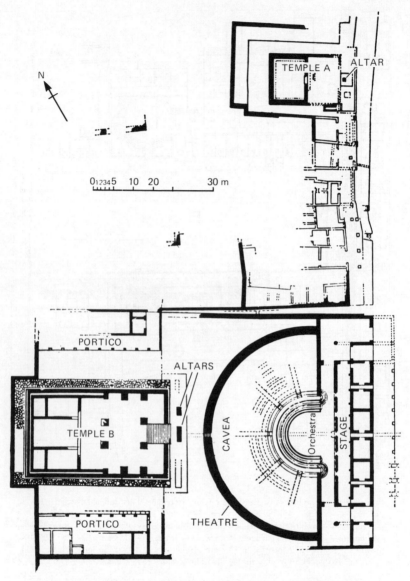

Fig. 6. Plan of the sanctuary of Pietrabbondante. (After Strazzulla 1971, 11, fig. 1: (H 265).)

colonization or conquest, town planning and architectural activity proceeded very unevenly in the various regions. Magna Graecia had not recovered from the wars of the first decades of the third century; Central and Southern Etruria had been severely tried. Northern Campania, on the other hand, at sites like Teano or Cales, showed a vitality attested not by

dwellings, about which very little is yet known, but by sanctuaries with
rich votive deposits. However, what must be noted especially is the
emergence of a region like Samnium, which henceforth became receptive
to Greek influence. On the future site of the great temple of
Pietrabbondante (temple B), erected towards the end of the second
century, there was constructed in the second half of the third century a
sanctuary of a very highly developed type, composed of porticoes around
a temple with Ionic capitals (Fig. 6). The terracotta elements of these have
been recovered and a *favissa* containing, among others, arms which were
probably of Tarentine origin. This sanctuary was being built at the very
time when in the Latin colony of Isernia, quite close at hand, Italian
models which were unmistakably archaic were still being adopted for the
podium of the principal temple.[24]

Generally speaking, it is important to observe at this time the use –
which was largely to disappear subsequently in the face of a certain
tendency towards unification – of local and traditional methods of
construction, such as a structure of dry stone at Bolsena, or the *opus
craticium* at Aufidena, which consisted of a clay structure supported by an
armature of wood, on a stone base.[25] Again, the Circus Flaminius, built by
Gaius Flaminius who was censor in 221/20, is a reminder, with its
probably wooden structure,[26] that technical innovations and new
materials still remained the exceptions, even in the *Urbs*.

(iii) Art

The last three-quarters of the third century were not, in Italy, a particularly
brilliant period for art; it did not even benefit from the thrust of Roman
expansion, which spread architectural achievements throughout Italy at
the same time. Moreover, it was not long before the rare art-forms which,
about the middle of the century, still testified to the competence and
originality of certain regions of Italy, began to decline or to disappear. The
second half of the third century saw the extinction of the soft-stone reliefs
of Tarentum and of the Etruscan cista and carved mirrors, and the decline
of the painted tombs of Tarquinia, the rock cemeteries of inner Etruria
and the limestone busts of Praeneste. The capitals with human or divine
figures to be seen then at Paestum, Teggiano, Sovana and Vulci
disappeared at the end of the century.[27] At this period there was no longer
much pottery of any artistic pretensions, apart from the last off-shoots of

[24] Strazzulla 1972, 42–4: (H 265); La Regina, *HIM*, 1.223–6: (H 142).
[25] Bolsena: Balland and others 1971, 55: (B 148); Alfedena: La Regina, *HIM*, 1.219: (H 142).
[26] This is at least the view of Zevi 1976, 1048–9: (B 208).
[27] On these various kinds of evidence, see in particular Bianchi Bandinelli, *RIGS*, 547; Carter,
Atti Taranto x (1970) 288; Coarelli, *RIGS*, 299; *id.* 1977, 35–6: (H 239); Colonna Di Paolo and
Colonna 1978, 511: (B 162). Greco Pontrandolfo and Greco 1981, 1.50: (H 95); Torelli, *RIGS*, 301 and
437: (H 268); *id. HIM*, 1.100: (H 269).

North Etruscan production called 'Malacena' ware, sometimes decorated in relief, and the Cales ware, also in the Etruscan tradition despite its place of manufacture – of considerable interest, but numerically insignificant.

One of the most widely distributed forms of artistic expression, often the most significant of this period, is represented by the *ex-voto* of the innumerable votive deposits dispersed about Central Italy. These terracotta statues, heads and statuettes, in all their diversity, are evidence that their creators, the craftsmen of the small towns of Campania, Latium and Samnium, possessed if not great originality at least an effective assimilation of the Hellenistic forms which had invaded Italy at the end of the fourth century and at the beginning of the third century.[28] In the course of the third century, however, these naturalistic forms tended to disintegrate and a preference became apparent for an Italic canon which flattened the heads, making them almost two-dimensional, stiffened postures and merged the lines of bodies into vague masses – developments which are to be observed also in the Etruscan and Italic 'bronzetti' with their increasingly elongated and unreal shapes. In both instances, compared with what had preceded them, 'it was, in short, something different'.[29]

It was as if, since the Magna Graecia models had ceased to exist and the new models to be presented by Greece and the eastern world were not yet easily available, there was a kind of pause or a period of confusion in artistic creation – at least if measured by the standard of hellenization. Pliny dates the 'death of art' to 296; R. Bianchi Bandinelli adduces good reasons for preferring to set the essential turning-point in the middle of the third century.[30]

This void is to be observed even in the case of Rome, where artistic activity was almost confined to 'borrowings' or rather plunder, as with the 2,000 statues from Volsinii. The few genuinely Roman works known from texts to date to this period, from which hardly any concrete evidence has survived in the realm of art, belong to the most traditional form of Roman 'triumphal' art, designed to commemorate. Examples include the battle-scene, *tabula proelii*, set up in the Curia of the Senate by Manius Valerius Maximus Messalla, the consul of 262, to celebrate his victory over Hiero II of Syracuse, the statues of *imperatores*, such as the one of himself which Gaius Duilius caused to be erected after 260, or the famous rostrated column of that same Duilius, which shows the direction taken by the Roman quest for originality in architectural ornamentation at that time.[31]

[28] Bonghi Jovino 1976: (H 230).
[29] Torelli, *RIGS*, 301. For a clear synthesis of the development of Italian bronzes see Colonna 1971: (H 236).   [30] Pliny, *HN* XXXIV.52; Bianchi Bandinelli 1977, 490: (H 229).
[31] Pliny, *HN* XXXIV.20, XXXV.22; Quint. 1.7, 12; Serv. *Georg.* III.29; Martina 1980, 143–4: (H 50).

II. FROM THE SECOND PUNIC WAR TO THE GRACCHI, 218–133 B.C.

a. A new context

The year 200 or, more exactly, the end of the Second Punic War might well be considered a crucial turning-point in the history and consequently in the archaeology of Italy. On closer scrutiny, however, it might be more proper to trace back to the actual outbreak of this war, in 218, the origin of the numerous upheavals which affected both economic conditions and art, and the beginning of what P. Veyne has called the 'second hellenization' of Rome.[32]

It is well known what major social changes took place during these critical years, characterized notably by the widening of the gulf between an oligarchy, which from this time was closing its ranks ever more completely, and the most exposed and proletarian social strata, by the recrudescence of the 'triumphal' ideology, by the slave mode of production, by the severe blows inflicted on smallholdings and by the conflicts between tradition and innovation, between *religio* and *superstitio*. The question to be resolved here is how these new conditions are revealed in the archaeological evidence.

These changes were essentially attributable to the oncoming triumphant tide of Roman imperialism. *Devicta Asia* (Pliny) and *Graecia capta* (Horace) were recognized by Romans of later generations as the most obvious causes of the cultural upheaval attending the end of the Republic.[33] The conquests achieved by Rome made their impact in a surge of new possibilities and incentives, firstly in the form of material riches at its disposal (primarily in money, but also in precious ores or materials hitherto almost unavailable, like marble). Cultural wealth also resulted from the convergence on Rome of the spoils of war and the plundering of celebrated cities and regions of ancient civilization, from Syracuse, Capua and Tarentum to Corinth and Carthage, not to mention Macedonia and Asia Minor.[34] Some key dates established by the historians are reflected in the archaeological evidence: for example, the end of the Third Macedonian War in 168 had its echo a year later in the construction of the *Porticus Octavia*, which introduced a hellenic style of architecture to Rome. The year 146 marked the fall of Corinth and of Carthage (the concurrence of these two events was given a symbolic sanction, so to speak, by the joint censorship of Scipio Aemilianus and Lucius Mummius in 142); it was also,

---

[32] Veyne 1979, 11: (H 216).
[33] Pliny, *HN* xxxiv.34 (see also xxxiii.148, and Livy xxxix.6.7–9); Hor. *Epist.* ii.1.156.
[34] Bianchi Bandinelli 1969, 36–9: (H 226); for Syracuse see Gros 1979: (H 191).

as will be seen, the date of the construction of the first marble temple in Rome, that of Jupiter Stator.

The forcible importation of works of art and the arrival of Greek artists (for whom henceforth Rome was to be the most reliable and most profitable source of patronage) brought to Rome a great range of examples and models; and this diversity was to stamp Roman art indelibly with the seal of eclecticism. At the same time an unprecedented traffic in slaves[35] (the number of captives increasing tenfold between the third and the second centuries, with Delos becoming the hub from 167 onwards) caused the convergence on Rome both of experts in various art-forms and of a miscellaneous workforce which in certain fields was to revolutionize conditions of production.

Rome did not confine herself to accepting merchandise, prototypes and craftsmanship. Having become by degrees mistress of the western and then of the eastern Mediterranean, she multiplied her ventures there; perhaps the most characteristic instance was the activity on Delos of the *Rhomaioi*, in the widest sense of the term. They demonstrated the power of penetration of the Italian economy and in return were themselves subjected to influences which, in some cases, affected even rather modest social strata – manifested above all in a certain type of portrait or a certain type of house.

As mistress of the Mediterranean, Rome was more than ever disposed to exercise her predominance in Italy, and archaeological evidence makes this quite clear. For example, modern scholarship agrees in dating the introduction of the *denarius* to the period of the Second Punic War. The *denarius* initially circulated alongside the *victoriatus*, a lighter denomination struck in debased silver, and these coins were minted in widely dispersed workshops. However, the *victoriatus* had ceased to be struck by 165, which resulted in the *denarius* circulating throughout Italy, while at the same time the provincial workshops were being gradually closed down and the whole of the minting concentrated in Rome[36] – an obvious indication, in this sphere, of the primacy of the *Urbs*.

In certain regions of Italy, some of which had already suffered hardship at the time of the Pyrrhic War, the Second Punic War marked the beginning, or the renewal, of a deep recession, attested by a complete gap in archaeological documentation – a gap which has perhaps been sometimes exaggerated, but which it would be even more misleading to try to deny too systematically (as often happens through failure to take account of pottery dating). It is the case in Apulia, for sites such as Monte Sannace, Herdonea, Tarentum, Venusia. It is the case in Bruttium as a

---

[35] Hoffmann, *RIGS*, 501: (H 98).
[36] Zehnacker 1976, 1042–3: (B 147). For a general review of this period see Zehnacker 1973, 1.323–476: (B 146).

whole, at Picentia in Southern Campania, and finally in Southern or Central-Southern Etruria, for sites such as Tarquinia (at least from the middle of the second century) and Lucus Feroniae.

At the same time, here and there and occasionally even in regions affected by the post-Hannibalic *Italiae solitudo*, islands of prosperity survived or asserted themselves, as for example Canusium, Brundisium, Luceria and Lupiae in Apulia or Volterra in Northern Etruria.[37] Among them were isolated pockets of hellenism, including Naples, of course, but also Ancona, where archaeology has uncovered funerary deposits that show some astonishingly original features for an increasingly Romanized Central Italy.[38]

The second century B.C. marked in Italy the beginning and, with the following century, also the culmination of the slave mode of production, which was obviously favoured by the incredible influx of slaves already mentioned and by the growing class-differentiation at the heart of Roman society which in turn it tended to promote. At the same time as this innovation there appeared another, indissolubly linked with it and resulting from the same social climate: this was the development of *luxuria*, with all the reactions and controversies arising from it. The period extending from the Second Punic War to the middle of the second century witnessed a proliferation of sumptuary laws, from the *lex Oppia* of 215 to the *lex Licinia* of 140,[39] and these were indicative of an intense debate within a ruling class divided in face of the innovations which were invading the *Urbs*. Expenditure was encouraged only for public purposes. It remains to examine the archaeological data for traces of all these changes.

b. Production

(i) Agricultural production

Despite its preponderant importance in the economy of ancient Italy, little is yet known about agriculture in its specific aspects, especially for the period under review. Of three possible approaches to the subject – nature of landed property, agrarian technique and trade in agricultural products – only the last has been made the subject of relatively extensive study.

The *villa* of the Catonian type where, thanks to slave labour, fairly

---

[37] For examples of opposing views on the decadence or prosperity of these various zones see Coarelli, *Atti Taranto* x (1970) 201–2 (Taranto); Harris 1977: (H 96) (a carefully differentiated account of Northern Etruria); Mertens 1965: (B 183); Morel, *Atti Taranto* x (1970) 412 (Taranto); Potter 1979, *passim*: (B 188) (with perhaps too optimistic a view of the state of Southern Etruria in the second century); Sgubini Moretti and Bordenache Battaglia 1975, 95: (B 199) (Lucus Feroniae); Torelli, *RIGS*, 439 (Apulia); *id. HIM*, 1.103–4: (H 269) (Volterra).

[38] Mercando, *HIM*, 1.161–70: (H 252).   [39] Clemente 1981, III.1–14: (H 85).

specialized agriculture was practised on quite a large scale and the products in great measure sold, is beginning to be familiar to archaeologists, but chiefly in relation to subsequent periods. No attempt will be made here to embark on a discussion as to whether in the second century the smallholding was driven out by the large estate[40] – a question which obviously must receive varying answers in different decades and different regions. Moreover, a form of co-existence may have persisted for some time here and there. (There remains, however, an archaeological problem which it is hard to solve with certainty, for a farm of which traces can be discovered in the ground, whether walls or potsherds, may equally well represent the whole of a small property or part of a large one.) In any case, the limited persistence of the smallholding is much less significant than the innovation represented by the appearance, sometimes concurrently with the former system, of large-scale cultivation based on slave labour.

What in fact seems certain is that in some regions, dating from the second century and perhaps even from the end of the third century, there are remains of *villae* which can be described as Catonian in type and which existed on the one hand in Campania and on its borders (at Buccino, at Pompeii, in the Sarno valley, in the *ager Campanus*, in the *ager Falernus* and at Venafrum) and on the other hand in coastal Etruria (at Castrum Novum and at Cosa). Such archaeological evidence, together with the literary sources confirmed and completed by it, provides grounds for conjecturing that there occurred an 'extraordinary development of Italian agriculture in the second century B.C.'.[41]

Cato is insistent that the landowner whose property he describes must seek to sell his produce: he must be *vendax*,[42] and it is on this precise point that archaeology is now able to supply the most detailed information, as a result of the study of wrecks and of amphoras.

The ships in which Italian agricultural produce was exported overseas are a perfect illustration of this new or at any rate consolidated tendency (the Graeco-Italic amphoras must not be forgotten which, as already mentioned, had their origins in the third century) to regard agricultural produce as *merchandise* intended primarily for sale. The examination of wrecks found in the western Mediterranean in fact reveals the unquestionable predominance of those which can be dated to the second and first centuries B.C. (representing, as they do, more than half of the

---

[40] See especially Frederiksen, *RIGS*, 330–57: (H 41); and the general discussion at 359–62.
[41] Torelli 1977, 541: (H 270). On the whole subject of archaeological traces of the existence of *villae* see e.g. Frederiksen, *RIGS*, 359–62 (to be treated sometimes with reserve in the matter of dating); Holloway 1974, 25–32: (B 173); Johannowsky 1981, 307: (H 245); Torelli, *RIGS*, 435: (H 268); cf. also Polyb. III.91.2–3 and 92; Livy XXII.15.   [42] Cato, *Agr.* II.7.

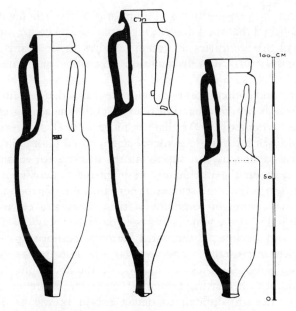

Fig. 7. Profiles of Dressel I amphoras. (After Morel 1976, 476, fig. 4: (H 256).)

discoveries), and among them an overwhelming majority of wrecks with a cargo mainly of wine amphoras.[43]

It is in fact these amphoras, whether found on land or under the sea, which must now be examined and they indicate a change of trend in the first decades of the second century. Hitherto, Italy had already been exporting wine, in Graeco-Italic amphoras, but in very small quantities. She was also importing wine, in amphoras chiefly from Rhodes but some also from Cos. Now, these latter disappeared, except perhaps from certain more conservative regions like the Adriatic coast and its hinterland, after the beginning of the second century.[44] Conversely, the production – and export – of Italian wine amphoras (and naturally of their contents) increased at a bewildering rate. The amphoras were at first Graeco-Italic and then of the type known as Dressel I (Fig. 7). The manner and the chronology of the change from one type to the other are not yet known exactly, but it appears certain that, until the end of the Republican era, the Dressel I amphora was to provide the most tangible evidence of Italian agriculture based on slave labour and of its ability to secure distant markets, especially in Africa and in Gaul. Now it must be noted that this amphora, which was clearly created to symbolize an increasingly successful product of Tyrrhenian Italy, represents in its

[43] Lequément and Liou 1975: (H 162).   [44] Baldacci, *RIGS*, 323.

whole form the very antithesis of amphoras of the hellenic type. It has been established that the Dressel I type amphoras were produced in the second and first centuries at numerous sites in Campania, Southern Latium and Etruria, not to mention imitations of it manufactured overseas.[45]

A similar and contemporary development was that certain regions of peninsular Italy began at that time to export oil. Archaeological evidence shows this particularly for Apulia[46] or, more precisely, for certain coastal areas around Brundisium – evidence again based on amphoras, which were in use particularly for supplying the markets for Cisalpine Gaul.

There was, on the one hand, an intensive system of agriculture, directed towards the large-scale commercialization of produce requiring complex processing. In complete contrast, there also existed in many regions of Italy – those which have been described above as undergoing recession and decline in the third century, comprising, essentially, Bruttium, the interior of Lucania and a large part of Apulia – an economy founded on extensive stock-rearing and on the development of forests yielding timber for construction and for heating, charcoal and pitch.[47] These activities are difficult to detect except by means of negative evidence, that is to say by the gap in the archaeological record which they leave in the areas concerned. It is, however, certain that some of the indications which can be mustered here and there by a cross-checking of the few available sources apply also to the second century B.C., and these affirm that never was the contrast so marked as at this time and in the following century between regions practising advanced agricultural techniques and that other Italy, colonized so to speak from within.

(ii) Craft production

For craft products, the pattern remained that of scattered small workshops; archaeological traces of them have survived here and there, but little progress has been made with the study of them. Against this background, which changed very little from one period to another, it is easier to distinguish the few exceptions which in themselves reveal the peculiarities of this period: several important manufacturing centres producing goods largely for export.

With regard to metalwork, an essential activity, for which archaeological evidence is all too often elusive (since objects disappear over the centuries as a result of melting-down or oxydization), it is necessary to have recourse to a body of literary, epigraphical and archaeological

[45] Hesnard and Lemoine 1981, 243–8 and 257: (B 172); Manacorda 1981, 13–24: (H 248). On the stylistic tendencies of the Dressel I amphoras see Morel, *HIM,* II.477–80: (H 256).
[46] Baldacci 1972, 9: (H 223).
[47] Morel 1975, 301–4: (H 255); Giardina 1981, I.87–113: (H 94).

information which often leaves much to be desired, especially in the matter of chronology. At Pozzuoli the working of iron with ore from the island of Elba presents all the appearance of a highly organized and standardized industry, the products of which were widely exported.[48] The geographical concentration, the juxtaposition of numerous workers and the distribution of functions (between groups of workmen, between middlemen and traders) are all indications of an organization that went far beyond craft level. It is possible that the production of the famous bronzes of Capua was accomplished in such conditions at this same period (which also, incidentally, saw the increasing use of furniture and dishes made of bronze). However, the actual chronology is still poorly attested. What is certain in any case is the regrouping of the coinage workshops, which from this time onward were concentrated in Rome, for silver as well as for bronze, as has been indicated. But once again it is pottery which gives the best insight into the development of Italy in about the year 200, thanks to its having been better preserved over the centuries. (Texts, on the other hand, contain nothing on the subject, which shows what gaps exist in the information available on the Roman economy.)

As in the third century, there is evidence of a host of small pottery workshops over the whole of Italy, the products of each being distributed within a radius of only a few kilometres. These conditions were the same for all types of pottery – black-glazed, red-glazed, utilitarian, etc. The fame of some of them may be misleading in relation to the insignificance of their economic and commercial impact. A typical case is that of the 'Popiliusbecher', bowls ornamented in relief which were manufactured in Umbria.[49] These vessels are interesting for their marks, which represent both free men and slaves, and also for their patterns. It would, however, be quite wrong to regard them as indicating an 'important industrial development' in Umbria at the end of the third century and at the beginning of the second century,[50] for their number remains negligible. The same argument applies to the production of other bowls decorated in relief which have been discovered at various places in Italy: in all cases only a few examples are known, or at most only a few dozen. Certain workshops producing black-glazed ware, by contrast, have left signs of immeasurably greater activity, as will be seen later.

Pottery production in second-century Italy confirms the break with hellenic tradition which has already been noted in respect of the second half of the third century. This applies *a contrario* to bowls decorated in relief, which were very Greek in appearance (though not without some

---

[48] Diod. Sic. v.13. On metallurgical production see Morel 1975, 287–93: (H 255).

[49] See most recently Verzar, *HIM*, 1.121–2: (H 272); Morel, *ibid.* 11.486–8: (H 256). On this and other similar products see Marabini Moevs 1980: (H 250).   [50] Verzar 1981, 1.376: (H 273).

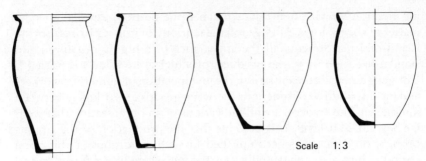

Scale   1:3

Fig. 8. Typical profiles of thin-walled pottery of the Republican period. (After Marrabini Moevs, 1973: (H 249).)

important points of difference) but which did not properly take root in the Italian environment at the time when they were plentiful in Greece. It applies also, as has been observed, to the Dressel I amphoras. It applies to lamps, which are black-glazed products, turned on a wheel, undecorated and usually unsigned, as distinct from the grey-glazed, moulded, decorated and signed lamps prevalent among the Greeks. Finally, it applies to those thin-walled vases which made their appearance in the first half of the second century and which also departed from the secular traditions of hellenism both in decoration and in shape (Fig. 8). These last, in particular, were reunited with continental traditions, 'Nordic' and especially 'Celtic', thus providing a typical example of the appropriation by Italian workshops of a new market in full swing.[51]

However, the originality of the second century – and of the first century – is revealed most of all in two or three important series of black-glazed pottery.[52] The most characteristic of them is the 'Campanian Type A', manufactured, with clay obtained from Ischia, in Naples (where a workshop has been discovered) and possibly also in Ischia. Without going into details, the essential features may be noted as follows. With regard to technique, a non-calcareous paste was used, a process which was relatively elementary for that period. In the matter of shape and decoration, there were simple outlines not requiring an elaborate finish and the shapes were generally 'open', with few vessels designed for pouring or for drinking (with a view to convenience not only of manufacture but also of transport, since such vessels could be stacked in piles without difficulty); patterns were repeated indefinitely, without major variations. As for production there was an absolute geographical concentration for more than a century and a half (from 200 to 40 B.C.

[51] On these various types of pottery see Marabini Moevs 1973: (H 249); Morel, HIM, II.491–7: (H 256); Torelli, ibid. II.497; Pavolini 1981, II.144–52: (H 262); Ricci 1981, II.126–7: (H 264).

[52] For general information on these products see Morel 1980, 100–5: (H 258); Morel 1981, II.87–97: (H 259).

approximately); total anonymity, no mark having been observed on any one of tens of thousands of fragments; a high degree of standardization; and an enormous output. With regard to trade, the exports went almost exclusively overseas, being shipped as merchandise accompanying agricultural produce, a practice which considerably reduced the cost of transport; and they were distributed on a large scale, were being transported over great distances throughout the whole of the western Mediterranean, and even – most exceptionally for products of Italian manufacture – reaching Delos.

Campanian Type A pottery thus presents in exemplary fashion the characteristics of production methods based on slave labour. It is a typical instance of a product regarded primarily as merchandise, that is to say, considered in terms of its exchange value rather than its usage value. At the same time, however, it must be realized that it remained an exception among Italian ceramic products, to which it continued to be subsidiary in Italy itself except in certain coastal locations.

There existed other black-glazed pottery similar to it, but with less pronounced features, as, for example, Campanian Type C, manufactured in Syracuse or its neighbourhood, the export of which to distant markets began at some time yet to be determined in the second century (but in much smaller quantities than Type A). More important was a group centred around Campanian Type B, which was a black-glazed ware from the north or north-central coastal area of Etruria, later to be imitated by workshops in various regions of Italy and particularly in Northern Campania. (It is probable that of these workshops some were branch establishments of the original manufacturers, others competitors imitating a successful product.) However, this pottery, although manifesting many of the characteristics which have been defined above as belonging to Campanian Type A, nevertheless departs from the latter in certain other features which in some respects place it in another world and which presage a turning-point to be amply confirmed in the Augustan era (perfection of technique, more varied shapes, distribution less exclusively by sea, etc.). Campanian Type A thus remains as unique as it is indicative of the changes which took place in certain Italian communities in about the year 200.

It may be noted that the most important of the products just described (Campanian Type B and its imitations, Campanian Type A) came from areas where at the same time agriculture specializing in wine production was being developed with the greatest success, that is to say the central and northern parts of the Etrurian coast, Southern Latium and Northern Campania. It was in these areas that production by means of slave labour (and this applies to other forms of craftsmanship also) was most prevalent, surrounding the city of Rome which was inclined to confine herself to more traditional activities, and to a role as a consumer rather than a producer of goods for profit.

On another plane there is also a marked break between two types of craft product: luxury artifacts and artifacts for daily use, a distinction often still difficult to make a century earlier. Thus pottery renounced all pretensions to art or luxury, except in products which were dying out (the last pieces of ceramic ware from Cales or Malacena) or which were strictly marginal (the bowls decorated in relief). At the same time the use of bronze and silver vessels (and also of valuable furniture) became more general among the well-to-do social classes, even in ordinary daily life.

The Romans were well aware of the upheavals of this kind brought about by conquest, in Italy and elsewhere. *Luxuria* was expressed in terms of craftsmanship (and, as will be seen, the same applied to art), not so much by general raising of the standard of products as by the disparity between luxury objects, notable for the sometimes dazzling opulence of materials or workmanship, and miscellaneous objects devoid of all artistic pretensions (thus objects in 'popular' use ceased to imitate luxury objects, such for example as metal drinking vessels of typical and complex shape).[53] This division was to continue until the Augustan era, when the *sigillata* of Arretium were to mark a rehabilitation of ceramic craftsmanship (though only for a few decades).

c. Architecture and art

(i) General observations

In this field also the Second Punic War signalled a fundamental break with the preceding period. The reasons were mainly the same as applied to the development of craft and agricultural production, but the visible results were different.

Italy, which at this time played an active pioneering part in economic affairs, was much more receptive (which does not mean passive) in respect of art and architecture, where the influx of specialists and of extra-Italian models was most noticeable. After the closing years of the third century these came not so much from Magna Graecia and Sicily – henceforth mere shadows of themselves, although the plundering of Verres demonstrated that their resources would continue to attract the covetous for a long time to come – as from Greece proper, Macedonia, the Aegean islands and Asia Minor. Booty flowed in from Greece and the Near East, together with the artists whom conquering generals brought back with them or who were drawn by the numerous commissions offered by Rome, now predominant in Italy and even in the Mediterra-

[53] On this whole question see Coarelli, *RIGS*, 264–5; Morel 1981, 503–8: (B 185).

nean world as a whole. Italians of all social classes and all types of specialization (including architects such as Dekmos Kossoutios Popliou Rhomaios who in 174 was working on the construction of the Athens Olympieium) were circulating throughout the countries of the eastern Mediterranean. These were all factors which combined to open up for Italy the range of opportunities and of novel experiences.[54]

This process of hellenization was a very complex phenomenon – complex in its motivation, in which were united a sense of frustration at the spectacle of a dazzling civilization and, on the part of certain members of the *nobilitas*, an 'arrogant desire for a break with tradition'[55] (an element which served appreciably to accentuate the split between academic art and everyday artistic production, analogous, *mutatis mutandis*, to that which has been indicated in relation to the craftsmen, and also to create a gulf between 'urban' art and that of the Italic communities). It was also complex in its modes of application, so that pure and simple transpositions of hellenic models in Italy (and in this case the graft was not usually very successful) were to be found side by side with adaptations of these models to the new conditions. It was symbolic of this process of adaptation, and also of its slowness, that while in 263 the first sundial introduced into Rome was – as has been described – left with the same setting as had been required for the latitude of Catana, whence it came, it was necessary to wait until 164 for Rome to be at last provided, by the censor Quintus Marcius Philippus, with a correctly regulated sundial.[56]

(ii) Architecture

Techniques and materials; marble and 'opus caementicium'   There are two innovations which adequately sum up this mixture of loans of Hellenic origin and strictly Roman innovations which characterized second-century architecture: the use of marble and the introduction of *opus caementicium*.

Marble, which in Italy was always an import until such time as the quarries of Luna (Carrara) began to be exploited under Augustus, came to be used in Rome only at a late date (a marble cist of the fifth century being merely the exception which proves the rule).[57] Not until 190 were two marble fountain-basins (*labra*) installed in the *Urbs* by Publius Cornelius Scipio Africanus.[58] In 173 the theft – or, if preferred, the impounding – of the marble tiles from the sanctuary of Hera Lacinia at

[54] On spoils and on artists see Bianchi Bandinelli, *RIGS*, 215: (H 228); Coarelli, *ibid.* 249–50: (H 233); also Livy xxxix.22.2 and 10; on Cossutius: Cassola, *RIGS*, 306; Torelli 1980: (H 118).
[55] Gros 1976, 402: (H 241).   [56] Pliny, *HN* vii.214.
[57] Colini, *RMR*, 196–7.   [58] Livy xxxvii.3.7.

Croton by the censor Quintus Fulvius Flaccus, who wished to use them
to adorn the temple of Fortuna Equestris which he was building in
Rome, illustrates simultaneously the envious fascination which this
material aroused in the Romans of that time, the dearth of it which
prevailed on the banks of the Tiber and, generally speaking, the lack of
experts in Italy. In fact, there was no one capable of putting these tiles
back into place when at last the scandalized Roman Senate had ordered
their restitution.[59] Marble became relatively familiar in Central Italy, and
particularly in Rome, only as one kind of booty among others accruing
from conquests in Greece and in Asia Minor. In this connection it is
highly significant that the first temple to be constructed entirely of
marble, the temple of Jupiter Stator, coincided in date with the capture of
Corinth.

Opus caementicium, on the other hand, was an Italian innovation – one
of those which were to have most productive results. This method of
construction consisted of dipping into a mortar of lime and sand small
pieces of stone of irregular shapes, within a wooden casing which could
be removed as soon as the filling had set. If the surface of the wall was to
be visible, the stones, although irregular, could be given a smoother,
more compact finish. It was a case then of *opus incertum*, in which the
degree of finish might be variable.

The date and the exact place of the advent of this new technique in Italy
have given rise to discussion. Campania and Latium are the two possible
candidates for the region of origin. As to date, the podium of the temple
of Cybele on the Palatine, constructed between 204 and 191, is probably
one of the first, if not the very first, examples of the use of *opus
caementicium*. In any case it has to be conceded that this technique
originated in Central Italy at about the end of the third or the beginning
of the second centuries.[60]

This was an innovation of very great importance, being easy and
adaptable in use. For its application, and especially in the preparation of
the materials, it required a less highly qualified, less specialized
workforce than did the *opus quadratum*, which used dressed blocks of
stone. *Opus caementicium* was also, perhaps, a more rapid process, though
it was none the less used in general with the greatest care, as is attested by
the fussily detailed provisions of the *lex parieti faciendo* drawn up at
Pozzuoli in 108 B.C.[61] It could be effected with materials which were less
difficult to obtain – since the stones required were small and of irregular
shapes – and, if necessary, with reclaimed materials. As a method, it
permitted new feats of daring in the realm of the arch and the vault, and it
achieved economies of time and means in the execution of large-scale

[59] Livy XLII.3.
[60] Coarelli 1977, 9–16: (H 36); Johannowsky, *HIM*, I.270: (H 244); Rakob, *ibid.* II.370–2: (H 263).
[61] *CIL* I².577 = X.1781.

building schemes with repetitive components, thanks to the employment of wooden casings which could be re-used many times. In short, it made possible the flourishing development of 'moulded architecture' which, over the centuries, was to endow the Roman world with so many bold constructions. In the distinctive manner in which it brought together technique, economy and art, *opus caementicium* not only marked a total break with Greek models and decisive progress in comparison with the traditional Italian construction types, whether in dry stone or polygonal blocks, or in *opus quadratum*; it also represented a 'creation of Roman capitalism',[62] which was to establish itself first not only in Rome and its vicinity but also in those regions of Tyrrhenian Italy where other forms of slave-labour production were being developed.

At the same time there appeared, though more tentatively, another innovation which afterwards was also to have a spectacular spread: the intensive use of baked bricks, employed particularly in Northern Italy, as, for example, in the first perimeter wall with which Aquileia was provided after its foundation in 181.[63]

The new infrastructure of Rome and Italy   The economic and political hold of Rome on Italy demanded and inspired a certain number of large-scale public works relating to the needs of land, sea and river communications and the provisioning of Rome. The network of roads continued to weave its web, centred more than ever on Rome and conceived more than ever in terms of her requirements or, which amounted to the same thing, to those of her colonies. These roads often disregarded the ancient centres, thus condemning them to decline (or sometimes, conversely, reviving certain cities which, hitherto somnolent, found themselves on the new highway – a phenomenon which has been closely studied in Southern Etruria and also in Bolsena, where the creation of the Via Cassia brought new life to the city together with a complete revolution in its urban plan, which had to be differently orientated in order to cope with the new conditions to which its activities were subjected.[64]

Within the framework of the *Urbs*, it was again the requirements of communication or transport which led to the building of the first stone bridge, the *Pons Aemilius*, begun in 179 and completed in 142, and the construction of new aqueducts in 179, in 144 (the *Aqua Marcia*, with an output of some 190,000 cubic metres a day) and in 125 (the *Aqua Tepula*).[65] However, the works which best revealed the opening-up of Rome to the Mediterranean world were those of a new port and of new commercial infrastructures.[66]

[62] Delbrück 1907–12, 180: (H 238). This expression is however modified by Torelli, *HIM*, II.377.
[63] Strazzulla 1981, II.194: (H 266).   [64] Gros 1981, 23–4: (B 169).
[65] Livy XL.51.6; Coarelli, *HIM*, 24: (H 234).
[66] Coarelli, *ibid.* 23: (H 234); *id.* 1980, 348–50: (B 161); Gabba, *HIM*, II.316: (H 91); Gros 1978, 12–17: (H 242).

The ancient Forum Boarium, for many years the centre of Roman business, had been repeatedly ravaged by water and fire. After a major fire in 213 and various floodings, it became the object of important works to raise it higher, but the site was too central and also too much encumbered with sanctuaries to be suitable for adequate extension. The magistrates of 193 chose the level area on the left bank of the Tiber, south of the Aventine, for the creation of new port installations to which Latin authors gave the significant name of *emporium* (this occurred, it should be noted, a year after the foundation of a colony at Pozzuoli, another 'lung' of Rome). The new installations were flanked by an enormous dock-warehouse, the *Porticus Aemilia*, begun in the same year and resumed in 174. This market-hall, 487 m long and 60 m wide, covering an area of almost 30,000 m², was composed of fifty vaulted aisles, each of them 8.50 m wide, the arches of which rested on 294 pillars. It was the first application of *opus caementicium* on such a grand scale, which exploited to the full the potentialities of moulded architecture of a repetitive character. At about the same time and slightly to the rear of the new port, Monte Testaccio may have begun to take shape, an immense dump of imported amphoras which was to become one of the most striking examples of the way in which Rome attracted the trade of the Mediterranean countries. It should be noted also that the censors of 179 reconstructed the market (*macellum*) of Rome, on the future site of the Forum Pacis.[67]

Finally, it was to the new use that Rome made of it, as its principal port, that Pozzuoli, frequented by the Romans since 215/14, owed its prodigious development from the time of the Second Punic War, whereas archaeology has not succeeded in discovering consistent traces of Samnite Pozzuoli.

Temples and the architecture of the nobilitas   The construction of sacred buildings was one of the activities pursued in Rome with the least interruption throughout the third and the second centuries, which makes the changes in the divinities honoured and the designs used all the more apparent. Thus, as an extension of the economic infrastructure just described, certain temples of the second century, especially a group in the area of the Forum Boarium,[68] were to acquire a definitely economic connotation. One example was the temple of Hercules Olivarius (the famous round 'Temple of Vesta'), which was built during the last decades of the second century by the rich oil merchant Octavius Herrenus and is the most ancient marble temple in Rome to have survived to the present day; another was the temple of Portunus, the so-called Temple of Fortuna Virilis. A different trend can be seen in the

[67] Coarelli, *HIM*, II.364–5.   [68] Coarelli 1980, 313–22: (B 161); Rakob 1969: (B 190).

erection on the Palatine of a sanctuary in honour of Cybele and Attis, reflecting the upheavals at the time of the Second Punic War that induced the Romans to admit into the *pomerium* cults apparently quite alien to the Roman tradition.

In design, certain of these temples were faithful copies of Greek models. In fact Strabo describes the temple of Venus Erycina, dedicated in 181 by Lucius Porcius Licinus in Rome, as a copy (*aphidryma*) of the temple on Mount Eryx.[69] Moreover, it may be noted that the stone entablature was introduced in Rome and superseded the traditional Italian use of timber beams.

It was the southern part of the Campus Martius which especially became, in the second century, the show-case and the trial ground of new architectural styles, introduced from the shores of the Aegean to the banks of the Tiber by an elite of *viri triumphales* eager to parade new riches and a new type of culture.[70]

In 221/20, as has been mentioned, Gaius Flaminius had created in this district, which was still on the outskirts of the city with ample space available, a new circus which was to be named after him. It was probably constructed in wood and no archaeological traces of it remain. Its exact site, which has long been a matter of controversy, is now thought to have been north-west of the Theatre of Marcellus, by the Tiber; indeed it was in relation to it that numerous monuments were subsequently sited in this district *in Circo*, and a plan of the whole lay-out can now be traced with reasonable probability and completeness. First, there were isolated temples and then – and this is the real innovation – groups of buildings combining porticoes and temples, which before long had converted the southern part of the Campus Martius into a truly Greek quarter of Rome. The first of these complexes was the *Porticus Octavia* (Gnaeus Octavius, *cos.* 165, with the *manubiae* of the Third Macedonian War); it consisted of a *porticus duplex*, probably a portico with a double nave, apparently with capitals of that Corinthian type which was to establish itself in Rome in the course of the century (in this case they were capitals covered in bronze and brought from Greece: this use of *spolia* makes it clear that this type of architecture had not yet become established in Rome). It was followed by the *Porticus Metelli*, begun in 146 (Quintus Metellus Macedonicus, *cos.* 143, likewise with the *manubiae* of Macedonia). This was a four-sided portico – 'the first Greek *temenos* in Rome',[71] though a similar plan, but with a portico on only three sides, had possibly made its appearance at Minturnae in the first decades of the century. Inside this enclosure there

[69] Strabo VI.2.5.
[70] Coarelli, *RIGS*, 262: (H 233); *id.* 1980, 266–84: (B 161); Gros 1976, 388–95: (H 241); Martina 1981: (H 209); Zevi 1976, 1061: (B 208); *id. HIM*, II.34–6: (B 209).
[71] Gros 1976, 395: (H 241).

was built the first marble temple to be constructed within the *Urbs*, the
temple of Jupiter Stator, created by the Cypriot architect Hermodorus of
Salamis, whose activity and influence were of importance in Rome
during the second half of the century.[72] This peripteral building, Greek
in type and made of Pentelicon marble, was erected shortly after the fall
of Corinth and well illustrates the famous maxim *Graecia capta ferum
victorem cepit*, which does not become any the less true for being frequently quoted.[73] Other temples in Greek marble were to follow, including the temple of Mars *in Circo Flaminio* beneath the church of S.
Salvatore in Campo (Decimus Brutus Callaicus, *cos.* 138) and that of
Hercules Olivarius already mentioned. In their plan (peripteral or tholos
as the case might be), their materials, their decoration and cult statues
(which will be discussed later) and their architectural detail, these buildings were, despite small variations, purely and simply Greek temples
transplanted to the banks of the Tiber.

Other new architectural forms are also related to the triumphal and
commemorative spirit which was so much alive in Rome at this time,
after she had become 'an important Mediterranean capital'.[74] We may
mention the first triumphal arches, erected in 196 in the Forum Boarium
and the Circus Maximus by Lucius Stertinius, or the façade added about
the middle of the second century to the ancient tomb of the Scipios,
which had originally simply been dug out of the tufa along the Via Appia.
Ornamented with marble statues, it is one of the first known examples of
this order of arches and attached half-columns which was subsequently
to be developed on a spectacular scale in Roman architecture.[75] It
remains, however, an exception in a period that still admired most of all
'Hallenfassaden' of Hellenistic type with pediment and rectilinear
entablature, regarded as being better suited to the purposes of prestige
and public display.[76]

In other regions of Italy which, as a result of participation of several
great families in the profit of maritime trade, collected a share of the by-
products of the Roman conquest, the sanctuaries built in the second
century played, on a local scale, a part analogous to that of the new
complexes of the Campus Martius; they were places for 'religious assembly, propaganda and political persuasion'.[77] This phenomenon has been
studied in relation to the region of the Samnite Pentri, who enjoyed at
this period, under the impetus of certain enterprising *gentes*, a recovery of

[72] Vell. Pat. I.11.5; Vitr. III.2.5; Gros 1973: (H 190).
[73] Hor. *Epist.* II.1.156, and Nenci's commentary, 1978: (H 210).
[74] Torelli 1977, 539: (H 270).   [75] Coarelli 1972, 62–82: (B 158); *id. HIM*, 25–6: (H 234).
[76] Kraus, *RIGS*, 228: (H 204).   [77] La Regina, *HIM*, I.243; see also 229–30: (H 142).

prosperity, the archaeological traces of which can be seen at Pietrabbondante and other sites.[78]

Innovation and resistance to change in Rome and throughout Italy   Other innovations made their appearance in this very fruitful century, resulting in a mixture of new techniques applied to buildings of ancient type and well-tried techniques applied to new types of plans and elevations, as has been already noted in relation to temples. In the former category are the *carceres*, probably in *opus caementicium* (and no longer in wood), with which the ancient Circus Maximus was provided in 174.[79] The second category is exemplified in Rome by the construction, in an *opus quadratum* of tufa, of several buildings of a new type, the basilica[80] (*Basilica Porcia*, 184; *Basilica Aemilia et Fulvia*, 179; *Basilica Sempronia*, 170/69). However controversial their origin may be, the evidence shows that they owe much, and not least their name, to Greek inspiration.

Generally speaking, it was exceptional for innovation of plan, architectural ornament, materials or building technique to be introduced without some modification or blending in of other elements. Thus in all spheres there are hybrid monuments, to mention only the moulded decoration of an Etruscan altar at Bolsena or of 'Samnite' temples of the second century, where hellenic styles and native Italian survivals existed side by side; a sanctuary in Buccino, which combines a very traditional base of polygonal blocks with a temple constructed according to principles which are clearly Greek, a 'phenomenon neither purely Greek nor purely Roman'; and certain temples in Campania which were of Etruscan-Italic type, but provided with hellenic architectural decoration.[81]

New ideas were accepted more or less readily according to the field in which they were applied. Private dwellings presented hardly any problems in this respect. Plautus in certain passages describes with envy some amenities and comforts still unknown to the Roman audience, which were already quite commonplace in Greece during the fourth and third centuries, such as baths, covered walks, colonnades and the versatile design of buildings to suit all times of year.[82] These Greek prototypes, particularly that of the house with peristyle, appeared in Campania during the first half of the second century and were to be adopted in Italy without much opposition. Luxurious town-houses were then being built (remains have been discovered particularly in Paestum and Pompeii) and

---

[78] *Sannio, passim*: (H 153).   [79] Livy XLI.27.6.
[80] Rakob, *HIM*, II.369: (H 263); Drerup, *ibid*. II.376: (B 163).
[81] Balland and others 1971, 259: (B 148) (Bolsena); Morel, *HIM*, I.259: (H 257) (Samnium); Holloway 1974, 25–32: (B 173) (Buccino); Johannowsky, *HIM*, I.273: (H 244) (Campania). In general: Bianchi Bandinelli, *RIGS*, 298.   [82] Grimal 1976, 371–86: (H 189).

these were provided with tetrastyled *atria* and with peristyles; essentially they differed very little from the contemporary Hellenistic palaces.[83] At about the same time there appeared the first leisure *villae*.[84]

On the other hand, innovations were less acceptable, especially in Rome, insofar as they impinged on what might be called public morality. The most striking example is that of the permanent theatre-buildings.[85] From about the middle of the second century (or a little later?), Campania was provided, in Sarno and in Pompeii, with theatres constructed in masonry, which were to multiply rapidly in the ensuing decades. Even the Samnite site of Pietrabbondante was equipped before the Social War with a complete theatre. Rome too acquired her first stone-built theatre in 154, erected by the censor Gaius Cassius Longinus, and traces of it have possibly been discovered in front of the temple of Magna Mater, on the south-west slope of the Palatine. However, Publius Cornelius Scipio Nasica immediately persuaded the Senate to order its demolition in the name of *pudicitia*, thus demonstrating, before an innovation which was contrary to *standi virilitas* and conducive to *desidia*, a reserve which was not to be finally overcome – and in any case not without difficulty – until a century later, with the theatre of Pompey.[86] It appears that public thermal baths may also have been introduced more readily in Campania, where they are known to have existed in Capua, Cumae and Pompeii from the end of the third century or the beginning of the following century, than in the *Urbs* itself.[87]

An analogous trend is apparent in the religious or politico-religious sphere, which was essentially traditionalist. When the Regia was reconstructed in 148, its traditional plan, regarded as sacred, was respected scrupulously. After the cult of Cybele was introduced into Rome, the goddess was housed in a temple which certainly contained an innovation in respect of its *opus caementicium* podium, as has been mentioned, but which followed the traditional native Italian prostyle plan. A subterranean area laid out at Bolsena for the celebration of the Bacchic mysteries, which well conveyed the atmosphere of this cult, abhorrent to the Roman moral code, was destroyed, most probably at the time of the great repression which followed the *senatus consultum* of 186 relating to the Bacchanalia.[88] Just as the theatre was regarded as an enervating influ-

---

[83] The exact date of the first appearance of houses with peristyles is controversial. See e.g. Johannowsky, *HIM*, I.275: (H 244); Rakob, *ibid.* II.370: (H 263).

[84] Here too the chronology is still uncertain. Coarelli, *RIGS*, 476 and 478; Frederiksen 1981, I.272: (H 89); Johannowsky, *RIGS*, 461–2: (H 243); id. *HIM*, I.276: (H 244).

[85] Johannowsky, *RIGS*, 469: (H 243); Lauter, *HIM*, II.413–22: (H 246).

[86] Livy, *Per.* XLVIII; Val. Max. II.4.2; Vell. Pat. I.15.3; App. *B.Civ.* I.28.125; Aug. *Civ.D.* I.31–3; Oros. IV.21.4.　　[87] Johannowsky, *RIGS*, 468: (H 243).

[88] Pailler 1976, 739–42: (H 109); Gros 1981, 65: (B 169). On the reconstruction of the Regia see Coarelli 1980, 80: (B 161).

ence, so Dionysiac practices were held to be incompatible with the Roman tradition.

(iii) Plastic arts

In the domain of art, the second century saw a polarization similar to that which has been noted in the economy between the production using slave labour and more traditional production, and in architecture between innovations (in themselves very varied) and obstinate survivals. The gulf deepened between art that was 'aristocratic' and 'urban' and impoverished popular art. This impoverishment was symbolized by the falling standards of offerings – statues, statuettes and heads – assembled in the votive deposits of the sanctuaries. The most characteristic decorative elements, architectural terracottas, declined in number and in quality throughout the whole of Italy, the best examples to be found henceforward being concentrated among the products of Rome. It has been said of this period that it was one in which a general spread of hellenization could have been expected *a priori*, but in fact it did not take place.[89] There was without question at that time a break in Italian art, though it had its antecedents largely in the preceding era.

Greek influence was in fact limited to the circle of the *nobilitas* (which amounts in essence to saying that it was therefore restricted to the urban art of Rome). It is important at this point to emphasize the part played by patronage in the development of a Roman Hellenistic art. The artists of this period may well have been mostly, if not almost entirely, Greeks; the critical factor was the patron who commissioned the work and who often influenced it in accordance with his personal ideology. 'The monument of Aemilius Paullus', as later 'Trajan's column', was spoken of without reference to the identity and origin of the artists and workmen, just as the portraits of the *viri triumphales* of the time, although Greek in inspiration, are in fact Roman portraits.

As a result of the conquest of the eastern Mediterranean, Rome had at her disposal a vast reservoir of artists and models which caused Italy to be flooded with a variety of influences, with eclectic results. It remains none the less true that the artistic current for which the *nobilitas* as a whole showed a preference was neo-Attic. During these decades Rome maintained continuous links with Athens, either directly or through Delos as the intermediary, an island of which she had taken control and which the Italians visited in large numbers. At a deeper level, neo-Attic art, in essence scholarly, academic and faultless, was in accord with the new political and ideological demands of the *nobilitas*, who had appropriated it to define more clearly the gulf between itself and the common people.

[89] Coarelli, *HIM*, II.498.

It was, in fact, the art-form that was the most remote from the spontaneous trends of native Italian expression and, in consequence, the one best
calculated to highlight the 'difference' of the elite, who borrowed from it
the artistic themes for self-celebration. Roman patrons set to work in
their own service whole dynasties of artists of the neo-Attic school, the
most studied and probably the most characteristic of them being the one
which throughout the second century provided the succession of sculptors named Timarchides, Polycles, Dionysius and Scopas.[90] These artists, and others like them, filled with their works the porticoes and
temples erected by the *imperatores* to immortalize their conquests, to
dazzle their fellow-citizens and to show their desire to break with an
artistic past which, whether sincerely or not, for reasons of taste,
ingenuousness or pride, they regarded as mediocre and outdated.

Two fields which would appear to reflect these tendencies more than
others are reliefs and statuary. Less is known about painting and mosaic,
whatever significance they too may have had.

The first half of the second century saw the parallel development of
marble relief, already Roman through its patrons although situated in
Greece (monument of Aemilius Paullus), and of terracotta relief, shaped
in Italy from models which were Hellenistic in style (represented by a
series of friezes and decorated pediments). These two currents converged, several decades later, in marble reliefs, now carved in Italy itself,
of which the 'altar of Domitius Ahenobarbus' is the earliest example still
preserved. Once more it may be observed how slowly these newly
acquired features were absorbed and what a mixture of models prevailed
at the beginning.

It was at Delphi that the first 'Roman' bas-relief recording an historical
event was created. Aemilius Paullus converted to his own use there, in
167, an unfinished carved pillar in Pentelicon marble, being erected in
honour of Perseus whom he had just defeated at Pydna. The general
inspiration, the style and the material were entirely Greek, but the
inscription which the Roman general caused to be added to it, (*L(ucius)
Aimilius L(ucii) f(ilius) inperator de rege Perse Macedonibusque cepet*),[91]
shows clearly who is its titulary owner and accordingly, in the Roman
view, its true originator – a concept which continued to be prevalent in
the future.

In Italy itself a whole series of decorative reliefs belonging to the first
three-quarters of the second century honoured the gods or celebrated
victories. They were executed in terracotta, a traditional material of
native Italian art, but unmistakable Hellenistic influence is perceptible in

---

[90] Coarelli 1970: (B 157); *id.*, *RIGS*, 250–8: (H 233).   [91] *CIL* I².622 = III.14203²².

them, sometimes of neo-Attic origin (as in the pediments of S. Gregorio in Rome and of Luna) and sometimes – especially in works of the first half of the century – deriving from Asia Minor (as in the reliefs of Talamone, Civitalba and Pozzuoli, and also in the immense series of alabaster urns from Volterra).[92] These examples show once again the variety of influences at this period of artistic ferment. Ultimately, however, the neo-Attic stream predominated, for the reasons explained above.

It culminated, just at the close of the period under review, in a significant monument known as the 'altar of Domitius Ahenobarbus',[93] which is probably a carved base from the temple of Mars *in Circo Flaminio* mentioned earlier. On three of its sides a marine procession advances, carved in marble with virtuosity and elegance. The fourth side, in contrast, reproduces with many precise details the scene of a census, in a style which is far more stiff and awkward. This last relief calls to mind 'an administrative prose following on the academic lyricism of the procession of Amphitrite', and it could be said to mark the first appearance of Roman or even Western art.[94] Nothing could appear more different than these two groups of reliefs; nevertheless it has been forcefully demonstrated that they are almost certainly the products of the same workshop. There could be no clearer sign of the effort made by artists of the neo-Attic stream to adapt themselves to the demands of a Roman patron, anxious to have an exact representation of events in which he was illustriously involved. In this case the patron was probably Decimus Junius Brutus Callaicus, *cos.* 138 and conqueror of Lusitania, who erected the temple to Mars in 132.

If Pliny is to be believed, there can have been hardly any statues in Rome before the conquest of Asia Minor apart from those in wood or terracotta.[95] The odds are that this statement is fairly close to the truth; nevertheless it underestimates an important aspect of Italian sculpture: statues in bronze. Whereas in 207 the Roman matrons carried in procession in honour of Juno two statues of cypress-wood, it was a bronze statue which they had offered to the goddess in 217.[96] Portraits of eminent personages were also executed in bronze occasionally, and this had been so for a long time. The 'Brutus' in the Museo dei Conservatori has already been mentioned in this connection. The fine male head from S. Giovanni Scipioni, of the second century, is scarcely inferior to it in

[92] Coarelli 1970, 85–6: (B 157); *id. HIM*, 25–6: (H 234); *id.* 1977, 37–8: (H 235); Johannowsky, *HIM*, I.130; Torelli 1977, 541: (H 270). With special reference to the urns of Volterra: *CDE*; and Pairault 1972: (H 261).
[93] Kähler 1966: (H 101); Zevi 1976, 1063: (B 208); in particular the essential article of Coarelli 1968: (B 156).   [94] Bianchi Bandinelli, *RIGS*, 217: (H 228); Charbonneaux 1948, 25: (I 5).
[95] Pliny, *HN* XXXIV.34.   [96] Livy XXVII.37.12 and XXI.62.

quality. However, in the course of the same century many statues and portraits were still fashioned out of local stone such as tufa (for example 'Ennius', Orpheus) or, most frequently, were modelled in clay.[97] This is probably true of most of those statues of important people, which became so invasive of the squares of Rome – in the Forum, on the Capitol – that it was necessary on several occasions, in the first half of the century, to have them removed by magisterial decree.[98]

It is in any case a fact, as stated by Pliny, that marble was beginning to supersede these traditional materials, both for private portraits like those of Scipio Africanus, Scipio Asiagenus or Ennius which adorned the new façade of the tomb of the Scipios[99] and also, above all, for the statues of divinities which occupied the temples erected by the *nobilitas*. These were often colossal statues, carved by the sculptors of the neo-Attic school already mentioned.

The Italians, of course, had long been familiar with the art of portraiture. It is significant, however, that the first portrait of a Roman to be identified with certainty should be of Greek origin. The subject was Flamininus, represented on Macedonian gold staters which explicitly give his name, and this has made it possible, by comparison, to identify hypothetically as a portrait in the round of this same Flamininus a celebrated bronze statue which had long been regarded as that of a Hellenistic prince.[100] In fact, many so-called portraits of 'Hellenistic princes' are probably nothing other than portraits of Roman aristocrats.[101]

These portraits of Flamininus are as Roman (or Greek, according to the point of view adopted) as the monument of Aemilius Paullus is Roman (or Greek). The question is whether they opened up a new avenue for the Romans, and it would seem that they did not, inasmuch as these staters were an isolated phenomenon, part of a Greek tradition which created no school in Italy. Indeed, it was necessary to wait until Caesar, more than a century later, for the next certain portrait of a living Roman, identified by the legend, this time on coins which were themselves Roman. As for the first Roman portraits in the round which can be identified with confidence, they were those of Pompey – a chronological disparity with Greece which reveals much about the differences between the two cultures.

In painting, scarcely any figurative works of this period are known, except indirectly. We know that the poet Pacuvius, for example, about

[97] On the head from S. Giovanni Scipioni see Bianchi Bandinelli 1969, 73–4: (H 226); for Orpheus, *ibid*. 28–9; 'Ennius': Coarelli 1972, 97–105: (B 158); *id. HIM*, 25: (H 234).
[98] For example, Pliny, *HN* XXXIV.30.
[99] Cic. *Arch*. 22. See Coarelli's observations: 1972, 78, 81–2 and 105: (B 158).
[100] Balty 1978: (H 225); *id*. 1980, 96: (B 149); Crawford 1974, 1.544: (B 88).
[101] Zanker, *HIM*, II.589: (H 274).

the middle of the century decorated the *Aedes Aemiliana Herculis*, one of the temples erected to Hercules on the Forum Boarium.[102] At about the same time a Greek painter of the name of Demetrios was living in Rome (exact dates unknown, but he was certainly there in 165).[103] Such individuals could have introduced into Italy more varied types of painting than the purely triumphal, represented by the Esquiline fragment noted at the beginning of this chapter, and which seems moreover to have declined after the first decades of the third century. An example which comes to mind is the pathetic baroque of the Tomb of the Typhon at Tarquinia.[104] The fact remains that, between the beginning of the third century and the birth of the 'second Pompeian style' in the first century, existing information on Roman and Italian painting is very incomplete. As regards mosaic, it was after the period now under review, in the last quarter of the second century, that masterpieces of Hellenistic inspiration were to be produced in Italy, the most famous of them being the mosaic of Alexander in the House of the Faun at Pompeii and the great Nilotic mosaic of Praeneste.

III. CONCLUSION

Rome was the intermediary through which Greek art conquered the West and fundamentally shaped its civilization. This simple statement is enough to demonstrate the importance of the third and second centuries, during which the influence of Greece on Italy was so strong.

It was, however, a more limited phenomenon than might be imagined. Chronological discrepancies and differences of culture between Greece and Italy were often considerable and were less the result of the inadequacy of Rome than of her habitual concern to borrow only what she wanted to borrow and only to the extent that she wished. In this respect a useful comparison has been made with modern Japan.[105] Developments deemed to be excessive or too rapid in the progress along the path of hellenization were unfailingly blocked by counter-action, which was sometimes violent. In relation to the second century B.C., examples may be cited as various as the *senatus consultum* on the Bacchanales, the expulsions of rhetoricians and philosophers, the demolition of the first stone theatre and the removals of statues. There was also the break, or at any rate the slowing-down, in hellenization which occurred at the end of the period under consideration, at the time of the Gracchan crisis.

[102] Pliny, *HN* xxxv.19.
[103] Diod. Sic. *Exc.* 31, 18 (that is, if *topographos* signifies 'painter' here).
[104] Torelli, *HIM*, 1.98: (H 269).
[105] Gallini 1973, 180–1: (H 182); Veyne 1979, *passim*: (H 216).

Moreover, hellenization could not of itself be held solely responsible for all the fundamental changes taking place in Italy in the third and second centuries. Hellenization cannot explain the profound changes in economic life: the establishment of production based on slave labour and of long-distance trade alongside the survivals of smaller-scale activities. Tyrrhenian Central Italy in the last centuries of the Republic thereby passed through an economic experience known to few other regions in the history of humanity, and perhaps to none in a similar way or to the same degree.

THREE HELLENISTIC DYNASTIES
(See also the tables appended to Chapter 11, pp. 420–1.)

Seleucus I Nicator	305–281
Antiochus I Soter	281–261
Antiochus II Theos	261–246
Seleucus II Callinicus	246–226/5
Seleucus III Soter	226/5–223
Antiochus III Megas	223–187
Seleucus IV Philopator	187–175
Antiochus IV Epiphanes	175–164
Antiochus V Eupator	164–162
Demetrius I Soter	162–150
Alexander Balas	150–145
Demetrius II Nicator	145–140
Antiochus VI Epiphanes	145–142/1 or 139/8
Antiochus VII (Sidetes)	138–129
Demetrius II Nicator (restored)	129–126/5
Cleopatra Thea	126/5–123
Antiochus VIII Grypus	126/5–96
Seleucus V	126
Antiochus IX Philopator (Cyzicenus)	114/13–95
Seleucus VI	95
Antiochus X Eusebes Philopator	95
Demetrius III Philopator Soter	95–88 (at Damascus)

twins {
Antiochus XI Epiphanes Philadelphus — 95 } (in Cilicia)
Philip I — 95–84/3

Antiochus XII Dionysus	87 (at Damascus)
Philip II	84/3

2. THE ANTIGONIDS

Antigonus I (Monophthalmus)	306–301
Demetrius I (Poliorcetes)	307–283
Antigonus II (Gonatas)	283–239
Demetrius II	239–229
Antigonus III (Doson)	229–221
Philip V	221–179
Perseus	179–168

3. THE ATTALIDS

(Philetaerus	283–263)
(Eumenes I	263–241)
Attalus I Soter	241–197
Eumenes II Soter	197–159/8
Attalus II	159/8–139/8
Attalus III	139/8–133
(Eumenes III (Aristonicus)	133–129)

GENEALOGICAL TABLES

THE ATTALIDS

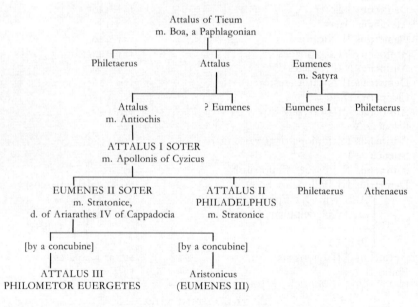

Attalus of Tieum
m. Boa, a Paphlagonian

Philetaerus   Attalus   Eumenes
m. Satyra

Attalus   ? Eumenes   Eumenes I   Philetaerus
m. Antiochis

ATTALUS I SOTER
m. Apollonis of Cyzicus

EUMENES II SOTER   ATTALUS II   Philetaerus   Athenaeus
m. Stratonice,   PHILADELPHUS
d. of Ariarathes IV of Cappadocia   m. Stratonice

[by a concubine]   [by a concubine]

ATTALUS III   Aristonicus
PHILOMETOR EUERGETES   (EUMENES III)

THE ANTIGONIDS

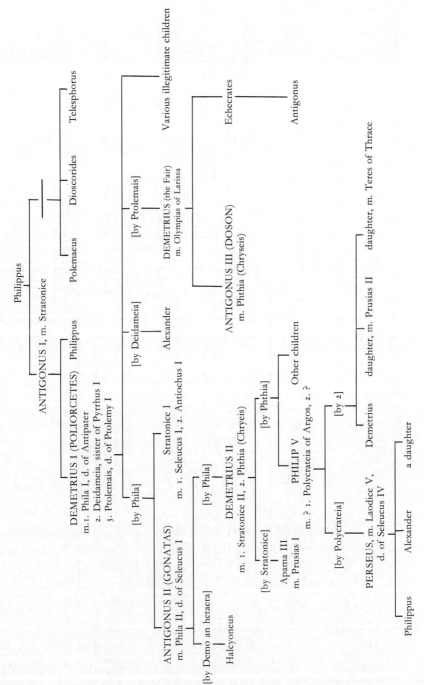

520

THE SELEUCIDS

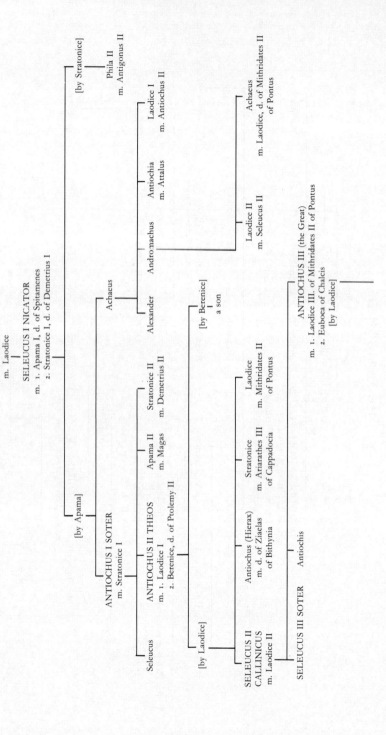

Antiochus
m. Laodice

SELEUCUS I NICATOR
m. 1. Apama I, d. of Spitamenes
2. Stratonice I, d. of Demetrius I

[by Apama]

[by Stratonice]

Phila II
m. Antigonus II

ANTIOCHUS I SOTER
m. Stratonice I

Achaeus

Seleucus

ANTIOCHUS II THEOS
m. 1. Laodice I
2. Berenice, d. of Ptolemy II

Apama II
m. Magas

Stratonice II
m. Demetrius II

Alexander

Andromachus

Antiochia
m. Attalus

Laodice I
m. Antiochus II

Achaeus
m. Laodice, d. of Mithridates II
of Pontus

Laodice II
m. Seleucus II

[by Berenice]
a son

[by Laodice]

SELEUCUS II
CALLINICUS
m. Laodice II

Antiochus (Hierax)
m. d. of Ziaelas
of Bithynia

Stratonice
m. Ariarathes III
of Cappadocia

Laodice
m. Mithridates II
of Pontus

SELEUCUS III SOTER

Antiochis

ANTIOCHUS III (the Great)
m. 1. Laodice III, of Mithridates II of Pontus
2. Euboea of Chalcis

[by Laodice]

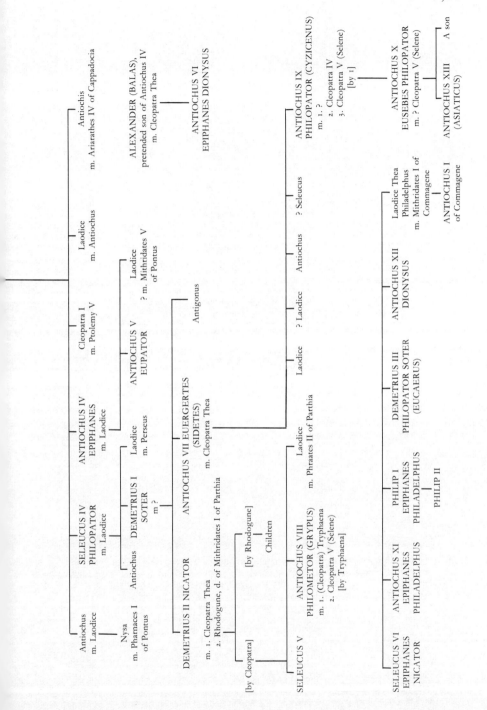

CHRONOLOGICAL TABLE

The table displays the chronological relationship between selected events which are mentioned in this volume. A few events which are discussed in other volumes are included but entries are placed between parentheses.

	ROMAN CONSULS	ROME AND ITALY	THE WEST	THE EAST
237	L. Cornelius Lentulus Caudinus Q. Fulvius Flaccus		Hamilcar Barca goes to Spain. (237–229) Hamilcar conquers much of southern and south-eastern Spain; he founds Akra Leuke.	
231	M. Pomponius Matho C. Papirius Maso		Hamilcar probably receives a Roman embassy.	
229	L. Postumius Albinus II Cn. Fulvius Centumalus		Death of Hamilcar. Hasdrubal takes command of Carthaginian forces in Spain.	First Illyrian War.
228	Sp. Carvilius Maximus II Q. Fabius Maximus Verrucosus II		(c. 228) Hasdrubal advances to the upper Guadiana. He founds Carthago Nova.	Roman envoys in Greece.
227	P. Valerius Flaccus M. Atilius Regulus	(Praetorships increased to four.)	Roman agreement with Saguntum (before 226?).	
226	M. Valerius Messalla L. Apustius Fullo		Roman envoys arrange the 'Ebro treaty' with Hasdrubal.	
225	L. Aemilius Papus C. Atilius Regulus	(Romans defeat Gauls at Telamon.)		
224	T. Manlius Torquatus II Q. Fulvius Flaccus II			
223	C. Flaminius P. Furius Philus	(Flaminius defeats Insubres.)		
222	M. Claudius Marcellus Cn. Cornelius Scipio Calvus	(Insubres defeated at Clastidium and surrender to Rome.) (15 March becomes beginning of the consular year (probably this year).)		Accession of Antiochus III to the Seleucid throne.

221	P. Cornelius Scipio Asina M. Minucius Rufus (?M. Aemilius Lepidus II, *suffectus*)	Roman expedition against the Histri. *Ludi plebei* instituted at Rome.	Hasdrubal killed; he is succeeded in command by Hannibal. Hannibal attacks the Olcades and winters in Carthago Nova. (*c.* 221–220) Saguntum invites Roman arbitration in an internal dispute.	Accession of Philip V as king of Macedonia.
220	(a) M. Valerius Laevinus Q. Mucius Scaevola (these either abdicated or more probably never entered office, presumably because they were faultily elected.) (b) C. Lutatius Catulus L. Veturius Philo		Hannibal defeats the Vaccaei, captures Salamanca and conquers central Spain. (220–219) Roman envoys meet Hannibal in his winter quarters in Carthago Nova.	Expedition of Demetrius and Scerdilaidas in the Adriatic. Outbreak of the 'Social War' in Greece. Achaeus takes the royal title in Asia Minor.
219	L. Aemilius Paullus M. Livius Salinator		Hannibal besieges and (late autumn) captures Saguntum.	Second Illyrian War.
218	P. Cornelius Scipio Ti. Sempronius Longus	Foundation of Placentia and Cremona. War declared between Rome and Carthage. Hannibal invades Italy; battles of the Ticinus and the Trebbia. *Lex Claudia* concerning the ownership of ships by senators.	Roman envoys deliver ultimatum at Carthage. Hannibal crosses the Ebro and marches to the Alps. Cn. Scipio gains control of the area north of the Ebro. Hiero of Syracuse warns Rome of a Carthaginian plan to capture Lilybaeum. Roman naval victory off Lilybaeum.	
217	Cn. Servilius Geminus C. Flaminius II M. Atilius Regulus II, *suffectus*	Battle of Lake Trasimene. Beginning of the 'Fabian strategy'. Equalization of the *imperium* of Fabius and Minucius. Suspension of the *lex Genucia* under which second consulships within ten years were forbidden.	Roman naval victory off the Ebro. Cn. Scipio sails south of Carthago Nova and to Ebusus. He is joined by his brother, P. Scipio. Servilius demands hostages in Sardinia.	Peace of Naupactus between Philip V and Aetolia.

	ROMAN CONSULS	ROME AND ITALY	THE WEST	THE EAST
216	C. Terentius Varro L. Aemilius Paullus II	Battle of Cannae. Large-scale defections in southern Italy.	Hasdrubal ordered to Italy and replaced by Himilco. Roman victories south of the Ebro. Carthaginian fleet ravages Syracusan territory.	Philip's operations in the Adriatic disturbed by Roman ships. (216–213) Campaigns of Antiochus III against Achaeus.
215	L. Postumius Albinus III (killed before he could enter office) M. Claudius Marcellus II, *suffectus* (abdicated when election declared invalid) Q. Fabius Maximus Verrucosus III, *suffectus* Ti. Sempronius Gracchus	Hannibal fails to take Nola and Cumae. Rome recovers some towns in Campania and Samnium. *Lex Oppia.*	Death of Hiero of Syracuse. Hieronymus makes approaches to Carthaginians. Unsuccessful attack on Sardinia by Hasdrubal the Bald.	Philip V's negotiations and agreement with Hannibal.
214	Q. Fabius Maximus Verrucosus IV M. Claudius Marcellus III	Rome recovers Casilinum. Hannibal fails to take Tarentum.	Hieronymus assassinated; defection of Syracuse to the Carthaginians Syphax revolts from Carthage.	Outbreak of First Macedonian War; Philip driven from the Adriatic.
213	Q. Fabius Maximus Ti. Sempronius Gracchus II	Rome recovers Arpi.	Marcellus lays siege to Syracuse.	Philip captures Lissus.
212	Q. Fulvius Flaccus III Ap. Claudius Pulcher	Hannibal captures Tarentum, Metapontum, Thurii and Heraclea. Claudius and Fulvius begin the siege of Capua. (*c.* 212) Reform of the Roman monetary system.	Rome captures Saguntum and Castulo. Marcellus captures Syracuse.	(212–211) Roman alliance with Aetolia against Philip V. (212–205) 'Anabasis' of Antiochus III.
211	C. Fulvius Centumalus Maximus P. Sulpicius Galba Maximus	Hannibal marches on Rome. Capua recovered by Rome.	The Scipios defeated and killed. Carthaginians regain control of large areas of Spain.	

210	M. Claudius Marcellus IV M. Valerius Laevinus (II?)	Roman successes in Apulia and Samnium. Roman fleet defeated off Tarentum.	Scipio (Africanus) arrives in Spain. Valerius Laevinus captures Agrigentum. Carthaginians raid Sardinia. Syphax sends embassy to Rome. Massinissa in the service of Carthage.	Aegina bought by Attalus from the Aetolians.
209	Q. Fabius Maximus Verrucosus V Q. Fulvius Flaccus IV	Twelve Latin colonies refuse contingents for Rome. Fabius recaptures Tarentum.	Scipio captures Carthago Nova.	
208	M. Claudius Marcellus V T. Quinctius Crispinus	Both consuls killed near Venusia.	Battle of Baecula, Hasdrubal crosses Pyrenees *en route* to Italy.	
207	C. Claudius Nero M. Livius Salinator II	Hasdrubal invades Italy and is defeated at the battle of the Metaurus.		
206	L. Veturius Philo Q. Caecilius Metellus	Rome recovers Lucania. Resettlement of Placentia and Cremona.	Battle of Ilipa. Capture of Ilourgeia and Castulo. Mutiny in Roman army. Mago attacks Carthago Nova and sails to Italy. Foundation of Italica. Scipio returns to Rome. Syphax visited by both Scipio and Hasdrubal. Massinissa changes sides. Syphax occupies Massinissa's kingdom.	Peace treaty between Aetolia and Philip V.
205	P. Cornelius Scipio (Africanus) P. Licinius Crassus Dives	Fabius and Fulvius oppose Scipio's plans to invade Africa. Mago lands at Genoa. Scipio recovers Locri.	Final defeat of Andobales and Mandonius. Laelius raids the coast of Africa. Carthaginian ships captured off Sardinia.	Peace of Phoenice. (c. 205) Outbreak of 'Cretan War'.
204	M. Cornelius Cethegus P. Sempronius Tuditanus	Roman successes in Bruttium. (c. 204–184) The plays of Plautus.	Scipio lands near Utica.	Death of Ptolemy Philopator. (204 or 203) Antiochus III in Asia Minor.

	ROMAN CONSULS	ROME AND ITALY	THE WEST	THE EAST
203	Cn. Servilius Caepio C. Servilius Geminus	Roman forces defeat Mago.	Carthaginian and Numidian camps destroyed. Battle of the Great Plains. Syphax captured by the Romans. Peace negotiations between Rome and Carthage. Hannibal and Mago return to Africa.	Roman embassy investigates Greek complaints about Philip V. Collapse of Agathocles' regime in Alexandria.
202	M. Servilius Pulex Geminus Ti. Claudius Nero	Last appointment of a dictator (until the appointment of Sulla).	Carthage attacks Roman supply ships. Hannibal offers terms for peace. Battle of Zama. Peace agreed on Roman terms.	Antiochus III in Coele Syria. Philip takes Lysimacheia, Chalcedon, Cius, Perinthus and Thasos.
201	Cn. Cornelius Lentulus P. Aelius Paetus	Peace settlement with Carthage ratified at Rome. Beginning of series of consular commands in northern Italy. (201–199) Veterans settled in Apulia and Samnium.		Siege of Gaza. Philip in the Aegean: capture of Samos, battles of Chios and Lade. Embassies sent to Rome by Attalus and Rhodes. Athenian embassy to Rome. (Winter 201/200) Philip at Bargylia.
200	P. Sulpicius Galba Maximus II C. Aurelius Cotta	First conflict of Cenomani with Rome. Roman assembly first rejects, then accepts proposal to declare war on Philip V of Macedonia.		Battle of Panium. Philip in Thrace; siege of Abydus. Roman envoys in Greece. Roman decision to make war on Philip. (Autumn) Arrival of Roman troops at Apollonia. Achaeans refuse to provide troops for Philip.
199	L. Cornelius Lentulus P. Villius Tappulus	Censorship of Scipio Africanus.		Sulpicius Galba attacks Upper Macedonia.
198	Sex. Aelius Paetus Catus T. Quinctius Flamininus	12,000 Latins and Italians required to return from Rome to their own communities.		T. Quinctius Flamininus takes command in the war against Philip. Achaean League joins Rome in the war.

197	C. Cornelius Cethegus Q. Minucius Rufus	Number of praetors increased to six. Tenure of the praetorship made a prerequisite for the consulship (probably in this year). Submission of Cenomani. New colonists recruited to Cosa.	Demarcation of the division between the two Spanish provinces. Spanish rebellion; beginning of continuous Roman wars in Spain.	Battle of Cynoscephalae. Antiochus III in Asia Minor.
196	L. Furius Purpurio M. Claudius Marcellus		Hannibal sufete at Carthage (196/5).	Proclamation of freedom at the Isthmian Games. Settlement in Greece and Macedonia. Abortive negotiations between Rome and Antiochus III.
195	L. Valerius Flaccus M. Porcius Cato	Repeal of the *lex Oppia*.	M. Porcius Cato's campaigns in Spain. First Roman invasion of Celtiberia. Roman envoys sent to Carthage. Hannibal flees to the eastern Mediterranean.	The war against Nabis.
194	P. Cornelius Scipio Africanus II Ti. Sempronius Longus	Roman defeat of Insubres. Eight citizen colonies established in southern Italy.		Roman evacuation of Greece.
193	L. Cornelius Merula Q. Minucius Thermus		First evidence of Lusitanians, Vettones and Vaccaei as enemies of the Romans; victories of M. Fulvius Nobilior. Carthaginian envoys to Rome complain about the activities of Massinissa in a boundary dispute; the Senate sends a mission led by Scipio Africanus to investigate but the issue is left unresolved.	Failure of negotiations at Rome between Flamininus and Antiochus' envoys. Roman envoys sent to Antiochus. War in the Peloponnese between Achaea and Sparta.
192	L. Quinctius Flamininus Cn. Domitius Ahenobarbus	Fines imposed on usurers.		Roman envoys in Greece. Roman fleet crosses to Greece. Aetolians invite the assistance of Antiochus, who crosses to Greece.

	ROMAN CONSULS	ROME AND ITALY	THE WEST	THE EAST
191	P. Cornelius Scipio Nasica M'. Acilius Glabrio	Roman defeat of Boii.	Rome refuses a Carthaginian offer to pay immediately the whole of the outstanding indemnity from the Second Punic War.	Rome declares war on Antiochus. Battle of Thermopylae. Antiochus driven from Greece.
190	L. Cornelius Scipio Asiaticus C. Laelius	Additional settlers sent to Placentia and Cremona.		Roman army crosses to Asia. Battle of Magnesia.
189	M. Fulvius Nobilior Cn. Manlius Vulso	Prosecution of M'. Acilius Glabrio. Foundation of Bononia on Boian land.		Expedition of Manlius Vulso in central Anatolia. Sack of Ambracia by Fulvius Nobilior.
188	M. Valerius Messalla C. Livius Salinator	Foundation of Forum Livii. Full Roman citizenship granted to Arpinum, Formiae and Fundi.		Peace of Apamea. Achaeans under Philopoemen force the submission of Sparta.
187	M. Aemilius Lepidus C. Flaminius	Political attacks on L. Cornelius Scipio Asiaticus. Construction of a *Via Flaminia* and a *Via Aemilia*.		Death of Antiochus III; Seleucus IV becomes king. (*c.* 187–183) War between Eumenes II of Pergamum and Prusias I of Bithynia.
186	Sp. Postumius Albinus Q. Marcius Philippus	Suppression of the 'Bacchanalian Conspiracy'.	Military successes of C. Calpurnius Piso and L. Quinctius Crispinus on the Tagus.	
185	Ap. Claudius Pulcher M. Sempronius Tuditanus			Embassy of Q. Caecilius Metellus to Macedonia and Greece.
184	P. Claudius Pulcher L. Porcius Licinus	Censorship of M. Porcius Cato and L. Valerius Flaccus. Political attack on Scipio Africanus.		Embassy of Ap. Claudius to Macedonia and Greece. Demetrius, son of Philip V, goes to Rome. Eumenes defeats Prusias and his allies.

531

	Consuls	Rome and Italy	The provinces	The East
183	M. Claudius Marcellus Q. Fabius Labeo	Death of Scipio Africanus. Citizen colonies founded at Mutina and Parma.	Celtiberians invade Roman-controlled territory.	Embassy of Q. Marcius Philippus to Macedonia and Greece. Messene revolts from the Achaean League. Death of Philopoemen. Peace between Eumenes and Prusias. Death of Hannibal. Pharnaces I of Pontus captures Sinope.
182	Cn. Baebius Tamphilus L. Aemilius Paullus	*Lex Orchia*, sumptuary law.	Q. Fulvius Flaccus invades Celtiberia. Conflict between Carthage and Massinissa.	Messene brought back into the Achaean League by Lycortas. Death of Prusias I; Prusias II becomes king of Bithynia. (*c.* 182–179) War between Eumenes and Pharnaces.
181	P. Cornelius Cethegus M. Baebius Tamphilus	*Lex Cornelia Baebia* concerning electoral corruption. *Lex Baebia* reduces the number of praetors in alternate years. Foundation of Aquileia. Beginning of deportation policy in Liguria; intensification of Roman military effort against the Ligurians.	Q. Fulvius Flaccus extends his invasion to more distant parts of Celtiberia.	Celebration of the first panhellenic *Nikephoria* in Pergamum. Eumenes supports Rhodes against the Lycians.
180	A. Postumius Albinus Luscus C. Calpurnius Piso	*Lex Villia annalis*. Founding of Luca as a Latin colony.	(180–178) Campaigns of Ti. Sempronius Gracchus in Celtiberia.	Embassy of Callicrates at Rome. Philip V puts to death his son Demetrius. Assassination of Ptolemy V Epiphanes of Egypt.
179	Q. Fulvius Flaccus L. Manlius Acidinus Fulvianus		L. Postumius Albinus defeats Lusitanians and Vaccaei.	Death of Philip V; accession of Perseus as king of Macedonia. Peace between Eumenes and Pharnaces.

	ROMAN CONSULS	ROME AND ITALY	THE WEST	THE EAST
178	M. Iunius Brutus A. Manlius Vulso	War in Istria	Treaties made by Ti. Sempronius Gracchus with the Celtiberians. Foundation of Gracchuris and (?)Iliturgi.	The Seleucid Antiochus, hostage in Rome, released in exchange for his nephew Demetrius.
177	C. Claudius Pulcher Ti. Sempronius Gracchus	Restrictions imposed on citizens of Latin and allied states. Foundation of Luna as a citizen colony. War in Istria.		Perseus of Macedon married to Laodice, daughter of Seleucus IV. (c. 177). Prusias II married to Apame, sister of Perseus.
176	Cn. Cornelius Scipio Hispallus C. Valerius Laevinus, *suffectus* Q. Petillius Spurinus			Death of Cleopatra, regent of Egypt.
175	P. Mucius Scaevola M. Aemilius Lepidus II	*Via Aemilia* built from Bononia to Aquileia.	Short-lived Celtiberian rebellion.	Seleucus IV murdered by Heliodorus. Eumenes supports Antiochus, who becomes king as Antiochus IV.
174	Sp. Postumius Albinus Paullulus Q. Mucius Scaevola		Cessation of Spanish wars. (174–172) Attacks by Massinissa on Carthaginian territory.	Jason appointed high-priest of the Jews by Antiochus IV; 'hellenistic reform' in Jerusalem.
173	L. Postumius Albinus M. Popillius Laenas	Latins in Rome required to return to their own cities. High-handed conduct of A. Postumius Albinus at Praeneste. M. Popillius Laenas in Liguria subjugates the Statellates; his treatment of the survivors generates political controversy. Commission led by M. Aemilius Lepidus appointed to distribute land in Cisalpine Gaul and Liguria to Romans and Latins, and possibly to other allies.		Final payment of indemnity due to Rome from the war with Antiochus III.

Year	Consuls	Rome and Italy	The West	Greece, Macedon and the East
172	C. Popillius Laenas P. Aelius Ligus		Carthaginian envoys complain to the Roman Senate about the encroachment of Massinissa.	Eumenes of Pergamum attacks Perseus of Macedon in a speech to the Senate at Rome. Attempt on the life of Eumenes at Delphi. Embassy of Q. Marcius Philippus to Greece. Boeotian Confederacy dissolved. (c. 172) Menelaus appointed high-priest of the Jews by Antiochus IV.
171	P. Licinius Crassus C. Cassius Longinus	Prosecution of three former governors of Spanish provinces.	Foundation of Carteia.	Beginning of war between Rome and Perseus (the Third Macedonian War). Perseus successful in cavalry engagement at Callicinus. (c. 171) Mithridates I becomes king of the Parthians.
170	A. Hostilius Mancinus A. Atilius Serranus		Rebellion in Nearer Spain.	Indecisive campaigns in Third Macedonian War. Perseus regains northern Thessaly. Epirote plot to kidnap the Roman consul. Antiochus, son of Seleucus IV, assassinated.
169	Q. Marcius Philippus II Cn. Servilius Caepio	Death of Ennius. Ti. Sempronius Gracchus as censor attempts to restrict the registration of most freedmen.		Roman army under Q. Marcius Philippus enters Macedonia. Rhodes, Pergamum and Bithynia waver in their support of Rome. The Molossians in Epirus and King Genthius of Illyria join Perseus. Sixth Syrian War; Antiochus IV invades Egypt.

	ROMAN CONSULS	ROME AND ITALY	THE WEST	THE EAST
168	L. Aemilius Paullus II C. Licinius Crassus	(c. 168?) Arrival of Crates in Rome.		Genthius of Illyria defeated by L. Anicius Gallus. Perseus defeated by L. Aemilius Paullus at Pydna (22 June) and later surrenders. Rome renounces friendship of Rhodes. Rebellion of Galatia against Eumenes of Pergamum. Second invasion of Egypt by Antiochus IV, who then evacuates Egypt and Cyprus in response to a Roman ultimatum. War in Jerusalem between Jason and Menelaus. Antiochus in Jerusalem. He prohibits the Jewish religion; Jewish martyrs.
167	Q. Aelius Paetus M. Iunius Pennus	Speech of M. Porcius Cato concerning the Rhodians.		Macedonia divided into four, Illyria into three, separate republics. Deportation to Italy of Rome's opponents in Greece, including 1,000 Achaeans (among them Polybius). 70 towns plundered and 150,000 persons enslaved in Epirus. Prusias before the Senate; Eumenes prohibited from coming to Rome. The Senate declares Caria and Lycia free. Delos given to Athens and made a free port by the Romans.
166	M. Claudius Marcellus C. Sulpicius Galus	Debate in the Senate concerning bribery. (166–160) The plays of Terence.		Eumenes defeats the Galatians; Galatia declared free by the Senate. Antiochus' celebrations in Daphne.

165	T. Manlius Torquatus Cn. Octavius		Antiochus IV begins his eastern campaign; Artaxias of Armenia defeated. Judas Maccabaeus recaptures Jerusalem and the temple.
164	A. Manlius Torquatus Q. Cassius Longinus		Embassy of C. Sulpicius Galus to Greece. He invites accusations against Eumenes. The Senate grants Rhodes a treaty. Lysias' first campaign against the Jews; Roman ambassadors contact the Maccabee rebels. Death of Antiochus IV; Antiochus V becomes king with Lysias as guardian. Death of Ariarathes IV; Ariarathes V becomes king of Cappadocia.
163	Ti. Sempronius Gracchus II M'. Iuventius Thalna		Antiochus V grants the Jews all former privileges; Menelaus executed; Alcimus appointed high-priest. Lysias' second campaign against the Jews. He concludes peace and defeats Philippus.
162	P. Cornelius Scipio Nasica Corculum C. Marcius Figulus (both abdicated in consequence of faulty election) P. Cornelius Lentulus, *suffectus* Cn. Domitius Ahenobarbus, *suffectus*	Disputes between Massinissa and Carthage (perhaps since 174).	Cn. Octavius murdered in Laodicea. The Seleucid Demetrius escapes from Rome; Antiochus V and Lysias executed; Demetrius I becomes king. Timarchus proclaims himself king.

536

	ROMAN CONSULS	ROME AND ITALY	THE WEST	THE EAST
161	M. Valerius Messala C. Fannius Strabo	Expulsion of philosophers from Rome. Lex Fannia, sumptuary law.		(161 or 160) Demetrius defeats Timarchus. Judas defeats Nicanor and concludes a treaty with Rome; he is defeated and killed by Bacchides.
160	L. Anicius Gallus M. Cornelius Cethegus			(161/60) Ariarathes of Cappadocia declines to marry Laodice, sister of Demetrius and widow of Perseus. (160/59) Eumenes of Pergamum appoints Attalus his co-ruler with the title of king. (c. 160) Nysa, daughter of Antiochus IV, married to Pharnaces of Pontus.
159	Cn. Cornelius Dolabella M. Fulvius Nobilior	Consular law concerning bribery.		Embassy of Demetrius in Rome. (159/8) Demetrius invades Cappadocia, expels Ariarathes and establishes Orophernes as king.
158	M. Aemilius Lepidus C. Popillius Laenas II			Death of Eumenes of Pergamum; Attalus II becomes sole king. Ariarathes V in Rome.
157	Sex. Iulius Caesar L. Aurelius Orestes		Roman envoys visit Africa to investigate a territorial dispute between Carthage and Massinissa.	Senate decrees that Cappadocia be divided between Ariarathes and Orophernes.
156	L. Cornelius Lentulus Lupus C. Marcius Figulus II			Attalus II defeats Orophernes and reinstates Ariarathes as king of Cappadocia. Prusias of Bithynia invades Pergamene territory and defeats Attalus. Roman campaign against Dalmatian pirates.

155	P. Cornelius Scipio Nasica Corculum II M. Claudius Marcellus II	Athenian 'philosophic' embassy to Rome. Conquest of Cisalpine Liguria completed.		Prusias besieges Pergamum. (155/4) Abortive attempt of Demetrius to take over Cyprus from Ptolemy VI. (155–153) War between Rhodes and Crete.
154	Q. Opimius L. Postumius Albinus M'. Acilius Glabrio, *suffectus*	Censors initiate the construction of a permanent theatre, subsequently demolished before completion.	Rome at war with Lusitanians and Celtiberians. Lusitanian successes.	Peace concluded between Prusias and Attalus. Attalus and Ariarathes ravage the territory of Priene; Rome intervenes. Coalition of Ptolemy, Attalus and Ariarathes against Demetrius.
153	Q. Fulvius Nobilior T. Annius Luscus	1 January becomes the beginning of the consular year.	Unsuccessful campaign of Q. Fulvius Nobilior against the Celtiberians. Roman envoys visit Africa in response to Carthaginian unrest directed at Massinissa. (c. 153–151) A further Roman mission sent to Carthage.	Alexander Balas of Syria in Rome.
152	M. Claudius Marcellus II L. Valerius Flaccus	Third consulship of M. Claudius Marcellus. Now or soon after, second consulships prohibited.	M. Claudius Marcellus takes command in Hither Spain and opens negotiations with the Celtiberians.	
151	L. Licinius Lucullus A. Postumius Albinus	Dispute concerning the levy; temporary imprisonment of the consuls.	Surrender of Celtiberians to M. Claudius Marcellus. Campaign of L. Licinius Lucullus against the Vaccaei and others. Carthage sends an army to resist Massinissa; suffers a major defeat. A further Roman mission arrives during the campaign.	Decree of the Senate in favour of Alexander Balas, who begins war against Demetrius. Alexander concludes an alliance with the Maccabean Jonathan and appoints him high-priest.

	ROMAN CONSULS	ROME AND ITALY	THE WEST	THE EAST
150	T. Quinctius Flamininus M'. Acilius Balbus		Ser. Sulpicius Galba defeats the Lusitanians and massacres a large number of them. Carthaginian attempts to appease Rome are met with evasions. Formal submission of Utica to Rome.	Achaean detainees released from Italy and return to Greece. Death of Callicrates. Demetrius defeated and killed in Syria. Alexander married to Ptolemy's daughter Cleopatra.
149	L. Marcius Censorinus M'. Manilius	Attempt to prosecute Ser. Sulpicius Galba for misconduct in Spain. Lex Calpurnia to provide a standing court for extortion cases. Death of M. Porcius Cato.	Rome declares war on Carthage; Roman army in Africa. Carthage disarmed but resists demands to evacuate the site of the city. Roman army begins the siege of Carthage.	Rising of Andriscus in Macedonia. He has initial success against a Roman army under P. Iuventius Thalna. Sparta seeks to secede from the Achaean League. Prusias defeated and killed by Nicomedes and Attalus; Nicomedes (II) becomes king of Bithynia.
148	Sp. Postumius Albinus Magnus L. Calpurnius Piso Caesoninus	Construction of the *Via Postumia* from Genua to Aquileia.		Attalus supports the Romans against Andriscus. Andriscus defeated and captured by Q. Caecilius Metellus (Macedonicus). (148/7) Media invaded and occupied by Mithridates I of Parthia; Susiane occupied by the Elamites.
147	P. Cornelius Scipio Africanus Aemilianus C. Livius Drusus	Scipio Aemilianus elected consul despite legal impediments.	Emergence of Viriathus as leader of the Lusitanians against Rome. Scipio Aemilianus in command in Africa; tightens the siege of Carthage.	Roman embassy under L. Aurelius Orestes authorizes secessions from the Achaean League. A further embassy to Greece, led by Sex. Iulius Caesar. Rhodes assists Rome against Carthage. Demetrius (II), son of Demetrius I, begins war against Alexander B...

146	Cn. Cornelius Lentulus L. Mummius	Capture and destruction of Carthage. Annexation of its territory as the province of Africa.		War between Rome and the Achaeans; victories of Q. Metellus Macedonicus and L. Mummius. Sack of Corinth; disbanding of the Achaean League. Creation of Roman province of Macedonia. Attalus, having supported the Romans in the Achaean War, defeats Diegylis in Thrace (146 or 145). Political events disrupt the Museum at Alexandria.
145	Q. Fabius Maximus Aemilianus L. Hostilius Mancinus			Ptolemy invades Syria (146 or 145) and concludes an alliance with Demetrius II, who marries Ptolemy's daughter Cleopatra. Ptolemy in Antioch; declines the Seleucid crown. Alexander Balas defeated by Ptolemy and Demetrius; death of Alexander and Ptolemy. Uproar in Antioch. Diodotus Tryphon proclaims Antiochus VI king.
144	Ser. Sulpicius Galba L. Aurelius Cotta	Building of the *Aqua Marcia*.	(144 or 143) Beginning of new Celtiberian rebellion. Successes of Q. Fabius Maximus Aemilianus against Viriathus.	(145/4) Demetrius retreats to Seleuceia. Alliance of Tryphon with Jonathan; Jonathan's brother Simon is satrap of Antiochus VI.
143	Ap. Claudius Pulcher Q. Caecilius Metellus Macedonicus	*Lex Didia* extends sumptuary legislation to Italy.	Renewed successes of Viriathus.	Jonathan killed by Tryphon; Simon becomes high-priest.

	ROMAN CONSULS	ROME AND ITALY	THE WEST	THE EAST
142	L. Caecilius Metellus Calvus Q. Fabius Maximus Servilianus	Censorship of Scipio Aemilianus.		Antiochus VI assassinated by Tryphon, who proclaims himself king. Alliance of Demetrius with Simon; Simon recaptures the citadel of Jerusalem. Simon's ambassadors in Rome. Tryphon rebuked by the Senate.
141	Cn. Servilius Caepio Q. Pompeius		Variathus' successes enable him to negotiate a treaty with Rome on favourable terms.	The Senate passes a decree in favour of Simon. Judea proclaimed independent. Mithridates I of Parthia occupies southern Mesopotamia.
140	C. Laelius Q. Servilius Caepio	Probable year of Laelius' agrarian proposal.	Rome repudiates the treaty with Viriathus and renews the war.	Demetrius sets out against the Parthians. Mithridates I defeats the Elamites at Kut-el-Amara. (140/39) Roman embassy led by Scipio Aemilianus in the east.
139	Cn. Calpurnius Piso M. Popillius Laenas	*Lex Gabinia*, ballot law. 'Chaldaeans' and Jews expelled from Rome.	Assassination of Viriathus. The Senate repudiates terms negotiated by Q. Pompeius with the Aravaci in Celtiberia.	Demetrius captured by the Parthians. (139/8) Antiochus VII proclaimed king, marries Cleopatra, and defeats Tryphon.
138	P. Cornelius Scipio Nasica Serapio D. Iunius Brutus Callaicus	Tribunate of Curiatius; agitation concerning the grain supply. Dispute about the levy; temporary imprisonment of the consuls.	Foundation of Valentia. (138/7) Campaigns of D. Brutus in north-western Spain.	Death of Attalus II; Attalus III becomes king of Pergamum. Death of Mithridates I; Phraates II becomes king of Parthia.
137	M. Aemilius Lepidus Porcina C. Hostilius Mancinus	*Lex Cassia*, ballot law.	Military disaster of C. Hostilius Mancinus at the hands of the Numantines. Treaty negotiated between him and the Numantines repudiated by the Senate.	

136	L. Furius Philus Sex. Atilius Serranus	Slave rebellion in Sicily.	M. Aemilius Lepidus and D. Brutus make war on the Vaccaei.	
135	Ser. Fulvius Flaccus Q. Calpurnius Piso			Decree of the Senate settles dispute between Samos and Priene. Simon assassinated; his son John (Hyrcanus) becomes high-priest at Jerusalem. Antiochus VII besieges Jerusalem.
134	P. Cornelius Scipio Africanus Aemilianus II C. Fulvius Flaccus	Second consulship of Scipio Aemilianus.	Scipio Aemilianus takes command in Celtiberia.	Jerusalem surrenders to Antiochus; the fortifications of the city are dismantled.
133	P. Mucius Scaevola L. Calpurnius Piso Frugi	(Tribunate of Tiberius Gracchus.)	Scipio Aemilianus ends the Celtiberian War by capturing and destroying Numantia.	Death of Attalus III, who bequeaths his fortune to Rome.

BIBLIOGRAPHY

Abbreviations

*AAN   Atti dell' Accademia di Scienzi morali e politiche della Società nazionale di
Scienze, Lettere ed Arti di Napoli*
AAnt. Hung.   Acta Antiqua Academiae Scientarum Hungaricae
AE   L'Année épigraphique
AFLPad.   Annali della Facoltà di Lettere e Filosofia di Padova
AIPh   Annuaire de l'Institut de philologie et d'histoire orientales et slaves
AJAH   American Journal of Ancient History
AJArch.   American Journal of Archaeology
AJPhil.   American Journal of Philology
AM   Annales du Midi
Amer. Hist. Rev.   American Historical Review
ANRW   Aufstieg und Niedergang der römischen Welt, ed. H. Temporini and
W. Haase. Berlin and New York, 1972–
ANSMN   American Numismatic Society, Museum Notes
Ant. Class.   L'Antiquité classique
Ant. Journ.   Antiquaries Journal
Arch. Anz.   Archäologischer Anzeiger (in *JDAI*)
Arch. Delt.   'Αρχαιολογικὸν Δελτίον
Arch. Eph.   'Αρχαιολογικὴ 'Εφημερίς
*ASAA   Annuario della Scuola Archeologica di Atene e delle Missioni Italiane in
Oriente*
ASNSP   Annali della Scuola Normale Superiore di Pisa
Atti Taranto   Atti dei Convegni di studi sulla Magna Graecia. Taranto
AvP   Altertümer von Pergamon (Museen zu Berlin and Deutsches Archäolo-
gisches Institut). Berlin, 1885–   (13 volumes so far published)
BASOR   Bulletin of the American Schools of Oriental Research
BCH   Bulletin de Correspondance Hellénique
BEFEO   Bulletin de l'École française d'Extrême-Orient
BICS   Bulletin of the Institute of Classical Studies (London)
BMQ   British Museum Quarterly
BSA   Annual of the British School at Athens
BSFN   Bulletin de la Société française de Numismatique
Bull. Com. Arch.   Bullettino della Commissione Archeologica Comunale in Roma
Bull. épigr.   J. and *L.* Robert, *Bulletin épigraphique* (in *REG*)
Bull. Rylands Libr.   Bulletin of the John Rylands Library

CAH   The Cambridge Ancient History
C&M   Classica et Mediaevalia
CDE   Caratteri dell'ellenismo nelle urne etrusche (Atti dell' incontro di studi.
   Università di Siena. 28–30 aprile 1976). Florence, 1977
CE   Chronique d'Égypte
CIL   Corpus Inscriptionum Latinarum
CJ   Classical Journal
CPh   Classical Philology
CQ   Classical Quarterly
CRAI   Comptes rendus de l'Académie des Inscriptions et Belles-lettres
CT   Les Cahiers de Tunisie
DArch.   Dialoghi di Archeologia
Denkschr. Akad. Wien   Denkschriften der Akademie der Wissenschaften in Wien
Ep. Ind.   Epigraphia Indica
ESAR   An Economic Survey of Ancient Rome, ed. T. Frank. 6 vols. Baltimore,
   1933–40
FD   Fouilles de Delphes
FGrH   F. Jacoby, Fragmente der griechischen Historiker. Berlin and Leiden, 1923–
FIRA   S. Riccobono, Fontes Iuris Romani Anteiustiniani. 3 vols. Florence,
   1940–3
G&R   Greece & Rome
Gramm. Rom. Frag.   H. Funaioli, Grammaticae Romanae fragmenta (Vol. 1 only).
   Leipzig, 1907
GRBS   Greek, Roman and Byzantine Studies
GWU   Geschichte in Wissenschaft und Unterricht
Harv. Stud.   Harvard Studies in Classical Philology
Hesp.   Hesperia. Journal of the American School of Classical Studies at Athens
HIM   Hellenismus in Mittelitalien (Kolloquium in Göttingen vom 5 bis 9 Juni 1974),
   ed. P. Zanker. 2 vols. Göttingen, 1976
Hist.-fil. Medd. Kgl. Da. Vid. Selsk. Historisk-filologiske Meddelelser, Kgl.
   Danske Videnskabernes Selskab.
HZ   Historische Zeitschrift
IBulg.   G. Mihailov, Inscriptiones Graecae in Bulgaria repertae. Sofia, 1958–
IC   M. Guarducci, Inscriptiones Creticae. 4 vols. Rome, 1935–50
ID   L'Italia Dialettale
IDélos   F. Durrbach and others, Inscriptions de Délos. Paris, 1926–50
IG   Inscriptiones Graecae
IGCH   M. Thompson, O. Mørkholm, C. M. Kraay, An Inventory of Greek Coin
   Hoards. New York, 1973
IGRom.   R. Cagnat and others. Inscriptiones Graecae ad res Romanas pertinentes.
   Paris, 1906–27
IHQ   Indian Historical Quarterly
ILampsakos   P. Frisch, Die Inschriften von Lampsakos. Bonn, 1978
ILindos   Ch. Blinkenberg, Lindos II: Les inscriptions. 2 vols. Berlin and Copen-
   hagen, 1941
ILLRP   A. Degrassi, Inscriptiones Latinae Liberae Rei Publicae, 2 vols. 2nd edn.
   Florence, 1963–5

ILS H. Dessau, *Inscriptiones Latinae Selectae.* 3 vols. Berlin, 1892–1916
Inscr. Italiae *Inscriptiones Italiae*
IPE B. Latyschev, *Inscriptiones Antiquae Orae Septentrionalis Ponti Euxeni Graecae et Latinae.* 2nd edn. St Petersburg, 1916
IPriene F. Hiller v. Gaertringen, *Die Inschriften von Priene.* Berlin, 1906
ISyrie L. Jalabert, R. Mouterde and J. P. Rey-Coquais, *Inscriptions greques et latines de la Syrie.* Paris, 1929–
IvP M. Fränkel, *Inschriften von Pergamon.* 2 vols. Berlin, 1890–5
IvP III Ch. Habicht, *Inschriften von Pergamon* III: *Die Inschriften des Asklepieions.* Berlin, 1969
JA *Journal Asiatique*
JAOS *Journal of the American Oriental Society*
JDAI *Jahrbuch des [kaiserlich] deutschen archäologischen Instituts*
JEg. Arch. *Journal of Egyptian Archaeology*
JHS *Journal of Hellenic Studies*
JNG *Jahrbruch für Numismatik und Geldgeschichte*
JNSI *Journal of the Numismatic Society of India*
JÖAI *Jahreshefte des Österreichischen archäologischen Instituts in Wien*
JRAS *Journal of the Royal Asiatic Society*
JRS *Journal of Roman Studies*
JS *Journal des Savants*
JSHRZ *Jüdische Schriften aus hellenistisch-römischer Zeit*, ed. W. G. Kümmel. Gütersloh, 1976
Le arti figurative *Storia e civiltà dei Greci* V: *La cultura ellenistica*, 10, *Le arti figurative* (ed. R. Bianchi Bandinelli). Milan, 1977
LEC *Les Études classiques*
LW Ph. Le Bas, W. H. Waddington, *Inscriptions grecques et latines recueillies en Asie-Mineure.* 2 vols. Paris, 1870
MAAR Memoirs of the American Academy in Rome
MAL *Memorie della classe di Scienze morali e storiche dell' Accademia dei Lincei*
MDAFA *Mémoires de la Délégation archéologique française en Afghanistan*
MDAI *Mitteilungen des deutschen archäologischen Instituts*
(A) *Athenische Abteilung*
(I) *Instanbuler Abteilung*
(M) *Madrider Abteilung*
Mélanges d'arch. *Mélanges d'archéologie et d'histoire de l'École française de Rome*
Mélanges Heurgon *L'Italie préromaine et la Rome républicaine, Mélanges offerts à Jacques Heurgon.* 2 vols. Rome, 1976
MH *Museum Helveticum*
Michel, *Recueil* Ch. Michel, *Recueil d'inscriptions grecques.* Brussels, 1900
Milet T. Wiegand, *Milet. Ergebnisse der Ausgrabungen und Untersuchungen seit 1899*
Moretti, *ISE* L. Moretti, *Iscrizioni storiche ellenistiche.* 2 vols. Florence, 1967 and 1976
MRR T. R. S. Broughton, *The Magistrates of the Roman Republic.* 2 vols. and suppl. New York, 1951–60
NAC *Numismatica e antichità classiche*

Neue Jahrb. Neue Jahrbücher (für das klassische Altertum, 1898–1925; *für Wissenschaft und Jugendbildung*, 1925–36)

NNM Numismatic Notes and Monographs, American Numismatic Society, New York

Num. Chron. Numismatic Chronicle

OGIS W. Dittenberger, *Orientis Graeci Inscriptiones Selectae*. 2 vols. Leipzig. 1903–5

ORF⁴ H. Malcovati, *Oratorum Romanorum Fragmenta*. 2 vols. 4th edn. Turin, 1976–9

PACA Proceedings of the African Classical Association

PBA Proceedings of the British Academy

PBSR Papers of the British School at Rome

PCPS Proceedings of the Cambridge Philological Society

Peek, *GVI* W. Peek, *Griechische Versinschriften* I: *Grabepigramme*. Berlin, 1955

PEQ Palestine Exploration Quarterly

Peter, *HRRel.* H. W. G. Peter, *Historicorum Romanorum Reliquiae*. 2 vols. Leipzig, 1906–14

PHerc. Papyri Herculanenses

Philol. Philologus

PJ Palästinajahrbuch

PP La Parola del Passato

Proc. Amer. Phil. Soc. Proceedings of the American Philosophical Society

PW A. Pauly, G. Wissowa and W. Kroll, *Real-Encyclopädie der classischen Altertumswissenschaft*

QC Quaderni Catanesi di Studi classici e medievale

RD Revue historique de droit français et étranger

REA Revue des études anciennes

REG Revue des études grecques

REJ Revue des études juives

REL Revue des études latines

Rend. Inst. Lomb. Cl. Lettere Rendiconti del Istituto Lombardo, Classe di lettere, scienze morali e storiche

Rev. Arch. Revue archéologique

Rev. Arch. Narbonnaise Revue archéologique de Narbonnaise

Rev. Hist. Rel. Revue de l'histoire des religions

Rev. Num. Revue numismatique

Rev. Phil. Revue de philologie

Rh. Mus. Rheinisches Museum für Philologie

RIGS Incontro di studi su "Roma e l'Italia fra i Gracchi e Silla" (Pontignano. 18–21 settembre 1969). DArch. 4–5 (1970–1) 3–4, 163–562

Riv. Fil. Rivista di filologia e d'istruzione classica

RMR Roma medio repubblicana, aspetti culturali di Roma e del Lazio nei secoli IV e III a.C. Rome, 1973

RSA Rivista storica dell' Antichità

RSI Rivista storica italiana

SCI Scripta Classica Israelica

SCO Studi classici e orientali

SDAW   *Sitzungsberichte der Deutschen Akademie der Wissenschaften zu Berlin*
Sherk, *Documents*   R. K. Sherk, *Roman Documents from the Greek East*.
    Baltimore, 1969
SIFC   *Studi italiani di filologia classica*
SIG   W. Dittenberger, *Sylloge Inscriptionum Graecarum*. 4 vols. 3rd edn. Leipzig,
    1915–24
SRPS   *Società romana e produzione schiavistica*, ed. A. Giardina and A. Schiavone.
    3 vols. Rome and Bari, 1981
Stud. Clas.   *Studii clasice*
Stud. Etr.   *Studi etruschi*
TAPA   *Transactions of the American Philological Association*
VDI   *Vestnik Drevnej Istorii*
Welles, *RC*   C. B. Welles, *Royal Correspondence in the Hellenistic Period*. New
    Haven, 1934
YCIS   *Yale Classical Studies*
ZATW   *Zeitschrift für die alttestamentliche Wissenschaft*
ZDPV   *Zeitschrift des Deutschen Palästinavereins*
ZNTW   *Zeitschrift für die neutestamentliche Wissenschaft*
ZPE   *Zeitschrift für Papyrologie und Epigraphik*

Bibliography

A. GENERAL STUDIES AND WORKS OF REFERENCE

1. Alvar, M. and others. *Enciclopedia linguistica hispanica* 1. Madrid, 1960
2. Austin, M. M. *The Hellenistic World from Alexander to the Roman Conquest.* Cambridge, 1981
3. Badian, E. *Foreign Clientelae (264–70 B.C.).* Oxford, 1958
4. Badian, E. *Studies in Greek and Roman History.* Oxford, 1964
5. Badian, E. *Roman Imperialism in the Late Republic.* 2nd edn. Oxford, 1968
6. Beloch J. *Die Bevölkerung der griechisch-römischen Welt.* Leipzig, 1886
7. Beloch, K. J. *Römische Geschichte bis zum Beginn der punischen Kriege.* Berlin, 1926
8. Bengtson, H. *Die Strategie in der hellenistischen Zeit* II. Munich, 1944
9. Bengtson, H. *Griechische Geschichte.* 5th edn. Munich, 1977
10. Broughton, T. R. S. *The Magistrates of the Roman Republic.* 2 vols. and Supplement. New York, 1951–2 and 1960
10A. Burstein, S. M. *The Hellenistic Age from the Battle of Ipsos to the Death of Kleopatra VII.* Cambridge, 1985
11. Carcopino, J. *Les étapes de l'impérialisme romain.* Paris, 1961
12. Crawford, M. H. *The Roman Republic.* London, 1978
13. De Martino, F. *Storia della costituzione romana.* 5 vols. 2nd edn. Naples, 1972–5
14. De Sanctis, G. *Storia dei Romani.* 4 vols. 2nd edn. Turin and Florence, 1907–64
15. Earl, D. *The Moral and Political Tradition of Rome.* London, 1967
16. Errington, R. M. *The Dawn of Empire. Rome's Rise to World Power.* London and Ithaca, 1971
17. Frank, T. *Roman Imperialism.* New York, 1914
18. Frank, T. *Economic Survey of Ancient Rome.* 6 vols. Baltimore, 1933–40
19. Gelzer, M. *Kleine Schriften.* 3 vols. Wiesbaden, 1962–4
20. Gruen, E. S. *The Hellenistic World and the Coming of Rome.* 2 vols. Berkeley, 1984
21. Harris W. V. *War and Imperialism in Republican Rome, 327–70 B.C.* Oxford, 1979
22. Lesky, A. *Geschichte der griechischen Literatur.* 2nd edn. Bern and Munich, 1973
23. Lintott, A. W. 'Imperial expansion and moral decline in the Roman Republic', *Historia* 21 (1972) 626–38
24. McDonald, A. H. Review of T. R. S. Broughton, *The Magistrates of the Roman Republic,* in *JRS* 43 (1953) 142–5
25. Mommsen, T. *Römisches Staatsrecht.* 3 vols. Leipzig, 1887–8
26. Mommsen, T. *Römische Geschichte* I–III, V. 12th edn., 1921–3
27. Nicolet, C., ed. *Rome et la conquête du monde méditerranéen 264–27 avant J.-C.* 2 vols. Paris, 1977–8
28. North, J. A. 'The development of Roman imperialism', *JRS* 71 (1981) 1–9
29. Pais, E. *Dalle guerre puniche a Cesare Augusto* II. Rome, 1918

30. Richardson, J. S. 'Polybius' view of the Roman Empire', *PBSR* 47 (1979) 1–11
31. Rostovtzeff, M. *A Social and Economic History of the Hellenistic World.* 3 vols. Oxford, 1941 (2nd edn, 1957)
32. Schmitt, H. H. *Die Staatsverträge des Altertums* III: *Die Verträge der griechisch-römischen Welt von 338 bis 200 v. Chr.* Munich, 1969
33. Sherwin-White, A. N. 'Rome the aggressor?', *JRS* 70 (1980) 177–81
34. Sherwin-White, A. N. *Roman Foreign Policy in the Near East, 168 B.C.– A.D. 1.* London, 1984
35. Ste Croix, G. E. M. de. *The Class Struggle in the Ancient Greek World.* London, 1981
36. Tarn, W. W. and Griffiths, G. T. *Hellenistic Civilization.* 3rd edn. London, 1955
37. Toynbee, A. J. *Hannibal's Legacy.* 2 vols. London, 1965
38. Veyne, P. 'Y-a-t-il eu un impérialisme romain?', *Mélanges d'arch.* 87 (1975) 793–85
39. Werner, R. 'Das Problem des Imperialismus und die römische Ostpolitik im zweiten Jahrhundert v. Chr.', *ANRW* 1.1 (1972) 501–63
40. Will, E. *Histoire politique du monde hellénistique.* 2 vols. 2nd edn. Nancy, 1982 (1st edn, 1966–7)

B. SOURCES

a. Commentaries and other works concerning ancient authors

1. Boissevain, U. P., de Boor, C. and Büttner-Wobst, T. *Excerpta Historica Iussu Imp. Constantini Porphyrogeniti Confecta.* 4 vols. in 5. Berlin, 1903–10
2. Brink, C. O. and Walbank, F. W. 'The construction of the Sixth Book of Polybius', *CQ* n.s. 4 (1954) 97–122
3. Briscoe, J. *A Commentary on Livy Books XXXI–XXXIII.* Oxford, 1973
4. Briscoe, J. *A Commentary on Livy Books XXXIV–XXXVII.* Oxford, 1981
5. Bunge, J. G. *Untersuchungen zum 2. Makkabäerbuch.* Diss. Bonn, 1971
6. Derow, P. S. Review of F. W. Walbank, *A Historical Commentary on Polybius* III, in *JRS* 74 (1984) 231–5
7. Gabba, E. *Appiano e la storia delle Guerre Civili.* Florence, 1956
8. Gabba, E. *Appiani Bellorum Civilium Liber Primus.* Florence, 1958
9. Gauger, J.-D. *Beiträge zur jüdischen Apologetik. Untersuchungen zur Authentizität von Urkunden bei Flavius Josephus und im 1. Makkabäerbuch.* Cologne and Bonn, 1977
10. Habicht, Ch. *2. Makkabäerbuch.* Gütersloh, 1976 (*JSHRZ*)
11. Hanhart, R. 'Zur Zeitrechnung des ersten und zweiten Makkabäerbuches', in A. Jepsen and R. Hanhart, *Untersuchungen zur israelitisch-jüdischen Chronologie,* 55–96. Berlin, 1966
12. Jacoby, F. *Die Fragmente der griechischen Historiker.* Berlin and Leiden, 1923– (*FGrH*)
13. Klotz, A. *Livius und seine Vorgänger.* Berlin and Leipzig, 1940–1

14. Lehmann, G. A. *Untersuchungen zur historischen Glaubwürdigkeit des Polybios.* Münster, 1967
15. Luce, T. J. *Livy. The Composition of his History.* Princeton, 1977
16. Malcovati, H. *Oratorum Romanorum Fragmenta.* 2 vols. 4th edn. Turin, 1976–9
17. Martina, M. 'La "vita Antiochi" dell' annalista Liciniano', *Athenaeum* 62 (1984) 190–209
18. Momigliano, A. 'Linee per una valutazione di Fabio Pittore', in *Terzo contributo alla storia degli studi classici*, 55–68. Rome, 1966
19. Momigliano, A. 'The second book of the Maccabees', *CPh* 70 (1975) 81–8
20. Momigliano, A. *Polybius between the English and the Turks.* The Seventh J. L. Myres Memorial Lecture. Oxford, 1974 = *Sesto contributo alla storia degli studi classici e del mondo antico* I, 125–41. Rome, 1980
21. Münscher, K. *Xenophon in der griechisch-römischen Literatur*, *Philol.* Suppl. 13.2 (1920)
22. Musti, D. *Polibio e l'imperialismo romano.* Naples, 1978
23. Nissen, H. *Kritische Untersuchungen über die Quellen der vierten und fünften Dekade des Livius.* Berlin, 1863
24. Norden, E. *Ennius und Vergilius.* Leipzig, 1915
25. Ogilvie, R. M. *A Commentary on Livy, Books 1–5.* Oxford, 1965
26. Pédech, P. *La méthode historique de Polybe.* Paris, 1964
27. Peter, H. G. W. *Historicorum Romanorum Reliquiae.* 2 vols. Leipzig, 1906–14
28. Pritchard, J. B. *Ancient Near Eastern Texts relating to the Old Testament.* 2nd edn. Princeton, 1955 (3rd edn, 1969)
29. Raschke, W. J. 'The chronology of the early books of Lucilius', *JRS* 69 (1979) 78–89
30. Rubinsohn, Z. 'The "bellum Asiaticum". A reconsideration', *Rend. Inst. Lomb. Cl. Lettere* 107 (1973) 546–70
31. Salem, M. S. 'Ennius and the "Isiaci Coniectores"', *JRS* 27 (1938) 56–9
32. Schröder, W. A. M. *Porcius Cato: Das erste Buch der Origines.* Meisenheim am Glan, 1971
33. Schulten, A., ed. *Fontes Hispaniae Antiquae* III, IV. Barcelona, 1935, 1937
34. Schulten, A. and Bosch Gimpera, P. *Fontes Hispaniae Antiquae* I: *Avieni Ora Maritima.* Barcelona, 1922
35. Skutsch, O. *Studia Enniana.* London, 1967
35A. Skutsch, O. *The Annals of Quintus Ennius.* Oxford, 1985.
36. Till, R. *La lingua di Catone.* Rome, 1968 (tr., with addit. notes, by C. de Meo of *Die Sprache Catos.* Leipzig, 1935)
37. Timpanaro, S. 'Per una nuova edizione critica di Ennio', *SIFC* 23 (1948) 5–58
37A. Vahlen, J. *Ennianae Poesis Reliquiae.* 3rd edn. Leipzig, 1928
38. Walbank, F. W. *A Historical Commentary on Polybius.* 3 vols. Oxford, 1957–79.
39. Walbank, F. W. *Polybius.* Berkeley, 1972
40. Walsh, P. G. *Livy.* Cambridge, 1961
41. Walsh, P. G. *T. Livi ab Urbe Condita Liber XXI.* London, 1973
42. Warrior, V. M. 'Livy, Book 42: structure and chronology', *AJAH* 6 (1981) 1–50

43. Weissenborn, W. and Müller, H. J. *Titi Livi ab Urbe Condita*. Berlin, 1880–1911

44. Welwei, K.-W. *Könige und Königtum im Urteil des Polybios*. Diss. Cologne, 1963

b. *Epigraphy*

(For most of the principal collections of inscriptions see Abbrevations)

44A. Blümel, W. *Die Inschriften von Iasos*. 2 vols. Bonn. 1985

45. Crampa, J. *Labraunda: Swedish Excavations and Researches* III.1: *The Greek Inscriptions* Part 1, 1–12 (Period of Olympichus). Skrifter utgivna av Svenska Institutet i Athen v.iii.1. Lund, 1969

46. Crampa, J. *Labraunda: Swedish Excavations and Researches* III.2: *The Greek Inscriptions* Part II, 13–133. Skrifter utgivna av Svenska Institutet i Athen v.iii.2. Lund, 1972

47. Degrassi, A. *Fasti Consulares et Triumphales. Inscriptiones Italiae* XIII.1. Rome, 1947

48. Degrassi, A. 'Epigraphica, III', *Memorie dell' Accademia nazionale dei Lincei* (*Classe di scienze morali e storiche*)[8] 13 (1967) 1–53 (reprinted in *Scritti vari di Antichità* III. Venice and Trieste, 1967)

49. Dupont-Sommer, A. 'Deux inscriptions araméennes trouvées près du lac de Sevan (Arménie)', *Syria* 25 (1946–8) 53–66

50. Durrbach, F. *Choix d'inscriptions de Délos*. Paris, 1921

50A. Errington, (R.)M. 'Antiochus III, Zeuxis and Euromos', *Epigraphica Anatolica* 8 (1986) 1–8

51. Habicht, Ch. 'Samische Volksbeschlüsse der hellenistischen Zeit', *MDAI(A)* 72 (1957) 152–274

52. Holleaux, M. 'Une inscription de Séleucie-de-Pierie', *BCH* 57 (1933) 6–67

53. Mazzarino, S. 'L'iscrizione di Toutonenstein è un'incompiunta?', *QC* 1 (1979) 567–602

54. Mellor, R. 'The dedications on the Capitoline hill', *Chiron* 8 (1978) 319–30

55. Moretti, L. 'Ancora su Hagemonidas di Dyme', *Riv. Fil.* 93 (1965) 283–7

56. Moretti, L. *Iscrizioni storiche ellenistiche*. 2 vols. Florence, 1967–75

57. Moretti, L. 'Chio e la lupa capitolina', *Riv. Fil.* 108 (1980) 33–54

58. Peek, W. *Griechische Versinschriften* I: *Grabepigramme*. Berlin, 1955

59. Petzl, G. 'Inschriften aus der Umgebung von Saittai (I)', *ZPE* 30 (1978) 249–79

60. Poccetti, P. 'Iscrizione umbra su meridiana', *Aiôn* 1 (1979) 77

61. Robert, J. and L. *Hellenica* VI. Paris, 1948

62. Robert, L. 'Notes d'épigraphie hellénistique', *BCH* 52 (1928) 426–43

63. Robert, L. 'Décret de Tralles', *Rev. Phil.* 60 (1934) 279–91

64. Robert, L. 'Décret d'Athènes pour un officier d'Antiochos Epiphane', *Hellenica* XI–XII, 91–111. Paris, 1960

65. Robert, L. Review of *Samothrace* II.1, in *Gnomon* 35 (1963) 50–79

66. Robert, L. *Nouvelles inscriptions de Sardes*. Paris, 1964

67. Robert, L. 'Décret d'Athènes pour un courtisan Séleucide', *Arch. Eph.* 1969, 1–6

68. Robert, L. 'Sur des inscriptions de Délos', *Études Déliennes. BCH* Supplement 1, 435–89. Paris, 1973
69. Robert, L. 'Documents d'Asie Mineure', *BCH* 102 (1978) 395–543
70. Robert, L. 'Catalogue agonistique des Romaia de Xanthos', *Rev. Arch.* (1978) 77–90
71. Robert, L. 'Documents d'Asie Mineure', *BCH* 108 (1984) 457–532 ('Documents pergaméniens', pp. 472–99)
72. Segre, M. 'Iscrizioni di Licia', *Clara Rhodos* 9 (1938) 179–208
73. Sherk, R. K. *Roman Documents from the Greek East.* Baltimore, 1969
74. Welles, C. B. *Royal Correspondence in the Hellenistic Period.* New Haven, 1934
75. Wilhelm, A. 'Eine Inschrift des Königs Epiphanes Nikomedes', *JÖAI* 11 (1908) 75–82

                            c. Numismatics

                          (See also Section F)

76. Adams, J. P. 'Aristonikos and the cistophori', *Historia* 29 (1980) 302–14
77. Bauslaugh, R. A. 'The unique portrait tetradrachms of Eumenes II', *ANSMN* 27 (1982) 39–51
78. Bellinger, A. R. 'Hyspaosines of Charax', *YClS* 7 (1942) 51–67
79. Bellinger, A. R. 'The bronze coins of Timarchus', *ANSMN* 1 (1945) 37–44
80. Ben-David, A. 'When did the Maccabees begin to strike their first coins?', *PEQ* 104 (1972) 93–103
81. Blázquez, J. M. 'Consideraciones históricas en torno a los supuestos retratos bárquidas en las monedas cartaginesas', *Numisma* 26 (1976) 39–48
82. Boehringer, Chr. *Zur Chronologie mittelhellenistischer Münzserien.* Berlin, 1972
83. Brett, A. B. 'Seleucid coins of Ake-Ptolemais', *ANSMN* 4 (1950) 17–35
84. Brett, A. B. 'The mint of Ascalon under the Seleucids', *ANSMN* 4 (1950) 43–54
85. Bunge, J. G. 'Münzen als Mittel politischer Propaganda: Antiochos IV. Epiphanes von Syrien', *Stud. Clas.* 16 (1974) 43–52
86. Crawford, M. H. 'War and finance', *JRS* 54 (1964) 29–32
87. Crawford, M. H. *Roman Republican Coin Hoards.* London, 1969
88. Crawford, M. H. *Roman Republican Coinage.* 2 vols. Cambridge, 1974
88A. Crawford, M. H. 'Le monete romane nelle regioni d'Italia', *Les 'Bourgeoisies' municipales italiennes aux IIe et Ier siècles av. J.-C.*, 47–50. Colloques Int. CNRS 609. Paris and Naples, 1983
89. De Guadan, A. M. *Numismática ibérica e ibero-romana.* Madrid, 1969
90. Fischer, Th. 'Die Berliner Goldmünze des Seleukiden Antiochos V. (164–162 v. Chr.)', *Schweizer Münzblätter* 21 (1971) 37–9
91. Furtwängler, A. 'Griechische Vieltypenprägung und Münzbeamte', *Schweizerische Numismatische Rundschau* 61 (1982) 5–25
92. Giovannini, A. *Rome et la circulation monétaire en Grèce au II siècle avant Jésus-Christ.* Basel, 1978
93. Grant, M. *From Imperium to Auctoritas.* Cambridge, 1946

94. Hanson, R. S. 'Toward a chronology of the Hasmonean coins', *BASOR* 216 (1974) 21–3

95. Heichelheim, F. M. 'Numismatic comments, II. A Seleucid pretender Antiochus in 151/0 B.C.', *Hesp.* 13 (1944) 363–4

96. Hill, G. F. *Notes on the Ancient Coinage of Hispania Citerior.* NNM 50. New York, 1931

97. Houghton, A. *Coins of the Seleucid Empire from the Collection of A. Houghton.* New York, 1983

98. Jahn, J. 'Literaturüberblick der griechischen Numismatik. Karthago und westliches Nordafrica', *Chiron* 7 (1977) 411–85

99. Jenkins, G. K. 'Notes on Seleucid coins', *Num. Chron.*[6] 11 (1951) 1–21

100. Jenkins, G. K. 'Hellenistic coins from Nimrud', *Iraq* 20 (1958) 158–68

101. Jenkins, G. K. and Lewis, R. B. *Carthaginian Gold and Electrum Coins.* London, 1963

102. Kienast, D. 'Cistophoren', *JNG* 11 (1961) 159–88

103. Kleiner, F. S. 'The dated cistophori of Ephesus', *ANSMN* 18 (1972) 17–32

104. Kleiner, F. S. 'Further reflections on the early cistophoric coins', *ANSMN* 25 (1980) 45–52

105. Kleiner, F. S. and Noe, S. P. *The Early Cistophoric Coinage (166–133).* New York, 1976

106. Knapp, R. C. 'The date and purpose of the Iberian denarii', *Num. Chron.*[7] 17 (1977) 1–18

107. Kraay, C. M. *Greek Coins and History.* London, 1969

108. Küthmann, C. 'Bermerkungen zu einigen Münzen des hellenistischen Ostens', *Schweizer Münzblätter* 1 (1950) 63–9

109. Küthmann, C. 'Münzen als Denkmäler seleukidischer Geschichte des II. Jahrhunderts v. Chr.', *Blätter für Münzfreunde und Münzforschung* 78 (1954) 1–20

110. LeRider, G. 'Monnaies grecques récemment acquises par le Cabinet de Paris', *Rev. Num.*[6] 11 (1969) 7–27

111. LeRider, G. 'Un tétradrachme d'Athéna Niképhoros', *Rev. Num.*[6] 15 (1973) 66–79

112. Mørkholm, O. *Studies in the Coinage of Antiochus IV of Syria*, Hist.-fil. Medd. Kgl. Da. Vid. Selsk. 40 no. 3 (1963)

113. Mørkholm, O. 'Seleucid coins from Cilicia ca. 220–150 B.C.', *ANSMN* 11 (1964) 53–62

114. Mørkholm, O. 'The Seleucid mint at Antiochia on the Persian Gulf', *ANSMN* 16 (1970) 31–44

115. Mørkholm, O. 'The Ptolemaic "coins of an unknown era"', *Nordisk Numismatisk Årsskrift* (1975–6) 23–58

116. Mørkholm, O. 'Some reflections on the early cistophoric coinage', *ANSMN* 24 (1979) 50–62

117. Mørkholm, O. 'The Hellenistic period', in *A Survey of Numismatic Research 1972–1977*, 60–97. Berne, 1979

118. Mørkholm, O. 'Sculpture and coins; the portrait of Alexander Balas of Syria', *NAC* 10 (1981) 235–45

119. Mørkholm, O. 'Some reflections on the production and use of coinage in ancient Greece', *Historia* 31 (1982) 290–305
120. Navascues, J. M. De. 'Ni Barquidas ni Escipion', in *Homenaje al Professor Cayetano de Mergelina*, 1–22. Murcia, 1961–2
121. Newell, E. T. *The Seleucid Coinage of Tyre. A Supplement.* NNM 73. New York, 1936
122. Newell, E. T. *Late Seleucid Mints in Ake-Ptolemais and Damascus.* NNM 84. New York, 1939
123. Pautasso, A. *Le monete preromane dell' Italia settentrionale.* Varese, 1966 (= *Sibrium* VII)
124. Pautasso, A. 'Sulla cronologia delle monetazioni padane', *NAC* 4 (1975) 45–54
125. Pfeiler, H. 'Wann erreichten die Karthager die Azoren?', *Schweizer Münzblätter* 15 (1965) 53
126. Pfeiler, H. 'Eine Drachme Demetrios' I. aus Soloi', *Schweizer Münzblätter* 19 (1969) 42–3
127. Regling, K. *Die Münzen von Priene.* Berlin, 1927
128. Robinson, E. S. G. 'Carthaginian coins', *BMQ* 12 (1937–8) 141–3
129. Robinson, E. S. G. 'Cistophors in the name of King Eumenes', *Num. Chron.*⁶ 14 (1954) 1–8
130. Robinson, E. S. G. 'Punic coins in Spain', in *Essays on Roman Coinage presented to H. Mattingly*, ed. R. A. G. Carson and C. H. V. Sutherland, 34–53. London 1956
131. Seyrig, H. *Notes on Syrian Coins.* NNM 119. New York, 1950
132. Seyrig, H. 'Antiquités syriennes 67: Monnaies contremarquées en Syrie', *Syria* 35 (1958) 187–97
133. Seyrig, H. 'Le monnayage de Ptolemais en Phénicie', *Rev. Num.*⁶ 4 (1962) 25–50
134. Seyrig, H. 'Le traité d'Apamée et le monnayage des villes d'Asie', *Rev. Num.*⁶ 5 (1963) 19–22
135. Seyrig, H. 'Questions cistophoriques', *Rev. Num.*⁶ 5 (1963) 22–31
136. Seyrig, H. 'Monnaies hellénistiques, XII: Questions aradiennes', *Rev. Num.*⁶ 6 (1964) 9–50
137. Spaer, A. 'Monnaies de bronze palestiniennes d'Antiochos VII', *Rev. Num.*⁶ 13 (1971) 160–1
138. Spaer, A. 'A hoard of Seleucid silver coins from Jericho: addenda', *Num. Chron.* 142 (1982) 140–2
139. Strauss, P. 'Un trésor de monnaies hellénistiques trouvé près de Suse', *Rev. Num.*⁶ 13 (1971) 109–40
140. Thompson, M., Mørkholm, O. and Kraay, C. M. *An Inventory of Greek Coin Hoards.* New York, 1973 (*IGCH*)
141. Villaronga, L. *Las monedas hispano-cartaginesas.* Barcelona, 1973
142. Volkmann. H. 'Zur Münzprägung des Demetrios I. und Alexander I. von Syrien', *Zeitschrift für Numismatik* 34 (1924) 51–66
143. Volkmann, H. 'Demetrios I. und Alexander I. von Syrien', *Klio* 19 (1925) 373–412
144. von Fritze, H. *Die Münzen von Pergamon.* Abh. Akad. Berlin, 1910

145. Waggoner, N. M. 'The Propontis hoard (*IGCH* 888)', *Rev. Num.*[6] 21 (1979) 1–29
146. Zehnacker, H. *Moneta. Recherches sur l'organisation et l'art des émissions monétaires de la République romaine (289–31 av. J.-C.).* 2 vols. Rome, 1973
147. Zehnacker, H. 'Les "nummi novi" de la "casina"', in *Mélanges Heurgon* II, 1035–46

d. Excavation reports and archaeological studies
(See also Section Hh)

148. Balland, A., Barbet, A., Gros, P. and Hallier, G. *Fouilles de l'École Française de Rome à Bolsena (Poggio Moscini)* II: *Les architectures (1962–67).* Rome, 1971
149. Balty, J.-Ch. 'Le portrait romain. Textes et monuments; archéologie et histoire', in *Grec et latin en 1980*, Études et documents dédiés à Edmond Liénard et édités par Ghislaine Viré, 89–109. Brussels, 1980
150. Beltrán Lloris, M. *Las anforas romanas de España.* Saragossa, 1970
151. Beltrán Lloris, M. *Arqueología e historia de las ciudades antiguas del Cabezo de Alcalá de Azaila (Teruel).* Saragossa, 1976
152. Beltrán Lloris, M. 'La cerámica campaniense de Azaila', *Caesaraugusta* 47–8 (1979) 141–232
153. Callaghan, P. J. 'On the date of the Great Altar of Zeus at Pergamon', *BICS* 28 (1981) 115–21
154. Callaghan, P. J. 'The Medusa Rondanini and Antiochus III', *BSA* 76 (1981) 59–70
155. Callaghan, P. J. 'On the origins of the Long Petal Bowl', *BICS* 29 (1982) 63–8
156. Coarelli, F. 'L' "ara di Domizio Enobarbo" e la cultura artistica in Roma nel II secolo a.C.', *DArch.* 2 (1968) 302–68
157. Coarelli, F. 'Polycles', *Studi Miscellanei* 15 (1970) 77–89
158. Coarelli, F. 'Il sepolcro degli Scipioni', *DArch.* 6 (1972) 36–105
159. Coarelli, F. 'Due tombe repubblicane dall'Esquilino', in *Affreschi romani dalle raccolte dell'Antiquarium communale*, 3–11. Rome, 1976
160. Coarelli, F. 'Il comizio dalle origini alla fine della Repubblica; cronologia e topografia', *PP* 174 (1977) 166–238
161. Coarelli, F. *Roma* (Guide archeologiche Laterza). Rome and Bari, 1980
162. Colonna Di Paolo, E., and Colonna, G. *Norchia* I. Rome, 1978
163. Drerup, H. 'Zur Plangestaltung römischer Fora', in *HIM* II, 398–412
164. Duval, R. 'Mise au jour de l'enceinte extérieure de la Carthage punique', *CRAI* 1950, 53–9
165. Ferron, J. and Pinard, H. 'Les fouilles de Byrsa: 1953–1954', *Cahiers de Byrsa* 5 (1955) 31–81
166. Fischer, Th. 'Ein Bildnis des Tryphon in Basel?', *Antike Kunst* 14 (1971) 56
167. Forti, L. *La ceramica di Gnathia.* Naples, 1965
168. Greco, E. and Theodorescu, D. *Poseidonia-Paestum* I: *La 'Curia'.* Rome, 1980

169. Gros, P. *Bolsena. Guide des fouilles*. Rome, 1981
170. Hauschild, T. 'Die römischer Stadtmauer von Tarragona', *MDAI(M)* 20 (1979) 204–37
171. Herzfeld, E. 'Sakastan. Geschichtliche Untersuchungen zu den Ausgrabungen am Kūh ī Khwadja', *Archäologische Mitteilungen aus Iran* 4 (1932) 1–116
172. Hesnard, A. and Lemoine, Ch. 'Les amphores du Cécube et du Falerne: prospections, typologie, analyses', *Mélanges d'arch.* 93 (1981) 243–95
173. Holloway, R. R. 'The Sanctuary at San Mauro, Buccino', *AJArch.* 78 (1974) 25–32
174. Hurst, H. 'Excavations at Carthage 1977–1978. Fourth Interim Report', *Ant. Journ.* 59 (1979) 19–49
175. Kähler, H. *Der grosse Fries von Pergamon*. Berlin, 1948
176. Kyrieleis, H. *Ein Bildnis des Königs Antiochus IV. von Syrien.* Winckelmannsprogramm der Archäologischen Gesellschaft zu Berlin 127. Berlin, 1980
177. Lambrino, S. 'Fouilles d'Histria', *Dacia* 3–4 (1927–32) 378–410
178. Lancel, S. 'Fouilles de Carthage 1976–1977. La colline de Byrsa et l'occupation punique', *CRAI* 1978, 300–31
179. Lancel, S. and others. 'Fouilles françaises à Carthage (1974–1975)', *Antiquités Africaines* 11 (1977) 11–130
180. Maricq, A. 'Inscriptions de Surkh-Kotal (Baghlan)', *JA* 246 (1958) 378–84
181. Martin, R. *Recherches sur les agronomes latins*. Paris, 1971
182. Meischner, J. 'Beobachtungen zu einem bärtigen Reliefkopf in Pergamon', *MDAI(I)* 22 (1972) 113–32
183. Mertens, J. 'Rapport provisoire sur les campagnes de 1962/63 and 1963/4', in *Ordona* 1, ed. J. Mertens. Brussels and Rome, 1965
184. Morel, J.-P. 'Les vases à vernis noir et à figures rouges d'Afrique avant la deuxième guerre punique et le problème des exportations de Grande-Grèce', *Antiquités Africaines* 15 (1980) 29–75
185. Morel, J.-P. *Céramique campanienne: les formes.* 2 vols. Rome, 1981
186. Morel, J.-P., Torelli, M. and Coarelli, F. 'La ceramica di Roma nei secoli IV e III a.C.', in *RMR*, 43–72. Rome, 1973
187. Pellicer Catalán, M. 'La cerámica ibérica del Valle del Ebro', *Caesaraugusta* 19–20 (1962) 37–78
188. Potter, T. W. *The Changing Landscape of South Etruria*. London, 1979
189. Raddatz, K. *Die Schatzfunde der iberischen Halbinsel vom Ende 3. bis Mitte 1. Jhdt.*, Berlin, 1969
190. Rakob, F. 'Zum Rundtempel auf dem Forum Boarium in Rom', *Arch. Anz.* (1969) 275–84
191. Ramos Folques, A. and Ramos Fernández, R. *Excavaciones en la Alcudia de Elche*. Madrid, 1976
192. Richter, G. M. A. *The Portraits of the Greeks.* 3 vols. London, 1965
193. Robert, J. and L. *Fouilles d'Amyzon en Carie* 1. Paris, 1983
194. Roussel, P. 'Fouilles de Délos', *BCH* 34 (1910) 355–423

195. Sanmartí-Grego, E. *La cerámica campaniense de Emporion y Rhode* I. Barcelona, 1978
196. Schober, A. *Die Kunst von Pergamon.* Vienna, 1951
197. Schrammen, J. *Der Grosse Altar. Der Obere Markt. AvP* III.1. Berlin, 1906
198. Schulten, A. *Numantia. Die Ergebnisse der Ausgrabungen 1905–1912* I–IV. Munich, 1914–31
199. Sgubini Moretti, A. M. and Bordenache Battaglia, G. 'Materiali archeologici scoperti a Lucus Feroniae', in *Nuove scoperte e acquisizioni nell' Etruria meridionale.* Rome, 1975
200. Solier, Y. 'Découverte d'inscriptions sur plombs en écriture ibérique dans un entrepôt de Pech Maho (Sigean)', *Rev. Arch. Narbonnaise* 12 (1979) 55–123
201. Stähler, K. P. *Das Unklassische im Telephosfries. Die Friese des Pergamonaltars im Rahmen der hellenistischen Plastik.* Münster, 1966
202. Swoboda, R., Keil, J. and Knoll, F. *Denkmäler aus Lykaonien, Pamphylien und Isaurien.* Brünn and Vienna, 1935
203. Thompson, H. A. and Wycherley, R. E. *The Agora of Athens.* Princeton, 1972
204. Tuchelt, K. 'Buleuterion und Ara Augusti. Bemerkungen zur Rathausanlage von Milet', *MDAI(I)* 25 (1975) 91–140
205. Wattenberg, F. *Las cerámicas indígenas de Numancia.* Madrid, 1963
206. Winnefeld, H. *Die Friese des Grossen Altars. AvP* III.2. Berlin, 1910
207. Wycherley, R. E. *The Stones of Athens.* Princeton, 1978
208. Zevi, F. 'L'identificazione del tempio di Marte "in Circo" e altre osservazioni', in *Mélanges Heurgon* II, 1047–66
209. Zevi, F. 'L'identificazione del tempio sotte S. Salvatore in Campo', in *HIM* I, 34–6

e. Other

210. Bagnall, R. S. and Derow, P. *Greek Historical Documents: The Hellenistic Period.* SBL Sources for Biblical Study 16. Chico, Ca, 1981
211. Forni, G., and others, eds. *Fontes Ligurum et Liguriae Antiquae.* Genoa, 1976
212. Greenidge, A. H. J. and Clay, A. M. *Sources for Roman History 133–70 B.C.* 2nd edn. Oxford, 1960 (Revised paperback edn, 1986)
213. Olmstead, A. T. 'Cuneiform texts and hellenistic chronology', *CPh* 32 (1937) 1–14
214. Parker, R. W. and Dubberstein, W. H. *Babylonian Chronology 626 B.C.–A.D. 75.* Providence, 1956
215. Pritchett, W. K. and Meritt, B. D. *The Chronology of Hellenistic Athens.* Cambridge, Mass., 1940
216. Ray, J. D. *The Archive of Hor.* London, 1976
217. Sachs, A. J. and Wiseman, D. J. 'A Babylonian king list of the Hellenistic period', *Iraq* 16 (1954) 202–12
218. Schulten, A. *Iberische Landeskunde. Geographie des antiken Spanien* I–II. Strasbourg, 1955–7

219. Seyrig, H. *Trésors du Levant*. Paris, 1973
220. Shore, A. F. and Smith, H. S. 'Two unpublished demotic documents from the Asyut archive', *JEg. Arch.* 45 (1959) 52–60
221. Skeat, T. C. *The Reigns of the Ptolemies*. Munich, 1955
222. Skeat, T. C. 'Notes on Ptolemaic chronology, II. "The twelfth year which is also the first." The invasion of Egypt by Antiochus Epiphanes', *JEg. Arch.* (1961) 107–12
223. Tovar, A. *Iberische Landeskunde* I–II. Baden-Baden, 1974–6

C. ROME AND CARTHAGE

1. Arnold, C. J. C. *Oorzaak en schuld van den tweeden Punischen oorlog*. Diss. Nijmegen, 1939
2. Astin, A. E. 'Saguntum and the origins of the Second Punic War', *Latomus* 26 (1967) 577–96 (German translation in Christ 1974: (C 9))
3. Badian, E. 'Two Polybian treaties', in *Miscellanea di studi classici in onore di E. Manni*, 161–9. Rome, 1980
4. Bénabou, M. *La résistance africaine à la romanisation*. Paris, 1976
5. Bickerman, E. 'Hannibal's covenant', *AJPhil.* 73 (1952) 1–23
6. Brisson, J.-P. *Carthage ou Rome?* Paris, 1973
7. Carcopino, J. 'Le traité d'Hasdrubal et la responsibilité de la deuxième guerre punique', *REA* 35 (1953) 258–93
8. Caven, B. *The Punic Wars*. London, 1980
9. Christ, K., ed. *Hannibal*. Darmstadt, 1974
10. Cuff, P. J. 'Polybius, iii, 30.3: a note', *RSA* 3 (1973) 163–70
11. De Sanctis, G. 'Annibale e la Schuldfrage d'una guerra antica', in *Problemi di storia antica*, 162–86. Bari, 1932 (German translation in Christ 1974: (C 9))
12. Dorey, T. A. 'The dictatorship of Minucius', *JRS* 45 (1955) 92–6
13. Dorey, T. A. 'The treaty of Saguntum', *Humanitas* 8 (1959) 1–10
14. Drachmann, A. B. *Sagunt und die Ebro-Grenze*. Hist.-fil. Medd. Kgl. Da. Vid. Selsk. 3. Copenhagen, 1920
15. Errington, R. M. 'Rome and Spain before the Second Punic War', *Latomus* 29 (1970) 24–57
16. Fulford, M. 'Pottery and the economy of Carthage and its hinterland', *Opus* 2 (1983) 5–14
17. Gauthier, Ph. 'L'Èbre et Sagonte. Défense de Polybe', *Rev. Phil.* 42 (1968) 91–108
18. Gelzer, M. 'Nasicas Widerspruch gegen die Zerstörung Karthagos', *Philol.* 86 (1931) 261–99 (= *Vom Römischen Staat* 1, 78–124. Leipzig, 1943 = *Kleine Schriften* II, 39–72. Wiesbaden, 1962–4)
19. Gómez, N. P. *Guerras di Anibal preparatories del sitio de Saguntum*. Valencia, 1951
20. Groag, E. *Hannibal als Politiker*. Vienna, 1929
20A. Gruen, E. S. 'The consular elections for 216 B.C. and the veracity of Livy', *California Studies in Classical Antiquity* 11 (1978) 61–74
21. Gsell, S. *Histoire ancienne de l'Afrique du Nord* I–VIII. Paris, 1913–28

22. Hallward, B. L. 'The Fall of Carthage', in *CAH*[1] VIII, 466–84. Cambridge, 1930

23. Hampl, F. 'Vorgeschichte des ersten und zweiten punischen Krieges', *ANRW* 1.1, 427–41. Berlin, 1972

24. Heichelheim, F. M. 'New evidence on the Ebro Treaty', *Historia* 3 (1954) 211–19

25. Hoffmann, W. 'Die römische Kriegserklärung an Karthago in Jahre 218', *Rh. Mus.* 94 (1951) 69–88 (reprinted in Christ 1974: (c 9))

26. Hoffmann, W. 'Die römische Politik des 2. Jahrhundert und das Ende Karthagos', *Historia* 9 (1960) 309–44 (reprinted in R. Klein, ed., *Das Staatsdenken der Römer*. Darmstadt, 1966)

27. Huss, W. 'Vier Sufeten in Karthago?', *Museon* 90 (1977) 427–33

28. Koch, M. 'Observaciones sobre la permanencia del sustrato púnico en la península ibérica', in *Actas del I Coloquio sobre lenguas y culturas preromanas de la península ibérica*, 191–9. Salamanca, 1976

29. Kolbe, W. *Die Kriegsschuldfrage von 218 v. Chr. Geb.* Sitz. Heidelberger Akademie der Wissenschaft. Heidelberg, 1934

30. Kramer, F. R. 'Massilian diplomacy before the Second Punic War', *AJPhil.* 49 (1948) 1–26

31. Lazenby, J. F. *Hannibal's War. A Military History of the Second Punic War.* Warminster, 1978

32. Liebmann-Frankfort, Th. 'Du traité de l'Èbre à la paix de Dardanos', *Latomus* 30 (1971) 585–97

33. Liebmann-Frankfort, Th. 'Le traité de l'Èbre et sa valeur juridique', *RD* 50 (1972) 193–204

34. Mazzarino, S. *Introduzione alle guerre puniche*. Catania, 1947

35. Meltzer, O. 'Zur Vorgeschichte des dritten punischen Krieges', *Neue Jahrb.* 143 (1891) 685–8

36. Meltzer, O. and Kahrstedt, U. *Geschichte der Karthager* I–III. Berlin, 1879–1913

37. Meyer, Ed. 'Untersuchungen zur Geschichte des zweiten punischen Krieges', in *Kleine Schriften* II, 331–405. Halle, 1924

38. Millar, F. 'Local cultures in the Roman Empire: Libyan, Punic and Latin in Roman Africa', *JRS* 58 (1968) 126–34

39. Oertel, F. 'Der Ebrovertrag und der Ausbruch des zweiten punischen Krieges', *Rh.Mus.* 81 (1932) 221–31

40. Otto, W. 'Eine antike Kriegsschuldfrage. Die Vorgeschichte des zweiten punischen Krieges', *HZ* 145 (1932) 498–516 (reprinted in Christ 1974: (c 9))

41. Patterson, M. L. 'Rome's choice of magistrates during the Hannabalic War', *TAPA* 73 (1942) 319–40

42. Pfiffig, A. J. 'Die Haltung Etruriens im 2. Punischen Krieg', *Historia* 15 (1966) 193–210

43. Picard, G. Ch. 'Le traité Romano-Barcide 226 av. J.-C.', in *Mélanges offerts à J. Carcopino*, 747–62. Paris, 1966

44. Proctor, D. *Hannibal's March in History*. Oxford, 1971

45. Reid, J. S. 'Problems of the Second Punic War', *JRS* 3 (1913) 175–90

46. Reyniers, F. 'Remarques sur la topographie de Carthage à l'époque de la troisième guerre punique', in *Mélanges d'archéologie et d'histoire offerts à André Piganiol* III, 1281–90. Paris, 1966

47. Röllig, W. 'Das Punische im Römischen Reich', in *Die Sprache im Römischen Reich der Kaiserzeit* = *Bonner Jahrbücher* 40 (1980) 285–99

48. Romanelli, P. *Storia delle province romane dell' Africa*. Rome, 1959

49. Ruschenbusch, E. 'Der Beginn des 2. punischen Krieges', *Historia* 27 (1978) 232–4

50. Sancho Royo, A. 'En tomo al tratado del Ebro entre Roma y Asdrubal', *Habis* 7 (1976) 75–110

51. Santos Yanguas, N. 'El tratado del Ebro y el origen de la segunda guerra punica', *Hispania* 37 (1977) 269–98

52. Schnabel, P. 'Zur Vorgeschichte des zweiten punischen Krieges', *Klio* 20 (1920) 110ff.

53. Schulten, A. *Tartessos*. Hamburg, 1922

54. Scullard, H. H. 'Rome's declaration of war on Carthage in 218', *Rh. Mus.* 95 (1952) 209–16 (German translation in Christ 1974: (C 9))

55. Sumner, G. V. 'The chronology of the outbreak of the Second Punic War', *PACA* 9 (1966) 5–30

56. Sumner, G. V. 'Roman policy in Spain before the Hannibalic War', *Harv. Stud.* 72 (1967) 205–46

57. Sumner, G. V. 'Elections at Rome in 217 B.C.', *Phoenix* 29 (1975) 250–9

58. Täubler, E. *Die Vorgeschichte des 2. punischen Krieges*. Berlin, 1921

59. Ungern-Sternberg, J. von. *Capua im Zweiten Punischen Krieg: Untersuchungen zur römischen Annalistik*. Munich, 1975

60. Untermann, J. *Sprachräume und Sprachbewegungen im vorrömischen Hispanien*. Wiesbaden, 1961.

61. Vogt, J., ed. *Rom und Karthago*. Leipzig, 1943

62. Walsh, P. G. 'Massinissa', *JRS* 55 (1965) 149–60

63. Warmington, B. H. *Carthage*. 2nd edn. London, 1969

64. Welwei, K. W. 'Die Belagerung Sagunts und die römische Passivität im Westen 219 v. Chr.', *Talanta* 8–9 (1977) 156–73

65. Whittaker, C. R. 'The Western Phoenicians. Colonisation and assimilation', *PCPS* 20 (1974) 58–79

D. ROME, GREECE AND MACEDONIA

1. Aymard, A. *Les premiers rapports de Rome et de la confédération achaienne (198–89 av.J.-C.)*. Bordeaux, 1938

2. Aymard, A. *Les assemblées de la confédération achaienne*. Bordeaux, 1938

3. Aymard, A. 'Tutelle et usurpation dans les monarchies hellénistiques', *Aegyptus* 12 (1952) 85–96

4. Badian, E. 'Notes on Roman policy in Illyria (230–201 B.C.)', *PBSR* 20 (1952) 72–93 (= *Studies in Greek and Roman History*, 1–25. Oxford, 1964)

5. Badian, E. 'The treaty between Rome and the Achaean League', *JRS* 42 (1952) 76–80

6. Badian, E. 'Aetolica', *Latomus* 17 (1958) 197–211

7. Bernhardt, R. *Imperium und Eleutheria: Die römische Politik gegenüber den freien Städten des griechischen Ostens*. Diss. Hamburg, 1971
8. Briscoe, J. 'Q. Marcius Philippus and *nova sapientia*', *JRS* 54 (1964) 66–77
9. Briscoe, J. 'Eastern policy and senatorial politics 168–146 B.C.', *Historia* 18 (1969) 49–70
10. Briscoe, J. 'The Antigonids and the Greek states', in *Imperialism in the Ancient World*, ed. P. D. A. Garnsey and C. R. Whittaker. Cambridge, 1978
11. Cabanes, P. 'Les inscriptions du théâtre de Bouthrotos', *Annales littéraires de l'université de Besançon* 163. 1974
12. Cabanes, P. *L'Épire de la mort de Pyrrhos à la conquête romaine (272–167)*. Paris, 1976
13. Colin, G. *Rome et la Grèce de 200 à 146 av. J.-C.* Paris, 1905
14. Daux, G. 'Décret de Delphes en réponse à une ambassade de Sardes', in *Mélanges G. Glotz*, 289–97. Paris, 1932
15. Daux, G. *Delphes au IIe et au Ier siècle depuis l'abaissement de l'Étolie jusqu'à la paix romaine, 191–31 av. J.-C.* Paris, 1936
16. Deininger, J. *Der politische Widerstand gegen Rom in Griechenland 217–86 v. Chr.* Berlin and New York, 1971
17. Dell, H. J. 'Antigonus III and Rome', *CPh* 62 (1964) 94–103
18. Dell, H. J. 'The origin and nature of Illyrian piracy', *Historia* 16 (1967) 344–58
19. Derow, P. S. 'Polybius and the embassy of Kallikrates', in *Essays presented to C. M. Bowra*, 12–24. Oxford, 1970
20. Derow, P. S. 'Kleemporos', *Phoenix* 27 (1973) 118–34
21. Derow, P. S. 'Polybius, Rome and the East', *JRS* 69 (1979) 1–15
22. Derow, P. S. and Forrest, W. G. 'An inscription from Chios', *BSA* 77 (1982) 79–92
23. Errington, R. M. *Philopoemen*. Oxford, 1969
24. Errington, R. M. 'The alleged Syro-Macedonian pact and the origins of the Second Macedonian War', *Athenaeum* 49 (1971) 336–54
25. Etienne, R. and Knoepfler, D. *Hyettos de Béotie et la chronologie des archontes féderaux entre 250 et 171 avant J.-C. BCH* Suppl. III. Paris, 1976
26. Ferguson, W. S. *Hellenistic Athens*. London, 1911
27. Fuks, A. 'The Bellum Achaicum and its social aspect', *JHS* 80 (1970) 78–89
28. Giovannini, A. 'Les origines de la 3e guerre de Macédoine', *BCH* 93 (1969) 853–61
29. Giovannini, A. 'Philipp V, Perseus und die Delphische Amphiktyonie', in *Ancient Macedonia* I, 147–54. Thessalonica, 1970
30. Habicht, Ch. *Studien zur Geschichte Athens in hellenistischer Zeit. Hypomnemata* 75. Göttingen, 1982
31. Hammond, N. G. L. 'The opening campaigns and the battle of the Aoi Stena in the Second Macedonian War', *JRS* 56 (1966) 39–54
31A. Hammond, N. G. L. *Epirus*. Oxford, 1967
32. Hammond, N. G. L. 'Illyris, Rome and Macedon in 229–205 B.C.', *JRS* 58 (1968) 1–21

33. Holleaux, M. *Rome, la Grèce et les monarchies hellénistiques au IIIe siècle avant J.-C. (273–205)*. Paris, 1921
34. Holleaux, M. 'Rome and Macedon. The Romans against Philip. Rome and Antiochus', in *CAH*[1] VIII, 138–240. Cambridge, 1930
35. Holleaux, M. *Études d'épigraphie et d'histoire grecques*. 6 vols. Paris, 1938–68
36. Hopital, R. G. 'Le traité romano-aetolien de 212 avant J.-C.', *RD* 42 (1964) 18–48, 204–46
37. Klaffenbach, G. *Der römisch–ätolische Bündnisvertrag vom Jahre 212 v.Chr. SDAW* 1. Berlin, 1954
38. Kramolisch, H. *Die Strategen des Thessalischen Bundes vom Jahr 196 v.Chr. bis zum Ausgang der römischen Republik. Die deutschen archäologischen Forschungen in Thessalien: Demetrias* II. Bonn, 1978
39. Lanzilotta, E. 'Cn. Ottavio e gli Argivi', in *Sesta Miscellanea Greca e Romana* (1978) 233–47
40. Larsen, J. A. O. 'Roman Greece', in *ESAR* IV. Baltimore, 1940
41. Larsen, J. A. O. *Greek Federal States*. Oxford, 1968
42. Launey, M. *Recherches sur les armées hellénistiques*. 2 vols. Paris, 1949–50
43. Mattingly, H. B. 'Some problems in second-century Attic prosopography', *Historia* 20 (1971) 24–46
44. McDonald, A. H. and Walbank, F. W. 'The origins of the Second Macedonian War', *JRS* 27 (1937) 180–207
45. Meloni, P. *Perseo e la fine della monarchia macedone*. Rome, 1953
46. Niese, B. *Geschichte der griechischen und makedonischen Staaten seit der Schlacht bei Chaeronea* III. Gotha, 1910
47. Oost, S. I. *Roman Policy in Epirus and Acarnania in the Age of the Roman Conquest of Greece*. Dallas, 1954
48. Oost, S. I. 'Amynander, Athamania, and Rome', *CPh* 52 (1957) 1–15
49. Petzold, K.-E. 'Rom und Illyrien', *Histroria* 20 (1971) 199–223
50. Schleussner, B. 'Zur Frage der geheimen pergamenisch–makedonischen Kontakte im Perseuskrieg', *Historia* 22 (1973) 119–23
51. Schwertfeger, T. *Der Achaiische Bund von 146 bis 27 v. Chr.* Vestigia 19. Munich, 1974
52. Stier, H. E. *Roms Aufstieg zur Weltmacht und die griechische Welt*. Cologne, 1957
53. Thompson, H. A. 'Athens and the Hellenistic princes', *Proc. Amer. Phil. Soc.* 97 (1953) 254–61
54. Walbank, F. W. *Philip V of Macedon*. Cambridge, 1940
55. Werner, R. 'Quellenkritische Bemerkungen zu den Ursachen des Perseuskrieges', *Grazer Beiträge* 6 (1977) 149–216

E. THE SELEUCIDS AND THEIR NEIGHBOURS

a. Seleucids and the Seleucid kingdom

1. Baldus, H. R. 'Der Helm des Tryphon und die seleukidische Chronologie der Jahre 146–138 v. Chr.', *JNG* 20 (1970) 217–39
2. Bar-Kochva, B. *The Seleucid Army. Organization and Tactics in the Great Campaigns*. Cambridge, 1976

3. Bellinger, A. R. 'The end of the Seleucids', *Transactions of the Connecticut Academy of Arts and Sciences* 38 (1949) 51–102
4. Bevan, E. R. *The House of Seleucus* II. London, 1902
5. Bickerman, E. 'Notes sur Polybe. I. Le statut des villes d'Asie après la paix d'Apamée', *REG* 50 (1937) 217–39
6. Bickerman, E. *Institutions des Séleucides*. Paris, 1938
7. Bickerman, E. 'Sur la chronologie de la sixième guerre de Syrie', *CE* 27 (1952) 396–403
8. Bouché-Leclerq, A. *Histoire de Séleucides* I. Paris, 1913
9. Bunge, J. G. '"Theos Epiphanes" in den ersten fünf Regierungsjahren des Antiochos IV. Epiphanes', *Historia* 23 (1974) 57–85
10. Bunge, J. G. '"Antiochos Helios"', *Historia* 24 (1975) 164–88
11. Bunge, J. G. 'Die Feiern Antiochos' IV. in Daphne im Herbst 166', *Chiron* 6 (1976) 53–71
12. Burstein, S. M. 'The aftermath of the Peace of Apamea', *AJAH* 5 (1980) 1–12
13. Charbonneaux, J. and Laumonier, A. 'Trois portraits d'Alexandre Balas', *BCH* 79 (1955) 528–38
14. Cohen, G. M. *The Seleucid Colonies. Studies in Founding, Administration and Organization*. Wiesbaden, 1978
15. Downey, G. *A History of Antioch in Syria from Seleucus to the Arab Conquest*. Princeton, 1961
16. Edson, Ch. 'Macedonicum Imperium: the Seleucid empire and the literary evidence', *CPh* 53 (1958) 153–70
17. El-Zein, M. *Geschichte der Stadt Apameia am Orontes von den Anfängen bis Augustus*. Diss. Heidelberg, 1972
18. Fischer, Th. *Untersuchungen zum Partherkrieg Antiochos' VII. im Rahmen der Seleukidengeschichte*. Diss. Munich, 1970
19. Fischer, Th. 'Zu Tryphon', *Chiron* 2 (1972) 201–13
20. Gruen, E. 'Rome and the Seleucids in the aftermath of Pydna', *Chiron* 6 (1976) 73–95
21. Habicht, Ch. 'Der Stratege Hegemonides', *Historia* 7 (1958) 376–8
22. Helliesen, J. M. 'Demetrius I Soter: a Seleucid king with an Antigonid name', in *Ancient Macedonian Studies in Honor of Charles F. Edson*, ed. H. Dell, 219–29. Thessalonica, 1981
23. Holleaux, M. 'La mort d'Antiochos IV Epiphanès', *REA* 18 (1916) 77–102
24. Holleaux, M. 'Le décret de Bargylia en l'honneur de Poseidonios', *REA* 21 (1919) 1–19
25. Houghton, A. 'Timarchus as king of Babylonia', *Rev. Num.*[6] 21 (1979) 213–17
26. Houghton, A. 'The second reign of Demetrius II of Syria at Tarsus', *ANSMN* 24 (1979) 211–16
27. Jansen, H. L. *Die Politik Antiochos' IV*. Oslo, 1943
28. Kiechle, F. 'Antiochos IV. und der letzte Versuch einer Konsolidierung des Seleukidenreiches', *GWU* 14 (1963) 159–70

29. Mendels, D. 'A note on the tradition of Antiochus IV' death', *Israel Exploration Journal* 31 (1981) 51–6
30. Mendels, D. 'The Five Empires: a note on a propagandistic topos', *AJPhil.* 102 (1981) 330–3
31. Mooren, L. 'Antiochos IV. Epiphanes und das ptolemäische Königtum', in *Actes du XVe Congr. Internat. de Papyrologie*, 78ff. Brussels, 1978
32. Mørkholm, O. 'The accession of Antiochos IV of Syria', *ANSMN* 11 (1964) 63–76
33. Mørkholm, O. *Antiochus IV of Syria*. Copenhagen, 1966
34. Musti, D. 'Lo stato dei Seleucidi', *SCO* 15 (1966) 59–201
35. Paltiel, E. 'The treaty of Apamea and the later Seleucids', *Antichthon* 13 (1979) 30–41
36. Paltiel, E. 'Antiochus IV and Demetrius of Syria', *Antichthon* 13 (1979) 42–7
37. Paltiel, E. 'Antiochus Epiphanes and Roman politics', *Latomus* 41 (1982) 229–54
38. Reuter, F. *Beiträge zur Beurteilung des Antiochos Epiphanes*. Diss. Münster, 1938
39. Rigsby, K. J. 'Seleucid notes', *TAPA* 110 (1980) 233–54
40. Swain, J. W. 'Antiochus Epiphanes and Egypt', *CPh* 39 (1944) 73–94
41. Will, Ed. 'Rome et les Séleucides', *ANRW* 1.1 (1972) 590–632

b. Antiochus the Great and the war with Rome

42. Errington, R. M. 'Rom, Antiochos der Grosse und die Asylie von Teos', *ZPE* 39 (1980) 279–84
43. Giovannini, A. 'La clause territoriale de la paix d'Apamée', *Athenaeum* 60 (1982) 224–36
44. Giovannini, A. 'Téos, Antiochos III et Attale Ier', *MH* 40 (1983) 178–84
45. Herrmann, P. 'Antiochos der Grosse und Teos', *Anadolu* 9 (1965) 29–159
46. Holleaux, M. 'Un prétendu décret d'Antioche sur l'Oronte', *REG* 13 (1900) 258–80
47. McDonald, A. H. 'The treaty of Apamea (188 B.C.)', *JRS* 57 (1967) 1–8
48. McDonald, A. H. and Walbank, F. W. 'The treaty of Apamea (188 B.C.): the naval clauses', *JRS* 59 (1969) 30–9
49. Pagnon, B. 'Le récit de l'expédition de Cn. Manlius Vulso contre les Gallo-Grecs et de ses prolongements dans le livre 38 de Tite-Live', *LEC* 50 (1982) 115–28
50. Schmitt, H. H. *Untersuchungen zur Geschichte Antiochos' des Grossen und seiner Zeit. Historia*, Einzelschriften 6. Wiesbaden, 1964
51. Walser, G. 'Die Ursachen des ersten römisch–illyrischen Krieges', *Historia* 2 (1954) 308–18

c. The Attalid kingdom (including Aristonicus)

52. Allen, R. E. *The Attalid Kingdom. A Constitutional History*. Oxford, 1983
53. Cardinali, G. *Il regno di Pergamo*. Turin, 1906

54. Dunst, G. 'Die Bestimmungen des Vertrages zwischen Eumenes II. und den kretischen Städten vom Jahre 181 v. Chr.', *Philol.* 100 (1956) 305–11
55. Fontenrose, J. 'The crucified Daphidas', *TAPA* 91 (1960) 83–99
56. Habicht, Ch. 'Über die Kriege zwischen Pergamon und Bithynien', *Hermes* 84 (1956) 90–110
57. Hansen, E. V. *The Attalids of Pergamum.* 2nd edn. Ithaca, 1971
58. Herrmann, P. 'Der Brief Attalos' II. an die Ephesier', *ZPE* 22 (1976) 233–4
59. Holleaux, M. 'Le décret des Ioniens en l'honneur d'Eumènes II', *REG* 37 (1924) 305–30, 478–9
60. Hopp, J. *Untersuchungen zur Geschichte der letzten Attaliden.* Munich, 1977
61. Jones, C. P. 'Diodoros Pasparos and the Nikephoria of Pergamon', *Chiron* 4 (1974) 183–205
62. McShane, R. B. *The Foreign Policy of the Attalids of Pergamon.* Urbana, 1964
63. Ohlemutz, E. *Die Kulte und Heiligtümer der Götter in Pergamon.* Diss. Giessen, 1940
64. Rohde, E. *Pergamon. Burgberg und Altar.* Munich, 1982
65. Rostovtzeff, M. 'Pergamum', in *CAH*[1] VIII, 590–618. Cambridge, 1930
66. Schleussner, B. 'Die Gesandtschaftsreise des P. Scipio Nasica im Jahre 133/2 v. Chr. und die Provinzialisierung des Königreichs Pergamon', *Chiron* 6 (1976) 97–112
67. Segre, M. 'L'institution des Nikephoria de Pergame', in L. Robert, *Hellenica* v (1948) 87–128
68. van Looy, H. 'Apollonis, reine de Pergame', *Ancient Society* 9 (1976) 151–76
69. Vavřinek, V. *La révolte d'Aristonicos.* Prague, 1957
70. Vavřinek, V. 'Aristonicus of Pergamon: pretender to the throne or leader of a slave revolt?', *Eirene* 13 (1975) 109–29
71. Virgilio, B. 'Strabone e la storia di Pergamo e degli Attalidi', *Studi Ellenistici* 1 (1984) 21–37
72. Vogt, J. 'Pergamon und Aristonikos', in *Atti del terzo congresso internazionale di epigrafia Greca e Latina,* 45–54. Rome, 1959

d. Rhodes

73. Berthold, R. M. *Rhodes in the Hellenistic Age.* Ithaca, NY, 1984
74. Börker, Chr. 'Der rhodische Kalender', *ZPE* 31 (1978) 193–218
75. Fraser, P. M. and Bean, G. E. *The Rhodian Peraea and Islands.* Oxford, 1954
76. Gruen, E. 'Rome and Rhodes in the second century B.C.: a historiographical inquiry', *CQ* 25 (1975) 58–81
77. Schmitt, H. H. *Rom und Rhodos.* Munich, 1957

e. Palestine and the Maccabees

78. Abel, F.-M. *Géographie de la Palestine* II. Paris, 1938
79. Abel, F.-M. *Les livres des Maccabées.* Paris, 1949

80. Abel, F.-M. *Histoire de la Palestine depuis le conquête d' Alexandre à l'invasion arabe* 1. Paris, 1952

81. Arenhoevel, D. *Die Theokratie nach dem 1. und 2. Makkabäerbuch.* Mainz, 1967

82. Avi-Yonah, M. *The Holy Land. From the Persian to the Arab Conquests (536 B.C. to A.D. 640). A Historical Geography.* Grand Rapids, Mich., 1966

83. Bevan, E. R. 'Syria and the Jews', in *CAH*[1] VIII, 495–533. Cambridge, 1930

84. Bickermann, E. 'Ein jüdischer Festbrief vom Jahre 124 v. Chr.', *ZNTW* 32 (1933) 233–54

85. Bickerman, E. 'La charte séleucide de Jérusalem', *REJ* 100 (1935) 4–35

86. Bickerman, E. *Der Gott der Makkabäer. Untersuchungen über Sinn and Ursprung der makkabäischen Erhebung.* Berlin, 1937

87. Bickerman, E. 'Un document relatif à la persécution d'Antiochos IV Epiphane', *Rev. Hist. Rel.* 115 (1937) 188–223

88. Bickerman, E. 'Héliodore au temple de Jérusalem', *AIPh* 7 (1939/44) 7–40

89. Bickerman, E. 'Une proclamation séleucide relative au temple de Jérusalem', *Syria* 25 (1946–8) 67–88

90. Bickerman, E. *Studies in Jewish and Christian History* 11. Leiden, 1980

91. Bringmann, K. 'Die Verfolgung der jüdischen Religion durch Antiochos IV. Ein Konflikt zwischen Judentum und Hellenismus?', *Antike und Abendland* 26 (1980) 176–90

92. Bringmann, K. *Hellenistische Reform und Religionsverfolgung in Judäa. Eine Untersuchung zur jüdisch-hellenistischen Geschichte (175–163 v. Chr.).* Göttingen, 1983

93. Cardauns, B. 'Juden und Spartaner', *Hermes* 97 (1967) 117–24

94. Fischer, Th. 'Zu den Beziehungen zwischen Rom und den Juden im 2. Jhdt. v. Chr.', *ZATW* 86 (1974) 90–3

95. Fischer, Th. *Seleukiden und Makkabäer. Beiträge zur Seleukidengeschichte und zu den politischen Ereignissen in Judäa während der ersten Hälfte des 2. Jhdts. v. Chr.* Bochum, 1980

96. Fischer, Th. 'Rom und die Hasmonäer', *Gymnasium* 88 (1981) 139–50

97. Galling, K. 'Judäa, Galiläa und der Osten im Jahre 164/3 v. Chr.', *PJ* 36 (1940) 43–77

98. Giovannini, A. and Müller, H. 'Die Beziehungen zwischen Rom und den Juden im 2. Jhdt. v. Chr.', *MH* 28 (1971) 156–71

99. Goldstein, J. A. 'The tales of the Tobiads', in *Studies in Judaism and Late Antiquity* XII, vol. 3 (1975) 85–123

100. Habicht, Ch. 'Hellenismus und Judentum in der Zeit des Judas Makkabäus', *Jahrbuch Heidelberger Akademie* 1974, 97–110

101. Habicht, Ch. 'Royal documents in II Maccabees', *Harv. Stud.* 80 (1976) 1–18

102. Hengel, M. *Judentum und Hellenismus. Studien zu ihrer Begegnung unter besonderer Berücksichtigung Palästinas bis zur Mitte des 2. Jhdts. v. Chr.* 2nd edn. Tübingen, 1973

103. Kolbe, W. *Beiträge zur syrischen und jüdischen Geschichte. Kritische*

Untersuchungen zur Seleukidenliste und zu den beiden ersten Makkabäerbüchern.
Stuttgart, 1935

104. Liebmann-Frankfort, Th. 'Rome et le conflict judéo-syrien (164–161 avant notre ère)', *Ant. Class.* 38 (1969) 101–20

105. Momigliano, A. *Prime linee di storia della tradizione maccabaica.* Rome, 1930

106. Momigliano, A. 'Ricerche sull'organizzazione della Giudea sotto il dominio Romano (63 a.c.–70 d.c.)', *ASNSP*² 3 (1934) 183–221

107. Plöger, O. 'Hyrkan im Ostjordanland', *ZDPV* 71 (1955) 70–81

108. Plöger, O. 'Die makkabäischen Burgen', *ZDPV* 71 (1955) 141–72

109. Plöger, O. 'Die Feldzüge der Seleukiden gegen den Makkabäer Judas', *ZDPV* 74 (1958) 155–88

110. Rajak, T. 'Roman intervention in a Seleucid siege of Jerusalem?', *GRBS* 22 (1981) 65–81

111. Schaumberger, H. B. 'Die neue Seleukidenliste BM 35603 und die makkabäische Chronologie', *Biblica* 36 (1955) 423–35

112. Schürer, E. *A History of the Jewish People in the Age of Jesus Christ (175 B.C.– A.D. 135)* i, revised and edited by G. Vermes and F. Millar. Edinburgh, 1973

113. Sevenster, J. N. *The Roots of Pagan Antisemitism in the Ancient World.* Leiden, 1975

114. Stiehl, R. 'Das Buch Esther', *Wiener Zeitschrift für die Kunde des Morgenlandes* 53 (1956) 4–22

115. Tcherikover, V. *Hellenistic Civilization and the Jews.* Philadelphia, 1961

116. Timpe, D. 'Der römische Vertrag mit den Juden 161 v. Chr.', *Chiron* 4 (1974) 133–52

117. Tushingham, A. D. 'A hellenistic inscription from Samaria Sebaste', *PEQ* 104 (1972) 59–63

118. Vidal-Naquet, P. 'Les Juifs entre l'état et l'apocalypse', in *Rome et la conquête du monde méditerranéen* ii, ed. C. Nicolet, 846–82. Paris, 1978

119. Wacholder, B. Z. 'The date of the death of Antiochus IV Epiphanes and I Macc. 6:16–17', in *Panhellenica. Essays in Ancient History and Historiography in Honor of Truesdell S. Brown*, ed. S. M. Burnstein and C. A. Okin, 129–32. Kansas, 1980

120. Wirgin, W. 'Simon Maccabaeus' embassy to Rome – its purpose and outcome', *PEQ* 106 (1974) 141–6

121. Zambelli, M. 'La composizione del secondo libro dei Maccabei e la nuova cronologia di Antioco Epifane', *Miscellanea Greca e Romana* (1965) 195–299

f. Other

122. Altheim, F. *Weltgeschichte Asiens im griechischen Zeitalter.* 2 vols. Halle, 1947–8

123. Astin, A. E. 'Diodorus and the date of the embassy to the East of Scipio Aemilianus', *CPh* 54 (1959) 321–7

124. Bickermann, E. 'Rom und Lampsakos', *Philol.* 87 (1932) 277–99

125. Braund, D. C. 'Three Hellenistic personages: Amynander, Prusias II, Daphidas', *CQ* 32 (1982) 350–7

126. Braund, D. C. 'Royal wills and Rome', *PBSR* 51 (1983) 16–57
127. Braunert, H. 'Hegemoniale Bestrebungen der hellenistischen Gross-mächte in Politik und Wirtschaft', *Historia* 13 (1964) 80–104
128. Breglia Pulci Doria, L. 'Diodoro e Ariarate V. Conflitti dinastici, tradizione e propaganda politica nelle Cappadocia del secondo secolo A.C.', *PP* 33 (1978) 104–29
129. Broughton, T. R. S. 'Stratoniceia and Aristonicus', *CPh* 29 (1934) 252–4
130. Carrata-Thomes, F. *La rivolta di Aristonico e le origini della provincia Romana d'Asia.* Turin, 1968
131. Collins, F. 'Eutropius and the dynastic name Eumenes of the Pergamene pretender Aristonicus', *Ancient World* 4 (1981) 39–43
132. Debevoise, N. C. *A Political History of Parthia.* Chicago, 1938
133. Delplace, Chr. 'Le contenu sociale et économique du soulèvement d'Aristonicos', *Athenaeum* 56 (1978) 20–53
134. Drew-Bear, Th. 'Three senatus consulta concerning the province of Asia', *Historia* 21 (1972) 75–87
135. Dumont, J. C. 'A propos d'Aristonicos', *Eos* 5 (1966) 181–96
136. Fischer, Th. *'Βασιλέως Καμνισκ(ε)ίρου'*, *Chiron* 1 (1971) 169–75
137. Fraser, P. M. *Ptolemaic Alexandria.* 3 vols. Oxford, 1972
138. Gutschmid, A. von. *Geschichte Irans und seiner Nachbarländer von Alexander dem Grossen bis zum Untergang der Arsaciden.* Tübingen, 1888
139. Habicht, Ch. 'Über eine armenische Inschrift mit Versen des Euripides', *Hermes* 81 (1953) 251–6
140. Heberdey, R. and Wilhelm, Ad. *Reisen in Kilikien.* Denkschr. Akad. Wien 44 (1896)
141. Herrmann, P. *Ergebnisse einer Reise in Nordostlydien.* Denkschr. Akad. Wien 80 (1962)
142. Herrmann, P. 'Neue Urkunden zur Geschichte von Milet im 2. Jhdt. v. Chr.', *MDAI(I)* 15 (1965) 71–117
143. Herrmann, P. 'Cn. Domitius Ahenobarbus, patronus von Ephesos und Samos', *ZPE* 14 (1974) 257–8
144. Hommel, H. 'Ein König von Milet', *Chiron* 6 (1976) 119–27
145. Keil, J. and Wilhelm, Ad. 'Vorläufiger Bericht über eine Reise in Kilikien (1914)', *JÖAI* 18 (1915) 16–21
146. Knibbe, D. 'Die Gesandtschaft des jüngeren Scipio Aemilianus im Jahre 140 v. Chr.; ein Höhepunkt der Weltreichspolitik Roms im 2. Jahrhundert', *JÖAI* 4 (1960) 33–8
147. Levy, I. 'Ptolemée fils de Makron', *AIPh* 10 (1950) 688–99
148. Liebmann-Frankfort, Th. *La frontière orientale dans la politique extérieure de la République romaine (189–63 av.J.-C.).* Brussels, 1969
149. Le Rider, G. *Suse sous les Séleucides et les Parthes.* Paris, 1965
150. Magie, D. *Roman Rule in Asia Minor.* 2 vols. Princeton, 1950
151. Meyer, Ed. *Geschichte des Königreichs Pontos.* Leipzig, 1879
152. Meyer, Ed. *Blüte und Niedergang des Hellenismus in Asien.* Berlin, 1925
153. Meyer, Ed. *Die Grenzen der hellenistischen Staaten in Kleinasien.* Zürich and Leipzig, 1925

154. Mørkholm, O. 'Eulaios and Lenaios', *C&M* 22 (1961) 31–43
155. Müller, H. *Milesische Volksbeschlüsse. Eine Untersuchung zur Verfassungsgeschichte der Stadt Milet in hellenistischer Zeit.* Göttingen, 1976
156. Otto, W. *Zur Geschichte der Zeit des 6. Ptolemäers.* Abh. Akad. München, N.F. 11. 1934
157. Passerini, A. 'Studi di storia ellenistico-romana, v: L'ultimo piano di Annibale e una testimonianza di Ennio', *Athenaeum* 11 (1933) 10–28
158. Piejko, F. 'A decree of Cos in honor of the Cappadocian royal couple', *PP* 38 (1983) 200–7
159. Rey-Coquais, P. *Arados et sa pérée aux époques grecque, romaine et byzantine.* Paris, 1974
160. Rigsby, K. 'The era of the province of Asia', *Phoenix* 33 (1979) 39–47
161. Robert, L. *Villes d'Asie Mineure.* Paris, 1935 (2nd edn, 1962)
162. Robert, L. *Études anatoliennes.* Paris, 1937
163. Robert, L. and J. *La Carie* II. Paris, 1954
164. Segre, M. and Pugliese-Carratelli, G. 'La regina Antiochide di Cappadocia', *PP* 27 (1972) 182–5
165. Seyrig, H. 'Arados et Baetocaece', *Syria* 18 (1950) 191–206
166. Seyrig, H. 'Arados et sa pérée sous les rois Séleucides', *Syria* 18 (1950) 206–20
167. Sherwin-White, A. N. 'Roman involvement in Anatolia', *JRS* 67 (1977) 62–75
168. Sherwin-White, S. *Ancient Cos.* Göttingen, 1978
169. Stähelin, F. *Geschichte der kleinasiatischen Galater.* 2nd edn. Leipzig, 1907
170. Stiehl, R. 'Chronologie der Frātādara', in F. Altheim, *Geschichte der Hunnen* I, 375–9. Berlin, 1959
171. Sullivan, R. 'Die Stellung der kommagenischen Königsdynastie in den Herrscherfamilien der hellenistischen Staatenwelt', *Antike Welt* 6 (1975), *Sondernummer Kommagene* 31–9
172. Trever, K. V. *Contribution à l'histoire de la civilisation de l'Arménie antique.* Moscow, 1953 (in Russian)
173. Tuchelt, K. *Frühe Denkmäler Roms in Kleinasien* I: *Roma und Promagistrate. MDAI(I),* Beiheft 23, 1979
174. Turner, E. G. 'A Ptolemaic vine-yard lease', *Bull. Rylands Libr.* 31 (1948) 148–61
175. Virgilio, B. *Il 'tempio stato' di Pessinunte fra Pergamo e Roma nel II–I secolo A.C.* Pisa, 1981
176. Vitucci, G. *Il regno di Bitinia.* Rome, 1953
177. Willrich, H. 'Von Athen über Pergamon nach Jerusalem', *Hermes* 59 (1924) 246–8
178. Wolski, J. 'Arsace II et la généalogie des premiers Arsacides', *Historia* 11 (1962) 38–54

F. THE GREEKS OF BACTRIA AND INDIA

1. Allan, J. *A Catalogue of Indian Coins in the British Museum, Coins of Ancient India.* London, 1934

2. Audouin, R. and Bernard, P. 'Trésor de monnaies indiennes et indo-grecques d'Aï Khanoum (Afghanistan)', *Rev. Num.*[6] 16 (1974) 7–41
3. Audouin, R. 'Trésor de monnaies indiennes et indo-grecques d'Aï Khanoum (Afghanistan)', *CRAI* 1971, 238–89
4. Allouche-Le Page, M.-T. *L'art monétaire des Royaumes bactriens: essai d'interprétation de la symbolique religieuse gréco-orientale du IIIe au Ier siècle avant J.-C.* Paris, 1956
5. Bayer, T. S. *Historia Regni Graecorum Bactriani.* St Petersburg, 1738
6. Bellinger, A.R. 'Greek coins from the Yale Numismatic Collection', *YCIS* 11 (1950) 307–16
7. Bernard, P. 'Ai Khanoum on the Oxus: a hellenistic city in Central Asia', *PBA* 53 (1967) 71–95
8. Bernard, P. 'La campagne de fouilles de 1970 à Aï Khanoum (Afghanistan)', *CRAI* 1971, 385–453
9. Bernard, P. 'La campagne de fouilles à Aï Khanoum (Afghanistan)', *CRAI* 1973, 280–307, 605–32
10. Bernard, P. and others. *Fouilles d'Aï Khanoum* I: *Campagnes 1965, 1966, 1967, 1968. MDAFA* 21. Paris, 1973
11. Bernard, P. and Audouin, R. 'Trésor de monnaies indiennes et indo-grecques d'Aï Khanoum (Afghanistan) I: les monnaies indiennes', *Rev. Num.* 15 (1973) 238–89
12. Bernard, P. and Audouin, R. 'Trésor de monnaies indiennes et indo-grecques d'Aï Khanoum (Afghanistan) II: les monnaies indo-grecques', *Rev. Num.* 16 (1974) 6–41
13. Bernard, P. 'Fouilles d'Aï Khanoum (Afghanistan), campagnes de 1972 et 1973', *CRAI* 1974, 280–308
14. Bernard, P. 'Campagne de fouilles 1974 à Aï Khanoum (Afghanistan)', *CRAI* 1975, 167–97
15. Bernard, P. and others. 'Fouilles d'Aï Khanoum (Afghanistan), campagne de 1974', *BEFEO* 63 (1976) 5–51
16. Bernard, P. and Francfort, H. P. *Études de géographie historique sur la plaine d'Aï Khanoum (Afghanistan).* Paris, 1978
17. Bernard, P. 'Campagne de fouilles 1978 à Aï Khanoum (Afghanistan)', *CRAI* 1980, 435–59
18. Bernard, P. and others. 'Campagne de fouilles 1978 à Aï Khanoum (Afghanistan)', *BEFEO* 68 (1980) 1–103
19. Bernard, P. and Guillaume, O. 'Monnaies inédites de la Bactriane grecque à Aï Khanoum (Afghanistan)', *Rev. Num.* 22 (1980) 9–32
20. Bernard, P. 'An ancient Greek city in Central Asia', *Scientific American* 246 (1982) 148–59
21. Bernard, P. 'Alexandre et Aï Khanoum', *JS* 1982, 125–38
22. Bernard, P. 'Diodore XVII.83.1, Alexandrie du Caucase ou Alexandrie l'Oxus', *JS* 1982, 217–42
23. Vacat
24. Bernard, P. and others. *Fouilles d'Aï Khanoum* IV: *Les monnaies, trésors, questions d'histoire gréco-bactrienne. MDAFA* 28. Paris, 1985

25. Bikerman, E. 'Notes on Seleucid and Parthian chronology', *Berytus* 8 (1944) 73–83
26. Bivar, A. D. H. 'The death of Eucratides in medieval tradition', *JRAS* (1950) 7–13
27. Bivar, A. D. H. 'The Bactra coinage of Euthydemus and Demetrius', *Num. Chron.*⁶ 15 (1955) 22–39
28. Bivar, A. D. H. *The Bactrian Treasure of Qunduz*. Numismatic Society of India, NNM 3. Bombay, 1955
29. Bivar, A. D. H. 'The Indo-Bactrian problems', *Num. Chron.*⁷ 5 (1965) 69–108
30. Bivar, A. D. H. 'The sequence of Menander's drachmae', *JRAS* (1970) 123–36
31. Bongard-Levin, G. M. *Mauryan India*. New Delhi, 1985
32. Briant, P. 'D'Alexandre le Grand aux Diodoques: le cas d'Eumène de Kardia', *REA* 75 (1973) 42–81, esp. 63ff.
33. Briant, P. '"Brigandage", dissidence et conquête en Asie achéménide et hellénistique', *Dialogues d'histoire ancienne* 2 (1976) 163ff.
34. Briant, P. 'Colonisation hellénistique et populations indigènes. La phase d'installation', *Klio* 60 (1978) 56–92
35. Cammann, S. V. R. 'The Bactrian nickel theory', *AJArch.* 62 (1958) 409–14
36. Colledge, M. A. R. *The Parthians*. New York, 1967
37. Cozzoli, U. 'La Beozia durante il conflitto tra l'Ellade e la Persia', *Riv. Fil.* 86 (1958) 264–87
38. Cribb, J. W. 'The earliest Ganesa: a case of mistaken identity', *Numismatic Digest* 6 (1982) 30–3
39. Curiel, R. and Fussman, G. *Le trésor monétaire de Qunduz*. *MDAFA* 20. Paris, 1965
40. Dalton, O. M. *The Treasure of the Oxus*. 3rd edn. London, 1954
41. Dandamayev, M. A. 'Noviye documenti tsarskogo khoziastva v. Irane (509–494 gg. do n.e.)', *VDI* 119 (1972) 25ff.
42. Dani, A. H. Review of A. K. Narain, *The Indo-Greeks*, in *Journal of the Asiatic Society of Pakistan* 2 (1957) 197–200
43. Dani, A. H. *Indian Palaeography*. Oxford, 1963
44. De la Vallée-Poussin, L. *L'Inde aux temps des Mauryas et des barbares, Grecs, Scythes, Parthes et Yue-tchi*. Paris, 1930
45. Demivielle, P. 'Les versions chinoises du Milindapañha', *BEFEO* 24 (1924–5) 1–255
46. Engels, D. W. *Alexander the Great and the Logistics of the Macedonian Army*. Berkeley, 1978
47. Filliozat, J. 'Représentations de Vasudeva et Samkarsana au IIe siècle avant J.-C.', *Arts Asiatiques* 26 (1973) 113–21
48. Francfort, H.-P. 'Deux nouveaux tétradrachmes commémoratifs d'Agathocle', *Rev. Num.*⁶ 17 (1975) 19–22
49. Fraser, P. M. 'The son of Aristonax at Kandahar', *Afghan Studies* 2 (1979–80) 9–21

50. Fry, R.N. 'Greco-Bactrians, Sakas and Parthians', in *The History of Ancient Iran*, ch. 7. Munich 1983

51. Fussman, G. 'Nouvelles inscriptions Saka: ère d'Eukratide, ère d'Azes, ère d'Vikrama, ère de Kanishka', *BEFEO* 67 (1980) 1–43

52. Gardner, P. 'New coins from Bactria', *Num. Chron.*[2] 19 (1879) 1–12

53. Gardner, P. *A Catalogue of Indian Coins in the British Museum. The Greek and Scythic Kings of Bactria*, London, 1886 (reprint, Chicago, 1966)

54. Grenet, F. 'L'onomastique iranienne à Aï Khanoum', *BCH* 107 (1983) 373–81

55. Grousset, R. *Histoire de l'Extreme-Orient* I. Paris, 1929

56. Guépin, J. P. 'Apollodotus et Eukratidès', *Jaarbook voor Munt- en Penningkunde* 43 (1956) 1–19

57. Guillaume, O. 'An analysis of the modes of reconstruction of the Graeco-Bactrian and Indo-Greek history', *Studies in History* n.s. 2.1 (1986) 1–16

58. Guillaume, O. 'Coins and small finds of Indian origin in Aï Khanoum (Afghanistan)', MS of a paper read at the 14th Annual Conference of the Indian Archaeological Society. New Delhi, 1986

59. Gupta, P. L. 'Kushanas in the Yamuno-Gangetic region, chronology and date', *Annali: Rivista del Dipartimento di Studi Asiatici e del Dipartimento di Studi e Ricerche su Africa e Paesi Arabi*, Istituto Universitario Orientale, Napoli 45 (1985) 199–222

60. Haughton, H. L. 'A note on the distribution of Indo-Greek coins', *Num. Chron.*[6] 3 (1943) 50–9

61. Haughton, H. L. 'The silver coinage of Strato and of Strato and Agathocleia', *Num. Chron.*[6] 8 (1948) 134–41

62. Haughton, H. L. *Haughton Sale Catalogue*, Sotheby & Co. (April–May 1958). London, 1958

63. Head, B. V. 'The earliest Graeco-Bactrian and Graeco-Indian coins', *Num. Chron.*[4] 6 (1906) 1–16

64. Hegyi, D. 'The historical background of the Ionian revolt', *A Ant. Hung.* 14 (1966) 285–302

65. Holt, F. L. 'The Euthydemid coinage of Bactria: further hoard evidence from Ai Khanoum', *Rev. Num.* 23 (1981) 7–44

66. Holt, F. L. 'Alexander's settlements in Central Asia', in *Ancient Macedonia* IV, (Thessalonica, 1986) 315–23

67. Holt, F. L. 'Ai Khanoum and the question of Bactrian independence', *AJArch.* 88 (1984) 248

68. Holt, F. L. 'The so-called Pedigree coins of the Bactrian Greeks', in W. Heckel and R. Sullivan, eds., *Ancient Coins of the Graeco-Roman World*, 69–91. Laurier, 1984

69. Holt, F. L. 'Beyond Plato's pond: the Greeks and barbarians in Bactria'. Unpublished diss. University of Virginia, Charlottesville, 1984

70. Houghton, A. and Moore, W. 'Some early Far Northeastern Seleucid mints', *ANSMN* 29 (1984) 1–9

71. Howorth, H. 'The eastern capital of the Seleucidae', *Num. Chron.*[3] 8 (1888) 293–9

72. Jenkins, G. K. Review of A. K. Narain, *The Indo-Greeks*, in *The Journal of the Central Asian Society*, 1957

73. Jenkins, G. K. 'The Apollodotus question: another view', *JNSI* 21 (1959) 20–31

74. Jenkins, G. K. 'Some recent Indo-Greek accessions of the British Museum', *JNSI* 30 (1968) 23–7

75. Jenkins, G. K. 'Indo-Greek tetradrachms', *BMQ* 32 (1968) 108–12

76. Jenkins, G. K. and Narain, A. K. *The Coin-Types of the Saka-Pahlava Kings of India*. Numismatic Society of India, NNM 4. Varanasi, 1957

76A. Kalidasa. *Malavikagnimitra*, ed. R. C. Misra, Varanasi, 1951.

77. Klima, O. Review of A. K. Narain, *The Indo-Greeks*, in *Archiv Orientální* 26 (1958) 173–5

78. Konow, S. *Corpus Inscriptionum Indicarum* II. 1: *Kharosthi Inscriptions with the Exception of those of Asoka*. Calcutta, 1929

79. Koshelenko, G. A. 'The revolt of the Greeks in Bactria and Sogdiana in the light of 4th century social and political theory', *VDI* 119 (1972) 59–78 (in Russian)

80. Koshelenko, G. A. *Grecheskiy Polis na ellinisticheskom vostoke (The Greek Polis in the Hellenistic East)*. Moscow, 1979

81. Kraay, C. M. *The Hellenistic Kingdoms, Portrait Coins and History*. London, 1973

82. Kraay, C. M. 'Demetrius in Bactria and India', *NAC* 10 (1981) 219–33

83. Lahiri, A. N. *Corpus of Indo-Greek Coins*. Calcutta, 1965

84. Lazarus, E. J., ed., *Abhayanandi's Commentary* Mahāvritti *on Jainendra's* Vyākaraṇa. Varanasi, 1918

85. Le Rider, G. 'Un octodrachme d'or d'Euthydème I de Bactriane', *BSFN* 21 (1966) 94

86. Le Rider, G. 'Monnaies grecques recemment acquises par le Cabinet de Paris', *Rev. Num.* 11 (1969) 7–27

87. Levi, S. 'Alexander and Alexandria in Indian literature', *IHQ* 12 (1936) 121–33

88. Litvinskiy, B. A. and Pichikiyan, I. R. 'The Temple of the Oxus', *JRAS* (1981) 133–67

89. Macdonald, G. 'The hellenistic kingdoms of Syria, Bactria and Parthia', in *Cambridge History of India* I, ed. E. J. Rapson, ch. 17. Cambridge, 1922

90. MacDowall, D. W. and Wilson, N. G. 'Apollodoti reges Indorum', *Num. Chron.*[6] 20 (1960) 221–8

91. MacDowall, D. W. 'The copper denominations of Menander', in *Acta Iranica* (Deuxième série, vol. II) *Hommages et Opera Minora, Monumentum H. S. Nyberg*, 39–52. Leiden/Téhéran – Liège, 1975

92. MacDowall, D. W. 'Excavations at Kandahar 1975: coin finds', *Afghan Studies* 1 (1978) 50–1

93. Vacat

94. MacDowall, D. W. and Ibrahim, M. 'Pre-Islamic coins in Kandahar Museum', *Afghan Studies* 1 (1978) 67–77

95. MacDowall, D. W. 'Pre-Islamic coins in Herat Museum', *Afghan Studies* 2 (1979) 45–53

96. Majumdar, N. G. 'The Bajaur Casket of the reign of Menander', *Ep. Ind.* 24 (1937–8) 1–10

97. Mankad, D. R. *Yuqapuranam*, Vallabhvidyanagar, 1951

98. Marshall, J. *Taxila, An Illustrated Account of Archaeological Excavation.* 3 vols. Cambridge, 1951

99. Masson, V. M. 'Demetrij Baktrijskij i zavoievanie Indii', (Demetrius of Bactria and the conquest of India), *VDI* 76 (1961) 39–45

100. *Milindapañha*, ed. V. Trenckner. London, 1928. (Trans. by T. W. Rhys Davids. Sacred Books of the East xxv and xxxvi. Oxford, 1890, 1894)

101. Mitchiner, M. *Indo-Greek and Indo-Scythian Coinage.* 9 vols. London, 1975

101A. Musti, D. 'Syria and the East', in *CAH*[2] vii.i. 175–220. Cambridge, 1984

102. Narain, A. K. *The Coin-types of the Indo-Greek Kings.* Numismatic Society of India, NNM 2. Varanasi, 1955 (3rd reprint, Chicago, 1976)

103. Narain, A. K. *The Indo-Greeks.* Oxford, 1957 (3rd reprint, 1980)

104. Narain, A. K. 'Apollodotus and his coins', *JNSI* 19 (1957) 121–34

105. Narain, A. K. and Jenkins, G. K. *The Coin-types of the Saka-Pahlava Kings of India.* Numismatic Society of India, 4. Varanasi, 1957

106. Narain, A. K. 'Alexander and India', *G&R* 12 (1965) 155–65 (= *The Impact of Alexander the Great, Civilizer or Destroyer*, ed. E. G. Borza, 57–65. Hinsdale, Ill., 1974)

107. Narain, A. K. 'The two Hindu divinities on the coins of Agathocles from Ai Khanum', *JNSI* 35 (1973) 73–7

108. Narain, A. K. 'On the earliest Ganes', in the *Senarat Paranavitana Commemoration Volume.* I. Prematilake and J. E. Van Lohuizen-de Leeuw, 142–4. Leiden, 1978. Also 'Ganesa on Hermaeus' coin', *Num. Dig.* 6 (1982) 26–9

109. Narain, A. K. 'Iconographic origins of Ganesa and the evidence of the Indo-Greek coinage', in *Orientalia Iosephi Tucci Memoriae Dicata*, ed. G. Gnoli and L. Lanciotti (*Orientale Roma* 56.3. Rome forthcoming

110. Narain, A. K. 'The earliest Brahmi inscription outside India', *JAOS* 106.4 (1986) 797–801

111. Narain, A. K. 'The Greek monogram and Ai-Khanum: the Bactrian Greek city', *Num. Dig.* 10 (1986) 5–15

111A. Narain, A. K. 'Notes on some inscriptions from Ai Khanum (Afghanistan)', *ZPE* 69 (1987) 277–82

112. Narain, A. K. 'On the foundation and chronology of Ai Khanum: a Greek-Bactrian city', *India and the Ancient World*, ed. G. Pollet (Orientalia Lovaniensia Analecta 25), 115–30. Leuven, 1987

113. Narain, S. 'The twenty-stater gold piece of Eucratides', *JNSI* 18 (1956) 217–18

114. Newell, E. T. *The Coinage of the Eastern Seleucid Mints.* Numismatic Studies 1. New York, 1938

115. Newell, E. T. *The Coinage of the Western Seleucid Mints.* Numismatic Studies 4. New York, 1941

116. Nilakanta Sastri, K. A. *Foreign Notices of South India.* Madras, 1972

117. Olmstead, A. *History of the Persian Empire.* Chicago, 1948

118. Panini, *Ashṭādhyāyī*, ed. O. Böhtling, *Pāṇiṇi's Grammatik*. Leipzig, 1887
119. Pargiter, F. E. *The Purana Text of the Dynasties of the Kali Age*. Oxford, 1913
120. Patañjali, *The Vyākaraṇa-Mahābhāshya of Patañjali*, ed. F. Kielhorn. 3 vols. 1892–9
121. Pelliot, M. P. 'Les noms propres dans les traductions chinoises du *Milindapañha*', *JA*[11] 4 (1914) 379–419, esp. 413ff.
122. Petitot-Biehler, C.-Y. 'Trésor de monnaies grecques et gréco-bactriennes trouvé à Ai Khanoum', *Rev. Num.* 17 (1975) 23–57
123. Pichikiyan, I. R. and Litvinskij, B. A. 'Découvertes dans un sanctuaire du dieu Oxus de la Bactriane septentrionale', *Rev. Arch.* 00 (1981) 195–216
124. Pugachenkova, G. A., 'K stratigrafiy novykh moetykh nakhodok iz severnoi Baktrij' (New coin finds from North Bactria), *VDI* 3 (1967) 74–88
125. Pugachenkova, G. A. 'Herakles in Bactria', *VDI* 10 (1977) 77–92
126. Pugachenkova, G. A. and Rtveladze, E. V. 'Novye monetye nakhodki iz pravobereinoi Baktrij' (New coin finds from North Bactria), *VDI* 4 (1971) 101–13
127. Rapin, Cl. 'Inscriptions économiques de la trésorerie hellénistique', *BCH* 107 (1983) 315–72
128. Rapson, E. J. 'The successors of Alexander the Great', in *Cambridge History of India* 1, ed. E. J. Rapson, ch. 22. Cambridge, 1922
129. Rawlinson, H. G. *Bactria, the History of a Forgotten Empire*. London, 1912
130. Robert, L. 'Encore une inscription grecque de l'Iran', *CRAI* 1967, 281–96
131. Robert, L. 'De Delphes à l'Oxus', *CRAI* 1968, 416–57
132. Robert, L. 'Les inscriptions', in P. Bernard, *Fouilles d'Aï Khanoum* 1, 207–37. Paris, 1973
133. Rtveladze, E. V. 'The location of the Greek crossing on the Oxus river', *VDI* 4 (1971) 108–16
134. Sarianidi, V. *The Golden Hoard of Bactria*. Leningrad and New York, 1985
135. Schlumberger, D. 'The excavations at Surkh Kotal and the problem of Hellenism in Bactria and India', *PBA* 47 (1961) 77–95
136. Schlumberger, D. 'Une nouvelle inscription grecque d'Asoka', *CRAI* 1964, 120–40
137. Schlumberger, D. 'Ai Khanoum, une ville hellénistique en Afghanistan', *CRAI* 1965, 36–46
138. Schlumberger, D. and Curiel, R. *Trésors monétaires d'Afghanistan*. *MDAFA* 14. Paris, 1953
139. Schlumberger, D. and Bernard, P. 'Ai Khanoum', *BCH* 89 (1965) 590–637
140. Sedlar, J. W. *India and the Greek World. A Study in the Transmission of Culture*. Totowa, NJ, 1980
141. Senior, R. C. *Sale List* 4. Somerset, England, January 1983
142. Sharma, G. R. *Reh Inscription of Menander and the Indo-Greek Invasion of the Ganga Valley*. Allahabad, 1980
143. Simonetta, A. 'An essay on the so-called "Indo-Greek" coinage', *East and West* 8 (1957) 44–66

144. Simonetta, A. 'A new essay on the Indo-Greeks, the Sakas and the Pahlavas', *East and West* 9 (1958) 154–83

145. Simonetta, A. 'Some hypotheses on the military and political structure of the Indo-Greek kingdom', *JNSI* 22 (1960) 56–62

146. Smith, R. M. 'On the ancient chronology of India (III)', *JAOS* 78.3 (1958) 174–92

147. Smith, R. M. 'Greek kings in India: a synopsis', *Annals of Bhandrakar Oriental Research Institute* 1977–8, 327–36

148. Smith, V. A. *A Catalogue of Coins in the Indian Museum* 1. Oxford, 1906

149. Staviski, B. J. 'The capitals of Ancient Bactria', *East and West* 23 (1973) 265–77

150. Taranatha. *Taranathas Geschichte des Buddhismus in India*, ed. A. Schiefner. St Petersburg, 1879

151. Tarn, W. W. *Alexander the Great.* 2 vols. Cambridge, 1948

152. Tarn, W. W. *The Greeks in Bactria and India.* 2nd edn. Cambridge, 1951 (reprinted with an introductory note by F. L. Holt, Chicago, 1984)

153. Thomas, F. W. 'Notes on "The Scythian Period"', *JRAS* (1952) 108–16

153A. Töttössy, C. 'Graeco-Indo-Iranica', *AAnt. Hung.* 25 (1977) 129–35

154. Trever, K. B. *Pamyatniki Greko-Baktriyskogo Iskusstva.* Moscow and Leningrad, 1940

155. Verma, T. P. 'A note on the Reh Inscription', in *Rangavalli, Recent Researches in Indology*, 77–80. Bombay, 1981

156. Von Sallet, A. *Die Nachfolger Alexanders des Grossen in Baktrien und Indien.* Berlin, 1879

157. Walbank, F. W. Review of A. K. Narain, *The Indo-Greeks*, in *History* (1958) 125–6

158. Walbank, F. W. *The Hellenistic World*, Cambridge, Mass, 1982

158A. Walbank, F. W. 'Monarchies and Monarchic ideas', ch. 3 in *The Cambridge Ancient History*, 2 ed. vol. 7.1 (1984): 62–100.

159. Wheeler, R. M. *Charsada, A Metropolis of the North-west Frontier.* Oxford, 1962

160. Whitehead, R. B. *Catalogue of the Coins in the Punjab Museum, Lahore* 1: *Indo-Greek Coins.* Oxford, 1914

161. Whitehead, R. B. 'Notes on Indo-Greek numismatics', *Num. Chron.*[5] 3 (1923) 294–343

162. Whitehead, R. B. 'Notes on the Indo-Greeks', *Num. Chron.*[5] 20 (1940) 89–122

163. Whitehead, R. B. 'The dynasty of the General Aspavarma', *Num. Chron.*[6] 4 (1944) 99–104

164. Whitehead, R. B. *Indo-Greek Numismatics.* Chicago, 1970

165. Widemann, F. 'Une surfrappe de Gondopharès sur Hermaios et une autre de Kozoulo Kadphises sur Gondopharès qui apportent deux jalons numismatiques à la chronologie entre les Indo-Grecs et le début de l'empire Kouchans', *Bulletin de la Société française de Numismatique* 27.1 (1972) 147–51

165A. Wolski, J. 'L'effondrement de la domination des Séleucides en Iran au IIIe

siècle av. J.-C., *Bull. Internat. de l'Académie Polonaise des Sciences et des Lettres* Suppl. v, 13–70. Cracow, 1947
166. Wolski, J. 'The decay of the Iranian empire of the Seleucids and the chronology of the Parthian beginnings', *Berytus* 12 (1956/7) 35–52
167. Wolski, J. 'Le problème de la fondation de l'état gréco-bactrien', *Iranica Antiqua* 17 (1982) 131–46
168. Woodcock, G. *The Greeks in India.* London, 1966

G. THE ROMANS IN SPAIN

1. Albertini, E. *Les divisions administratives de l'Espagne romaine.* Paris, 1923
2. Astin, A. E. 'The Roman commander in Hispania Ulterior in 142 B.C.', *Historia* 13 (1964) 245–54
3. Badian, E. 'The prefect at Gades', *CPh* 49 (1954) 250–2
4. Balil, A. 'Un factor difusor de la Romanización: las tropas hispánicas al servicio de Roma (siglos III–I a. de J.C.)', *Emerita* 24 (1956) 108–34
5. Bernhardt, R. 'Die Entwicklung römischer amici et socii zu civitates liberae in Spanien', *Historia* 24 (1975) 411–24
6. Blázquez, J. M. 'El impacto de la conquista de Hispania en Roma (218–154 a. J.C.)', *Estudios Clásicos* 7 (1962–3) 1–29
7. Blázquez, J. M. 'El impacto de la conquista de Hispania en Roma (154–83 a.C.)', *Klio* 41 (1963) 168–86
8. Blázquez, J. M. 'Causas de la Romanización de Hispania', *Hispania* 24 (1964) 5–26, 165–84, 325–47, 485–508
9. Blázquez, J. M. 'Economía de los pueblos prerromanos del área no ibérica hasta la época de Augusto', in *Estudios de Economiá Antigua de la Península Ibérica*, ed. M. Tarrandell, 191–269. Barcelona, 1968 (reprinted in J. M. Blázquez, *Economía de la Hispania Romana*. Bilbao, 1978)
10. Blázquez, J. M. 'Economía de Hispania durante la República Romana', *Revista Internacional de Sociología* 32 (1974) 19–57 (reprinted in J. M. Blázquez, *Economia de la Hispania Romana*. Bilbao, 1978)
11. Blázquez, J. M. and others. *Historia de España Antigua* i–ii. Madrid, 1978 (vol. II), 1980 (vol. I)
12. Develin, R. 'The Roman command structure and Spain, 218–190 B.C.', *Klio* 62 (1980) 355–68
13. Domínguez Arranz, A. *Las cecas ibéricas del Valle del Ebro.* Saragossa, 1979
14. Fatás, G. *Contrebia Belaisca (Botorrita, Zaragoza)* ii: *Tabula Contrebiensis.* Saragossa, 1980
15. Galsterer, H. *Untersuchungen zum römischen Städtewesen auf der iberischen Halbinsel.* Berlin, 1971
16. García y Bellido, A. 'Las colonias romanas de Hispania', *Anuario de Historia del Derecho Español* 29 (1959) 447–512
17. García y Bellido, A. *Resumén histórico del urbanismo en España.* 2nd edn. Madrid, 1968
18. García y Bellido, A. 'Die Latinisierung Hispaniens', *ANRW* i.1 (1972) 462–500

19. Griffin, M. 'The Elder Seneca and Spain', *JRS* 62 (1972) 1–19
20. Knapp, R. C. *Aspects of the Roman Experience in Iberia, 206–100 B.C.* Valladolid, 1977
21. Maluquer de Motes, J. *Epigrafía prelatina de la Península ibérica.* Barcelona, 1968
22. Martínez Gázquez, J. *La campaña de Catón en Hispania.* Barcelona, 1974
23. Menéndez Pidal, R., ed. *Historia de España* I. 3; II, 4th edn. Madrid, 1954 and 1980
24. Richardson, J. S. 'The Spanish mines and the development of provincial taxation in the second century B.C.', *JRS* 66 (1976) 139–52
25. Richardson, J. S. 'The Tabula Contrebiensis: Roman law in Spain in the early first century B.C.', *JRS* 73 (1983) 33–41
26. Rickard, T. A. 'The mining of the Romans in Spain', *JRS* 18 (1928) 129–43
27. Sánchez-Albornoz, C. 'Proceso de la romanización de España desde los Escipiones hasta Augusto', *Anales de Historia Antigua u Medieval* (1949) 5–36
28. Schulten, A. 'The Romans in Spain', in *CAH*[1] VIII, 306–25. Cambridge, 1930
29. Simon, H. *Roms Kriege in Spanien, 154–133 v. Chr.* Frankfurt-am-Main, 1962
30. Sumner, G. V. 'Proconsuls and Provinciae in Spain, 218/17–196/5 B.C.', *Arethusa* 3 (1970) 85–102
31. Sumner, G. V. 'Notes on *Provinciae* in Spain (197–133 B.C.)', *CPh* 72 (1977) 126–30
32. Torres, C. 'La fundación de Valencia', *Ampurias* 13 (1951) 113–21
33. Van Nostrand, J. J. 'Roman Spain', in *ESAR* III, 119–224
34. Wattenberg, F. *La región vaccea. Celtiberismo y romanización en la Cuenca media del Duero.* Madrid, 1959
35. Wiegels, R. 'Liv. per. 55 und die Gründung von Valentia', *Chiron* 4 (1974) 153–76
36. Wiegels, R. 'Iliturgi und der "deductor" Ti. Sempronius Gracchus', *MDAI(M)* 23 (1982) 152–221

H. ROME AND ITALY

a.   Constitutional studies and the nature of Roman politics

1. Afzelius, A. 'Zur Definition der römischen Nobilität vor der Zeit Ciceros', *C&M* 7 (1945) 150–200
2. Astin, A. E. *The Lex Annalis before Sulla.* Collection Latomus XXXII. Brussels, 1958
3. Astin, A. E. *Politics and Policies in the Roman Republic* (Inaugural lecture). Belfast, 1968
4. Broughton, T. R. S. 'Senate and senators of the Roman Republic: the prosopographical approach', *ANRW* I.1 (1972) 250–65
5. Brunt, P. A. 'Amicitia in the Late Roman Republic', *PCPS* 191 (1965) 1–20

6. Brunt, P. A. 'Nobilitas and novitas', *JRS* 72 (1982) 1–17
7. Finley, M. I. *Politics in the Ancient World*. Cambridge, 1983
8. Gelzer, M. *Die Nobilität der römischen Republik*. Leipzig and Berlin, 1912
9. Gelzer, M. and Seager, R. *The Roman Nobility* (trans. of Gelzer 1912: (H 8)). Oxford, 1969
10. Greenidge, A. H. J. *Roman Public Life*. London, 1901
11. Gruen, E. S. *Roman Politics and the Criminal Courts, 149–78 B.C.* Cambridge, Mass, 1968
12. Jashemski, W. F. *The Origins and History of the Proconsular and Propraetorian Imperium to 27 B.C.* Diss. Chicago, 1950
13. Lippold, A. *Consules*. Bonn, 1963
14. Millar, F. G. B. 'The political character of the classical Roman Republic, 200–151 B.C.', *JRS* 74 (1984) 1–19
15. Münzer, F. *Römische Adelsparteien und Adelsfamilien*. Stuttgart, 1920
16. Nicolet, C. 'Polybe et les institutions romaines', in *Polybe* (Entretiens sur l'antiquité classique, Fondation Hardt, 20), 209–65. Geneva, 1973
17. Nowak, M. *Die Strafverhängungen der Censoren*. Breslau, 1909
18. Pieri, G. *L'histoire du cens jusqu'à la fin de la république romaine*. Paris, 1968
19. Poeschl, V. *Römischer Staat und griechisches Staatsdenken bei Cicero*. Berlin, 1936
20. Rich, J. W. *Declaring War in the Roman Republic in the Period of Transmarine Expansion*. Collection Latomus CXLIX. Brussels, 1976
21. Rilinger, R. *Der Einfluss des Wahlleiters bei den römischen Konsulwahlen von 366 bis 50 v. Chr.* Munich, 1976
22. Schleussner, B. *Die Legaten der römischen Republik*. Munich, 1978
23. Schmähling, E. *Die Sittenaufsicht der Censoren*. Stuttgart, 1938
24. Scullard, H. H. 'Roman politics', *BICS* 2 (1955) 15–21
25. Shatzman, I. 'The Roman general's authority over booty', *Historia* 21 (1972) 177–205
26. Staveley, E. S. 'The conduct of elections during an interregnum', *Historia* 3 (1954–5) 193–211
27. Staveley, E. S. *Greek and Roman Voting and Elections*. London, 1966
28. Suolahti, J. *The Roman Censors*. Helsinki, 1963
29. Taylor, L. R. *The Voting Districts of the Roman Republic*. Rome, 1960
30. Taylor, L. R. *Roman Voting Assemblies*. Ann Arbor, Mich., 1966

b. Political and public life

31. Albert, S. *Bellum Iustum*. Kallmünz, 1980
32. Badian, E. *Publicans and Sinners. Private Enterprise in the Service of the Roman Republic*. Oxford, 1972
33. Badian, E. 'Tiberius Gracchus and the beginnings of the Roman revolution', *ANRW* I.1 (1972) 608–731
34. Calboli, G. *Marci Porcii Catonis Oratio pro Rhodiensibus: Catone, l'oriente greco e gli imprenditori Romani*. Bologna, 1978
35. Cassola, F. *I gruppi politici romani nel III secolo a.C.* Trieste, 1962

36. Coarelli, F. 'Public buildings in Rome between the Second Punic War and Sylla', *PBSR* 45 (1977) 1–23

37. Cova, P. V. 'Livio e la repressione dei Baccanali', *Athenaeum* 52 (1974) 82–109

38. Dihle, A. 'Zum s.c. de Bacchanalibus', *Hermes* 90 (1962) 376–9

39. Earl, D. C. 'Political terminology in Plautus', *Historia* 9 (1960) 235–43

40. Earl, D. C. 'Terence and Roman politics', *Historia* 11 (1962) 469–85

41. Frederiksen, M. 'The contribution of archaeology to the agrarian problem in the Gracchan period', in *RIGS*, 330–57

42. Gabba, E. *Republican Rome. The Army and the Allies.* Oxford, 1976

43. Gabba, E. 'Esercito e fiscalità a Roma in età repubblicana', in *Armées et fiscalité dans le monde antique*, 13–33. Paris, 1977

44. Gabba, E. 'Richezza e classe dirigente romana fra II e I sec. a.C.', *RSI* 93 (1981) 541–58

45. Gelzer, M. 'Römische Politik bei Fabius Pictor', *Hermes* 68 (1933) 129–66 (= *Kl. Schr.* III, 51–92. Wiesbaden, 1964)

46. Gelzer, M. 'Die Unterdrückung der Bacchanalia bei Livius', *Hermes* 71 (1936) 275–87 = (*Kl. Schr.* III, 256–69. Wiesbaden, 1964)

47. Heuss, A. *Die völkerrechtlichen Grundlagen der römischen Aussenpolitik in republikanischer Zeit.* Leipzig, 1933

48. Hill, H. *The Roman Middle Class in the Republican Period.* Oxford, 1952

49. Hopkins, K. *Death and Renewal.* Sociological Studies in Roman History 2. Cambridge, 1983

50. Martina, M. 'I censori del 258 a.C.', *Quaderni di Storia* 12 (July–December 1980) 143–70

51. Nicolet, C. *The World of the Citizen in Republican Rome.* London, 1980

52. Rawson, E. 'The eastern clientelae of Clodius and the patrician Clodii', *Historia* 22 (1973) 219–39

53. Rich, J. W. 'The supposed Roman manpower shortage of the later second century B.C.', *Historia* 32 (1983) 287–331

54. Scullard, H. H. *Roman Politics, 220–150 B.C.* 2nd edn. Oxford, 1973

55. Shatzman, I. *Senatorial Wealth and Roman Politics.* Collection Latomus CXLII. Brussels, 1975

56. Sherwin-White, A. N. 'The date of the Lex Repetundarum and its consequences', *JRS* 62 (1972) 83–99

57. Sordi, M. 'La tradizione storiografica su Tiberio Sempronio Gracco e la propaganda contemporanea', *Miscellanea Greca e Romana* 6 (1978) 299–330

58. Tarditi, G. 'La questione dei Baccanali a Roma nel 186 a.C.', *PP* 9 (1954) 265–87

59. Taylor, L. R. 'Forerunners of the Gracchi', *JRS* 52 (1962) 19–27

60. Thiel, J. H. *Studies on the History of Roman Sea-power in Republican Times.* Amsterdam, 1946

61. Venturini, C. *Studi sul 'crimen repetundarum' nell'età repubblicana.* Milan, 1979

62. Walbank, F. W. 'Political morality and the friends of Scipio', *JRS* 55 (1965) 1–16

63. Wiseman, T. P. 'Roman Republican road-building', *PBSR* 38 (1970) 122–52
64. Wiseman, T. P. *New Men in the Roman Senate 139 B.C.–14 A.D.* Oxford, 1971
65. Wiseman, T. P. 'Legendary genealogies in late-Republican Rome', *G&R* 21 (1974) 153–64
66. Wiseman, T. P. *'Domi Nobiles* and the Roman cultural élite', in *Les 'Bourgeoisies' municipales italiennes aux IIe et Ier siècles avant J.-C.*, 299–307. Naples, 1983

c. Biographical studies

67. Astin, A. E. *Scipio Aemilianus*. Oxford, 1967
68. Astin, A. E. *Cato the Censor*. Oxford, 1978
69. Badian, E. T. *Quinctius Flamininus: Philhellenism and Realpolitik* (Lectures in Memory of Louise Taft Semple). Cincinnati, 1970
70. Badian, E. 'Ennius and his Friends', in *Ennius* (Entretiens sur l'antiquité classique, Fondation Hardt, 17), 149–208. Vandoeuvres–Geneva, 1972
71. Della Corte, F. *Catone Censore: La vita e la fortuna*. Florence, 1969
72. Haffter, H. 'Cato der Ältere in Politik und Kultur seiner Zeit', in *Römische Politik und Politiker*. Heidelberg, 1967
73. Kammer, U. *Untersuchungen zu Ciceros Bild von Cato Censorius*. Diss. Frankfurt am Main, 1964
74. Kienast, D. *Cato der Zensor, seine Persönlichkeit und seine Zeit*. Heidelberg, 1954
75. Nicolet, C. 'Arpinum, Aemilius Scaurus et les Tullii Cicerones', *REL* 45 (1967) 276–304
76. Scullard, H. H. 'Scipio Aemilianus and Roman politics', *JRS* 50 (1960) 59–74
77. Scullard, H. H. *Scipio Africanus: Soldier and Politician*. London, 1970
78. Strasburger, H. 'Der "Scipionenkreis"', *Hermes* 94 (1966) 60–72
79. Walbank, F. W. 'The Scipionic Legend', *PCPS* n.s. 13 (1967) 54–69

d. Social life and institutions

80. Afzelius, A. *Die römische Kriegsmacht*. Copenhagen, 1944
81. Bonner, S. F. *Education in Ancient Rome*. London, 1977
82. Brunt, P. A. *Italian Manpower 225 B.C.–A.D. 14*. Oxford, 1971
83. Carandini, A. 'Sviluppo e crisi delle manifatture rurali e urbane', in *SRPS* II, 249–60
84. Castagnoli, F. 'Note al Liber Coloniarum', *Bull. Com. Arch.* 72 (1946–8) Appendice, 49–58
85. Clemente, G. 'Le leggi sul lusso e la società romana tra III e II secolo a.C.', in *SRPS* III, 1–14
86. Dahlheim, W. *Struktur und Entwicklung des römischen Völkerrechts im 3. und 2. Jahrhundert v. Chr.* Munich, 1968
87. Evans, J. K. 'Plebs rustica. The peasantry of Classical Italy', *AJAH* 5 (1980) 19–47, 134–73

88. Frederiksen, M. 'Changes in the patterns of settlement', in *HIM* II, 341–55
89. Frederiksen, M. 'I cambiamenti delle strutture agrarie nella tarda repubblica: la Campania', in *SRPS* I, 265–87
90. Gabba, E. *Esercito e società nella tarda repubblica romana.* Florence, 1973
91. Gabba, E. 'Considerazioni politiche ed economiche sullo sviluppo urbano in Italia sui secoli II e I a.C.', in *HIM* II, 315–26
92. Gabba, E. 'Riflessioni antiche e moderne sulle attività commerciali a Roma nei secoli II e I a.C.', in *The Seaborne Commerce of Ancient Rome*, ed. J. H. D'Arms and E. C. Kopff, 91–102. MAAR 36. Rome, 1980
93. Gabba, E. and Pasquinucci, M. *Strutture agrarie allevamento transumante nell' Italia romana (III–I sec. a.C.).* Pisa, 1979
94. Giardina, A. 'Allevamento ed economia della selva in Italia meridionale: traformazioni e continuita', in *SRPS* I, 87–114
95. Giardina, A. and Schiavone, A., eds. *Società romana e produzione schiavistica.* 3 vols. Rome and Bari, 1981. (*SRPS*)
96. Harris, W. V. 'Economic conditions in Northern Etruria in the second century B.C.', in *CDE*, 56–63
97. Heurgon, J. 'Classes et ordres chez les Étrusques', in *Recherches sur les structures sociales dans l'antiquité classique* (Caen 25–26 April 1969), 29–41. Paris, 1970
98. Hoffmann, W. 'Probleme der Sklaverei und ihre Bedeutung für die inneritalische Entwicklung um die Wende von 2. zum 1. Jhdt. v.Z.', in *RIGS*, 498–514
99. Hopkins, K. *Conquerors and Slaves.* Cambridge, 1978
100. Jory, E. J. 'Associations of actors in Rome', *Hermes* 98 (1970) 224–53
101. Kähler, H. *Seethiasos und Census.* Berlin, 1966
102. Laffi, U. *Adtributio e contributio.* Pisa, 1966
103. Maroti, E. 'The vilicus and the villa-system in ancient Italy', *Oikoumene* I (1976) 109–24
104. Neeve, P. W. de. *Colonus. Private Farm-tenancy in Roman Italy during the Republic and Early Principate.* Amsterdam, 1984
105. Neeve, P. W. de. *Peasants in Peril. Location and Economy in Italy in the Second Century B.C.* Amsterdam, 1984
106. Nicolet, C. 'Armée et société à Rome sous la république: à propos de l'ordre équestre', in J.-P. Brisson, ed., *Problèmes de la guerre à Rome*, 117–56. Paris and The Hague, 1969
107. North, J. 'Conservation and change in Roman religion', *PBSR* 44 (1976) 1–12
108. North, J. 'Religious toleration in Republican Rome', *PCPS* 205 (1979) 85–103
109. Pailler, J.-M. '"Raptos a diis homines dici . . ." (Tite-Live XXXIX, 13). Les bacchanales et la possession par les nymphes', *Mélanges Heurgon* II, 731–42
110. Piganiol, A. *Recherches sur les jeux romains.* Strasbourg, 1923
111. Schiavone, A. *Nascita della giurisprudenza.* Bari, 1976
112. Schilling, R. *La religion romaine de Vénus depuis les origines jusqu'au temps d'Auguste.* Paris, 1954
113. Sherwin-White, A. N. *The Roman Citizenship.* 2nd edn. Oxford, 1973

114. Smith, R. E. 'Latins and the Roman citizenship in Roman colonies: Livy, 34, 42, 5–6', *JRS* 44 (1954) 18–20
115. Tibiletti, G. 'Il possesso dell' ager publicus e le norme de modo agrorum sino ai Gracchi', *Athenaeum* 26 (1948) 173–236; 27 (1949) 3–42
116. Tibiletti, G. 'Ricerche di storia agraria romana', *Athenaeum* 28 (1950) 183–266
117. Tibiletti, G. 'Lo sviluppo del latifondo dall' epoca graccana al principio dell' impero', in *X Congresso Internazionale di Scienze Storiche, Relazioni* II. Florence, 1955
118. Torelli, M. 'Industria estrattiva, lavoro artigianale, interessi economici: qualche appunto', in *The Seaborne Commerce of Ancient Rome: Studies in Archaeology and History*, ed. J. H. D'Arms and E. C. Kopff, 313–23. MAAR 36. Rome, 1980
118A. Treggiari, S. *Roman Freedmen during the Late Republic*. Oxford, 1969
119. Watson, A. *Rome of the XII Tables. Persons and Property*. Princeton, 1975
120. White, K. D. *Roman Farming*. London, 1970
121. Wilson, A. J. N. *Emigration from Italy in the Republican Age of Rome*. Manchester, 1966
122. Wissowa, G. *Religion und Kultus der Römer*. 2nd edn. Munich, 1912
123. Zevi, F. 'Ostia', *Stud. Etr.* 41 (1973) 507–29

e. Rome and the Italians

124. Badian, E. 'Roman politics and the Italians (133–91 B.C.)', in *RIGS*, 373–409
125. Beloch, K. J. *Der italische Bund unter Roms Hegemonie*. Leipzig, 1880
126. Bernardi, A. *Nomen Latinum*. Pavia, 1973
127. Brunt, P. A. 'Italian aims at the time of the Social War', *JRS* 55 (1965) 90–109
128. Cassola, F. 'Romani e italici in oriente', in *RIGS*, 305–22
129. Crawford, M. H. 'Italy and Rome', *JRS* 71 (1981) 153–60
130. Gabba, E. 'Le origini della Guerra Sociale e la vita politica romana dopo l'89 a.C.', *Athenaeum* n.s. 32 (1954) 41–114, 293–345 (translated in Gabba 1976: (H 42))
131. Gabba, E. 'Il problema dell'unità dell'Italia romana', in *La cultura italica*. Pisa, 1978
132. Galsterer, H. *Herrschaft und Verwaltung im republikanischen Italien*. Munich, 1976
133. Ghinatti, F. 'Economia e romanizzazione della Campania', *AFLPad.* 2 (1977) 93–159
134. Giuffrè, V. 'Esigenze militari romane ed Italici', *Labeo* 21 (1975) 215–38
135. Göhler, J. *Rom und Italien*. Breslau, 1939
136. Harris, W. V. *Rome in Etruria and Umbria*. Oxford, 1971
137. Harris, W. V. 'Was Roman law imposed on the Italian allies?', *Historia* 24 (1972) 639–45
138. Humbert, M. 'Libertas id est civitas. Autour d'un conflit négatif de citoyennetés au IIe s. av. J.-C.', *Mélanges d'arch.* 88 (1976) 221–42

139. Humbert, M. *Municipium et civitas sine suffragio*. Rome, 1978
140. Ilari, V. *Gli Italici nelle strutture militari romane*. Milan, 1974
141. Klingner, F. 'Italien, Name, Begriff und Idee im Altertum', in *Römische Geisteswelt*, 11–33, 5th edn. Munich, 1965
142. La Regina, A. 'Il Sannio', in *HIM* 1, 219–44
143. Luraschi, G. *Foedus Ius Latii Civitas*. Pavia, 1979
144. Luraschi, G. 'A proposito dei Ligures Statellates transducti trans Padum nel 172 a.C. (Liv. 42.22.5–6)', *Annali Benacensi di Cavriana* 7 (1981) 73–80
145. McDonald, A. H. 'Rome and the Italian Confederation (200–186 B.C.)', *JRS* 34 (1944) 11–33
146. Nagle, D. B. 'An allied view of the Social War', *AJArch.* 72 (1973) 367–78
147. Nicolet, C. 'Le *stipendium* des alliés italiens avant la Guerre Sociale', *PBSR* 46 (1978) 1–11
148. Pais, E. 'La persistenza delle stirpi sannitiche nell'età romana e la participazione di genti sabelliche alla colonizzazione romana e latina', *AAN* n.s. 7 (1918) 415–57
149. Richardson, J. S. 'The ownership of Roman lands: Tiberius Gracchus and the Italians', *JRS* 70 (1980) 1–11
150. Salmon, E. T. 'The "Coloniae Maritimae"', *Athenaeum* 41 (1963) 30–8
151. Salmon, E. T. *Samnium and the Samnites*. Cambridge, 1967
152. Salmon, E. T. *Roman Colonization under the Republic*. London, 1970
153. *Sannio. Pentri e Frentani dal VI al I sec. a.C.* Catalogo della Mostra della Soprintendenza Archeologica e per i Beni Ambientali, Architettonici Artistici e Storici del Malise, Isernia, Museo Nazionale, Ottobre-Dicembre 1980. Rome, 1980
154. Sartori, F. 'I praefecti Capuam Cumas', in *I Campi Flegrei, Atti dei Convegni Lincei* 33, 149–71. Rome, 1977
155. Tibiletti, G. 'La politica delle coloniae e città latine nella guerra sociale', *Rend. Ist. Lomb. Cl. Lettere* 86 (1953) 45–63
156. Wegner, M. *Untersuchungen zu den lateinischen Begriffen socius und societas*. Göttingen, 1969

f. Cisalpine Gaul

157. Arslan, E. A. 'Spunti per lo studio del celtismo cisalpino', *Notizie dal Chiostro del Monastero Maggiore* 7–10 (1971–4) 43–57
158. Arslan, E. A. 'Centi e romani in Transpadana', *Études Celtiques* 15 (1976–8) 441–81
159. Chilver, G. E. F. *Cisalpine Gaul*. Oxford, 1941
160. Gabba, E. 'Caio Flaminio e la sua legge sulla colonizzazione dell'agro Gallico', *Athenaeum* 57 (1979) 159–63
161. Hoyos, B. D. 'Roman strategy in Cisalpina, 224–222 and 203–191 B.C.', *Antichthon* 10 (1976) 44–55
162. Lequement, R. and Liou, B. 'Les épaves de la côte de Transalpine. Essai de dénombrement, suivi de quelques observations sur le trafic maritime aux IIe et Ier siècles avant J.-C.', *Cahiers Ligures de Préhistoire et d'Archéologie* 24 (1975) 76–82

163. Mansuelli, G. A. 'La civiltà gallica nell' area lombardo-piemontese', in *Arte e civiltà romana nell' Italia settentrionale* II, 45–55. Bologna, 1965
164. Peyre, C. *La cisalpine gauloise du IIIe siècle av. J.-C.* Paris, 1979
165. Robson, D. O. 'The Samnites in the Po Valley', *CJ* 29 (1934) 599–608
166. Tozzi, P. *Storia padana antica.* Milan, 1972
167. Tozzi, P. 'L'Italia settentrionale nell' età antica', *Athenaeum*, Fascicolo speciale (1976) 28–50

g. Roman literature and culture: Greek influences

168. Besançon, A. *Les adversaires de l'hellénisme à Rome pendant la période républicaine.* Paris and Lausanne, 1910
169. Bilinski, B. *De veterum tragicorum Romanorum notitiis geographicis observationes.* Wroclaw, 1952
170. Boscherini, L. *Lingua e scienza greca nel 'De agri cultura' di Catone.* Rome, 1970
171. Bowra, C. M. 'Orpheus and Eurydice', *CQ* n.s. 2 (1952) 113–26
172. Boyancé, P. 'Fulvius Nobilior et le dieu ineffable', *Rev. Phil.* 29 (1955) 172–92
173. Brink, C. O. 'Ennius and the Hellenistic worship of Homer', *AJPhil.* 93 (1972) 547–67
174. Büchner, K. *Das Theater des Terenz.* Heidelberg, 1974
175. Chalmers, W. R. 'Plautus and his audience', in *Roman Drama*, ed. T. A. Dorey and D. K. Dudley, 21–50. London, 1965
176. Delatte, A. 'Les doctrines pythagoriciennes des Livres de Numa', *Bull. de l'Acad. royale de Belg.* 22 (1936) 19–40
177. Della Corte, F. *La filologia latina dalle origini a Varrone.* Turin, 1937
178. Della Corte, F. 'Stoicismo in Macedonia e in Roma', in *Opuscula* I, 173–83. Genoa, 1971
179. Fraenkel, E. 'Some aspects of the structure of Aeneid VII', *JRS* 35 (1945) 1–14
180. Fraenkel, E. *Elementi Plautini in Plauto.* Florence, 1960 (translation, with addenda, of *Plautinisches im Plautus.* Berlin, 1922)
181. Gagé, J. *Apollon romain. Essai sur le culte d'Apollon et le développement du 'ritus Graecus' à Rome.* Paris, 1955
182. Gallini, C. 'Che cosa intendere per ellenizzazione. Problemi di metodo', *DArch.* 7 (1973) 2–3, 175–91
183. Garbarino, G. *Roma e la filosofia greca dalle origini alla fine del II secolo.* Turin, 1973
184. Gelzer, M. 'Der Anfang römischer Geschichtsschreibung', *Hermes* 69 (1934) 46–55 (= *Kl. Schr.* III, 93–103)
185. Gelzer, M. 'Nochmals über den Anfang der römischen Geschichtsschreibung', *Hermes* 82 (1954) 342–8 (= *Kl. Schr.* III, 104–10)
186. Gigante, M. 'L'epicureismo a Roma da Alcio e Filisco a Fedro', in *Ricerche Filodemee*, 13–21. Naples, 1969
187. Graillot, H. *Le culte de Cybèle mère des dieux à Rome et dans l'empire romain.* Paris, 1912

188. Grimal, P. *Le siècle des Scipions: Rome et l'hellénisme au temps des guerres puniques*. Paris, 1953

189. Grimal, P. 'La maison de Simon et celle de Théopropidès dans la "Mostellaria" de Plaute', in *Mélanges Heurgon* I, 371–86

190. Gros, P. 'Hermodoros et Vitruve', *Mélanges d'arch.* 85 (1973) 137–61

191. Gros, P. 'Les statues de Syracuse et les "dieux" de Tarente (la classe politique devant l'art grec à la fin du IIIe siècle avant J.-C.)', *REL* 57 (1979) 85–114

192. Gross, W. H. 'Zum sogennanten Brutus', in *HIM* II, 504–75

193. Haffter, H. *Terenz und seine künstlerische Eigenart*. Darmstadt, 1967

194. Heurgon, J. 'Caton et la Gaule Cisalpine', in *Mélanges W. Seston*, 231–47. Paris, 1974

195. Horsfall, N. 'The Collegium Poetarum', *BICS* 23 (1976) 79–95

196. Jocelyn, H. D. *The Tragedies of Ennius*. Cambridge, 1967

197. Jocelyn, H. D. 'The poems of Q. Ennius', *ANRW* I.2 (1972) 987–1026

198. Jocelyn, H. D. 'The ruling class of the Roman Republic and Greek philosophers', *Bull. Rylands Libr.* 59 (1976) 323–66

199. Kennedy, G. *The Art of Rhetoric in the Roman World*. Princeton, 1972

200. Kierdorf, W. 'Catos "Origines" und die Anfänge der römischen Geschichtsschreibung', *Chiron* 10 (1980) 205–24

201. Klingner, F. 'Cato Censorius und die Krisis Roms', in *Römische Geisteswelt*, 34–65. 5th edn. Munich, 1965

202. Kolendo, J. *Le traité d'agronomie de Saserna*. Wroclaw, 1973

203. Köves, T. 'Zum Empfang der Magna Mater in Rom', *Historia* 12 (1963) 321–47

204. Kraus, Th. 'Strömungen hellenistischer Kunst', in *RIGS*, 224–40

205. Latte, K. *Römische Religionsgeschichte*. Munich, 1960

206. Laughton, E. 'The prose of Ennius', *Eranos* 49 (1951) 35–46 (with additional note by E. Fraenkel)

207. Leeman, A. D. *Orationis Ratio*. Amsterdam, 1963

208. Letta, C. 'L'Italia dei *mores romani* nelle *Origines* di Catone', *Athenaeum* 62 (1984) 3–30

209. Martina, M. 'Aedes Herculis Musarum', *DArch.* n.s. 3 (1981) 49–68

210. Nenci, G. 'Graecia capta ferum victorem cepit', *ASNSP*³ 8 (1978) 1007–23

211. Rawson, E. 'Architecture and sculpture: the activities of the Cossutii', *PBSR* 43 (1975) 36–47

212. Rawson, E. 'The first Latin annalists', *Latomus* 35 (1976) 689–71

213. Rawson, E. 'The introduction of logical organization into Roman prose literature', *PBSR* 46 (1978) 12–34

214. Traina, A. *Vortit barbare*. Rome, 1970

215. Tränkle, H. 'Micio und Demea in den Terenzischen Adelphen', *MH* 29 (1972) 241–55

216. Veyne, P. 'L'hellénisation de Rome et la problématique des acculturations', *Diogène* 106 (April–June 1979) 3–29

217. Wardman, A. *Rome's Debt to Greece*. London, 1976

218. Weber, E. 'Die Trojanische Abstammung der Römer als politisches Argument', *Wiener Studien* 85 (1972) 213–25
219. Webster, T. B. L. *Hellenistic Poetry and Art*. London, 1964
220. Weippert, O. *Alexander-imitatio und römische Politik in republikanischer Zeit*. Diss. Augsburg, 1972
221. Wülfing-von Martitz, P. 'Ennius als hellenistischer Dichter', in *Ennius* (Entretiens sur l'antiquité classique, Fondation Hardt, 17), 253–89. Vandoeuvres–Geneva, 1972
222. Zetzel, J. E. G. 'Cicero and the Scipionic circle', *Harv. Stud.* 76 (1972) 173–9

h. Roman and Italian culture: archaeological evidence

(See also Section Bd)

223. Baldacci, P. 'Importazioni cisalpine e produzioni apule', in *Recherches sur les amphores romaines*, 7–28. Rome, 1972
224. Balty, J.-Ch. 'Une nouvelle réplique du Démosthène de Polyeuctes', *Bull. des Musées Royaux d'Art et d'Histoire* 50 (1978) 49–74
225. Balty, J.-Ch. 'La statue de bronze de T. Quinctius Flamininus *ad Apollinis in Circo*', *Mélanges d'arch.* 90 (1978) 669–86
226. Bevilacqua, G. *Tituli* II: *Miscellanea*. Rome, 1980
227. Bianchi Bandinelli, R. *Rome: le centre du pouvoir*. Paris, 1969
228. Bianchi Bandinelli, R. 'Problemi dell'arte figurativa', in *RIGS*, 213–23
229. Bianchi Bandinelli, R. 'La pittura', in *Le arti figurative*, 461–53. Milan, 1977
230. Bonghi Jovino, M. 'Breve nota in margine al problema dell'ellenismo italico: tipi ellenistici nella coroplastica capuana', in *Mélanges Heurgon* I, 41–7
231. Brown, F. E. *Cosa: The Making of a Roman Town*. Ann Arbor, Mich., 1979
232. Cianfarani, V. *Santuari nel Sannio*. Rome, 1960
233. Coarelli, F. 'Classe dirigente romana e arti figurative', in *RIGS*, 241–65
234. Coarelli, F. 'Architettura e arti figurative in Roma: 150–50 a.C.', in *HIM* o, 21–32
235. Coarelli, F. 'Arte ellenistica e arte romana: la cultura figurativa in Roma tra II e I secolo a.C.', in *CDE*, 35–40
236. Colonna, G. 'Problemi dell'arte figurativa di età ellenistica nell' Italia adriatica', in *Atti del II Convegno di Studi sulle antichità adriatiche* (Chieti-Francavilla al Mare, 1971), 172–7. Pisa, n.d.
237. Conta Haller, G. *Ricerche su alcuni centri fortificati in opera poligonale in area campano-sannitica*. Naples, 1978
238. Delbrück, R. *Hellenistische Bauten in Latium*. Strasbourg, 1907–12
239. Greco Pontrandolfo, A. and Greco, E. 'L'Agro Picentino e la Lucania occidentale', in *SRPS* I, 137–50
240. Grelle, F. 'Canosa. Le istituzioni, la società', in *SRPS* I, 181–226
241. Gros, P. 'Les premières générations d'architectes hellénistiques à Rome', in *Mélanges Heurgon* I, 387–410

242. Gros, P. *Architecture et société à Rome et en Italie centro-méridionale aux deux derniers siècles de la république.* Brussels, 1978
243. Johannowsky, W. 'Contributo dell'archeologia alla storia sociale: la Campania', in *RIGS*, 460–71
244. Johannowsky, W. 'La situazione in Campania', in *HIM* I, 267–99
245. Johannowsky, W. 'Testimonianze materiali del modo di produzione schiavistico in Campania e nel Sannio Irpino', in *SRPS* I, 299–309
246. Lauter, H. 'Die hellenistischen Theater der Samniten und Latiner in ihrer Beziehung zur Theaterarchitektur der Griechen', in *HIM* II, 413–22
247. Luchi, O. 'I territori di Volterra e di Chiusi', in *SRPS* I, 413–20
248. Manacorda, D. 'Produzione agricola, produzione ceramica e proprietari nell'ager Cosanus nel I a.C.', in *SRPS* I, 3–54
249. Marabini Moevs, M. T. *The Roman Thin-walled Pottery from Cosa (1948–1954).* MAAR 32. Rome, 1973
250. Marabini Moevs, M. T. *Italo-Megarian Ware at Cosa.* MAAR 34, 157–227. Rome, 1980
251. Mercando, L. 'Area sacra di S. Omobono, esplorazione della fase repubblicana', *Bull. Com. Arch.* 79 (1963–4) 43–52
252. Mercando, L. 'L'ellenismo nel Piceno', in *HIM* I, 161–218
253. Montagna Pasquinucci, M. 'La ceramica a vernice nera del Museo Guarnacci di Volterra', *Mélanges d'arch.* 84 (1972) 269–498
254. Morel, J.-P. 'Études de céramique campanienne. 1. L'atelier des petites estampilles', *Mélanges d'arch.* 81 (1969) 59–117
255. Morel, J.-P. 'Aspects de l'artisanat dans la Grande Grèce romaine', in *Atti Taranto* 15 (1975) 263–324
256. Morel, J.-P. 'Céramiques d'Italie et céramiques hellénistiques', in *HIM* II, 471–97
257. Morel, J.-P. 'Le sanctuaire de Vastogirardi (Molise) et les influences hellénistiques en Italie centrale', in *HIM* I, 255–9
258. Morel, J.-P. 'La céramique companienne: acquis et problèmes', in *Céramiques hellénistiques et romaines*, 85–122. Paris, 1980
259. Morel, J.-P. 'La produzione della ceramica campana: aspetti economici e sociali', in *SRPS* II, 81–97
260. Morel, J.-P. 'Les producteurs de biens artisanaux en Italie à la fin de la République', in *Les 'Bourgeoisies' municipales italiennes aux IIe et Ier siécles av. J.-C.*, 21–39. Paris and Naples, 1983
261. Pairault, F.-H. *Recherches sur quelques séries d'urnes de Volterra à représentations mythologiques.* Rome, 1972
262. Pavolini, C. 'Le lucerne nell'Italia romana', in *SRPS* II, 139–85
263. Rakob, F. 'Hellenismus in Mittelitalien: Bautypen und Bautechnik', in *HIM* II, 366–86
264. Ricci, A. 'I vasi potori a pareti sottili', in *SRPS* II, 123–38
265. Strazzulla, M. J. *Il santuario sannitico di Pietrabbondante.* 2nd edn. Campobasso, 1972
266. Strazzulla, M. J. 'Le terrecotte architettoniche. Le produzioni dal IV al I a.C.', in *SRPS* II, 187–208

267. Torelli, M. 'Il donario di M. Fulvio Flacco nell'area di S. Omobono', in *Studi di topografia antica*, 71–5. Rome, 1968

268. Torelli, M. 'Contributo dell'archeologia alla storia sociale: l'Etruria e l'Apulia', in *RIGS*, 431–42

269. Torelli, M. 'La situazione in Etruria', in *HIM* i, 97–109

270. Torelli, M. 'L'ellenismo fuori del mondo classico', in *Le arti figurative*, 536–55. Milan, 1977

271. Torelli, M. 'Osservazioni conclusive sulla situazione in Lazio, Umbria ed Etruria', in *SRPS* i, 421–6

272. Verzar, M. 'Archäologische Zeugnisse aus Umbrien', in *HIM* i, 116–42

273. Verzar, M. 'La situazione in Umbria dal III a.c. alla tarda antichità', in *SRPS* i, 374–406

274. Zanker, P. 'Zur Rezeption des hellenistischen Individualporträts in Rom und den italischen Städten', in *HIM* ii, 581–619

i. Other

275. Alföldi, A. *Römische Frühgeschichte*. Heidelberg, 1976

276. Campanile, E. 'La latinizzazione dell' osco', in *Scritti in onore di G. Bonifante* i, 109–20. Rome, 1976

277. Campanile, E. and Letta, C. *Studi sulle magistrature indigene e municipali in area italica*. Pisa, 1979

278. Camporeale, G. 'La terminologia magistratuale nelle lingue osco-umbre', *Atti Accad. Toscana di Scienze e Lett.* 1956, 33–108

279. Cristofani, M. 'Società e istituzioni nell'Italia preromana', *Popoli e civiltà dell'Italia antica* 7 (1978) 51–112

280. Dahlheim, W. *Gewalt und Herrschaft. Das provinziale Herrschaftssystem der römischen Republik*. Berlin, 1977

281. De Simone, C. 'Italien', in *Die Sprachen im römischen Reich der Kaiserzeit*, 65–81. Cologne, 1980

282. Derow, P. S. 'The Roman calendar, 190–168 B.C.', *Phoenix* 27 (1973) 345–56

283. Derow, P. S. 'The Roman calendar, 218–191 B.C.', *Phoenix* 30 (1976) 265–81

284. Goar, R. J. *Cicero and the State Religion*. Amsterdam, 1972

285. Lazzeroni, R. 'Le più antiche attestazioni del nom. pl. -ās in latino e la provenienza dei coloni pesaresi', *Studi e saggi linguistici* 2 (1962) 106–22

286. Lejeune, M. *L'anthroponomie osque*. Paris, 1976

287. Prosdocimi, A. L. 'Il lessico istituzionale italico. Tra linguistica e storia', in *La cultura italica*, 29–74. Pisa, 1978

288. Prosdocimi, A. L., ed. *Lingue e dialetti dell' Italia antica*. Rome, 1978

289. Rawson, E. 'Scipio, Furius, Laelius and the ancestral religion', *JRS* 63 (1973) 161–74

290. Rix, H. *Die etruskischen Cognomen*. Wiesbaden, 1953

291. Rix, H. 'L'apporto dell'onomastica personale alla cognoscenza della storia sociale', in *CDE*, 64–73

590 I. MISCELLANEOUS

I. MISCELLANEOUS

1. Bickerman, E. J. 'Origines Gentium', *CPh* 47 (1952) 65–81
2. Bleicken, J. Review of Badian, 1958: (A 3), *Gnomon* 36 (1964) 176–87
3. Capasso, M. and others. 'In margine alla vita di Filonide', *Cronache Ercolanesi* 6 (1976) 55–9
4. Casson, L. 'The grain trade of the hellenistic world', *TAPA* 85 (1954) 168–87
5. Charbonneaux, J. *L'art au siècle d'Auguste*. Lausanne, 1948
6. Coarelli, F. 'La Sicilia tra la fine della guerra annibalica e Cicerone', in *SRPS* 1, 1–18
7. Crönert, W. 'Der Epikureer Philonides', *SDAW* 1900, 942–59
8. Crönert, W. 'Die Epikureer in Syrien', *JÖAI* 10 (1907) 145–52
9. Franke, P. R. Review of Westermark, *Das Bildnis des Philetairos*, *Gnomon* 34 (1962) 589–96
10. Freeman, E. A. *A History of Federal Government in Greece and Italy*. 2nd edn by J. B. Bury. London, 1893
11. Gabba, E. 'Sui senati delle città siciliane nell' età di Verre', *Athenaeum* 37 (1959) 304–20
12. Gabba, E. 'Mario e Silla', *ANRW* 1.1 (1972) 764–805
13. Gawantka, W. *Isopolitie*. Vestigia 22. Munich, 1975
14. Gow, A. S. F. and Schofield, A. F. *Nicander. The Poems and Poetical Fragments*. Cambridge, 1953
15. Gratwick, A. Chapters in *The Cambridge History of Classical Literature* II, 60–171. Cambridge, 1982
16. Gruben, G. *Die Tempel der Griechen*. Munich, 1966
17. Guthrie, W. K. C. *Orpheus and Greek Religion*. London, 1935
18. Harris, W. V. 'On war and greed in the second century B.C.', *Amer. Hist. Rev.* 76 (1971) 1371–85
19. Hatzfeld, J. *Les trafiquants italiens dans l'orient hellénique*. Paris, 1912
20. Healey, J. F. *Mining and Metallurgy in the Greek and Roman World*. London, 1978
21. Heurgon, J. 'The date of Vegoia's prophecy', *JRS* 49 (1959) 41–5
22. Heurgon, J. 'Tityre, Alfenus Varus et la 1re Églogue de Virgile', *CT* 15 (1967) (= *Mélanges Saumagne*) 39–45
23. Köhler, U. 'Nachtrag zum Lebenslauf des Epikureers Philonides', *SDAW* 1900, 999–1001
24. Lane, E. N. 'Sabazius and the Jews in Valerius Maximus; a re-examination', *JRS* 69 (1979) 35–8
25. Mellor, R. Θεὰ Ῥώμη. *The Worship of the Goddess Roma in the Greek World*. Göttingen, 1975
26. Meyer, Ed. *Ursprung und Anfänge des Christentums* II. Stuttgart, 1921
27. Momigliano, A. *Alien Wisdom: The Limits of Hellenization*. Cambridge, 1975
28. Nilsson, M. P. *The Dionysiac Mysteries of the Hellenistic and Roman Age*. Lund, 1957

29. Olshausen, E. *Prosopographie der hellenistischen Königsgesandten* I. Louvain, 1974
30. Pritchett, W. K. *Studies in Ancient Greek Topography* II. Berkeley, 1969
31. Ritter, H.-W. *Diadem und Königsherrschaft*. Munich, 1965
32. Seibert, J. *Historische Beiträge zu den dynastischen Verbindungen in hellenistischer Zeit*. Wiesbaden, 1967
33. Simon, E. *Pergamon und Hesiod*. Mainz, 1975
34. Swain, J. W. 'The theory of the four monarchies', *CPh* 35 (1940) 1–21
35. Tcherikower, V. *Die hellenistischen Städtegründungen von Alexander dem Grossen bis auf die Römerzeit*. Leipzig, 1927

INDEX

Numidia, *9 Bb*; and Carthage, 21, 27, 40,
150–1, 153, (Rome arbitrates in disputes),
143–7, 149–51, 529, 533, 536, (trade
relationship), 147, 156; Syphax' revolt, 57;
and Second Punic War, 60, 62–3, 65, 160,
528; coinage, 147–8; *see also*: Massinissa
Nysa, queen of Pontus, 357, 536

obligation: of allies to Rome, 75–8, 201–2,
221–3, 228, 229, 230, 232, 239, 289, 443;
personal, in Roman politics, 168–70, 171,
173, 204, 424, 435, 450–1
Octavius Herrenus (merchant), 506
Octavius Lampadio, C. (*grammaticus*), 472
Octavius, Cn. (*cos.* 165): embassy to Greece,
313; and Third Macedonian War, 315, 316;
embassy to Syria, 334, 355, 384; murder of,
354, 358, 443, 535; builds *Porticus Octavia*,
507; hellenism, 443
Oeniadae, *6 Ee*, 102
Oenoparas, R., battle of, 365
oil, olive, 148, 234, 239, 498, 506
Olcades (Iberian tribe), *1 Ec–Fc*, 32, 525
oligarchy: Roman, 78, 168–72, 174–96, 231,
239–40; Rome favours in other states,
310–11
olives, 148, 234, 239, 498, 506
Olympia, 100, 342, 427, 443, 462
Onias (Jewish high priest), 348
opus caementicium, 503, 504–5, 506, 509,
510
opus craticium, 491
opus intertum, 504
opus quadratum, 504–5, 509
opus signinum, 487
oracles, *see*: Delphi; Sibylline
oratory, 436, 457–9, 461
Orchomenos, Arcadia, *12 Bd*, 322
Orestae, 273n
Oretani (Iberian tribe), *1 Ec, 8 Ec–d*, 36, 124
Oreus, *11 Bc*, 262, 263, 273
Oricum, *6 Dd*, 98, 106
Orissi (Iberian tribe), *1 Ec–d*, 23, 28
Orongis, *4 Ed*, 60
Orophernes (Cappadocian pretender), 359,
360–1, 374, 536
Oropus, 472
Oroscopa, 150
Orosius (historian), 10, 11, 17n
Orthosia, *13 Ed*, 366, 369n
Ortiagon, king of Galatia, 325, 328
Osca, 202, 228; language, 231, 428, 444
Ostia, *16 Cd*, 219, 436, 480, 487, 488
Osuna, 17, 136
Otacilius Crassus, T., 66–7, 70
Otranto, Straits of, *6 Dd–e*, 84, 86, 88, 89, 90,
95, 244

Oxthracai, 133
Oxus Treasure, 395, 396

Pacuvius, M. (tragedian and painter), 463,
469–70, 514–15
Pacuvius Calavius (Capuan rebel leader), 72
Paeligni, 217, 242
Paestum, *16 Dd*, 481, 483, 488, 489, 491,
509–10
Pagasae, *11 Bc*
Pahlavas (Indian term for Scytho-Parthians),
413n, 414, 415, 416
painting: Italian, 481, 491; Roman, 469, 475,
481, 492, 494, 514–15
Pakistan, *17, 20*, 406, 408, 421
Palestine, 251, 364–5; *see also* Jews
Palibothra, 394, 409
Pallantia, *8 Da*, 137n
palliatae (drama), 438, 468–9
Pamphylia, *11 Fd, 13 Dc*, 289, 369, 376
Panaetius (philosopher), 381, 473
Pāṇini of Gandhara, 388–9
Panium, battle of, 252, 528
Panormus, 27n
Pantaleon, king of Greek Bactria, 405, 406n,
420, 421
Paphlagonia, *13 Db*, 329, 380
Papirius Maso, C. (*cos.* 231), 69n, 524
papyri, 9, 13
Paraetacene, 352
parasiti Apollinis (actors), 430
parchment, 472
Parma, *7 Cb*, 114, 215, 531
Paropamisadae, *14 Cd–Dd, 15 Ab*, 398, 399,
400, 407, 421
Paros, *11 Cd*, 252, 259
Parthia, *13 Hd–Jd, 14 Bc*; under Arsaces II,
249, 397, 398, 402; under Mithridates I,
353, 533, (wars against Syria), 351, 352–3,
368, 371, 538, 540; under Phraates II, 371,
540, (and Syria), 368, 369, 371–3, (and
Scythians), 413; Rome favours, 386;
nomads and, 403, 413
Parthini (Illyrian tribe), *6 Dd–Ed*; and Illyrian
wars, 89, 90; Demetrius of Pharos and, 92;
and Macedonian Wars, 97, 98, 100, 104,
273
Parthyene, satrapy of, 398
Patalene, *14 De*, 393
Patañjali (Indian grammatician), 409
Patavium, 226
patriotism, concept of Roman, 211–12
patronage: of arts, 435, 441, 444, 492, 494,
502–3, 511, (patron as originator of work),
511, 512; political, 168–70, 204, 424, 435,
450–1; of provinces, 114n, 127n, 435, 440,
442, 462